MIND TRAINING: THE GREAT COLLECTION

The Library of Tibetan Classics is a special series being developed by the Institute of Tibetan Classics aimed at making key classical Tibetan texts part of the global literary and intellectual heritage. Eventually comprising thirty-two large volumes, the collection will contain over two hundred distinct texts by more than a hundred of the best-known authors. These texts have been selected in consultation with the preeminent lineage holders of all the schools and other senior Tibetan scholars to represent the Tibetan literary tradition as a whole. The works included in the series span more than a millennium and cover the vast expanse of classical Tibetan knowledge—from the core teachings of the specific schools to such diverse fields as ethics, philosophy, linguistics, medicine, astronomy and astrology, folklore, and historiography.

Mind Training: The Great Collection

Compiled by Shönu Gyalchok (ca. fourteenth–fifteenth centuries)
and Könchok Gyaltsen (1388–1469)

Compiled in the fifteenth century, *Mind Training: The Great Collection (Theg pa chen po blo sbyong rgya rtsa)* represents the earliest anthology of a special genre of Tibetan spiritual literature known simply as "mind training" or *lojong* in Tibetan. Tibetans revere the mind training tradition for its pragmatic and down-to-earth advice, especially the teachings on "transforming adversities into favorable opportunities." This volume contains forty-three individual texts, including the most important works of the mind training cycle, such as Serlingpa's *Leveling out All Conceptions*, Atiśa's *Bodhisattva's Jewel Garland*, Langri Thang-pa's *Eight Verses on Mind Training*, and Chekawa's *Seven-Point Mind Training*, together with the earliest commentaries on these seminal texts as well as other independent works. These texts expound the systematic cultivation of such altruistic thoughts and emotions as compassion, love, forbearance, and perseverance. Central to this discipline are the diverse practices for combating our habitual self-centeredness and the afflictive emotions and way of being that arise from it.

THE LIBRARY OF TIBETAN CLASSICS • VOLUME 1
Thupten Jinpa, General Editor

MIND TRAINING

The Great Collection

Compiled by Shönu Gyalchok
and Könchok Gyaltsen

Translated and edited by Thupten Jinpa

in association with the Institute of Tibetan Classics

Wisdom Publications, Inc.
132 Perry Street
New York, NY 10014 USA
www.wisdomexperience.org

©2006 The Institute of Tibetan Classics
All rights reserved.

Library of Congress Cataloging-in-Publication Data
Theg pa chen po blo sbyon rgya tsa. English.
    Mind training : the great collection / compiled by Shonu Gyalchok and Konchok
Gyaltsen ; translated and edited by Thupten Jinpa.
        p. cm. — (Library of Tibetan classics; v. 1)
    Includes bibliographical references and index.
    ISBN 0-86171-440-7 (hardcover : alk. paper)
    1. Blo-sbyon—Early works to 1800. 2. Spiritual life—Buddhism—Early works to
1800. 3. Buddhism—China—Tibet—Doctrines—Early works to 1800. I. Gzon-nu-
rgyal-mchog, Sems-dpa'-chen-po, 14th/15th cent. II. Dkon-mchog-rgyal-mtshan, Sems-
dpa'-chen-po, 1388–1469. III. Thupten Jinpa. IV. Title. V. Series.
BQ7800. T513 2005
294.3'444—dc22   2005024910

First Edition
25 24
6 5 4

ISBN 9780861714407
eBook ISBN 9780861717118
Cover & interior design by Gopa &Ted2, Inc.
Set in Garamond Premier Pro 10.5/13.5

Message from the Dalai Lama

THE LAST TWO MILLENNIA witnessed a tremendous proliferation of cultural and literary development in Tibet, the "Land of Snows." Moreover, due to the inestimable contributions made by Tibet's early spiritual kings, numerous Tibetan translators, and many great Indian paṇḍitas over a period of so many centuries, the teachings of the Buddha and the scholastic tradition of ancient India's Nālandā monastic university became firmly rooted in Tibet. As evidenced from the historical writings, this flowering of Buddhist tradition in the country brought about the fulfillment of the deep spiritual aspirations of countless sentient beings. In particular, it contributed to the inner peace and tranquility of the peoples of Tibet, Outer Mongolia—a country historically suffused with Tibetan Buddhism and its culture—the Tuva and Kalmuk regions in present-day Russia, the outer regions of mainland China, and the entire trans-Himalayan areas on the southern side, including Bhutan, Sikkim, Ladakh, Kinnaur, and Spiti. Today this tradition of Buddhism has the potential to make significant contributions to the welfare of the entire human family. I have no doubt that, when combined with the methods and insights of modern science, the Tibetan Buddhist cultural heritage and knowledge will help foster a more enlightened and compassionate human society, a humanity that is at peace with itself, with fellow sentient beings, and with the natural world at large.

It is for this reason I am delighted that the Institute of Tibetan Classics in Montreal, Canada, is compiling a thirty-two-volume series containing the works of many great Tibetan teachers, philosophers, scholars, and practitioners representing all major Tibetan schools and traditions. These important writings are being critically edited and annotated and then published in modern book format in a reference collection called *The Library of Tibetan Classics*, with their translations into other major languages to follow later. While expressing my heartfelt commendation for this noble project, I pray and hope that *The Library of Tibetan Classics* will not only make these important Tibetan treatises accessible to scholars of Tibetan studies, but will create a new opportunity for younger Tibetans to study and take interest in their own rich and profound culture. Through translations into other languages, it is my sincere hope that millions of fellow citizens of the wider human family will also be able to share in the joy of engaging with Tibet's classical literary heritage, textual riches that have been such a great source of joy and inspiration to me personally for so long.

The Dalai Lama
The Buddhist monk Tenzin Gyatso

Special Acknowledgments

THE INSTITUTE OF TIBETAN CLASSICS expresses its deep gratitude to Barry J. Hershey, Connie Hershey, and the Hershey Family Foundation for funding the entire cost of this translation project. We also thank the Ing Foundation for its longstanding patronage of the Institute of Tibetan Classics, which has, in addition to supporting other translation projects in the series, helped support the work of the Institute's chief editor, Dr. Thupten Jinpa.

Publisher's Acknowledgments

THE PUBLISHER wishes to extend a heartfelt thanks to the following people who have contributed substantially to the publication of *The Library of Tibetan Classics*:

Pat Gruber and the Patricia and Peter Gruber Foundation
The Hershey Family Foundation
The Ing Foundation

We also extend deep appreciation to our other subscribing benefactors:

Anonymous, dedicated to Buddhas within
Anonymous, in honor of Dzongsar Khyentse Rinpoche
Anonymous, in honor of Geshe Tenzin Dorje
Anonymous, in memory of K. J. Manel De Silva—may she realize the truth
Anonymous, in memory of Gene Smith
Dr. Patrick Bangert
Nilda Venegas Bernal
Serje Samlo Khentul Lhundub Choden and his Dharma friends
Nicholas Cope
Kushok Lobsang Dhamchöe
Diep Thi Thoai
Tenzin Dorjee

Richard Farris
Gaden Samten Ling, Canada
Evgeniy Gavrilov & Tatiana Fotina
Petar Gesovic
Great Vow Zen Monastery
Ginger Gregory
the Grohmann family, Taiwan
Gyaltsen Lobsang Jamyang (WeiJie) and Pema Looi
Rick Meeker Hayman
Steven D. Hearst
Jana & Mahi Hummel
Curt and Alice Jones
Julie LaValle Jones
Heidi Kaiter
Paul, Trisha, Rachel, and Daniel Kane
Land of Medicine Buddha
Dennis Leksander

Diane & Joseph Lucas
Elizabeth Mettling
Russ Miyashiro
Kestrel Montague
the Nalanda Institute, Olympia, WA
Craig T. Neyman
Kristin A. Ohlson
Arnold Possick
Magdalene Camilla Frank Prest
Quek Heng Bee, Ong Siok Ngow, and family
Randall-Gonzales Family Foundation
Erick Rinner
Andrew Rittenour
Dombon Roig Family
Jonathan and Diana Rose
the Sharchitsang family

Nirbhay N. Singh
Wee Kee Tan
Tibetisches Zentrum e.V. Hamburg
Richard Toft
Alissa KieuNgoc Tran
Timothy Trompeter
Tsadra Foundation
the Vahagn Setian Charitable Foundation
Ellyse Adele Vitiello
Jampa (Alicia H.) Vogel
Nicholas C. Weeks II
Richard and Carol Weingarten
Claudia Wellnitz
Bob White
Kevin Michael White, MD
Eve and Jeff Wild

and the other donors who wish to remain anonymous.

Contents

Preface

THIS VOLUME CONTAINS the most important early works of the Tibetan spiritual genre of *mind training (lojong)*. Compiled in the first half of the fifteenth century, *Mind Training: The Great Collection* features texts from the eleventh to the fifteenth century, many of which have had a lasting impact on the landscape of Tibetan culture, literature, and spiritual life, as well as on the psyche of the Tibetan people. The publication of this first-ever English translation of the *Great Collection* marks the realization of a long-held personal dream. This translation, volume 1 in *The Library of Tibetan Classics*, is actually the second volume to be issued in the series.

Two primary objectives have driven the creation and development of *The Library of Tibetan Classics*. The first aim is to help revitalize the appreciation and the study of the Tibetan classical heritage within Tibetan-speaking communities worldwide, the younger generation in particular who struggle with the tension between traditional Tibetan culture and the realities of modern consumerism. To this end, efforts have been made to develop a comprehensive yet manageable body of texts, one that features the works of Tibet's best-known authors and covers the gamut of classical Tibetan knowledge.

The second objective of *The Library of Tibetan Classics* is to help make these texts part of the global literary and intellectual heritage. In this regard, we have tried to make the English reader-friendly and, as much as possible, keep the body of the text free of unnecessary scholarly apparatus, which can intimidate general readers. For specialists who wish to compare the translation with the Tibetan original, page references of the critical edition of the Tibetan text are provided in brackets.

The texts in the thirty-volume series span more than a millennium—from the development of the Tibetan script in the seventh century to the first part of the twentieth century, when Tibetan society and culture first encountered industrial modernity. The volumes are thematically organized and cover sixteen categories of classical Tibetan knowledge: (1) teachings specific to each Tibetan school, (2) the bodhisattva's altruistic ideal, (3) presentation of the ethics of the three codes, (4) generation and completion stages of the highest yoga tantra, (5) Perfection of Wisdom studies, (6) buddha-nature theory, (7) the Middle Way philosophy of emptiness, (8) logic and epistemology, (9) Abhidharma psychology and phenomenology, (10) the tenets of classical Indian philosophical schools, (11) advice on worldly affairs, (12) "gateway for the learned," which includes linguistics, poetry, and literature, (13) medicine, (14) astronomy and astrology, (15) Tibetan opera, and (16) history.

The first category includes teachings of the Kadam, Nyingma, Sakya, Kagyü, Geluk, and Jonang schools, of miscellaneous Buddhist lineages, and of the Bön school. Texts in these volumes have been largely selected by senior lineage holders of the individual schools. Texts in the other categories have been selected primarily on recognition of the historical reality of the individual disciplines. For example, in the field of epistemology, works from the Sakya and Geluk schools have been selected, while the volume on buddha-nature features the writings of Butön Rinchen Drup and various Kagyü masters. Where fields are of more common interest, such as the three codes or the bodhisattva ideal, efforts have been made to represent the perspectives of all four major Tibetan Buddhist schools. *The Library of Tibetan Classics* can function as a comprehensive library of the Tibetan literary heritage for libraries, educational and cultural institutions, and interested individuals.

Today I feel a profound sense of joy, satisfaction, and more importantly an honor to be able to offer this volume of most inspiring Tibetan spiritual texts in English translation. Numerous individuals and organizations have helped make this possible. First of all I would like to express my deepest appreciation and respects to all my teachers, especially His Holiness the Dalai Lama and Kyapjé Zemey Rinpoché. Both introduced the beautiful world of mind training to me in my years as a young novice monk in India. I would especially like to thank Barry J. Hershey, Connie Hershey, and the Hershey Family Foundation for their most generous support, without which the dream of creating *The Library of Tibetan Classics* could not have even begun to be realized. Barry's conviction in the value of The Institute of Tibetan Classics' work and his continued support have helped keep my own translation work on this volume on course.

I owe deep gratitude to several other individuals and organizations. Catherine Moore helped in the editing of some texts in their early drafts.

Gene Smith and his Tibetan Buddhist Resource Center (TBRC) helped in obtaining some key texts, especially a scanned copy of Lechen's *History of the Kadam Tradition*. Geshe Lobsang Choedar, my co-editor for the critical edition of the Tibetan volume of the anthology, helped in comparing the different editions of the individual texts as well as assisted in the difficult task of sourcing the countless numbers of citations found in the Tibetan texts. The Central Institute of Higher Tibetan Studies, Sarnath, India, provided full access to its library to the Tibetan editors of *The Library of Tibetan Classics*, including myself. My wife Sophie was always there with her warmth and emotional support, and has taken on the endless logistical and administrative chores of the Institute. Finally, I thank my editor at Wisdom David Kittelstrom for his most valuable and incisive editorial assistance that has helped improve the language of this volume. Whatever merit we may have gathered—by all of us who have been involved with this project—through these may all beings enjoy peace and happiness. May these Tibetan texts become a genuine offering of peace and happiness to all.

Thupten Jinpa
Montreal, 2005

Introduction

WITHIN THE VAST CORPUS OF Tibetan Buddhist literature is a genre of writings that stands out for its inspirational power, poignant fervor, and down-to-earth practicality, all of which have made these teachings dear to the Tibetan people for generations. I am referring to a collection of texts and their associated spiritual practices known simply as *lojong,* or "mind training," which first appeared in the land of snows almost a millennium ago. The present volume is the first-ever complete English translation of *Mind Training: The Great Collection (Thekpa chenpo lojong gyatsa),* the earliest anthology of the most important works of mind training. The heart of Tibetan mind training is the cultivation and enhancement of Mahayana Buddhism's highest spiritual ideal, the generation of the awakening mind *(bodhicitta)*— the altruistic aspiration to attain perfect enlightenment for the benefit of all beings. More specifically, "mind training" or *lojong* refers to a specific approach to cultivating the awakening mind. That approach entails a disciplined process for radically transforming our thoughts and prejudices from natural self-centeredness to other-centered altruism.

The meaning of mind training

The Tibetan term *lojong* (spelled *blo sbyong*) is composed of two syllables, *lo* and *jong. Lo* stands for "mind," "thought," or "attitudes," while *jong* connotes several interrelated but distinct meanings. First, *jong* can refer to training whereby one acquires a skill or masters a field of knowledge. *Jong* can also connote habituation or familiarization with specific ways of being and thinking. Third, *jong* can refer to cultivating specific mental qualities, such as universal compassion or the awakening mind. Finally, *jong* can connote cleansing or purification, as in purifying one's mind of craving, hatred, and delusion. All these different meanings carry the salient idea of transformation, whereby a process of training, habituation, cultivation, and cleansing induces a profound transformation—a kind of metanoesis—from the ordinary deluded state, whose modus operandi is self-centeredness, to a fundamentally changed perspective of enlightened, other-centeredness.[1]

Broadly speaking, all the teachings of the Buddha and their associated commentarial explanations can be characterized as "mind training" in all four senses described above. However, what we are concerned with here is the emergence in Tibet of a specific genre of teaching. In this special usage, *mind training* refers to specific approaches for cultivating the altruistic awakening mind, especially through the practice of equalizing and exchanging of self and others as found in Śāntideva's eighth-century classic, *A Guide to the Bodhisattva's Way of Life*. When used in this sense, the term *mind training* represents an abbreviation of the fuller expression "mind training in the Mahayana (Great Vehicle)" or "Mahayana mind training."[2]

Two famous short works of the Tibetan mind training genre are today well known to the English-speaking world, with numerous commentaries by contemporary Tibetan teachers translated into different languages. These are Langri Thangpa's *Eight Verses on Mind Training* and Chekawa's *Seven-Point Mind Training*, both of which are contained in the present volume together with translations of their earliest commentaries. Historically, the Tibetan mind training teachings evolved within the context of the emergence of the Kadam school following the founding of Radreng Monastery near Lhasa in 1056.

What are the early scriptural sources for the instructions of mind training? Sangyé Gompa's *Public Explication of Mind Training* contains a memorable passage that describes a brief exchange between Chekawa (1101–75) and his teacher, Sharawa. Having been intrigued by the powerful altruistic sentiments expressed in Langri Thangpa's *Eight Verses*—such as "May I accept upon myself the defeat / And offer to others the victory"—Chekawa asks Sharawa whether these teachings have a scriptural basis. The teacher then cites some stanzas from Nāgārjuna's *Precious Garland* and asks if there is anyone who does not accept the authority of Nāgārjuna.[3] It is in this work of Sé Chilbu, which is effectively a compilation of notes taken from Chekawa's lectures, that we have the earliest known discussion of the scriptural sources of the mind training instruction. According to Chekawa, several sutras and early Indian treatises stand out as the primary sources of mind training teachings. Among the Mahayana sutras, those singled out are the *Ākāśagarbha Sutra*,[4] the *Teachings of Vimalakirti Sutra,* the *Flower Ornament Scripture,* the *Teachings of Akṣayamati Sutra,* as well as the *Collection of Aphorisms* (sometimes referred to as the Tibetan *Dhammapada*). Of the classical Indian treatises, those singled out are Nāgārjuna's *Precious Garland*, his *Discourse on the Wish-Fulfilling Jewel Dream*, Āryaśūra's *Garland of Birth Stories*, Maitreya's *Ornament of Mahayana Sutras*, Asaṅga's *Levels of the Bodhisattva*, and Śāntideva's *Guide to the Bodhisattva's Way of Life* and *Compendium of Training*. Of these, the two most important sources are undoubtedly Nāgārjuna's *Precious Garland* and Śāntideva's *Guide to the Bodhisattva's Way of Life*.

Key features of mind training

A central theme of mind training practice is the profound reorientation of our basic attitude both toward our own self and toward fellow sentient beings, as well as toward the events around us. Presently, we tend not only to grasp at some kind of intrinsically real "self" that constitutes our true being but also to cherish the welfare of this true "me" at the expense of all others. The mind training teaching challenges us to reverse this process. The training involves a deep understanding of others as true friends—as "more precious than a wish-fulfilling jewel," as Langri Thangpa puts it in his *Eight Verses on Mind Training*—and the recognition that our true enemy lies inside ourselves, not outside. We feel hurt when someone insults us, disappointed when someone we love betrays us, outraged when provoked for no reason, pangs of jealousy when others are successful, all because of deep-seated self-cherishing. It is self-cherishing that opens us to these painful and undesirable experiences. So the mind training teachings admonish us to "Banish all blames to the single source. / Toward all beings contemplate their kindness."

One of mind training's most memorable contributions to world spirituality is the practice of *tonglen,* or "giving and taking." *Tonglen* is a seemingly simple meditation practice of giving away one's own happiness and good fortune to others and taking upon oneself their suffering and misfortune. Traditionally, the meditation is designed to enhance the cultivation of loving-kindness and compassion, two central ideals in Mahayana Buddhism. According to mind training, this practice is combined with our respiration, whereby when we breathe in, we imagine taking from all other beings their pain and misfortune, all their negative traits and behaviors. These are visualized in the form of streams of dark clouds, smoke, or even brackish water, which enter our body. Then, when we exhale, we imagine giving to others all our happiness and good fortune, as well as our virtuous traits and behaviors. These are visualized in the form of white clouds, bright lights, and streams of nectar, which enter the bodies of other beings. The *Seven-Point Mind Training* presents this practice most succinctly: "Train alternately in giving and taking; / Place the two astride your breath."

Since a key goal of mind training is the radical transformation of our thoughts, attitudes, and habits, the application of remedies against the various ills of the mind is a dominant theme. To begin with, there is the highly practical approach of tackling one's coarsest mental afflictions first. Then comes the admonition to "overcome all errors through a single means," namely compassion. In addition, one finds the critically important injunction to ensure the purity of both the initial motivation and the state of mind at the conclusion of a specific act. The *Seven-Point* expresses this injunction as "There are two tasks—one at the start and one at the end." Finally, we are advised to make our own self the primary witness to our thoughts and actions, a principle aptly presented in the line "Of the two witnesses, uphold the primary one." If, despite all of this, we still fail to recognize the ultimate nature of things as devoid of substantial reality and continue to fall prey to self-grasping, we are advised to learn to view all things from their ultimate perspective, as dreamlike and devoid of substantial reality. Given our deeply ingrained tendency to reify anything we deem worthy of attention, once our application of remedies proves successful, there is the danger of grasping at the remedies themselves and once again being caught in bondage. So we are told, "The remedy too is freed in its own place."

On the path of spiritual transformation we are bound to confront all kinds of circumstances, both positive and negative. To be successful, we need a method whereby we can remain steadfast on our course. In this context, the mind training teaching excels brilliantly with the principle of transforming all adversities into the path. The *Seven-Point Mind Training* puts it this way: "When the world and its inhabitants are filled with negativity, / Transform adverse conditions into the path of enlightenment." For example, if we are slandered by someone without any justifiable basis, we can see the situation as a precious opportunity to cultivate forbearance. If we are attacked by someone, we can view the assailant with compassion, seeing that he is possessed by the demon of mental afflictions, such as anger. The masters of the mind training teachings extend this principle to all possible situations. They speak of taking both success and misfortune onto the path, both joy and pain onto the path, both wealth and poverty onto the path, and so on.

In a beautiful stanza, the Kashmiri master Śākyaśrī, who came to Tibet at the beginning of the thirteenth century, writes:

When happy I shall dedicate my virtues to all;
May benefit and happiness pervade all of space!
When suffering I shall take on the pains of all beings;
May the ocean of suffering become dry![5]

When we as spiritual practitioners learn to relate to all events in this radically transformed manner, we will then be able to fulfill the injunction "Cultivate the joyful mind alone." We will possess something akin to the philosopher's stone, for we will be able to transform every circumstance or event, whether positive or negative, into a condition favorable to our enhancement of altruism. No wonder the early mind training masters compare this teaching to an indestructible diamond, to the all-powerful sun, and to the mythological wish-granting tree. If we lived our lives according to the principles of mind training as instructed by the great masters of the tradition, we could then certainly relate to the sentiments expressed in the following by Chekawa:

Because of multiple aspirations,
I have defied the tragic tale of suffering
And have taken instructions to subdue self-grasping;
Now, even if I die, I have no remorse.

For me, and perhaps for many others too, one of the greatest attractions of the mind training teachings is their down-to-earth practicality. These teachings are unlike many other established teachings of the Tibetan Buddhist tradition, such as the rigorously systematized approach of the *lamrim,* or stages of the path teachings, the somewhat mystical approach of Vajrayana-related mahāmudrā (great seal) and dzokchen (great perfection) teachings, or the highest yoga tantra meditations, with their ritualized deity-yoga visualizations. In fact, the masters of mind training extol its simplicity, lack of systematic organization, and absence of elaborations, such as poetic embellishment or verbosity. They rightly proclaim that all the transformations that take place through mind training do so discreetly yet in great strides. Even a single line can be seen as encapsulating the entire teaching of the Buddha, for even a single statement of mind training has the power to subdue self-cherishing and the mental afflictions. Unlike in other teachings, in mind training there are no complicated structure, no confusing outlines, nor is any complex reasoning process called for.

Right from the earliest stages of their development, the mind training teachings became a shared heritage of all the major schools of Tibetan Buddhism. It is no wonder today, as interest in Tibetan spiritual teaching and insights grow worldwide, that the mind training teachings are the ones most shared with the outside world by the Tibetan teachers, including His Holiness the Dalai Lama. I vividly remember the beautiful morning of August 15, 1999, when nearly one hundred thousand people from all walks of life gathered in New York's Central Park to listen to the Dalai Lama's exposition of the *Eight Verses on Mind Training.* As on many of the Dalai Lama's trips to English-speaking countries, on that day too I had the privilege to sit beside him as his official translator. The atmosphere was pervaded by a stillness of attention, deep spiritual presence, and a shared experience of warmth toward all things living, and those present felt—at least for an hour and a half—that they had touched something deep within themselves. [6]

Origin of the mind training teachings

The Tibetan tradition attributes the origin of mind training to the Indian master Atiśa Dīpaṃkara of Vikramaśīla Monastery, who came to Tibet in the first half of the eleventh century. Atiśa's journey to Tibet, his long and close relationship with his principal disciple Dromtönpa, his composition of the highly influential work *Lamp for the Path to Enlightenment,* his contributions to the translation into Tibetan of major Indian Buddhist classics, and his critical role in what came to be later defined as the "latter dissemination of Buddhism in Tibet" are all well chronicled. What is not clear is whether Atiśa is personally responsible for the emergence of the mind training teaching we know today. Atiśa did not use the expression *mind training* in the manner defined above in any of his more well-known writings. Even Atiśa's own short mind training text, entitled the *Bodhisattva's Jewel Garland,* the first entry in our present volume, does not carry the term in its title or colophon. Similarly, the expression does not appear in any of the "mind training" works attributed to Atiśa's Indian teachers, such as the *Wheel of Sharp Weapons,* all of which are featured in our volume. The earliest known texts that explicitly carry the term are Langri Thangpa's *Eight Verses on Mind Training*[7] and Chekawa's *Seven-Point Mind Training,* both of which appeared about a century after Atiśa.

So who exactly is the author of the first mind training work? How far back can we trace the usage of the expression *mind training* in the manner defined above? We can defer the first question for now, as addressing it requires an analysis of the origin of the *Seven-Point Mind Training,* and look instead at the origin of modern use of the expression *mind training.*

There do appear to be clear references to "mind training" in the writings of Dromtönpa, Atiśa's chief disciple, in the manner we understand today. Chekawa, in his commentary to the *Eight Verses,* cites the following from Dromtönpa:

> In Kham, I went to visit the teacher Sherapbar, a friend close to my heart. I went knowing he had not invited me, and he took offense at this and sent me away. He ordered others to remove all my belongings, and he himself locked me in a dark room. That was when it became clear whether I had trained my mind in loving-kindness and compassion, and whether the lines "May their sufferings ripen upon me; / May all my happiness ripen upon them" had remained a lie for me.[8]

The use of the term *mind training* or *lojong* for a specific approach to the cultivation of the awakening mind, especially on the basis of equalizing and exchanging self and others, is even more explicit in the writings of Potowa, a primary student of Dromtönpa. In his letter to a student, the famous Kadam master Neusurpa, Potowa writes:

> The stages of mind training, once taught in secret,
> Are today being proclaimed in public.
> The stages of the path meditations that begin with death—
> Today not even their names exist anymore.[9]

So the understanding that within Atiśa's instructions there are two distinct approaches—stages of the path (which was taught publicly) and mind training (which was taught in secret)—goes back to the earliest framing of Atiśa's instructions. In other words, the tradition of distinguishing between two specific sets of instructions stemming from Atiśa—the stages of the path approach, grounded upon Atiśa's work *Lamp for the Path,* and the mind training approach, based on equalizing and exchanging self and others— seems to have evolved early in the development of the Kadam school. Later historians identify two distinct lineages of Atiśa's Kadam school—(1) the

Kadam lineage of treatises and (2) the Kadam lineage of instructions. Sometimes this list is expanded to include three, with (3) being the Kadam lineage of pith instructions.[10] Both stages of the path and mind training belong to the second of these three lineages.

Atiśa's three masters of the awakening mind

One critical element of the traditional account of the origins of the mind training teaching is the story of the "three masters" from whom Atiśa is said to have received instructions on awakening mind. Once again, Chekawa's teaching, as penned by his student Sé Chilbu, is an important source for the legend. According to this story, Atiśa received instructions on the generation of awakening mind from three different Indian masters. The first is the teacher Dharmarakṣita, a yogi who happened to uphold the philosophical standpoint of the Vaibhāṣika school and whose compassion was so great that he once cut off a piece of his own flesh and gave it to a sick man as medicine.[11] The second is Kusalī Jr., a dedicated yogi of Maitreya, who is therefore sometimes called Maitrīyogi. Finally, there is Serlingpa Dharmakīrti, whom Atiśa is said to have deliberately sought by braving a twelve-month sea voyage to the Indonesian island of Sumatra. The question is, what was Chekawa's source for his account of the three distinct lineages of awakening mind that Atiśa is believed to have received? How early can we trace the story?

The story may be traceable to Atiśa himself, at least as told by his student Dromtönpa. In an extract from Atīśa's advice to Naljorpa Sherap Dorjé and Jvalamati, Dromtönpa identifies two distinct approaches in the training of one's mind in the cultivation of great compassion. One is to first cultivate a deep sense of equality between self and others and then move on to the next stage of exchanging self and others. This, Dromtönpa states, is the tradition of the teacher Dharmarakṣita. In contrast, he says, exchanging self and others right from the start is the approach of master Serlingpa.[12] Interestingly, no mention is made of the approach of Atiśa's remaining teacher on awakening mind, Maitrīyogi or Kusalī, Jr. However, we find in Chekawa, and especially later in Thokmé Sangpo, an allusion to a statement by Chengawa that first equalizing and then exchanging self and others is the approach of the teacher Maitrīyogi.[13] In the absence of further evidence, it is difficult to speculate who is responsible for introducing the legend of Atiśa's three awakening mind gurus. My own feeling is that it is traceable at least to Dromtönpa, if not directly to Atiśa himself. In any case, all textual sources agree in recognizing Serlingpa as Atiśa's most important awakening mind teacher and therefore the true source of his mind training teachings.

Who, then, is Serlingpa?[14] All biographies of Atiśa state that whenever he would utter Serlingpa's name, tears would fall down his cheeks. They report that Atiśa exclaimed that whatever degree of good heart he possessed was due entirely to Serlingpa.[15] The present volume contains an interesting if somewhat mythological account of Atiśa's long sea voyage to Sumatra, where he went to meet with Serlingpa.[16] Apart from this account, few texts provide any clear depiction of Serlingpa. That he was a Buddhist scholar of great stature in the tenth and eleventh centuries remains beyond doubt.[17] Six works by Serlingpa Dharmakīrti, most of which were in fact translated under the personal supervision of Atiśa himself, are included in the Tengyur, the Tibetan collection of canonical treatises. Of these, the most notable works are Serlingpa's commentary on Maitreya's *Ornament of Clear Realizations* and various treatises on Śāntideva's *Guide to the Bodhisattva's Way of Life* and *Compendium of Trainings*. So, regardless of how much of the narrative of Atiśa's voyage to Sumatra and his subsequent tutelage under Serlingpa in the later biographies is true, there is no doubt that it is Serlingpa's teaching on the awakening mind that forms the core of Atiśa's mind training instructions.

From the beginning of the twelfth century, especially after the codification of Atiśa's scattered teachings on mind training by Sharawa and Chekawa into the well-known seven points, master Serlingpa's instructions on the cultivation of awakening mind as transmitted to Atiśa have effectively formed the kernel of the Tibetan mind training teachings. This seven-point approach became so influential that for many later authors, especially after the fifteenth century, Chekawa's *Seven-Point Mind Training* became almost equivalent to mind training itself.[18] It is to this influential short text that we now turn our attention. In doing so, we can also begin to address the question of the authorship of the first mind training work.

Seven-Point Mind Training

Without a doubt, Chekawa was one of the first teachers, if not the first, who presented the key elements of Atiśa's mind training instructions in terms of seven key points. The earliest work we have that presents this is Chekawa's teachings on the seven points as compiled by his student Sé Chilbu. This, however, does not mean that Chekawa was the first to organize the teaching of mind training according to this schema.[19] The seven points are as follows: (1) presentation of the preliminaries, (2) training in the two awakening minds, (3) taking adversities onto the path of enlightenment, (4) presentation of a lifetime's practice in summary, (5) the measure of having trained the mind, (6) the commitments of mind training, and (7) the precepts of mind training.

That Chekawa did not actually write all the lines of the *Seven-Point* in the sense of an author composing his own original work appears fairly certain. To begin with, at least two versions of so-called root lines of mind training exist—almost all lines of which find their way into the *Seven-Point*. Both versions are attributed to Atiśa and appear in our present anthology. In addition, at least two different pre–fourteenth-century expositions of mind training are featured in this volume, and neither makes any reference to the seven-point framework. One is the beautifully succinct work entitled simply *A Mahayana Mind Training*, which appears to come from the lineage of Jayülwa, which is different from that of Chekawa. The other work is the famous *Public Explication* of Sangyé Gompa, where the root lines are explained in terms of (1) the bodylike main part and (2) its branches. The first part is in turn divided into the preliminary, the actual, and the concluding practices. The root lines embedded within these two guide texts are different enough from Chekawa's *Seven-Point* to warrant their recognition as representing different redactions of the root lines on mind training. So, effectively, we have the following extant redactions of the root lines on mind training, all but the last of which appears in the present anthology:

1. *Root Lines*
2. *Annotated Root Lines*
3. Root lines embedded in Chekawa's *Seven-Point Mind Training*
4. Root lines embedded in *A Mahayana Mind Training*
5. Root lines embedded in Sangyé Gompa's *Public Explication*
6. Versified redaction root lines in Shönu Gyalchok's *Compendium of All Well-Uttered Insights*

These root lines differ significantly from each other in terms of their length, ordering of the lines, subtle divergences even in what appear to be the same lines, differences in versification, and so on. However, it seems fairly certain that all these redactions originate from a common source. It is difficult, however, to determine who the actual author of these seminal lines may be and who first compiled them together into a cohesive text. It does appear that Atiśa never actually explicitly authored a mind training text in the sense of a coherently organized work. These lines are most probably based on spontaneous instructions that Atiśa gave to different individuals on numerous occasions and that were later compiled by various teachers into oral transmissions so that they would not be lost.[20] Their origin in oral transmissions is evident from their brevity and vernacular style. It is perhaps also due to this oral origin that so many redactions of the root lines came about, some of which do not demonstrate any familiarity with the others. Based on the antiquity of their style of presentation, my own guess is that the two versions of the root lines featured in the present anthology may be the earliest versions. It is on the basis of some of these different redactions that Chekawa, drawing on the instructions of his teacher Sharawa, organized the root lines according to the so-called seven points of mind training. Over the years, this seven-point instruction came to dominate both the pedagogy and the commentarial tradition of Atiśa's mind training teachings.

That the mind training teaching originated in a scattered oral tradition of Atiśa's instructions appears to be recognized also by the author of what is effectively the earliest history of the Kadam tradition. In his *History of the Precious Kadam Tradition*, Tibetan author Sönam Lhai Wangpo (fifteenth century) lists four different categories of master Atiśa's teachings: (1) those pertaining to the stages of the path, (2) scattered sayings, (3) epistles, and finally (4) the various pith instructions. Within this fourfold division, the author lists the entire collection of mind training teachings as belonging to the second class, namely scattered sayings.[21] It is probably also for this reason that the root lines on mind training do not appear among the works attributed to Atiśa in the Tengyur. For until these scattered sayings were compiled together into a coherent text, no such work called the *Root Lines on Mind Training* existed. Almost all Tibetan sources agree that Langri Thangpa, and later Chekawa, were responsible for bringing the "secret" mind trainings teaching into the wider public domain.[22]

Following the organization of the root lines on mind training into the seven key points, the *Seven-Point Mind Training* effectively became the root text of Atiśa's mind training teachings. This short text attracted numerous commentaries from many great Tibetan teachers, such as the following well-known ones:

1. Sé Chilbu's (twelfth century) commentary compiled from Chekawa's own lectures (featured in this anthology)

2. Thokmé Sangpo's (fourteenth century) commentary
3. Shönu Gyalchok's (fourteenth century) *Compendium of All Well-Uttered Insights*
4. Könchok Gyaltsen's (fifteenth century) *Supplement to Oral Transmission* (featured in this anthology)
5. Radrengpa's (fifteenth century) *Stream of the Awakening Mind*
6. Hortön Namkha Pal's (fifteenth century) *Mind Training: Rays of the Sun*
7. The First Dalai Lama Gendün Drup's (fifteenth century) *Lucid and Succinct Guide to Mind Training*
8. Khedrup Sangyé Yeshé's (sixteenth century) *How to Integrate into One's Mind the Well-Known Seven-Point Mind Training*
9. Kalden Gyatso's (seventeenth century) *Dispelling the Darkness of Mind*
10. Yongzin Yeshé Gyaltsen's (eighteenth century) *Essence of Ambrosia*
11. Ngülchu Dharmabhadra's (eighteenth century) *Heart Jewel of the Bodhisattvas*
12. Jamyang Khyentse's (nineteenth century) *Seeds of Benefit and Well-Being*

The historian Lechen identifies two distinct traditions of the teaching of *Seven-Point Mind Training*. One is the so-called northern lineage that stems from Rampa Lhadingpa and later Radrengpa, while the other, the southern lineage, stems from Thokmé Sangpo.[23] The key difference between these two lineages lies in their interpretation of the following well-known line from the root text: "Place your mind on the basis of all, which is the actual path." The southern-lineage proponent, such as Thokmé Sangpo, reads "the basis of all" as the uncontrived natural mind, while the northern-lineage proponents, such as Radrengpa, read it as emptiness. According to Yeshé Döndrup, Shönu Gyalchok's approach combines both lineages, thus making a third approach to the teaching of *Seven-Point*.[24] At the beginning of the fifteenth century, thanks to Namkha Pal and Radrengpa's composition of their commentaries on the *Seven-Point Mind Training*, a unique transmission of the *Seven-Point* based upon the ear-whispered teachings of the great Tsongkhapa came into being.

Due to this diversity in the presentation of the instructions of the *Seven-Point Mind Training*, several different redactions of the *Seven-Point* evolved.[25] There are some variations in the length of these different versions, with certain lines appearing in some yet not in others. In addition, some versions present the training in the cultivation of the ultimate awakening mind in the beginning part, while others follow Sangyé Gompa's approach and present the ultimate awakening mind toward the end.[26] Atiśa's mind training teachings became a particularly dominant element of pedagogy and practice in the Geluk school, giving rise to some noteworthy original works on mind training. These include Tsongkhapa's beautiful verse work *Mind Training in Ornamental Words,* Chenga Lodrö Gyaltsen's *Opening the Door of Dharma,* his *Mind Training on Forbearance,* his root text and autocommentary on *Mind Training in Altruistic Aspirations,* and Yongzin Yeshé Gyaltsen's *Ornament of Lobsang's Thought.*

Compilation of the present anthology

A few words about the compilation of our present anthology are in order. The original Tibetan xylograph text, which was the basis of the critical edition produced by the Institute of Tibetan Classics, appears to have been printed during the reign of the Thirteenth Dalai Lama, probably at the beginning of the twentieth century. Unfortunately, we have no information as to what texts that edition was based upon. The colophon simply refers to the volume as "The instructions on awakening mind known as *Mind Training: The Great Collection,* which was compiled together by the great bodhisattva Shönu Gyalchok and the great Mü master Könchok Gyaltsen." To date, I have failed to locate any biographical material on Shönu Gyalchok other than the brief note in Lechen's *History of the Kadam Tradition* (p. 307a–b). He is said to have studied with numerous noted fourteenth-century thinkers, including Tsongkhapa and Yakdé Paṇchen, but received the mind training instructions from a direct student of Thokmé Sangpo called Tsültrim Pal. As for Kön-chok Gyaltsen (1388–1469), there is an "official" biography in volume 1 of the *lamdré* cycle of texts. This biography contains a brief reference to how Shönu Gyalchok conferred the entire transmission of mind training teachings on Könchok Gyaltsen and effectively appointed him his successor in the transmission of these mind training teachings.

Whether the present version of our mind training anthology really is the original volume compiled by the two masters or is a later expanded and modified version is unclear. There appear to be at least three different versions of *The Great Collection.* First is the present version. However, the eighteenth-century Geluk author Longdöl Ngawang Lobsang enumerates seventeen sets of mind training texts within the great collection compiled by Shönu

Gyalchok.[27] His list does not contain many of the entries of the present volume, including Atiśa's *Bodhisattva's Jewel Garland,* Sé Chilbu's commentary on the *Seven-Point Mind Training,* and Sangyé Gompa's *Public Explication* along with its supplement by Könchok Gyaltsen. Longdöl's enumeration is corroborated by Yeshé Döndrup, who states that Shönu Gyalchok compiled around thirty extant mind training texts into a single volume.[28] Finally, Jamgön Kongtrül appears to use a different version of the anthology as the basis for the mind training cycle of texts included in volume 2 of his *Treasury of Instructions.* Unfortunately, Kongtrül does not tell us what edition he used. We do not even know whether the texts he included in his *Treasury of Instructions* represent the entire anthology or a further selection. The *Treasury* collection does not include Sangyé Gompa's *Public Explication* and its supplement by Könchok Gyaltsen, Yangönpa's short mind training instruction, *Heart of Dependent Origination,* as well as the entire set of texts on *Parting from the Four Clingings.*[29] In the absence of further textual resources and after consultation with the records of teachings received by numerous Tibetan masters, it is difficult to make an informed determination on this question of the earliest version of the anthology.

I propose that the original basis for our present anthology of mind training texts is the final section of Shönu Gyalchok's *Compendium of All Well-Uttered Insights.* Toward the end of this long work, the author provides an extensive list as well as extracts, and in some cases complete renderings, of numerous mind training texts. If we read Shönu Gyalchok's treatment of the various mind training texts carefully, we can recognize the overall structure and theme of the present anthology. After providing a version of Atiśa's *Root Lines* (equivalent to entries 4 and 5 of our anthology), he lists five broad categories of what he calls essential supplementary instructions: (1) In the first category, Shönu Gyalchok includes the short biographical works on Atiśa, such as his renouncing of his kingdom and his voyage to Sumatra (entries 2 and 3 in our present anthology), (2) while in the second he includes supplementary instructions on the practice of ultimate awakening mind but does not list any specific texts. (3) In the third category he lists the instruction of the *Eight Sessions of Mind Training* (entry 22 of our volume) as well as *Samantabhadra's Mind Training* (entry 21). (4) In the fourth category, Shönu Gyalchok includes the well-known teaching *Leveling Out All Conceptions,* both the root text and its commentary (entries 12 and 32), which are believed to have been given to Atiśa by Serlingpa specifically to tame people in barbarian borderlands. (5) The fifth category of instructions he calls miscellaneous mind instructions, which include Virvapa's mind training (entry 28); Kusulu's merit accumulation (entry 18); Śākyaśrī's instruction on taking joys and suffering onto the path (entry 19); instructions on taking afflictions onto the path (entry 13), on purifying grudges (entry 16), and on purifying negative karma (entry 15); as well as advice to Namdak Tsuknor (entry 27) and Chim Namkha Drak's mind training in one session (entry 26). This is then followed by extracts from the mind training works attributed to Atiśa's three Indian awakening mind teachers (entries 8, 9, 10, and 11), which in turn is followed by a full citation of Langri Thangpa's *Eight Verses on Mind Training.*[30]

Since Shönu Gyalchok offers only a list or extracts of most of these texts in his *Mind Training: Compendium of All Well-Uttered Insights,* it was probably either his student Könchok Gyaltsen or both teacher and student together who brought into a single volume the complete texts of all the mind training works listed. To this were then added (either by them or by a later editor) Atiśa's *Bodhisattva's Jewel Garland* and the remaining additional texts. Whatever the actual facts of these diverse redactions, today the present anthology is universally recognized as the authentic *Mind Training: The Great Collection (Lojong gyatsa).*[31]

The texts in *Mind Training: The Great Collection* represent the flowering of an important spiritual culture dedicated to the perfection of the human heart by cultivating the altruistic intention. In their birthplace of Tibet, these spiritual writings have inspired, nurtured, and transformed the hearts of millions of individuals across many generations. Even though the first mind training text emerged nearly a millennium ago, these simple yet profound teachings have retained their appeal and poignancy. By making these teachings available in translation, my hope is that many more individuals will be able to share in the wonderful insights of the Tibetan mind training teachings.

Technical Note

The name of the Tibetan text is *Theg pa chen po blo sbyong rgya rtsa,* and the original xylograph edition used as the basis of this translation is a rare copy of the Lhasa Shöl edition archived by the library of the Central Institute for Higher Tibetan Studies, Sarnath, Varanasi, India (acquisition no. 16767). In the publisher's dedication of the Tibetan text, Shönu Gyalchok and Müchen Könchok Gyaltsen are listed as the compilers of this volume.

Bracketed numbers embedded in the text refer to page numbers of the new critical and annotated Tibetan edition published in modern book format by The Institute of Tibetan Classics in New Delhi (2004, ISBN 81-89165-01-1) as volume 1 of the series entitled *Bod kyi gtsug lag gces btus.*

All Tibetan names in the main body of text are rendered phonetically in accordance with a style sheet developed by the Institute of Tibetan Classics and Wisdom Publications especially for the *Library of Tibetan Classics* series. There is a correspondence table at the back of the book where transliterated spellings can be found. Sanskrit diacriticals are used throughout, except for naturalized Sanskrit terms such as *sutra, mandala,* and *nirvana.*

Pronunciation of Tibetan phonetics:
ph and *th* are aspirated *p* and *t,* as in *pet* and *tip.*
ö is similar to the *eu* in French *seul.*
ü is similar to the *ü* in the German *füllen.*
ai is similar to the *e* in *bet.*
é is similar to the *e* in *prey.*

Pronunciation of Sanskrit:
Palatal *ś* and retroflex *ṣ* are similar to the English unvoiced *sh.*
c is an unaspirated *ch* similar to the *ch* in *chill.*
The vowel *ṛ* is similar to the American *r* in *pretty.*
ñ is somewhat similar to a nasalized *ny* in *canyon.*
ṅ is similar to the *ng* in *sing* or *anger.*

In the Tibetan original of three texts (entries 5, 34, and 37), there are annotations inserted into the main body of the text in small fonts. While the annotations to entry 5 are extensive and may in fact be considered an integral part of the actual text, the annotations inserted in entries 34 and 37 appear to be, for the most part, attempts (by a later editor) to identify the texts from which citations are made yet whose titles are not mentioned by the author. In my transltion I have treated the annotations of entry 5 as integral to the text and have therefore faithfully produced an equsivalent annotated root text in English. For this, I have highlighted the actual "root lines" in bold while keeping the annotations inserted in between the root lines in normal fonts so that the two—the root text and the annotations—can be read interspersed. All other annotations inserted in the various Tibetan texts appear in my translation in parentheses. In contrast, additions made to help faciliate the reading of the English translation are provided in brackets.

In the critical edition of the volume published by the Institute of Tibetan Classics, the individual texts of the collection have been compared against those found in the collected works of the individual authors, their commentaries, or in other anthologies, especially Jamgön Kongrül's *Gdams ngag mdzod* (vol. 2), where many of the mind training texts are featured. The variant readings of these different editions are fully annotated in the critical Tibetan edition. In my translation I have only referred to those variances that are significant and alter the reading of the texts. The referencing of the numerous citations from Kangyur and Tengyur and the works of Tibetan masters has been, on the whole, based on The Institute of Tibetan Classics' new critical edition.

Mind Training:
The Great Collection

Compiled by Shönu Gyalchok
and Könchok Gyaltsen

1. Bodhisattva's Jewel Garland[32]
Atiśa (982–1054)

Sanskrit title: *Bodhisattvamaṇyāvalī*
Homage to great compassion.

Homage to the teachers.
Homage to the faith divinities.

1
Discard all lingering doubts,
And strive with dedication in your practice.
Thoroughly relinquish sloth, mental dullness, and laziness,
And strive always with joyful perseverance.

2
With mindfulness, vigilance, and conscientiousness,
Constantly guard the gateways of your senses.
Again and again, three times both day and night,
Examine the flow of your thoughts.

3
Reveal your own shortcomings,
But do not seek out others' errors.
Conceal your own good qualities,
But proclaim those of others.

4
Forsake wealth and ministrations;
At all times relinquish gain and fame.
Have modest desires, be easily satisfied,
And reciprocate kindness.

5

Cultivate love and compassion,
And stabilize your awakening mind.
Relinquish the ten negative actions,
And always reinforce your faith.[33]

6

Destroy anger and conceit,
And be endowed with humility.
Relinquish wrong livelihood,
And be sustained by ethical livelihood.

7

Forsake material possessions,
Embellish yourself with the wealth of the noble ones.
Avoid all trifling distractions,
And reside in the solitude of wilderness.

8

Abandon frivolous words;
Constantly guard your speech.
When you see your teachers and preceptors,[34]
Reverently generate the wish to serve.

9

Toward wise beings with Dharma eyes
And toward beginners on the path as well,
Recognize them as your spiritual teachers.
[In fact] when you see any sentient being,
View them as your parent, your child, or your grandchild.

10

Renounce negative friendships,
And rely on a spiritual friend.
Dispel hostility and unpleasantness,[35]
And venture forth to where happiness lies.

11
Abandon attachment to all things
And abide free of desire.
Attachment fails to bring even the higher realms;
In fact, it kills the life of true liberation.

12
When you encounter the causes of happiness,
In these always persevere.
Whichever task you take up first,
Address this task primarily.
In this way, you ensure the success of both tasks,
Where otherwise you accomplish neither.

13
Since you take no pleasure in negative deeds,
When a thought of self-importance arises,
At that instant deflate your pride [4]
And recall your teacher's instructions.

14
When discouraged thoughts arise,
Uplift your mind
And meditate on the emptiness of both.[36]
When objects of attraction or aversion appear,
View them as you would illusions and apparitions.

15
When you hear unpleasant words,
View them as [mere] echoes.
When injuries afflict your body,
See them as [the fruits of] past deeds.

16
Dwell utterly in solitude, beyond town limits.
Like the carcass of a wild animal,
Hide yourself away [in the forest]
And live free of attachment.

17
Always remain firm in your commitment.
When a hint of procrastination and laziness arises,
At that instant enumerate your flaws
And recall the essence of [spiritual] conduct.

18
However, if you do encounter others,
Speak peacefully and truthfully.
Do not grimace or frown,
But always maintain a smile.

19
In general when you see others,
Be free of miserliness and delight in giving;
Relinquish all thoughts of envy.

20
To help soothe others' minds,
Forsake all disputation
And be endowed with forbearance.

21
Be free of flattery and fickleness in friendship,
Be steadfast and reliable at all times.
Do not disparage others,
But always abide with respectful demeanor.

22
When giving advice,
Maintain compassion and altruism.
Never defame the teachings.
Whatever practices you admire,
With aspiration and the ten spiritual deeds,
Strive diligently, dividing day and night.[37]

23
Whatever virtues you gather though the three times,
Dedicate them toward the unexcelled great awakening.
Disperse your merit to all sentient beings,
And utter the peerless aspiration prayers
Of the seven limbs at all times.

24
If you proceed thus, you'll swiftly perfect merit and wisdom
And eliminate the two defilements.[38]
Since your human existence will be meaningful,
You'll attain the unexcelled enlightenment.

25
The wealth of faith, the wealth of morality,
The wealth of giving, the wealth of learning,
The wealth of conscience, the wealth of shame,
And the wealth of insight—these are the seven riches.

26
These precious and excellent jewels
Are the seven inexhaustible riches.[39]
Do not speak of these to those not human.
Among others guard your speech;
When alone guard your mind.

This concludes the *Bodhisattva's Jewel Garland* composed by the Indian abbot Dīpaṃkaraśrījñāna.

2. How Atiśa Relinquished His Kingdom and Sought Liberation[40]

Dromtönpa (1005–64)[41]

[5] Sanskrit title: *Guruguṇadharmākaranāma*
Tibetan title: *Bla ma'i yon tan chos kyi 'byung gnas*
English title: *The Qualities of My Teacher, Which Are the Source of Dharma*
Homage to the excellent masters, friends of the doctrine.

For beings tormented by heat waves of the afflictions,
You send forth clouds of love in the space of ultimate expanse
And dispel grief through a rain of great compassion—
To you, O Dharma king, I bow with reverence.

From the stainless ocean of his life's events,
As I respectfully extract here mere drops,
Uncluttered by words of exaggeration and denigration,
And relate them with the skills of my intelligence, please listen.

In the supreme land of Sahor[42] in eastern India
Is a town called Bangala.[43]
Its sovereign is the Dharma king Kalyāṇaśrī,
[In whose dominion] prosperity showers like rain.

His palace is adorned with golden victory banners
And encircled by a hundred thousand households.
It has twenty-five thousand bathing pools
Enclosed within seven hundred and twenty gardens.

He has more than fifty-six thousand banyan trees
And thirty-five thousand subjects.

This town has seven perimeter fences
And three hundred and sixty-seven bridges.

There golden victory banners number twenty-five thousand.
The central palace sports thirteen gilded roofs.
His wealth and power rival that of the Eastern emperor.[44]
His majesty resembles that of the celestial Indra himself.

The population rivals the city of Gandhava's;[45]
The flourishing of Dharma wealth resembles Dharmodgata's.[46]
The queen of this Dharma king is
The glorious Śrīprabhā, who is like a goddess.

Shy, conscientious, and glowing with beauty,
She propitiates the Three Jewels and is a mother to all.
To this goddess was born three sons:
Śrīgarbhā, Candragarbhā, and Padmagarbhā.

Their numbering three is mentioned as an aside.[47]
The middle one, Candragarbhā,[48]
Is today my sublime spiritual teacher.

When the fortunate one was born to his mother, [6]
Showers of blossoms rained upon the kingdom;
The center of the sky was filled with rainbow tents;
Heavenly songs and melodies were heard by all.

Everyone was joyful and experienced a sense of purity.
For eighteen months he stayed in the palace,
Nurtured and cared for by eight wet nurses.
To the north of this kingdom
Lay the monastery of Vikramalapūri.[49]

To make offerings at this religious site,
The parents, ministers, and subjects set forth in fifty carriages,
With young men and women adorned in beautiful clothes.
All were encircled by hundreds of skilled musicians.

[The entourage] carried countless precious offerings.
As they ventured forth with dancing and song,
Our teacher looked three years of age, with an attractive physique
And a beautiful face, which even constant gazing upon could not sate.

Adorned with celestial clothes and jewelry
And dressed in *pāñcālika* silk, he was carried in the king's lap.
As people saw this celestial being,
They gasped with joy and glowed with happiness.

It's said they gazed upon him with affection and could not pull
    themselves away.
Thus those who saw him uttered these words:
"When you were born, flowers rained down,
The sun shone like a tent, and enchanting tunes were heard.

"Thinking 'When will we see your face?' our hearts felt pangs;
Today we have seen you, and it is truly a miracle."
Then the excellent prince uttered the following:
"O my parents, who are these people?"

Both his parents replied thus:
"O prince, these are your loyal subjects."
To this the prince responded:
"May they have perfect parents like me;
And possessing kingdom, power, and blazing merit,
May they be born as the chief sons of kings;
May they all be sustained by the sublime Dharma."

Then, as they arrived with their entire retinue
At the monastery of Kamala,[50]
The prince paid homage to the Three Jewels
And, in a melodious tune, uttered the following praise:

"I've obtained the human life of leisure and opportunity,
Free from any deficiencies; I follow you, the Three Jewels.
Always I take you to my crown;
From this very day, pray be my refuge."

When he uttered these words,
Everyone, his parents, ministers, and subjects,
As well as many monks heard them.
Utterly delighted, they felt a sense of wonder. [7]
Unanimously, all agreed he was a sublime being.

Then his parents, together with their retinues,[51]
Gathered merit by making offerings, service, and reverence.
And they prayed: "May we throughout this and all other lives
Make offerings to the Three Jewels,
Serve the spiritual community, and reveal the sublime Dharma.
May we dispel the pain of afflictions and enjoy freedom."

As he heard these words of aspiration,
While looking at his parents, the prince uttered:
"May I never be chained by the lifestyle of a householder
But attain Dharma wealth in the midst of ordained monks;
Free of conceit, may I make offerings to the [Three] Jewels
And look on all beings with [the eyes of] compassion."

When they heard the prince's words,
His parents and all the others felt deeply awed.
Those words were the first lesson of my teacher.

When the prince reached the age of three,
He became versed in arithmetic, letters, and Sanskrit.
When he reached the age of six,
He could differentiate Buddhist and non-Buddhist tenets.

From this point till he reached the age of ten,
He went for refuge to the Three Jewels,
Observed day-long precepts, and gave charity;
He read scriptures and committed them to recitation.

He made supplications and sought the sublime Dharma,
Served his parents and honored them.
All his songs and dances were rooted in Dharma;
Upon seeing spiritual practitioners, he would receive them from afar.

He looked after his subjects and nurtured them with compassion.
He protected those who were bereft of refuge.
Thus he engaged in countless deeds of a sublime being.

When the prince reached the age of eleven,
The ministers and his subjects offered as his bride
Twenty-two girls of noble patronage;[52]
The [prince's] parents showered them with gifts.

One day the king summoned all his ministers and ordered:
"At dawn, prepare well thirteen horse-drawn carriages;
Adorn them with various ornaments of beauty.
Atop the center, on an especially beautiful and compliant carriage,
Pitch an umbrella of peacock feathers with cooling screens.
In the center below, on a beautiful throne made of precious jewels,
You should place Candragarbhā, attired in rich silks.

"On thirteen horse-drawn carriages bedecked with ornaments,
The ministers should be seated beautifully clothed;
Singing joyful songs, they should play all kinds of music.
Three horse-drawn white carriages should take the lead,
Three red carriages should bring up the rear,
Three yellow carriages should flank on the right, [8]
While three green carriages should flank on the left.

"Within these carriages should sit five hundred youths,
With celestial ornaments matching their direction's color.
The prince's carriage should be of five different colors,
With its four corners adorned with carved arching peacock heads.

"These should be encircled by offering goddesses;
And surrounded, too, by subjects who rob people's hearts
By playing lutes, flutes, drums, and cymbals,[53]
All of which creates a symphony of most melodious tunes.

"At the outskirts of the great city,
In the great parks, which are places of utter joy,
People should be captivated with spectacles and games.

For the duration, a half a month or so,
Make everyone happy and keep them entertained.

"Then everywhere, in all directions,
You should seek out girls who might please the prince.
When the ministers see the girls,
They should summon them and extract firm pledges."

Once the king had issued these firm orders,
The ministers made all the preparations in seven days—
Thirteen carriages bedecked with ornaments,
Three thousand five hundred youths adorned with jewels.

The prince was at the center of a carriage adorned with jewels.
Twelve carriages were filled with skilled musicians,
Who played varieties of musical instruments.
Then at the outskirts of the great city,
At the crossroads and in the spacious town squares,
Games were staged that captured the minds of the people.

Candragarbhā and his retinue of two thousand five hundred
Were seated in the carriages.
At that time, in all directions and in all the towns,
At the outskirts and in the lotus groves,
And at all the wide crossroads here and there,
Crowds gathered as if he were a universal monarch.
All went there to see the emanation body.

The assembly of celestial girls such as Kiraṇdevī,[54]
Those of noble lineage and their close friends,
All of them said, "Let's go watch."

As the throngs of people gathered there,
There arrived, too, the daughters of King Sönamzin,[55]
The daughters of King Mukhyüzin,
The daughters of King Chudakzin,
The daughters of King Tumbula,
Twenty-two girls excelling in nobility, physique, wealth, and power,
Who had all been broached as prospective brides.[56]

In each carriage sat seven girls,
And each girl was accompanied by seven maids.
Thus there were twenty-two stunning carriages,
All adorned with diverse ornaments. [9]

With melodious tunes and ecstatic hearts they arrived.
None could take their eyes off the prince,
For, like the celestial maidens, they too were attached.
Thoroughly amorous, the hairs stood up from their pores.

At that point an emanation of a ḍākinī,
Assuming the form of a girl with dark bluish skin,
Exhorted the prince thus in a melodious singing voice:

"Do not be attached, O sole lord, fortunate one.
If, like elephants enamored with muddy waters,
You should become entrapped in the mires of desire,
Will this not veil the one enrobed with ethical discipline?

"Through five hundred and fifty-two lives,
You have led the life of a pure, learned monk;
So, like swans plunging into a lotus lake,
You'll become a renunciant in this life.

"In the city are girls devoted to cleanliness;
They are but messengers of Māra stealing away morality's glow.
With seeming love they will seduce and deceive you.
Know this, O prince of beguiling appearance.

"Like the clear reflection of the moon in a lake,
O exalted body, clear, transparent, and unblemished,
Who wears his hair in five locks and is adorned with heavenly jewels,
O beautiful one, you've robbed the minds of all people.

"At this time when you've obtained the precious human life so rare,
Since you must expend your life in study, reflection, and meditation,
Thoroughly seek a spiritual guide, which is their principal condition,
So that all knots of lingering doubts can be cut."

As the ḍākinī uttered these words,
The prince brightened with a smile and responded:
"Well said, well said! Extremely well said!
The prince of wisdom is happier in the forests;[57]
Peacocks' well-being lies in the forest of poisonous trees;
Due to the force of habit, swans are happier in lakes.

"How can crows plunge into a lotus lake
As they would into a mire of filth?
How can persons with the noble lineage
Immerse themselves in towns like mere ordinaries?

"In the past the prince Siddhārtha[58]
Felt revulsion toward the kingdom and wealth
Of King Śuddhodana[59] as if it were a mire of filth;
Forsaking sixty thousand queens, he sought liberation.

"Acclaimed and revered as 'the Able One,'
He was hailed by the entire world, including the gods.
This Dharma king endowed with major and minor noble marks
Attained awakening through the twelve great deeds.[60]

"So if I do not renounce my kingdom,
Attachment will proliferate in this mire of desire.
All friends are but Māra's tricksters; [10]
I'll recognize all sense objects as salt water.[61]

"Now I shall search for many learned teachers;
And throughout this life I'll seek supreme awakening.
No matter how joyfully one indulges in the sense objects,
Like the moon's reflection in water, they are devoid of essence.

"Like echoes, they have no content;
Like emanations, they lack identifiable nature;
Like reflections, they are devoid of self-subsistence.

"In this vast ocean of afflicted foundational consciousness,
The rivers of birth, aging, sickness, and death flow perpetually;

If, in the past, I lacked power over the lower realms due to karma,
Why don't I search today when all the conditions are perfect?

"Reflecting deeply upon cyclic existence in general,
I will seek a teacher and strive in the sublime Dharma."
As the prince uttered these words of teachings,
The people of the kingdom all felt, "With such manner of speech,
Will he ever reign over the kingdom?

"If he does, doubtless he will be a Dharma king;
Otherwise he will seek the learned and realized teachers
And will reign over the kingdom like the king of the Śākyas.[62]
Amazing indeed is this!" Such shouts were echoed.

Feeling attached, circumambulating, they gazed at him over and over;
The girls of noble lineage who came to strengthen familial standing,
Though delighted to see him, were saddened by his words.
Approaching their parents, they exclaimed:

"The great prince says that he is disenchanted by samsara;
He says he will forsake the kingdom and become a renunciate monk;
He says that Prince Siddhārtha left behind his queens;
He says he is not attached to his retinue and subjects.

"So, O parents together with your retinues,
Pray venture forth to the royal palace;
Engage in various activities to attract the prince's mind;
With wealth and various resources captivate him."

Thus the girls exhorted their parents.
So the parents, ministers, and subjects
Strove hard with songs, dances, and clusters of girls.
As the caravans approached the kingdom,[63]
The prince, taking with him one hundred and fifty horsemen,
Dressed in battle costume and roamed the hills.

On one cliff sat the mendicant Jetari.
In the manner of a mendicant, he was reciting verses of poetry;

Jetari was honoring sages of pure conduct with his crown,
And the prince saw him [as someone] utterly victorious over the
    afflictions.

Without dismounting from his horse,[64]
The prince offered the following words to the sage:
"You practice the ascetic life and what is taught in the scriptures in
    solitude;
As pure conduct you consume food borne of untainted livelihood; [11]
Apart from renouncing sense objects and venerating the sages,[65]
What other higher qualities have you attained?"[66]

As he asked this,
The prince felt that the mendicant, without even looking,
Responded in the following manner:
"Even if the king prohibits the mendicant's provisions,
Other than casting me by karma's power to the lower realms,
Like a flower in a garden at season's end,
I see no long-term result, so I shall remain here [in the wilderness].

"Fearing that, like cattle, dogs, and pigs,
I may be reborn as a worm living in mires of filth,
I strive in the ascetic life and practice pure conduct.
Failing to see any essence in illusory material possessions,
I contemplate the other shore[67] and honor sages with my crown."

When the prince heard the mendicant's words,
He uttered the following response to test the mendicant:
"Monks are even more conceited than others.[68]
Why did you not rise when the lord of the land arrived?"

The great mendicant responded:
"O lord of the land, who are you? And from where do you hail?
As I've neither friends nor enemies, I failed to recognize you;
As I've no possessions, I am happier in the forest;
The [sole] foe of this body and mind is the lord of death;
As I've no conceit, I have forsaken all distracting pursuits."

Hearing the mendicant's words, the prince replied:
"I have come from the palace with golden victory banners;
I am a scion of [the king] Kalyāṇaśrī.
Who can rival me in this forest today?
Not recognizing the lord of the land, you've transgressed the law."

To this the great mendicant replied:
"I am an outcast to human ranks and I am outside the law;
I have no ruler, no servants, nor anyone to act with deference toward.
O lord of the land, when one departs to the other shore,
One does so alone on foot, with no horses and no companions.

"With no food, no clothes, naked, one will roam in the intermediate
   state;
With no place, no country, none familiar, the journey will be long.
Even a prince has no guarantee on how long he may live.
Because of this I prefer to live in the forest."

As the prince heard the mendicant's words,
Dismounting his horse, he offered him the three spheres.[69]
With deep reverence and palms folded, he made the following plea:
"To test your higher qualities, O learned one,
As if with arrogance I uttered these insolent words.[70]

"However, six times throughout day and night
I contemplate samsara's defects and feel disenchanted by it.
So since I wish to renounce my kingdom and achieve true liberation,
O great mendicant, sustain me under your care." [12]

To this the great mendicant replied:
"Come here, come here! I'll bless you so that,
Unassailed by conceit, you'll become a master of the doctrine."

Stating thus:

He conferred the blessing of the Three Jewels and the awakening mind.
Rising up, the prince once again offered the master

His horse-drawn carriages[71] as gifts for granting refuge and the
  awakening mind;
To perfect the prince's merit, he accepted the gifts for a while,
And he gave the following instruction:

"O prince, even ghosts can pursue for a while
The mundane ambitions of those who are unreflective;
The pursuit of self-interest is done even by falcons and wolves.
Even self-realized ones seek a partial awakening.

"Even serfs consume food adequate to fill their stomachs;
How can anyone, even a king, have a full stomach in all lives?
O prince, devote your mental continuum to Dharma practice.
Relinquish your kingdom and seek true liberation."

Again, the excellent prince made further supplication:
"Teacher, I am a prisoner under house arrest,
As if tied with silk scarves inside a royal palace.
First, caught tightly in a marriage of afflictions and karma,

"I fear being deceived by everyone under the guise of love,
Leading me further into the mires of cyclic existence.[72]
Bless me, teacher, O bless me,
So that I cannot be harmed by my king."

To this the great mendicant stated:
"Family lineage is samsara's strong chain;
Kingdom is the great mire of filth and refuse;
'Kinghood' is the great, endearing title of Māra;
Ministers are the great family members of Māra.

"Certainly and swiftly you must remain vigilant;
Do not remain here, but depart to Nālandā.
There resides the teacher Bodhibhadra,
With whom you've had close connections since beginningless time;
Receive mind generation teaching and create karmic connections.
This learned master will benefit you greatly."

Thereupon the great mendicant returned all the offerings
And offered the prince the following advice:
"Leave home, and come forth to me;
I will nourish you with various instructions."

Then the prince returned to his palace.
He gathered various articles, such as gold and silver,
And together with his retinue, ventured forth to Nālandā.

Frightened, the king of Nālandā welcomed from afar
The prince and his retinue of soldiers.
When they met, the king offered these words:
"O lord of the land, from where do you hail? [13]
Where do you venture forth, you who resemble a universal monarch?
Wearing battle attire, to where are you off to crush your enemy?
Since I saw you from afar, I've come to meet you."

To this the prince replied:
"I hail from the east, the land of Sahor;
I have come from the palace with golden victory banners;
I am journeying to conquer the foe of cyclic existence;
I am traveling to destroy the Māra foe, the lord of death."

The king of Nālandā responded:
"You are the son of the Sahor king in the east,
The lord of the land, the Dharma king Kalyāṇaśrī.
The universal monarch is victorious over the forces of evil;
Fortunate it is that his son has visited our region.

"In your Vikramaśīla, the palaces of the Three Jewels are
Like the gods' celestial mansions;
Inconceivable numbers of ordained monks reside there,
As well as a great [many] learned paṇḍitas resembling the sun and moon.
O lord of the land, which learned master do you seek?"

To this the excellent prince replied:
"The great learning center of Nālandā is,
Like an ocean, a source of precious jewels;

In it is found a multitude of starlike mahāpaṇḍitas.
Bodhibhadra, most highly acclaimed, is my teacher,
As prophesied by the mendicant [Jetari].
O lord of the land, pray help remove my obstacles."

To this the great king replied:
"The great hero Bodhibhadra is unwavering,
Like the king of mountains clad in snow.
He abides resplendent, brilliant, and at ease.

"Affluent like Vaiśravaṇa,[73]
He has found the fortune of the noble ones' riches.[74]
O come, come near the environs of my palace.
With pleasant tales and material gifts I'll entertain you."

The prince said "Wonderful" to this invitation,
And, led by the king's welcoming procession
And amid an offering of music, they ventured forth to Nālandā.

To its south, in the region of lotuses,
Was the palace called Samantabhadra,
Surrounded by a hundred thousand homes;
It was to this the noble prince was invited.
Seated on an expansive throne adorned with precious jewels,
He was accorded the honor befitting a royal prince.

Then they departed to the monastery of Nālandā,
To the presence of the teacher Bodhibhadra.
Upon entering the monastic complex,
The prince saw the teacher and felt immeasurable joy,
A joy that was most extraordinary.

Upon hearing of the excellent prince's arrival, [14]
Bodhibhadra, too, felt great joy and rose from his seat.
He uttered the following teaching in eloquent words:
"You have arrived, O son of a Dharma king.
Is the Dharma jewel flourishing in the land of Sahor?
Are you not tired from the long journey?"

At this point the excellent prince replied:
"Yes, my father is well and he lives in accord with Dharma;
Though the road was long, I have now met you.
O learned master, are you not exhausted due to
Study, reflection, and meditation on the Buddha's teaching?"

To this the teacher replied, "I too am happy
Through day and night thanks to the sublime Dharma.
O prince, be seated and tell me what you seek."

Then, with deep reverence, the prince prostrated
And pleased the teacher with offerings of precious jewels;
He also respectfully made the following plea:
"O teacher of sentient beings, listen to this tale with compassion.

"Afraid of being harmed by great kingdom, the Trickster,
In the bottomless mire of filth that is samsara,
I fled to the forest with my soldiers.
There I found residing a teacher totally victorious over foes.

"When I appealed to him to confer the awakening mind,
With his vision of compassion the great learned master advised:
'Go to Nālandā, the great center of learning;
There resides the excellent teacher Bodhibhadra,
Who has sustained you with compassion in past lives.
Receive from him the instructions on awakening mind.'

"Immediately I gathered offering articles from my palace
And have arrived here today;
So, with compassion, kindly grant me now
The various instructions on the awakening mind."

Instantly, as he sat down on the cushion,
The teacher entered into deep meditative absorption
And blessed the three doors[75] to make them serviceable;
He then gave many instructions on awakening mind.

Such were the instructions conferred:
"O prince, to achieve meaning in this life,
Renounce your kingdom and seek liberation. If you do not,
When you fall to lower realms due to the power of karma,
You will regret it intensely; but then it will be too late.

"At this point while you are laying the foundation of your ultimate
    welfare,
If you fail to persevere with great hardships,
Then, when you have definitely squandered your chance for liberation,
O son of good family, there is no hope to regain it in the future.

"Even if you are courageous, firm, and well-armored,
When you are led through the narrow gorges of the afterlife by Yama,[76]
Simply feeling the remorse of a powerless desperate person [15]
Will be of no benefit and purpose at all.
Contemplate this sublime teaching, O prince.

"Over there, to the north of Nālandā
Lives the one known as the bodhisattva Vidyākaukila,
Who has been your father since beginningless time.
Transcending life and abiding in solitude,
He is untainted by elaborations of the eight mundane concerns.[77]
Wearing the attire of ethical discipline, he possesses unobstructed
    clairvoyance.
Go to him and receive instructions of Dharma."

When he heard these words of the master Bodhibhadra,
While reluctant to part from him,
He ventured forth to meet the noble Vidyākaukila.
Prostrating and making offerings, he uttered the following plea:

"I live in the east in the land of Sahor;
I am a son of the king of Bangala;
I come from the palace with golden victory banners;
I have been to the monastery of Nālandā
And have received the awakening mind from Bodhibhadra.

"Having granted the instruction, he advised me thus:
'Do not remain here but go to the north;
For there resides a bodhisattva called Vidyākaukila,
Who has been your father since beginningless time;
Go forth to him and request the awakening mind.
He will benefit you.'

"Immediately, though reluctant to part from the master,
I came here to you with joy rising in my heart.
O teacher, take me within your fold
So that I may not be harmed by my father."

The sublime teacher was thoroughly pleased.
"Wonderful indeed that the lord of the land has come!
Come here, I shall bless you within nonduality;
I'll expound the truthful words of reality's unchanging nature;
With compassionate heart, I will teach you the sublime Dharma."

Then respectfully the prince made offerings of articles.
He prostrated at the teacher's presence and folded his palms.
Forsaking pride, he sat down on a cushion.
The excellent Kaukila revealed the instructions of the awakening mind.

The key instruction, hailed to be supreme, was this:
"O prince, even if you enjoy all the prosperities in this life,
If you fail to plant the seed for life's ultimate welfare,
Obtaining a human life of leisure and opportunity has little meaning.
To lose this jewel would be an immense loss for the future.

"O prince, the conqueror Nāgārjunagarbha stated the following:
'The nature of all, dreamlike, illusionlike, is devoid of elaborations.
The mind itself is uncontrived and abides in the innate nature.
He who fails to contemplate these two in his thoughts
Will remain entrapped in the mires of cyclic existence.'[78]

"O prince, abide in meditative equipoise on the spacelike ultimate. [16]
In the illusionlike subsequent periods, reflect on karma and its fruits."

When the teacher revealed this profound teaching, [the prince] attained
The path of preparation[79] and realized the "heroic" meditative absorption.

He then recounted his realization to the teacher thus:
"When I remain in equipoise, one-pointed in meditative absorption,[80]
Like the sky that is totally free of clouds,
Everything is clear, translucent, and devoid of obscurations.
O teacher, is this reality's true mode of being?

"Then as I rise from this meditative absorption,
Without clinging to appearances, thoughts of sentient beings arise;
Though [appearances are] false, I find respect for the minute facets of karma.
O teacher, are these experiences of mine deluded?"

In response, the teacher stated:
"Well done, prince, you are indeed a fortunate son;
I am an ordained monk free of exaggeration and denigration.
Though being cleansed in the spacelike meditative equipoise,
Out of compassion I lead sentient beings in subsequent periods.
Yes, this is indeed the mode of being of the two truths.
This, then, is my excellent instruction.

"So if you wish to be free from your kingdom,
Then to the south of the dark rocky mountain called Summit,
There resides my teacher, Avadhūti.
He was your teacher [too] in the past.

"Go to him and receive the instructions of the awakening mind.
Receive from him the instructions for renouncing your kingdom."
When the prince heard the teacher's words,
Though saddened to depart from the master, he felt deep joy.

Together with his retinue, he paid his farewell homage,
And entered the road with the demeanor of a hero.
The great king of Nālandā as well
Gathered together manifold provisions.

And, followed by his retinue, he accompanied them up to three *yojana*.[81]
As the king turned his back to return [home],
The prince, reluctant to part, uttered the following words:

"O king, though you've found the joys of higher rebirth,
If you fail to vanquish the enemy of cyclic existence,
When you are later led away chained by Yama,
Remorse will be too late, so seek the wealth of Dharma.

"With warmth in our hearts we have bonded for a few days,
Yet, like merchants gathered at a market, this is all transient.
Though I may be leaving, do not cast me from your affection.
I shall meet you soon, in full accord with the Dharma."

The king, too, responded in the following manner:
"By my good fortune I have met you today.
My heart has been moved by meeting you, O prince of a Dharma king.
I feel saddened since you, my son, are leaving today.
But I pray that we will meet again in the near future." [17]

Then the prince went forth to find the teacher Avadhūti,
Venturing toward the south of Summit Mountain.
At that time the sublime teacher, the excellent being,
Was living in a cave on a dark rocky cliff.

Draped over his body was a black woolen shawl;
He was seated on a *kṛṣṇasāra*[82] pelt;
And around his chest hung a large meditator's belt;
His body stout, he had an extremely large, round belly.

His eyes red and his skin a slight blue,
With a sense of abandon he sat in half-lotus posture,
And the entire world and its contents were distilled in a single skull cup.[83]
The prince saw the teacher living thus, free of attachment.

Dismounting his horse, the prince prostrated from a distance.
Together with his retinue he sat down in the teacher's presence.
Suddenly the teacher looked at them and uttered:
"Has the bubble of your pride not yet burst?

"Have you not been afflicted by the forces of darkness?
Are you not sunk in the mires of a household?
Have you not been seduced by Māra's daughters?
Have you not wasted the perfect human existence?
Where do you hail from, you who resemble a prince?"

With folded palms, the prince replied:
"I hail from the palace with golden victory banners;
I come here disenchanted with the life of royalty;
I come seeking refuge from the ways of cyclic existence.

"I have been to the great monastery of Nālandā
And have sought refuge in Vidyākaukila.
That elder sent me here to your presence.
So, master, please grant me your protection now."

Avadhūti uttered the following response:
"Though I was born in the royal lineage,
As I feared greatly the army of afflictions and karma,
I shunned my kingdom as if it were a drop of spit.
Can you follow Avadhūti's lifestyle?

"The riches of royalty are like a poisonous sea:
The instant you drink from it, the life of freedom is threatened.
The riches of royalty are like a barrier of fire:
The instant you cross it, suffering is engendered.

"Go! Go back to your palace today;
Observe the defects of a householder's life and return soon."
When the prince heard the teacher's words,
He made offerings, paid his respects, and swiftly returned home.

When the subjects saw the prince,
They shouted his praise, offering songs, dance, and music.
As the prince reached his home,
His parents, the king and queen, were utterly overjoyed.

"O Candragarbhā, where did you go?
Are you not exhausted after such a journey?

Seeing the problems, were you not saddened? [18]
Wonderful it is that you're back," they exclaimed joyfully.

The prince answered them in great detail:
"I went to [different] places to pursue my aspirations;
I went to vanquish with skill the enemy of doctrine;
I went seeking an able teacher for my refuge.

"I went searching for solitude in mountains and in cliffs.
Wherever I went I saw the defects of cyclic existence;
Whoever I met spoke of samsara's flaws;
No matter what I did, my mind remained restless.

"So open the way, for I shall go forth to Dharma practice."
In response his parents said:
"O prince, if you are saddened by the samsaric realm,
Uphold the kingdom and make offerings to the Three Jewels.

"With compassion make the poor and the destitute content;
Create sacred books and always support the monastic community;
Cultivate love and compassion free of discrimination.
If you conduct yourself in this manner, you will always be happy."

To this, the prince replied:
"If you love me, my sole father, listen to me.
In this palace of precious gems and gold,
I'll be bound tightly with unyielding silk knots;
I will be afflicted in this palace indeed.

"As I observe well [the nature of] this cyclic existence
And reflect on the sufferings of all sentient beings,
I feel no sense of attachment to this kingdom,
Not even the size of a saliva drop.

"Six times during day and night,
I reflect on the extensive defects of a householder's life.
Toward the seductive daughters of Māra, though enchanting,
I feel not even a fleeting instant of attraction.

"When I view all of this false appearance [of the world],
I see no distinction, not even the slightest,
Between the three sweets—sugar, molasses, and honey—
And impurities like a leper's brain, dog's meat, pus, and blood.[84]

"If there is not even the slightest difference
Between being richly adorned—with beautiful silk clothes
And heavenly ornaments of turquoise and coral—
And wearing a woolen cloak found in the midst of filth,

"I shall go, I shall go to the forest to engage in meditative absorptions;
I shall go to the eight cemeteries to play [all kinds of] sports.
I shall go, I shall go to the land of the ḍākinīs;
I shall go to secret places to generate bliss;
I shall go to seek a fortress in the realm of nonattachment.

"I shall go, I shall go to Summit Mountain;
I shall go to the presence of the most holy Avadhūti.
I shall go, I shall go to the lands of the ḍākinīs;
I shall go savor the supreme taste of Vajrayana.

"I shall go, I shall go to the land of Udhyāna;[85]
I shall go attract the wisdom ḍākinīs as my partners. [19]
I shall go, I shall go to the realm of Akaniṣṭha;[86]
I shall go touch the feet of Vairocana with my crown.

"I shall go, I shall go to the land of Tuṣita;[87]
I shall go seek supreme Maitreya as my teacher.
I shall go, I shall go to all the buddha fields;
I shall go celebrate the joyful feast of Dharma.

"I shall go, I shall go to the land of the noble ones;
I shall go to Sukhāvatī[88] to nurture ecstatic experience.
Do not chain me, do not chain me, O Kalyāṇaśrī.
If you love your son, my sole father, take me to a secure place.

"Do not bind me, do not bind me, O Śrīprabhā.
Mother, if you love your son, connect me to the Dharma.

With affection prepare for me this day
A few provisions—some rice beer and meat,
Some milk, sugar, and honey as well.

"I shall go to the presence of most holy Avadhūti;
I shall go to serve him and to discipline my mind."
Thus sang the excellent prince these words in a song;
He offered these [words] to his parents' ears.

Just as the king of the gandharvas'[89] singing
Stirs the hearts of many,
The parents' hearts were deeply stirred.
Unable to reply, they gave the prince all he desired.

Then with various provisions, such as rice beer,
He left for the forest along with a thousand riders.
Satisfying Avadhūti with all the offerings,
With palms folded, the prince touched the feet of the teacher.
The teacher initiated him into the Mahayana awakening mind.

At that instant, like a universal monarch
Protected from all threats by his surrounding retinue,
The prince was encircled by his riders, none dismounting,
And they shouted merrily ha! ha! and ku! ku!

Setting torches aflame, they offered melodious songs.
After such merriment the teacher said:
"Go to the temple of the dark mountain;
Go to the yogi of glorious Hevajra.[90]

"Go to the yogi of the oath-bound guardian Yama;
Enter the presence of glorious Rāhula;
Take from him initiations and awakening mind instructions.
He, too, was your sublime teacher in the past.
Depart with joy; linger not, but leave straight away."

When the prince heard the teacher's words,
[He set forth] like a great hero embarking on a campaign.

Surrounded by a thousand horsemen wearing full armor,
Wielding axes, hatchets, hammers, and spears,
Shooting arrows into the sky while shouting battle cries and
Singing songs of joy, he and his retinue all charged toward the temple.

At the temple of the dark mountain [20]
Lived the yogi of glorious Hevajra
Teaching an assembly of countless yogis and yoginīs
Classes of tantra from the secret mantra [vehicle].
He saw the arrival of youthful Prince Candra.

Though psychically he knew the prince had come for Dharma,
Out of great compassion he issued a threatening gesture,
Sending forth a lightning bolt upon the prince.
The lightning, reluctant to descend, hovered [momentarily] in the sky
And instead crashed upon the mountain of the tīrthikas'[91] black
    reliquary.
Deeply surprised by this, the yogis asked the prince:
"Against whom is the royal prince waging battle?"

To this the teacher immediately responded:
"For five hundred and fifty-two lives,
He lived the life of a pure learned monk;
Today in Bangala he has been born
As the son of the Dharma king Kalyāṇaśrī.

"Not being attached to his retinue and great kingdom,
He desires to endure the hardships of an ascetic.
From Summit Mountain the master Avadhūti
Prophesied my name, and today he has come here.
Is this not amazing, O fortunate men and women?"

When he spoke thus,
All exclaimed "A la la! Amazing this is indeed;
Wonderful indeed that this great hero has come today!"
From everywhere, near and far, they welcomed him.

The great prince dismounted from his horse;
The thousand riders did the same.
Approaching the abode of the teacher,
The prince respectfully pleaded:

"O sublime teacher, most excellent one, pray listen to me.
Though I wish to renounce home and seek true liberation,
I find myself today in a renowned high family,
And there is a danger I may be trapped in Bangala.

"Although I have sought teachers realized in higher attainments,
Such as Jetari and Bodhibhadra,
Vidyākaukila and Avadhūti,
Still I am not free from the realm of kingship.
I have now been sent to your presence, O teacher.
Initiate me into the Mahayana awakening mind;
Release me decisively from this bondage."

Then the teacher, the excellent hero,
Led the prince alone into the mandala palace[92]
And conferred the Hevajra empowerment,
Giving him the secret name Jñānaguhyavajra.
Day and night showers of instruction rained;
For thirteen days empowerments were performed;
All concluding rites were fully performed as well.

Throughout this time all the members of the retinue
Did not sleep; they strolled around, played sports,
Sang songs, danced, and played various musical instruments.
Apart from the wish "When will the prince come out?" [21]
No other thoughts entered their minds.

On the thirteenth day,
The prince appeared wearing the apparel of Heruka.[93]
Gazing on his subjects, he sang a song of impermanence;[94]
Observing the three spheres, he saw their lack of essence.

Then he sang this melodious song:
"In the sky of ultimate expanse utterly free of elaborations
Resound empty words echoing [reality's] unborn nature.
My kingdom, which resembles a dream object, is devoid of essence.
Subjects are mere deceptions, illusions.

"If I fail to renounce all this and seek enlightenment,
Then I am not a fortunate one who has amassed great merit.
Day and night I shall contemplate the meaning of ultimate nature;
I shall always seek vast and extensive learning."

Then the yogis of [glorious] Hevajra,
The activity yoginīs who represent impermanence,
And the heroes, the yogis who have gained higher attainments—
Eight such terrifying naked male and female adepts—

Holding trumpets of human thigh-bones in their right hands,
Their left hands grasp a human hand whose flesh they tear with their
    teeth,
Shouting aloud from their throats the sounds of *Hūṃ* and *Phat,*
And sprinting fast, they circled around the prince.

"Go to Bangala and transform the king's mind;
Change his mind so that the prince is spared from statecraft;
Take the prince to the presence of excellent Avadhūti;
Dress him in a woolen cloak, and send him with the few provisions of a
    commoner;
Free him from rich silk cushions and give him instead a *kṛṣṇasāra* pelt;
Free him from retinues and horses and let him learn to journey alone.

"Lose no heart, lose no heart, this is the time to seek liberation;
Definitely, this is the time to vanquish [afflictions] with antidotes;
Go this moment," ordered the [excellent] teacher.
Then the prince, in the guise of a realized adept,
And surrounded by a thousand horsemen, mounted his horse.
As he entered the road, he sang the following vajra song:

"In the unborn vajra[95] mind
I have found the immutable Vajra Vehicle;
In the extremely blissful vajra of experience,
Visions of vajra experience dawn [vividly].

"In the vajra of meditation deities, clear and lucid,
Reflections of action free of defects appear;
In the precious vajra mandala of body,
Manifestations of fearlessness, the vajra of no-self, arise.
This secret vajra, the nonconceptual wisdom,
Has certainly won the battle against samsara."

When the prince sang his vajra song,
The great internal minister Vīryavajra,
The great minister Phegöl Rapjom,
The great minister Karmarāja,
And the great minister Abhaya—[22]
These four sang the following lament:

"Emaho! The domain of karma is most powerful indeed;
In the excellent land of Sahor praised by all,[96]
In the town of Bangala, affluent with riches,
Is the palace of golden banners striking to behold.

"Abandoning the extraordinary king Kalyāṇaśrī,
The goddess Śrīprabhā, a mother to all,
And ministers and subjects that are as apparitions,
The excellent prince hastens to the forest.

"Forsaking his horses, elephants, and carriages,
He hastens to journey on foot like a lowly person.
Forsaking heavenly ornaments and silk garments,
He hastens to wear a woolen cloak, a garment of the poor.

"Forsaking his peacock-supported throne and cushions,
He hastens to spread out a *kṛṣṇasāra* pelt inside a hut.
Instead of taking a beautiful goddess for his wife,
He hastens to roam in cemeteries and live on the food of the dead.

O you who shone with light the moment you were born,
Can you part from your loved ones who've gathered here?"

Singing songs of lament, they approached the vicinity.
Everyone, on arriving near the palace,
Sensed this [resolve] as they looked upon the prince.
Like the ten directions' guardians embarking on a campaign,
Dressed in solid armor, the prince inspired awe by his heroism.
Attractive, breathtaking, he was a spectacle of wonder.

Sounds like cymbals and drums resounded.
The ministers felt awed by their own prince,
And for three months even they attired themselves
In combat gear and kept their horses saddled.

Some competed in horsemanship while others sang and danced;
Yet others stood on guard as if engaged in battle;
Male and female yogis jumped and sprinted about;
The prince displayed acts of insanity in the midst of town.

Everyone concluded that the prince would renounce his kingdom;
Saddened to lose [him], they all shed tears wherever they lived.
Like a flock of deer fawns chased by animals of prey,
The prince's parents erupted in cries of grief for their son.

In particular the father uttered the following words:
"*Ema!* O son, when you were born amid auspiciousness,
We observed wondrous signs and felt you would rule the kingdom.
With this thought our hearts were filled with joy and hope.
How is it that now you wish to seek the forests?"

To this the prince replied thus:
"O Dharma king, pray listen.
If I were to rule the kingdom as you advise,
I may live close to you in this brief life, my father;
But in all future lives we would not recognize each other as father
   and son.
With no benefit, it will be a source of grave consequences. [23]

"If, in contrast, I thoroughly renounce the great kingdom
And seek the path of enlightenment that holds definite freedom,
Through all lives we'll join each other with joy and happiness;
So grant me today such an opportunity."

Then his mother uttered the following words:
"What can we do? Though it's most difficult to part from my son,
For all beings the power of karma is the most important force.
O supreme master, permit him to go to Dharma where he is happy;
Let's pray that we will be together perpetually in the future."

Early at dawn the next day, together with the yogis,
The prince ventured forth to the forest;
In Avadhūti's presence he embraced the life of an ascetic.
Free of desire, he studied the Middle Way teachings;
From the age of twelve till he reached eighteen,
While adopting the lifestyle of Avadhūti,
He accomplished study, reflection, and meditation on one seat.

In this way, our most venerable teacher, great compassionate one,
Through persevering despite hundreds of hardships,
Thoroughly renounced his unimaginably great kingdom
As if expelling gobs of spit.
He sought true liberation, the unmistaken freedom.

Therefore as none can rival him,
He is the master of doctrine who has realized all the aims.
To him, I, Dromtönpa, bow my head extremely low
And pay respectful homage until samsara is emptied.
For any stains of exaggeration and omission herein,
O most compassionate one, I seek your forbearance.

From the oceanlike events of the teacher's liberating life, [Dromtönpa]
presented here a broad sketch of the teacher's excellent qualities of how he
renounced his kingdom and sought true liberation.[97]

3. The Story of Atiśa's Voyage to Sumatra[98]
Attributed to Atiśa

I

[24] Homage to the most holy Maitreya and Avalokiteśvara!

I, the monk Dīpaṃkaraśrījñāna, was aboard a ship for thirteen months when I went to the see the teacher Serlingpa. About five months into the journey, to create obstacles for my awakening mind, Maheśvara, the son of the gods, sent hostile storms, and assuming the form of a large sea monster *makara*,[99] he obstructed the boat's bow and sent thunderbolts down upon me from above. At that point, I meditated on loving-kindness and extraordinary compassion, and the hostile storms subsided. I even saw six powerful lightning bolts freeze in the sky. Still the large sea monster makara blocked our passage forward, and because of the storm, the sea had become turbulent. Like a flag fluttering violently in the wind, the large ship tossed about—bouncing, at times lifted high in the air and at others feeling as though thrown into the ocean's depths. Even though the sails in each of the four directions were lowered and four cast-iron balls dropped to the ocean depths [to anchor], gales of wind blew and rattled thunderously, like massive drums being pounded in the four cardinal directions. Powerful and massive lightning bolts continued to strike. Because of this, the members of the retinue grew extremely frightened and trembled with fear.

As I remained balanced in meditative absorption on loving-kindness and compassion, the learned monk Kṣitigarbha supplicated his teacher:[100]

> Rise, rise, O teacher of great compassion!
> As you have no rival on this earth, I beseech you;
> Pray pacify with your great compassion
> These terrors and threats posed today by dark forces.

As I strive to free all beings from the ocean of existence,
The forces of darkness today defy me.
Alas! They send turbulent storms and blazing lightning bolts;
A monstrous makara threatens us from the front.
Most holy teacher, protect us from this grave danger.

The sea is racked by storms, and waves jump high in the air;
Disturbing noises blare, red lightning bolts dance around. [25]
Violently tossed, the ship too is turbulent and unstable;
It jumps high in the air and is thrown down into the water's depths.
O most holy teacher, protect us now from this danger.

In the spacelike [expanse] of your excellent qualities,
Oath-bound guardians hover like garuḍa birds;[101]
Circling about, they dispel all obstacles.
Not protecting us today when we are facing obstacles,
But abiding instead in solitary expanse, how can your compassion be
   so meager?

Now, ḍākinīs, Dharma protectors of inner and outer mantra,
Arhats, and the assembly of heroes and heroines, wisdom deities—
All of you who delight in the forces of light,
From all directions come encircle us here on this great ocean.
Teacher, avert this [danger] with your power of compassion.

The lord Red Yamāntaka,[102] undefeated by anyone,
Who is surrounded by a retinue of terrifying yamas,
The guardian Acala[103] together with the ten wrathful deities,
And the goddess of blazing auspiciousness who guards from eight
   dangers,[104]
O teacher, Dharma king, help avert this [danger] through your
   might.

Most holy blessed Buddha, the master of doctrine,
Most venerable Avalokiteśvara of the stainless mandala circles,
Dharma king father and son,[105] who dispel the sufferings of
   sentient beings,

The time has come now to exert the power of your great
   compassion.
Pray help long perpetuate the river of untainted blessings.

I heard clearly and very well this supplication being delivered. I too saw
Lord Yamāntaka, who was red[106] with a large round belly. His dark brown
hair stood upward, and his bloodshot eyes, open wide, peered in all ten directions. The instant I saw him, it was as if all the hand implements of other
wrathful deities had fallen into his hands, and he wielded his vajra-cudgel in
the sky. With his left hand in a threatening gesture, and circling a lasso over
his head, he swung his vajra-cudgel, which struck Mount Meru, splitting it
down to its base and up to the golden ground beneath. This shook the great
ocean, causing it to boil violently and turning the makara into a mere skele-
ton. [26] The makara then assumed the form of a young boy with bluish face
but with no flesh at all [on his body]. He entered the ship and made prostrations and, with his palms folded, made the following plea:

O king of wrathful deities, most mighty one,
O great compassionate one, the sole refuge of all beings,
I have wronged you by causing grave danger.
Protect me today through your great compassion.

As he pleaded in this manner, I too picked up a cudgel in my hand and
exclaimed:

Hūṃ! I'm the grand master of the life of all beings.
Due to the power of my great compassion,
I have mercifully not annihilated you.
From now on never teach my students
The false paths of the heretics,
Or false practices such as divination and animism,[107]
For I now own your very being and life force.

After I uttered these words, he offered this penitent reply:

O great compassion, pray attend to me.
I shall never show your students
Any of the false teachings.

Bear me in your thoughts with compassion.
You are [now] the master of my life force.

Then from the furnace arose a white man who was heard to utter this:

You've not traveled across the land of snows
Confined in this Nepalese ship;[108]
You've not traveled to the small islands,
Such as the island of copper [mines],
For they all are barred by water.
Bhrūm hri yakṣa

Thereupon the entire storm calmed down; the [violent] waves, the lightning, and the noises disappeared, and the ship regained its course. Everyone sighed with relief and began joyfully conversing with each other.

Still, without dismantling my generation stage [visualization] of wrathful Yamāntaka, I stood by, leaving rainbow beams around the ship's deck, and swung down my vajra-cudgel as if it were a staff. The ship became as stable as a vast landmass with no turbulence. As I looked about, wondering what was happening, I heard the laughter of youthful maidens. When I looked, there in the ocean was the king of wrathful deities Acala standing with his two legs submerged up to his knees. Like a strong young man holding a container in his arms, he held the ship from its two ends and lifted it to his crown, which was up in the clouds. On the edge of the ship were twenty-one young maidens with their faces turned outward. They were exclaiming, "O brothers and sisters, had it not been for us, there could have been a great crisis today." [27]

Then I made the following supplication:

Homage to the lady who protects from the eight dangers;
Homage to the lady who sets ablaze the glory of auspiciousness;
Homage to the lady who closes the doors to the lower realms;
Homage to the lady who leads us on the path to the higher realms;
You have always sustained me in your care;
Guard me still with your great compassion.

As I appealed thus, the maidens replied, "If it were not for your son Kṣiti-garbha, [we would have not known]. Just as we were entertaining the thought 'Let us reduce the heretic city Svabhāvanātha[109] to ashes,' we heard your prayer."

They continued: "Alas! Supreme among all beings is this great bodhisattva. We have come here to help him. If, in the future, this youth with a blue face recovers, strike him."

"Youth, from this day, do not attack this Nepalese ship," [they commanded].

Then they exhorted Kṣitigarbha: "O most venerable one, shoot this bolt of the sky[110] and strike Svabhāvanātha with it. We, the ladies, shall bear responsibility for [any possible transgression of] the precepts of refuge and the generation of the awakening mind."[111]

By holding one thunderbolt with a threatening gesture, the most learned Kṣitigarbha wielded it and shot it to the north of the heretic city Svabhāvanātha, where the goddess Cacika resides. The heretics' temple and the goddess were both annihilated. He shot forth another [bolt of lightning] and struck the image of Maheśvara, splitting it in two from the head down. A fragment from this hit the *tirthika* king, causing the right part of his body to become paralyzed. Another fragment struck the palace of the Turukas[112] in the hinterlands, and it is said that for thirteen years the incursions of Mongol hordes to Bodhgaya ceased. One fragment struck the Black Tent palace of the Shangshung king, causing the destruction of the teachings of Bön.[113] The one or two that were left were chased away and escaped, it is said, into the Kailash mountain range. With another fragment the palace of Dark Poison Sea in the south was demolished, which, it is said, brought an end to the disease of leprosy.[114] One fragment struck Laṅka, the land of rākṣasas,[115] reducing to ashes the palace of the rākṣasa king Laṅkapuri, and the lineage of the man-eating rākṣasas was brought to an end. Kṣitigarbha was then heard to exclaim the following words of pride:

I am the master of this mandala of earth;
Run, run, forces of evil, for I shall reduce you to ashes.
I, a great hero, am the lord of the land;[116]
In Udhyāna the neighing of the Hayagrīva horse [head] resounds
  aloud;
Annihilate! Annihilate! Annihilate Maheśvara to mere dust;
Steal away the powers of the gods of animism. [28]

Oṃ padmantakrita śvata hayaṃgriva hulu hulu hūṃ phat[117]

Then the king of wrathful deities Acala and the Blessed [Yamāntaka] both suddenly disappeared. I too found myself seated on my cushion in my [normal] form as a monk. All the members of my retinue felt deep admiration and exclaimed the following:

> Spontaneously arising and uncontrived,
> O Dharma king, you resemble Mount Meru.
> You, who bear the name of Jñāna,[118]
> Have [today] made us all content.

> Emaho! O mighty and glorious protector;
> O Tathāgata, as we are threatened
> With terror here in the ocean,
> Without fail pray protect us
> Within the fold of your great compassion.

They had been unable to move anywhere for twenty-one days, but the moment the retinue was freed from the terror, the sails were hoisted in all four directions, and the massive cast-iron anchors were pulled up. Assisted by favorable winds, the ship sailed for a month and a half both day and night without interruption.

Seven months into the journey, another storm arose, pushing them back to a distance of a day's voyage. However, as we prayed to the teachers, the Three Jewels, the ḍākinīs, and the protectors, the storm calmed down. However, the winds that could blow us in the right direction were not strong. Due to the [inadequate] merit among the sentient beings on the ship, we were thus stranded for about half a month. Then, by cultivating loving-kindness and compassion, we sailed in accord with a favorable wind. So in two months and twenty-six days, we went from shore to shore across the ocean.

Thus ends the story of how Atiśa conquered Maheśvara in the ocean and coped with adversities, which is part of the tale of how Atiśa endured hardships for the sake of finding his teacher. This is indeed a source of wonder.

II

Homage to the most venerable Maitreya and Avalokiteśvara!

Immediately after crossing the great ocean, I [Atiśa] went to the site of the golden reliquary of the Tathāgata built by a Tibetan king,[119] where lived six meditator monks,[120] students of the teacher Serlingpa. This reliquary was located to the west of the forests of Sumatra, to the south of the joyful lotuses, to the north of the dangerous mires, and to the east of the sea monster Kekeru.[121] [29] I spent fourteen days there enquiring after the liberating life story of the teacher Serlingpa. I found out what spiritual practices the teacher undertook as his heart practice, what scriptures he accepted as authoritative, what treatises and systems of thought he had mastered, what scriptural knowledge and reasoning methods he embodied, what levels of realization he had attained, and to what degree he had trained his mind. On all these points I questioned the meditators, and they explained these things to me without exaggeration or omission. Because of this, I experienced such joy as if I had attained a bodhisattva ground.

The meditators in turn asked the learned Kṣitigarbha and others the biographical details of the teacher. He explained how I [Atiśa] had renounced my kingdom and sought the life of a renunciate, how I had relied on countless teachers, how I had overseen countless monasteries, and how I had mastered great knowledge. To this the meditators responded, "Is it possible that this great paṇḍita is the Indian master known as Dīpaṃkaraśrījñāna?"

Kṣitigarbha replied:

> He is hailed in the entire world as the second Buddha;
> He is venerated by all fifty-two learned paṇḍitas;
> He is praised by the followers of both Great and Lesser Vehicles;
> He is known universally as the great Indian master.

All the meditators responded:

> O lord of the land, welcome to our abode.
> Though saddened before by only hearing your fame,
> Today we have become fortunate indeed.
> Welcome, O great scholar; you have arrived by ship.
> Were you disturbed by māras in your course?

Did the sea monster and storms throw up obstacles?
Did you long suffer any lack of provisions?

Kṣitigarbha replied:

For thirteen months we sailed aboard the ship.
Maheśvara harassed us with *makara* and violent storms.
In an instant, through love and compassion,
Māra was defeated, and we found the good fortune of safety.

Again as our sea voyage continued,
Since the most holy teacher has mastery over the sky treasury,[122]
The hundred and twenty-five passengers did not suffer [from hunger].
   [30]
Adversities were pacified with words of truth.

When Kṣitigarbha uttered these words, the meditators were delighted, and
with great joy they approached where I was sitting and respectfully uttered
the following plea:

When we heard your fame from afar,
With joy in our hearts we yearned to see you.
When the great scholar came here today,
We erred due to our veil of ignorance.[123]
Now with our body, speech, and mind,
With deepest respect, we pay you homage.

With this they prostrated in front of me; and abandoning pride, I also prostrated before them with respect. Again all the meditators exclaimed:

Please explain to us, O most excellent being,
What the purpose is of your visit here.
With reverence we shall help you to pursue your goal;
Do tell us what you seek.

I responded:

I've come here to be in the presence of the teacher of Serling;
I've come here to seek the essence of human existence;
Please go to the teacher and convey my request,
Thus opening the way for [the fulfillment of] my wish.

Then the meditators went to the teacher Serlingpa and pleaded:

O sublime teacher, pray listen to us. The Indian master known as Dīpaṃkaraśrījñāna is currently here in our region with his retinue of a hundred and twenty-five students. For thirteen months in the ocean, he chained Māra and the tīrthika god Maheśvara with loving-kindness and compassion. Now without loss of any majesty of his body, speech, and mind, he has arrived here. For fourteen days we engaged with him in conversations pertaining to Dharma; we developed deep admiration for him and feel content. Now to convey the main point, the great scholar has come to see you. He wishes to listen primarily to the mother [the Perfection of Wisdom scriptures] that gives birth to all the conquerors of the three times, to generate the aspiring and engaging aspects of the mind of supreme awakening, to train his mind in the Mahayana, and to immerse himself both day and night in the teacher's oceanlike treatises. So, out of great compassion, please open the way for him.

Hearing these words, the teacher Serlingpa said:

Welcome, O lord of the land;
Welcome, O royal prince; [31]
Welcome, O great scholar;
Welcome, O master of beings.

Welcome, O great hero;
Welcome! You've come with your retinue.
Wonderful indeed that you've endured great hardships;
Wonderful indeed that you've defeated Maheśvara;
Wonderful indeed that you were victorious over the adverse forces.

Wonderful indeed that the banner of your fame is fluttering;
Wonderful indeed that you've arrived unharmed.
O monks, put on your ceremonial robes
And welcome this most excellent being.

In this way, standing at the head of 535 monks all clad in the three robes of similar colors, holding small water bottles and staffs[124] and possessing the extremely peaceful demeanor of arhats, the teacher Serlingpa extended his welcome. He was joined also by 62 novices. In brief, in single file, 597 monastics welcomed me from a distance.

Instantly, I felt deeply moved and experienced a profound joy, thinking how the blessed Buddha must have been surrounded by arhats in this way when he was alive. At this point I loaded two elephants with various articles and had four lay practitioners take charge of all the possessions. To put on a display for the teacher, I had all the paṇḍitas learned in the five fields of knowledge and all the monks versed in the three scriptural collections—not excluding a single one—dressed in sandals and clad in the three robes excellently dyed with the Kashmiri saffron praised by the Mahāsāṃghika tradition. Due to the auspiciousness of the occasion, all of them held metal alms bowls of perfect size and free of cracks and holes, as well as copper water containers capable of carrying one *dre,*[125] according to the Magadha measurement system. They also carried the monk staffs praised by the Master of Doctrine and that contained all the required features intact with their corresponding symbolism. All the paṇḍitas wore hats symbolizing their absence of pride and held white tail-fans.

The congregation of great paṇḍitas included Drowa Sangpo, Dharma-mitra, Puṇyākara, Vīryavajra, Devamati, Sūryagupta, Kṣitigarbha, Jñāna-garbha, Vāgīśvara, Dhānaśrīmitra, Prajñābhadra, Candrabhadra, Samantabhadra, Guhyagarbha, Matinanta, [32] Gyatso Balap, Rirap Gyalpo, and Pawo Rölpa.[126] There were also one hundred and eight monks, such as Jñānabhadra, who were versed in the three scriptural collections. There were thirteen novice monks and four great fully ordained monks. Thus one hundred and twenty-five monks followed behind me, all in a close line, not touching but leaving a space of one person in between. Neither too close nor too far apart and resembling a five-colored rainbow, we all went to where teacher Serlingpa was residing. Since all the conditions were perfectly gathered, the gods let descend a rain of flowers.

Although I had close connections with the teacher in lives since beginningless time, I had not yet received instructions from him in this life. Behind me were many great learned paṇḍitas, and together we paid our homage. Since I had made sure that we all possessed complete higher qualities, beginning with the ethical discipline of individual liberation, it was as if all our hearts were one and the same. We shared the same view and conduct, and everyone was a student following in my footsteps. Unable to bear the majesty of my highly learned students and myself, the teacher and his retinue all made reciprocal prostrations as if falling to the ground.

Serlingpa then performed a consecration that caused me later to become revered by all, Indians and Tibetans. At that time, I filled a precious jewel vase—one with a large body, a firm flat base, a long neck, and a spout protruding from its mouth—with gold, silver, pearls, coral, and lapis lazuli, and offered the vase to the teacher. Everyone else each offered a gold coin. The teacher Serlingpa then queried in verse to determine if there were any obstacles on the path:

Welcome, O upholder of monastic ethics;
Welcome, the one clad in discipline;
Welcome, O great compassionate one;
O Dharma king, you have come here.

Your fame is great [even] from afar;
Welcome, it is indeed good to see you.
In the Dharma palace of India,
Performing vast deeds for sentient beings,
With compassion free of prejudice,
Have you been a refuge, an ally, and a friend?

Learned one, have you been industrious from your depths?
Have you been nurtured by many spiritual teachers?
Have you been honored by many learned scholars? [33]
Wonderful it is indeed that you have come here today.

O master of beings, I have heard that
For thirteen months you've sailed the ocean;
Amazing is your endurance of hardship.
I have heard that you defeated the black Īśvara.

Amazing indeed is the extent of your renown;
Amazing is your surmounting of dangers.
O learned one, were your mind and body
Not exhausted by this long journey?

With compassion, were you not saddened
By the jealousy of the dark forces?
Welcome, O most excellent being.
Here we are but a few scattered residents.

Most of us are engaged in learning and reflection;
Others have come here to see you.
Fortunate it is indeed that we meet today.
Now let us enter the monastery.

Let's go to the courtyard where congregations gather;
We can share tales of your journey in due course.
Let us converse in accord with the Dharma.

I then offered the following response:

Yes, I've come; I come from central India;
I come with freedom from obstructive factors.
I've flourished due to the glory of the Three Jewels' kindness.
Through powerful rites, black Īśvara was defeated.

Our three doors triumphed over the dark forces.
Unharmed, we have arrived in good health.
O conqueror, are you living splendidly,
Undeterred from the welfare of beings?

By perfectly elucidating the ocean of treatises,
Are you immersed in its brilliance?
By vanquishing the entire host of māras,
Are you residing in the ocean of wisdom?

You are the most learned in Sumatra.
With love and compassion you look after

The welfare of all beings both day and night
And reside as a master of doctrine, I've heard.

So, all-knowing one,
As I appeal to you to be my teacher,
Please expand my understanding
In the vast sphere of knowledge.

As I made this request, all the monks joined in unison:

Welcome, O most excellent one.
Together with you we too shall
Become sated by the bliss of sublime Dharma.

The residents and visitors together went to the courtyard of the monastic community. An elder was in the midst of teaching a group of monks. I prostrated to him, but he did not prostrate in return. Then, with a golden parasol hoisted above, [34] we entered the teacher's residence, and as we were seated, the elder completed his teaching session and prostrated to me in full accordance with the teachings, saying, "I did not welcome you when you arrived here, O most excellent one. However, I have no conceit, for I believe that to please a sublime being is to act according to the Dharma."[127]

When I heard these words, I admired him. I felt that it was an amazing expression of the greatness of the teacher [Serlingpa] and his teachings. Then, as the groundwork had been well laid, indicating the immensity of the interdependent factors that led to this auspicious occasion, the teacher gave a clear elucidation in fifteen sessions of the *Ornament of Clear Realizations*.[128] He thus perfectly conferred this teaching upon me. Following this, I set up residence in the palace of silver parasols and spent my time pursuing study, reflection, and meditation.

All of this relates the account of Atiśa's journey to Sumatra and his meeting with great joy the peerless great Serlingpa Dharmakīrti, the lord of all beings.[129]

Most excellent is this glorious ocean of wonders![130]
Bless me so that I may train in the awakening mind for all;
Bless me so that I may free the numberless beings from samsara;

Bless me so that renunciation and revulsion [toward samsara] arise
  in me.
Born of royal lineage, he was learned in all five fields of knowledge.
As prophesied by Tārā, he came to the glorious land of snows.
Trained in cherishing others more than self, he engaged in others'
  welfare—
To you, O unrivaled Atiśa, I make supplications.
Confer blessings upon me this very instant.

Instantly remove the sufferings of beings.
Eliminate all the miseries of cyclic existence.
Clear away the obstacles to Dharma practice.
Bless me so that I may have nothing to do but practice Dharma.

Due to making such fervent supplications without interruption, may the
uncontrived precious awakening mind exchanging self and others, which is
the pure altruistic thought that cherishes others more than one's own self,
arise in all sentient beings, both self and others, equal to [the expanse of]
space. May I [thus] be born soon as a great navigator who will liberate all
beings.

4. Root Lines of Mahayana Mind Training[131]

Attributed to Atiśa

[35] Homage to the sovereign who has accomplished all purposes and who is the glorious auspicious jewel swiftly endowing others with great happiness.

1

First, train in the preliminaries.
For the main practice, train alternately in giving and taking.
There are three objects, three poisons, and three roots of virtue—
This, in brief, is the instruction for subsequent practice.

2

Commence the sequence of taking from your own self.
Place the two astride your breath.
In brief, this is the distilled essence of instruction:
In all actions, train by means of the words.

3

Relate whatever you can to meditation right now.
When both are present, take them all.
Train constantly toward the chosen objects.

4

Banish all blames to the single source.
Toward all beings contemplate their great kindness.
Train in the three difficult challenges.
There are two tasks—one at the start and one at the end.

5

Contemplate the three that are free of degeneration.
Train constantly in the three general points.
Transform your attitudes but remain as you are.
Adopt the three principal conditions.
Train in the five powers.

6

The intent of all teachings converges on a single point.
Of the two witnesses uphold the principal one.[132]
Cultivate constantly the joyful mind alone;
If this can be done even when distracted, you are trained.

    i.   Do not torment with malicious banter.
    ii.   Do not boast of your good deeds.
    iii.   Do not be ill-tempered.
    iv.   Do not be boisterous.
    v.   Do not be fickle.
    vi.   Do not lie in ambush.
    vii.   Do not place the load of a dzo onto an ox.
    viii.   Do not sprint to win a race.
    ix.   Do not maintain inappropriate loyalty.
    x.   Do not be sporadic.
    xi.   Do not abuse this practice.
    xii.   Be released through the two: investigation and close analysis.
    xiii.   Train with decisiveness.
    xiv.   Be endowed with the three inseparable factors.

7

Accomplish all yogas through a single means.
If relapsed, meditate on it as the very remedy.
Whichever of the two arises, bear them both;
Do not speak of the defects [of others].

8

Do not dwell on others' shortcomings.
Do not turn the gods into demons.
Do not seek misery as a means to happiness.
Do not depend on other conditions.

xv. Recognize what is primary.
xvi. Forsake all expectations of reward.
xvii. Discard poisonous food.
xviii. Do not strike at the heart.

9
This proliferation of the five degenerations
Is transformed into the path of enlightenment.
When stability is attained, reveal the secret.

10
This distilled essence of pith instructions
Stems from the lineage of most sublime masters.

These are the root lines. This was composed by Atiśa.

5. Annotated Root Lines
of Mahayana Mind Training[133]

[36] Homage to the sovereign who has accomplished all purposes and who is the glorious auspicious jewel swiftly granting all happiness.

1

First, a trainee whose mind is trained in the three scopes and who, having taken the aspiring and engaging [aspects of the awakening mind], is cognizant of the precepts should[134] train in the preliminaries by reflecting on the human existence of leisure and opportunity, on karma and its fruits, and on the defects of cyclic existence.

Contemplate all phenomena—encompassed by self and others, the outer environment, and the inner sentient beings—as dreamlike, nonexistent but appearing to exist due to the force of the deluded mind.[135]

Experience, free of identification, the thoroughly unborn nature of awareness, which cognizes in such manner.

The remedy, which cuts across both body and mind, is itself freed in its natural place, free of grasping at existence and nonexistence.

During the interval between sessions, that is, afterward, create the illusion-like person as it arises on the basis of the above two.

2

Train alternately in the two—giving (to others of your body, resources, and roots of virtue) and taking.

Place the two (giving and taking) astride your breath as it exits.

There are three objects (the desirable, the undesirable, and the neutral), three poisons (attachment, anger, and delusion), and (their exterminations) three roots of virtue.

In all your actions (such as when gathering [merit] and so on) train by directing the focus of your mind by means of the words.

3
The negativities (and their fruit) of the world (the external) and beings (the inner) within cyclic existence and the afflictions[136]—

Transform the adverse conditions (derived from either sentient beings or the natural elements) into aids on the path of enlightenment.

How is this so? Whatever undesirable events befall, banish all the blames to the single source, which is not others but rather self-grasping.

Toward all beings (humans, nonhumans, enemies, friends, and in particular the perpetrators of harm), contemplate their great kindness.

4
Contemplating the illusions arising from your mind as the four (as presented in your palms) buddha bodies, that is, the adverse forces and their antidotes[137]—

Emptiness (all in the nature of mind) is among protection unsurpassed.

The fourfold practice (making offerings to meditation deities and teachers, purifying negative karma, giving offerings to the harmful forces, and propitiating the Dharma protectors) is the most excellent method.

Relate whatever you can (adverse conditions such as the arising of intense suffering or afflictions) to your meditation right now.[138]

5
In brief, to present the points of the practice of a lifetime, the essence of instruction is this:[139]

Apply yourself to the five powers[140]—intention, familiarity, positive seed, eradication, and aspiration.

As the Perfection Vehicle, **Mahayana's transference instruction is** [37] **the five powers** (noted above) **alone, their practice** in particular **is vital**, that is, treat this with critical importance.[141]

The intent of all teachings converges on a single point: whether or not it can help subdue you.

6

Of the two witnesses (between others' speech and your own mind, train your mind by ensuring that you do not disgrace yourself, but train in accordance with your aspiration) **uphold the principal one.**

Cultivate constantly the joyful mind alone.

If this can be done even when distracted, you (your mind) **are trained in** the remedies.

Train constantly in the three general points[142] to ensure that your mind training does not violate your precepts and that it does not become sarcastic.

7

Transform your attitudes (the aspirations of self-grasping) **but remain as you are** with respect to the objectives that have not been assigned.

Do not speak of the defects [of others] in conduct of body and speech.

Do not dwell on others' (those who have entered the spiritual order, in particular) **shortcomings.**

Discard all expectations of reward as a fruit of practicing mind training, in either this life or the future life, including even the attainment of buddhahood.

    i. **Discard poisonous food** (the virtues mixed with the false views and self-grasping).

ii. **Do not maintain** [inappropriate] **loyalty** that retaliates against harms caused by others.
iii. **Do not torment with malicious banter** that hurts others in the heart.
iv. **Do not lie in ambush** to take revenge.
v. **Do not strike at the heart** anyone, whether human or nonhuman.
vi. **Do not place the load of a dzo** (the undesirable accusations and their burden) **onto an ox.**[143]
vii. **Do not sprint** (by giving an advantage to yourself when what you desire is owned communally) **to win the race** but instead accept the defeat.
viii. **Do not abuse the practice,** seeking victory for yourself.
ix. **Do not turn gods** (the mind training) **into demons.**
x. **Do not seek misery for others as a means to happiness** for yourself.

8
Accomplish all yogas (the yoga of eating and so on) **through** not others but **a single means.**

There are two tasks to pursue—**one at the start** (in the morning) **and one at the end** (in the evening).

Whichever of the two (benefit and so on) **arises, bear them both** without conceit or dejection.

Guard the two (the precepts revealed in the teachings in general and the precepts presented in this [mind training teaching] in particular) **even at the cost of your life.**[144]

9
Train (on the basis of a qualified teacher, the ability to channel your mind, and the coming together of the external and internal conditions) **in the three difficult challenges:** the difficulty of recalling the antidotes of the afflictions [at the beginning], the difficulty of averting them in the middle, and the difficulty of exterminating their continuum.

Adopt the three principal conditions.

Contemplate the three ([undiminished] reverence for your teacher [and so on]) **that are free of degeneration.**

Be endowed with the three inseparable factors, as if your body, speech, and mind were competing [among themselves in their accumulation of] the three virtuous activities.[145]

10

Train constantly toward the chosen objects: those living together [with you], those hostile toward you, and those unappealing to you.

Those who have the good fortune to practice this mind training should adopt a standpoint such that they **do not depend on other conditions.**

If relapsed, take this inability to realize when practicing mind training as your very basis, and **meditate on it as the remedy itself.** [38]

Engage in the principal practices right now—especially bodhisattvas on the beginner's level—now that you have obtained the human life of leisure and opportunity and encountered the sublime spiritual teacher.[146]

 xi. **Do not apply misplaced understanding.**[147] Learn to cultivate joy in the virtuous activities and do not engage in the six [distorted understandings], such as [misplaced] heedfulness.
 xii. **Do not be sporadic,** sometimes training and sometimes not.
 xiii. **Train with decisiveness** the task of measuring whether you can do this.
 xiv. **Be released,** whether or not your mindstream has attained familiarity with the examples, **through the two: investigation and close analysis** (when self-grasping arises).
 xv. **Do not boast** to anyone, ever, when you engage in the practice **of your good deeds.**
 xvi. **Do not be ill-tempered,** regardless of how others treat you.
 xvii. **Do not be fickle,** fluctuating in your expressions of likes and dislikes.
 xviii. **Do not be boisterous,** [even] in words of thanks.

11

Like a diamond, like the sun, and like a tree in full blossom, including even medicines—[148]

Understand (such as the purpose of practice and so on) **the words, their meanings** (the words and their contents), **and so on.**

Through this proliferation of the five degenerations due to the abundance of conditions for practicing mind training

[Everything] is transformed into aids to the path of enlightenment.

The heart practice of Atiśa, the instruction that has stemmed from Maitreya (The Blessed One transmitted it to Maitreya; he to Asaṅga; he to Vasubandhu; he to Kusalī the elder; he to Kusalī Jr.; and he transmitted it to the teacher Serlingpa.) is concluded.

II

12
Relinquish all biases (those negative acts—done out of attraction to the gods' realms, or related to wealth or loss—that are the causes [of suffering] of yourself and others).[149]

Transform everything (the degenerate era and the afflictions, which are the underlying motives) into the Mahayana path.

Cherish your training toward the entire human race (all yogas, and all conduct), all its breadth and depth, for as each moment of consciousness arises, this [training sees it as] in the nature of suffering and so on.

Train in both the main (the two—giving and taking—and the precepts; [Combat] not the gods, demons, and so on, but rather the self-grasping) and the secondary practices.

13
Apply abstention and adoption forcefully with regard to the fierce one.[150]

Transform the adverse factors into aids of practice.

Destroy all rationalizations, for example, losing your enthusiasm for giving and taking because of thoughts like "Others are harming me."

Purify first whichever affliction is strongest by examining your mind and applying the antidotes against whatever is strongest. [Purify also]

discriminatory thoughts, such as "near and distant," "love and hate," "high and low."

14
Train without partiality toward [any] **object,** for if you settle your mind in this [training], everything turns into an aid.[151]

This greatly surpasses all other virtues; even merely hearing about it as news again and again [enhances] its potency.

When both are present, [39] since you have discarded sufferings, you can **take them all** (those of others).

Learn to ensure ease in your practice. Although this is advice pertaining to an achieved objective, you must integrate it right from the start.

15
Begin the sequence of taking from your own self such as those [sufferings] you are likely to experience toward the latter part of your life, [the sufferings of] your actual mother, [and so on].

The defining characteristic of the act (the practice of exchanging self and others) **is that of letting go** of attachment and clinging to all—to this life and future lives, to cyclic existence and its transcendence [nirvana].[152]

The sign that you are trained is when you are endowed with the five [marks of] **greatness,** the foremost of which is the practice of a fully ordained monk, an upholder of monastic ethics).

    xix. **Do not be a stranger,** but instead relate to others affectionately with the awakening mind.[153]
    xx. **Do not give "clarifications"** of [others'] negative acts and shortcomings, for this prevents your realization.
    xxi. **Do not harbor expectations** (of others).

This is the end.

III

  xxii. **Take many,** for you are aware of the discarding of others' sufferings.

  xxiii. **In the future, always put on the armor** with the thought "I shall not allow myself to fall prey to all the conditions that preoccupy me in my life."

  xxiv. **When stability is attained, reveal the secret:** the two (giving and taking), the profound meaning (the experience of the exchanging of self and others) [the relation between] negative karma and suffering, and so on.

This concludes the treatise on mind training. This was composed by master Atiśa. May goodness prevail!

6. Seven-Point Mind Training[154]
Chekawa Yeshé Dorjé (1101–75)

I. Presentation of the preliminaries, the basis
First, train in the preliminaries.

II. Training in the awakening mind, the main practice
A. Training in ultimate awakening mind
Train to view all phenomena as dreamlike.

Examine the nature of the unborn awareness.
The remedy, too, is freed in its own place.
Place your mind on the basis-of-all, the actual path.

In the intervals be a conjurer of illusions.

B. Training in conventional awakening mind
Train in the two—giving and taking—alternately.

Place the two astride your breath.
There are three objects, three poisons, and three roots of virtue.
In all actions, train by means of the words.

III. Taking adverse conditions onto the path of enlightenment
When the world and its inhabitants boil with negativity,
Transform adverse conditions into the path of enlightenment.
Banish all blames to the single source.
Toward all beings contemplate their great kindness.

With the three views and treasury of space,
The yoga of protection is unexcelled.
By meditating on illusions as the four buddha bodies,
Emptiness is protection unsurpassed.

The fourfold practice is the most excellent method.
Relate whatever you can to meditation right now.

IV. Presentation of a lifetime's practice in summary
In brief the essence of instruction is this:
Apply yourself to the five powers.
As Mahayana's transference method is
The five powers alone, their practice is vital.

V. Presentation of the measure of having trained the mind
The intent of all teachings converges on a single point.
Of the two witnesses uphold the principal one.
Cultivate constantly the joyful mind alone.
If this can be done even when distracted, you are trained.

VI. Presentation of the commitments of mind training
Train constantly in the three general points.
Transform your attitudes but remain as you are.

Do not speak of the defects [of others].
Do not reflect on others' shortcomings.
Discard all expectations of reward.
Discard poisonous food.
Do not maintain inappropriate loyalty.
Do not torment with malicious banter.
Do not lie in ambush.
Do not strike at the heart.
Do not place the load of a dzo onto an ox.
Do not sprint to win a race.
Do not abuse this [practice] as a rite.
Do not turn the gods into demons.
Do not seek misery as a means to happiness.

VII. Presentation of the precepts of mind training
Accomplish all yogas through a single means.
Overcome all errors through a single means.
There are two tasks—one at the start and one at the end.
Forbear whichever of the two arises.

Guard the two even at the cost of your life.
Train in the three difficult challenges.
Adopt the three principal conditions.
Contemplate the three that are free of degeneration.

Be endowed with the three inseparable factors.
Train constantly toward the chosen objects.
Do not depend on other conditions.
Engage in the principal practices right now.

Do not apply misplaced understanding.
Do not be sporadic.
Train with decisiveness.
Be released through the two: investigation and close analysis.
Do not boast of your good deeds.
Do not be ill-tempered.
Do not be fickle.
Do not be boisterous.

Through this proliferation of the five degenerations
Transform [every event] into the path of enlightenment.

Because of my numerous aspirations,
I have defied the tragic tale of suffering
And have taken instructions to subdue self-grasping.
Now, even if death comes, I have no regrets.

7. A Commentary on the "Seven-Point Mind Training"[155]

Sé Chilbu Chökyi Gyaltsen (1121–89)

[41] Your precious body is the source of all goodness;

In the midst of the darkness of ignorance of the three worlds
You uphold the pure light that illuminates the path to liberation—
To you, Serlingpa, who are true to your excellent name,[156] I bow
my head.

Following his full enlightenment Lord Śākyamuni turned the wheel of Dharma three times, and after his entry into nirvana, the authors of the commentarial treatises elucidated these [three turnings]. Through the combination of the Buddha's sacred words and the commentarial treatises, [the teachings] flourished extensively in the world.

The doctrine is taught in two vehicles, namely the Great Vehicle and the Lesser Vehicle; the Great Vehicle is divided further into two—Mantra[157] and Perfection. As far as their subject matter is concerned, all of these vehicles present, either directly or indirectly, the elimination of self-grasping and the cherishing of others—the two themes. Since there is only the self-grasping to be eliminated and the well-being of others to be sought, those engaged in the practice of the Buddha's teaching must understand how to relate whatever practice they undertake to these two endeavors. You should practice in such a manner. If you are able to, your Dharma practice will then be free of error, and you will arrive at the enlightened intent of the Buddha.

"Can these two points be practiced adequately on the basis of reading the treatises?"

No. The tantras are tangled, the main treatises are disorganized, and the pith instructions remain concealed. Sealed within six parameters,[158] they require dependence on the teacher's instructions [to understand]. In particular, in the context of our present uncommon Mahayana instruction, Atiśa possessed the instructions of three teachers. First, he possessed what he received from his teacher Dharmarakṣita. This teacher gave away even parts of his own body by cutting flesh from his thighs. Atiśa stated that although Dharmarakṣita's philosophical views were inferior, based on this practice alone, one can be certain that he had attained the great seal [of perfection]. His philosophical standpoint was that of the Vaibhāṣika tenets of the Disciple's School, his scriptural authority was *Garland of Three Clubs*,[159] while his analytic reasoning was [based on] Aśvaghoṣa's *Ornament of Sutras*[160] and the *Jātaka Tales*.[161] [42]

Second, Atiśa possessed the instructions received from Maitrīyogi.[162] He was the junior Kusalī brother, and he was known as Maitrīyogi because he meditated solely on Maitreya with special focus. His philosophical standpoint was that of nonabiding [Middle Way], his scriptural authority was the sutra on the *Questions of Ākāśagarbha;*[163] while in his analytic reasoning he followed Śāntideva's *Guide to the Bodhisattva's Way of Life*[164] and the *Compendium of Trainings*.[165]

Third, Atiśa also possessed the instruction he received from his teacher Serlingpa. Serlingpa's philosophical standpoint was akin to that of the non-Buddhist schools that, without relinquishing self-grasping, use it as the very ground for training. His scriptural authority was the *Teachings of Vimalakirti*,[166] while in his analytic reasoning he followed the *Levels of the Bodhisattva*.[167] This instruction stems from Ārya Maitreya. The present teaching belongs to the instructions received from teacher Serlingpa.

This, in turn, is based on the following statement from the *Teachings of Vimalakirti*:

> [Egoistic] viewing of the perishable composite is the seed of the tathāgata.[168]

Just as a lotus does not grow out of a well-leveled soil but from the mire, in the same way the awakening mind is not born in the hearts of disciples in whom the moisture of attachment has dried up. It grows instead in the hearts of ordinary sentient beings who possess in full all the fetters of bondage. Therefore, in dependence upon this self-grasping, it is possible to cultivate the awakening mind that exchanges self and others, which is the uncommon cause for attaining buddhahood. This very self-grasping is, therefore, the "bone" of the buddhas.

Since the teacher Serlingpa gave this to him as the kernel of his spiritual practice, Atiśa accorded great respect and reverence to this particular teacher, more so than to his other teachers. Atiśa stated, "The little warm-heartedness that I possess is due to the kindness of my teacher Serlingpa. Because of this, my lineage has blessings." Again, Atiśa is reported to have asserted that no remedy in either the Mantra or the Perfection vehicles can be an adequate substitute for entering the gateway of this spiritual practice. Atiśa bestowed this [teaching] upon the spiritual mentor Dromtönpa as his heart remedy practice. Although Dromtönpa had many disciples, his principal students were the three brothers.[169]

Chenga Rinpoché is said to have stated that one must first equalize and then practice the exchange. "This," it is taught, "is the tradition of Maitrī-yogi." Potowa is reported to have stated, [43] "As for me, when I received it from the old layman from Radreng's forest of junipers,[170] I heard that, in the tradition of teacher Serlingpa, one must practice the exchange right from start." Here I shall present the instruction of Potowa.

This has seven points:

    I. Presentation of the preliminaries, the basis
    II. Training in the two minds of awakening, the main practice
    III. Taking adverse conditions onto the path of enlightenment
    IV. Presentation of a lifetime's practice in summary
    V. Presentation of the measure of having trained the mind
    VI. Presentation of the commitments of mind training
    VII. Presentation of the precepts of mind training

I. Presentation of the preliminary practices, the basis

The first point, the presentation of the preliminaries, which is the basis, is stated by the following:

First, train in the preliminaries.

The practitioner of this mind training must be someone who, by relying on a qualified teacher whose lineage stems from Atiśa, has trained his or her mind in the three scopes in a systematic order and has thus reached a certain level. The practitioner, having generated the two awakening minds, aspiring and engaging, is cognizant of including even [the minute] precepts of these practices. These are the prerequisites.

To engage in the practice of the two minds of awakening, you, the practitioner, should first induce enthusiasm at the beginning of your meditation session by earnestly contemplating the following points.

Reflect on the meaningfulness of having obtained a human existence of leisure and opportunity. To prevent yourself from wasting it, think: "I must practice Dharma. And among Dharma practices, this [mind training] is the most excellent." Then reflect, "Even though I may have found a human existence of leisure and opportunity, within my life's span there is no time to spare. Since in future lives I must experience happiness and suffering as fruits of my virtuous and negative karma, this [mind training] is the most excellent virtuous activity. Even for the goal of freedom from cyclic existence, no path is more profound than this. This [training] is also the supreme cause for attaining buddhahood for the benefit of self and others." Contemplate these points not only when your enthusiasm for the training of mind is strong but also when such enthusiasm is lacking. [44]

II. Training in the two minds of awakening, the main practice

The second point, the training in the two minds of awakening, is the main practice. It has two parts: the ultimate [mind] and the conventional [mind]. Given the sequence in which meditative equipoise and post-meditation stages arise within a single person, these two [minds] are presented here in the following order. First, to train in the ultimate awakening mind, there are two parts: the actual meditation session and the subsequent period [practices].

A. Training in the ultimate awakening mind
1. The actual meditation session

The meditation session divides into three—preparatory practices, the main practice, and the concluding practice. As for preparation, undertake the seven-limb practice inside your chamber of divinities,[171] make supplications to meditation deities and your teachers, and having seated yourself comfortably on your meditation cushion, count your respiration—exhalation and inhalation—twenty-one times. With these practices, you enable your body, speech, and mind to become a fit vessel for meditative concentration. Then generate, as a precursor, the conventional awakening mind accompanied by the beneficial qualities of meditative stabilization.

During the main session, given that all of these [mind training practices] adhere to the tradition of "simultaneous engagement," you should simultaneously meditate on the emptiness of all phenomena, including that of your own self and the self of others. Although this is true, during the preparatory stage you must relate to these phenomena in a gradual manner, enumerating each phenomenon by means of the pristine cognition of discriminative awareness. This, the master said,[172] has the benefit of allowing the moisture of tranquil abiding to give birth to the shoots of realization.

Next, the initial meditation on the absence of intrinsic existence of perceived objects is presented in the following line:

Train to view all phenomena as dreamlike.[173]

This entire world of the external environment and the beings within it, which are by nature mere appearances, are nothing but apparitions of your own deluded mind. Thus not even a single atom exists with a reality separate from the mind. When you examine thus, you will come to realize that even on the conventional level no referent of your awareness is established as possessing substantially true existence. Contemplate in this manner.

Next, the meditation on the absence of the intrinsic existence of perceiving subjects is presented in the following line:

Examine the nature of the unborn awareness.[174]

Contemplate thus: Similar [to the preceding meditation], the very mind that negated the intrinsic existence of the perceived objects [1] in terms of its past is no more, [2] in terms of its future is yet to be, and [3] in terms of its present is composed of three parts. It is devoid of color, shape, and spatial location; it cannot be said to be located in any specific point of the body; when analyzed, it is empty of all identifiable characteristics. [The perceiving mind too] abides as primordially unborn. [45]

Next, the meditation on the absence of the intrinsic existence of phenomena is presented by the following line:

The remedy, too, is freed in its own place.

Thus, the very mind that performs the act of applying the remedies through experiencing the emptiness of all phenomena, including your body and mind, is not established. [In general,] all objects of knowledge are subsumed within the class of either objects or minds. Furthermore, since the mind in its generality has already been examined, you should think, "Certainly nothing is established primordially as possessing substantial reality." Free the mind of conceptualization in this manner and release it in this state of nongrasping at intrinsic nature in terms of any of the three times. Focus the mind with ease, lucidity, and vibrancy, not allowing it to fall under the influence of either dullness or excitation. This is presented by the following line:

Place your mind on the basis-of-all, the actual path.[175]

You should identify the ordinary mind and place it in a state free of negation or affirmation. Since all seven types of consciousness are conceptual minds, relinquish them. The essential point is to avoid being tainted by a conceptualization of subject-object duality. Subsequently, whenever conceptualization arises, by observing awareness with awareness, let it rest free within reality itself. Since this constitutes actual meditation of clear light, keep your sessions intense but of short duration; within one session, you can have many subsessions. As for the length of the meditation session, it is said that "the best session should have a stable base and should end in a joyful state." At the conclusion, after dissolving your visualizations, cultivate great compassion for those without such realization. Thinking, "I shall place all beings in the undistorted truth of such ultimate mode of being," dedicate all virtues to the benefit of others. Then slowly undo your crossed legs and perform the seven-limb rites inside the chamber of divinities.

2. The subsequent period [practices]

How to train in the subsequent practices is presented by the following:

In the intervals be a conjurer of illusions.

The subsequent periods must be cultivated without losing the flavor of your meditative equipoise [on emptiness]. Therefore, even though perceptions of self and others, the external environment and the beings within it, and so on arise, it is your delusion that causes nonexisting things to appear [as existing]. Contemplating such things as indistinguishable from illusory horses and elephants, relinquish clinging to substantial reality. Although you perceive yourself in terms of your five aggregates, you are but an appearance of the mere aggregation of dependently originated things. Apart from this, no self possesses an eternal and unitary nature. [46] Contemplate and see [yourself] as an illusory person who engages in the activity of going and coming and interacts with objects. Do not remain blank, thinking nothing, but instead be sustained by mindfulness, and the instant something appears to the senses, think, "This too is illusionlike, it is dreamlike." In this way, you experience objects by relying upon such adages [as well].

As you view [everything] in this manner, during the subsequent periods your mind will not become remote from the dreamlike experience of the meditation session. In this way, during the intervals between sessions, turn all your virtuous activities into the path. Abide thus in the great union, not losing the experience of the meditation session throughout all activities. To make these points, the master cited the following stanza and explained the practices of the relevant points together with their beneficial qualities:

> Thus ensure that all your practices remain
> Untainted by the clinging of grasping at real entities
> And spread them across the vast spacelike great emptiness;
> You will [then] travel in the sphere of immortal great bliss.[176]

B. Training in the conventional awakening mind

Second, the conventional awakening mind of exchanging self and others is presented. This has been taught by Śāntideva. [For example] he states:

> He who wishes to quickly rescue
> Both himself and others
> Should practice the secret instruction:
> The exchanging of self and others.[177]

> If you do not thoroughly exchange
> Your own happiness with others' suffering,
> You will not become a buddha.
> Even in samsara there will be no happiness.[178]

> Hence to assuage your own injuries
> And to pacify others' sufferings,
> You should give your own self to others
> And protect others as you would yourself.[179]

This, in turn, has two parts: the actual meditation session and the subsequent periods.

1. The meditation session

How to practice during the meditation session is presented by the following:

> **Train in the two—giving and taking—alternately.**

Seated on a comfortable cushion, visualize your dear mother vividly in front. First, to cultivate loving-kindness and compassion, reflect in the following manner:

"Because she, my mother, first gave me this human existence of leisure and opportunity, which she nurtured without any negligence, I have encountered the Buddha's teachings. Because of this [today] it is possible to grab happiness by its very snout.[180] She has thus helped me. Throughout all stages, when I was in her womb and after birth, she nurtured me with impossible acts of kindness. Not only that, since samsara's beginningless time, she has constantly watched me with eyes of love, perpetually held me with affection [47], and repeatedly protected me from harm and misfortune. She has given me so much benefit and happiness and has thus embodied true kindness."

Reflect thus and cultivate a depth of emotion such that tears fall from your eyes and the hairs of your pores stand on end.

You should reflect "How sad that she, my kind mother, has been wandering in the infinite cycle of existence with so many kinds of sufferings, all the while working for my benefit. In return, I shall now help her by providing her benefits and happiness. I shall protect her from harm and all misfortune." You should reflect in this manner.

What harms this dear mother? Suffering harms her directly, while the origin of suffering injures her indirectly. So while thinking, "I shall take all these upon myself," take into your own heart in clean swaths—as if layers sheared off by a sharp knife—all the sufferings, their origin, the afflictions, and the subtle defilements to knowledge along with their propensities, all of which exist in your dear mother. This is the meditation on the "taking" aspect of awakening mind.

Again, thinking, "I shall myself seek the complete happiness of my dear mother," unconditionally offer your body, wealth, and all your virtues to your mother. This is the meaning of the following lines of *A Guide to the Bodhisattva's Way of Life:*

> To accomplish the welfare of sentient beings,
> I shall turn my body into a wish-fulfilling [jewel].[181]

Imagine therefore your body, wealth, and roots of virtue as precious [wish-fulfilling] jewels. From these emerge for your dear mother all the conditions for engaging in spiritual practice, such as food, clothing, shelter, assistants, as well as reliance on a spiritual teacher—all the conditions favorable to the attainment of enlightenment—whatever she wishes. Imagine, because of this, that your dear mother accomplishes the accumulations and attains buddhahood. This is the meditation on the "giving" aspect of awakening mind.

In this manner, first cultivating loving-kindness and compassion, combine giving and taking; undertake their practices so that your heart becomes even more moist and ripe than before. As you train in this manner and become capable of making an actual exchange [48]—that is, allaying your dear mother's sufferings and seeking her happiness without calculating the cost to yourself—you have reached a degree of success in this practice. The measure is that if your mother were to be reborn in the hells, for example, you would without hesitation plunge into the burning flames to rescue her.

Then proceed to the second session. First cultivate love and compassion toward all sentient beings, and then reflect: "When I generated the mind of awakening, I gave away my wealth and roots of virtue to all sentient beings; I pledged to accomplish their welfare, taking this responsibility upon myself. I must now undertake this in actuality." As before, you should combine giving and taking and train in them. Here, when you engage in the giving, imagine each and every sentient being receiving a complete set of your body, wealth, and virtues. Give these away wholeheartedly and with no conceptual elaborations. Thinking, "Whosoever desires, take them; do with them whatever you wish," regard yourself as a medicinal tree. Discarding joy and sadness, train with the mind and recite the words aloud.

You should pray, "May my body, wealth, and roots of virtue that I have unconditionally given away become food, drink, and clothing for those who lack them; may they become shelter for those who lack shelter." In this way, think, "May I become the sole cause of the happiness of both samsara and nirvana for all sentient beings; may I become the cause for eliminating all their sufferings; may all higher qualities and fruits of the path of all sentient beings come into being in dependence upon me." Train with your mind and recite these [aspirations] as well.

When training in such manner, you should rejoice with the following thought: "Given that even the buddhas have no aim other than the welfare of sentient beings, joyful indeed is it that I have the opportunity to implement from this very instant the heart practice of the great lord of the ten levels."[182] Again, take upon yourself the subtle obscurations to knowledge that exist within the disciples, the self-realized ones, and the noble bodhisattvas abiding on the levels, and as you give them your three factors [body, wealth, and roots of virtue], imagine that, as a result, they accomplish their accumulations and attain buddhahood. [49] All these noble ones can also be included within the general category of sentient beings; or alternatively, they can be visualized separately. Choose whichever is most convenient.

Place the two astride your breath.

You should train in the two, giving and taking, in relation to respiratory exhalation and inhalation. This makes it easier to maintain your mental focus, because the breath is readily available, and this method combats many [false] conceptualizations.

2. *The subsequent period [practices]*

The subsequent period [practices] are presented by the following line:

There are three objects, three poisons, and three roots of virtue.

In the subsequent periods, train the mind by purifying the fields of your experience. When, in relation to forms, sounds, and so on that are either attractive, unattractive, or neutral, you experience emotions such as attachment, anger, and delusion, train the mind in the following manner: "Sadly, just as I indulge in sensual desires now, countless beings in the universe are dominated by desire and thus indulge in infinite [negative] acts." Extract all of these [attachments of other beings] in one fell swoop, taking them into your heart and praying, "May all these sentient beings be endowed with the virtuous root of nonattachment." In the same manner, extend this practice to all five poisons.

In all actions, train by means of the words.

This line pertains to training the mind [even] by means of mere words. You can undertake this, for instance, by reciting the following lines from a treatise:

> May the sufferings of all beings ripen upon me.
> Through my virtues, may they all achieve happiness.[183]

Alternatively, you can recite the following when no one is around: "May the sufferings of all sentient beings and those sufferings' causes ripen upon me, and may my own self be subdued and annihilated. May my virtues ripen on all sentient beings, and may they become endowed with happiness." From the depth of your bones, cultivate the thought "O my dear mother, my dear brother [and sister] sentient beings! Most dear indeed are all these beings!"

This training by means of words in your four daily activities[184] involves following the sutra's admonition to cultivate loving-kindness by means of mere words. [50]

III. Taking adverse conditions onto the path of enlightenment

The third, taking adverse conditions onto the path of enlightenment, is presented by the following [lines]:

> **When the world and its inhabitants boil with negativity,**
> **Transform adverse conditions into the path of enlightenment.**[185]

Whatever harms befall you, whether caused by living beings or caused by natural elements, they are fruits of your own past negative actions. Harms are seen as adversities and obstacles by those unfamiliar with Dharma. But for someone who has entered the gateway of Dharma, the master said, they are [exactly] like what Chengawa explained to Shawo Gangpa: "If someone possesses mind training, all of this—physical illness and mental suffering— is skillful means through which the teachers and the Three Jewels bestow their blessings and higher attainments." Therefore, you should transform all circumstances into factors conducive for training in the awakening mind.

This has two parts: (A) training in the two awakening minds (the extraordinary thoughts) and (B) striving in the dual practice of accumulation and purification (the extraordinary activities).

A. Training in the two awakening minds, the extraordinary thoughts

1. Taking adverse conditions onto the path of enlightenment by means of training in the conventional awakening mind

Taking adverse conditions onto the path by means of the conventional awakening mind is taught first. So how does one take these [adverse conditions] onto the path?

Reflect, "Since beginningless time I have failed to distinguish between enemies and friends, and as a result I have failed to recognize what is to be relinquished and what is to be adopted. I have erred, because whatever spiritual practices I may have pursued have all been endeavors of self-grasping. I have come no closer to establishing familiarity with liberation and [the Buddha's] omniscience. Today I shall therefore differentiate enemies from friends and shall ensure the success of my Dharma practice. Now my own self is the enemy, and sentient beings are the friends. So, other than viewing my own self as my enemy and relinquishing myself, and viewing others as friends and cherishing them, nothing else is to be done."

a. Recognizing your own self as the enemy[186]

As for the reason why your own self is the enemy, this is presented by the following [line]:

Banish all blames to the single source.

This line presents the perceiving of your own self as the enemy. Whatever calamities befall you, without blaming others, you should think, "This is due to my own self-grasping." In this manner, scatter all the accusations [fomenting] within yourself. It has been taught:

> Whatever harms exist in the world,
> Whatever dangers and sufferings are in the world—
> All of these arise from grasping at self;
> What use is this great demon for me?[187]

Also:

> If there is "self," recognition of "others" arises; [51]
> On this division of self and others, grasping and anger arise;
> And in relation to these two [emotions],
> All calamities come into being.[188]

Also:

> Recognizing myself as flawed
> And others as an ocean of higher qualities,
> I will thoroughly discard grasping at self
> And practice embracing others.[189]

Reflect, "All shortcomings and defects I may possess, originate from my grasping at selfhood. From beginningless time, I have held onto a self when there was none. Wherever I was born, though there was no self, I have grasped at my body as [the basis of my] selfhood. Taking its side, I have resorted to rejection and affirmation depending on whether I deemed something desirable or undesirable. In this manner I have committed all three — deception, duplicity, and deviousness—toward others and, as a consequence, have accumulated afflictions and negative karma over and over again. This has compelled me, since beginingless time, to endure the incalculable sufferings of cyclic existence in general and the immeasurable sufferings of the three lower realms in particular. Still, as stated in the following,

> Although countless eons have passed
> With such great hardships,
> You have sought only suffering.[190]

"So long as I fail to view this [the self] as the enemy, so long will I continue to seek the well-being of this self. Consequently I will accumulate negative karma that will compel me in the future to wander in this infinite cycle of existence, where I will suffer even more and for longer than before. So this cherishing of self brings about all the sufferings of the three times. Since this [self] has been my own executioner and my enemy from beginningless time, then in all the deaths I have experienced in the beginningless cycle of existence, no one else has done the killing. Rather I have been killed by my own self!" As if biting your lower lip,[191] firmly hold your own self as the enemy.

Where is this enemy? It is in your own heart. Śāntideva taught, for example:

> If this ancient enemy long settled,
> The sole cause of steadily increasing hosts of harms,
> Has found its home within my very heart,
> How can there be joy for me within this cyclic existence?[192]

Think that this kind of behavior—living on the head yet not giving victory to the eyes—is most inappropriate.[193] [52] Thus the focus or the site of this self-grasping, which is the source of [all] defects, is the very body you are born into. Since beginningless lifetimes you have held on to an "I" when there was none and have held on to a self when there was none. [Self-grasping] is fraught with defects and is the source of all sufferings. So to cherish, look at, and protect this discolored human corpse—a lump of pus and blood and a sack of mucus—is like carrying a bag of thorns on your back while naked! Happiness could result if you let go, but [instead] you believe that pursuing self-interest will bring happiness and thus sink ever deeper into suffering as though you craved it. Śāntideva, too, states:

> Whatever suffering is in the world
> Arises from wishing for one's own happiness;
> Whatever happiness is in the world
> Arises from the wish for others' happiness.

> What need is there to say more?
> The childish pursue their own interests,
> While the buddhas act for the welfare of others:
> Observe the difference between these two.[194]

Among all the afflictions that have harmed you since beginningless time, this self-grasping [is the worst]. This jealous, evil-ridden [force] that [makes beings] commit negative acts against all other beings, from high spiritual teachers to lice, resides right here [in you]. It obstructs the attainment of freedom from cyclic existence and ties beings further into bondage. This [force] welcomes all human and nonhuman agents of harm. This owl-headed betrayer[195] is the very mind that grasps on to "I" or "self" and seeks only its own selfish ends. Thinking in this manner, you should recognize the enemy as the enemy. Śāntideva states:

Within all the hundreds of world systems
Of cyclic existence, this has harmed me.
Rouse your vengeance thus
And destroy thoughts of self-interest.[196]

If you still feel unable to eradicate this [self-grasping], then cultivate the following thought: "This time it is different. Today I have sought a spiritual teacher, I have read the sutras, and as a result I have now recognized the enemy!" It has been stated:

The old days when you could
Ruin me at will are now gone;
I can see you now, so where are you off to?
I shall tear down your arrogance.[197]

Contemplate along these lines, and whenever any self-centered thought arises, the master said, you should be cognizant and strike at the snout of this boar with a cane. [53] Therefore it was taught that as far as the subject matter of all the teachings of the Great Vehicle is concerned, there are only the two themes: (1) totally letting go of self-grasping and (2) upholding sentient beings with deep concern and, on this basis, crippling this self-grasping as much as you can and nurturing sentient beings as much you can.

Furthermore, since all the sacred scriptures and treatises were taught for the purpose of subduing the afflictions, it is the afflictions that must be subdued by means of them. In general there are 84,000 afflictions, all of which, when subsumed, fall into 212 classes.[198] When subsumed, they in turn fall into the class of six root afflictions and twenty derivative afflictions. These, too, can be further subsumed into the five or three poisons. When subsumed further, they are reduced into a single affliction, namely the self-grasping alone. He who has subdued it to the highest degree enjoys the highest degree of happiness; to a medium degree, a medium degree of happiness; and to a minimal degree, a minimal degree of happiness. He who has not subdued it to any degree will enjoy no happiness at all. So the root of suffering is self-grasping; and since all faults and defects are contingent upon this, you must from now on abandon any clinging to your body and mind and instead regard them as your enemies. Most importantly you must abandon your clinging to the body. On this point Śāntideva states:

> If I am attached to my body,
> Fear arises from even slight dangers.
> This body that brings so much fear—
> Who would not detest it like an enemy?[199]

Reflect, "Although I have striven hard since beginningless time to benefit this body, it is in the nature of a material object, and feels no joy or pain in relation to any benefit or injury. As for the mind, it is devoid of substantial reality and empty. Since what appears conventionally right now comes into being from causes and conditions, it is devoid of [self-defining] identity. Furthermore, since the causes and effects cease every moment, there is nothing that is established following its origination. Therefore you should think, "In the past I have been preoccupied with worthless, ruinous pursuits. Now I shall regard my own self as the enemy and shall call upon all eight classes of worldly gods, demigods, and demons, and all eighty thousand families of obstructive forces to withdraw their support of this self." Train with the thought "Be my ally and help vanquish this self-grasping; help make my five aggregates devoid of substantial reality and empty."

By engaging in these practices, [54] the master entreated, strive to the best of your ability to subdue this self-grasping demon during your brief life.

Shawopa states: "So long as we fail to see our own self as the enemy, no one, including our teachers, can save us. If we see it as the enemy, benefits will ensue."[200]

So if you view your own self as the enemy, even when harms caused by hosts of nonhumans and malevolent elemental spirits befall you, these become harms perpetrated against the enemy. They become aids in your battle against self-grasping. Since they are a powerful army on your side, it is inappropriate to generate anger toward these agents of harm; rather, you should look on them with joy. At some point in the future, the master said, there will emerge a true spiritual practice that can free you from the narrow gorges of adverse conditions. At that point you should train in [the recognition of others as] friends.[201] In this manner, train now to distinguish between self and others as enemy and friends, respectively.

Occasionally, you should train your mind also by drawing a distinction between enemy and friend even within yourself. You can give your lay name to your thoughts and actions concerned with the pursuit of your own welfare and your ordination name to your thoughts and actions concerned with the pursuit of others' welfare.[202] Then, following the example of the spiritual mentor Ben, correlate your arms, right and left, to avoidance [of nonvirtue] and adoption [of virtuous acts]. The spiritual mentor Ben states: "I have no other task than to stand guard with a short spear of antidote at the entrance of my mind. When they [the afflictions] are vigilant, I too am vigilant; when they are relaxed, I too am relaxed."[203] Also, "You should be vigilant and strike at the snout of each boar with a cane and chase it."[204] All the sutras and the commentarial treatises [too] demonstrate that there is no task other than eliminating self-grasping.

These, then, present the viewing of one's own self as the enemy and the elimination of self-grasping. Because of Shawopa's teachings, the expression "the practice for smashing the demon's head" evolved.

b. Recognizing sentient beings as friends and cherishing them

Second, the viewing of sentient beings as friends and cherishing them is presented by the following line:

Toward all beings contemplate their great kindness.

Shawopa calls this "the spiritual practice of carrying the flesh and carrying the blood."[205] It is called "the practice of accepting all ill omens as charms."[206] Here one deliberately focuses on the perpetrators of harm and cultivates loving-kindness and compassion and then trains in giving and taking.

First, the meditation on loving-kindness is as follows. Reflect, "These humans and nonhumans, who perpetrate harms against me, have been related to me so many times as my parents, as siblings, and as friends— [55] the frequency of which is greater than the [quantity of] *kolāsita* nuts [required to cover the face of the earth].[207] They have constantly looked at me with eyes of love, perpetually sustained me with affectionate hearts, and constantly guarded me from harms and inexpedient situations. They have helped me with all kinds of benefits and happiness and are thus embodiments of true kindness." Reflecting thus, develop deep and earnest empathy and feel as though, were you able to place them deep within your heart, you would still not be content. View them as if they were pieces of your own heart. Atiśa refers to [sentient beings] as "my divinities" and "my spiritual teachers."

The meditation on compassion is as follows. Reflect, "They harm me today not willfully but out of a deluded mind. I have pursued my own self-interest since beginningless time, without regard to negative karma, suffering, or disrepute, and I have thus accumulated afflictions and negative karma. Because of this I have wandered in this infinite cycle of existence, embracing misery as practice. The blame for all of this lies in the self. Even at present, in my quest for enlightenment for the benefit of self and others, as I uncontrollably exploit and create obstacles for my dear mothers because of my negative karma, I am causing obstacles to the happiness of all sentient beings. So the blame for their departing to the hells in their future lives lies also in me. This is most sad indeed." Cultivate compassion as intense as a spark of fire on your bare flesh. In this manner, cultivate loving-kindness and compassion focused specially on the perpetrators of harm.

If you cultivate [loving-kindness and compassion] in this manner, because nonhumans have some karmically acquired clairvoyance, the moment you recognize them as your mothers, they will recognize you as their children. When this mother-child attitude emerges, how can they perpetrate harm? It is a law of nature that when I relate to someone as my mother, she will in turn relate to me as her child. This alone can alleviate your suffering. The *Condensed [Perfection of Wisdom]* states:

> The world of humans is replete with element spirits and diseases,
> But these are pacified with power of truth by those who care and have
>   compassion.[208]

When you cultivate loving-kindness and compassion toward the perpetrators of harm, you arrive at the following realization: "Since beginningless time, they have only benefited me, yet I have given only harm in return. [56] Therefore, from now on, I shall help them and protect them from harm." With this thought, combine the two practices of giving and taking and train your mind. Take upon yourself all leprosy and sickness in the world.[209] Heap upon your present sickness all the negative karma within your own life, all that you are likely to reap in the remainder of your life or in your future life, and rejoice.

Again, train as follows. Invite the malevolent nonhuman spirits in front of you and declare: "The number of times you have been my mother is beyond count. Also, if I were to pile together the number of times I ate your flesh, drank your blood, chewed your bones, wore your skin, and sucked your milk, even the entire trichiliocosm universe would be too small to contain it all. I have also killed you, assaulted you, and robbed you countless times. Today you have thus come to collect the debt. Today please take [in return] all these debts of kind acts and dues. It is appropriate that you own me, for you have been most kind indeed."

Reflecting thus, declare: "Devour my flesh if you like flesh! Drink my blood if you like blood! Chew my bones if you like bones! Peel away my skin and wear it if you like skin! Eat me raw if you are in haste! Eat me cooked if you are not in haste!" Potowa is reported have expressed the following:

> To all beings of the six realms
> I offer ritual cakes in the four directions.
> How much I yearn for the time
> When I'm devoured and carried away by insects! [210]

Then [imagine that] the nonhuman spirit rises up instantly and devours you from head to heels, smearing his mouth with your blood. His body full, his harmful intentions disappear, and he becomes endowed with altruistic thoughts. Imagine that, as a by-product, your negative karma becomes cleansed. Imagine that a moment later, your body rematerializes and is again devoured. Visualize this over and over. Imagine that your body is cut into a hundred or a thousand pieces, and these are then given away everywhere. In particular, share this body and mind in places of special sensitivity [such as cemeteries]. Then, with the thought "This body [of mine] belongs to him," undertake all virtuous practices for [the nonhuman spirit's] sake. Even the concluding dedication should be done on his behalf. In particular, where such nonhuman forces reside, mentally discard your body, [57] and cutting it open right there, with blood soaking everything, offer it with the thought "Now eat!"

Then let go of cherishing your body as stated:

> I have already given this body
> To all beings to do with as they please;
> Let them do whatever they wish, such as beating it;
> Why should I be concerned? [211]

These [citations] present the [practice of] regarding sentient beings as friends and cherishing them. Thus it is necessary to train your mind by distinguishing between the two classes—enemy and friend.

Shawopa states: "Search for the enemy in oneself; search for a god in the

demons; search for virtues in nonvirtues; and search for happiness in suffering."²¹²

Langri Thangpa, too, says: "No matter what profound scriptures I open, I
find none that do not suggest that all faults are one's own, and that all higher
qualities belong to brother and sister sentient beings. Because of this, you
must offer all gain and victory to others and accept all loss and defeat for
yourself. I have found no other meaning."²¹³

Shawopa states: "If someone finds a meaning other than this, it is an
error."²¹⁴ In brief, the master said, no other intent can be found in all the
scriptural collections. With this, the taking of adverse conditions onto the
path of enlightenment by means of conventional awakening mind has now
been presented.

2. Taking adverse conditions onto the path by means of training in ultimate awakening mind

Following this, the second, taking adverse conditions onto the path of enlightenment by means of training in ultimate awakening mind is presented
in the following:

> With the three views and treasury of space,
> The yoga of protection is unexcelled.
> By meditating on illusions as the four buddha bodies,
> Emptiness is protection unsurpassed.²¹⁵

Conclude decisively that everything in this world of appearance, both the
external environment and the beings within—such as the object of impairment and the agent of impairment²¹⁶—are only deluded perceptions of your
own mind. As mere deceptive, deluded appearances, both [polarities] will
cease within moments, with no time either to injure or to engage in any
negation or affirmation. So even conventionally, nothing exists as an object
or agent of harm. On the ultimate level no phenomenon is primordially
established. Like the center of a spotless sky, [phenomena] are all one.

Since self is an awareness devoid of substantial reality, and the agent of
harm is an awareness devoid of substantial reality as well, neither exists as the
object of impairment or the agent of impairment. Everything is empty, and
emptiness cannot be attacked by emptiness. Just as the eastern part of the sky
[58] cannot cause harm to the western part, they [the object of impairment

and the agent of impairment] cannot injure each other. Therefore, since your current perceptions are illusions of a deluded mind—the self, the object of impairment, and the illnesses—other than being constructs of your mind, nothing can be established in terms of identity. It is taught:

> Your own mind is māra;
> Your own mind is the obstructive force;
> All obstructive forces arise from conceptualization;
> Therefore relinquish conceptualization.[217]

Because you have grasped your concepts as real, as true, as something separate from the mind, and as fault-ridden, this has produced all the sufferings of cyclic existence. Apart from your own conceptualization, nothing outside is an obstructer; therefore your own conceptualization is the sole object of elimination. When examined in this manner, everything comes down to your mind; and the mind too, when examined, is found to be emptiness. There is no difference between the clear-light nature of your own mind, the clear-light nature of the minds of all sentient beings, and the pristine cognition of the Buddha's enlightened mind; they are equally dharmakāya—the buddha body of reality. So who can be harmed? Who causes the harm? And how is anyone harmed? Ultimately, nothing exists as a separate reality. Conventionally, however, all illnesses and malevolent forces exist as your own concepts. Reflecting that "The concepts [too] exist as dharmakāya," place the mind naturally at rest, free of any conceptualization. Like throwing up vomit, place your mind free of all clinging. Like the corpse of a leper, discard it as if it were of no use. Like a dead person's empty house, release it without clinging.

Reflect: "Although phenomena are not established primordially, yet I remain bound, as though unable to undo knots made in the sky or strangled by a tortoise-hair noose.[218] As such, my mind has arisen as a demon, and chained by conceptualization, I remain bewildered in suffering." All hopes and fears, such as fearing illness or harm from ghosts, or hoping to be cured of illnesses, as well as all thoughts of negation and affirmation in emptiness, place them all within the sphere of emptiness and release them within ultimate reality itself. [59]

Imagine that, unable to bear this, you react violently, pulling at the hem of your clothes and shouting your name aloud. You tremble, the hairs on your body stand up, and you experience the dissolution of the ten classes of consciousness.[219] At that instant [although] there are two [streams of] awareness, think that they are both your own mind; they are but [different] modes of perception. As you contemplate thus, your thoughts and awareness will calm, and your body and mind will rest in their own natural states. When the thought arises spontaneously, "Oh, everything is my mind," nonconceptuality dawns in its nakedness.

Therefore, when sickness, malevolent forces, and your own self are examined with the pristine cognition of discriminative awareness, none [are found to have] ever come into being; this is the unborn dharmakāya. The unborn has no cessation, and this absence of cessation is the unceasing enjoyment buddha body. Between origination and cessation is no abiding, and this absence of abiding is the nonabiding emanation buddha body. That which does not exist in any of the three times is devoid of substantial reality, and this absence of substantial reality is the natural buddha body.

View this absence of four resultant buddha bodies—which are separate from the three factors of sickness, malevolent forces, and your own mind— as the [actual] four buddha bodies. In this way you recognize that every conceptualization places the four buddha bodies in your very palms. View every conceptualization as a resounding signal of ultimate reality. View all illnesses and malevolent forces as embodiments of kindness. This is the "instruction on introducing the four buddha bodies," which presents the transformation of adverse conditions into the path by means of the ultimate awakening mind.

To conclude the practice of the two awakening minds, or as a meditation implicit within it, cultivate the following viewpoint to help cut [the knots of] expectations and apprehensions: "Since this perpetrator of harm has led me to train in the two awakening minds, it is placing enlightenment in my very palms. It is thus most kind indeed. Furthermore, like a messenger it bears a warning: 'Since a suffering like the present one comes about as a consequence of a cause—a negative, nonvirtuous karma—if you wish to avoid suffering you should purify its cause, the negative karma. In the future, forsake all negative acts.' [The perpetrator of harm] is therefore kind indeed."

Think, "These perpetrators of harm [60] expose my lack of antidotes, my failure even to notice afflictions arising, and are thereby definitely emanations of my teacher." Thinking thus, view them with joy from the depths of your heart. Think, furthermore, "This perpetrator of harm reveals within this very life the sufferings of a future lifetime in the lower realms—the fruit of past lives' negative karma. He holds the drawstring [of the sack] of the lower realms and is therefore most kind indeed." Reflecting, "If he has bene-fited me this much, he must definitely be [an expression of] the enlightened activities of the teachers and the Three Jewels," view the perpetrator of harm as desirable, endearing, and close to your heart. You should view sickness and suffering as possessing similarly beneficial qualities.

Even if you contract leprosy, you should reflect, "This will bring future sufferings to the fore. This life is but a momentary event, and if I were not afflicted by leprosy and illness, my mind would be embroiled in the chores of this life, leading me to accumulate negative karma. Given that [illnesses and so on] end this [mundane way of life] abruptly and enable me to encounter Dharma, they help me take the essence of this bodily existence." View lep-rosy and sickness with heartfelt, uncontrived joy. Furthermore, think, "Sick-ness and suffering engender true renunciation in me; for without suffering, there can be no true renunciation. Since they definitely help dispel the afflic-tions of my mind, they help me realize the teachings' intent. So they are most kind indeed!" For it is stated:

With disenchantment arrogance is dispelled.[220]

Furthermore [suffering] brings forth compassion, which is the root of the Great Vehicle. For it is stated:

Toward samsaric beings, generate compassion.[221]

Reflect: "Suffering dispels all my suffering and secures all my happiness and therefore brings me benefit." Just as your teachers and preceptors are most kind in conferring vows upon you and giving teachings, sentient beings and malevolent elemental forces, too, assist you in attaining enlightenment. You should therefore view all of them, too, as your spiritual teachers and contemplate their great kindness.

When you learn to train your mind in this manner, all activities of your body, speech, and mind, and everything that appears in the field of your senses will be transformed into the two accumulations. From that point onward, you will obtain the spiritual practice that ensures nothing is wasted. [61] It is from here that the three innumerable eons start. With this, the train-ing in the two awakening minds—the special thoughts—has been presented.

B. Striving in the dual practice of accumulation and purification, the extraordinary activities

Transforming adverse conditions into the path of enlightenment by means of striving in the dual practice of accumulation and purification—the extraordinary activities—is presented as follows:

The fourfold practice is the most excellent method.

When you encounter suffering, thoughts desiring happiness arise uncontrollably. Experience such moments as motivating you in the following manner.

1) The first practice, the accumulation of merit, is as follows. "If you wish for happiness free of suffering, cultivate faith and respect toward the teachers and the Three Jewels, which are the causes of all happiness; gather the accumulations." Think that [the experience of suffering] admonishes you to think such thoughts. Engage extensively in making offerings to the Three Jewels, offer alms and services to the spiritual community, make torma offerings to the elemental spirits, give charity to ordinary folk, and, making prayers for the cessation of your [cyclical] expectations and apprehensions, offer mandalas and other articles to the teachers and the Three Jewels. Cultivate faith and respect toward them, go for refuge and generate the awakening mind, and make the following appeal with fervent joy: "Since I am ignorant, please care for me in the best way possible." Make the following supplication as well:

> If being sick is best, please make me ill;
> If being cured is best, please restore my health;
> If being dead is best, please make me die;
> If long life is best, please prolong my life;
> If shorter life is best, please shorten my life.
> May all enjoy the fortune of enlightenment.[222]

2) The second practice, the purification of negative karma, is as follows. Again, imagine that suffering comes as a messenger, exhorting you, "If you do not desire suffering, abandon its cause, which is negative karma." With this thought, purify negative karma through the four powers.[223] In the presence of the Three Jewels, engage also in the rites requesting forbearance and in the extensive purification rites.

3) The third practice, making offerings to the malevolent forces, is as follows. Offer torma to the perpetrators of harm. Those who can mentally cope should also do the following meditation:

Summon in front of you the perpetrator of harm, visualized as a meditation deity, and reflect, "You are kind indeed, for you have led me to the two awakening minds; you have helped me in my quest to find happiness and dispel suffering. [62] I request you further to cause all the sufferings of sentient beings to ripen in my current illness. Please do not depart. Instead stay inside this body of mine and ensure that this sickness is not cured but endures."

Thus joyfully let go of your body and mind, and cut [the rope of] all expectations, apprehensions, and desire for happiness. Without dwelling on sadness, from the depth of your heart, experience a blissful enthusiasm. Those unable to contemplate along these lines should here cultivate loving-kindness and compassion with special emphasis. Reflect, "Since you obstruct my work for the benefit of all sentient beings, you will be reborn in the hells in your next life. I shall help you with material and spiritual gifts; cease harming me, therefore, and leave." Exhorting thus, confront them with words of truth. Visualizing the perpetrators of harm as deities is like placing an evil person in the domain of the king. They cannot then do any harm. This is another approach.

4) The fourth practice is offering torma to the Dharma protectors and supplicating them as follows: "Please ensure that no obstacles arise in my meditative practice. Remember the promises and the solemn oaths you have taken in the presence of the buddhas."

In this way, you should train with effort in these four practices—(1) making offerings to the deities and the spiritual teachers and supplicating them, (2) purifying your negative karma, (3) making offerings to the malevolent forces, and (4) making offerings to the Dharma protectors.

Having presented the practice of taking adverse conditions onto the path, the following is now stated to present the yoga of in-between sessions:

Relate whatever you can to meditation right now.

When adverse circumstances unexpectedly strike, train in the two awakening minds right there and then. For instance, if you are struck with leprosy or a severe infectious disease,[224] if you are lynched by a crowd, beaten up, robbed, or attacked with weapons, or if you simply fail to meet your desired conditions (by encountering harms caused by nonhuman forces or acute, unbearable sufferings), think how the vast universe contains infinite cases like your own, and generate compassion for those [enduring these sufferings]. As you mentally take all of these in one fell swoop upon your own suffering, imagine your suffering increasing to such an intensity that your heart could break open. [63]

Following this, reflect, "This perpetrator of harm has been my spiritual teacher for training in the awakening mind and the practice of forbearance, and has thus been most kind to me." The moment you see these sufferings in others, right there and then take them upon yourself. Also when an intense, unbearable affliction arises because of attachment and anger, contemplate as before and take them upon yourself. After this imagine all other beings as free of both suffering and its causes and enjoying happiness.

Langri Thangpa states, "All of what is called 'transforming adverse conditions into enlightenment' entails the cessation of expectations and apprehensions. So long as these two do not cease, one cannot take adverse conditions onto the path. Even if one were eventually led to the path that is free of expectations and apprehensions, training in the differentiation of enemy and friends at such a time would be like trying to straighten a crooked tree."[225]

IV. Presentation of a lifetime's practice in summary

The fourth point, which is the presentation of a lifetime's practice in summary, is presented in the following:

> **In brief the essence of instruction is this:**
> **Apply yourself to the five powers.**

The yogi of this teaching should engage in all mind training by means of a condensed [practice of the] five powers.

1) First is the *power of propelling intention*. "From now until my full enlightenment I shall never be divorced from the two awakening minds, and I shall not allow my mind training to lose its continuity. I shall make sure to never be divorced from the two awakening minds until my death." Bless yourself by resolving in terms of "this year" and "this month," and so on. Repeatedly propel your thoughts in this way with great force.

2) The *power of acquaintance* refers to cultivating the two awakening minds at all times, free of distraction.

3) The *power of positive seed* means striving during the period in between sessions in virtuous activities—such as engaging in the ten spiritual practices, free of any damaging interferences from your body, wealth, and so on—for the purpose of engendering those [experiences of] this teaching that have not yet arisen and enhancing those already arisen. [64]

4) The *power of eradication* is the actual eradication of self-grasping. How long have you wandered in cyclic existence in general and in the three lower realms in particular? This is brought about by cherishing your self and desiring its happiness. Even within this life, all undesirable events—being incapable of maintaining a relationship with your partner, failing to have integrity with respect to your promises and vows, and having no interest in cultivating the realizations of such spiritual attainments, from the [recognition of the rarity of] precious human existence to [the realization of] no-self—all are due to cherishing your self and desiring its happiness. Every one of your defects is therefore contingent upon this. With the thought "From hereon I shall never seek the self's welfare for even a single instant; instead, I must totally eliminate this," view [self-cherishing] in this manner and regard it as the enemy.

5) The *power of aspirational prayer* is this. At the conclusion of all virtuous activities, make the following aspiration: "From this moment until I have attained buddhahood, throughout all my lives, may I never be divorced from the two awakening minds, and may I instead train in them. May I know how to take all circumstances that befall me, whether positive or adverse, into this training." [Then] make offerings to the teachers and the Three Jewels, and offer a torma to the Dharma protectors and the elemental spirits, supplicating them thus: "Help me so that I am never divorced from the two awakening minds throughout all my lives. Help me to meet sublime teachers who reveal this teaching." This, the master said, is a teaching that folds everything into a single [utterance of] *Hūṃ*.

As Mahayana's transference method is
The five powers alone, their practice is vital.

Thus when he [or she] who has trained his mind throughout his entire life contracts a fatal illness and becomes aware of his imminent death, he must apply this very [mind training] teaching as the time-of-death instruction and effect the transition while engaged in such practice. Practices such as tantra cannot be practiced at this juncture; he [or she] should go through the transition by means of the five powers alone.

1) First undertake the practice of the power of *positive seed.*[226] To do this, you offer your belongings to the teachers and the Three Jewels as the gifts of the deceased.[227] It is inappropriate to give these [belongings] to beings who might be your objects of clinging. [65] Prepare so that even in your aftermath, your possessions do not become conditions for accumulating negative karma. Make excellent offerings to those worthy of veneration. It is not appropriate to offer [only] tokens of your belongings to those who are embodiments of kindness.[228] Then, without any attachment to your possessions of this life, generate a fearless attitude with regard to your future life.

2) The power of *aspirational prayer* is as follows. Lay out an excellent array of offerings in the presence of the Three Jewels, request forbearance for your shortcomings, and declare and purify your negative karma. Review as well the pledges you have taken, such as that of going for refuge. Then make offerings to the Three Jewels, offer tormas to the Dharma protectors, and make this fervent request to be led to the threshold of the path: "Bless me so that in the intermediate state and the next life I will remember the two awakening minds and engage in their practice. Help me to encounter sublime teachers who reveal this teaching. Lead me to the beginning of my path of happiness. Today I place my hope in you." Then invoke the following aspirations again and again: "May I train in the two awakening minds during the intermediate state; may I train in the two awakening minds throughout all lives; may I meet sublime teachers who reveal this teaching."

3) The power of *eradication* is as follows. "That which grasps at self and 'I' has made me suffer since beginningless time. This has also brought about my present suffering. So long as I am not divorced from this, no happiness can arise. How have I allowed it to ruin me? This happened because I have assumed a [corporeal] body. So I shall definitely not assume a [corporeal] body in the intermediate state. I shall allow my mind to fade into space." Reflecting in this manner repeatedly, eradicate self-grasping.

4) Next is the power of *propelling intention*. "In the past I have enhanced the two awakening minds so that their continuity did not cease. I shall now recall the two awakening minds in the intermediate state and engage in their training." Reflect along these lines and repeatedly recall [the two minds].

5) As for the power of *acquaintance*, the key is to first train uninterruptedly in the awakening mind.

Then, as you approach the moment of death, lie down on your right and, placing your right hand on your cheek, block the right nostril with your little finger [66] and breathe through the left nostril. This is transference in terms of your conduct.

Then, preceded by loving-kindness, train in the dual practice of giving and taking on the basis of your in- and out-breaths. While in this state, engage in the practice of ultimate awakening mind thus, contemplating, "Everything that shares the nature of samsara and nirvana has its root in the deluded mind.[229] As for the mind, it never deviates from its primordial nature of dharmakāya." Reflect how, in reality, even what is called death has no existence. Combine these two [contemplations], engage in their practice, and die while in that mindstate.

If this is unlikely to be feasible, then arouse the true nature of samsara and nirvana that is free of rejection and affirmation within the expanse of the ever-present innate dharmakāya, which is the uncontrived mind itself. Release your mind restfully in the ultimate expanse and place it upon the mind's ultimate nature, which is devoid of transference. Then, even if you are unable to die [in tune with the meditative state] because of temporarily losing your mindfulness, you will still die with the instruction [appropriate] for the moment of death. Although numerous celebrated moment-of-death instructions exist, the master said, nothing is more amazing than this [instruction presented here]. With these, the complete aspects of the path have been presented without omission.

V. Presentation of the measure of having trained the mind

The fifth point, the measure of having trained the mind is presented by the following:

The intent of all teachings converges on a single point.

The scriptures and the treatises were taught for the purpose of overcoming self-grasping, thus there is no target other than this for the trio of study, reflection, and meditation to destroy. When examined, the selfhood of persons is as nonexistent as the horn of a rabbit; [nevertheless] it has made us suffer since beginningless time. Observe and analyze whether all your endeavors of body, speech, and mind are directed toward reinforcing [your grasping at the selfhood of persons] or bringing its downfall. If they are reinforcing it, you are striving solely out of the eight mundane concerns and for the pursuit of greatness in this life. If this is the case, then even if you are observing ethical discipline with dedication, you have erred with regard to your paternal [spiritual] lineage. [67] Even if you are training the mind through study, reflection, and meditation, the practice has gone awry. On the other had, if your endeavors are toppling self-grasping, you are [achieving the] true purpose of ethical discipline with industry and you are training [the mind] with skillfulness. In this way, by giving rise to genuine mind-training realizations in your mind, you can likewise attain the full measure of Dharma practice. Since this is a benchmark for determining whether a Dharma practice has truly become a Dharma practice, the master said, this is the long bar of a scale on which the practitioner is weighed. Learn how to turn all your endeavors of body, speech, and mind into antidotes to self-grasping.

Of the two witnesses uphold the principal one.[230]

People might say of you, "This brother's heart has become softened, like a piece of wool that is taken out of water [after being washed].[231] Genuine spiritual practice has arisen in him. 'True Dharma practitioner' refers to all who are like him." Not being disapproved of by those who are reputedly sublime is a [form of] witness. But this should not be the principal one. Why? Because others may praise you when they observe one or two good actions or when you do a few things that please them, but other people cannot fully penetrate the depth [of your character].

What, then, is the principal [witness]? Regard it to be not becoming the object of your own disapproval. You should be able to feel that, even if you were to die this evening, you could have done nothing more. For you have striven to the best of your capacity with faith, intelligence, and perseverance, regardless of how weak these may have been, such that your guts become filled with air, and blood and water gushes out of them.[232] At that point you have attained a qualified stage of meditative practice. Therefore hold this fact of not being the object of your own disapproval as the principal witness.

Cultivate constantly the joyful mind alone.

This line suggests that, having trained your mind and tasted the flavor of

[true] Dharma practice, no matter what adverse circumstances befall you, you experience no disturbance within, for you [immediately] think: "I can cultivate its remedy, the two awakening minds." Remaining unassailed in such a manner is also a measure of having trained your mind.

Again, regarding the four desirable things and four undesirable things in the world, when you train the mind by focusing on the four undesirable things, everything becomes desirable. You will find thus no narrow mountain terrains or impediments, thus your mind will always be filled with joy, and the edifice [of your mind training practice] will not crumble. [68] This too is a measure of having trained the mind.

Again, when you have trained the mind in the dual practice of giving and taking, then whatever suffering afflicts your body and mind, you will [instantly] have the thought "Now, what I have taken from others in the past has its consequence," and you will experience once again an extraordinary sense of joy. In brief, whatever undesirable events occur, if they become factors conducive for training your mind and cause no disquiet, this is the measure of having trained the mind. At that point your remedy has reached its [true] depth.

If this can be done even when distracted, you are trained.

Just as a skilled horseman does not fall when distracted by the horse suddenly rearing up, in the same way, once your mind is trained, then even when unexpected adversities arise—such as unanticipated criticism and denigration—you instantly cope by [applying appropriate] antidotes. In this way, if [adversities] become factors conducive to the awakening mind, and if you do not fall prey to the adverse conditions, your mind is trained.

Furthermore, cultivate the thought, "The time of death is uncertain, and were it to come suddenly, I have no means [of facing it] other than this [practice]. This is true Dharma; wonderful indeed is my path!" In this manner, make sure you fortify the mind so that no matter when you die, you will do so joyfully and with a palpable warmth within. If you possess these signs of being trained, illnesses and [harms caused by] possessors will enhance your realizations. This doesn't mean that you need not train your mind further. This merely presents the measure of when [the application of] the remedy attains the measure of completeness.

VI. Presentation of the commitments of mind training

Train constantly in the three general points.

This line expresses that (1) your mind training should not contradict your pledges, (2) your mind training should not become offensive, and (3) your mind training should not be biased.

1) The first point entails relinquishing all behaviors that disregard the law of karma and its results. [This includes behaviors such as] defying the minor precepts with the assertion "Since I am training the mind, nothing can harm me," and engaging in actions that contradict the general [Dharma] practice with the assertion "If one has this mind training, one needs nothing else." [69] Engage in mind training by means of your thought, while in your actions observe, in a pure way, all the pledges and commitments you have taken, from the opening stanzas [of the ethical discipline texts] up to the Vajrayana. Make sure your practice and day-to-day way of life accord with and can withstand close scrutiny judged against the [three] scriptural collections.

2) The second point entails discarding such obnoxious behaviors as sleeping in harmful places, felling harmful trees,[233] visiting areas where you may contract contagious diseases, associating with people who are degenerate in their commitments, with lepers, or with those possessed by spirits. Do not act contrary to the Kadampa's way of life, a great tradition that has been established by Geshe Dromtönpa at Radreng. Practice the teaching instead as if [lifting all] four corners of square [cloth]. Shawopa states: "Examine where you might go wrong. You have erred when your spiritual practice becomes offensive."[234] Forsake consorting with those who are degenerate in their commitments or in their morality or who commit negative acts, and make sure your conduct does not become obnoxious.

3) The third point refers to the following. Some practitioners can tolerate harms caused by humans but are unable to do so in relation to nonhumans; they are obsessed with demonic harms. For others the reverse is true. Some practitioners are respectful toward important people but bully the weak. Some are affectionate toward their family but hostile toward outsiders. Others train their mind in relation to sentient beings but not in relation to elemental spirits. These attitudes are all biased. Train your mind to be free of such discriminations.

Transform your attitudes but remain as you are.

While practicing the exchange of self and others and reflecting on this yoga
—not divorced from it for even a single instant in your thought or in your
physical and verbal conduct—you must nonetheless maintain your conduct
the way it was before, with no [radical] shift. For instance, do not recite
[the words of mind training] in others' presence but strive to conform with
others. Maintain the level of spiritual activity that you normally engage in,
and leave your [external] behaviors unchanged from before. Some people, after listening to the teaching, become fickle, leaving behind their past
manner and practices. This is tantamount of forsaking your past, which is
extremely inappropriate. Since it is taught that your mind training should be
discreet yet effective, you should ripen your mind without others noticing.

Do not speak of the defects [of others].

This states that you should never speak of others' defects—neither their
worldly defects, for instance by calling them "That blind person," [70] nor
their spiritual defects, for instance by calling them "That morally degenerate
person."

Do not reflect on others' shortcomings.

It is inappropriate to ruminate about the shortcomings of sentient beings
in general and particularly of those who have entered the monastic order,
especially your fellow practitioners. At the least, you should be joyful toward
them, for you are training the mind. Even if you happen to feel that certain
associations may be inappropriate, since you are training the mind, contemplating others' shortcomings is inappropriate. If you do happen to lose
control and notice another's shortcoming, think, "This is my own deluded
perception; no such flaw exists in them. All sentient beings are endowed
with the nucleus of buddhahood." Reflect in this manner and judge this
[perception] to be your own flaw.

Discard all expectations of reward.

Discard all expectations, such as respect for your mind training; material
gifts, services, and fame; protection against harms caused by nonhumans in

this and future lives; the attainment of a joyful human or celestial existence; and the attainment of nirvana. Ensure that you have no expectation even of buddhahood for your own sake. Do not harbor impatience and excessive expectation even for the meditative qualities, for were the demons to become aware of this, they could create obstacles. Even if you exert strong effort with no loss of interest for a long time but still get no results, do not become discouraged.

Discard poisonous food.

[Poisonous food is] the harboring of self-interest in the depth of your heart. Never fail to perceive self-grasping as the enemy, or fail to let go of self-cherishing and the thoughts that grasp at the substantial reality of things. These make everything you do into a cause of cyclic existence, thus binding you [ever more] within cyclic existence and giving rise to suffering. Since these are all like poisonous food, you must discard them.

Do not maintain [inappropriate] loyalty.

This means you should not refrain from expressing condemnation out of disapproval of unjust acts committed by the other.

Do not torment with malicious banter.

Whatever tasks befall you, do not engage in malicious jokes that tear at others' hearts or cause them to lose their composure. Regardless of their culpability, avoid insulting and speaking harshly to others—whether close or distant, good or bad.

Do not lie in ambush.

Do not harbor vengeance for a wrong done to you, waiting for an opportune moment to retaliate. [71]

Do not strike at the heart.

Toward both humans and nonhumans, avoid delving into their weak points. With nonhumans, for instance, you should avoid uttering fierce life-extracting mantras; and in the case of humans, you should avoid unearthing, for instance, their moral lapses in situations where many people are around.

Do not place the load of a dzo onto an ox.

Avoid such negative behavior as attempting, by devious means, to shift blame and liabilities onto others that would otherwise fall on you.

Do not sprint to win a race.

Avoid such behavior as attempting, through unbecoming conduct and other means, to transfer the ownership of commonly owned desired objects to yourself. You should not be in a state of craving when you die, and since the "other shore" comes into being as a result of karma anyway, it is far more joyful instead to let go with a sense of ease, the master said.

Do not abuse this [practice] as a rite.

There is no [qualitative] difference between someone who, seeking well-being in the long term, accepts certain loss in interim and someone who engages in mind training as a ritual with the long-term motivation to conquer demonic harms. Therefore avoid [behavior] such as this that fails to root out the jaundice of self-centeredness from its depth. Some [practitioners] seem to think that mind training [practice] is beneficial for such a result or purpose. If this is true, there is no real difference between [practicing mind training] and engaging in shamanistic rites. To be called Dharma practice, [mind training] must become an antidote to afflictions and false conceptualization.

Do not turn the gods into demons.

When displeased, the worldly gods cause harm. The gods are supposed to be beneficial in general; so if they cause harm, they then become demons. Similarly, mind training is supposed to subdue self-grasping. Avoid, therefore, becoming inflated by its practice and generating conceited thoughts such as "I am an excellent practitioner of mind training; others lack this spiritual practice." Avoid ridiculing and insulting others out of a sense of superiority. If practitioners strengthen their grasping at the self-existence of phenomena, their practice becomes an endeavor of the enemy. It becomes the act of allowing a thief to escape into the forest while looking for his footprints on a rocky mountain. Avoid all such conduct and, by disgracing the self-grasping, ensure that the medicine is applied right where the illness is. Comport yourself as the lowest of the low among the servants of all sentient beings.

Do not seek misery as a means to happiness.

[72] This refers to not drawing personal gratification from others' miseries. Do not, for example, harbor thoughts such as, "If my spouse or this particular friend dies, their family lineage will come to an end," "If the wealthy benefactor becomes ill or dies, I will have the opportunity to accumulate merit and roots of virtue," "If my meditator colleague of this region dies, I alone will have the opportunity to accumulate merit," and "If this enemy dies, I will enjoy happiness." The master said that since sentient beings experience their own individual merits, no matter where you go, due to karma you will find enemies and friends.

VII. Presentation of the precepts of mind training

Since your mind training will not degenerate but will [in fact] take you to progressively higher levels, you should engage in the practice of this teaching.

Accomplish all yogas through a single means.

Other spiritual practices have their own particular dietary requirements, modes of conduct, and so on, in addition to their yogic practices. For those who have entered the door [of] this [mind training practice], it is sufficient to engage in all activities, such as [those pertaining to] food, solely by keeping in mind this [mind training practice]. So you should engage in this practice.

Overcome all errors through a single means.

Some who are under Māra's influence fail to develop confidence in this spiritual practice. They experience the false perceptions of misguided meditation practice, with thoughts like: "Since I began practicing mind training, illnesses have increased, harms from demons have increased, people have become more hostile, and afflictions such as self-grasping have increased as well." Based on such thoughts, or for no particular reason, they lose enthusiasm for mind training and are in danger of turning away. When this happens, you should become aware of it right there and then and think, "A misguided meditative practice has arisen in me." With a second thought you should reflect, "There must be many beings like me in the universe whose thoughts have deviated from [true] Dharma practice," and take all of these [deviations] upon yourself and offer your body, wealth, and virtues to others. Imagine that because of this, the thoughts of those others turn toward the Dharma, and these others enter the unmistaken path. [73]

There are two tasks—one at the start and one at the end.

In the morning, after getting up, you should project the thought "Throughout this day I shall make sure I don't become tainted by the clinging of self-cherishing. I shall make sure that thoughts cherishing others do not degenerate." Then, during the day, remain sustained by the vigilance that accompanies [everyday] activity. When going to bed at night, while in the meditative absorption "lion's majestic pose," sequentially review [the day] by recalling, "First I did this, then I did that, and so on." If you detect any transgression, it is stated, "At that instant enumerate your flaws / And recall your teacher's instructions."[235] Then cultivate the following thought: "Isn't it amazing that there are people like me who waste their precious human existence and bring harm upon themselves!" Thinking thus, appeal for forbearance, declare and purify your negative karma, and cultivate the resolve to forsake this in the future. If you have not committed any transgression, then rejoice, thinking "I have indeed made my human existence meaningful." Dedicate the virtues toward the aspiration to realize this practice in your mental continuum. [Also] make the aspiration prayer, "May I never be divorced from the two awakening minds throughout all my lives."

Forbear whichever of the two arises.

If you suddenly come into a great fortune, do not become arrogant or become attached to it; make sure you do not fall prey to the eight mundane concerns. You should take this [fortune] as a basis for your Dharma practice. Some people who attract followers and material gifts become conceited by this; they [then] despise others and do whatever comes to mind. You must discard such behavior.

Likewise, if you experience misfortune such that the only thing that seems beneath you is the water [flowing under a bridge], do not become depressed or demoralized, wondering how "such an unfortunate person like me" could exist. Do not be so downcast you are incapable of training [the mind].

Instead reflect, "Compared to the contrast in degree and intensity between the happiness of the higher realms and the suffering of the lower realms of existence, the contrast between pleasant and unpleasant states of human existence is not so immense. So, without further distraction, I shall focus on my spiritual practices." For it is taught:

> Even if you are prosperous like the gods,
> Pray do not be conceited.
> Even if you become as destitute as a hungry ghost,
> Pray do not be disheartened.[236]

Guard the two even at the cost of your life.

These are (1) the precepts and commitments presented in the teachings in general and (2) the commitments of this particular [mind training] teaching, [74] such as "Do not speak of the defects [of others]."[237] Since even the mundane happiness of this present life will elude you if these two commitments become degenerate, hold them more dearly than your life.

Train in the three difficult challenges.

When eliminating the afflictions, in the beginning it can be difficult to remember the antidotes, in the middle it can be difficult to overcome the afflictions, and at the end it can be difficult to eradicate the continuum of the afflictions. Therefore make sure you accomplish these three without [great] difficulty. To train, [first thing] in the morning put on the armor with respect to all three [stages]. When the afflictions [actually] arise, recall their antidotes, counter them, and cultivate the resolve "From here on I shall never allow the afflictions to arise in my mind."

Adopt the three principal conditions.

(1) There should be a qualified spiritual teacher who possesses the pith instructions and is endowed with higher realizations. The bond [between the teacher and you] should be so close that no dog can come between, and the teacher should be pleased with you. (2) Your state of mind should be such that [many realizations have arisen]—from [the rarity of] precious human existence to [the understanding of] no-self—and these should have arisen just as contemplated or as taught by your teacher. (3) Conditions conducive to Dharma practice must be gathered—such as faith, intelligence, joyous effort, a strong sense of disenchantment [toward cyclic existence], food and clothing, and other necessities.

Since these three are the principal conditions of Dharma practice, if you possess them, rejoice and strive especially to enhance them. If you do not possess them, contemplate: "How sad! The [vast] expanse of the universe must contain countless others like me who lack these three factors and have failed in their Dharma practice." Thinking thus, take upon yourself all their [deficiencies]. As you offer your body and so on to them, imagine they obtain the three conditions and that all experience the Great Vehicle.

> **Contemplate the three that are free of degeneration.**

Since all the attainments of the Mahayana depend upon the student's faith and respect [toward his or her teacher], make sure you are never divorced at any time from the perception of your teacher as a buddha. In this manner, make sure that your faith and respect toward your spiritual teacher remain undiminished. Furthermore, with the thought "This mind training [teaching] represents the quintessence of Mahayana and is like a potent seed of buddhahood," engage in this incomparable practice. Thus make sure your enthusiasm for mind training remains undiminished. As for the pledges of the Great and Lesser vehicles you have taken, [75] you should, by sailing the great ship of shame and conscientiousness, which are the [true] antidotes, learn to guard them undiminished, not tainted by even the slightest infractions.

> **Be endowed with the three inseparable factors.**

Make sure that your body is never divorced from such virtuous acts as offering services to your spiritual teachers, making offerings to the Three Jewels, offering torma cakes to the Dharma protectors and the elemental spirits, making prostrations, performing circumambulation, and so on. Make sure that your speech is never divorced from such virtuous acts as reciting [verses on] taking refuge, repeating mantras, and doing recitations. Make sure that your mind is never divorced from the two awakening minds and is endowed with inconceivable courage to vanquish all the conceptualizing afflictions, such as self-cherishing. In brief, make sure your body, speech, and mind are never divorced from virtuous activity at all times.

Train constantly toward the chosen objects.

It is stated that being angry and vengeful toward enemies and adversaries who are right there in your presence comes about on the basis of frequent interactions.[238] Thus, from one angle, there is a real risk of losing your mind training in relation to those who simply appear repulsive, those who harbor ill-will against you even though you have caused them no harm, and those you find undesirable even though they harbor no ill-will toward you. Therefore single these people out for special focus, and train your mind by perceiving them as parts of your own heart. Furthermore, because your spiritual teachers, parents, and bodhisattvas are objects of special significance—the fruitional effects are inconceivably [grave] if you accumulate negative karma in relation to them—single them out [for special focus] and engage in the training.

Do not depend on other conditions.

To engage in other spiritual practices, it is essential to gather various favorable conditions such as food, clothing, and so on; you also need to have good health, [access to] water that is suited to your body, and no excessive disturbances from humans and nonhumans [alike]. The practice of mind training, in contrast, does not depend on such conditions. Since the very absence of favorable conditions is itself a resource for this spiritual practice, today take all of these as [the ripening of] meritorious karma and as factors conducive to mind training.

Engage in the principal practices right now.

Since beginningless time you have roamed in the three lower realms of existence as if it were your ancestral home. Today, at this juncture, [76] when you have obtained the human existence of leisure and opportunity that is so rarely found in even a billion eons, instead of making all kinds of plans for this life, it is more important to engage in Dharma practice that aims for [the welfare of] future lives. Of the two aspects of Dharma, exposition and practice, the latter is more important. Compared to all other meditative practices, the practice of training in the awakening mind is more important. Compared to training [the mind] by applying the [two] paddles of scripture and reasoning, it is more important to persistently train in applying the appropriate antidotes on the basis of your teacher's pith instructions. Compared to other activities, training by remaining seated on your cushion is more important. Compared to avoiding the objects [of your afflictions], it is more important to probe within. It is critical for you to train in these points.

Do not apply misplaced understanding.

This refers to the avoidance of six misplaced understandings. If, instead of enduring the hardships entailed in Dharma practice, you forbear difficulties when seeking the objects of your desire, nurturing your friends, and subduing your foes—this is *misplaced forbearance.* If, instead of aspiring to purify your negative karma as much as you can, accumulate merit as much as you can, and strive to transform your thoughts as much as you can, you view the excellences of this life as admirable qualities and aspire to them—this is *misplaced aspiration.* If, instead of savoring your experience of the Dharma through striving in learning, reflection, and meditation, you savor the taste of sensual desire and pursue it and you dwell on and relish memories of past sexual experiences and triumphs over enemies—this is *misplaced savoring.* If, instead of cultivating compassion for those caught in suffering and its conditions, you have compassion for those who undergo sufferings as part of their ascetic life and meditative pursuits—this is *misplaced compassion.* If, instead of cultivating dedication to Dharma practice as a privilege, you have a sense of dedication to such endeavors as accumulating material wealth, nurturing friends, and pursuing mundane greatness—this is *misplaced dedication.* If, instead of rejoicing in those—from the buddhas to the sentient beings— who engage in virtue and enjoy its fruit, happiness, you rejoice when misfortunes and disasters befall your adversaries—this is *misplaced rejoicing.* You should relate to these six misplaced understandings with [appropriate] avoidance and affirmation.

Do not be sporadic.

At times you practice mind training while at others you engage in mantra repetitions; on some occasions you forsake both, yet on other occasions you guard both. Relinquish such a sporadic approach. Forsake also such sporadic approaches as sometimes making plans for this mundane life [77] and increasing negative karma and afflictions, and sometimes engaging in Dharma practice for the sake of your future life. Without being sporadic, engage in Dharma practice with single-pointed dedication. In particular, practice mind training, for mind training is the innermost essence of Dharma practice.

Train with decisiveness.

When a minor nerve is damaged, you treat it by cutting it clean. In the same way, when you engage in the training of mind, do not remain hesitant but direct your entire mind. You should remain resolute in your decision and train with no hesitation. Avoid such dilettantish attitudes as "First I will check to see if mind training is beneficial; if not, I will recite mantras." This indicates that you have failed to let go of yearning for [self-centered] happiness; this [kind of practice] can't even overcome sickness and malevolent possessions.

Be released through the two: investigation and close analysis.

[First] investigate which affliction is most dominant in your mind and earnestly apply its specific antidote, striving hard to subdue the affliction. Then analyze the way deluded mental projections arise in relation to the objects that act as their bases. By applying the antidotes, you reduce the force of the afflictions or prevent their arising. By repeatedly thinking "From here on I will never allow my mindstream to be tainted by these afflictions," you cultivate familiarity with the protective armor for the future. Thus, with these twin methods for applying antidotes to past and future [afflictions], strive diligently to eliminate the afflictions.[239]

Do not boast of your good deeds.[240]

Don't be boastful and arrogant toward others on any grounds, suggesting, for example, that another person is indebted to you, or that you engage in certain spiritual practices, or that you are learned, or that you are industrious in your ethical discipline, or that you are great, or that your family lineage is excellent. Radrengpa has said, "Don't place too much hope in humans; supplicate the gods instead."[241] In any case, if you have correctly distinguished between enemy and friend, you understand everyone to be a friend. Then [even] when you work for others' welfare, the jaundice of self-centeredness does not arise. Instead you recognize all such tasks as obligations, so boastfulness toward others simply does not occur. At this point your mind has become trained.

Do not be ill-tempered.

Whatever others may have done to you in the past, such as humiliating you or verbally abusing you, the blame lies within yourself. Do not react to others with contorted facial expressions or abusive words. [78] Even with your mind, restrain yourself from ill-temperedness. Because your Dharma practice has not yet become an antidote to self-grasping, your resilience is at present weak, and you are volatile due to ill-temperedness. Since such behavior makes your Dharma practice ineffective, ensure that [your Dharma practice] becomes an antidote to self-grasping.

Do not be fickle.

This means not displaying erratic responses to every situation out of a transient temperament. This causes great inconvenience to your companions and must therefore be relinquished.

Do not be boisterous.

Avoid seeking fame and praise through expressions of gratitude for assistance you may have rendered others or benefits you may have brought them. In brief, do not desire even to hear compliments for help or assistance rendered to others.

In this manner you should train, your entire life, in the two awakening minds by means of both meditative sessions and practices in the subsequent periods. There will [then] be no basis for dispute and no reason for conflict with the gods, demons, or your fellow humans. By making the gods at peace, the serpentine nāgas tranquil, and everyone happy as best as possible, when your last breath approaches, you will experience the beginning of [true] happiness, and you will turn your back on misery and travel from light to light, from joy to joy.

The effects or benefits of these spiritual practices are presented in the following:

Through this proliferation of the five degenerations,
Transform [every event] into the path of enlightenment.

Generally speaking, the teaching of Buddha Śākyamuni emerged during an era when the five degenerations were on the rise. In particular, it has emerged during this present age, the era of the last five-hundred-year cycle, when the degenerations are even more severe than the five degenerations. Because of this, sentient beings have only afflictions in their thoughts and only negative karma for their actions. They relish when others suffer and feel anguished when others are fortunate. So with all three doors—body, speech, and mind—sentient beings indulge only in deeds that are harmful to others. It is [therefore] an era when [harmful] sentient beings have gathered. Furthermore, those nonhuman agents that admire the positive white force have departed to the pure realms to benefit the bodhisattvas, whereas the strength and force of those who admire the dark side have increased. Because of this, misfortunes plague sentient beings.

Today, therefore, a multitude of adverse conditions cause all kinds of suffering for sentient beings, [79] and myriad obstacles particularly befall those who put the doctrine into practice. So at this time, when adverse conditions compete to form a thicket, if you do not train in this spiritual practice, though you may enter other systems of practice, you will fail to succeed in Dharma practice. By entering this practice and striving in it [on the other hand], you will transform all adverse conditions into factors conducive for training on the path to enlightenment.

As for other benefits, a year's pursuit of virtuous activities during this age—when the teachings of the Buddha face hostile threats—will help accomplish the accumulations better than eons pursuing virtuous activities in the pure realms. Therefore, those capable of training the mind are not vulnerable to the proliferation of the five degenerations and remain contented. If you know how to train the mind, even your body, the body of a mind training yogi, is known as the "city that is a source of joy." For all happiness—of this and future lives, of self and others—comes about on the basis of this very body.

Strive therefore by concentrating all your efforts in this endeavor. And if you make sure that the teachings are integrated with your mind—that the rule of Dharma is established as firmly as a stake driven through your heart—and that you experience the taste of Dharma, before long you will attain the perfect state, wherein the complete aims of self and others are accomplished. Thus said the master.

To illustrate these points in a definitive formulation, the author[242] himself wrote the following lines:

> **Because of my numerous aspirations,**
> **I have defied the tragic tale of suffering**
> **And have taken instructions to subdue self-grasping.**
> **Now, even if death comes, I have no regrets.**

These words were uttered as an expression of joy by the highly accomplished yogi Chekawa, who, having presented the method of practice, arrived at a decisively settled state of mind following a clear discrimination between enemy and friend.

Colophon

These words of my teacher, an ocean of goodness delighting everyone—
Through the merit of compiling them with a wish to help others
May the [giant] elephant of mind training carry all beings
And demolish the solid mountain of egoistic view.

As the rays of your fame pervade all directions,
Like a magnet pulling forth [all] iron objects, [80]
Stirred by your fame, [disciples] remain in your presence;
They've beheld your face so rare and have accomplished great aims.

In the sky of the exalted mind of Serlingpa's lineage,
Though the sun of mind training still shines brilliantly,
It is now obscured by clouds of negative conceptualization;
The line between gold and worn-out brass has become blurred.

O, those who wish to relinquish the sufferings of self and others—
Forsake the inferior paths described as incomplete
And enter this horse-drawn carriage path of the conqueror's supreme
    children.[243]

How can anyone hope to become enlightened without this?
[Extracted] from the distillation of all scriptures,
This innermost essence of Kadam is most amazing!

Sarva śubham

8. The Wheel of Sharp Weapons
Attributed to Dharmarakṣita[244]

Homage to the Three Jewels![245]

This is the wheel of weapons striking at the vital points of the enemy's body.
Homage to the wrathful Yamāntaka![246]

1
When peacocks roam through the jungle of virulent poison,
Though the gardens of medicinal plants may be attractive,
The peacock flocks will not take delight in them;
For peacocks thrive on the essence of virulent poison.

2
Likewise when heroes enter the jungle of cyclic existence,
Though the gardens of happiness and prosperity may seem beautiful,
The heroes will not become attached to them;
For heroes thrive in the forest of suffering.

3
Those who avidly pursue happiness and prosperity
Are brought to suffering due to their cowardice.
The bodhisattvas, who willingly embrace suffering,
Always remain happy due to their heroism.

4
Now here, desire is like the jungle of virulent poison;
The peacock-like heroes [alone] can digest this.
But for the crow-like cowards it spells death,
For how can the self-centered digest such poison?
When you extend this [analogy] to other afflictions,[247]
Each similarly assails liberation's life force, like [poison to] a crow.

5

Therefore peacock-like heroes must convert
Afflictions that resemble a jungle of poisons into an elixir
And enter the jungle of cyclic existence;
Embracing the afflictions, heroes must destroy their poison.

6

From now on I will distance myself from this demon's emissary—
Self-grasping—which [makes me] wander helplessly
And seeks [only] selfish happiness and prosperity;
I will joyfully embrace hardship for the sake of others.

7

Propelled by karma and habituated to the afflictions—
The sufferings of all beings who share this nature
I will heap them upon this self that yearns for happiness.

8

When selfish craving enters my heart,
I will expel it and offer my happiness to all beings.
If those around me rise in mutiny against me,
I will relish it, thinking, "This is due to my own negligence."

9

When my body falls prey to unbearable illnesses,
It is the weapon of evil karma returning on me
For injuring the bodies of others; [82]
From now on I will take all sickness upon myself.

10

When my mind falls prey to suffering,
It is the weapon of evil karma turning upon me
For definitely causing turbulence in the hearts of others;
From now on I will take all suffering upon myself.

11

When I am tormented by extreme hunger and thirst,
It is the weapon of evil karma turning upon me
For engaging in deception, theft, and miserly acts;
From now on I will take all hunger and thirst upon myself.

12

When I am powerless and suffer in servitude to others,
It is the weapon of evil karma turning upon me
For being hostile to the weak and subjugating them;
From now on I will employ my body and life in the service of others.

13

When unpleasant words reach my ears,
It is the weapon of evil karma turning upon me
For my verbal offenses, such as divisive speech;
From now on I will condemn flawed speech.[248]

14

When I am born in a place of impurity,
It is the weapon of evil karma turning upon me
For always cultivating impure perceptions;
From now on I will cultivate only pure perceptions.

15

When I become separated from helpful and loving friends,
It is the weapon of evil karma turning upon me
For luring away others' companions;
From now on I will never estrange others from their companions.

16

When the sublime ones become displeased with me,
It is the weapon of evil karma turning upon me
For renouncing the sublime ones and seeking bad companions;
From now on I will renounce negative friendships.

17

When others assail me with exaggeration, denigration, and so on,
It is the weapon of evil karma turning upon me
For disparaging sublime beings;
From now on I will never belittle others with disparaging words.

18

When my material resources waste away,
It is the weapon of evil karma turning upon me

For being disrespectful toward others' resources;
From now on I will help others find what they need.

19

When my mind becomes dull and my heart unhappy,
It is the weapon of evil karma turning upon me
For making others accumulate negative karma;
From now on I will shun enabling others' negative acts.

20

When I fail in my endeavors and feel deeply disturbed,
It is the weapon of evil karma turning upon me
For obstructing the work of sublime ones;
From now on I will relinquish all obstructive deeds.

21

When my gurus remain displeased no matter what I do,
It is the weapon of evil karma turning upon me
For acting duplicitously toward the sublime Dharma;
From now on I will be less duplicitous with respect to the Dharma. [83]

22

When everyone challenges what I say,
It is the weapon of evil karma turning upon me
For disregarding shame and my conscience;
From now on I will refrain from troubling behavior.

23

When disputes arise as soon as my companions gather,
It is the weapon of evil karma turning upon me
For peddling my destructive, evil character in all directions;
From now on I will maintain good character wherever I am.

24

When all who are close to me rise up as enemies,
It is the weapon of evil karma turning upon me
For harboring harmful, evil intentions within;
From now on I will diminish deceit and guile.[249]

25

When I am sick with a chronic ulcer or edema,
It is the weapon of evil karma turning upon me
For wrongfully and with no conscience using others' possessions;
From now on I will renounce acts such as plundering others' possessions.

26

When my body is struck suddenly by contagious disease,
It is the weapon of evil karma turning upon me
For committing acts that undermined my solemn pledges;
From now on I will renounce nonvirtue.

27

When my intellect becomes ignorant of all fields of knowledge,
It is the weapon of evil karma turning upon me
For persisting in activities that must be cast aside;
From now on I will cultivate the insights of learning and so on.[250]

28

When I am overwhelmed by sloth while practicing Dharma,
It is the weapon of evil karma turning upon me
For amassing obscurations to the sublime Dharma;
From now on I will undergo hardships for the sake of the Dharma.

29

When I delight in afflictions and am greatly distracted,
It is the weapon of evil karma turning upon me
For not contemplating impermanence and the defects of cyclic existence;
From now on I will increase my dissatisfaction with cyclic existence.

30

When I continue to regress despite all my efforts,
It is the weapon of evil karma turning upon me
For defying karma and the law of cause and effect;
From now on I will strive to accumulate merit.

31

When all the religious rituals I perform go amiss,
It is the weapon of evil karma turning upon me
For investing hope and expectation in forces of darkness;
From now on I will turn away from forces of darkness.

32

When my prayers to the Three Jewels are impotent,
It is the weapon of evil karma turning upon me
For not entrusting myself to the Buddha's way;
From now on I will rely solely on the Three Jewels.

33

When my imagination arises as veils and possessor spirits,
It is the weapon of evil karma turning upon me
For accumulating negative karma against deities and their mantras;
From now on I will vanquish all negative conceptions.[251]

34

When I am lost and wander like a powerless man,
It is the weapon of evil karma turning upon me
For driving others, such as my guru, away from their abodes; [84]
From now on I will expel no one from their home.

35

When calamities such as frost and hailstorms occur,
It is the weapon of evil karma turning upon me
For failing to properly observe my pledges and moral precepts;
From now on I will keep my pledges and vows pure.

36

When I am avaricious yet bereft of wealth,
It is the weapon of evil karma turning upon me
For failing to give charity and make offerings to the Three Jewels;
From now on I will strive in giving and offering.[252]

37

When I am ugly and am mistreated by my companions,
It is the weapon of evil karma turning upon me

For erecting ugly images while in the turmoil of anger;
From now on I will be patient when creating the images of gods.

38
When attachment and anger erupt no matter what I do,
It is the weapon of evil karma turning upon me
For allowing my untamed evil mind to become rigid;
From now on I will root out this obstinate heart.[253]

39
When all my meditative practices fail in their aims,
It is the weapon of evil karma turning on me
For allowing pernicious views to enter my heart;
From now on whatever I do will be solely for others' sake.

40
When my mind remains untamed despite spiritual practice,
It is the weapon of evil karma turning upon me
For eagerly pursuing mundane ambitions;
From now on I will concentrate on aspiring for liberation.

41
When I feel remorse as soon as I sit down and reflect,
It is the weapon of evil karma turning upon me
For being shamelessly fickle and clamoring for high status;
From now on I will be vigilant in my associations with others.

42
When I am deceived by others' treachery,
It is the weapon of evil karma turning upon me
For being conceited and greedy;
From now on I will be discreet with respect to everything.[254]

43
When my studies and teaching fall prey to attachment and anger,
It is the weapon of evil karma turning upon me
For failing to reflect on the ills of demons in my heart;
From now on I will examine adverse forces and overcome them.

44

When all the good I have done turns out badly,
It is the weapon of evil karma turning upon me
For repaying others' kindness with ingratitude;
From now on I will respectfully repay others' kindness.[255]

45

In brief, when calamities befall me like bolts of lightning,
It is the weapon of evil karma turning upon me,
Just like the ironsmith who is slain by his own sword;
From now on I will be heedful against negative acts.

46

When I undergo sufferings in the lower realms,
It is the weapon of evil karma turning upon me,
Like an archer slain by his own arrow; [85]
From now on I will be heedful against negative acts.[256]

47

When the sufferings of the householder befall me,
It is the weapon of evil karma turning upon me,
Like parents slain by their own cherished children;
From now I will rightly renounce worldly life.

48

Since that's the way things are, I've seized the enemy!
I've caught the thief who steals and deceives with stealth.
Aha! There is no doubt that it's this self-grasping indeed;
This charlatan deceives me by impersonating me.

49

Now, O Yamāntaka, raise the weapon of karma over his head—
Spin the wheel three times fiercely over his head.
Your legs of two truths spread apart and eyes of method and wisdom
    wide open,
With your fangs of four powers bared, strike the enemy!

50
The king of spells who confounds the enemy's mind;
Summon this oath breaker who betrays self and others—
This savage called "self-grasping demon"—
Who, while brandishing the weapon of karma,
Runs amok in the jungle of cyclic existence.

51
Summon him, summon him, wrathful Yamāntaka!
Strike him, strike him, pierce the heart of this enemy, the self!
Dance and trample on the head of this betrayer, false conception!
Mortally strike at the heart of this butcher and enemy, Ego!

52
Hūṃ! Hūṃ! Great meditation deity, display your miraculous powers;
Dza! Dza! Bind this enemy tightly;
Phat! Phat! Release us from all bondage;
Shik! Shik! I beseech you to cut the knot of grasping.

53
Appear before me, O Yamāntaka, my meditation deity!
Tear it! Tear it! Rip to shreds this very instant—
The leather sack of karma and the five poisonous afflictions
That mire me in karma's samsaric mud.

54
Even though he leads me to misery in the three lower realms,
I do not learn to fear him but rush to his source—
Dance and trample on the head of this betrayer, false conception!
Mortally strike at the heart of this butcher and enemy, Ego!

55
Though my desire for comfort is great, I do not gather its causes;
Though I have little endurance for pain, I am rife with the dark craving of
    greed—
Dance and trample on the head of this betrayer, false conception!
Mortally strike at the heart of this butcher and enemy, Ego!

56

Though I want immediate results, my efforts to achieve them are feeble;
Though I pursue many tasks, I never complete a single one—
Dance and trample on the head of this betrayer, false conception!
Mortally strike at the heart of this butcher and enemy, Ego!

57

Though I am eager to make new friends, my loyalty and friendship are
    short-lived; [86]
Though I aspire for resources, I seek them through theft and
    extortion[257]—
Dance and trample on the head of this betrayer, false conception!
Mortally strike at the heart of this butcher and enemy, Ego!

58

Though skilled at flattery and innuendo, my discontent runs deep;
Though assiduously amassing wealth, I am chained by miserliness—
Dance and trample on the head of this betrayer, false conception!
Mortally strike at the heart of this butcher and enemy, Ego!

59

Though rarely rendering help to others, I remain most boastful;
Though unwilling to take risks, I am bloated with ambition—
Dance and trample on the head of this betrayer, false conception!
Mortally strike at the heart of this butcher and enemy, Ego!

60

Though I've many teachers, my capacity for pledges remains weak;
Though I've many students, my patience and will to help are scant—
Dance and trample on the head of this betrayer, false conception!
Mortally strike at the heart of this butcher and enemy, Ego!

61

Though eager to make promises, I remain weak in actual assistance;
Though my fame may be great, when I am probed, even gods and ghosts
    are appalled—
Dance and trample on the head of this betrayer, false conception!
Mortally strike at the heart of this butcher and enemy, Ego!

62

Though I am weak in learning, my temerity for empty words is great;
Though slight in scriptural knowledge, I meddle in all kinds of topics—
Dance and trample on the head of this betrayer, false conception!
Mortally strike at the heart of this butcher and enemy, Ego!

63

Though I may have many friends and servants, none with dedication;
Though I may have many leaders, I have no guardian I can rely on—
Dance and trample on the head of this betrayer, false conception!
Mortally strike at the heart of this butcher and enemy, Ego!

64

Though my status may be high, my qualities remain less than a ghost's;
Though I may be a great teacher, my afflictions remain worse than a
    demon's—
Dance and trample on the head of this betrayer, false conception!
Mortally strike at the heart of this butcher and enemy, Ego!

65

Though my views may be lofty, my deeds are worse than a dog's;
Though my qualities may be numerous, the fundamental ones are lost to
    the winds—
Dance and trample on the head of this betrayer, false conception!
Mortally strike at the heart of this butcher and enemy, Ego!

66

I harbor all my self-centered desires deep within;
For all my disputes I blame others for no reason—
Dance and trample on the head of this betrayer, false conception!
Mortally strike at the heart of this butcher and enemy, Ego!

67

Though clad in saffron robes, I seek protection from the ghosts;
Though I've taken the precepts, my conduct is that of a demon—
Dance and trample on the head of this betrayer, false conception!
Mortally strike at the heart of this butcher and enemy, Ego!

68

Though the gods create my happiness, I propitiate malevolent spirits;
Though the Dharma acts as my savior, I deceive the Three Jewels—
Dance and trample on the head of this betrayer, false conception!
Mortally strike at the heart of this butcher and enemy, Ego!

69

Though always living in solitude, I am carried away by distractions;
Though receiving sublime Dharma scriptures, I cherish divination and
    shamanism[258]—[87]
Dance and trample on the head of this betrayer, false conception!
Mortally strike at the heart of this butcher and enemy, Ego!

70

Forsaking ethical discipline, the liberation path, I cling to paternal
    home;[259]
Casting my happiness into the river, I chase after misery—
Dance and trample on the head of this betrayer, false conception!
Mortally strike at the heart of this butcher and enemy, Ego!

71

Forsaking the gateway to liberation, I wander in the wilderness;[260]
Though obtaining a precious human birth, I seek the hell realms—
Dance and trample on the head of this betrayer, false conception!
Mortally strike at the heart of this butcher and enemy, Ego!

72

Putting aside spiritual developments, I pursue the profits of trade;
Leaving my teacher's classroom behind, I roam through towns and
    places—
Dance and trample on the head of this betrayer, false conception!
Mortally strike at the heart of this butcher and enemy, Ego!

73

Forsaking my own livelihood, I rob others of their resources;
Squandering my own inherited wealth,[261] I plunder from others—
Dance and trample on the head of this betrayer, false conception!
Mortally strike at the heart of this butcher and enemy, Ego!

74
Alas! Though my endurance for meditation is poor, I've sharp
    clairvoyance;[262]
Though I've not even reached the edge of the path, my legs are needlessly
    fast—
Dance and trample on the head of this betrayer, false conception!
Mortally strike at the heart of this butcher and enemy, Ego!

75
When someone gives useful advice, I view them as a hostile foe;
When someone fools me with treachery, I repay the heartless one with
    kindness—
Dance and trample on the head of this betrayer, false conception!
Mortally strike at the heart of this butcher and enemy, Ego!

76
When someone treats me as their family, I reveal their secrets to their
    foes;
When someone befriends me, I betray their trust with no pangs of
    conscience—
Dance and trample on the head of this betrayer, false conception!
Mortally strike at the heart of this butcher and enemy, Ego!

77
My ill temper is intense, my paranoia more coarse than everyone's;
Hard to befriend, I constantly provoke others' negative traits—
Dance and trample on the head of this betrayer, false conception!
Mortally strike at the heart of this butcher and enemy, Ego!

78
When someone asks for favor, I ignore him yet covertly cause him harm;
When someone respects my wishes, I don't concur but seek disputes from
    afar—
Dance and trample on the head of this betrayer, false conception!
Mortally strike at the heart of this butcher and enemy, Ego!

79

I dislike advice and am always difficult to be with;
I am easily offended, and my grudge is always strong—
Dance and trample on the head of this betrayer, false conception!
Mortally strike at the heart of this butcher and enemy, Ego!

80

I crave high status and regard sublime beings as foes;
Because my lust is strong, I eagerly pursue the young—
Dance and trample on the head of this betrayer, false conception!
Mortally strike at the heart of this butcher and enemy, Ego!

81

Because of fickleness I cast far away my past friendships;
Infatuated with novelty, I talk animatedly to everyone—[88]
Dance and trample on the head of this betrayer, false conception!
Mortally strike at the heart of this butcher and enemy, Ego!

82

Having no clairvoyance, I resort to lies and deprecation;
Having no compassion, I betray others' trust and cause their hearts
    pain—
Dance and trample on the head of this betrayer, false conception!
Mortally strike at the heart of this butcher and enemy, Ego!

83

Though my learning is feeble, I guess wildly about everything;
As my scriptural knowledge is scant, I engender wrong views about
    everything—
Dance and trample on the head of this betrayer, false conception!
Mortally strike at the heart of this butcher and enemy, Ego!

84

Habituated to attachment and anger, I insult all those who oppose me;
Habituated to envy, I slander and denigrate others—
Dance and trample on the head of this betrayer, false conception!
Mortally strike at the heart of this butcher and enemy, Ego!

85

Failing to study, I have forsaken the vast [scholarly disciplines];
Failing to rely upon teachers, I defame the scriptures—
Dance and trample on the head of this betrayer, false conception!
Mortally strike at the heart of this butcher and enemy, Ego!

86

Instead of teaching the discourses, I expound lies of my own invention;
Failing to cultivate pure perception, I utter insults and threats—
Dance and trample on the head of this betrayer, false conception!
Mortally strike at the heart of this butcher and enemy, Ego!

87

Refusing to condemn deeds that are contrary to Dharma,
I level various criticisms against all well-spoken words[263]—
Dance and trample on the head of this betrayer, false conception!
Mortally strike at the heart of this butcher and enemy, Ego!

88

Failing to regard signs of disgrace as a source of shame,
Perversely I hold what are signs of honor as a source of shame—
Dance and trample on the head of this betrayer, false conception!
Mortally strike at the heart of this butcher and enemy, Ego!

89

Failing to pursue any suitable deeds,
I perform instead all that is inappropriate—
Dance and trample on the head of this betrayer, false conception!
Mortally strike at the heart of this butcher and enemy, Ego!

90

Powerful one, you who possess the Bliss Gone's[264] dharmakāya
And destroy the demon of egoistic view,
O wielder of club, the weapon of no-self wisdom,[265]
Twirl it over your head three times, without hesitation!

91

With your great ferocity obliterate this enemy!
With your great wisdom dismantle this false conception!

With your great compassion protect me from my karma!
Help destroy this Ego once and for all!

92
Whatever suffering exists for the beings in cyclic existence,
Pile it all decisively upon this self-grasping.
Wherever the poisons of five afflictions are found,
Heap them decisively upon that which shares the same nature.

93
Though having thus recognized the root of all evil
Through critical reasoning and beyond any doubt,
If I continue to abet it and act in its defense,
Then destroy the very person, the grasper himself! [89]

94
Now I will banish all the blames onto one source;
And to all beings I'll contemplate their great kindness.[266]
I will take into myself the undesirable qualities of others
And dedicate my virtuous roots for the benefit of all beings.

95
Thus, as I take on myself all [negative] deeds of others
Committed through their three doors throughout all three times,
So, like a peacock that has colorful feathers because of poison,
May the afflictions be transformed into factors of enlightenment.

96
As I offer my roots of virtue to sentient beings,
Like the crow that has consumed poison and is cured by its antidote,
May I hold the lifeline of liberation of all beings
And swiftly attain buddhahood of one gone to bliss.

97
Until all who have been my parents and I have attained
[Full] enlightenment in the Akaniṣṭha realm,
As we wander through the six realms due to our karma,
May we all hold each other in our hearts.

98

During that period, even for the sake of only a single being,
May I immerse myself in the three lower realms,
And, without compromising the conduct of a great bodhisattva,
May I relieve the sufferings of the lower realms.

99

At that very instant, may the guardians of hells
Relate to me as their spiritual teacher, and
May their weapons turn into a cascade of flowers;
And free of harms, may peace and happiness prevail.

100

May the beings of the lower realms, too, obtain clairvoyance and mantra,
And may they attain human or celestial birth and generate the awakening
    mind;
May they repay my kindness through spiritual practice,
And may they take me as their teacher and rely upon me.

101

At this time, too, may all the beings of the higher realms
Meditate thoroughly on no-self just like me,
And without contrasting existence and pacification,[267]
May they meditate on their perfect equanimity;[268]
May they recognize their self-identity as perfect equanimity.

102

If I do this, the enemy will be vanquished!
If I do this, false conceptions will be vanquished!
I'll meditate on the nonconceptual wisdom of no-self.
So why would I not attain the causes and effects of [Buddha's] form
    body?

103

Listen! All of this is but dependent origination.
Dependent and empty, they are devoid of self-subsistence.
Changing from one form into another, they are like apparitions;
Like a fire ring [seen in a rotating torch], they are mere illusions.

104

Like the plantain tree, life force has no inner core;
Like a bubble, life has no inner core;²⁶⁹
Like a mist, it dissipates when one bends down [to look];
Like a mirage, it is beguiling from a distance;
Like a reflection in a mirror, it appears tangible and real;
Like a fog, it appears as if it is here to stay.

105

This butcher and enemy, Ego, too, is just the same: [90]
Though ostensibly it appears to exist, it never does;
Though seemingly real, nowhere is it really;
Though appearing, it's beyond reification and refutation.

106

So how can there be a wheel of karma?
It's thus: Though they are devoid of intrinsic existence,
Just as moon's reflection appears in a cup of water,
Karma and its effects appear as diverse falsehoods.²⁷⁰
So within this mere appearance I will follow the ethical norms.

107

When the fire at the end of the universe blazes in a dream,
I feel terrified by its heat, though it has no intrinsic reality.
Likewise, although hell realms and their likes have no intrinsic reality,
Out of trepidation for being smelted, burnt, and so on, I forsake [evil].

108

When in feverish delirium, although there is no darkness at all
One feels as if plunged and trapped inside a deep, dark cave.
So, too, although ignorance and so on lack intrinsic reality,
I will dispel ignorance by means of the three wisdoms.²⁷¹

109

When a musician plays a song with his violin,²⁷²
If probed, there is no intrinsic reality to the sound.
Yet melodious tunes arise through aggregation of unprobed facts
And soothe the anguish that lies in people's hearts.

110

Likewise when karma and its effects are thoroughly analyzed,[273]
Though they do not exist as intrinsically one or many,
Vividly appearing, they cause the rising and cessation of phenomena.
Seemingly real, they experience birth and death of every kind.
So within this mere appearance I'll follow the ethical norms.

111

When drops of water fill a vase,
It is not the first drop that fills it,
Nor the last drop or each drop individually;
Through the gathering of dependent factors the vase is filled.

112

Likewise, when someone experiences joy and suffering—the effects—
This is not due to the first instant of their cause;
Nor is it due to the last instant of the cause.
Joy and pain are felt through coming together of dependent factors.
So within this mere appearance I will observe ethical norms.

113

Ah! So utterly delightful when left unanalyzed,
This world of appearance is devoid of any essence;
Yet it seems as if it really does exist.
Profound indeed is this truth so hard for the weak to see.

114

Now as I place my mind on this truth in total equipoise,
What is there that retains definite appearance?
What exists and what does not exist?
What thesis is there anywhere of *is* or *is not*?

115

There is no object, no subject, nor no ultimate nature [of things];
Free of all ethical norms and conceptual elaborations,
If I abide naturally with this uncontrived awareness
In the ever-present, innate state, I will become a great being.

116

Thus by practicing conventional awakening mind
And the ultimate mind of awakening,
May I accomplish without obstacles the two accumulations
And realize perfect fulfillment of the two aims.

Colophon

This text entitled *The Wheel Weapon Striking at the Vital Points of the Enemy* was composed by the great Dharmarakṣita, a yogi of scriptural knowledge, reasoning, and realizations, in accordance with the instructions of the sublime teachers. He composed this in a jungle where terrifying animals of prey roam free and undertook its practice in the terrifying jungle of our degenerate era.

He gave this teaching to Atiśa, who, in order to transform many sentient beings so difficult to tame, undertook this practice throughout all places where sentient beings lie, whether in cardinal or intermediate directions. As he experienced the realizations of this practice, he uttered the following lines:

When I renounced my kingdom and practiced austerity,
I accumulated merit and met with my supreme teacher.
He revealed to me this sublime Dharma nectar and initiated me into it.
Having mastered the antidotes today, I commit the words to my heart.

By casting wide my intelligence free of prejudice
Upon a detailed study of diverse doctrinal systems,
I have witnessed immeasurable wonders,
But I've found this teaching most helpful to our degenerate age.

From among his countless disciples in India and Tibet, Atiśa bestowed this teaching to the most qualified vessel, Upāsaka [Dromtönpa], who was prophesied by many meditation deities such as the Bhagavatī Tārā. This teaching was given to help tame the hardened people of Tibet, a land outside the bounds of civilization. The father conqueror [Atiśa] and his son [Dromtönpa] themselves acted as the scholar and translator of this text.

Atiśa [gave this teaching] to Dromtönpa, [who then transmitted it to]

Potowa, and thence, in a lineal order, to Sharawa, Chekawa, Chilbupa, Lha Chenpo, Lha Drowai Gönpo, Öjopa, Khenpo Martön, Khenpo Sherap Dorjé, Buddharatna, Kīrtiśīla, Gyalwa Sangpo, Nup Chölungpa Sönam Rinchen, and he to myself, Shönu Gyalchok Könchok Bang.

This belongs to the cycle of Dharmarakṣita's mind training [teachings].

9. The Peacock's Neutralizing of Poison
Attributed to Dharmarakṣita

I

The Peacocks Roaming in the Jungle of Virulent Poison[274]

Homage to Lord Yamāntaka!

1
Just as when he was born as Prince Viśvāntara[275]
He gave away his son, daughter, and kingdom,
So, too, must you give away entirely, without reservation,
Your wealth, friends, and so forth, which you hold so dear.

2
Just as when he was born as Prince Mahāsattva[276]
He nourished a tigress with his own flesh,
So, too, must you joyfully give to the flesh-eating demons
This illusory body of yours that you hold so dear.

3
Just as when he was born as King Maitrībala[277]
He nourished a yakṣa with his own blood,
So, too, must you lovingly give to the blood-drinkers
Warm blood from your heart, so hard to extract.

4
Just as when he was born as the chief merchant's son, Jalavahana,[278]
He rescued fish by reciting the name of the sugatas,
So, too, must you give gifts of the sublime Dharma
To all those who are impoverished of Dharma.

5

Just as when he was born as Prince Mahākalyāṇārtha[279]
He bore Pāpārtha's ingratitude with great compassion,
So, too, must you be especially kind and compassionate
Toward your companions' ingratitude and stirrings of negative traits.

6

Just as when he was born as the monkey bodhisattva[280]
He pulled an evil person from a well,
So, too, must you save those ridden with evil compassionately,
With no thought of reward or recognition for your help.

7

Alas! There is no one who has not been your parent.
There is not one instant of happiness in this jungle of cyclic existence.
Responding with evil to evildoers is [as senseless] as a donkey's horn.

8

Now, despite respectfully embracing the heroic example
Of the great Sage,[281] if you fail to cultivate the antidotes,
Engaging in the practice of the hero's way becomes impossible.
So embrace the practice of austerity even at the cost of your life.

9

After the display of the Sugata's transcendence [from the world],
If you who aspire to follow in his footsteps
Fail to cultivate these practices in your heart,
There is a risk that beings' happiness will evolve no more.

10

This, then, is the hero's happy way of life:
Come what may, endure hardships even at the cost of your life. [93]
This is the practice of the hero's path:
Chapter I of *Extracting the Essence of Poison*.[282]

II

The Peacocks Roaming in the Jungle of Virulent Poison

Homage to Lord Yamāntaka!

11
Heroes, you who are enthusiastic, listen to this teaching.
In the jungle of cyclic existence delight not in the beautiful peacocks;
Or at the feet of a poisonous tree of the five afflictions,
Delight not in medicinal fruits ripened with poison.

12
If you fail to counter the boiling poisonous potion
Of lustful acts with something akin to lust,
The threat looms of this lust inciting injury;
So destroy this poison through simulated lust!

13
If you fail to display your wrath as Yamāntaka
To the blossoming poisonous flowers of anger,
The threat looms of the hostile ones impeding you;
So slay this enemy and obstacle through simulated anger!

14
If you fail to engender forbearance like a corpse
Toward the muddy poisonous mire of delusion,
The threat looms of the evil ones accumulating negative acts;
So meditate on equanimity through simulated delusion!

15
If you fail to distinguish between inner and outer as "I" and "you"
Toward the blossoming poisonous tree of envy,
The threat looms of the heretics destroying the Dharma;
So uphold the sublime Dharma through simulated envy!

16

If you fail to react hostilely as though haughty
To the blossoming poisonous tree of conceit,
The threat looms of deception by the demons;
So crush your opponents when upholding the Buddha's teaching!

17

Thus you must bind together in this one fetter of self, or "I,"
Within the experience of unreal, illusion-like appearance and emptiness,
The entire army of poisons without excepting one,
And, like a peacock, consume all such poisons as nourishment.

18

Though you may present yourself in diverse ways to others' mind,
Deep inside do not lose the secure discipline of antidotes,
And guard the ethics of virtue versus evil dearer even than your life;
Even if it entails suffering, you should eagerly embrace enlightenment.

19

Thus even if you are expert in all forms of knowledge,
If you fail to forgo your own happiness and prosperity,
The danger of afflictions entering [your heart] still exists because of
    craving; [94]
So beat this self-centeredness as you might a [charging] dog or a thief.

20

Although you may be at the feet of learned ones,
If you fail to cultivate your knowledge of the vast treatises,
You risk defaming and denigrating the learned ones;
So cultivate familiarity with all fields of knowledge.

21

Even if you suffer throughout day and night,
If you do not contemplate the defects of cyclic existence in general,
The danger of indulging in the causes of suffering still exists;
So torment your heart with thoughts of karma's ill consequences.

22

Though this is so, seek all undesirable sufferings
As counterforces in vanquishing self-grasping.
Even if a million or a billion demon armies rise up against you,
Abandon the fear that rises from the thought "I am."

23

In working for others, you may fall into the lower realms;
Embrace this experience without regret.
Even if the executors of death come to rob you of your life,
Do not have beneficial rites performed for your sake.

24

Even if you must bear the evil karma of every being,
Since your burden will be most worthy, you must not complain.
Even if a virulent contagion ravages your body,
Since it is your own fault, do not seek to revert it.

25

Thus if unwanted calamities fail to befall you,
You will have no means to obtain the wanted.
When the wise examine, all calamities are seen as
Sources of fulfillment; thus you must eagerly embrace them.

26

If, through eagerly embracing others' ingratitude,
heroes fail to wear the protective armor,
The one within cyclic existence will find no joy.
Therefore embrace all calamities willingly.

27

From the example of the life of the great Sage,
Such is the teaching to be practiced by the sublime ones.
This is a gateway worthy of the heroic ones:
Chapter II of *Extracting the Essence of Poison*.

III

The Peacocks Roaming in the Jungle of Virulent Poison

Homage to Lord Yamāntaka!

28
The intelligent one who six times, day and night,
Peruses and analyzes the general and specific defects [95]
Of the cycle of existence and is utterly fearful of them
Will take and guard the precepts of individual liberation.[283]

29
Having thus made firm the precepts of liberation,
Until you reach the state of enlightenment,
View all beings as fathers and mothers, and for their sake
Take the precepts of "aspiration" and "engagement."[284]

30
When aspiration and engagement are made firm through love and
    compassion,
Even though you suffer in the jungle of cyclic existence,
Think of this as nothing, and for the benefit of others
Resolutely endure austerities even at the cost of your life.

31
When you experience infinite encounters with
Beings of negative character and those who act ungratefully,
Like a dream, or like an illusion, view them as devoid of elaboration;
Probe their nature and perceive them as reality's expanse.

32
When their unreality and nonappearance become manifest,
Generate heightened confidence; as for the dangers entailed,
Harbor no concepts of them of any kind;
Work solely and spontaneously for the benefit of others.

33

When such spiritual practice is the load you carry,
The forces of darkness become ever more pernicious,
And when thick clouds of impediments amass before you,
Scatter them across pure space with gales of mantra.

34

When you shout a loud *Hūṃ!* of wrathful mantras,
Your identity can arise as a fierce wrathful deity;
Therefore recognize the sounds as fanciful musical tunes
Resounding inside a body resembling an illusory town.

35

In this mind of yours amid its diverse apparitions
Nothing is tangible; it is like the mind of a chimera.
As it has never existed, let it rest in its natural place;
Release it within the truth of those who see the ultimate expanse.

36

Even if everything arises as an enemy or a demon in every way,
Think nothing of this, make no attempts to reverse it,
And trample upon thoughts of attachment and hostility, self and others;
View all memories and perceptions as wrathful Yamāntaka.

37

At that point, see all beings as your parents
And draw them forth together without hesitation.
Without far and near, nestle them in the heart of your compassion.
With no prejudice, sustain them with the two truths.

38

To cultivate in this way is the liberating life of the Sage;
If you conduct yourself thus, the Three Jewels will smile;
On such a person the Dharma protectors converge naturally;
Know this well, O children of the Sage.

39

I spit on the way of life that is bereft of conscience;
As I reflect, I feel revulsion for the heedless conduct.
This, too, is a practice worthy of entry by the heroes:
Chapter III of *Extracting the Essence of Poison.* [96]

IV

The Peacocks Roaming in the Jungle of Virulent Poison

Homage to Lord Yamāntaka!

40

Though you may be a perfect monk like Upāli[285]
And possess wonderful heedfulness like Aśvajit,[286]
If you fail to guide your parents on the path to enlightenment,
This liberation of self-joy must be trampled underfoot.

41

Though you may achieve expertise in all fields of knowledge
And impress all fools with your reputation,
If you do not uphold with your crown the great burden of the teachings,
This should all be dismissed like the dance of a mad man.

42

Though everyone may honor you as a spiritual teacher,
If you do not bear the great responsibility of the entire teaching
But eagerly pursue your own self-centered interests,
You should be spat on by the noble ones.

43

Though all may elevate you as excellent,
When the self-grasping view stirs in the jungle of wrong views,
You'll remain a threat, like a tigress devouring her own cubs.
You should be slain by the oath-bound protectors.

44
Though you may be clad in saffron and have an appealing, tranquil
     countenance,
If you still harbor ill-will like a cat [left in the midst of pigeons],
This is irredeemable conduct for someone in a holy guise.
You should be thrust into the mouth of the she-demons.

45
Though you may command ninety thousand,
If your heart remains untamed like Viṣṇu,[287]
Emitting rays of attachment and anger to the ten directions,
You should be thrust into Yamāntaka's mouth.

46
Though you may reign with a smile and affability,
If you enhance the defilements of those who follow you
And become hailed as a chief of those who are faithless,
You should be cast into a den sealed shut with truth.

47
Though you may renounce the householder's life and enter the order,
If, like a householder, you retain infinite chores,
And if you disregard all ethical injunctions,
You should certainly be cursed by wise sages.

48
Though clad in monk's robes, you do not observe the precepts,
Your senses remain immersed in diverse acts of lustfulness,
And you criticize and denigrate the noble ones—
You should be expelled by ḍākinīs to the life beyond.

49
For the sake of material gain you assume the guise of a noble one;
Like dogs and pigs you indulge in lustful acts,
Deceiving all with the claim that this is tantra—
You should be burned in a hearth by vajra holders.[288] [97]

50

In the pretense of Mahayana you defy karma and its effects;
In the boast of emptiness you deceive the assembly of students;
Like a demonic ghost you inhabit sacred images—
You should be slain with incantations by those pure in oath.

51

Since they bring no benefit to the Buddha's teaching as a whole,
Those proudly peddled as tantras or profound pith instructions
And evil verses strung together through conceptual fabrications—
They should be denigrated as trivial by sublime ones.

52

If [an instruction] definitely harms the Buddha's teaching as a whole,
Even though it may bring some benefit to a few at certain times,
Like rice beer for someone suffering from severe fever,
This is a detrimental help that deserves to be thrown into water.

53

When dangerous mystics who possess little learning
See common visions, they acquire arrogance of attaining supreme feats.
Those who lead the foolish with no graduated stages of the path
Should be brought to the level of dogs by the learned ones.

54

When hostile enemies appear for the Buddha's teaching,
With pretensions of excellence in the individual liberation vows,
Some fail to defend the well-uttered insights [of the Buddha]—
Such "sublime ones" that undermine the doctrine are most intriguing!

55

Let alone [breaking] the vows of individual liberation,
If you fail to vanquish the destroyers of doctrine,
You will depart for the vast realms of lower migration.
Such oath-breaking enemies, obstructive forces, should be sent to their
    afterlife.

56
The deluded who are chased by afflictions and karma
Are careless of the doctrine and sentient beings as a whole,
Yet they angrily drive enemies who harm them
To their afterlife with incantations.
Whether lapsed in morality or not, they are most intriguing!

57
In brief you should relinquish at all times
The pursuit of selfish ends so abhorrent to conquerors.
If praised by conquerors of all ten directions,
Whatever such a deed may be, it's worthy of pursuit.

58
O intelligent ones, be cognizant of this!
Undertake all your practices scrupulously;
Even at the cost of your life renounce anything that contradicts Dharma;
Never harm the collective, and do what is beneficial to yourself.

59
Though the foolish may not see even after a passage of time,
To the wise these truths are immediately clear and evident.
This, too, is a gateway for the heroic ones:
Chapter IV of *Extracting the Essence of Poison*. [98]

V

The Peacocks Roaming in the Jungle of Virulent Poison

Homage to Lord Yamāntaka!

60
You who harbor harmful intentions and are consumed with hate,
You who are of the dark force, all of you, appear before me!

Millions and billions of flesh-eating and blood-drinking demons,
Appear before me in front of this mortal being today!

61
Appear before me O assembly of gods, nāgas, and yakṣas,
Smell-eaters, demigods, and belly-crawlers,
Countless hungry ghosts who roam the skies,
And the elemental spirits that are karmic debtors.

62
Simultaneously born gods[289] and sages,
Obstructers, false gods, and the eighteen great possessors,[290]
The she-demons and all the action guardians, as well as
The noble ones, such as the Three Jewels: stand before me.

63
Thus, in the presence of all samsara and nirvana,
Present today to bear witness,
I shall recount here without the slightest wavering
The most expansive tale of my pledges; so listen to me.

64
Thanks to its conditions, my virtues of the past,
Today I've obtained human life endowed with ten opportunities.
This is most wondrous, but days and nights pass [with no results];
Why am I not enjoying the glory of benefit and joy today?

65
With pure aspirations I will transcend the householder's life;
Discarding selfish desires, I will clad myself in aspiration and
    engagement;
Finding the supreme thought, I will bear the burden of others' welfare;
Entering the [noble] path, I will nourish myself on supreme bliss.

66
Listen again, O you who've gathered.
Such is the savagery of the dark forces!
Such is the poverty of merit of the unfortunate ones!
I aspire no more for [birth in] the pure lands.

67

Countless are the elemental spirits bereft of merit,
Heavy is the burden of beings' suffering in the lower realms,
Repulsive is the conduct of those who commit evil acts,
So I find no joy in the places of tranquillity [now].

68

Easily ambushed are the antidotes of the childish,
Powerful are the thoughts and deeds of demonic forces;
As there is no time for pause in this transient life of mine,
I feel no attraction for abiding in places of solitude.

69

Foes hostile to this doctrine are numerous;
Realized mystics who have gained secure grounds are few;
Since the appearance of the world in this degenerate age is so bad,
I find no attraction for the realm of the ḍākinīs.

70

Now even if all the mighty ones of this universe
Were to rise up as my sworn enemies,
I will not waver, not even a hair on my body will move;
I will don armor in this realm of cyclic existence.

71

In places where people suffer contagious diseases
And when serious epidemics threaten the entire world,
I shall put on the great and powerful armor
By becoming the physician or the nurse myself.

72

When I nurture all sentient beings with acts of kindness,
If someone vexes with extreme ingratitude,
I shall especially help him and generate thoughts of kindness;
I shall [thus] wear the armor of the heroic ones.

73

When a ferocious man-eating tigress awaits in ambush
And pounces on people, threatening their lives,

I shall don the armor of charging without hesitation
For the sake of those threatened sentient beings.

74
The diverse misfortunes that blanket the world like a dense jungle,
Such as the calamities least desired,
I shall put on the armor of wearing them as charms
To help destroy the evil character, the enemy Ego.

75
Everything utterly useless in this universe—
The turbulence of karma, afflictions, and confusions—
I shall wear the armor of eagerly embracing them
To help forcibly rob self-grasping of its life.

76
Phat! Hurrah! Mortally strike, O lord of death!
Set fire to the life force of this demon, the joy-seeking desire!
Dance and trample upon the head of procrastination!
Cut completely the thread that binds to cyclic existence!

77
We all suffer in this cycle of existence;
As I search down to its foundation for the root,
I see the king, the thought "I am," which resides
In the palace of my heart in the midst of false conceptions.

78
When I banish all blame onto this and combat it, what does it say?
"I have been here since beginningless time.
I pervade everywhere—inner, outer, and in between;
Ask all the chiefs, the six classes of consciousness, whether this is true
    or false!"[291]

79
With whom shall I battle, for I am my own enemy?
Who will save whom, for I am my own savior?
I am my own witness for my actions and inaction.
I will be free when I tame my own self.[292]

80

When someone tames another, conflict and disputes arise;
Where conflict and disputes arise, evildoers gather;
The lustful and hateful have no chance of freedom;
Thus a yogi free of false conceptions is blissful.[293]

81

A la la! What more can be said?
Mortally strike at the life force that grasps at existence!
Set fire to the life force that grasps at nonexistence! [100]
Since the self-grasping king is to blame, vanquish the chief![294]

82

If I fail to tame the principal mental consciousness,
I risk being led away by the self-grasping king.
Once the principal mental consciousness is subdued,
The other chiefs, such as the eyes, will also be vanquished.

83

So tame this mental consciousness,
And then forms, sounds, smells, and so on will be no more;
Grasping at self and its belongings, too, shall be no more;
The conceptualization king will starve for want of conditions.

84

When one has spoken to the king in this way,
Conceptions will be naturally freed and understood as reality's expanse;
The six classes [of consciousness] are unreal like illusory elephants;
Subjects and objects are unreal like the actions of a chimera.

85

Since this is so, eliminate false conceptions from their roots;[295]
Since there is no subject or object, transform egoistic view into the
    expanse;
Since there is neither "I" nor "you," leave attachment and anger in their
    innate states.

86

Like the horn of a rabbit, neither sharp nor dull faculties exist;
So free those of higher and middling faculties from their chains of
    bondage.²⁹⁶
Like the child of a barren woman, there is nothing to discard or adopt;
So integrate all of samsara and nirvana into perfect equanimity.²⁹⁷

87

Like the turtle's hair, no shortness or length exists;
So set free all births and deaths in the great middle way.
Like echoes that are primordially empty,
Integrate all conventional facts into one sublime truth.²⁹⁸

88

Āḥ! Āḥ! In this sphere of unborn spacelike nature,
Ee! Ee! This body free of conceptual elaboration is fearless;
Oṃ! Oṃ! By recognizing this as the utterly pure dharmakāya,²⁹⁹
May I be sustained by the kindness of the great compassionate one.

Colophon

This work entitled *The Peacocks Roaming in the Jungle of Virulent Poison* was motivated by a great nonobjectifying compassion for all sentient beings. It was composed by me, Dharmarakṣita, a yogi dwelling in the Dark Mountain Cave, who has trained his eyes of intelligence in the myriad fields of knowledge, has gained powers over the undeceiving laws of karma, and is free of doubts pertaining to the meaning of the nondual view. May it be auspicious! May it be auspicious for all! *(Sarva śubham)*

10. Melodies of an Adamantine Song: A Chanting Meditation on Mind Training[300]

Attributed to Maitrīyogi

Alas! To guide all beings who've been my parents,
I'll extract without exception the five poisons of each being
By means of the five poisonous afflictions present in me;
Whatever virtue I may possess, such as an absence of attachment,
I will distribute equally to all beings of the six realms.

Using the painful fruits [of my karma] such as sickness and so on
I will extract all similar sufferings of sentient beings;
Whatever joy and benefit I may possess, such as absence of illness,
I will distribute equally to all beings of the six realms.

If I do this, what occasion is there for me, even for a single instant,
To wander aimlessly in this ocean of cyclic existence?
Yet until I have attained [full] enlightenment,
Whatever class of the five poisons and their fruits may lie in store,
I will exhaust entirely in this very lifetime.

I will extract them this very year and this very month;
I will exhaust them this very day and this very instant;
I will seek the means to cut even the thread of minor sufferings.
O Maitrīyogi, make sure that your mind becomes trained![301]

I, Maitrīyogi, regularly recite this song, wherein loving-kindness, compassion, and awakening mind are sung as a diamond song, and on one occasion, near the river Ganges, Bhagavan Maitreya, the embodiment of great compassion, appeared in the form of a king and approached me. He then uttered the following lines:

This song that dispels sufferings of the lower realms through mere
    hearing,
This song that cuts down the tree of cyclic existence through mere
    reflection,
This song that swiftly grants enlightenment through mere meditation—
Wondrous indeed is this song of love, compassion, and awakening mind!

Though the five poisonous afflictions must be destroyed as enemies,
Amazing indeed that you still uphold them in your heart!
Though sickness and suffering are hard to endure in all respects,
Amazing indeed is your current way of being!

Who would not find it hard to wander selflessly through samsara
By discarding self-interest and embracing other's well-being? [102]
So to take others' misfortune upon oneself without being tied
By thoughts of self-interest even for an instant is sublime indeed!

Though the Mahayana scriptures are numberless,
Not even an atom-sized portion is missing from this [teaching].
So this diamond song of yours, O yogi,
Whether it's heard, reflected upon, expounded, or meditated upon,
Is a sublime refuge for the entire world, including the gods.

Wondrous indeed that the innermost essence of the mind
Of the buddhas of all ten directions shines within you!

As [Maitreya] uttered these lines in response to the words of the diamond
song, Maitrīyogi experienced great ecstasy, and with the knots of his doubts
undone, he entered the great battle of the heroic ones. *Kye Ho!*

Furthermore, as [Maitrīyogi] trained his mind in this spiritual practice three
times in the day and three times at night, with full mindfulness of time and
context, and free of forgetfulness, singing this diamond song to rejuvenate
his elements, like a mother who loves her only son, all the gods, yakṣas, smell-
eaters, demigods, garuḍas, semihumans, the great belly-crawlers, flesh-eating
demons, ogres, and so on were brought under his influence and revered him.
Similarly, the king of the land, his ministers, his queens, the brahmin priests,
householders, young men and women, ordinary people, and so on, came

under his influence as well. They joyfully followed him, and anyone who saw this or heard of this became endowed with loving nature. Horses, elephants, water buffaloes, monkeys, winged creatures, water-borne creatures, mountain creatures, predators, all beings of the six classes, including even small insects like the ants, remained unafraid of him, and peacefully they converged in the presence of the yogi.

Then the yogi felt, "I cultivated in my heart love, compassion, and awakening mind; I have recited the words as incantations and have sung the melodious diamond song. Because of this Blessed Maitreya, the embodiment of great compassion, revealed bare his face to me and uttered words of delight, which severed the entire network of doubts. [103] As a consequence, my practices of forbearance, joyous effort, and so on became enhanced like a waxing moon. By the force of this, like a mother gazing on her only son, all beings of the six classes became delighted in me."

In grateful response, and with thoughts of making offerings to Buddha Maitreya, Maitrīyogi sang this song:

Those closely related to me since beginningless time,
All sentient beings who've been my parents,
I recall my pledge to lead them to supreme enlightenment.
I make offerings to Maitreya with this spiritual practice.

At that point, not entangled in self-interest for even an instant,
I contemplate in my heart others' welfare alone—
This is the principal cause for attaining [full] enlightenment.
I make offerings to Maitreya with this spiritual practice.

Whatever experiences I may undergo—joyful, painful, or neutral—
I will eagerly embrace them as aids to enlightenment.
Whatever merits I may accumulate over many eons,
I will prevent them from ripening as the disciple's cowardly path.
I make offerings to Maitreya with this spiritual practice.

Whatever undesirable events may befall me on such occasions,
May my armor of forbearance never be lost for even an instant.
Even if someone I've nurtured with kindness
Acts against me with ingratitude, I will nurture him with a smiling face.
I make offerings to Maitreya with this spiritual practice.

Even though the hateful, on their part, engage in negative acts,
May I never give in to negative thoughts for even an instant.
Even when the entire universe rose up as demons, ghosts, or enemies,
I never guarded the binding chains of self-centeredness.
I make offerings to Maitreya with this spiritual practice.

Even when afflicted with an illness certain to kill me,
I never entrust myself to nonvirtuous endeavors.
Even when my resources are meager because of my habituation to
    miserliness,
I never seek hope in the wrong means of livelihood.
I make offerings to Maitreya with this spiritual practice.

Even when surrounded by negative companions,
I never forsake the resolution of the remedies.
In brief, whatever I do—going, sitting, and so on—
I never do without careful examination.
I make offerings to Maitreya with this spiritual practice.

Though this is so, not even an atom has ever existed
That has been affirmed to be substantially real.
This, then, is the principal cause for attaining enlightenment.
I make offerings to Maitreya with this spiritual practice.

Through this sublime offering of meditative practice,
To help train this yogi's mind,
O soldiers of loving-kindness,
Accept this [offering] and help transform my mind.

As this offering was made, the five offering goddesses appeared in space with
an infinity of diverse offerings, such as music, lights, and other attractive
objects. At that moment, the sublime masters who have trained their mind
in Mahayana recognized this spiritual practice as a source of great wonder.
They observed that although many have engaged in the austerity of this
spiritual practice—received the teaching and undertaken its practice—[it
was Maitrīyogi who] gave the instruction to Atiśa. He was the master of
one hundred and eight highly holy places, the crown jewel among fifty-two
learned pundits, a heroic being venerated by sixty-two religious kings, the

preceptor of countless upholders of ethical discipline, the teacher of countless upholders of scriptural discourses, an object of reverence by numberless upholders of higher knowledge, and the spiritual mentor of oceans of knowledge bearers—in brief, he is an unrivaled sublime being and the protector of [all] sentient beings. This embodiment of great compassion undertook the practice [of this teaching]. This is as stated in the following lines:

> He who discards his own interests and naturally accomplishes
> The welfare of others, he is my spiritual teacher.[302]

This sublime being gave this instruction both in India and Tibet as a hidden guide to those sublime ones who shared deep interest [in the practice].

As for its lineage: Maitreya, Maitrīyogi, who [in turn] transmitted it to master Atiśa.

11. Stages of the Heroic Mind[303]
Attributed to Serlingpa

Homage to the yogi of loving-kindness![304]

I

Teaching on the presentation of the ground, the afflictions

1

In samsara's realms you endure the hardships,
You help vanquish the selfishness of all beings,
You do not cower before dangers and calamities—
To you, O heroes, I respectfully bow my head.[305]

2

To nurture the tradition of the sugatas,
Just like the great courageous king,[306]
I shall think only of others' welfare
And definitely exchange self and others.

3

For this I, whose heart is hardened,
Call upon the sugatas and scriptures as my witness,
And in your presence, O heroes who embody the essence,
In words of desperation I beseech you for this instruction.

4

Ah! Heroes of great compassion,
I've relinquished the objects of attachment
And endured hardships on hazardous paths;
Victorious over [the dark] force, I've arrived here.[307]

5

Now to help endure beings of ingratitude[308]
Who are tormented by illness,
I seek a teaching that helps conquer incapacitation
While in this filthy mire of samsara.

6

To this the great compassionate one[309] replied:
For you who've come here with great hardship,
I offer the mind training called *Stages of the Heroic Mind*
To help overcome fear and fatigue.

7

Through learning, the upturned vessel is averted;
Through reflection, the broken vessel is repaired;
Through meditation, the tainted vessel is cleansed—
Discard these defects and take this inner nourishment.

8

Alas! Since time without beginning,
As you've failed to subdue your own mental continuum,
In this demonic house of your untamed heart,
Apostles of afflictions and karma enslave you.

9

Because you failed to care for your parents,
Now when all sentient beings are suffering
You [callously] remain at ease and joyful—
Alas! Will you not wear the armor of antidotes?

10

This [self-centeredness] is the notorious source of disputes.
From now on learn to turn it away.
If you fail to conquer the demon of your mind,
Alas, will you not pose a threat to your parents' lives?

11

Alas! This is sure to destroy your happiness.
Alas! This is the anchor of cyclic existence.
If you do not bind the head of your negative traits,
All beings may rise up as your enemies.

12

And when the poisonous arrow strikes at your heart,
Alas, you are certain to be betrayed.
If you fail to expel selfishness, the stray dog and a thief, [106]
Alas, even though your armor of antidotes may be tight,

13

When disturbances occur within,
Alas, even medicinal wine may turn into poison.
Without slaying the life force of the five poisons,
Even if you generate courage out of laziness,

14

When you are swept away by the gale of short life span,
Alas, you will feel remorse from the depths of your heart.
This, then, is the great advice:
In the future, examine your thoughts.

15

Conceptualization is the king of all māras;[310]
Destructive traits are the executive lord of death;
Self-cherishing is a tree of poisonous fruits—
You who procrastinate, contemplate these defects.

16

Mundane ambitions are a field of betrayal;
Abundance of support is but mere deception;
The multitude of gods and demons are not other than tricksters—
Conceptualizations, rise not as enemies!

17

There is no end to the mundane tasks you undertake;
No conscience and integrity exist in those you've nurtured;
The wealth you've hoarded is without essence—
Relinquish these sources of betrayal and downfall.

18

The lord of death resides in your own heart;
Your life is being cut short by you yourself;
It is you who drinks the poisonous water—
WIth certainty, beware of this demon!

19

These defects of the self
I've explained from my vast experience.
Reflect deeply on this tale with terror,
And in the future understand it well.

20

Those that definitely occupy your heart,
These multitudes of chores threaten your life.
Lacking the thought to help others,
Many a great teacher attracts disdain.

21

The valorous who are bereft of antidotes:
These negative friends threaten your spiritual practice.
Those never sated of sensory objects and complaints:
These mirror-image practitioners[311] threaten material resources.

22

He who is cognizant yet fails to return others' kindness:
Such lack of conscience is a threat to all.
He who has failed to discard self-interest:
Alas, he may deceive others through words of altruism.

This concludes the "Teaching on the presentation of the ground, the afflictions," from the mind training entitled *Stages of the Heroic Mind*.

II

Teaching on the contrary forces, the antidotes

23
You're the sole medicine for compassion's anguish;
You're the sole friend to help vanquish the egoistic view;
You're the sole god to protect from attachment and anger—
I bow to you who has severed the root by means of its antidotes.

24
When false afflictive conceptualizations arise, [107]
Then just as a flock of birds is chased away by a falcon,
You should target them and chase them away;
Grab them with your hands and crush them.

25
When negative conceptualizations cling to your heart,
Then just as one identifies enemies and thieves,
You should discern their shapes and characteristics
And ensure that in the future [false] conceptions are no more.

26
When positive conceptualizations rise as enemies,
Then just like catching an assailant disguised as a son,
The moment they're apprehended, hammer down on their heads
And take their life so that the [false] conceptions are no more.

27
When craving for pleasure and laziness arise,
Then just like waking a servant caught taking a nap,
You should repeatedly engage in the liberating deeds
With such intense striving as if there were no time even to pause.

28
When you [notice yourself] aspiring for mundane greatness,
Then as though seeing a man-eating monster,
Petrified, you should instantly forsake your efforts
And run far away from the realms bereft of leisure.

29

When swept away by your spouse and distractions,
Then as though seeing a dead body in a battle zone,
Feel revulsion for being entrapped with companions
And seek the solitude of forest in the wilderness.

30

When distracted by demons of attachment and aversion,
Then as though seeing a rabid dog or a venomous snake,
Turn your back on the pleasures of cyclic existence
And run away to a secure ground, the expanse of nirvana.

31

When you are chained in the prison of grasping at permanence,
Then as though being tortured in a king's dungeon,
You should contemplate the uncertainty of the time of death
And cultivate fervent thoughts of renunciation and disenchantment.

32

When your learning and reflection fall prey to a desire for fame,
Understand them to lack implementation,
Like the words of an actor in a play,
And make yourself an object of ridicule.

33

If, despite striving in Dharma practice throughout day and night,
The foul odor of [self-cherishing] still lingers,
See this as a sign of possession by Māra,
Reverse it, and apply the remedies.

34

If, despite an intention to do something spiritual,
Everything you do becomes the opposite,
See this as a sign of possession by Māra,
And decisively call upon the Three Jewels as your allies.

35
If, residing at your teacher's seat of learning
With pretensions of being an abbot, a preceptor, or a colleague,
You become tainted by rivalry in spiritual practice,
See this as Māra's doing and seek the solitude of the forest.

36
If, despite engaging single-pointedly in meditative practice,
You still fail to find the freedom you seek,
This is the fault of not discerning the pitfalls through learning;
Thinking thus, you should read the profound scriptures.

This concludes the "Teaching on the contrary forces, the antidotes," from the mind training entitled *Stages of the Heroic Mind*. [108]

III

Teaching on humiliating one's own negative mental continuum

37
Since the craving of self-interest has not entered your heart,
You have not fallen into the views of the Lesser Vehicle;
You are not chained in the prison of cyclic existence.
To you who are free, I pay homage.

38
"I am" is but a deception;
"I want" is but an appeasement [of ego];
"The other" is but an enemy's word;
"I do not want" is a hindrance.

39
"Self and others" are terms of division;
"Attachment and aversion" words of conflict;
He who makes such distinctions
Has become deficient in profound Dharma.

40

If the wise wish to conquer enemies,
They should first sacrifice "I" and "self."
So when someone insults or belittles them,
They will not react with insults and profanity.

41

Even when someone injures them,
They do not take the [self's] side and fight for its sake.
Even if someone strips them of body, life, and possessions,
Thinking, "This is so due to my own karma,"
They savor this as especially satisfying.

42

Even if someone casts spells of demons and possessions on them,
They harbor no resentment,
But help fulfill the wishes of others.
For this helps trample any thoughts of inadequacy.

43

Even if someone close to them steals away
Their circle of friends so dear to their heart,
Taking no offense, they savor it as most satisfying.

44

If someone responds to their acts of kindness negatively,
They do not become perturbed for even an instant,
But recall it as kindness for inspiring forbearance.

45

Now, as a means to avert negative karma,
I present here the divisions of nonaversion:
Contemplate others' kindness and cultivate loving-kindness;
Taunt your own self and spit on it.

46

Thus until you've achieved forbearance,
Associate with friends of negative traits,
And taking them as your focus of meditation,
Contemplate the defects of cyclic existence.

47 .

Cultivate great compassion especially.
For your shelter and bed seek
A cave, a crevice, a ruin, or a house with leaky roof,
A temple, a cattle yard, or a discarded nomadic site,
Or reside in a gorge that displeases the mind.

48

At such times you may feel unhappy within:
When in the plains you long for the mountains,
But you don't enjoy residing there either.
You search for a shelter, a roof, or a corner.

49

When you move like this from place to place
And feel unhappy and discouraged,
Conduct this self-confession:
Judging by your attitude and conduct, [109]

50

Even the present shelter and bed are too good;
Your thoughts and feelings are too good, as well.
For you will be lucky if
Your restlessness does not give birth to the hells!

51

You'll be lucky if you're not set ablaze and burnt;
You'll be lucky if you're not born for eons
In cities of perpetually hungry and thirsty ghosts;
You'll be lucky if you're not born for eons

52

In the foul towns of [ravenous] ogres,
Where huge mires of filth swirl around.
You should reflect further on the terror
And make self the object of ridicule and correction.

53

Accepting loss of food, you should adopt austerities;
Accepting loss of clothing, you should adopt humility;
Sacrificing pleasure, you should meditate on its antidotes;
Abandoning chores entirely, you should seek nondoing
And turn whatever you do into aids to enlightenment.

This concludes the "Teaching on humiliating one's own negative mental continuum," from the mind training entitled *Stages of the Heroic Mind*.

IV

Teaching on cultivating the power of tainted virtues

54

You have no concern for your body and life,
You never seek kingdom and rewards for acts done,
And you practice austerities and forbearance—
To you, O hero, I pay homage.

55

Listen to this tale, O those who grasp at permanence.
Think of this task, O those who are burdened.
If you wish to attain in this short life
The seed of your life's ultimate aim,

56

Why do you lack the will despite your opportunity?
What demonic force has come to possess you?
Though you are consistently let down by excessive yearning for pleasure,
The turn of your thoughts remains coarse.

57
If you persist in failing to relinquish your negative traits,
You'll be let down even further.
If you persist in failing to care for others' welfare
And seek only your own needs and desires,

58
You'll betray everyone—both self and others—
And definitely enter the Avīci hell.
By siding with this life and fighting for its sake,
Your thoughts and demonic preconceptions are coarser than anyone's.

59
Your pain and suffering are greater than everyone's;
The torment of piercing wounds and agony is intense indeed;
The pains of heat and cold resemble those of the hells;
The misery of poverty and deprivation seems greater than anyone's.

60
The terror of hunger and thirst is as intense as the hungry ghosts';
You are like a poisonous snake or a rabid dog. [110]
When you have [a possession], you suffer from having to guard it;
When you don't have, you wander about searching for it.

61
So however you act, you seek pain and suffering;
Whatever you do, you lose your real purpose.
This is so because excessive self-grasping lies at the root.
This is so because of inadequate forbearance and courage.

62
This is so because the soil of loving-kindness is made barren.
This is so because the root of compassion has been cut.
This is so because the virtuous awakening mind is lost.
This is so because of consorting with unruly, negative friends.

63

All these are now things of the past.
The paths lost must now be offered to those above.
From here on you place high hopes in no one;
Locate not your needs either within or without;

64

Hail not the rise of unnecessary conceptions;
Follow not the trail of past negative deeds.
O mountain of demonic self-grasping, swear now!
O mountain of demonic negative traits, swear now!

65

O mountain of blaming others, swear now!
O mountain of craving for sensual objects, swear now!
Contemplate the dear beings as your mothers
And shoulder all their misfortunes upon yourself.

66

Take all their suffering upon yourself
And make your own self the object of intense ridicule.
Think! Think of the terror!
Reverse! Reverse all your negative deeds.

67

In this way cut the continuum of afflictions.
Both within, without, and at all times,
Never hold on to the suffering of this self.
If you gather negative karma, declare this in public.

68

If you act with duplicity, you'll suffer others' insults.
Empty yourself within and destroy your inner secrets;
Call forth your negative acts and spit on them.
When obsession for cleanliness arises, tame it with a leper's corpse.[312]

69

When thoughts of goal-seeking arise, strive to pass through numerous
 hazards.[313]
When feelings of revulsion arise, suck pus and blood.
Be not boisterous, but relinquish grasping at self.
Take not blessings [from the gods], but give alms to the ghosts.

70

Entrust your faith in the mighty ones;
Settle not your mind on diviners and shamans;
Place not your hopes in wrathful incantations,
But make yourself the substance and scapegoat [of exorcism].

71

When afflicted by demons, possessions, or sickness,
May Vajrapāṇi and his like—
All such wrathful deities—instantly appear.
May Mahākāla and his like—
All fierce ones—appear as paternal lineage.

72

Today I will pay my dues and debts;
The protective fence [around self] is today no more;
Today samsaric bark and the core wood of nirvana are separated.
O gather here, gather here, all flesh-eating beings.

73

O gather, all you who rob others of their breath.
May you appear here as helpers to skin me alive;
May you appear here as companions to share the meat.
You are my fathers and mothers;

74

Devour with pleasure the flesh and blood of this child of yours.
Appear here today to accept gifts for your kindness.
In the past I've cherished my own body and mind,
And due to this I still wander in cyclic existence.

75
In the past I took for myself the rewards for good deeds, [111]
And I am plagued with sickness now as a result.
In the past I caused much harm to others,
And my burden [today] is accordingly heavier than a mountain.

76
With the remorse I feel for my past actions,
I am buried under a load and might die under its weight.
In the past I guarded my self-grasping at all times
And sought refuge merely through mouth and [empty] words.

77
From here on, O powerful Three Jewels,
Do not be an ally of this self.
Do not give depth to this agent of downfall;
Should you, out of mercy, be its refuge, however,

78
Help me destroy the grasping from within
And dismantle the objects of grasping from without.
Help me sever attachment and aversion at their very sites;
Help me ensure freedom from aversion henceforth.

79
I will arrange a feast for my debts and dues;
All guests, from the summit of cyclic existence
To the bottom of the eighteen hells,
Gather here, all who would like to possess

80
My body, wealth, and rewards, my breath, radiance, and dignity.
Come here, O class of eighty thousand obstructive forces,
Relish [this feast of] flesh and blood
That I have cherished with such care since beginningless time.

81

Devour these debts and dues, and disturb me no more.
Come, O eighty-thousand classes of guests;
Come, O fifteen major possessions of children;[314]
Come, O yakṣas, carnivores, and elemental spirits;

82

Come, O messenger of the male demons;
Come, O demonesses, the ogresses that execute karma's fruits;
Come, O demons, the spirits of dead kings and earth spirits;
Come, all of you, and partake in [this feast of] flesh and blood.

83

From the top, the opening of my crown,
Down to the tip of the nails on my toes,
I shall be attached to [my body] no more.
O all of you, leisurely devour it with relish.

84

Tear the flesh, drink the blood, and chew the bones.
Take away my head, my limbs, and my heart;
Take away my joints, my offal, and my fluids;
In brief, my brain, my skin, and so on,

85

Whatever parts of my body, within or without,
That you may wish to devour or slice into pieces,
Enjoy them till you're satiated, for I shall bear no grudge.
Pacify them, utterly destroy them;

86

Heap them together and sever them from their roots;
Stir them and churn them—stir and churn this very self;
Rip apart the flesh and blood of this self;
Kill it, kill it, and wrap it, wrap this self.

87

With incantations of *Hūṃ! Jaḥ!* make this self no more.
End the circling of this samsaric wheel;
Cross the rapids of aggregates born of negative karma.
In the past I've cherished this body [of mine] with care;

88

Help me today to destroy its very self.
O mighty ones with the power to destroy evil,
O fierce ones immersed in the feast of flesh and blood,
O breath-snatchers bound by their solemn oath—

89

O all of you, help me destroy this self.
You'll [then] be greater than the buddhas of the three times.
If you fail to help vanquish this self,
We will all be destroyed by our individual karma.

90

So today, through fear born of knowledge,
I yearn to perfect the accumulations and undo the bondage. [112]
If through this I fail to gain liberation,
O hostile forces gathered here,

91

Cause me illnesses of wind, bile, and phlegm,
Or a combination of these [three humors];
Cause me other unbearable sufferings as well.
Whatever undesirable events there may be

92

In this world of appearance and experience,
Help direct them all upon this very self;
Help bring an end to afflictions and karma,
The suffering and birth of all beings.

93
May the suffering of all sentient beings
Definitely ripen upon me
This very instant in my heart.
Through this, may all beings without exception

94
Root out the causes and fruits of negative karma
And attain perfect abandonment of them.
Whatever virtues I may possess,
I dedicate them all for sentient beings.

95
Through this, may all beings without exception
Perfect their realization.
When all beings have thus attained
Perfect abandonment and realization—

96
The glory of loving-kindness and compassion
And the sole [state of] dharmakāya—
Then through the resulting two accumulations,
How can the self wander [any longer] in cyclic existence?

97
Whatever the situation, until my enlightenment
May I experience in the present lifetime
All future causes and effects of my afflictions;
May the causes and effects of afflictions of this life

98
Come to fruition in this very year;
May this occur this very month;
May this occur this very day;
May this occur this very moment.

99

When I today experience intense pain,
Such as acute aches and injuries,
With such sickness I will take on the illnesses of all beings
As a worthy duty, honor, and purpose.

100

The day of reckoning has now arrived!
Giving and taking have hit their mark!
Ah! Ah! I am ecstatic!
Certainly all beings are now overjoyed.

101

I have taken their suffering upon myself.
With the thought "Today I will serve my purpose,"
The moment a sickness strikes,
I will take on all that is unwanted.

102

I shall then have served the purpose of being ill;
I shall then have served the purpose of being burnt,
And of suffering thirst, hunger, and cold.
Though my body may burn with sickness,
My mind will be waxing with joy.

This concludes entirely the "Teaching on cultivating the power of tainted virtues," from the mind training *Stages of the Heroic Mind*.

12. Leveling Out All Conceptions[315]
Attributed to Serlingpa[316]

Herein is contained a teaching conferred by Serlingpa on Atiśa to help him subdue the barbarian borderlands.

The guardian and teacher Serlingpa said to master Atiśa, "Son, to subdue the barbarian borderlands, you will need the following teachings:"

1
Level out all [false] conceptions;
Carry forth the force of all antidotes;
Concentrate all aspirations into one;
And seek the path where all paths converge—

2
These are the four enlightened factors, the antidotes.
They are vital if you are to tame barbarian borderlands;
They are essential, too, in the age of degeneration
To bear with misguided ways of negative companions.

3
Adverse conditions are your spiritual teacher;
Demons and possessor spirits, the Buddha's emanations;
Sickness is a broom for negative karma and defilements;
Sufferings are displays of ultimate reality's expanse—

4
These are the four thoroughly afflicted factors;
They are vital if you are to tame the barbarian borderlands;
They are essential, too, in the era of degeneration
To bear with misguided ways of negative companions.

5

This [training] is the great counterpoint to happiness;
This is the great successor to misery;
This is the charm that attracts misfortune;
And this is a capping of wishes that are least useful[317]—

6

These are the four antidotes to misguided ways;
They are vital if you are to tame the barbarian borderlands;
They are essential, too, in the age of degeneration,
To bear with misguided ways of negative companions.

7

"Self" is the root of negative karma;
It is to be discarded decisively.
"Other" is a source of enlightenment;
It is to be embraced enthusiastically—

8

These two teachings draw the remedies to a close;
They are vital if you are to tame the barbarian borderlands;
They are essential, too, in the age of degeneration
To bear with misguided ways of negative companions.

9

Cast away decisively, let go with ease;
Dismantle thoroughly, and let be with gentleness—
These are the four aspects of the sealing of emptiness;[318]
They are vital if you are to tame the barbarian borderlands.

10

They are essential, too, in the age of degeneration
To bear with misguided ways of negative companions.
If you engage in the practices in this way,
Beings will not be fettered but will attain freedom.

Thus it was taught.

13. A Teaching on Taking Afflictions onto the Path[319]

Namo Ratna Guru!
[Homage to the Precious Teachers!]

It is said that the instruction for transforming forceful mental states, such as attachment and aversion, into the path on the basis of the two awakening minds—how to take afflictions onto the path—is presented in the tantras. It is impossible [however] for the ordinary afflictions themselves to become [aspects of] the path. As far as taking afflictions onto the path by means of selecting them as your meditation focus and turning them away is concerned, this has been taught repeatedly in the sutras. The instruction for this [sutra approach] is as follows.

Take attachment, for instance. First, when you observe yourself experiencing attachment to either an internal experience or to a specific external object, contemplate the following: "This is the affliction of attachment. If not relinquished, not purified, and not conquered, it will give rise to immeasurable suffering, such as birth in the lower realms. If transformed and conquered, it can become a condition for full enlightenment. I will therefore conquer it so that it becomes a condition for buddhahood."

Thinking thus, take into your mind your enemies' afflictions of attachment. Then, as you do when meditating on loving-kindness, cultivate this toward a larger sphere. Finally, take upon yourself all the attachments, including their propensities, existing in all beings. As you do this, imagine that your own attachment becomes so great as to be unfathomable. Imagine that all sentient beings become free of attachment and attain buddhahood. This is the [practice of taking afflictions upon yourself on the basis of the] conventional awakening mind.

Take upon yourself this attachment of yours, [now] the size of Mount Meru, and heap others' attachment upon it as well. Then reflect, "Attachment is by nature mental; apart from the mind there is no attachment, not even an atom's breadth. So when the mind observes itself, past and future states become no more. The past has ceased to be, while the future is, though [subject to] cessation, yet to be; and the present is devoid of any identifiable characteristics, such as shape, [color,] and so on. Not existing in any manner, [the mind] abides like space. So what is called 'attachment' [115] is a mere name with no referent at all." Place your mind in this state as long as it abides. This is the [practice of the] ultimate awakening mind.

From these two, respectively, arise the form body *(rūpakāya),* the mere hearing of whose name gives rise to the enlightened activities that help pacify the afflictions, and the dharmakāya, which helps eliminate all afflictions including their propensities that lead to more contaminated states. We should know how to extend this practice similarly to all afflictions, such as hatred, the master said.

This has been written on the basis of my teacher's words alone, with no omissions or additions. May the goodness of the content of this extremely profound instruction for taking afflictions onto the path equal [the measure of] space!

14. Guru Yoga Mind Training[320]

[116] Homage to the teachers!

In general, because [reliance on] a spiritual teacher is critical, the qualifications of the spiritual teacher and the proper manner of relating to him have been stated extensively in all the teachings of both the Great and Lesser Vehicles. The *Array of Trees Sutra* states:

> Without holding the paddles,
> The boat cannot cross to the other shore.
> Even if all other conditions are present,
> Without a teacher's presence, the end is not reached.[321]

Even if you possess such mundane qualities as being born into a high caste and so on, or such spiritual qualities as [being endowed with] faith, joyous effort, and so on, without relying on a teacher who blesses your mind, realizations will not arise. If realizations do not arise, you will not gain freedom from cyclic existence, so it is necessary to rely on a teacher. As for the qualifications of the teacher, it is stated:

> As for the teacher's qualifications, if he possesses
> The lineage and the realizations, he is qualified.[322]

You must rely on someone who is in a sacred lineage such as that of master Atiśa, one who possesses a transmission unbroken from the fully enlightened Buddha and who holds a firm conviction in the awakening mind. There are two aspects to such a manner of reliance. First is the reliance by means of actual [practice], which is to put the teachings into action through all three doors just as they are found in the teacher's words.

[Second] is the secret reliance by means of symbols, which refers to

visualizing the teacher at your heart or at your crown and making supplications to him with admiration and reverence. There are three parts to this:
(1) the preliminary, (2) the main practice, and (3) the concluding practices.

1. The preliminary

The preliminary has two elements: first you prepare the mind by cultivating
loving-kindness, compassion, and the awakening mind. Second, on the basis
of hollow-body meditation, contemplate your body as an appearance devoid
of intrinsic existence, like a form's reflection in a mirror, and then imagine
your heart as a mass of light.

2. The main practice

For the main practice, visualize your teacher at your crown, one teacher you
admire most, seated on a cushion of lotus and moon. Regardless of his actual
body size, which you may or may not have seen in the past, here imagine him
the size of a thumb. Recall everything about him—his face, his sitting posture,
the cadence of his voice, his aspirations, and so on. Imagine that, in reality, he
is inseparable from all the teachers from whom you have received Dharma
teachings, the lineage of which goes back to the Buddha himself, as well as
from the meditation deities, and from all the buddhas and bodhisattvas. [117]
Then make whatever offerings you can afford. With palms folded, you should
then, to your utmost capacity, seek refuge in the exalted body, speech, and
mind of the teacher. As for the true meaning of this [practice of going for ref-
uge], contemplate like this: "Although free of faults and perfect in all enlightened qualities, like space, he is devoid of any ultimate intrinsic existence. He
appears for the benefit of all beings, including me."

Then make the following supplication: "O most precious spiritual guide,
my teacher, bless me so that the two awakening minds—just as they are
found in your heart and in the hearts of those in your lineage, just as found
in the minds of the buddhas and bodhisattvas, who are the core expression of
the definitive scriptures—arise in me this very instant. Bless me so that awakening mind remains manifest in me throughout all times—of prosperity, of
misfortune, of success, of failure, of happiness, of sadness, at times of sickness, death, transition, and birth. Bless me so that I will know how to take
all adverse conditions and obstacles as factors complementary to this [mind
training] practice." Make this supplication three times.

Then, while maintaining the hand gesture of meditative equipoise, you should imagine that your crown aperture has opened. From it emerges, like a shooting star, a luminous image of the teacher, which then enters your heart. Recognizing this to actually be the teacher and a buddha, cultivate faith and respect to the best of your ability. Then let your mind rest, and as the teacher's body, speech, and mind dissolve into your body, speech, and mind, imagine that your body, speech, and mind assume the nature of clear light and space, and then rest your mind in this state for as long as possible.

3. The concluding practices

Third, the concluding practices are as follows. When your mind abides no more in the preceding state, visualize your body and the teacher at your heart as before. Alternately, you can imagine that he dissolves into your crown or that he departs to his natural abode. You should dedicate all your virtues of the three times toward the goal of fulfilling your teacher's aspirations and toward the birth of this spiritual practice [within you], and make aspiration prayers [to this end].

Although the benefits of such practice are inconceivable, you will obtain the common and uncommon benefits. In brief, you will be protected against harms caused by both humans and nonhumans, you will attain both mundane and supramundane excellences, [118] and you will receive all instructions and subsequent instructions. Since you will experience the transference [of consciousness] into clear light specifically by means of the two visualizations, this alone is the instruction to be applied at the moment of death. If you consolidate your efforts in this practice, the master said, you will be able to gain whatever realization you aspire for, and you will need no other realizations of meditative absorption. The precious Chilbupa says: "Even if I were to cut open my heart, there would be nothing but a pulsating lump of red meat. The distilled essence of my practice lies in this [mind training] alone."[323]

This guru yoga is drawn from my teacher's words and put into letters.[324]

The following is the lineage of this teaching: The Blessed Buddha gave this to Ārya Maitreya, he to Asaṅga, he to Vasubandhu, [then through to] Kusalī elder, Kusalī Jr., Serlingpa, the sole lord Atiśa, Geshe Dromtönpa, Sharawa, Chekawa, Chilbupa, Lopön Lha, Lhadingwa, Pön, Dharma Siṅha, Gyatön Jangchup Gyaltsen, Khenpo Shönu Jangchup, the glorious

Rinchen Jungné, he to Buddharatna, he to Kīrtiśīla, he to Jayabhadra, and he to Puṇyaratna.

Sarva he! Smile!

15. An Instruction on Purifying Negative Karma[325]

[119] Homage to the precious teacher!

As for the means to purify negative karma, although many methods, such as the four powers, the [recitation of] *kaṃkani* mantra,[326] and the hundred syllables [mantra recitations],[327] have been taught in both Tantric and Perfection [vehicles], here you should generate awakening mind by cultivating the thought "I shall purify, without exception, all the negative karma and obscurations of beings."

View your own body as a rainbow or composed of light, and visualize an opening at the point of your nose. As you recite the three syllables [*Oṃ Āḥ Hūṃ*], visualize that three syllables like a long thread of white fat emerge from this opening. Imagine that all your negative karma and obscurations flow out in the form of black liquid. With this thought, repeat [the three syllables].

As you end the session, imagine that all [negative karma] is thoroughly purified. Recognize all of these as mere expressions of the mind, dedicate the virtues, and make aspiration prayers.

Since [through the force of this meditation] the body, speech, and mind of the tathāgatas will descend in the form of three syllables, this is a source of great blessing. It is said that through this [practice], even such grave negative acts as causing dissension within a spiritual community can be purified.

16. Mahayana Purification of Grudges[328]

[120] Homage to the bodhisattvas!

Whether beings are humans or nonhuman animals, when they become objects of your grudges and when you experience reluctance to train in [cultivating] awakening mind in relation to them, you fail to gain realization of awakening mind. So the following is an instruction to purify grudges.

Seat yourself on a comfortable cushion in whatever posture is most convenient, then stir your heart with fervent loving-kindness and compassion. Then visualize the object of your grudge inside the hollow space of your heart; on his lap is your meditation deity, who physically resembles you. Visualize that these two are touching each other at their hearts, mouths, and foreheads and that their arms are in embrace.

At your crown, visualize, appearing from a white *Āḥ*, a white Vajrasattva seated on a moon disk. He has one face and two arms; in his right arm he holds a vajra at his heart, while in his left he holds a bell at his [left] hip. He is adorned with all [varieties of] ornaments. He is seated in the posture of a bodhisattva; his big toes touch your crown aperture. Then visualize at his heart, appearing from the *Āḥ*, a white vajra marked by *Hūṃ*.

As you recite the hundred-syllable mantra, drops of bodhicitta—manifestations of loving-kindness and compassion—that represent the mind of Vajrasattva (who in turn is the mind of all the buddhas and bodhisattvas) descend in the form of milklike nectar from the vajra and the *Hūṃ*. These flow from Vajrasattva's toes, enter through your crown aperture, and dissolve into the figure at your heart. When this occurs, imagine that your grudges, malevolent forces, harmful intentions, competitiveness, and jealousy, which have existed since beginningless lifetimes, are purified. Imagine that [the objects of your grudges] take birth as your parents, as your relatives, or as your friends.

As you end your session, and as Vajrasattva dissolves down through your crown, meditate on the spacelike equanimity of all beings, both self and others.

This is a sublime instruction of Mahayana mind training.

17. Two Yoginīs' Admonition to Atiśa to Train His Mind[329]

[121] *Namo Ratna Guru!*
[Homage to the precious teachers!]

On one special occasion, when master Atiśa was doing circumambulations while training his mind in the awakening mind, he encountered two women in the sky to the east of Bodhgaya [stupa]. Their physical appearance transcended that of the human realm but was not fully perfected like celestial gods. They were adorned with all kinds of ornaments.

The younger woman inquired of the elder one the following: "In what method should those who wish to swiftly attain full enlightenment train?"

[The elder one] replied: "Those who wish to attain full enlightenment should train their minds in awakening mind." Responding thus, she taught the method of [training in the awakening mind according to] secret mantra.[330] The two women were said to be Tārā and Bhṛkuṭī.

Atiśa transmitted this to Geshe Dromtönpa, he to Chengawa, he to Jayülwa, he to Tsangpa Rinpoché, he to Langlungpa, he to Sangyé Gompa, he to Samtsé Ringsangpa, he to Sangyé Gompa Jangchup Kyap, he to Yeshé Shap Śīlavajra, he to Dönyö Shap, he to Buddharatna at Lo Monastery, he to Kīrtiśīla, he to Jayabhadra, he to Puṇyaratna, and he to [me] Shönu Gyalchok Könchok Bang.

18. Kusulu's Accumulation Mind Training[331]

[122] Master Atiśa said: "This practice of Kusulu's accumulation is a source of great merit. It shakes the very trunk of cyclic existence."[332] He stated that there are the following eight benefits to Kusulu's accumulation [practice]:

1. It helps you sever grasping at the body as ordinary.
2. It helps you deceive death.
3. It helps you restore damaged commitments.
4. It helps you to effortlessly recognize dreams [as dreams].
5. It guards against persecution.
6. It helps you recognize pure illusory body during the intermediate state.
7. It helps you realize both common and supreme attainments.
8. It helps you accomplish others' welfare effortlessly through the power of your aspiration prayers and great compassion.

When you undertake this meditation, sit on a comfortable cushion and make sure that you have adopted the appropriate physical and mental postures. While generating the thought "I shall attain full enlightenment for the sake of all beings and to this end I shall engage in the practice of Kusulu's yogi instruction," cultivate the awakening mind.

Visualize your body as hollow like a baked earthen vase, your throat up to your crown aperture resembling the clear and hollow neck of a vase. Then, inside your hollow body, at your heart, visualize a blue *Hūṃ,* which is the nature of your mind. Imagine that as this letter is pushed upward by the wind, it exits from your crown aperture and floats in space about four finger-widths above [your crown]. Now, focusing on this [letter], recite three times *Oṃ svabhāvaśuddhāḥ sarvadharmāḥ svabhāvaśuddho haṃ* and perceive this as a mere dream or a mere magical illusion. Then, while reciting *Oṃ śūnyatā jñāna vajra svabhāva ātma ko haṃ* three times, imagine that the *Hūṃ* dissolves into emptiness.

From within this state, visualize that an orange lotus appears in space, melts into light, and becomes a lotus cushion. On this, evolving from *A,* visualize a moon disk upon which stands a red *Bam.* This melts into light and becomes a curved knife, and on its handle is, arising from *A,* a red *Bam* standing on moon disk. Light rays emanate from this [curved knife], touching all sentient beings. As this cleanses their negative karma and obscurations, imagine that all sentient beings become sister yoginīs. [123] Then visualize that the light rays are drawn back and dissolve into the handle of the curved knife. As *Bam* together with the curved knife melts, imagine that your mind transforms into a yoginī as depicted in the painted icon.[333] At her heart is a *Bam* standing on a moon disk, which is evolving from *A.* As light rays radiate from this, imagine that they invite wisdom-being yoginīs from the Blissful western [Buddha] realm, who arrive [in front of you].

[With] *Jah* she descends onto your crown; with *Hūm* she dissolves into you; with *Bam* she merges inseparably [with you]; and with *Hoh* you rejoice while generating the thought "I am the sister Varayoginī, who is the distilled embodiment of the great compassion of all the buddhas of the three times."

[Now] visualize at her heart, evolving from *A,* a red *Bam* on a moon disk; and at her crown, evolving from *A,* a white *A* on a moon disk; at her throat, evolving from *A,* a red *A* on a moon disk; and at her heart, evolving from *Ram,* a smoky-blue *Hūm* on a sun disk. Focusing your attention of these [letters], recite *Om Āh Hūm* three times.

Now imagine that your human body lies inert as a corpse in front of the yoginī. At its front is a green *Yam,* which melts into light and becomes a wind mandala in the form of a luminous bow, its two sides each adorned with a blue wind banner. On this is an orange *Ram* [which melts and becomes a red triangular fire mandala].[334] On the points [of the triangle] you should visualize three light blue *Hūms,* which melt into light and become a tripod made of three freshly severed human heads.

Now visualize that your mind as Vajrayoginī slices off the corpse's skull at its base and places it [with its open side facing up] upon the tripod of human heads. Imagine that this skull is wide and spacious and has a white exterior and a red interior. Visualize that the corpse is now placed inside the skull cup and upon it, evolving from *A,* is a *Bam* on a moon disk. This melts into light and transforms into a curved knife; at its handle, evolving from *A,* is a *Bam* on a moon disk. Light rays emanate from this, which transform the corpse into nectar; again light rays emanate, causing nectar to descend from the hearts of the buddhas and bodhisattvas, [124] filling the skull cup. Light rays emit from the *Baṃ* that is at Vajrayoginī's heart; at the tip of these rays are dense cloudlike clusters of nectar from which [streams of] nectar descend, filling the skull cup with a whitish fluid. As [Vajrayoginī] stirs the nectar with her curved knife, you should imagine that the commitment-being and wisdom-being nectars merge inseparably into one. [Now] the curved knife and the letters [too] transform into nectar. Then, as the yoginī recites *Hūṃ* three times, a forceful wind blows continuously from her nose that touches the two banners, which then fan the *Raṃ,* setting the fire ablaze. This causes the nectar to boil forcibly. As *Oṃ Āḥ Hūṃ* bless it, the nectar settles into a pink color.

Then light rays emanate from the *Hūṃ* at your heart as the yoginī, which invites countless sister yoginīs from the Blissful western [buddha] realm. They scoop nectar from the skull cup and travel to the hell realms. Imagine that on the head of each hell being appears a [replica] yoginī, who forcibly pours nectar into the mouth of that hell being, thus relieving it of the pains of [acute] heat and cold. Imagine that they all transform into yoginīs. The remaining nectar spills out and transforms [the hell realm] into the world of the Blissful [buddha] realm. This example can be extended to all the six realms, the master said.

Although it is [generally] inappropriate to offer leftovers to the Three Jewels, since [here] all food and drink is being offered to the Three Jewels without exception, it is said that this offering can be made. [In conclusion] you should dedicate your virtue toward the [attainment of] enlightenment and make prayers of aspiration.

19. Mind Training Taking Joys and Pains onto the Path[335]

[125] Homage to the spiritual teachers!

For this instruction on taking joys and pains onto the path, you should [first] generate the awakening mind. Then, when experiencing joy, identify clearly what it is that experiences the joy—whether it is your body or your mind. Since your corporeal body is like a corpse, it does not exist as the enjoyer of that happiness. Yet the mind is empty like the sky, and as such, it is devoid of itself, so it [too] cannot be the enjoyer of that joy. Therefore, since that which conceives of joy is devoid of itself, recognize what is empty as empty. Then place your mind—lucid, pure, relaxed, and settled—for as long as you can in this expanse of emptiness. This is the method for attaining the uncontrived, uncontaminated dharmakāya (the buddha body of reality).

While in this state, vividly conceive what you experience as joy to be in essence your meditation deity; and irrespective of whether your mind is distracted, seal yourself inseparably with your meditation deity. This is the method for attaining the enjoyment body, which is the means for taming the pure trainees.[336]

Not divorced from this identity, you should dedicate what you perceive as joy for the benefit of all sentient beings and recite the following three times:

> When happy, I shall dedicate my virtues to all;
> May benefit and happiness pervade all of space!

This is the method for attaining the emanation body, which is the means for taming the impure trainees.[337]

[Now] if you experience pain, vividly identify what it is that experiences the suffering—whether it is your body or your mind. Since your corporeal body is like a corpse, it does not exist as the subject of suffering. Yet the mind is empty like the sky; as such, it is devoid of itself, so it cannot be the subject of that suffering. Then affirm the emptiness of that which conceives of suffering to be devoid of itself, and while in this expanse of emptiness, place your mind—lucid, pure, relaxed, and settled—for as long as you can. This is the method for attaining the uncontrived, uncontaminated dharmakāya.

While in this state, vividly contemplate what you conceive of as suffering to be in essence your meditation deity; and irrespective of whether your mind is distracted, seal yourself inseparably with your meditation deity. This is the method for attaining the enjoyment body, which is the means for taming the pure trainees.

Not divorced from this identity, dedicate what you perceive as suffering for the benefit of sentient beings and recite the following three times:

> When suffering, I shall take on the pains of all beings;
> May the ocean of suffering become dry! [126]

This is the method for attaining the emanation body, which is the means for taming the impure trainees.

This, then, is the instruction for taking joy and suffering onto the path.

The lineage of this is as follows: Paṇchen Śākyaśrī, Trophu Lotsāwa, Khenchen Lhodrakpa, Khenchen Dewa Jamchenpa, Rinchen Drakpa Shenyen, Chöjé Sönam Rinchen, and Shönu Gyalchok.

20. Sumpa Lotsāwa's Ear-Whispered Mind Training[338]

[127] *Guru Namo!*
[Homage to the spiritual teachers!]

The realized siddha Sumpa Lotsāwa traveled to India and undertook extensive study of most of the secret mantra [systems]. Just before his return to Tibet, he brought his leftover gold to offer to the great enlightenment monument at Bodhgaya. As he was circumambulating this stupa, two women, one reddish and the other bluish, were circumambulating the stupa [as well]; at times they [hovered] above in the sky, and at other times they appeared to be walking on the ground.

The bluish woman then said to the reddish one, "Last night I felt mentally restless; I felt like going somewhere. I hope this is not some premonition about my death, for I am terrified of dying." Exclaiming this, she asked her companion four questions. To this, the reddish woman, casting side glances at Lotsāwa, responded to her companion as follows:

1. If you have a sense of abandonment, O lady, everything you do will bring happiness. Your mind suffers because it lacks this quality of abandonment.
2. If your mind rests where it is placed, O lady, it will be okay even if you travel [elsewhere]. Your mind suffers because it cannot rest where it is placed.
3. If your mind is turned to Dharma, O lady, you can die with ease. Your mind suffers because it is not usually turned to Dharma.
4. If you have recognized your mind as unborn, O lady, there will be no death. Your mind suffers because you have failed to recognize your mind as unborn.

She was said to have responded to her companion with these four statements. At that point it is said that Lotsāwa overcame his sadness, the practices he had learned in the past became effective, and extraordinary realizations arose in his mind.

The following is the introduction to this [practice]:

It is taught that if you have a sense of acceptance, you will remain content with whatever degree of material resources you may enjoy commensurate with the [karmic potential] you have stored for yourself. You will not envy others' prosperity, and you will ensure that [immediate] circumstances, whether happy or painful, will not burden your heart. It is necessary to recognize the nature of your own mind, guard your own place, and attain freedom on the basis of blessings from your spiritual teachers and on the basis of [applying] special meditation techniques. [128] The fusion of your mind with Dharma is this very lucid awareness [of yours]; it is vital that you recognize its [true] nature. To realize the mind as unborn is to realize its origination and to cease its death. The realization where you no longer differentiate between the actual meditation session and subsequent periods insofar as the cognition of mind as free of origination, cessation, and abiding is concerned—this [realization] has no death.

The lineage of this teaching is that the most holy Vajravārāhī and two Tārās revealed it to Sumpa Lotsāwa, he to Sapaṇ, he to the great siddha Tsotrangwa, he to Khedrup Chöjé, he to Ritrö Rechen, he to Prajñābodhi, he to Dönshakpa Buddharatna, he to Kīrtiśīla, he to Chöjé Gyalwa Sangpo, he to Chöjé Sönam Rinchen, and he to [me], Könchok Bang.

21. Bodhisattva Samantabhadra's Mind Training[339]

[129] *Guru maitrī namo!*
[Homage to my teacher Maitreya!]

The teacher said:

All phenomena are [manifestations of] your own mind, so you must bring them all together and then engage in your practice. Furthermore, since this lineage of sacred words is the path of your spiritual teacher, you should recognize that all the offerings of the three times are the creative play of your teacher and engage in the training of your mind. So pay homage to the teacher and make outer, inner, and secret offerings to him and make supplications to him as well. Entrust your tethers to the teacher and then engage in the practices—from [contemplations on] impermanence to the ultimate nature of reality.

For this you should establish the perfect spacelike view, [wherein] all phenomena of cyclic existence and beyond are primordially devoid of origination and cessation and transcend all boundaries of conceptual elaboration. You should train in the skills of noncessation, and cultivate the three [types of compassion]: (1) focusing on sentient beings, (2) focusing on their mere phenomenal nature, and (3) devoid of objectified focus. You should cultivate the three equanimities [toward others]: free [of discrimination] of closeness and distance, [free of discrimination] in your respect, and free of discrimination of [the qualities of] good and bad. Cultivate these three qualities. Furthermore you should train to cultivate the "expansive thought," the "resolute thought," and the "diamondlike thought."

I. Expansive thought

The first refers to some attitudes of the Great Vehicle. As the younger brother generated the aspiration "May I achieve equality with all my elder brothers, especially in their enlightened activities, such as turning the wheel of Dharma," he attained equality with all. The Buddha Śākyamuni, too, generated the expansive thought "May I tame all those sentient beings who are unattractive, who possess a negative nature and have failed to become trainees of all the [previous] buddhas." He [then] engaged in immeasurable austerities. The teacher spoke also of how, owing to the great compassion of the lords of the three families, the Buddha became the embodiment of the great compassion of all the buddhas. He spoke also of how the Buddha's emanations pervade the entire trichiliocosm and how immeasurable are the waves of his great compassion.

When he was born as the bodhisattva Vegadharin, Vajrapāṇi had the thought that the Great Vehicle is not for the swift attainment of buddhahood. [So] as a bodhisattva he remained always within cyclic existence, [130] endured great hardships to assist suffering sentient beings, and pleased the buddhas through veneration. He realized the qualities of the Buddha and became the custodian of the secrets of all the buddhas of the three times. He [then] engaged in such expansive conduct as subduing Māra and guarding against the obstacles.

As for Ārya Mañjuśrī, when he first generated the awakening mind, he took a vow to lead all beings to the state of buddhahood while still engaged in bodhisattva deeds. He took the vow that until he had led all sentient beings in all the ten directions to enlightenment and they had individually attained buddhahood, he would not himself become fully enlightened. He vowed that even for the sake of a single being he would remain till the end, and he vowed that for the sake of every single being, he would never become disheartened by sufferings such as those of the Avīci hells. Thus he vowed to engage in the enlightened activities of the Buddha even while remaining as a bodhisattva, and made the aspiration "May it be a betrayal of the tathāgatas to realize full enlightenment before my vows are fulfilled!" since this would be tantamount to committing [one of the] five heinous acts.

Bodhisattva Samantabhadra was even more expansive than all these [bodhisattvas].[340] When he first generated the awakening mind, he did so in a manner that included, without exception, the aspirations of all the buddhas. Also, when engaging in the bodhisattva deeds, he did so by embracing all the austerities, without exception, undertaken by all the bodhisattvas of the three times. He cultivated the aspiration to usher all sentient beings without exception and equal to the limits of space to buddhahood. He vowed that he would perfect the enlightened activities of all the buddhas while still a bodhisattva, and that when he performed in each buddha realm the inconceivable enlightened activities of the respective buddha, he would undergo such sufferings as those of Avīci hells for countless eons even for the sake of a single being, and he pledged that he would perform the enlightened deeds of the buddhas of the three times. He generated such altruistic thoughts as "I shall generate the altruism of the bodhisattvas of the three times that I have not generated so far. I shall endure the austerities associated with conduct that lies beyond the capacity [of many bodhisattvas]." He generated the altruistic intention to lead to the state of buddhahood those sentient beings who had been abandoned even by those with great compassion and skillful means. [131]

By emanating bodies equal in number to all atoms in the universe, he made outer, inner, and secret offerings in the presence of each and every buddha. Each of these bodies cultivated countless buddha realms. Similarly he made aspiration prayers to help discipline those trainees whose conduct is so hard to reign in. He pledged to engage in the enlightened deeds of all the buddhas, and he vowed to try every single instant to accomplish the activities of all the buddhas of the three times. He prayed, "If I realize buddhahood before these aspirations are fulfilled, may this be betrayal of all the buddhas of the three times." So his courage is as infinite as space and transcends words.

So you should generate a mind even more expansive than that of the buddhas and bodhisattvas. It is on this basis that the awakening mind will first arise, will abide in the middle, and will finally culminate in buddhahood. Do not become disheartened.

This [awakening mind] is a catalyst for suffering, a counterpoint to joy, a walking companion for those who are afraid, a remedy for sickness and malevolent harms, and it levels the afflictions flat. To follow in the footsteps of the buddhas and bodhisattvas, perform the following visualization.

At your heart, with yourself in your ordinary form, visualize, evolving from an *A,* a white *Maṃ* on a moon disk. Light rays radiate profusely from this and touch all sentient beings pervading the limits of space. The light rays extract karma and afflictions, such as attachment, anger, delusion, pride, envy, and miserliness, as well as the six root and the twenty derivative afflictions. They [also] extract the negative acts motivated by [the afflictions] that obstruct higher rebirth and liberation and force beings to experience the sufferings of cyclic existence and the lower realms. [These negative acts] include the ten negative actions committed through body, speech, and mind, the five heinous acts, the five approximate heinous acts, the root infraction of precepts, showing disrespect to the Three Jewels, abandoning the teachings, and belittling the noble beings. Imagine that all of these dissolve into you like rain falling on your body and that the minds of all sentient beings thereby become cleansed and free of obscuration.

Then with the thought "I shall purify all this negative karma," you should visualize another stream of light rays shooting forth [132] that touches all sentient beings. Imagine that all future sufferings of cyclic existence that may harm and afflict their body, speech, and mind—such as the heat and cold of the hell realms, the thirst and hunger of the hungry ghosts, the ignorance and confusion of the animal realms, the conflicts of the demigods, the death and fall of the celestial gods, and the eight and the eleven categories of suffering of the human realm—all these sufferings are dispelled. Imagine that the instant light rays touch the beings, their bodies and minds become blissful. Then as the light rays dissolve back into your body, imagine that all these sufferings descend upon your body like rain and that every single pore of your body becomes permeated by the inconceivable sufferings of the six realms of existence, such as the Avīci hells. Cultivate the thought, "If sentient beings gain freedom from suffering, then what I've shouldered as my responsibility will become a truly great objective." Reflect further, "Since all sentient beings have placed their trust in me to be their guarantor and protector, I shall offer myself as their protector and obtain their release. I shall undergo all the sufferings but lead them to happiness."

Now visualize another stream of whitish light rays, which depart and touch the hearts of your teacher and all his lineage, of the buddhas, of the bodhisattvas, of the meditation deities, of the disciples, and of the self-realized ones, drawing forth their obstacles to meditative practice, the damages caused to their body, their failure in realizing their enlightened aspirations, and the disruptions caused to their completion of liberating life deeds. These are visibly drawn forth on the tip of the light rays, which then dissolve into your body like a rain. Then rejoice: "It is indeed a great fortune that I have the honor to shoulder such responsibility."

At all times, never deviate from the spacelike expanse; at all times, never be divorced from contemplating your teachers; offer them as gifts your body, your wealth, and your roots of virtue. To the obstructive forces who are vengeful and to whom sentient beings owe karmic debts, conjure many effigies of yourself as scapegoats with pleasing appearance and delicious flavor, and offer these to them. Similarly you should conjure immeasurable meat, blood, bones, internal organs, limbs, and toes and offer these to them, or whatever they desire. Exhort them to consume [these] raw if they are in haste, and if not, to devour them cooked. By their eating these, imagine their afflictions of craving are overcome and they experience enhanced bliss. [Then] make prayers for these [obstructive forces] to become your disciples [in future]. [133]

Some may assert that now is not the time to give [away your body]. However, since guarding this impure body is like carrying a sack of prickly thorns, greater happiness comes if you let go of it, the master said. You should then utter: "As I have accumulated immeasurable merit, through the power of my unsullied intentions and through the blessings of my teachers, may my two accumulations increase immeasurably, and may the enlightened aspirations of all noble beings be fulfilled. May all sentient beings be relieved of suffering and endowed with perfect happiness."

When [reciting] essence mantras and engaging in wrathful rites, you should generate yourself as a meditation deity, and, through diverse threatening displays of magical power, you should crush all mundane bodies into dust and imagine that all beings are led to the wisdom of omniscience. When chronic illness or harmful spells strike you, free of mental agony, cultivate the conviction that they are all devoid of origin. Recognize all experiences as mirror reflections, placing your mind in meditative equipoise on loving-kindness. Thus taught the master.

If afflictions arise in your mind, recognize their nature to be devoid of origin and transform the afflictions into wisdom. Whatever adverse circumstance or conflict may arise, train your mind to transform these into a means for completing the two accumulations. In this manner, then, you should partake in everything—food, clothing, and shelter—as factors conducive to [the practice of] the awakening mind. You should strive in the causes that help all sentient beings who see, hear, think, or speak about you, to exhaust their three obscurations[341] and thus attain the buddha bodies. You should take all adverse circumstances onto the perfect path and engage in the deeds of Samantabhadra. You should [then] cultivate the intention "I shall help realize the enlightened intentions, the enlightened activities, and the aspirations and expansive deeds of all the buddhas and bodhisattvas."

II. Resolute thought

This refers to cultivating the courage "If fishermen, farmers, and traders can bear the pains of heat and cold [in the course of their work], why cannot someone like me bear them for the sake of sentient beings' well-being?"[342]

With such an attitude, when working for the welfare of other sentient beings, it is necessary to remain resolute and unshaken by negative karma, the afflictions, mundane concerns, [the outlook of] the Lesser Vehicle, and all forms of grasping at substantial existence, and [instead] seek omniscience.

III. Diamondlike thought

This refers to engaging in the practice of the awakening mind uninterrupted by any false conceptions from now until you have attained buddhahood. This, too, must be [accomplished through] an indivisible union of method and wisdom. When you practice one, the other naturally follows, thus you practice the two in union.

At the time of your full enlightenment, given that the scope and extent of your buddha realm are enlightened qualities that evolve from the distinctive features of your present capacity, strength, and aspirations, then those to whom your loving-kindness extends at present will become your disciples in the future. Therefore, as you cultivate the illusionlike person's awakening mind, endure the austerities, and train in the paths, you will attain full enlightenment in the spacelike expanse and, through your emanations, help free sentient beings from cyclic existence. This is simply a case of space occupying space.

Having thus determined everything as spacelike, you should recognize everything as expressions of illusion and train in the skills of noncessation, which is the expansive thought of awakening, and thus amass the two illusionlike accumulations. This, then, is the union [of method and wisdom]. Since the essential points will dawn within, you will not be disheartened by cyclic existence, and you will remain not too far from nirvana, the master said.

At that point, you are free of expectations and apprehensions. Since you have recognized the dharmakāya, even if you descend to the Avīci hell, you perceive it as the Blissful buddha realm. Since you have perceived samsara and nirvana as nondual, you are free of any thoughts of affirmation and abandonment. Since you have perceived buddhas and sentient beings as indivisible, your grasping at good and bad is dismantled. Since you have perceived all phenomena as equal, you are free of biased thoughts such as regarding some to be superior and others inferior. So, without [deliberately] traveling there, you will have arrived at Nāgārjuna's intention!

Those who wish to engage in such spiritual training should, in terms of their actions, gather the accumulations and, in terms of their thoughts, train their minds. They should embrace this [practice] as their object of admiration and embark on it with deep conviction. Once you have become connected [with this practice], it will not let you down, and gradually you will gain its realization.

Now, to avoid forgetting the awakening mind throughout all your lives, relinquish the four negative factors and always learn to acquire the four positive factors.[343] Train your mind to never abandon sentient beings and learn to relinquish the four conditions that lead to such abandonment, which are as follows:

1. If you entertain the thought "How can I work for the welfare of so many sentient beings?" [think instead,] "The more there are, the greater my awakening mind will become enhanced." [135]
2. Relinquishing the negative functions: Although it may not be possible to physically befriend [all beings], you should [nonetheless] attempt to at all times and mentally gather them.
3. Relinquishing through perceiving the objects of cyclic existence: Just as there are numerous sufferings, you should correspondingly eliminate them and remove them [from sentient beings].
4. Relinquishing through perception of emptiness: If you do not recognize what is empty to be empty and grasp at it as substantial reality, you undergo suffering. What a pity!

In this manner, relinquish the four conditions that lead to abandonment [of sentient beings] and enhance your compassion for sentient beings as much as possible. When the awakening mind equalizing all sentient beings arises, it is stated:

> When the awakening mind has arisen in them,
> Instantly the wretched, captives in samsara's prison,
> Are hailed as children of the sugatas;
> They're revered by the worlds of gods and humans.[344]

Such bodhisattvas train to be modest in their desires and to seek inner contentment. In their guarding of mindfulness and introspective vigilance, they train just like Ārya Kātyāyana.[345] Those who conduct themselves in the manner of an illusion, because they are free of arrogance, are like mirror reflections of a person. Like one's own hand feeding one's mouth, they are free of any expectation of reward. Like an illusory person, they harbor no hopes of results. Since they have unconditionally given their bodies, wealth, and roots of virtue away, they are said to be like the Buddha.

Although this is not yet the time to actually give [away your body], make sure that your will to give is perfected through pure thought, the master said. In future the time will come when, even as a bodhisattva, you will perform the enlightened deeds of the Buddha. Becoming fully enlightened and having attained the dharmakāya, the fulfillment of your own interest—the fulfillment of the welfare of the three types of realms (pure, impure, and mixed)—will take place until the end of cyclic existence through the two form bodies—which constitute the perfection of others' interests.

Iti. This has been hidden as a secret.

Master Atiśa gave this [teaching to] glorious Gönpawa, [he to] Rinchen Naburpa,[346] [then through to] Gyergom Sangyé Wön, Sang Gönpa, Khenpo Chöden, Lopön Śhākya Tashi, Gyamapa Tashi Gyaltsen, to Buddharatna, to Kīrtiśīla, to Jayabhadra, to Puṇyaratna, and he to Mipham Chöjé.[347]

22. Eight Sessions Mind Training³⁴⁸

[136] Homage to the Mahayana spiritual teachers!

In general, Atiśa had seventy-two teachers from whom he received teachings on tantra and the Perfection Vehicle. Three teachers in particular revealed [the teachings of] the awakening mind—Maitrīyogi, Dharmarakṣita, and Serlingpa. Among them it is his teacher Serlingpa that Atiśa held in highest reverence. The basis for this claim is the following: While Atiśa did not have reliquaries for the others, he had one with a silver parasol for Serlingpa; while there were no monthly commemoration rites for the others, there was one for Serlingpa; while Atiśa would place his folded palms at his heart whenever he heard the names of his other teachers, he would place his folded palms at his crown whenever he heard the name of his teacher Serlingpa; and while no tears would fall when Atiśa recalled the memory of his other teachers, this would happen the moment he recalled the memory of his teacher Serlingpa.

Atiśa was once asked, "Though you have many teachers, why is that you have such depth of reverence for Serlingpa?" Atiśa replied, "It is from none other than my teacher Serlingpa that I received the awakening mind that equalizes and exchanges self with others."

In the teacher Serlingpa's lineage, [there is] the perfectly enlightened Buddha, Maitreya, Asaṅga, Vasubandhu, Ārya Muktisena, Vadanta Vimuktisena, he to Paramasena, he to Vinītasena, he to the abbot Paramārthavairocana, he to Haribhadra, he to Ratnasūtra, he to the teacher Serlingpa, he to glorious Atiśa, he to Geshe Dromtönpa, who [in turn] transmitted it to the three brothers and, in particular, to Chengawa. He transmitted it to Langri Thangpa and Shawo Gangpa. Langri Thangpa gave it to Shangshung and Lugu; these two transmitted it to the latter Jowo. He transmitted it to the abbot Lungnangpa Rinpoché; he transmitted it to Draktön Sherap Rinchen; he to the master Shönu Samten, the custodian of the Buddha's doctrine; he to Buddharatna; he to Kīrtiśīla; he to the one with the conqueror's name;[349] he to Puṇyaratna; and he transmitted it to Shönu Gyalchok. This is the lineage of spiritual teachers up to the present. All of them, it has been taught, attained higher realizations on the basis of this teaching and experienced the arising of extraordinary spiritual experiences. [137]

What is referred to as the "Mahayana mind training" has been taught in general in all the teachings, such as the scriptural collections that compose the sacred words. In particular, in the chapter on meditation in *A Guide to the Bodhisattva's Way of Life,* the following has been stated:

> Recognizing oneself as flawed
> And seeing others as an ocean of virtues,
> You should relinquish self-grasping
> And practice as well the embracing of others.[350]

To distill the meaning of verses such as these, engage in the following contemplation:

"Generally speaking, there are eighty-four thousand afflictions that cause us to wander in the cycle of existence. When condensed, they are subsumed under six root afflictions and twenty derivative afflictions, and at the root of all of these lies self-grasping. Where no intrinsic reality exists, I have grasped at "I" or "self" and have taken its side and fought for its sake. Because of this, what ought to have been positive karma has turned into negative karma, and as a consequence I have fallen into suffering. This is because, on my part, I took the self's side and fought with others for its sake. In the future, too, if I do not relinquish this self-grasping, I will roam in the cycle of existence, as I do now. I have no doubt that it is this self-cherishing demon, the so-called "I" or "self," that forces me to suffer in all three times—in the past, at present, and in the future—all because of taking its side and fighting on its behalf. There is nothing in what I see, hear, or think about that I have not harnessed [for the sake of the self]. It has not enabled me to get any farther from cyclic existence, so I must now let go of it as best as I can. I must let go of it for the sake of [becoming a] heroic bodhisattva."

Thinking thus, let go of it entirely, let go of it naturally and with ease, and let go of it by thoroughly dismantling it.

You can't say that sentient beings are, by themselves, generally not worthy, for they are all our kind parents. Therefore imagine that you take away the negative actions (the causes) and the sufferings (the fruits) that persist in sentient beings; take them away as if sheering them off with a sharp razor, and imagine that they come to be realized upon your own body. Then imagine that your own happiness and virtues ripen upon sentient beings. Meditate on the reversal and exchange of these two situations. You should also mentally sow the roots of virtue of all the buddhas and bodhisattvas so that they come to fruition on sentient beings. This is the real meaning of "Mahayana training of mind," the master said.

Khenpowa states, [138] "What is called *mind training* is sacrificing oneself and having respect for other sentient beings. 'Sacrificing oneself' implies, if necessary, even allowing this very ground [of self] to become lost, since this demon of self-cherishing has caused us to suffer since beginningless cyclic existence."[351] So it connotes many things, the master said. "Cultivating respect for other sentient beings" refers, in general, to never abandoning the beings of the three realms of cyclic existence. Since all have been our kind parents, we should cultivate respect for them and strive to be of benefit to them through gifts of our body, speech, and mind free of any sense of caution, the master said.

1. Mind training pertaining to food

Now, in order to put into practice the instruction of Geshe Dromtönpa, to accumulate merit for your benefactors, and to help you to digest food offered by others out of faith and reverence, you should engage in mind training pertaining to food.

[First] cultivate the thought "I will attain buddhahood for the benefit of all beings. In particular, I will nurture the eighty-four thousand classes of microorganisms that inhabit my body this very instant through material gifts, and in the future I shall nurture them through Dharma."

Then as you swallow food, visualize that, as if sheered off by a sharp razor, the causal negative karma and their resultant suffering of all beings are taken away and converge instead upon you. As you exhale, contemplate that your own happiness and virtues ripen upon other sentient beings. Meditate thus on the reversal and exchange of these two situations.

Imagine also mentally transferring the roots of virtue of all the buddhas and bodhisattvas, which then come to fruition on other sentient beings. Thus, you imagine sentient beings becoming free of their causal negative karma and resultant suffering. They generate the awakening mind that aspires for supreme enlightenment, and they attain buddhahood by accomplishing the two accumulations. Again imagine that sentient beings become free from causal negative karma and resultant sufferings. They generate the awakening mind that aspires for supreme enlightenment, and, accomplishing the two accumulations, they visibly transform into the blessed Akṣobhya. [139]

Then imagine that a thumb-size wisdom-being Akṣobhya arrives from his natural abode and descends on the crown of your head. Focused on this, cultivate devotion and reverence with your mind, and with your speech recite the praise hymns. Then make offerings and supplications to him. After entering through your crown aperture, he descends and arrives at the level of your heart; think that he dissolves spontaneously into emptiness there. Place the mind in this state blissfully, freely, at ease, and lucidly. If your mind abides in this state, let it do so. If your mind enters into sleep while in this state, this is the instruction of taking sleep into the ultimate expanse. If you die while in this state, this is the instruction [for application] at the point of death. You will then actualize the supreme attainment of the great seal during the intermediate state, the master said. While in this state, if you engage in mantra recitation, this will be a source of extremely great blessings, for it will become a mantra repetition of the enlightened body, speech, and mind. This is because the visualization of the meditation deity is the mantra repetition of body, the recitation of essence mantra is the repetition of speech, while meditation on emptiness is the mantra repetition of mind, the master said.

When you wish to rise out of this state, then like a rainbow appearing in the sky, you should instantaneously generate [yourself as] a blessed Akṣobhya, and visualize that the thumb-size wisdom-being that dissolved [into you] earlier reappears at your crown. Focused on this, cultivate devotion and reverence with your mind, and with your speech recite the praise hymns. Then make offerings and supplications to him. Then, if you have a drawing of him, dissolve him into this. If not, dissolve him into a sculpture or a reliquary stupa. If none of these is present, then request him to depart to his natural abode. Then, on the basis of the stanza "To the Buddha, Dharma, and the supreme assembly," you should make dedications three times by means of taking refuge and generating the awakening mind. You should meditate on this world of appearance as illusionlike, the master said.

This is the first chapter, the chapter pertaining to food. [140]

2. Mind training pertaining to breathing

Second, the mind training pertaining to breathing is as follows: Cultivate the thought "I shall attain buddhahood for the benefit of all beings and, to this end, I shall engage in the meditation on mind training pertaining to breathing."

Then, as you inhale, imagine that the sufferings of all sentient beings ripen upon you; and as you exhale, imagine that your own happiness and virtues come to fruition upon sentient beings. Meditate thus on the reversal and exchange of these situations.

Mentally take the roots of virtue of all the buddhas and bodhisattvas and imagine that they come to fruition upon sentient beings. In the same way, imagine yourself, too, to be free of negative karma and sufferings and, generating the mind aspiring for supreme enlightenment as before, engage in the meditation and mantra recitation of your meditation deity.

This is the second chapter, the chapter pertaining to breathing.

3. Training the mind by multiplying your body into the number of grains of sand in the Ganges and taking upon yourself the sufferings of the beings of the six realms

Third, to engage in mind training by multiplying your body into the number of grains of sand in the Ganges[352] and taking upon yourself the sufferings of the beings of the six realms, cultivate the thought "I will attain buddhahood for the benefit of all beings and, to this end, I will train my mind by multiplying my body equal to the number of grains of sand that exist in the Ganges and take upon myself the sufferings of the beings of the six realms."

Then imagine emanating into the hell realms bodies equal to the number of grains of sand in the river Ganges. Imagine that all the negative karma and sufferings of the hell beings converge in their entirety upon these bodies. Imagine that all your happiness and virtues come to fruition upon the hell beings. Meditate thus on the reversal and exchange of these two situations.

Now mentally take the roots of virtue of all the buddhas and bodhisattvas and imagine that they come to fruition upon sentient beings. Imagine that the hell beings become free from negative karma and suffering and, [141] having generated the mind aspiring for supreme enlightenment, they accomplish the two accumulations and attain higher states of existence, such as birth as humans or celestial gods. In the same way, imagine that the hungry ghosts, animals, and demigods also attain the existence of human or celestial gods.

Imagine that you emanate in the human realm bodies equal to the number of grains of sand in the Ganges and that all the negative karma and the sufferings of beings converge upon these bodies. Imagine that all your happiness and virtues come to fruition upon human beings. Meditate thus on the reversal and exchange of these two situations.

Now mentally take the roots of virtue of all the buddhas and bodhisattvas and imagine that they come to fruition upon sentient beings. Imagine that the human beings become free from negative karma and suffering, and, having generated the mind aspiring for supreme enlightenment, they accomplish the two accumulations and attain buddhahood.

Now visualize this world—the external environment and the beings within it—as an expansive and wide container made of precious jewels. Imagine that your body is then cut into pieces and that this [container] becomes filled with meat and blood. Focusing on this, as you recite *Oṃ Āḥ Hūṃ* three times, imagine that this all transforms into ambrosia. Imagine that the container is filled, too, with wisdom-being nectars that descend from the hearts of all the buddhas and bodhisattvas. Imagine that the container is also filled with the nectars and vital essences of Tuṣita,³⁵³ the northern continent Uttarakuru,³⁵⁴ and the entire world system. Then as you offer the ambrosia first to the teachers and meditation deities, next to the buddhas and bodhisattvas, and then to the beings of the six realms, imagine that, as a result, all of them attain the nonconceptual wisdom of the dharmakāya.

Now your body is no more, for it has been taken away by sentient beings; as for your mind, place it naturally in the absence of intrinsic existence. Then engage in the meditation and mantra recitation of the meditation deity as before and dedicate the roots of virtue.

This is the third chapter, the chapter on multiplying your body into the number of grains of sand that exist in the Ganges and eagerly embracing the sufferings of the beings of the six realms. [142]

4. Mind training pertaining to flesh and blood

Fourth, to engage in mind training pertaining to flesh and blood, cultivate the thought "I will attain buddhahood for the benefit of all beings and, to this end, I will engage in mind training pertaining to flesh and blood."

Then visualize your room filled with flesh and blood and imagine that, upon your summoning, all the hungry ghosts that are attached to flesh and blood gather [in your presence]. Imagine exhorting them: "Eat meat, O you who like meat! Drink blood, O you who like blood! O king of demons, take my head! O queen of demons, take my legs! O the nine gods and demons, you who are so easily provoked, take what is left in between! If you are in haste, eat them raw! If you are not in haste, eat them cooked! Do whatever pleases you!"

As you give thus, imagine that they devour the meat, drink the blood, and chew all the bones as well.

Now your body is no more, for it has been given to them; as for the mind, place it naturally in the absence of intrinsic existence. Then, as the scope of your mind increases, the master said, visualize flesh and blood pervading everywhere within the your perimeter fence, then the entire region, and then the entire expanse of the universe. When you wish to rise from this [meditation], dedicate the merit and meditate on [all things as] dreamlike.

This is the fourth chapter, the chapter on giving flesh and blood.[355]

5. Mind training pertaining to torma [356] [offering]

Fifth, to engage in mind training pertaining to torma, cultivate the thought "I will attain buddhahood for the benefit of all beings and, to this end, I will engage in mind training pertaining to torma."

Now visualize this world—the external environment and the beings within—as an expansive and wide container made of precious jewels. Imagine that your body is then cut into pieces and this [container] becomes filled with meat and blood. Focusing on this, as you recite *Oṃ Āḥ Hūṃ* three times, imagine that they transform into ambrosia.

Then as you recite the names of the four tathāgatas, such as Ratnaneka, imagine that all those who guard the sublime teaching, such as Mahākāla and Śrīdevi and so on, who have pledged to protect the teachings of the Buddha, and who utterly admire the side of the positive force, [143] congregate and partake [in the feast]. And as you recite *Nama sarva tathāgata ava lokete saṃbhara saṃbhara hūṃ* three times, imagine that they spontaneously partake of the offering. Then utter: "May all beings of the six realms accept this great feast of torma so that the accumulations may be accomplished in the hearts of all beings and myself." Then recite the stanza "May, by the power of my merit and so on...."[357]

Now your body is no more, for it has been taken away; as for your mind, place it naturally in the absence of intrinsic existence. Then when you wish to rise out of this [meditation], dedicate the merit and meditate on [all things as] dreamlike and illusionlike.

This is the fifth chapter, the chapter pertaining to torma [offering].

6. Mind training pertaining to the natural elements

Sixth, to engage in mind training pertaining to the natural elements, *A Guide to the Bodhisattva's Way of Life* states:

> Like great natural elements such as earth
> And like space, may I always become,
> For countless beings,
> Diverse forms of sustenance.[358]

[First] cultivate the thought, "I will attain buddhahood for the benefit of all beings and, to this end, I will engage in mind training pertaining to the natural elements."

Then imagine that your flesh and bones dissolve into the external element of earth, your blood and fluids dissolve into the water element, your breath into the wind, while your body heat dissolves into the fire element. This body, now transformed into the four elements of nature, serves the welfare of sentient beings—earth through its nature of solidity and firmness, water through its nature of moisture and fluidity, fire through its nature of heat and burning, and wind through its nature of lightness and mobility. The sun and moon become the two eyes and serve the welfare of sentient beings.

Imagine that sentient beings eating food are consuming your flesh, those wearing clothes are clad in your skin, and those quenching their thirst are drinking your blood. Then visualize that the negative karma and sufferings of sentient beings converge upon you [144] and that all your happiness and virtues come to fruition upon sentient beings. Thus meditate on the reversal and exchange of these two situations.

Mentally take the roots of virtue of all the buddhas and bodhisattvas and imagine that they come to fruition upon sentient beings. Imagine that human beings become free from negative karma and suffering, and having generated the mind aspiring for supreme enlightenment, they accomplish the two accumulations and attain buddhahood.

As you recite *Oṃ Āḥ Hūṃ* seven times on the body composed of four elements, imagine that your body transforms into ambrosia. Imagine that the container, too, is filled with wisdom-being nectars, which descend from the hearts of all the buddhas and bodhisattvas. Imagine that the container is also filled with the nectars and vital essences of Tuṣita, the northern continent Uttarakuru, and the entire world system. Then, as you offer the ambrosia first to the teachers and meditation deities, next to the buddhas and bodhisattvas, and then to the beings of the six realms, imagine that, as a result, all of them attain the nonconceptual wisdom of the dharmakāya.

Now your body is no more, for you have offered it to the teachers, meditation deities, buddhas, bodhisattvas, and the beings of the six realms; as for your mind, place it naturally in the absence of intrinsic existence. [Then] engage in the meditation and mantra recitation of the meditation deity as before and dedicate the roots of virtue.

This is the sixth chapter, the chapter on mind training pertaining to the natural elements.

7. Training the mind by transforming your body into a wish-fulfilling jewel

Seventh, to train the mind by transforming your body into a wish-granting jewel, *A Guide to the Bodhisattva's Way of Life* states:

> Like the wish-fulfilling jewel, like the excellent vase,
> Like the spell of an accomplished one, like the great medicine,
> And like the wish-fulfilling tree—
> May I become a source of wishes for all beings.[359]

[First] cultivate the thought "I will attain buddhahood for the benefit of all beings and, to this end, I will engage in the practice of mind training by transforming my body into a wish-fulfilling jewel." [145]

[Then] imagine that your body has transformed into a wish-fulfilling jewel that is blue, has eight sides, and is about the size of an average person's thigh. As you place this atop a victory banner, honor it with offerings, and make supplications to it, imagine that unequaled showers of rain descend, sprinkling the ground. Again, as you honor it with offerings and make supplications to it, an unequaled wind rises that sweeps the ground. Again, as you honor it with offerings and make supplications to it, rains of ambrosia descend that purify the karma, afflictions, and solidity of the ordinary flesh and blood of sentient beings. Generating the mind aspiring for supreme enlightenment, imagine that sentient beings accomplish the two accumulations and attain buddhahood.

Again, as you honor it with offerings and make supplications to it, imagine that rains of jewel descend, adorning sentient beings with precious ornaments. Again, as you honor it with offerings and make supplications to it, rains of five-textured celestial clothes descend, dressing them with silks. Again as you honor it with offerings and make supplications to it, rains of uncontaminated nectar descend, filling the entire expanse of the universe. Imagine that the container is filled with wisdom-being nectars that descend from the hearts of all the buddhas and bodhisattvas. Imagine that the container is filled, too, with the nectars and vital essences of Tuṣita, the northern continent Uttarakuru, and the entire world system. Then as you offer ambrosia first to the teachers and meditation deities, next to the buddhas and bodhisattvas, and then to the beings of the six realms, imagine that, as a result, all of them attain the nonconceptual wisdom of the dharmakāya.

Now your body has been offered to the teachers, meditation deities, buddhas, bodhisattvas, and beings of the six realms. As for your mind, since it is devoid of intrinsic existence, place it naturally in the absence of intrinsic existence. When you wish to rise out of this [meditation], dedicate the roots of virtue and meditate on [all things as] dreamlike and illusionlike.

This is the seventh chapter, the chapter on transforming your body into a wish-fulfilling jewel. [146]

8. Mind training as an instruction for the moment of death

Eighth, to engage in mind training as an instruction to be applied at the moment of death, you should die by means of the six perfections. At the point of death divide your three possessions[360] into three parts, and offer one part to the teachers and the Three Jewels, use another part for the accumulation of merit, and use the third part in whatever appropriate way you choose, such as distributing it as gifts [to the members of the monastic community], the master said. This is giving. For ethical discipline, declare and purify the infractions of the individual liberation class and reinforce your generation of the aspiring and engaging aspects of the awakening mind. This is ethical discipline. For forbearance, if you harbor any past grudges, seek forgiveness. If the person [who is the object of your grudge] is not within the immediate vicinity, you should [still] ask for his forgiveness by recounting the situation between yourself and him and offering him even a small article, such as an earring, [as a gift]. Even though he may not actually grant forgiveness, this ensures that there is no feeling of disquiet in you. Joyous effort is to engage in all of these with a sense of joyfulness. Concentration and wisdom are embedded in the body of these [previous four perfections].

Then, if you can afford it, prepare an elaborate array of offerings in the presence of the Three Jewels, perform the seven-limb practice extensively, and make the following supplication: "Bless me so that undistorted realizations of Mahayana mind training arise in me. Bless me so that I may never forget mind training during the four situations when it is most likely to be forgotten. Bless me so that I may never lose mind training during the four situations when it is most likely to be lost."[361]

Now, in the presence of the Three Jewels, visualize a golden *Baṃ,* which melts into light and from it appears a lotus with a stem. On the corolla of this lotus, which is adorned with jewels and silk garments, visualize your teacher as inseparable from your meditation deity. Then mentally take the offerings [imagined] earlier and offer these to him. Perform the seven-limb practice and make supplications as before.

Then, in a secluded environment, adopt what is called the seven bodily postures of Vairocana or the six characteristics of meditative concentration:[362] (1) Your feet should be in the crossed-legged position; (2) your spine should be straight and well-aligned like a stack of gold coins; (3) your two hands should be in the gesture of meditation at a distance of four finger-widths at the level of your navel; (4) your neck should be bent like a hook [147] while your front and back must remain even, the master said. [The posture should be] such that if you were to tilt [your head] three times to the left, nose drips would fall at about the level of your navel. (5) Your eyes should be left focusing on the tip of your nose; (6) your teeth should be open the space of a hair-width; and (7) your tongue should touch the upper palate of your mouth. Your eyes should not be kept closed, for this will lead to mental laxity; nor should they be left wide open, for this will lead to distraction. Like the eyes of the celestial gods, they should blink at a regular pace. Then you should focus your mind three times at the level of your navel, the master said.

Then cultivate the thought "I will attain buddhahood for the benefit of all beings and, to this end, I will engage in the practice of Mahayana mind training as an instruction to be applied at the point of death."

[Contemplate] "All these sufferings in cyclic existence arise from negative, positive, or unwavering karma.[363] They in turn arise on the basis of the afflictions, and the root of all eighty-four thousand classes of afflictions is self-grasping. By grasping at self where there is no intrinsic reality we always take its side and constantly fight with others for its sake, and because of this, we accumulate karma. Through karma we wander in cyclic existence and undergo the suffering of cyclic existence, which is limitless and has no discernable end. In this life, too, because of taking its side and fighting with others for its sake, instead of experiencing happiness we encounter suffering, and instead of being virtuous we remain nonvirtuous. This is because, on our part, we took the self's side and fought with others for its sake. In the future, too, if we do not relinquish this self-grasping, we will wander in the cycle of existence, as we do at present."

Then conclude, "There is no doubt that it is this so-called 'I' or 'self,'—the demon that compels me to cherish my own self—that causes me to suffer in all three times—the past, present, and future. This is because I take its side and fight with others for its sake. There is not a single thing that I have not pursued [for its sake] on the basis of what I have seen, heard of, or thought about. However, since this has not taken me farther away from cyclic existence in the past, I must let go of it to the best of my ability." Thinking that you will let go of it by casting it away completely, let go of it entirely, let go of it naturally with ease, and let go of it by thoroughly dismantling it.

In general, all other sentient beings of the three realms are not to be abandoned. As they are all, like your parents, embodiments of kindness, you should imagine that the sufferings of sentient beings come to fruition upon yourself and that your own happiness and virtues ripen upon other sentient beings. [148] Meditate on the reversal and exchanging of these two situations. Mentally take the roots of virtue of all the buddhas and bodhisattvas and imagine that they come to fruition upon sentient beings. Imagine that, in this way, sentient beings become free of their negative karma and suffering and attain full enlightenment, and that you, too, are free of negative karma and suffering. [Then,] as before, engage in the meditation and mantra recitation of your meditation deity.

Then if you can afford it, prepare an elaborate array of offerings in the presence of the Three Jewels, perform the seven-limb practice extensively, and make the following supplication: "Bless me so that the undistorted realizations of Mahayana mind training will arise in me. Bless me so that I may not forget mind training during the four situations when it is most likely to be forgotten. Bless me so that I may not lose mind training during the four situations when it is most likely to be lost."

At the actual moment of death, when respiration ceases, there dawns to all beings a clear state of consciousness, free of conceptualization, that resembles a clear sky on an autumn day. It is this that is brought into correlation with what was described earlier.[364] When properly correlated, they will merge like streams of water joining each other. You can abide in this state for a year, a month, and so on, and arise from this in the intermediate state as the enjoyment body. Those with perseverance can become fully enlightened within this lifetime [through using this method], the master said.

Should this fail, however, you will then arise with the full characteristics of an intermediate-state being. An intermediate-state being has the body of a five-year-old and possesses five colors. If, at that time, you can recognize these [colors] as indivisible from the eight metaphors of illusion,[365] the five poisons will [then] transform into the five wisdoms. The wisdom of ultimate expanse and that of perfect equanimity are the dharmakāya; the mirror-like wisdom is the enjoyment body; while the wisdom of accomplishment of deeds and that of discriminative awareness are the emanation body. If you become attached to the light of five colors and cling to them, the lights will revert to the five poisons, and [you] will revolve inside the nexus of six conditions,[366] thus [compelling you] to wander around taking birth in the six realms of existence. Nevertheless, within six or seven lifetimes from the present life, it is said, you will attain full enlightenment. Compared to the beginningless cycle of existence, this is equivalent to the distance of tomorrow or the day after, said the master. Those extremely lazy ones will attain full enlightenment in successive lives, the master said.

May the instruction of eight sessions bring virtue and excellence! *Mangalam.*

23. Mind Training Removing Obstacles³⁶⁷

[149] Homage to the greatly compassionate spiritual teachers!

[The instruction on] dispelling the obstacles of Mahayana mind training is, it has been taught, (1) to accept ill omens as charms, (2) to exterminate Māra at its very source, (3) to bring obstacles onto the path, and (4) to cap your least useful desires.

1. First, [accepting all ill omens as charms] is as follows:

When worldly people encounter bad omens, such as hearing owls crying or foxes howling [at night], they consult astrology, make divinations, and have rituals performed. You, on the other hand, should eagerly embrace ill omens and negative signs when they appear by cultivating the thought "Since it is self-grasping that causes me to suffer, may all the suffering that exists in the world arising from the fear of encountering ill omens befall upon this self. May this help vanquish the self-grasping."

2. Second, [exterminating Māra at its very source] is as follows:

It is taught that self-grasping causes us to suffer. So when you experience pain or injury to your bodies, caused either by humans or nonhumans, you should think, "It is this [body] that causes me to undergo suffering. If you desire it, take it away this very instant. O king of demons residing above, take away my head! Great indeed is your kindness in causing all the harms to it. Since you are my ally in subduing the [true] enemy, and my ally in subduing Māra, help me exterminate the very continuum of worldly gods, humans, and ghosts, and help me vanquish [this] demon to the best of my ability." Cut [self-grasping] from its root with the thought "It is not inconsistent to relish doing so."

3. Third, [bringing obstacles onto the path] is as follows:

Whatever unhelpful events, such as physical ailments, mental anxieties, and so on, occur, or when adversities afflict you, contemplate, "This is due to my own self-grasping. If today I do not discard this self-grasping, obstacles will continue to arise. So may all the adversities in the world and those feared to come be realized upon me. May this help subdue the self and utterly destroy it." Contemplating thus, bring them onto the path.

4. Fourth, [capping one's desires that are least useful] is as follows:

"What benefit has this brought me, if any? It has never made me go farther away from cyclic existence, so it must be destroyed [today]. Then, at least, I will have derived some purpose from its utter lack of usefulness. [If I achieve this,] it will be due to my teacher's blessing; it will be owing to his kindness. Pray help me so that in the future, too, I can gather upon this [self-grasping] everything that has no usefulness and vanquish them by subjugating them." Contemplating in this way, cap your least useful desires.

Iti.

24. Mahayana Mind Training Eliminating Future Adversities[368]

Mahayana training of mind eliminating future adversities has three parts: [(1) The preliminary, (2) the actual practice, and (3) the purpose of mind training.]

1. The preliminary

There are four occasions when mind training is likely to be forgotten: (1) during the agonizing moment of death, (2) during the intermediate state, (3) in the mother's womb, and (4) in the next life. There are four occasions when mind training is likely to be lost: (1) when suffering severe harms caused by humans, (2) [when suffering severe harms] caused by nonhumans, (3) when suffering a grave illness caused by the elements, and (4) when strong afflictions arise.

The antidote to these is as follows: Having made offerings to the teacher and the Three Jewels, make the following prayers of aspiration: "Bless me so that undistorted realizations of Mahayana mind training arise in me. Bless me so that I do not forget it [mind training] during the four occasions when it is likely to be forgotten and I do not lose it when it is likely to be lost."

Next, offer torma to the Dharma protectors and, as before, make aspiration prayers: "Having accumulated the merit, may Mahayana mind training arise in me. May it not be forgotten when this is likely to occur, and may it not be wasted during the four occasions when this is likely."

Make these aspiration prayers and repeat the same in relation to the collective merit of sentient beings.

The four decisions pertaining to the practice of Mahayana mind training, the master said, are as follows: (1) all paths are traversed by one, (2) all aspirations are concentrated into one, (3) all conceptions are leveled out, and (4) the remedies are instantly applied to vanquish [the opposing forces].

All paths are traversed by one, for there are no enumerations of levels and paths [in mind training practice]. One undermines self-grasping as fully as one can. If you annihilate it today, you attain buddhahood today; if you annihilate it tomorrow, you attain buddhahood tomorrow; if it remains undestroyed, there is no buddhahood; and when you annihilate it, at that instant you become fully enlightened, it has been taught.

All aspirations are concentrated into one, for whatever activities you might engage in, be it walking [toward a specific destination], strolling, sleeping, or sitting, you have no purpose other than to undermine self-grasping to the best of your ability and to help sentient beings as much as you can. Few other aspirations need be pursued, it has been taught.

All conceptions are leveled out. Some assert that [all] conceptions are to be eliminated; however, it is not necessary to eliminate them. [Instead] conceptions are taken onto the path, for they are the very stuff of the dharmakāya. As for afflictions, since they grow to a small degree when they first arise, it is vital to vanquish them the moment they are born. If not destroyed, they grow enormous and then cannot be overcome. When afflictions can be easily averted by simply applying the antidotes at their first appearance, [151] what a pity if you shy away and don't eliminate them, the master said. So when a conception arises, examine thus: "Where does it arise from? Where does it reside? Where does it go when it ceases?" and recognize that it is devoid of intrinsic existence. And, like meeting a past acquaintance, you take it onto the path, the master said. Or, like snowflakes falling onto hot rocks, dissolve it into emptiness.

The remedies are instantly applied to vanquish [the opposing forces], for the instant afflictions arise, just like hitting the head of each pig with a stick, you apply whatever is the most effective antidote [to that specific affliction], the master said.

2. *The actual practice*

The practice of Mahayana mind training has three methods of applying antidotes: (1) conjuring what is not there, (2) vanquishing through direct encounter, and (3) mocking [the afflictions].

The first method is like a Mongol taming a tiger:[369] First he rehearses by learning the skills of taming a tiger so that when he actually meets a tiger, he can subdue it. If he has not trained previously, he will be unable to tame it and may instead become its prey. Similarly, you should vividly conjure within yourself the powerful afflictions, such as attachment, and then imagine driving them away. By not neglecting your thoughts but training them, the antidotes will appear [spontaneously] whenever afflictions arise, and because of this you will not be overwhelmed by [adverse] conditions. [In other words] you will not fall under the power of the afflictions [at that time]. If you fail to train in this manner, the antidotes will not eliminate the [adverse] conditions, and you will fall under the power of afflictions, the master said.

[The second method,] vanquishing [the afflictions] through direct encounter, is this: Avoid acting like an elderly couple who are being robbed. Furthermore, when afflictions arise, they do not start out forcefully. They arise subtly at the beginning, so the moment they arise, you need to avert them by challenging them, thinking, "Who are you?" If you do this, you will not fall under their power; you will be able to overcome them through antidotes. If they are not averted at that point, their strength will increase, and it will then be difficult to overcome them with antidotes. As if striking pig heads with a stick, you should drive afflictions away the moment they arise.

[The third method, that of] mocking [the afflictions,] means to ridicule falling under the afflictions' power, thinking, "Alas! What kind of weakling are you? What point is there in such behavior?" In this way, you should mock yourself. Furthermore, when afflictions arise, think, "Because you behaved in this manner you are wandering in cyclic existence. Are you going to continue to behave like this?" Counter them and drive them away in this manner, the master said. [152]

So for the preliminary, one conjures what is not there; for the actual practice, one vanquishes [the afflictions] through direct encounter; and for conclusion, one mocks [the afflictions], the master said.

The essential points of mind training are, the master said, (1) to heap together, (2) to generate, and (3) to purify. "To heap together" means, for example, contemplating during an illness, "There are unimaginable illnesses in the universe; may all of these befall me at this very moment, and may their continuum come to an end." [In other words,] you heap upon yourself the sufferings of all sentient beings.

"To generate" refers to visualizing a hollow [light] where you are and imagining that this increases in size, eventually swallowing everything into emptiness. You should then place your mind naturally poised in this state, the master said.

"To purify" refers to visualizing a white *Āḥ*, which progressively diminishes and disappears, becoming devoid of intrinsic existence. You should then place your mind naturally poised in this state, the master said.

3. The purpose

There are four immediate purposes of Mahayana mind training, it has been taught: (1) It is the great counterpoint to happiness, (2) it is the great closure to your misery,[370] (3) it is the friend that commiserates if you live alone, and (4) it is the nurse when you are sick.

[It is the great counterpoint to happiness.] Without a teaching such as this [mind training], then generally, when things are going well, you do not practice, but when your fortune declines, you develop an interest in practice. Recognize that since cyclic existence is in the nature of suffering, the perception that it is joyful is a delusion. When such thought [that it is joyful] occurs, enquire, "Where does it arise from?" If it abides, ask, "Where does it abide?" If it ceases, analyze, "Where does it go when it ceases?" "What color and form does it have?" If you view [cyclic existence] in this manner, you will come to understand that it is devoid of intrinsic existence. This is the counterpoint to happiness.

[It is the great closure to your misery.] If you lack this type of spiritual practice, then when tragedy strikes, you tend to aggravate it further with such thoughts as "Why is this happening to me?" Whereas when you possess this mind training, usually [you recognize] self-grasping as the root cause of your suffering. The grasping at body as "mine" is to blame. The coming together of the causes and conditions for suffering is to blame. Arrows cannot hit a target not put up; birds cannot land on a roof not erected. Similarly, if you do not grasp the body as "mine," you simply have no basis for suffering to arise. So your self-grasping is to blame. Without grasping as "mine" at what you cherish so much in your heart, this situation will not arise. Can suffering exist in the earth, rocks, mountains, cliffs, or in empty space? As you probe in this manner, suffering is pacified. This is the closure to your misery.

It is the companion that commiserates if you live alone. Without a spiritual practice such as this, you cannot live alone [peacefully]. When indoors, you will feel like going out; when outside, you will feel like coming in. However, with a practice such as this, you recognize that, in general, self-grasping is the root cause of the suffering of all beings. [So think,] "Since grasping onto something as having intrinsic existence when in fact there is none makes me suffer, I shall let go of it as best as I can. I shall let go of it so that it is wiped clean."[371]

It is not true that the array of beings in cyclic existence are unconnected.

Since all are your kind and dear parents, you should take their suffering into your heart and dedicate your happiness and virtues to them. As you practice by exchanging these two and [even] once experience its taste, days and nights will seem very short. So if you live alone, this [mind training] becomes a commiserating friend.

It is the nurse when you become ill. If you lack this mind training, then when you become ill, no nurse will seem satisfactory. You will be plagued by such thoughts as "She could have done more for me, for she owes me a lot," and will thus remain consumed by thoughts about what others should have done for you. If [on the other hand] you possess this mind training, when you become ill, you will think like this: "No one is to blame for my illness; my own self-grasping is to blame. For without grasping onto self, sickness has no basis to arise. If I benefit from nursing, [then I can recall how] I have had nurses countless times in the past. There is no medicine I have not taken, no healing ritual that I have not had performed. As for treatment, there is no treatment I have not undergone. Whether I shall be free from cyclic existence or not, today I will vanquish this [self-grasping]. Help me destroy it. I will derive great satisfaction [from destroying it]. I will vanquish this self-grasping and let it go."

Without annihilating this [self-grasping] there is no attainment of buddhahood, the master said.

As you meditate with the thought "It is my grasping at body as 'mine' that is to blame," your feeling of conceit with respect to other beings will subside. This is how it [i.e., mind training] acts as your nurse, the master said.

It has been taught that Mahayana mind training leads to the following way of being of one's body, speech, and mind: [154]

> When suffering occurs, I will take on that of all beings;
> When virtue arises, I will dedicate it to all.
> Body and speech are like an illusion and an echo,
> While clear-light mind is devoid of going and coming.[372]

The first [taking the sufferings of all beings] is twofold: taking them from what is nearest and taking them from what is greatest. Of these, the first is to contemplate with the thought "May all the sufferings of my parents, friends, and relatives ripen upon me at this very instant. May the continuum of all these sufferings come to an end." The second is to contemplate with the thought "May all the sufferings of the hell realms ripen upon me. May the continuum of all these sufferings come to an end." Then extend this to all beings and take [their sufferings]—from the hungry ghosts, from the animals, from the demigods, from the celestial gods, and from human beings.

To dedicate your virtues when they arise to the assembly, whatever virtues arise, engage in meditation with the thought "May my root of virtue come to fruition upon my two parents and upon all the sentient beings of the six classes. May all beings enjoy happiness and be free from suffering."

Regarding viewing your body and speech as illusions and echoes, the body is said to be like an illusion. Through the power of mantra and [magical] substances, the magician casts a spell on the eyes of the spectators, thus making them perceive various illusory creations, though he [himself] does not apprehend them as real. Even at the moment perceptions appear, things do not exist as such. Taking this mere appearance that transcends the extremes of both permanence and annihilation as a metaphor for the body, meditate on the absence of intrinsic existence in the face of appearances.

[Likewise,] speech is like an echo. For example, if you shout in a gorge with high cliffs, "O lady echo," you will receive exactly the same response. However, you cannot say that this exists [as speech], for it is an echo. Yet you cannot say that it does not exist either, for it is obviously there. With this illustration of mere appearance, meditate on how [speech] is indistinguishable from an echo and, in this manner, meditate on the absence of intrinsic existence.

"The clear-light mind is devoid of going and coming" indicates that for this mind of clear light, you cannot say that it has gone somewhere, nor can you say that it abides somewhere. Devoid of origination, cessation, and abiding, and not existing with any identity, it is like space.

So the body is like an illusion, speech is like an echo, and the mind is devoid of intrinsic existence. Place your mind naturally poised in this state of absence of intrinsic existence, the master said.

May this instruction stemming from the glorious Dīpaṃkara remain ever excellent!

25. Atiśa's Seven-Point Mind Training[373]

[155] *Namo Guru!*
[Homage to the teachers!]
The supreme path of all the buddhas of the three times,
The union of loving-kindness, compassion, and emptiness,
Which equalizes self and others and exchanges happiness for suffering—
To the great compassionate awakening mind, I pay homage.

Emptiness, the equanimity of self and others,
And the awakening mind, which equalizes foes and friends—
He who generates these [two] attains enlightenment.
With no omissions and additions I shall write about these in accordance
    with my teacher's words.

Here I shall present the following:

1. An account of the lineage of the teachers that is credible and drawn
   from reliable sources
2. Guru yoga meditation for receiving blessings
3. Cultivating loving-kindness toward sentient beings
4. Cultivating compassion with three yogic exercises[374]
5. Introduction to the two minds—aspiration and engagement
6. Taking the obstacles onto the path
7. Single-pointed meditation on objects of special focus

1. An account of the lineage of the teachers that is credible and drawn from reliable sources

Although master Atiśa had many teachers, the following is the transmission lineage of this [instruction]: Vajradhara, Tilopa, Nāropa, Ḍombīpa, master Atiśa, Dzeng Wangchuk Gyaltsen,[375] Potowa, Gya Chakriwa, Lha Chakriwa, Lhari Tsagyepa, Dakpo Lhajé, Phakmo Drupa, Gya Gomriwa

Shikpo, Gyakhar Ri, Rinchen Drakmarwa, Shang Drakarwa, Lama Kön-chok Jangchup Pal, Shönu Drak, Lopön Shang, he transmitted it to Sherap Sönam, he to Tsöndü, he to Lopön Chöchok, he to Lopön Tsültrim Pal, he to Buddharatna, he to Kīrtiśīla, he to Chöjé Gyalwa Sangpo, he to Chöjé Sönam Rinchen, he to Shönu Gyalchok, and he to me.[376] [156]

2. Guru yoga meditation for receiving blessings

While generating the thought "I will cultivate the awakening mind for the benefit of all beings," visualize your teacher seated on a lotus cushion. From his heart, light radiates toward all those from whom you have received teachings. They are [then] drawn forth and absorbed into the teacher's heart. Likewise draw forth all lineage teachers, the assembly of meditation deities, the buddhas and bodhisattvas, all of whom dissolve into the teacher. Then offer your body, material resources, and the virtues of all three times to your teacher and cultivate fervent admiration and reverence for him. Then make the following ardent supplication: "Bless me so that loving-kindness, compassion, and the extraordinary attitude of the awakening mind arise in me."

This completes the section on guru yoga meditation.

3. Cultivating loving-kindness toward sentient beings

First, visualize your real-life mother[377] in front of you and reflect, "Her kindness toward me has been extremely great. [For instance] by offering her own body to conceive me she has placed me among the ranks of the humans. While I was in her womb for nine months, approaching ten, she nurtured me with loving and kind thoughts. With the wish 'May my child be unexcelled by anyone' she had all kinds of activities undertaken for my sake—divinations performed, charms made, clay imprints of sacred images constructed, water offerings made, and sacred scriptures read. In her con-duct, too, she gave up all that might harm her child. Even when I was a new-born, merely the size of a hand, a bundle of hair and wrinkles, so fragile that if left unattended for a single moment—the duration of a fingersnap—it could have proved fatal, she protected [me,] her child, from death. She drew me close to her warm flesh, cleaned my waste with her hands, broke my food by chewing it, and wiped my runny nose with her tongue.

"She took great joy in me, and so her child grew bigger. I became able to eat on my own [157] and to call my parents by their names, and I slowly learned to walk. She protected me, her child, more than she did her own body. She nurtured me, her child, with no regard for pleasure, pain, or fame. She called me her child with endearing names; she looked at me, her child, with loving eyes. As I, her child, grew older, she gave me, without any sense of possessiveness, all that she had hoarded through small accumulations, which often required struggle and produced hostility toward others. For her child's sake, she endured both good and bad circumstances, including negative reputation. Had she the power to make me, her child, a universal monarch, she would have considered even such highest excellence of the mundane realm inadequate. She would have considered such supermundane accomplishments inadequate even if her child were led to the bliss of full enlightenment. In this way, she nurtured me, her child, with kindness, watched me with loving eyes, and called me by endearing names. [In brief] she nurtured me as if I were a piece of her own heart existing outside. She gave me, her child, her food, clothes, and possessions, which she could have used for herself. In this way she held me dearer than her own self. She worried when I was away even for a day. This kind mother, who has helped me in so many ways and fought harms in so many ways [on my behalf], has been indeed a great embodiment of kindness."

Reflect in this manner until tears flow from your eyes and the hair stands up from the pores of your body.

[Again] reflect, "How can I benefit my kind mother? How can I make her achieve happiness?" Extend this same thought to your fellow practitioners, your family, and then extend it further to your neighbors and to all the sentient beings you have ever seen. Then extend the contemplation to the beings of all six realms wherever space pervades. If the force of your loving-kindness is weak, engage in this contemplation individually toward the beings of each of the six classes until loving-kindness toward them arises. It has been stated in the *Great Nirvana Sutra:*

Even if you were to count beads the size of *kolāsita* nuts,
The earth will fail to measure the extent of your mothers.[378]

Since this is not a case of contemplating someone who is not a mother as a mother, you should practice this until this [recognition of mother] arises as forcefully toward all sentient beings as it does toward your own real-life mother. [158]

4. Cultivating compassion with three yogic exercises

Meditate on compassion through all three [doors]—your body, speech, and mind—and perform their yogic exercises. The yogic exercise of mind refers to cultivating [compassion] until it arises for beings of each of the six classes. [Beginning with the first class,] the eight hot hell realms are as follows: the Reviving, the Black-Lined, the Crushing, the Howling, the Great Howling, the Hot, the Extremely Hot, and the Unrelenting. In the first is the heat of weapons, while in the rest are sufferings such as being burnt inside a metal house in a blazing furnace enclosed by three perimeter walls [one inside the other].

The eight cold hell realms are as follows: the Blistering, the Popping Blisters, the Screaming of "I am Cold!," the Chattering-Teeth, the Moaning, the Splitting Like a Water Lily, the Splitting Like a Lotus, and the Splitting Like a Large Lotus. Thus there are immeasurable sufferings in the cold hells. As for lifespan and body size, contemplate these as explained in the Abhidharma works and the sutra entitled the *Foundations of Mindfulness*.[379] Generate as great a compassion toward the hell beings as you would toward your real-life mother and feel "How tragic that my mothers undergo such unbearable suffering! Tragic indeed is that my mothers undergo such suffering due to their [past] accumulation of negative karma. How I wish that they could gain freedom from their suffering." Reflect in this way until tears flow freely.

The yogic exercise of body is this: Place your two palms to your cheeks and your elbows on your thighs. Then, in a squatting position, hold your head down and contort your face into a somber expression. Then shout, "My mother, my mother!" This is the yogic exercise of speech.

Likewise, there are hungry ghosts whose external obscurants prevent their even seeing food and water with their eyes for many years. Even when they do, they see it only as pus and blood, or as a heap of burning wheat husks, which makes it impossible for them to eat. Those with internal obscurations have stomachs the size of a vast plain, mouths as small as a needle's eye, and throats and limbs the width of straw. Food can hardly enter their mouths, and even when it does, it cannot pass through their throat. When their stomachs are full, their limbs can no longer support them. In this way, they suffer immeasurably. [159] Food and water themselves can be the obscurations. As a result of eating and drinking, [for instance, hungry ghosts] are consumed by a heap of burning wheat husks and burning metal balls, which reduce them to ash. Ponder these sufferings, as before, and thereby cultivate compassion.

Animals that live in the water are said to experience inconceivable types of suffering. Those we can see suffer, for example, by having their body penetrated by hands even before death. Birds and wild animals devour each other alive; in autumn, sheep and cattle are slaughtered; and Mongols and so on also hunt animals. Some animals have to carry loads beyond their strength; not wishing to dig, they are forced to pull plows. In addition are the immeasurable sufferings that come from being ignorant and confused. Focusing on these realities, cultivate compassion as before.

Humans have the sufferings of birth, aging, sickness, and death. They have the pains of not finding what they do not have, being unable to protect what they have, being separated from loved ones, and encountering those who are hostile. Then there is the immeasurable pain of the death of one's children, husband, wife, friends, and leader, all of whom are indispensable for coping with harsh words and hostility [of others] that rob one of happiness.[380] Furthermore, while alive, humans engage only in negative acts and hardly allow the flow of good thoughts, even for a moment. So when they die, they go nowhere but the lower realms. Think, "Tragic indeed are these humans," and as before, cultivate compassion for them.

Reflect that the demigods [too] have immeasurable sufferings, such as of war, conflict, killing, and death. As for the gods, they too experience immeasurable pain [observing] the signs of approaching death: They suffer from being shunned by their friends; and some gods suffer from having nothing but a single lute as their wealth. Focused on these beings, cultivate compassion as before. As for their lifespans and body sizes and so on, you should study the explanations in the Abhidharma texts.

In brief, contemplate all these beings as having been your kind mothers and feel compassion for these dear mothers undergoing such sufferings. Reflect, "These mothers, my mothers, have their eyes of intelligence blinded, their legs of skillful means broken; they are bereft of a spiritual teacher, a guide for the blind, and they also lack good companions and friends who could connect them with the Dharma. [160] May they be free of suffering." Contemplate in this manner until tears flow freely.

5. Introduction to the two minds—aspiration and engagement[381]

First, aspiration is as follows. Whatever sickness or discomfort befalls your body, at that time, make the aspiration, "May the sufferings of all sentient beings ripen upon my illness. As the sufferings of all sentient beings ripen upon me, may those beings never even hear the name of suffering." Then, whatever happiness, well-being, flourishing of virtuous activities, ability to direct your mind toward positive actions, and favorable conditions for spiritual practice that you may possess in relation to your body, speech, and mind, think that they are equal to the bliss and virtues of the Buddha. Reflecting thus, think, "May these qualities of mine be realized upon others. May happiness and virtue flourish for all sentient beings."

Second, engagement is as follows. Sentient beings are suffering great harm and also its seeds. So, as if slicing it off with a sharp razor, mentally collect in one gesture all their physical sickness, mental pains, afflictions, negative actions, and obscurations. Inhaling through the left nostril, imagine that these enter into you and are absorbed into the center of your heart. Whatever illness and sufferings appear, ideally, [if you can, imagine that] they too enter into your heart as before. Contemplate in this manner with respect to all, without any exceptions.

Whatever benefit sentient beings enjoy come in the immediate term due to the favorable conditions of spiritual practice and, in the ultimate term, due to the bliss of the buddhas. So, whatever happiness and virtues you may possess in relation to your body, speech, and mind, imagine them [as becoming], for the immediate term, the favorable conditions and, for the ultimate term, the inconceivable bliss of the buddhas. Imagine that all of this, without exception, exits [from you] when you exhale [161] from the right nostril and that this is realized upon sentient beings. Imagine that sentient beings enjoy temporary and ultimate well-being as well as [the flourishing of] virtues. [The realization of] emptiness and compassion now engendered within them, imagine that all their negative intentions and hostilities become pacified, the master said.

6. Taking the obstacles onto the path [382]

In brief, you should recognize all the conditions that are adverse to Dharma practice—illness, suffering, incidents that are contrary to your liking such as being unjustly accused or derided, being the object of spells, being paralyzed by your enemies, being hindered by harmful agents, failing to gather appropriate conditions, the arising of forceful afflictions within your mind, being unable to direct your mind to spiritual matters, the diminishing of your admiration and reverence toward the teacher and the Three Jewels, lacking enthusiasm for meditative practice and spiritual activities, having your quest for mind's nature being robbed by falcons because of excessive thinking, the arising of dislike, conceit, and self-importance, and the degeneration and infraction of the commitments—you should recognize all these as māras, for they are obstacles [caused by] māras. Thinking, "At such times I must reinvigorate my awareness,"383 cultivate fervent loving-kindness, compassion, and the awakening mind for sentient beings equal to the expanse of space until tears flow from your eyes. Cultivate these thoughts particularly toward your enemies, the obstructive forces who harm you.

Then, with renewed force, take upon the [obstacles] that you experience the obstacles and adverse conditions of all sentient beings—from bodhisattvas on the levels to sentient beings in the Avīci hells—and conclude decisively that the objects from whom you have done the taking and all the sufferings and factors that are taken, all are reflections of your own deluded mind. Then place the mind naturally with ease in this absence of origination, cessation, and abiding.

As you repeat this process and engage repeatedly in meditation, the obstacles caused by māras and all sufferings [162] become catalysts for enhancing your virtuous activities. You recognize all obstacles as blessings from your teachers and the Three Jewels, and the awareness of true ascertainment arises from your depths, the master said. When this occurs, you embrace ill omens as charms, understand māras as nature's expanse, and adversities arise as complementary factors. In this manner, the master said, all your perceptions become aspects of the path. When such things do occur, do not become inflated; for if you do, this [too] is a māra. Recognize your own virtues and the virtues of your body and mind in the manner [described] earlier. Thus decisively conclude that all appearances are your own mind, and throughout all times be sustained by mindfulness.

7. Single-pointed meditation on objects of special focus

For this, visualize the malevolent forces or enemies that cause you harm. Whether a malevolent spirit who has been hostile in the past or a force perpetrating harm in the present, examine the appearances it displays, such as in dreams, and the hallucinations it conjures, and recognize them for what they are. Then summon this enemy or malevolent force into your presence and visualize it with clear awareness. Then visualize all classes of malevolent spirits that are harmful and hostile toward sentient beings, visualize all beings of the six classes as well, and generate the altruistic mind by reflecting, "All sentient beings, especially these agents of harm, are my kind mothers. I will endeavor to make them achieve happiness and become free from suffering, and for their benefit I will attain buddhahood. For the sake of them I will cultivate the awakening mind."

You should then reflect, "She [the harmful being] is my kind mother; she has been my parent many times in my previous lives, and thus I am indebted to her. Having accumulated negative karma in her past lives, alas, my kind mother today assumes this current bodily existence. Based on this bodily existence, she has grasped onto an 'I' when there is none; she has grasped onto a self when there is none. [163] As such, today, she has done only harmful things to other sentient beings, so there is no escape for her from the great sufferings of cyclic existence, the lower realms [in particular]. How sad indeed!" Think of her as your own real-life mother and, in speech, call to her, "My mother!" cultivating a powerful compassion until tears flow freely from your eyes and the hairs stand up from your pores.

In one sweeping gesture, collect upon the mental ailments you possess the physical ailments and suffering of all beings, especially this agent of harm, and imagine that they merge with your own so that nothing is left for him. As you give him all your happiness and virtues of body, speech, and mind, imagine that all his negative intentions and hostile thoughts are pacified and that he generates the awakening mind in his heart. Perform this [meditation] many times.

Again, contemplate that all illnesses and malevolent possessions are a basis for kindness. Reflect, "Since they propel virtuous activities, they are indeed greatly kind; I will make sure I am never divorced from them, from now until the attainment of buddhahood." Furthermore, when unjust sufferings befall your body and mind, do not become disheartened. Think, "During such times I must reinvigorate my awareness" and reflect upon the sufferings and the immediate causes of suffering of all sentient beings, especially the agents of harm. Then reflect, "How sad that these beings who, like my mother, are sources of great kindness are undergoing such suffering. If I have no power to free them from suffering in this moment, how can I help them gain freedom from suffering?"

In this way, you engage in the yogic exercise of mind, contemplating the suffering of all sentient beings. The yogic exercise of the body is as follows: Your body in a seated position, with your right palm touch your cheeks while your elbow rests on your [right] thigh and then contort the muscles between your eyebrows as if shedding tears. As in the yogic exercise of speech, you repeat, "My mother!" like an incantation a hundred times, a thousand times, and so on.

Thus, due to cultivating loving-kindness, compassion arises uncontrollably. You may feel like crying [164] and experience such things as heartache, and whenever you see, hear about, and think about suffering beings, compassion may arise within you naturally. When this happens, imagine that all the sufferings of sentient beings are sliced away as if by a sharp razor and that, as you inhale, the [sufferings] enter through your left nostril and are absorbed into your heart. Imagine that not a single instance of suffering remains behind for sentient beings. Repeat this process again and again when any class of afflictions arises in you. Place your mind in the perfect meaning, the view that is devoid of "is" and "is not."

As you unconditionally give to sentient beings all your happiness and virtues, imagine that the harmful intentions and hostilities of all beings become pacified. As a result, all illnesses and malevolent possessions arise as complementary factors. [This practice] thus has inconceivable benefits. There are many explanations on how, in the near term, all illnesses and malevolent possessions become naturally liberated. I won't write them here, however. Whatever activities you engage in, if they are sustained by this [mind training practice], they become aspects of the path to buddhahood, the master said. If they are divorced from this, the master said, then even if you engage in mantra repetitions of profound secret tantra, these will be no different from reciting the wrathful mantras of non-Buddhist Indian traditions. You should also consult the sutras and the treatises of the Great Vehicle.

26. Mind Training in a Single Session[384]
Chim Namkha Drak (1210–85)

[165]
Homage to the teachers, the perfect spiritual friends!

There are three points to this instruction: [(1) the preparatory practice, (2) the main practice, and (3) the concluding practice].

1. The preparatory practice

The first, the preparatory practice, is as follows. In a solitary place, a site free of conditions nonconducive to observing pure ethical conduct, sit on a comfortable cushion and then go for refuge and generate the awakening mind. Then contemplate your body as devoid of substantial reality, like a balloon filled with air. Imagine your heart as a mass of white light, and at your crown visualize your root teacher seated on a cushion of a moon upon a lotus, and contemplate him to be the sole embodiment of all the lineage masters from the Buddha to the present, of the teachers from whom you have actually received teachings, of the meditation deities, and of all the buddhas and bodhisattvas. Prostrate to them mentally and make offerings to them.

The supplication is this:

> O my gurus, you who are perfect spiritual friends, please attend
> to me.
> Bless me, O my gurus, you who are perfect spiritual friends, so that
> unblemished realizations of Mahayana mind training may arise
> within me.
> Bless me so that I may subdue the grasping at "I" and "self" this very
> instant and that I may understand all adversities and obstacles as
> aids to Dharma practice.

Make this supplication three times.

While imagining "My mind is an actual buddha who has eliminated all defects, including their propensities, and who is endowed with every higher quality," take refuge in the body, speech, and mind of your teacher. Then imagine that your teacher descends through your crown aperture and enters your heart, which is a heap of light, and contemplate that this is an actual buddha. As your teacher's body, speech, and mind dissolve into you, they become the ultimate expanse, which is the great clear light. Leave your mind in this state for as long as it abides. When thoughts arise, visualize your teacher at your crown, make dedications toward the fulfillment of his enlightened aspirations, [166] and supplicate him. Engage in this [meditation] approximately six times during day and night, and so on. Then whatever meditative absorptions you aspire to will arise in your mental continuum.

First, train in the preliminaries.

This is threefold: (1) As for the rarity of attaining a human existence of leisure and opportunity, contemplate the qualities of leisure and opportunity and take their essence. Since mind training is the supreme Dharma practice, you should engage in this. (2) Even if you obtain a human existence of leisure and opportunity, you cannot remain permanently, and when the force of your karma is exhausted, there is no telling when you might die. At the time of death, there is no worse defeat than dying with remorse, bereft of any Dharma realization. Therefore train your mind. (3) After death you do not stop becoming; you must take rebirth. Wherever you may be reborn in cyclic existence will be subject to suffering. You should therefore relinquish cyclic existence, and to this end that you should practice mind training. Purify your mental continuum of negative karma and the obstructions you have accumulated, and toward others cultivate loving-kindness, compassion, and the awakening mind.

2. *The main practice*

The main practice has two parts, of which the first, the conventional awakening mind, is as follows.

Train alternately in the two—giving and taking.[385]
Commence the sequence of taking from yourself.

This states that you should imagine that all the sufferings and their origins that are likely to befall you in your future lives, including even those that might materialize tomorrow, bear fruit at this very instant. Reflecting in this way has the advantage of transforming adverse conditions into complementary factors. You should then cultivate loving-kindness and compassion toward your real-life mother and, from the depth of your heart, take all her sufferings and their origins upon yourself. Similarly, take the subtle obscuration to knowledge from all sentient beings and the three noble beings.[386] In brief, you should take upon your heart all the deficiencies of samsara and nirvana from all beings except your teachers and the buddhas. Taking these repeatedly, when your shoulders ache, you imagine your body to be a balloon filling with air that expands to pervade the entire expanse of space. You then place your mind in the absence of intrinsic existence.

As you meditate on emptiness, reflect, "How sad that all these mothers of mine are caught within the immediate conditions of suffering and cyclic existence. I shall free them from these immediate conditions of suffering and place them in unexcelled bliss and happiness, and to this end I will give away everything—my body, material resources, and my roots of virtue." Thinking in this manner, transform your body into a precious wish-fulfilling jewel and confer, to all your dear mothers, material resources equal to the wealth of all gods and humans [167] filling all of space, as well as your virtues accumulated throughout the three times. As you give these, imagine that [your dear mothers] enjoy the perfect gathering of all favorable conditions for Dharma practice and that they accomplish the two accumulations and attain perfect buddhahood. Make this contemplation in regard to all sentient beings.

Place the two astride your breath.

This indicates that when you exhale, you give all your wealth and virtues to sentient beings, and as you practice in this manner and experience the dawning of meditative absorptions, you then take on the sufferings and their origins of both yourself and others. When you engage in this way, it is said, you derive the benefit of attaining the realization of mind training as these [meditative absorptions] arise within you.

Second, the meditation on the ultimate awakening mind is as follows:

Having become trained, engage in the secret point.[387]

This suggests that when you are able to exchange your virtues with others' sufferings, you then meditate on emptiness, which is kept secret from the weak-minded. This is as follows:

All phenomena are [in general] subsumed into the two classes of object and subject. As you [then] examine individually all the objects that appear as material realities, they are [reduced to] subtle particles. Invariably, these turn out to be midpoints interfacing the six directions,[388] which means they are not established as substantially real singular entities. [And] since they do not exist as substantially real multiple entities [either], meditate on the nonsubstantiality of materially constituted realities.

As for inner awareness, the past is no more, the future is yet to be, and the present is devoid of color, shape, and spatial location. If it does not exist in such a manner, then it does not exist as a substantial reality. Therefore, contemplate inner awareness [too] as devoid of substantially real existence.

Since the external world of material realities does not exist, then the object of meditation does not exist; and since what appears as inner awareness [too] does not exist, then the meditating mind [too] does not exist. This freedom from the object of meditation and the meditating mind is called "exhausting knowable objects," and to abide unwavering in this state is "to meditate on suchness." As such, just as the objective world does not exist in any mode, the mind [too] does not grasp it in any way. So place your mind naturally with ease in the state of nonconceptuality. It has been taught:

> A mind entangled in knots,
> **If undone, no doubt it will be free.**[389]

When all acts of dissipation and withdrawal of conceptualization cease, this is "tranquil abiding"; and when the mind remains clear and lucid while free of conceptualization, with no grasping at any signs, this is referred to as "penetrative insight."

Initially, you should meditate in many short sessions, and when you have gained stability, you can remain there as long as your mind stays focused. [168] When you wish to rise, cultivate compassion toward all sentient beings and then dedicate the merit. During the actual meditation, you should alternate the practice of the conventional and ultimate awakening minds. As your familiarity grows, even if you cannot accomplish everything, you can engage in the practice of giving and taking at the level of mere illusionlike conventional reality, free of [belief in] substantial reality and clinging.

3. The concluding practice

"**Three objects, three poisons**" indicates that it is in relation to the three objects that the three poisons come into being, and you should transform these into the "**three roots of virtue.**" [For example] when you experience attachment toward attractive forms, which are objects of your eyes, you should take into the core of your heart the attachments of other sentient beings. Imagine that as you give your body, wealth, and roots of virtue to all sentient beings, all beings come to possess the root virtue of nonattachment. Toward the repulsive, imagine that you are free of aversion, and contemplate in a similar manner toward those who give rise to delusion. Likewise, you should contemplate in the same manner when each of the three [poisons] arises with respect to whatever occurs, such as sound to the ear, odor to the nose, taste to the tongue, and tactile sensations to the body.

In all actions, train by means of the words.

This suggests that during all your everyday activities—standing up, sitting down, or sleeping—you should recite whatever is most appropriate, such as "May the sufferings and their origins of all beings ripen upon me this very instant. May the 'self' suffer downfall; may the 'self' and 'real entities' become no more and be lost forever. May my body, wealth, and roots of virtue ripen upon sentient beings. May sentient beings attain all higher qualities of the path and the results of these at this very instant." Your actions will then follow after your speech, and, it is said, the benefit of [these realizations] will [then] arise swiftly in your mind.

This work entitled *A Single Session of Mind Training* was composed by the abbot of Narthang, the great Chim Namkha Drak. May the excellence [contained in this] equal space!

27. Advice to Namdak Tsuknor[390]

Atiśa Dīpaṃkara (982–1054)

[169] Though the sky of knowable objects is beyond measure,
You embrace them in terms of two: emptiness and compassion—
To you, O my gurus, Dīpaṃkara Śrījñāna and others,
I pay homage with my three doors and with a heart filled with devotion.

As the savior of beings was departing to Tibet,
He bestowed on me this most precious jewel.[391]

1

This sky is devoid of cause and conditions, my son;
Who would grasp that it does [have a cause] and who it does not?[392]
Know this to be true also of all phenomena, my son,
For there are numerous pitfalls if you fail to.
Remain in equipoise on this spacelike nature, my son.

2

When rainbows spread across the sky,
They seem so real and beautiful, my son.
Yet no one has observed their causes and conditions.
This is but a dependent origination, my learned son.

3

Rainbows appear in the sky, and they disappear in it too.
No one has observed the causes and conditions for this.
This is but a dependent origination, my learned son.
If you probe well, the rainbows are like the sky itself.
Is there any separation or division, my learned son?

4

In phenomena's primordially empty mode of being
Pulsates unbearable compassion that reaches out to beings.
When compassion arises, it does so from the ultimate expanse,
And when it ceases, it does so within the ultimate expanse, my son.

5

All phenomena of samsara and nirvana are but your own mind;
None has observed the causes and conditions for these.
When probed and analyzed, they are like the rainbows in the sky.
So just like the sky and the rainbows across it
Should you understand emptiness and compassion, my son.

6

From within an ocean deep and expansive,
Rise high and mighty waves.
When waves appear, they do so in the ocean itself,
And when they subside, they do so in the ocean itself, my son.

7

Between the dancing waves and the vast ocean,
None has observed any separation or division.
Similarly from the spontaneous coemergence of emptiness
Arises compassion that touches beings and stirs the heart.
When compassion arises, it does so from emptiness,
And when it ceases, it does so in emptiness, too, my son.

8

On the surface of a mirror free of blemishes
Varieties of forms appear in stark diversity. [170]
Do they come from the mirror or from the external objects?
Do they come from elsewhere or from no cause at all?
When probed, they cannot be posited; they're mere dependent
 origination.[393]

9

Between the face that never existed and its reflection,
None has observed any separation or division.

Likewise from the emptiness that resembles a mirror
Forms appear, though they were never real before.
Just so must you relate to emptiness and compassion, my son.

10
On the surface of clear, unperturbed water,
One may experience, like seeing a duality,
The illusion of a crystal-like reflection of the moon;
No one has observed that such a duality exists.

11
From emptiness that resembles a clear sky
Arises unbearable compassion toward sentient beings.
As compassion grows, it does so from within emptiness;
And when it ceases, it does so in emptiness, my son.

12
From the body of towering rocky cliffs
Echoes reverberate in succession;
What separation exists between the echoes and the cliffs?
Though resounding, who would grasp them to exist or not to exist?[394]

13
Likewise from primordially pure emptiness
Reverberates sounds of intense compassion for beings.
Just so contemplate emptiness and compassion, my son.

14
On the surface of an unblemished, resplendent sun
Arises light that actually benefits sentient beings.
None has observed the sun to be separate from its rays.

15
Though emptiness and great compassion appear as forms,
Compassion, too, is mere emptiness.
For no savior has ever taught of compassion
That is separate from emptiness, my learned son.

16

Ah! Listen to me while in the state of emptiness.
That beings eliminate their suffering
Is due only to emptiness: be cognizant of this.
Though there exist countless remedies,
It is emptiness alone, so engage in its meditation.

17

Though what is to be relinquished and its antidotes seem distinct,
Practice both in your meditation path by purifying the three aspects.[395]
Though countless people who fail to understand this
Are attracted to you, what need is there to shun them?[396]

18

View them as emptiness and compassion; how can this be confusion?
Is not compassion itself empty, my learned son?
Does not emptiness dawn as compassion, the discriminating one?
Is there a difference between emptiness and compassion?

19

Even when anger rises in me like a windstorm,
I perceive it undifferentiated from emptiness.
Likewise I see the countless instants of conceptualization[397]
As emerging definitely from emptiness. [171]

20

When I look nakedly at these conceptual thoughts,
I do not see them established as either true or false.
When I let go of them freely from within emptiness,
I do not see even the rising of mere concepts.[398]

21

So I see no difference or contradiction,
Even the size of an atom, between emptiness and compassion.
What need is there to say of the indivisibility of the two?

22

Ah! From here on, whether you are walking or sitting,
That very spot is the wilderness,[399] my learned son.

The mind's abiding in the middle way
Is emptiness' true mode of being, my learned son.

23

Meditating on compassion while in this state
Is the yoga of indivisibility, my son.
When you practice compassion with such knowledge,
Then even when in intense compassion, it is sheer emptiness.

24

There is no emptiness meditation not permeated by compassion;
For the practice of compassion is solely [the practice of] emptiness.
As for emptiness, even those seeking tranquil abiding must practice it.
For this vehicle, however, emptiness is compassion;
And the self-nature of this compassion is emptiness.
So understand that compassion is the essential nature.

25

Though you may command many disciplines of knowledge,
I reveal to you this great root [practice] of many essential points
From my teachings as my heart's final counsel.[400]
Now I shall linger no more and begin my journey to Tibet.

26

All activities are like clay [molds] and wax imprints;
The construct called life fluctuates like the [flickering of] lightning;
The meeting of body and mind, too, resembles a guesthouse and its
    guests;
Though it is possible I may return to this part [of the country],
It is nature's law that meeting ends in separation.

27

You'll indeed be my son if you take these instructions to heart.
You'll enjoy lasting joy if you follow these words of advice.
Soon I shall depart to the presence of Maitreya;
I shall depart to the Joyful realm[401] to realize fully
The words and meaning of the Perfection of Wisdom.[402]
On your part, too, you should pray to reach his presence
To discourse with him after this present life ends.

28
O all the buddhas and their children in all ten directions!
Pray attend to us here today with great compassion.
Whatever virtuous deeds we've engaged in with our three doors
In the three times, throughout all lives in this cycle of existence,
I dedicate them toward [the attainment of] great enlightenment.[403]

29
Until we realize the buddha bodies and the enlightened activities,
Regardless of whatever forms we assume in our births,
May we apply our three doors to [the practice of] the ten perfections,
And may we please our gurus and enhance their enlightened activities.

Colophon

This was bestowed as a general Dharma teaching to Namdak Tsuknor when
Atiśa, the savior of beings, was preparing to begin his journey to Tibet. The
lineage of this [teaching] is as follows: From master Atiśa to the abbot Matön
the lineage is the same as before;[404] and [through] to Joden Lungshöpa; he to
Kīrtiśīla; he to Chöjé Gyalwa Sangpo; he to Chöjé Sönam Rinchen; and he
to Chöjé Shönu Gyalchok.[405]

28. Glorious Virvapa's Mind Training[406]
Lo Lotsāwa (twelfth–thirteenth century)

[173] *Namo Guru!*
[Homage to the teachers!]

The glorious Virvapa said:

> To those who've nurtured you with affection,
> These embodiments of kindness, contemplate them with compassion.
> "This perpetrator of harm, too, is my mother!
> Though she has shown repeated kindness to me in the past,
> Like someone who is insane, she [today] has no self-control.
> Owing to her negative karma, she is suffering in the Avīci hell."

> As you contemplate thus, you perfect
> Your compassion for all three realms of existence.

1. The yoga of unparalleled compassion

The yoga of unparalleled compassion is as follows: Compassion is the root of Mahayana teachings. If this is absent, regardless of whatever aspects of the path you might have—such as the six perfections and the generation and completion stages of your solemn pledges—you will fall into the ranks of the Lesser Vehicle. You need, therefore, to possess loving-kindness, compassion, and the awakening mind. Loving-kindness brings benefits, while compassion is cultivated by starting with the perpetrators of harm.

So, in a secluded place, adopt a balanced physical lifestyle; take refuge [in the Three Jewels], and generate the awakening mind. Imagine yourself as a meditation deity and visualize your teacher at the crown of your head. Then visualize in front of you an enemy who causes serious harm to you and to others. Then engage in the meditative practice of compassion by combining both its continuum and its rationale.[407]

First, while maintaining a vigilant posture, focus your mind single-pointedly on your enemy. Then verbally recite the following a hundred or fifty times, as if it were an incantation: "Pitiable indeed is this enemy who causes me harm." This is the meditation on the continuum.

The second [the meditation on its rationale] is as follows: (1) Reflecting, "This enemy is bound to have been my mother in the past. Ah, my poor mother!" you cultivate compassion toward her repeatedly.[408]

(2) Why should I have compassion for her? "She has been my mother not just once or twice, but many times." Reflecting thus, develop compassion toward her repeatedly.

(3) Why should I have compassion for her? "Every time she was my mother, she showed me immeasurable kindness." Reflecting thus, develop compassion repeatedly.

(4) Why should I have compassion for her? "Mothers generally do only beneficial things, so why is this enemy causing harm? Although this enemy is indeed my mother, she has not mastered her consciousness and [today] is like an insane person. How sad! Not only does she harm other sentient beings, but she harms her own child [as well]!" Reflecting thus, develop compassion for her repeatedly. [174]

(5) Why should I have compassion for her? "Due to her harmful actions, she will be reborn in the Avīci hell and will be oppressed by intense suffering. Ah, my poor mother, this perpetrator of harm!" Repeat this many times.

As you meditate in this way—combining the object, incantations, and the five rationales for developing compassion—you generate compassion in full accordance with the appearance of the following signs: Tears flow from your eyes, the hair stands up from your pores, the force of your body and mind become indefatigable, and so on. Reflecting, "I will attain buddhahood for the benefit of all beings, especially the perpetrators of harm," generate the awakening mind and imagine that all sentient beings, including the perpetrators of harm, attain the state of meditation deities. Place your mind for a long period in this wisdom free of conceptual elaboration. When conceptualization begins to occur, perform the dedication.

When you have developed [compassion] toward one in this way, then extend it to others, such as medium and lesser perpetrators of harm. Then extend it to your relatives, fellow countrymen, [the people of] Tibet, of the earth, the four continents, and the [entire] trichiliocosm, pervading the expanse of space. Your compassion will [then] becomes immeasurable. Because of this, your hatred and anger will naturally diminish; and such enemies as leprosy and malevolent possessions will subside naturally of their own accord. Your mind will transform into affection for all beings, like a mother's love for her only child. The extraordinary wisdom that is free of conceptual elaboration will arise [as well].

2. *The yoga of root cause*

[Virvapa] said:

> Assailed by inner and outer elaborations,
> When your awareness is in turmoil,
> Recall this awakening mind
> That exchanges self and others.
> This will destroy the army of afflictions and māras,
> And transform them into wisdom free of elaboration.

As stated here, the awakening mind is the cause for attaining the state of omniscience. This is twofold—the conventional and ultimate awakening minds—of which the ultimate is the wisdom free of conceptual elaboration. Although the first [i.e., conventional awakening mind] has various forms, here we [focus on] the practice, as taught by our teacher, of exchanging self and others [which is] as follows:

When you are plagued by grave physical illness or a sorrowful heart, both of which are suffering, when [you are assailed by] enemies, harmful possessions, or an imbalance of natural elements, or when forceful afflictions arise [in you], take all these as ingredients of your path. For instance, when strong aversion arises, you should contemplate, "Through the arising of this aversion [175] may all the instances of aversion and its causes that exist in the hearts of hostile beings ripen upon me."

You should also aspire "May all the sufferings—which are the fruits of afflictions and are rooted in self-grasping—that exist in the minds of sentient beings manifest upon me. In particular, may the specific sufferings—such as the experience of being burned, inflamed, and so on of the hell beings; the hunger and thirst of the hungry ghosts; the killing and servitude of the animals; the quarrels and conflicts of the demigods; the sufferings of birth, aging, sickness, and death [of human beings], plus the illnesses of the sick, the poverty and deprivation of the poor, and the suffering of having defective organs—ripen upon my own suffering. May all the obstacles and conditions that obstruct my attainments—from the attainment of the human existence of leisure and opportunity to the realization of the grounds and paths—mature upon this aversion of mine."

In this way, concentrate your entire body, speech, and mind, and single-pointedly collect the sufferings of all sentient beings upon yourself. Meditate in this way for one, two, or three hours and so on while maintaining single-pointed focus. Meditate until the conceptual processes, such as the afflictions, are pacified. Turn these into [elements of] your path until the suffering of illness comes to cease. Recite aloud, "May the sufferings of all beings fall upon me."⁴⁰⁹

Then visualize that all your virtues—both their causes and their fruits—such as your two accumulations, emanate from your heart like the rays of a rising sun. Imagine that they touch the sentient beings, who are then led to the state of meditation deities, the nature of Buddha's body and wisdom. As you then place your mind in the wisdom free of conceptual elaboration, an extraordinary wisdom dawns [within]. When the continuum of conceptualization resurfaces, perform the dedication.

Those on the beginner's level should practice in this manner. Once you gain greater familiarity, then whatever thoughts arise—gross or subtle conceptual processes, fear, suffering, and so on—assimilate them as before and focus on them single-pointedly. Recite aloud, "Through my virtues, may all beings attain happiness."⁴¹⁰

You imagine that your body, material resources, and positive karma ripen upon sentient beings and that they thus attain uncontaminated bliss. The difference here lies in the pace of the visualization. With respect to purpose, there is no difference [between the meditations of beginners and those with greater familiarity]. As for the concluding practice, it is the same as the previous one [that is, to perform the dedication when conceptualization recurs].

The immediate [benefits] of the conventional awakening mind are that thought processes such as the afflictions subside, you gain release from sickness and harmful possessions, [176] you become beneficial to all beings, and you bring them under your sphere of influence. In the end term, you attain the states of Buddha's enjoyment body and emanation body and thus bring about the perfect welfare of others. Through the ultimate awakening mind you achieve the seed of dharmakāya and thus attain the great seal, which is the supreme attainment.

When such auspicious conditions are gathered, all kinds of signs associated with your body, speech, and mind emerge. In particular the mental states free of subject-and-object dualism—tranquil abiding and penetrative insight—arise in your mental continuum. You then abide in what is known as *the singular instance of reflexive awareness,* which is an instance [of cognition] that embodies the five wisdoms: The empty, nonconceptual mind is dharma body *(dharmakāya);* the self-cognition is the enjoyment body *(sambhogakāya);* while its luminosity is the emanation body *(nirmāṇakāya).* The indivisibility of these three is the self-nature body *(svabhāvakāya).* Since the mind itself is free from all conceptual elaborations, it is (1) the wisdom of the ultimate expanse; its cognition of itself as empty is (2) the mirrorlike [wisdom]; its self-cognition is (3) the discriminative awareness; its illumination of itself is (4) the wisdom accomplishing all deeds; and their indivisibility is (5) the wisdom of equanimity.

Colophon

The lineage of the transmission of this guide by Lo Lotsāwa on the instruction of unparalleled compassion—the intention of the glorious Virvapa and the teaching of Darpaṇa Ācārya—is as follows: Vajradhara, Virvapa, Jetsün Ḍombipa, Jetsün Matipa [Maitrīpa?], the siddha Ṇikalava, Jetsün Ravaintapa [Ravindra?], Chak Lotsāwa Chöjé Pal, Lama Dampa Shönu Gyaltsen, the vajra holder Matiśrī, Lama Yeshé Shap, Sangpoi Pal. He [passed the lineage on] to Buddharatna, he to Kīrtiśīla, he to Jayabhadra, he to Puṇyaratna, he to Shönu Gyalchok, and he to me.

Through whatever pure virtue may stem from this,
May all sentient beings residing in the cycle of existence
Attain the pure thought of emptiness and compassion,
And be led swiftly to the state of untainted bliss.

29. Eight Verses on Mind Training
Langri Thangpa (1054–1123)

1

With the wish to achieve the highest aim,
Which surpasses even a wish-fulfilling gem,
I will train myself to at all times
Cherish every sentient being as supreme.[411]

2

Whenever I interact with others,
I will view myself as inferior to all;
And I will train myself
To hold others superior from the depths of my heart.

3

During all my activities I will probe my mind,
And as soon as an affliction arises—
Since it endangers myself and others—
I will train myself to confront it directly and avert it.

4

When I encounter beings of unpleasant character
And those oppressed by intense negative karma and suffering,
As though finding a treasure of precious jewels,
I will train myself to cherish them, for they are so rarely found.

5

When others out of jealousy
Treat me wrongly with abuse and slander,
I will train to take the defeat upon myself
And offer the victory to others.

6

Even if one whom I have helped,
Or in whom I have placed great hope,
Gravely mistreats me in hurtful ways,
I will train myself to view him as my sublime teacher.

7

In brief, I will train myself to offer benefit and joy
To all my mothers, both directly and indirectly,
And respectfully take upon myself
All the hurts and pains of my mothers.

8

By ensuring that all this remains undefiled
From the stains of the eight mundane concerns,
And by understanding all things as illusions,
I will train myself to be free of the bondage of clinging.

30. A Commentary on "Eight Verses on Mind Training"[412]
Chekawa (1101–75)

[177] Herein is contained the *Eight Verses on Mind Training* together with the story of its origin.[413]

I pay homage to the sublime teachers!

Geshe Chekawa once remarked, "My admiration for the Kadampas first arose when I heard the eight verses from Chakshingwa.[414] Thereafter I studied the verses and meticulously memorized the words, repeating them until I arrived at Lungshö Gegong, yet I failed to realize [their meaning] in my heart. For if these verses had entered my heart, things would have been quite different by then. Nonetheless, whenever the fear of being attacked [by bandits and such] appeared in my mind during my journey, I reflected upon these verses and this helped. Also I was often in situations where I had to seek shelter with strangers when my mind turned wild and untamed. During times when I was confronted with seemingly unbearable situations, such as failing to secure a suitable shelter, or when I became the target of others' disparagement, these verses helped me."

What verses are these? They are the following eight verses:

1. **With the wish to achieve the highest aim,**
   Which surpasses even a wish-fulfilling gem,
   I shall train myself to at all times
   Cherish sentient beings as supreme.[415]

In general, in order to train yourself [to view] each sentient being as a wish-fulfilling gem, [you should recall] two [important] points of similarity shared by sentient beings and the precious gem. [First] if you submerge the wish-fulfilling gem in a muddy mire, the gem cannot cleanse itself of the mud; however, if you wash it with scented water on a full-moon day, adorn the tip of a victory banner with it, and make offerings to it, the gem can then become a source of all earthly wishes. In the same way, sentient beings afflicted with the various defects of cyclic existence cannot free themselves from the mire of this unenlightened state, nor can they wash away their sufferings and the origins of these sufferings. However, with our help, all the benefits, both immediate and ultimate, can issue from them. Without sentient beings how would you obtain even the immediate benefits—these would cease immediately; even ultimate happiness arises in relation to sentient beings. It is on the basis of sentient beings [178] that you attain the unexcelled state of buddhahood.

Second, in particular:

> 2. Whenever I interact with others,
>   I will view myself as inferior to all,
>   And I will train myself
>   To hold others superior from the depths of my heart.

As stated here, wherever we are and whomever we interact with, we should train to view ourselves, in all possible ways, as lower and to respect others from the depths of our heart. "Others" encompasses those who are higher than us, such as our spiritual teachers; those who are equal to us, such as our fellow monks; and those who are inferior to us, such as beggars. "In all respects" refers to our family lineage, mental capacity, and similar factors. We should reflect upon our own shortcomings in relation to these factors and avoid becoming proud. Thinking "They all belong to the lowly class of butchers," we generate pride on the basis of our physical existence. With skin the color of rusted gold, we are not even worthy of a sentient being's gaze!

With respect to our cognitive capacities, if we feel proud despite our [commonplace] lack of distinction, reflect, "I am ignorant of every one of the five fields of knowledge. Even in those fields where I have listened with care and attention, I fail to discern when I miss certain words and their explanations. In my behavior, too, though I am known to be a monk, there are hardly any negative deeds I have not committed. Even at this very moment, my thoughts embody the three poisons and my actions of body, speech, and mind remain mostly impure. Therefore, in the future, it will be difficult to attain birth in the higher realms, let alone liberation."

Śāntideva's *Guide to the Bodhisattva's Way of Life* states:

> By this type of behavior,
> Even the human form will not be obtained;
> If I fail to achieve human existence,
> There is only evil and no virtues.[416]

In this manner we should contemplate all our shortcomings and reflect, "Nothing falls beneath me but this river," and diminish our conceit and learn to respect others. This suggests that whenever we perceive positive qualities in others, or perceive qualities pertaining to family lineage, physical appearance, material resources, or spiritual realizations such as the six perfections, we should think, "How wondrous indeed that they possess these qualities despite their flawed natures!" [179] If, instead, they lack these qualities, we should reflect, "Who knows what higher qualities they may actually possess?" [Here] the story of the ugly mendicant is told.[417]

"From the depths or the very bone of my heart" indicates that our thoughts should not remain in our mouth as mere words. Instead, if we have the intention "I shall regard all beings as my family without discriminating on the basis of their family background," even the noble Avalokiteśvara will compliment us with the statement, "O child of noble family, this is excellent!" Just as, when the earth is leveled, oceans form upon it and draw forth the waters, in the same manner, the supramundane qualities flourish in the hearts of those free of pride. Therefore the *Condensed Perfection of Wisdom* states:

> Abide as if you were a servant of all beings.[418]

In essence, the three scriptural collections are a means to vanquish that conceit. When we are conceited, we are unable to live in harmony with others even in this present life. As for its detrimental consequences in the next life, [it is stated]:

> Some ignorant ones, owing to the force of their conceit,
> Take birth in the lower realms and in places bereft of leisure;
> They take birth as paupers or among the lowly castes;
> And they become blind, weak, or possessed of a vile demeanor.[419]

[Because of conceit] our propensities for afflictions will deepen further, and we will generate intense afflictions relative to those we deem inferior to ourselves. There is even a consequence more serious than this: we will fail to attain enlightenment. For it is written:

> The bodhisattva who is conceited
> Remains far away from enlightenment.[420]

So all the states of inferiority, degeneration, and suffering within the bounds of mundane existence arise from grasping at our own self as most precious. In contrast, all the joys—both mundane and supramundane—originate from sentient beings. We should therefore perceive all sentient beings as embodiments of higher qualities and vanquish our pride.

Third, since the afflictions impede us from proceeding in the above manner, eliminate them as follows:

> 3. **During all my activities I will probe my mind,**
>   **And as soon as an affliction arises—**
>   **Since it endangers myself and others—**
>   **I will train myself to confront it directly and avert it.**

Training ourselves to examine our mental continuum in all our activities and averting the afflictions as soon as they arise is as follows: Whichever of the four everyday activities we engage in,[421] with mindfulness and vigilance, we should analyze whether thoughts such as attachment arise in our mind. [180] With the thought "I will relinquish them the instant they arise," we should level them flat by observing them in this manner. Instead, if we act like an [elderly] couple being robbed by a thief, we procrastinate and then nothing happens. If afflictions proliferate in our mental continuum, emotions like anger will also increase exponentially. A sutra states:

> Likewise, those who place their faith in sleep
> Will procrastinate and fall further into slumber.
> This is true also of those who are lustful,
> And those who crave intoxicants.[422]

Our propensities for afflictions will deepen, and we will experience intense afflictive emotions toward all we perceive to be inferior. A more serious consequence is that we ourselves will experience acute suffering. If we relinquish the afflictions, their propensities too will become lighter. The past propensities will weaken, and only subtle propensities will be created anew toward desirable objects. Since the law of cause and effect is subtle, [the effects] will definitely be realized in our experience. So we should view the afflictions as our enemies and enhance the power of their antidotes.

Śāntideva states:

> I may be slain or burned alive;
> Likewise I may be decapitated;
> Under no circumstance shall I
> Bow before my enemy, the afflictions.[423]

As stated here, the conventional enemy can harm us only in this world and not beyond, but the enemy that is our afflictions can injure us throughout all our lives. It has been stated:

> This enemy of mine, the afflictions,
> Is long-lived, with neither beginning nor end;
> No other enemies can endure
> In this manner for so long.[424]

Furthermore, when we concede to our conventional enemies, they no longer harm us and may actually benefit us. If we assuage the afflictions in the same manner, however, they become even more destructive. It has been stated:

> If you relate to your enemies with friendship and gifts,
> These bring benefit and happiness.
> However, if you appease the afflictions,
> It causes ever more suffering and injury.[425]

Furthermore, conventional enemies harm only our body, life, and wealth, whereas the afflictions create immeasurable suffering in this cycle of existence. It has been stated:

> Even were all the gods and demigods
> To rise up against me as my enemies,

> They could not drag me and cast me
> Into the blazing fire of the eternal hells.
>
> Yet this powerful enemy, my afflictions,
> Can fling me instantly
> Where even mighty Mount Meru
> Would be crushed into dust upon contact.[426]

So we should view the afflictions as our enemy and discard them. [181] While conventional enemies can [return and] cause harm even after they have been banished, the afflictions enemy cannot resurface once they have been eradicated. It is like burnt seeds. The method for eliminating them is through conduct, meditation, and view.[427]

For beginners, given the weakness of their antidotes and their difficulty in countering afflictions that have already arisen, they must relinquish them [first] through their conduct. As for meditation, it is said that each affliction has a corresponding antidote. Since whatever meditative practice we undertake from among the three scopes becomes a remedy against all the afflictions, it is appropriate to engage in this practice. As our mental level advances, since afflictions are devoid of objects, it is sufficient simply to recognize that this is so. Thus there remains nothing to eliminate. [Śāntideva] states:

> Afflictions! Afflictions! Relinquish them with your eyes of insight.[428]

Fourth, training ourselves to regard beings of unpleasant character and those oppressed by powerful negative karma and suffering with special care and as something rarely found is presented in the following:

> 4. When I encounter beings of unpleasant character,
>   And those oppressed by intense negative karma and suffering,
>   As though finding a treasure of precious jewels,
>   I will train myself to cherish them, for they are so rarely found.

"Beings of unpleasant character" refers to those like the king Asaṅga[429] who, not having accumulated merit in the past, experience the arising of afflictions without even a trace of control. It also refers to beings such as the [ill-tempered] person who, while crossing a mountain pass, was given a plate of meat stew. But when the food burned his lips, he tossed the full plate away along with the pan, and then bellowed, "You dare burn me!" "[Intense] negative karma" refers to the five heinous crimes, degeneration of the vows, and [misappropriation of] offerings made to the Three Jewels. "Those oppressed by intense suffering" refers to those who are afflicted by leprosy, other serious illnesses, and so on.

We should not treat them as enemies by saying, "We cannot even look at them, and we must never allow them to come near us." Rather we should feel compassion toward them as though they were being led away by the king's executioners. Even if some among them are morally degenerate, we should feel, "What can I do to help them?" until our tears flow freely. This means that we should first console them with words, and if this proves ineffective, we should provide for their material needs and render help to cure their illness. If this, too, is unsuccessful, we should sustain them in our thoughts, and in action we should protect them even with shelter. Some people, thinking, "This will not benefit the other, but it could harm me," [182] cover their noses and walk away from those oppressed by acute suffering. Even so, there is no certainty that such suffering will never befall us. Therefore, in our actions, we should provide others with food, medicine, and the like, while with our thoughts we should contemplate the following and train the mind:

> Whatever sufferings beings have,
> May they all ripen upon me.[430]

The line "I will train myself to cherish them, for they are so rarely found" is explained as follows. Since it is rare to find a precious gem, we do not discard it but rather keep it and cherish it. In the same way, beings of unpleasant character are not so easy to find; yet in dependence upon them compassion arises, and in dependence upon them the awakening mind arises. Without making deliberate efforts, it is rare to encounter such objects as these that allow us to develop the Mahayana paths. Why? Because compassion does not arise toward the noble ones and those with worldly excellence, so they cannot help us enhance the awakening mind. They cannot therefore lead us to the attainment of buddhahood. This is stated in the following:

> Except for the awakening mind,
> The buddhas do not uphold any means.[431]

Fifth, training ourselves to accept the defeat without harboring any resentment, even when faced with misfortunes such as slander and so on, is presented in the following:

5. **When others out of jealousy**
   Treat me wrongly with abuse and slander,
   I shall train to take the defeat upon myself
   And offer the victory to others.

Regardless of whether we are to blame, if others slander us or speak ill of us out of jealousy or other motives, instead of harboring resentment, we should respond with a gentle mind. Free of resentment, we should refrain from claiming, for instance, "I am innocent. Others are to be blamed." Like Langri Thangpa, we should take the defeat upon ourselves. It is said that whenever misfortunes befell another, he would say, "I too am a part of him."[432] When we engage in giving and ethical discipline at present, we do so to purify our negative karma and accumulate merit. If we recognize those who slander us as sources of kindness, although this is not a substitute for the aforementioned two activities, [183] it nevertheless cleanses us of resentment and purifies our negative karma, the master said. Taking the defeat upon ourselves prevents us from adding to our [negative] karma.[433]

Langri Thangpa states, "In regard to purification of negative karma and accumulation of merit, it is more effective to recognize those who baselessly slander you as great sources of kindness than it is to offer butter-fried delicacies to each monk of the Phen region."[434] *A Guide to the Bodhisattva's Way of Life* states:

> Since it is in dependence upon
> His malign intention that forbearance arises,
> It's really he who is the cause of forbearance;
> Like the true Dharma, he is worthy of veneration.[435]

To substantiate this assertion, he [Śāntideva] states in the following that forbearance is more powerful than ethical discipline:

> There is no negativity like anger;
> And there is no fortitude like forbearance....[436]

This presents the forbearance of being unperturbed by harms.[437]

Sixth is the forbearance of voluntarily accepting suffering. When someone to whom we have rendered help in the past, or in whom we have placed great hope, betrays or slanders us, we should contemplate them as our teacher with a sense of gratitude. This is presented in the following:

> 6. Even if one whom I have helped
> Or in whom I have placed great hope
> Gravely mistreats me in hurtful ways,
> I will train myself to view him as my sublime teacher.

As for expectation, [Drom]tönpa once remarked,[438] "In Kham, I went to visit the teacher Sherapbar, a friend close to my heart. I went knowing he had not invited me, and he took offense at this and sent me away. He ordered others to remove all my belongings, and he himself locked me in a dark room. That was when it became clear whether I had trained my mind in loving-kindness and compassion, and whether the lines 'May these sufferings ripen upon me; / May all my happiness ripen upon them'[439] had remained a lie for me."[440] So we must never retaliate with resentment.

Furthermore, relating this to our own situation, were it not for inferior karma, such events would not befall us. For it has been stated:

> Previously I caused harms,
> Such as these, to other sentient beings;
> So it is right that [today] such injuries befall me,
> I who have harmed others.[441]

We should think that we ourselves are to blame [for whatever befalls us]; and in this manner, by maintaining a warm heart, we remain happy. [184] And because we do not transfer the blame to others, they too remain happy. We should reflect, "This is due to my own karma. It is established that no one harms the noble ones who have eliminated their negative karma." Even from the other's perspective, it is our own negative karma that caused them to injure us. Reflect, "Because of me, he will have to go to the lower realms. I am to blame for this." It has been stated:

Impelled by my own karma,
[The perpetrators] have brought this harm upon me;
Because of this they'll be in the pits of hell.
So is it not I who has destroyed them?[442]

Thus it is appropriate to protect these beings from their suffering. Again, it has been stated:

Those who falsely accuse me,
And others who cause me harm,
Likewise those who insult me:
May they all share in enlightenment.[443]

Also:

Even if others return kindness with harm,
I will practice responding with great compassion;
The most excellent beings of this world
Answer injury with benevolence.[444]

"To contemplate them gratefully as spiritual teachers" refers to the following: Our spiritual teachers are embodiments of great kindness, for they bestow on us the vows, provide us with the methods of meditative practice, and reveal to us the path to liberation. Of course, if we fail to contemplate this and fail to guard this contemplation, we will not tread the path. So reflect, "What this being has given me helps purify my negative karma and accomplish my accumulations. He has therefore benefited me. So I must view him as my spiritual teacher, no different from the one who has conferred on me the oral transmissions of the meditative practices." In this respect, [Atiśa's] *Songs of Blissfulness* states:

Whether someone is foe or friend —
These objects that give rise to afflictions—
He who sees them as spiritual teachers
Will be joyful wherever he resides.[445]

When such thoughts arise [spontaneously], our mind is trained; then even if we have no other practice, whatever acts we engage in turn into [aspects of the] path to enlightenment. This is like the saying, "One cannot find excrement in a land of gold."

Dharma refers to the transformation of your mind and not to the transformation of the external environment. For a trained person, even were the three worlds—of humans, celestial gods, and demons—to rise up as his enemies, his mind would not be afflicted by nonvirtue and suffering. Since no one can vanquish him, he is called a hero.

Seven, in brief, one must train to offer—both directly and indirectly—all the benefits and joys [185] to our dear mother sentient beings and to take all their hurts and pains into the depths of our hearts. This is presented in the following:

> 7. **In brief, I will train myself to offer benefit and joy**
>   **To all my mothers, both directly and indirectly,**
>   **And respectfully take upon myself**
>   **All the hurts and pains of my mothers.**

"In brief" refers to condensing all the preceding points. "Respectfully" suggests that we take these into the depths of our hearts while contemplating the kindness of our mothers. In other words, we should practice giving and taking not merely in words but from the depths of our heart. In practice, if we give away such factors of joy as food, medicine, and so on while taking upon ourselves all the hurts and pains of sentient beings, this is a cause for achieving birth in higher realms and attaining definitive goodness.[446] If, however, we are not yet able to actually practice this, we should instead perform the taking mentally by engaging in the meditation of giving and taking and dedicating all the joys of this life. When making aspiration prayers, we should utter from the depth of our hearts the following lines from *A Guide to the Bodhisattva's Way of Life:*

> My own happiness and others' suffering—
> If I do not thoroughly exchange them,
> I will not become fully enlightened;
> In this cyclic existence, too, I'll find no joy.[447]

Eight, since in all these practices it is possible to become defiled, we should make sure that they remain untainted by even the slightest mundane consideration of this life, and with the awareness that recognizes all phenomena as illusionlike, we should train to be utterly free of attachment. This is presented in the following:

8. **By ensuring that all this remains undefiled**
   From the stains of the eight mundane concerns,
   And by understanding all things as illusions,
   I will train myself to be free of the bondage of clinging.

Thus the remedy—the method—is this. When tainted with mundane concerns such as the desire to be perceived by others as praiseworthy, we fall under the influence of the eight mundane concerns, and our pursuits become those of self-interest. When this occurs, then the sacred teachings have been turned into demons. If we understand these [mundane concerns] as illusionlike, later we will relinquish them. Nothing within our present experience possesses substantial reality. [It has been stated:]

> So among these empty phenomena,
> What is there to gain or to lose?
> Who provides you with what service?
> And who subjects you to insults? [186]

> From whence do pleasure and pain arise?
> What is there to be sad or joyful about?[448]

And further,

> That all things are just like space,
> I, for one, shall accept.[449]

As for supplicating all [objects of refuge] and reciting this as an aspiration, it is as follows: We should make mandala offering to the teachers and the Three Jewels and make the following supplication:

"If you—my teachers, the buddhas of the three times, and all the bodhisattvas—possess blessings and compassion; if you—the ten male and ten female wrathful deities—possess power and might; and if you—the wisdom ḍākinīs—possess strength and abilities, bless me so that the meaning of these eight verses will be realized in me. Bless me so that all the suffering and its origin of all sentient beings ripens upon me and that all the fruits of my awakening mind ripen upon all beings." We should relate this [in the same manner] to all four truths and train [our mind].[450]

Whatever virtuous actions, such as these [mind training practices], we may perform, afterward we should recite this aspiration prayer of the eight verses. Making such an aspiration creates propensities for the awakening mind. We should recite the following aspiration prayer: "To such activities of root virtue I will dedicate all my time—all my months and all my years. In the future, too, I will make sure to encounter spiritual teachers and to associate with [virtuous] companions." We should recite these prayers of aspiration repeatedly.

This commentary on the eight verses of the bodhisattva Langri Thangpa was composed by Chekawa Yeshé Dorjé. This commentary on the root verses constitutes a profound instruction on mind training. Please strive in this. May [its realization] arise in the hearts [of all].

31. The Story of the Repulsive Mendicant[451]

[187] Once in India, among the beggars, a mendicant used to sit behind the doors [of taverns], and whenever drops fell on him from the tavern ladies spilling beer, he would utter, "Each on their own." At that time, proponents of the non-Buddhist schools had issued a challenge to debate, but no one who could rebuff their arguments could be found. The tavern lady mentioned that a mendicant behind her door would utter "Each on their own" whenever drops of beer fell on him. He was invited to debate, and the disputations were refuted. Thus it is taught that as far as inner knowledge is concerned, you cannot determine who possesses what.[452]

There is also the story of a couple who were robbed but failed to notice at [first]. Feeling they could get by anyway, they let it pass. However, from that night onward, [the looting] got even worse.[453]

Rājasaṅgha, a mendicant with an offensive character, met regularly with Atiśa. When Atiśa was requested [by his disciples] to stop seeing him, Atiśa responded, "It is in dependence on him that my practice of forbearance is being perfected!"[454]

A rumor once circulated that Langri Thangpa had transgressed the cardinal monastic precept [of celibacy]. Even though this was false, he nonetheless gave away his possessions—by making offerings of tea at Radreng Monastery and so on—and entered into a meditative retreat.

This is a supplement to the *Eight Verses*. Dzechenpa states:

> Reverence for the objects of refuge is the support of the path;
> Purity of ethical precepts of your vows is the basis of the path;
> Contemplating life's absence of leisure is the most excellent path;
> Accepting loss without despair is the way of the renunciate.[455]

The Middle Way work *Blaze of Reasoning* states:

Even if a bodhisattva engages in sensual desires,
Ordained members should pay him homage.[456]

The *Ear Ornament Sutra* states:

In the future, at the end of an era,
I will appear in the form of letters.[457]

If a deer and a predator live in close proximity in a forest, the deer will likely be killed. Likewise if a fully ordained monk and a woman live in close proximity, the life-thread of liberation will likely be severed. Atiśa said, "If a fully ordained monk who would otherwise have perceived the truth in half a month associates with someone degenerate in vows, he will not see the truth in this life." Therefore you should live far from those degenerate in vows and from women.[458] [188]

May I be able to extensively bring about the welfare of sentient beings. May I, on the basis of this profound Mahayana teaching, realize in my mental continuum an uncontrived awakening mind exchanging self and others, which is the pure altruistic intention.

32. A Commentary on "Leveling Out All Conceptions"[459]

[189] With great reverence I pay homage to and seek refuge in the precious teacher Lord Serlingpa, father and sons, including his entire lineage. Pray bless me!

Lord Serlingpa, the embodiment of wisdom and great compassion, once said to Atiśa, "My son, in order to serve others during this era of degeneration, you must distill the sacred words of the discourses, scriptures, and reasonings, and all the pith instructions of the teachers and undertake their practice in one sitting. For this you will require the following teaching, which makes you invulnerable to sickness, harm, interference from obstructive forces, demons, and upholders of false teachings, and all such adverse conditions and impediments." Then he taught the following:

> Level out all [false] conceptions;
> Carry forth the force of all antidotes;
> Concentrate all aspirations into one;
> And seek the path where all paths converge—
>
> These are the four enlightened factors, the antidotes.
> They are vital if you are to tame barbarian borderlands;
> They are essential, too, in the age of degeneration
> To bear with misguided ways of negative companions.

The meaning of these verses is as follows. It is essential to level out the conceptions at the very site of their origin. You should examine, "Where do these appear? To what sense faculties do they appear? In what shape and color do they appear?" They are like a venomous snake or a rabid dog; do not allow them to be near you. Rather, without giving in to procrastination, destroy them the moment they arise by applying their antidote. It has been stated in the sutra:

O attachment, I've now discerned your root:
You arise from the proliferation of concepts.⁴⁶⁰

Also:

Conceptualization is the great ignorance
That casts one into samsara's ocean.⁴⁶¹

Entering the Middle Way states:

Ordinary beings are chained by their conceptualization;
Yogis who are free of conceptualization gain freedom.
That which reveals the falsity of conceptualizations,
The learned ones taught, is the fruit of a thorough analysis.⁴⁶²

All the sacred scriptures and the treatises of the Great Vehicle, such as those cited here, assert conceptualization to be a great obstacle to attaining enlightenment. It is crucial, therefore, not to fall prey to procrastination. Since, as it says here, harboring too many thoughts prevents you from reaching far, do not engage in the proliferation of thoughts, even with respect to the profound truth. [190] Rather, consolidate your aspirations decisively on the single task of destroying [false] conceptions. Even the sutras describe all mental engagements as Māra's activity.

Therefore, until you attain omniscient buddhahood, concentrate all your aspirations and relate all the grounds and paths—such as the paths of accumulation, seeing, and meditation—to destroying false conceptions the instant they arise by applying their antidotes. In brief, every time a conceptualization arises, make sure that its antidote arrives there too. For it is through antidotes that your aspirations must be concentrated to destroy false conceptions; and all the paths, too, must be traversed by way of destroying these false conceptions. For this purpose, adopt four factors belonging to the class of enlightened phenomena.⁴⁶³

Again, the following was taught:

Adverse conditions are your spiritual teacher;
Demons and possessor spirits, the Buddha's emanations;
Sickness is a broom for negative karma and defilements;
Sufferings are displays of ultimate reality's expanse—

These are the four thoroughly afflicted factors;
They are vital if you are to tame the barbarian borderlands;
They are essential, too, in the era of degeneration
To bear with misguided ways of negative companions.

The meaning of these lines is as follows: Even if unwanted adverse conditions such as sickness and suffering befall you, turn these into catalysts and take on top of these the sickness and suffering of all sentient beings. Take these on mentally, without reservation, and rejoice for having taken them en masse. Similarly, as you give to sentient beings whatever favorable conditions you enjoy, such as your happiness, rejoice in [sentient beings] perfecting their accumulations of merit. Likewise, whatever conditions for sights, sounds, smells, tastes, and so on that arise, if probed, they are nowhere to be found. Place your mind in this truth of unfindability, and rejoice in [adverse conditions] [with the thought] "They are my spiritual teachers exhorting me to the ultimate expanse; they are conducive conditions for attaining enlightenment."

When harms from ghosts, ogresses, site spirits, and so on, befall you, place upon these, with your entire heart, whatever harms and sufferings sentient beings may possess. Thinking "I have definitely taken these," cultivate a sense of joy. By giving to the agents of harm whatever they desire—such as the flesh, blood, and so on of your body—out of compassion, out of loving-kindness, and out of the awakening mind, [191] [the harms] are turned into factors conducive to attaining enlightenment and therefore assist your journey to enlightenment. Given that all these malevolent forces are emanations of the buddhas, you should cultivate inconceivable joy and respect toward them.

When you are suffering from an illness, take all the sickness and pains of sentient beings into the very core of your heart and imagine that all sentient beings attain perfect abandonment. Thinking, "This has served its purpose," cultivate joy. When you are free of sickness, again motivated thus, give to sentient beings all your happiness and its causes and imagine that all sentient beings attain perfect realization. Thinking, "This has served its purpose," cultivate joy. This sweeps away negative karma and the obscurations, for it does not allow negative karma and obscurations to linger unchallenged for even a single moment. If a hundred sufferings arise, a hundred ways to search for [their true nature] will emerge. However, given that these [sufferings] never [truly] existed, there are a hundred [different] ways to not find them.

These are therefore the hundred abandonments and the hundred realizations—a great display of the ultimate expanse. Cultivate joy in this. These, then, are the objects to be relinquished, the four thoroughly unenlightened factors.

Again, the following was taught:

> This [training] is the great counterpoint to happiness;
> This is the great successor to misery;
> This is the charm that attracts misfortune;
> And this is a capping of wishes that are least useful[464]—
>
> These are the four antidotes to misguided ways.
> They are vital if you are to tame the barbarian borderlands;
> They are essential, too, in the age of degeneration
> To bear with misguided ways of negative companions.

The meaning of these lines is as follows: Harbor modest desires and contentment to counteract the longing for pleasures, such as for food, drink, wealth, fame, and so on, for these obstruct the pursuit of virtuous activities. On this basis follow up sufferings with [additional] pain: If your leg hurts, go for circumambulation; if your back hurts, do prostrations; if you suffer too much greed, give things away to others; if you suffer distractions, enter into retreat; and if you delight in gossip, cease speaking. When you suffer great unwanted omens—such as negative reputation, disputes, magical spells, and malicious gossip—since these are means for subduing the malevolent demon of self-grasping, welcome them as auspicious, as you would a charm that attracts good fortune. [192] Cultivate courage by shouting, "Send me more!" With the thought "As a consequence of all these events befalling me, events that are [normally] of no benefit, if I can [use them to] subdue this self, from here on I will not be reborn in cyclic existence." In this manner, you cap your desires and ensure that you achieve the strength of the three aspects of forbearance.[465]

These [four kinds of adverse conditions] are, then, the four misguided ways, the objects of thorough application of the [four] antidotes.

Again, the following was taught:

> "Self" is the root of negative karma;
> It is to be discarded decisively.

"Other" is a source of enlightenment;
It is to be embraced enthusiastically—

These two teachings draw the remedies to a close;
They are vital if you are to tame the barbarian borderlands;
They are essential, too, in the age of degeneration
To bear with misguided ways of negative companions.

The meaning of these lines is as follows: Given that the self is the source of all unwanted events and the root of all negative actions, we should never cherish it, but discard it with total abandon. We should reflect, "O enemies, if you like it, take it. O demons, if you like it, take it. If not in haste, eat it cooked; if in haste, just take it and run." In this way, totally discard your own self and serve the well-being of all. And since the joyful embracing of others' welfare through forsaking your own self-interest is the source of unexcelled goodness, nurture sentient beings with kindness and take their sufferings upon yourself. These two teachings, which bring closure to the objects to be relinquished and their remedies, are the practice of great beings.

Cast away decisively, let go with ease;
Dismantle thoroughly, and let be with gentleness—
These are the four aspects of the sealing of emptiness;[466]
They are vital if you are to tame the barbarian borderlands.

They are essential, too, in the age of degeneration
To bear with misguided ways of negative companions.
If you engage in the practices in this way,
Beings will not be fettered but will attain freedom.

The meaning of these lines is as follows: You should decisively cast away all dualistic thoughts of perceived objects and perceiving cognition, and let your mind rest free and radiant, absent of conceptualization and bondage in the ultimate expanse that is free of conceptual elaboration. Do not chase after earlier instants of cognition, [193] do not anticipate the future but, free of clinging, let the present remain as it is. Let it rest free in its natural state, uncontrived and free of any exaggeration or denigration. These are the four aspects of the sealing of emptiness. If you practice in this manner, you will not be chained by karma in cyclic existence; rather you will be free and you will attain liberation.

Some practice other than this would fail to tame the barbarous sentient beings of this era of degeneration. Yet, possessing this, you will be immune to obstacles, and will achieve the well-being of sentient beings with ease. Thus taught [Serlingpa]. I have here presented the teachings of the peerless Serlingpa in precise accordance with his words.[467]

The *Amoghapāśa Tantra* states:

> "Wisdom" refers to enlightenment, while "heroic being" indicates skillful means; with these two, the welfare of sentient beings will be achieved.[468]

Again, the Guhyasamāja tantra entitled *Drop of Freedom* states:

> Then with compassion as the sole basis,
> All enlightened qualities will arise.[469]

Again:

> If the root of compassion is absent,
> One cannot endure hardships.[470]

The sutra entitled *Perfectly Gathering the Qualities [of Avalokiteśvara]* states:

> Whosoever aspires to attain full enlightenment swiftly should not train in many practices. What is that sole [practice]? It is great compassion. For whosoever possesses great compassion possesses in his palms all the teachings of the Buddha. He shall achieve these without effort and without exertion. In brief, great compassion is the root of all the teachings.[471]

This instruction was given to Atiśa, the savior of beings, by his teacher Serlingpa Dharmakīrti to help tame [the people of] barbarian borderlands.

33. Mahayana Mind Training[472]

[194] To Maitreya, Asaṅga, and so on;
To Serlingpa and to master Atiśa;
To Dromtönpa, Potowa, and Sharawa;
And to Maldro[473] and Drakmarwa,[474] I pay homage.

Generally speaking, in order to attain full enlightenment through training your mind, nothing—from the beginning of practice up to the Vajrayana—is not encompassed within mind training. Yet, as if applying a general term to a particular, this [practice] is given the name "mind training." Atiśa possessed three traditions of mind training: the tradition of his teacher Dharmarak-ṣita, of his teacher Maitrīyogi, and of Serlingpa. Of these, the tradition of the teacher Serlingpa is presented here. In this tradition, it is accepted that one can even generate the awakening mind without relinquishing self-grasp-ing and without extinguishing manifest levels of clinging. In terms of philo-sophical standpoint, it is said that even if you are partial to a non-Buddhist school, there is no contradiction.

In terms of this instruction, it states:

First, train in the preliminaries.

If enumerated, this is fourfold: (1) contemplating the difficulty of finding a human existence of leisure and opportunity, (2) contemplating impermanence, (3) contemplating karmic cause and effect, and (4) contemplating the defects of existence.

First, by relying on both scriptural citations and reasoning, contemplate the difficulty of obtaining in hundreds and thousands of eons this [human existence], which is free of the eight types of nonleisure and endowed with the five personal and the five external opportunities. Reflect, "If I fail to appreciate the difficulty of obtaining it, whatever mundane pursuits I under-take will fail to make this existence meaningful. I must therefore engage in

Dharma practice. I will cultivate the awakening mind exchanging self and others, the supreme teaching."

When you feel that you have gained a reliable appreciation of this, then meditate on impermanence—that is, that you will not be around for long—by cultivating mindfulness of death. You will die: no one who has ever been born has escaped death so far. You will die: your life span will reach its end. You will die: the end of life is but a single moment. You must therefore definitely practice Dharma. The time when you will die is uncertain: the life span of an earthly being is unpredictable; unknown forces may still be present in your propelling karma; and, furthermore, there are many internal and external conditions [for death]. So you must engage in Dharma practice right from today.

When you die, no one can save you. When death approaches, even if Buddha Śākyamuni were to appear, even if the four wrathful deities were to guard you,[475] even if your family and friends were to encircle you, or even if you possessed lots of material goods and possessions, none of this will be of any benefit. You must therefore practice Dharma without wasting time appeasing anyone. Cultivate the awakening mind, the supreme teaching.

Does one become no more after death? No. You will have to take rebirth, and this you do depending on your karma. With positive karma, you will either be reborn in the higher realms or attain true liberation. Negative karma, on the other hand, causes suffering, [195] such as [birth in] the three lower realms of existence. So ensure the cessation of those negative deeds you may have committed in the past and resolve never to perform them again. With respect to positive karma, you should reactivate your past karma by engaging in virtuous actions from now on with utmost capacity. Since the awakening mind exchanging self and others is the best way of doing this, you should cultivate it.

Even if you are reborn in the higher realms because of your positive karma, you'll find no [lasting] happiness. Since the entire cycle of existence is unsatisfactory, distinctions between high and low within it is meaningless. Thus, following Nāgārjuna, reflect on the seven defects and so on, and in this way, cultivate renunciation toward the entirety of cyclic existence.[476] Transcend cyclic existence; attain liberation. If you do not do this [that is, reflect on the defects], you will fail foremost to transcend cyclic existence. Since self-grasping is the obstacle to attaining liberation, cultivating the awakening mind exchanging self and others is the supreme method for preventing its arising. You should therefore cultivate [the awakening mind].

For the main practice, cultivate alternately giving and taking;[477]

Take upon yourself the sufferings of sentient beings along with the origins of their suffering, transform your body into a precious wish-fulfilling jewel, and then give this to sentient beings.

Commence the sequence of taking from your mother.[478]

As is stated here, you should imagine in front of you sentient beings equal to the limits of space in all ten directions, such as your real-life mother, father, siblings, members of your community, the people of your region and of Tibet, of the four continents of the earth, of "a thousand world systems," of the "trichiliocosm" consisting of two thousand medium world systems,[479] to the extent that even when all ten directions are filled with beings like pods with mustard seeds, it extends still farther. Then reflect in the following manner:

"This sentient being, my real-life mother, gave me the human existence of leisure and opportunity. Whether I was in her womb, being born, or growing up, she fed me and clothed me. She gave me her most precious belongings. She acted as though the status of a universal monarch would be inadequate for me, in terms of mundane excellence, and as though the bliss of full enlightenment would be inadequate for me, in terms of supermundane accomplishments. She watched me, her child, with loving eyes, cared for me with affectionate heart, and called me with endearing names. To the best of her ability she protected me from dangers and led me to happiness. She is therefore a source of great kindness. So on my part, too, to reciprocate her kindness, I must protect her from suffering and lead her to happiness. Suffering harms her both immediately and long-term, and the origin of suffering prevents her from experiencing happiness. So I must help free her from these two."

Thinking thus, take from sentient beings their suffering and its origin as if you were slicing them off with a sharp razor; these then enter through your heart. Transform your body into a precious wish-fulfilling jewel and give it to all sentient beings. Since the fulfillment of all wishes flows from this jewel, imagine that all beings achieve, [196] in the immediate term, all the conditions favorable for Dharma practice and are led ultimately to the state of buddhahood. This is the practice of giving and taking within a single session.

As you gain conviction in this and achieve stability in this practice, it is stated:

Place the two astride your breath.

As you exhale, train in giving, and as you inhale, train in taking. Since it is impossible for the meditative absorption based on breathing not to arise, training the mind and seizing the gentle flow of breath can occur simultaneously. When practiced in this manner, giving is loving-kindness, while taking is compassion that aspires [for others] to be free of immediate and long-term suffering. As you are aspiring to lead [others] to happiness, it is joyfulness; as you are free of bias, it is equanimity; placing [beings] directly in the state of buddhahood is the awakening mind. This is, therefore, Serlingpa's instruction on training in the conventional awakening mind.

If, as you engage in these practices, they arise when you meditate and not when you do not, this is normal. If they arise whether or not you are meditating, this is great.[480] When the focal points—the objects, the attitudes (the meritorious thoughts), and their fruitions—are reversed [from your everyday ordinary pattern], they are then posited as immeasurable.[481]

Since subsequent cognitions determine whether the actual training of mind during meditative equipoise has been valid or erroneous, and whether [the realizations] have arisen, the following lines present the subsequent stage:

There are three objects, three poisons, and three roots of virtue;
This, in brief, is the subsequent instruction.

When, in relation to the three objects, the three poisonous afflictions arise in your mind, analyze the rationale [for their arising] and take upon yourself, without hesitation, the attachments and so forth of sentient beings. Transform your body into a precious wish-fulfilling jewel and give it to sentient beings. In this manner you give to sentient beings the virtue of nonattachment and lead them ultimately to the state of buddhahood. As with the three poisons, you should extend this [reflection] to all the afflictions, such as conceit, envy, and so on.

Relate whatever you can to meditation right now.

Take upon yourself the manifestations of immediate sufferings and their origins, which exist as one entity in sentient beings. As you transform your body into a precious wish-fulfilling jewel and give it to sentient beings, they enjoy, in the immediate term, the conditions conducive to Dharma practice, and they are led ultimately to the state of buddhahood. Whatever aspects of happiness you find in yourself, give these to sentient beings and imagine that they realize their immediate and ultimate aims.

In all actions, train by means of the words.

As described in the sutra entitled *Thoroughly Pure Spheres of Conduct*,[482] you should even reflect aloud, "May all the sufferings and negative karma of sentient beings ripen upon me. [197] May all my happiness and success ripen upon sentient beings."

At the start and at the end, engage in two trainings.[483]

First, prior to getting up in the morning and before initiating any tasks, you should armor yourself with the thought "I shall, in order to make my human existence purposeful, engage in the practice of the awakening mind by means of giving and taking." When going to bed or later [that day], look back and examine whether you have succeeded. If so, you should rejoice, and with admiration cultivate joy. If you have not succeeded, acknowledge your shortcomings and purify your negativity.

Banish all blames to the single source.

Given that all unhappiness and suffering, from beginningless time up to the present, have stemmed from self-grasping, reflect, "I shall undermine this [self-grasping] by applying whatever is most effective in wounding it."

Toward all beings contemplate their great kindness.

All temporary and ultimate benefits and happiness arise on the basis of taking sentient beings as the objects. Whether it is immediate needs such as food, clothing, and so forth, or whether it is the path of perfect enlightenment—the motivation of the awakening mind and its practical application, the six perfections—all can be accomplished in dependence upon sentient beings. They cannot be accomplished without sentient beings. Therefore contemplate [sentient beings'] kindness and practice giving and taking.

Train constantly toward those chosen objects.

In response to the kindness of your parents, your ordination masters and preceptors, and your spiritual teachers, cultivate compassion for and render help to those beings whose mental continuums are afflicted by grave negative karma. On the basis of their coming to harm you when you render them help, you will more easily appreciate [the kindness of the three objects].[484] You should therefore practice giving and taking especially by selecting these three objects for special attention.

Of the two, uphold the principal witness.

[Making sure] that your practice does not become an object of disapproval by sublime beings is the witness of persons. Observing whether you disapprove of yourself or whether you feel remorse is the witness of self-awareness.[485]

When both are present, take them all.

When you recognize for yourself the undesirability of suffering and its origin, you should recognize that they are equally undesirable for all other beings, sentient beings who are sources of kindness to you. Take these two [suffering and its origin] therefore from sentient beings and transform your body into a precious wish-fulfilling jewel and give it to them. Imagine that they immediately enjoy all the favorable conditions of Dharma practice and that they are ultimately led to buddhahood.

Train in the three challenges.

Taking as your cue your own afflictions, engage in the practice of giving and taking. In the beginning, when afflictions first arise in your mind, it is difficult to identify them—that is, it is difficult to grasp them with mindfulness. In the middle, it is difficult to overcome them with antidotes. And at the end, [198] it is difficult to exterminate these afflictions. So you should always train, as far as possible, to first identify [the afflictions], to overcome them in the middle, and to ultimately exterminate them.

Adopt the three principal conditions.

For those who engage in Dharma practice, the three principal conditions are (1) the meeting with a sublime spiritual teacher, (2) a serviceable mental continuum, and (3) the presence of favorable conditions such as food, clothing, shelter, and assistance. Take upon yourself all instances where [others] lack these conditions. Transform your body into a precious wish-fulfilling jewel from which emerge all wishes, and your giving these to sentient beings ensures no one is deprived of these three favorable conditions. [Imagine that] ultimately [all] are led to buddhahood.

Whichever of the two arises, bear them both.

When everything is perfect and all the right conditions present, practice giving and taking without distraction. When things are not perfect and misfortunes strike you, make sure this does not impede your practice of giving and taking and that you do not become demoralized. Instead engage in Dharma practice.

The intent of all teachings converges on a single point.

The purpose of engaging in all the practices—the contemplation of the difficulty of obtaining a human existence of leisure and opportunity; mindfulness of death; karma and its effects; the defects of cyclic existence; the cultivation of loving-kindness, compassion, and the awakening mind; the six perfections; and meditation on the two selflessnesses—is to eliminate self-grasping, which is the root of all misfortunes, and to cultivate the awakening mind cherishing others, which is the source of all higher qualities. This is the fundamental point and purpose of all the teachings, and nothing remains outside this.

Do not torment with malicious banter.

Since bodhisattvas work for the welfare of sentient beings, you must never utter harsh words to others.

Do not boast of your good deeds.[486]

Since bodhisattvas working for others' welfare are acting in accord with their vow to never do anything else, you have no basis for being boastful of your deeds. Therefore, never trumpet your good deeds.

Do not be ill-tempered.

When others cause a bodhisattva harm, this gives him the opportunity to take enlightenment into his very palms. So rejoice and never lose your temper toward such beings.

Do not boast of your good deeds.[487]

Again, since the bodhisattva working for the welfare of sentient beings is engaged in acts that he is supposed to do anyway, you should never harbor expectations of reward. For [if you do,] you are likely to eventually become excessively boisterous [as well]. So cast not even a second glance on what [beneficial deeds] you may have done for others.

Do not lie in ambush.

Never lie in ambush like a vicious person, with thoughts such as, "This person or that person did this or that wrong to me."

Do not maintain inappropriate loyalty.

The practice of the awakening mind [in terms of] giving and taking is incompatible with our beginningless fealty to the desire for revenge, so shun [the latter]. [199]

Do not sprint to win a race.

Pursuing the realization of your own personal enlightenment first is contrary to [the practice of] the awakening mind.

Do not place the load of a dzo onto an ox.

Since all misfortunes arise from self-grasping, never transfer blame onto others.

Do not seek misery as a means to happiness.

If you engage in trade, handicrafts, farming, and so on, in order to achieve happiness, you will be doing so merely out of self-grasping, which does not lead to finding happiness.

Train without depending on other conditions.[488]

The practice of the awakening mind [in terms of] giving and taking is not flawed by dependence upon the presence of either the best or the worst conditions. So regardless of whether you perceive a situation to be positive or negative, use however you perceive it as a rationale to practice.

Accomplish all yogas through a single means.

Whatever spiritual practice you undertake, make sure it becomes a condition for cultivating the awakening mind of giving and taking.

If relapsed, contemplate itself for its remedy.[489]

If problems arise in your meditation practice, do not seek their remedies elsewhere; instead, engage solely in the practice of giving and taking.

Be endowed with the three inseparable factors.

Whatever actions you undertake with your body, such as making prostrations and circumambulation; whatever words you utter through speech, such as [recitation of] sutras and essence mantras; and whatever thoughts you cultivate with your mind, such as deity meditation and so on, make sure that these do not deviate from the focus of giving and taking. In deity meditation, for example, if you visualize all the emanating and withdrawal of seed syllables and so on in terms of giving and taking, this then is a supreme yoga.

Guard the two even at the cost of your life.[490]

Guard the practice of the awakening mind [in terms of] giving and taking even at the cost of your life. Such is the measure of its critical importance. Make sure your [practice] accords with the general instructions of the sublime masters. Given that teachers who reveal the pith instructions on giving and taking are critically important, observing commitments [with respect to them] entails great hardship. This [practice of relating to them properly] should accord with such tantric and the Perfection Vehicle works as *Fifty Verses on the Guru.*[491]

Train in the three general points.[492]

When you practice giving and taking, train your mind in a way that does not contradict the teachings of the Buddha in general, does not contradict the sacred traditions of your spiritual teachers in particular, and especially does not contradict all the precepts and vows you have taken.

Contemplate the three that are free of degeneration.

Since you depend on their blessings, make sure that your faith and reverence toward your teachers remain undiminished. Since it is through habituation that mastery is attained, make sure that your interest in the practice of the awakening mind [in terms of] giving and taking remains undiminished. [200] And since pure ethical discipline is the foundation for all higher qualities to emerge, make sure that your respect for the precepts and vows you have taken remains undiminished. Train your mind in this manner.

Do not speak of defects.

A thousand others may criticize you even though you adopt pure conduct; however, never speak of the defects of others, whatever their behavior may be. This helps you maintain pure conduct.

Do not dwell on others' shortcomings.

Since it is necessary to train your mind through using whatever situations befall you as the very rationale [for training your mind]—whether good or bad, true or false, joyful or painful—embrace everything without making such distinctions as "this object of abandonment" and "this antidote," and practice giving and taking.

Do not be sporadic.

Since your mind will not be trained through mere momentary flashes of experience, train in the awakening mind of giving and taking at all times as if you were driving a stake through your heart.[493]

Do not be fickle.

Since the realization of perfect buddhahood requires three innumerable eons, practicing the awakening mind for a brief instant, or a single lifetime, or a single eon, cannot take you very far. Therefore you must practice through maintaining its continuum over a prolonged period.

Train with decisiveness.

In order to give away your body and so on and take on others' suffering and so on, it is not adequate to simply evoke the experience by entertaining the thought "Can I do this, or can't I do this?" Like severing a major artery or cutting the rope of a [heavy] load, you should apply yourself [to the task] decisively.[494]

Be released through the two: investigation and close analysis.

If you feel that you have attained stability in your realization of giving and taking, then examine whether or not you are able to give, whether or not you are able to take, and whether or not [your practice] has become a remedy against your afflictions. You should [also] examine your mind when you encounter objects of affliction, when you encounter suffering sentient beings, and when you experience happiness and suffering, and with clarity you should discard [any afflictions you discover].

Cultivate constantly the joyful mind alone.

Whatever situation befalls you, whether positive or negative, nothing cannot be turned into a condition, a vehicle, or a complement to the practice of the awakening mind of giving and taking. Therefore, whatever happens, remain joyful and make sure such situations do not become conditions for creating [more] suffering.

Discard all expectations of reward.

If your practice of awakening mind of giving and taking produces an appreciation of the immediate benefits or a yearning for the ultimate attainment of buddhahood, discard all yearning for happiness for your own sake and expectations of reward. In both the immediate and the long run, train your mind entirely for others' well-being and for their benefit.

Do not apply misplaced understanding.[495]

Do not maintain misplaced aspiration; [201] instead, you should forsake aspirations for your own interests and train your mind entirely in others' welfare. Forsake the misplaced compassion that belittles [others] or displays sarcasm. Forsake the misplaced forbearance that endures pains for your own benefit; seek instead to endure the hardships of the quest for enlightenment in order to benefit others. Forsake the misplaced joyous effort that perseveres in the pursuit of sensual pleasures or the fulfillment of your self-interest; strive instead with joyous effort to attain buddhahood for the benefit of others. Forsake the misplaced savoring of joy at the success of your own self-interest; cultivate joy instead in seeking others' welfare. Forsake the misplaced admiration that rejoices when misfortunes befall [other] sentient beings; cultivate instead [the ability to] rejoice when they attain excellence.

Do not strike at the heart.

If you are one who possesses power and so forth, do not torment and strike at the hearts of others, whether humans or nonhumans.

Do not turn the gods into demons.

Although the practice of the awakening mind [in terms of] giving and taking is by nature a positive quality, if you develop pride because of it, it becomes a basis for defects. So refrain from doing so.

Identify the principal cause.[496]

The practice of giving and taking, in other words the practice of the awakening mind, is the principal cause or seed for attaining full enlightenment. Overt physical and verbal actions are not much use, so make sure you can resist the temptation to be distracted by physical and verbal acts.[497] Train your mind at all times in the awakening mind of giving and taking without distraction.

Do not abuse this practice.

Since giving your body to others is not mere words, do so from the depth of your heart. Since taking others' negative karma and suffering is not mere words, take these in actual fact from the depths of your heart. Meditate on this to the point that you feel as if your self cracks, heaves, and disintegrates. In order to practice these points succinctly, it is stated:

Apply [yourself] to the five powers.[498]

Ceaselessly cultivating the wish to practice giving and taking is the *power of propelling intention*. Performing the rites of making offerings, offering gifts and honor, offering torma, and so forth in order to attain realization of the awakening mind of giving and taking is the *power of accumulating positive seeds*, which are the roots of virtue. Making supplication to the teachers and the Three Jewels, and making regular prayers of aspiration in order to attain realization of the awakening mind of giving and taking is the *power of aspirational prayer*. Gaining experience and self-mastery through habituating your mind to constant practice of the awakening mind of giving and taking is the *power of acquaintance*. Vanquishing thoughts of self-cherishing, such as "I cannot practice this kind of giving and taking," when they arise [202] is the *power of eradication*.

Contemplating this at the point of death and practicing it with the thought "I will strive to generate, to the best of my ability, the authentic awakening mind of giving and taking throughout all stages of the intermediate state" is the *power of propelling intention*. Distributing your possessions to those who are deserving, making offerings, giving torma cakes, and offering gifts and honor and so forth is the *power of virtuous seeds*, the accumulation of positive virtuous karma. Making offerings to your teachers and the Three Jewels, making supplications to the Dharma protectors ("Pray help me attain the realization of the awakening mind of giving and taking after the intermediate state"), and regularly making these kinds of prayers of aspiration is the *power of aspirational prayer*. You should [then] make supplications appropriate to the moment-of-death instructions.

Transform your attitudes but remain as you are.

If you encounter people who assert that such a transformation of intention cannot bring much progress in one's practice of giving and taking, make sure that your own mind remains convinced, for this is in actual fact the root [cause] of buddhahood.

The proliferation of five degenerations[499]

This era of five degenerations, when erroneous ways proliferate and when the force of afflictions is strong, whichever afflictions arise, they...

Are all transformed into the path to enlightenment.

Thus they are transformed into complementary factors, as champions of, or as conditions for, [the practice of] giving and taking.

This distilled essence of pith instructions

This essence distilled from the heart of all scriptural collections...

Stems from a lineage of sublime masters.

[This stemmed] from Maitreya to Serlingpa, Atiśa, Geshe Dromtönpa, Potowa, Sharawa, Maldrowa, and Drakmarwa. These masters are "sublime" because they are free of flaws, contamination, or pretensions in every sphere—their philosophical views, their conduct, their commitments, their ethical discipline, and so on. Because it was transmitted through them from ear to ear, it is an "instruction." Since it is the practice of the awakening mind of giving and taking by means of exchanging self and others, it is the instruction for ultimately taking everything—what is perceived or proclaimed, what is true or false—as conditions for training in the awakening mind.

The mind training instruction is complete. May auspiciousness prevail!

34. Public Explication of Mind Training[500]
Sangyé Gompa (1179–1250)

[203] Your omniscient mind ruled by compassion,
You are immersed in the single taste of others' welfare.
To you, O teachers descended from Maitreya, the Buddha's chief son—
I prostrate with a joyful mind steeped in faith.

I shall present here the essential instruction that opens
The great treasury of goodness that is the source of happiness,
The awakening mind that is the foundation of all Mahayana paths,
The exchanging of self and others, the teaching of all [great] teachers.

The teachings revealed by the perfectly enlightened Buddha—the three turnings of the wheel of Dharma, the twelve branches of sacred scripture, the three scriptural collections, the Great and Lesser Vehicles, and within the Great Vehicle, the Mantra and Perfection vehicles—since these are the very paths realized by himself and taught to others out of great compassion, they are all well-spoken sacred words. The elucidations by Maitreya and others of the intent of these scriptures constitute the commentarial treatises. Two key points constitute the essential subject matter of all these scriptures: to bring about the cessation of self and to cherish others. In terms of vehicles, the first is embodied by the disciples' and self-realized ones' vehicles, while the second encompasses the Great Vehicle.

In terms of implementing these, there are two systems, one based on the Mantra system and the other on the Perfection Vehicle system. For practice of the latter, master Atiśa possessed three traditions. The first was received from Dharmarakṣita, who remained a novice monk, but due to the force of his compassion, gave away parts of his own body by slicing them off. He followed the *Ornament of Sutras*[501] by master Aśvaghoṣa[502] for instructions on reasoning. For scriptural authority, he relied on the *Garland of Three Jewels*.[503] Neither of these works was translated into Tibetan, the master said.

His mode of embarking on the path was by means of the four noble truths; his philosophical view accorded with the Vaibhāṣika of the Disciples' Vehicle. In his tradition of meditation practice, the master said, one practices equalizing self and others right from the start. The teacher did not speak of the lineage of this first tradition.

The second tradition stems from Mañjuśrī and was received from the teacher Maitrīyogi, known as such because he always meditated on loving-kindness *[maitrī]*. He is the junior Kusalī, the one legend says bore the marks when a dog was being beaten with a stick. He relied on the *Ākāśagarbha Sutra*[504] for his scriptural authority, [204] while for his methods of analytic reasoning he followed the *Compendium of Trainings*.[505] His mode of embarking on the path relied on other sutras. His philosophical standpoint accorded with the Sautrāntika school, while his system of meditation is the same as the previous tradition's.

The third tradition stems from Maitreya and came through the teacher Serlingpa. His scriptural authority was the *Teachings of Vimalakirti Sutra*,[506] while his method of analytic reasoning followed *Levels of the Bodhisattva*.[507] His philosophical standpoint shared affinities with even non-Buddhist schools. His mode of embarking on the path was through entering the Perfection Vehicle. In his tradition of meditation practice, one practices exchanging [self and others] right from the start.

Thus, of these three traditions with their distinct lineages, this last tradition stems from Maitreya, and was transmitted from Maitreya to Asaṅga, Vasubandhu, and Sthiramati through to Serlingpa. As for its scriptural sources, the *Teachings of Vimalakirti Sutra* states:

[Egoistic] viewing of the perishable composite is the seed of the tathāgatas.[508]

Further it states:

Even if you generate an egoistic view perceiving the perishable composite the size of a mountain, the awakening mind will still arise, and from it will evolve the enlightened qualities of the Buddha.[509]

As for reasoning, *Levels of the Bodhisattva* states:

> If a bodhisattva departs to a place of solitude and with pure motive and thorough dedication generates interest from the depth of his heart in the diverse objects of giving—vast and immeasurable—and engages in giving them to sentient beings, he will enhance his merit immeasurably with minimal difficulty. This is because a bodhisattva is endowed with great wisdom....[510]

His philosophical affinity with non-Buddhist schools does not suggest that Serlingpa accepts a metaphysical conception of self. Rather it indicates that it is on the basis of innate self[-grasping]—which rouses the fear of suffering in cyclic existence and the recognition of one's mother's great kindness—that thoughts such as loving-kindness arise. This is why the egoistic view perceiving the perishable composite is called the seed of the tathāgatas. When asked why he always wept whenever he thought of his teacher [Serlingpa], Atiśa stated, "What little piece of the good heart I may possess is due the kindness of this teacher."[511]

Embarking on the path by entering the Perfection Vehicle is as follows. First, as a result of exchanging self and others, [205] cultivate familiarity with the method aspects of the path. Once this becomes stable, then practice wisdom. Atiśa's *Lamp for the Path* states:

> Whosoever cultivates wisdom thoroughly
> Through familiarity with the method,
> He will swiftly attain enlightenment,
> [But] not through meditating on no-self alone.[512]

Thus it is the power of the instructions of the Perfection of Wisdom [teachings] that lead you [on the path], the master said.

This [pith instruction] was given by master Atiśa to Geshe Dromtönpa alone and no one else. Dromtönpa asked Atiśa, "How is it that you gave this and that [teachings] to Khu and others, while you are giving this to me?" Atiśa is said to have replied, "Apart from you, I have found no one to whom I could give this." Geshe Dromtönpa, too, did not give this to anyone else other than Potowa, who in turn did not give this to anyone else other than Sharawa and Langri Thangpa.

The great Geshe Chekawa[513] possessed deep devotion to Dharma even from childhood and had received many teachings while still a layman. He became a monk and entered Geshe Chöbar's monastery at Nyal, and there he received many teachings. At Yarlung, he received commentaries on the *Compendium of Higher Knowledge*[514] about seven times from the two Nyek brothers. Together with Geshe Nyek, he listened to Yagepa's teaching on the *Udder*[515] on two separate occasions, but he failed to discover its exact sources. Then he asked Nyalpa Yönten Sherap, a student of Langri Thangpa, what kind of knowledge his spiritual teacher possessed and learned that he possessed mind training. Although Nyalpa was a student [of Langri Thangpa], it appears that he lacked this teaching. So there, at Nyal, he [Chekawa] heard the eight verses of Langri Thangpa's tradition from Nyang Chakshingwa.[516] This, too, caused Chekawa to develop admiration for the Kadam [lineage], the master said.

Chekawa met with Dölpa and Lungmepa and stayed [with them], seeking their guidance, for four years until he reached age thirty. Then Drai Sothangpa asked him to be his resident monk for performing prayers, and there he heard the same eight verses. Chekawa expressed his wish to leave, for he was deeply interested in seeking the Kadam teachings. Sothangpa made a ritual torma and uttered the following: "Now, even if you burn in the Avīci hells, you will not fail to encounter a teacher, or else [it means] I have no blessing power at all." So at the age of thirty-one, Chekawa left for Uru. Though Chekawa admired Langri Thangpa deeply, the latter had already passed away. He made inquiries as to who had the highest spiritual realization, and people said that Nyen's [realization] was the highest. [206] So, planning to visit Langthang Monastery, he sent three servants ahead with his books. They returned with the news that Nyen, the Vinaya master of Bawa, and the sutra master were in disagreement on how to run Langthang Monastery.

"This will not do, then. You three go to Sharawa's seat, Sho, and I will investigate Shang Drakmarwa's place." With this they parted company at Drompa, and Chekawa went to Serwakha. He sold a piece of cloth to the storekeeper at Serthok and stayed there for two months during the winter. In the spring, he departed for Jömo, and in Tsarna he lived on alms for twelve years. Then, as he was intending to depart to Jömo Keru, he encountered many monks from Sharawa selling merchandise. Offering his greetings, he asked them where they were going next, and they replied that they were going to Sho. They acquired a load at Dreurap Monastery and asked Chekawa to stay there while they went on a round of selling merchandise. After their return, they all went to Sho. During that summer *Levels of the Disciple*[517] was being read, and Chekawa listened. Apart from a vague understanding, he did not feel particularly inspired. Thinking that he had not yet discovered all the nooks and corners, he told an attendant who came to bring some provisions, "Since I need to follow after my interests, do not bring the provisions yet. If this teaching [I am looking for] exists here, I will stay; and if not, I must leave." He felt that it was not appropriate to remain wherever his body took him, like dogs and sheep. Yet he was not yet afforded an opportunity to make inquiries.

One day the monks were having a picnic. The spiritual mentor Sharawa was circumambulating the *[Perfection of Wisdom in a] Hundred Thousand Lines*[518] scripture that he had himself transcribed. With a deferential posture, Chekawa approached him and made prostrations. Laying down his cloak [as a seat], he requested, "Please be seated; I have something to ask you."

While counting the beads of his bodhi-seed rosary, Sharawa responded, "What unsettled questions do you have for the teacher?"

By prefacing his questions with the statement that he had heard that Geshe Potowa had something called Mahayana mind training, Chekawa asked, "I am deeply interested in this. There appears to be such a teaching; it helped me when I could not find shelter. At times I could not even begin to apply it. Does this practice constitute a [correct] path?"

Repeatedly showing his rosary and counting its beads, Sharawa said, "This is [certainly] not a question of a path that may be applied or not. If you do not wish to attain buddhahood, that is something else. But as long as you do aspire for it, it is impossible to become fully enlightened without relying on this path. This much is sufficient [to know]." Chekawa said that he felt that Sharawa definitely possessed extraordinary inner experiences. [207]

He then asked, "For those who rely on scriptural authority, are there scriptural citations if some are required? Will the line 'Whatever sufferings sentient beings may have' from *A Guide to the Bodhisattva's Way of Life*[519] be adequate?"

"Who does not accept Nāgārjuna as an authority? In Nāgārjuna's *Precious Garland*, toward the end, are said to be such passages as 'May their negative karma ripen upon me / May all my virtues ripen upon them.'[520] At this point, you must prostrate three times," replied Sharawa.

"Do you have a copy of the *Precious Garland?*" Chekawa asked, to which Sharawa replied that he did. Chekawa opened the text and found it. Sharawa said that earlier he checked but could not find it!

Delighted, Chekawa asked that his provisions be brought there [to

Sharawa's monastery]. He is reputed to have said that he had searched for this [instruction] alone for nine full years, including six years at Gegong. He had endeavored, as the saying goes, to "carry the merchandise around his neck with his moustache."[521]

He said that after leaving Sharawa, he went to Gangma Githok. And even though he stayed there for a very long time, he said that apart from [responses to his] discreet inquiries, he heard in the congregations only allusions [to mind training], such as "Where is the seed? If possible, plant this [tree]." Although those with the capacity to infer could understand this, the others could not even begin to comprehend. This saddened him, but his heart was known to be expansive. At times the congregation would have around two thousand eight hundred monks, but except for the master, all of them failed to detect the meaning. It is said that, for convenience, Sharawa would resort to merely citing the sutra of *Thoroughly Pure Spheres of Conduct*,[522] but he was said to remark that it would be beneficial for this sutra to be taught to more people.

With Chekawa, too, no one was initially aware of [his comprehension]. Later, as he imparted this [teaching] to some lepers, some of those with perfect devotion comprehended it. One told another, and they received the teaching. Thus it acquired the label "leper's teaching." While at his normal residence, Kyormo Lung, Chekawa would carry on his back, with assistance from his younger brother and Belpo Che, a leper woman who had lost her limbs. He gave the lepers food and taught them Dharma. At Lhading, he would cover [the leper woman] and Thöpa Ka with his cloak and let them sit behind him. He also taught methods and instructions for healing leprosy. [For all these reasons, then, mind training] became known as the "leper's teaching."

Chekawa later went to Dre, where he [initially] declared that this is not a teaching to be taught to a congregation, and he taught it discreetly to only a few capable of understanding it. However, he [later] announced that "Since it is not possible to determine who might have realization and who might not, it is not appropriate to expound this teaching only in secret. [208] I will now expound it at congregations to all." Saying this, he taught [mind training] publicly at gatherings.

So this is the uncommon Mahayana path not to be found elsewhere. Among the teachings, none is more profound and vast than this. Even the great spiritual teacher Chekawa sought guidance of nearly eighty teachers until he found this [teaching] through Sharawa. The more teachings and instructions he received, the more he felt "Where can I find some other instruction for the attainment of buddhahood," and thus he never felt completely satisfied. However, upon finding this [instruction] through Sharawa, he felt "This is it: No other teaching anywhere is superior to this," and felt decisive. He is then said to have remarked, "No more salivating for something else, no more urge to listen [to something else]; I feel a sense of relief."

If you possess this [instruction], even though you might appear ordinary to others' eyes, whatever you do can become nothing but a cause for attaining omniscience; everything turns into a great act. [Chekawa] embraced this as his sole heart practice such that even at the threshold of death he would say, "There is no more melodious sound in this world than the sound of mind training. Pray make this sound in my ears." And he would say, "From my childhood, when I first acquired language, I felt no apprehension about taking on others' pain; rather I felt joy. Thus today I experience no discomfort. I experience only visions of the pure land." Thus [even at the moment of death] he entertained the thought of collecting the sufferings of all beings upon himself. When his younger brother pleaded, "Your strength is weak now, so please begin the practice of the meditative absorptions," he recited few words of mind training and said, "Even though my physical strength is weak, I do not see how one can traverse the levels other than through this— [certainly not] through some hodgepodge of practices." This [instruction], then, is the extracted essence of Chekawa's heart practice.

* * *

In the case of the spiritual teacher Chilbu,[523] he first heard this instruction after arriving at Lhading of Gyeng and subsequently practiced it for twenty-four years. During this entire time he persevered by inquiring exclusively about it. In his practice, too, he engaged in this teaching alone from the very start. Whatever situations befell him, such as distractions, he suffered no harm. Chilbu seems to have trained only in this [mind training practice], even without a prayer room, the master said. His realizations also grew each time he repeated the recitation [of the instruction]. Later, he taught it even at large gatherings—at Cheka, Lhading, and many places.

Once, when Chilbu was residing at Gyeng, a monk called Kyeuchung from Chil asked [209], "Great spiritual teacher, although you have many disciples, they tend to have short lives. What is the cause of this? In my opinion, this is because nothing is more profound among the teachings of tantra and Perfection vehicles than this mind training, yet you expound it in public."

The great spiritual teacher responded, "This is true. Nothing is more profound than this. It is not appropriate to teach it in public, but since the master has now departed to far away, and since teaching it only in secret is impractical, it has been taught at gatherings. I am continuing this tradition."

Even during Chilbupa's time, it was given only to those who could please the teachers; one [teaching] was received in detail by Dreksumpa; and to the rest of the teachers and monks, he gave nothing other than this. Even to them, he said, "This is not appropriate for large gatherings. As for me, I was unable to turn down the requests from so-called important people [for the teaching]. However, it should not be taught in congregations. Please take serious note of this."

Given that we all follow in the footsteps of these masters and aspire to turn whatever we do into a cause for omniscience, it is critical that we develop conviction in this uncommon instruction and train our minds.

* * *

By what method do you train for buddhahood according to this [mind training] tradition? At what point in time, and in what manner, should you engage in the training?

This method of training is that of our teacher Buddha Śākyamuni. The *White Lotus of Compassion Sutra* states, for example, that in some remote past, eons in the past equaling the grains of sand on the shores of the river Ganges, was the eon called "Great Retainer." In this eon there was the brahmin Gyatsoi Dül, a minister of the universal monarch Aranemi, who had a son called Samudragarbha. [This son] became fully enlightened and was known as the Tathāgata Ratnagarbha, in whose presence, exhorted by the brahmin Samudra Parag, the eighty brothers of Tathāgata Ratnagarbha and two million disciples of the brahmin generated the awakening mind. They generated the thought to cultivate the buddha fields and made the following aspiration:

"In the degenerate age when there are sentient beings who are difficult to tame and have been abandoned by other brahmins, beings who do not respect their fathers as fathers, their mothers as mothers, and fail to duly honor the monks, the brahmins, and the elders, [210] may we attain full enlightenment at such a time and tame these beings."[524]

Rampopa said, "It is said that [at that moment] the rest of the buddhas cried out in astonishment." Therefore our tradition of training is that of the Buddha from the instant he took birth as the brahmin Gyatsoi Dül.

In addition, the way the Buddha trained throughout all of his previous lives, such as when he pulled a blazing fire carriage, when he made the sacrificial offering as Maitrībala, and when he was born as a tigress, can be all found in the sutras.[525] Although the savior Maitreya preceded Śākyamuni in generating the awakening mind by forty-two eons, that Śākyamuni attained buddhahood earlier is due to his having practiced this [mind training] with perfect joyous effort.

[PART I: THE MAIN PRACTICE]

The mode of engaging this practice that follows has two sections: (I) the trunk-like main practice and (II) the branch practices, which are like its limbs.

The first one [the trunk-like main practice] has three parts:

A. The preliminaries
B. The main practice
C. The concluding mind training methods

[A. The preliminaries]

First, train in the preliminaries.

This refers to:

1. Reflection on the difficulty of obtaining a human existence of leisure and opportunity
2. Reflection on impermanence by means of death
3. Reflection on the defects of cyclic existence

At all times—when first being led, when preparing to engage in the reflections, when plagued by loss of enthusiasm, and when distracted—contemplate these points and be motivated by them.

1. Reflection on the difficulty of obtaining a human existence of leisure and opportunity

The reflection on the difficulty of obtaining a human existence of leisure and opportunity is as follows: "Leisure" means having the leisure to practice Dharma by overcoming the eight types of absence of leisure. The eight are [birth in] the three lower realms and [as] a god of long life [211]—the four [absences] belonging to the nonhuman realms—and being born in a barbarian borderland, with deficient faculties, with wrong views, and in realms where the buddhas do not appear—the four [absences] belonging to the human realm. It is stated:

> The hells, hungry ghosts, and animals,
> Long-life gods, and barbarian lands,
> Where buddhas do not appear, with wrong views,
> And with deficient faculties—these are the eight bereft of leisure.[526]

"Opportunity" refers to the resources for Dharma practice, which include the five personal and the five external conditions. The five personal conditions are (1) being born as a human, (2) being born in a central region, (3) having full sensory faculties, (4) having faith in the objects [of refuge], and (5) having reversible karma. The five external conditions are (1) that the Buddha has appeared in the world, (2) that he has taught the Dharma, (3) that the teachings are still extant, (4) that there are others who follow the teachings, and (5) that a sense of caring exists for those who enter [the teachings]. In addition, Nāgārjuna's "four wheels,"[527] Asaṅga's "eight aspects of perfect fruition,"[528] and Vasubandhu's "seven higher qualities"[529] are all opportunities as well.

Reflection on the difficulty of obtaining this [life of leisure and opportunity] is threefold: from the perspective of (1) its nature and (2) its cause, and (3) by means of an analogy.

First, there are more flies in a pond or a lake than there are humans on this earth. Second, perfect ethical discipline is the cause of a human birth, and those who observe such discipline are extremely rare. Third, sutras such as the *Collection of Flowers*[530] and treatises such as those by Nāgārjuna, use many metaphors, such as the difficulty of a turtle's neck entering into the hole of a yoke. [For example, the *Friendly Letter*] states:

O King, since it is more difficult to obtain a human life than an animal
   life—
More even than for a turtle to meet the hole of a yoke
Floating aimlessly across a vast open ocean—
Please make this life fruitful by practicing sublime Dharma.[531]

And *A Guide to the Bodhisattva's Way of Life* states:

For this reason the Blessed One has stated,
Like a turtle's neck entering the hole
Of a yoke afloat in a vast, open ocean,
So rare is it to find human existence.[532]

And:

The advent of a tathāgata,
The possession of faith and a human life,
And the capacity to practice virtue such as this,
If these are rare indeed, when can one find them?[533]

Also *[Letter to a Student]* states:

That which illuminates the Sugata's path and helps you embark on
   saving beings,
A powerful, couragous spirit found by humans:
Gods, nāgas, or demigods cannot find this path, [212]
Nor can garuḍas, smell-eaters, human-or-what, or belly-crawlers.[534]

And *[A Guide to the Bodhisattva's Way of Life]* states:

This life of leisure and opportunity is so hard to find,
With it you can accomplish the great welfare of beings.
If you fail to reap benefits on the basis of this,
How can such good fortune be found again in the future?[535]

Also it is stated in *Array of Trees* that it is difficult to reverse the eight lacks
of leisure, it is difficult to obtain a human life, and it is also difficult to perfectly obtain all the [types of] leisure without omission.[536] Therefore, since
the difficulty of obtaining this [existence] has been stated in many sutras

and treatises, if you do not practice Dharma at this juncture when you have obtained it, this life of leisure and opportunity will be wasted. [*A Guide to the Bodhisattva's Way of Life* states:]

> Having found such life of leisure,
> If I fail to habituate myself with goodness,
> There is no greater betrayal than this!
> There is nothing more foolish than this![537]

And:

> If having the fortune to do good
> I fail to engage in good deeds,
> When I am thoroughly tormented by suffering
> In the unfortunate realms, what can I do then?[538]

Since such [sentiments] as these have been stated, it is vital that you strive in Dharma practice. *[Letter to a Student]* states:

> With the human life that is so hard to find
>   You can accomplish what you resolutely seek.[539]

Also it has been taught:

> If you can plant the precious seeds of supreme enlightenment—
> The attainment of which brings an end to the ocean of births—
> Who would make such human life bereft of fruit?
> For it far excels the qualities of a wish-fulfilling jewel.[540]

As for Dharma practice, since nothing is more excellent than the awakening mind, you must endeavor in its practice.

2. Reflection on impermanence by means of death

This has three parts:

    a. The certainty of death
    b. The unpredictability of the time of death
    c. The absence of anything that can benefit you at the time of death

a. The certainty of death

This first part is threefold: None who has been born has not died; life is a conditioned phenomenon; and you are certain to die, for life is momentary. The first is [stated in the following]:

> All things born
> Are faced with death.[541]

And *(Dispelling Sorrow)*[542] states: [213]

> Have you ever seen, heard of,
> Or harbored speculations of someone,
> Whether on the earth or in the heavens,
> Who was born but did not die?[543]

Also:

> If even the diamond bodies adorned with
> Major and minor noble marks are transient,
> What question is there of the embodied beings
> Who resemble the coreless banana trees?[544]

Second, because life is a conditioned phenomenon, one is certain to die. This is as follows:

> Even composite conditioned things disintegrate moment by moment;
> They possess the sufferings and afflictions of birth and so on.[545]

And (a discipline scripture) states:

> Is it possible at all that somewhere
> Conditioned things will ever be permanent?
> O Ānanda, lament not with sorrow;
> All conditioned things are transient.[546]

Also:

Alas! All conditioned things are transient:
They are subject to birth and cessation;
Since following birth they cease to exist,
Blissful is their thorough pacification.[547]

Third, because life is a momentary phenomenon, you are certain to die. This
is stated (in *A Guide to the Bodhisattva's Way of Life*):

Even if, like the sun, you are free of sickness,
Possess food, and are devoid of harm,
Life can instantly deceive you;
Our body is like a momentary reflection.[548]

Also (*Letter to a Student* states):

Like the flame of a lamp flickering due to a violent wind,
There is no certainty this life will remain for even an instant....[549]

b. The unpredictability of the time of death

If you still feel that you have sufficient time to avoid [preparing for] this,
contemplate the unpredictability of the time of death. This is threefold: the
body is devoid of essence, no extensions can be added to your life span, and
numerous conditions for death exist.

The first is as follows: Because the body is devoid of an essence—such as
permanence, purity, and so on—there is no time when death will certainly
not occur. (The *Friendly Letter* states:)

The end of the body is dust, decay, and disintegration;
In the end it is impure and devoid of any essence;
So it will fall apart completely and become rotten.
Recognize it as subject to disintegration.[550]

Also:

If by the blazing of seven suns even the earth,
Mount Meru, and the oceans are burned,
And if not even ashes remain of all these things,
What need is there to speak of utterly weak humans?

If life has many adversities and is more transient
Than even water bubbles blown by the wind,
Amazing indeed it is that we inhale after exhaling [214]
And wake up after going to sleep.[551]

(*The Tale of the Seven Maidens* states):

Toward the body that will be cast away,
Like the blade of a grass and the dewdrops on it....[552]

Second, since no extensions can be added to the life span, there is no time when death will certainly not occur. (*The Treasury of Higher Knowledge* states:)

In Kaurava continent the life span is one thousand years;
While in the other two, half is reduced in each case;
Here, there is no certainty [at all about the life span], and eventually
It will be ten years [at most], though it was at first immeasurable.[553]

Third, because there are numerous conditions that can cause death, there is no time when death will certainly not occur. (The *Precious Garland*) states:

There is not a single event
That cannot become a condition for death.[554]

And:

The conditions for death are numerous;
Those that sustain life are few.
Even they, too, are conditions for death.
So please practice Dharma.[555]

Since you cannot be certain about when you will die, it is vital to strive in Dharma practice. (The *Good Signs Sutra* states:)

Who can know that one won't die tomorrow?
So from this very day act as if this is so.
You are certainly not an ally
Of the lord of death and his great army.[556]

Also (*A Guide to the Bodhisattva's Way of Life* states):

> This unpredictable lord of death
> Does not hesitate because you have unfinished business.
> Whether you are ill or well,
> Do not put faith in such a transient life.[557]

c. The absence of anything that can benefit at the time of death

This is threefold: family and friends are of no benefit, material things and possessions are of no benefit, and even one's own body is of no benefit. The first is stated (in *A Guide to the Bodhisattva's Way of Life*):

> Though I lie here on my bed
> Circled by many friends and family,
> It's I alone who must endure
> The agony of the throes of death.[558]

The second, that material possessions are of no benefit, is (as *A Guide to the Bodhisattva's Way of Life* states):

> Even if I obtain vast resources
> And long enjoy happiness,
> Like someone robbed,
> I will leave naked and empty-handed.[559]

And (*The Tale of the Seven Maidens* states):

> The sovereign of land may at home hoard wealth
> Through a thousand different pursuits,
> [Yet] people could squander this [wealth] in an instant;
> Goodness alone is taught to be the [true] path.[560] [215]

Third, the body is also of no benefit. *A Guide to the Bodhisattva's Way of Life* states:

> If even the flesh and bones born with me
> Fall to pieces and disintegrate....[561]

When you fail to understand impermanence in these ways, you will act in the following manner, as (*A Guide to the Bodhisattva's Way of Life* states):

> Due to my failure to appreciate
> That I must depart leaving everything behind,
> For the sake of friendship and enmity
> I've committed all kinds of negative acts.[562]

If you understand impermanence in this manner, as stated in the sutra of *Advice to a King,*[563] you will recognize Dharma as your sole protector, your sole refuge, and your sole ally, and you will thus strive in Dharma practice. Since for Dharma practice, nothing is more excellent than the awakening mind, you will therefore strive to practice it.

3. Reflection on the defects of cyclic existence

Third, the reflection on the defects of cyclic existence is composed of [contemplations on] the defects of the individual realms and [on those of cyclic existence] in general. First is being born in the hells and undergoing suffering. (*Friendly Letter* states):

> Beings who engage in negative acts are born
> In such hells as the reviving, the black-lined,
> The intensely hot, the crushing, the howling, and Avīci—
> [There] they undergo perpetual suffering.[564]

As for their suffering, [it states]:

> However much pain arises here in a day—
> Say three hundred spears were to pierce your hands—
> This cannot rival or match even a portion
> Of the slightest suffering of the hells.[565]

And:

> If even seeing, hearing of, thinking of,
> Reading about, or giving shape to a mere drawing
> Of the hells generates fear, what need is there to speak
> Of the actual experience of the unbearable effects.[566]

You will thus be reduced to desperation by massive suffering. If you are born as a hungry ghost, numerous sufferings are mentioned:

> In the hungry ghost realm, too, you are deprived of your needs;
> The sufferings that arise are constant, with no end in sight.
> Hunger, thirst, cold, heat, exhaustion, and fear
> Arise unbearably; so seek [Dharma practice].[567]

If you are born an animal, its sufferings are stated thus: [216]

> In an animal birth, too, are diverse sufferings:
> Being killed, being bound, being beaten, and so on.
> Extreme, unbearable torments exist for those who have forsaken
> The tranquil virtue [of Dharma], such as one [animal] devouring
>   another.[568]

Even if you are born human, you still remain within the bounds of suffering. [Sufferings] such as the following have been described:

> Humans enjoy no perfect happiness;
> Recognize [human pleasures] as transient, devoid of self, and
>   impure.[569]

Birth as a celestial being, too, is still within the bounds of suffering, such as the [sufferings] stated here:

> In the higher realms, those with great joys
> [Experience] the agony of death and transition even more intensely.
> Knowing this, the well bred do not crave [rebirth in]
> The higher realms, which will come to an end [anyway].
>
> The attractive color of his body will start to change;
> He is revolted by his own cushion, and his flower garlands turn old;
> Bad odor begins to collect in his clothing;
> And his body perspires as never before—
>
> These five signs indicating death in the higher realms
> Occur for the gods residing in the celestial realms;

They parallel the signs that indicate death
For the humans on this earth.[570]

If you are born in the realm of the demigods, as for its sufferings, it is stated:

In the demigod realm, too, you undergo intense mental suffering;
By nature you become hostile toward the prosperity of the gods.
Although endowed with sharp intelligence, [demigods,]
Impeded by the migration defilement, are unable to perceive the
   truth.[571]

Therefore, no matter which of the six realms you are born into, you undergo suffering. It is stated:

Since such is cyclic existence, a birth in the realms
Of gods, humans, hell beings, animals, or hungry ghosts
Is certainly not a good birth, so pray recognize
That birth itself is a gateway to numerous harms.[572]

Second, as for the defects of cyclic existence in general, if you were to describe them in full, it would be beyond expression. It is stated:

Definite are the numerous and diverse pains—
Being deprived of your needs, death, sickness, and aging.
Be disenchanted with cyclic existence, the source of all these;
Recognize samsara's defects, and listen to me.[573]

So with respect to this source of all sufferings, the defects, roughly summarized, are as follows: (1) the defect of being subject to fluctuating highs and lows, (2) the defect of uncertainty, (3) the defect of having to take countless bodies, (4) the defect of being [perpetually] unsatisfied with sensory objects, and (5) the defect of being alone without any companions. [217] First, the defect of being subject to fluctuating highs and lows is [stated] in the following:

Having become Indra, an object worthy of veneration,
You fall back to the earth due to the power of karma.
Even having become a universal monarch,
In this cyclic existence you later become a servant's servant.[574]

The defect of uncertainty is as follows:

> Your father is the son, mother the spouse;
> He who was the enemy is now a friend—
> Everything is reversed, so therefore
> Nothing is definite in cyclic existence.[575]

The defect of having to take countless bodies is as follows:

> The skeletons of our each and every birth
> Together rival and transcend the mass of Mount Meru.[576]

Also (*Dispelling Sorrow* states):

> If you were to collect in a heap your heads
> Severed due to conflicts with others,
> The height of such a mountain would exceed
> The celestial world of the god Brahma![577]

The defects of being unsatisfied with sensory objects are suggested in the following:

> Though each one of us has drunk milk
> Greater in quantity than the four oceans,
> By following the way of the ordinary person,
> You will revolve in samsara and drink even more.[578]

Also:

> Even if *karśapaṇa* coins rain down,
> The greedy will have no contentment.[579]

The defect of being alone and without any companions is as follows (in *A Guide to the Bodhisattva's Way of Life*):

> When you are born, you do so alone;
> And when you die, you do so alone.[580]

There is also the defect of being conceived repeatedly, as stated in the following:

> Even if you were to count beads the size of *kolāsita* nuts,
> The earth will fail to measure the extent of your mothers.[581]

So, in this cycle of existence, no matter where you are born, you are caught within the bounds of suffering.

> All of this is transient and devoid of selfhood.
> Thus bereft of refuge, of savior, and of haven,
> O great personage, be disillusioned by cyclic existence.
> Like a banana tree, it has no essential core.[582]

If you contemplate and understand thus, you will be able to think in the following manner:

> As for the three realms I do not yearn for them, even in my dreams.[583]

If you are able to cultivate the attitude of someone disillusioned by an unfaithful woman, of a bird [disappointed by] a burnt forest, or of a merchant [trapped] in the land of ogresses, you will then engage in Dharma practice, which will liberate you from this [yearning for samsaric existence]. Liberation will never occur on its own, without your practicing Dharma. Nor can someone else undertaking it on your behalf be of any benefit. It is stated:

> Liberation depends upon your own self;
> There is nothing others can do to bring it.
> So through study, reflection, and meditation, [218]
> Pay heed to the four noble truths.[584]

As this states, you need to accomplish [liberation] by yourself alone. Although there are many spiritual practices, none is more excellent than the awakening mind. (*A Guide to the Bodhisattva's Way of Life* states:)

When the awakening mind has arisen in them,
Instantly the wretched—captives in samsara's prison—
Are hailed as children of the sugatas
And revered by the worlds of gods and humans.[585]

And (*Commentary on the Awakening Mind* states):

He who cultivates the awakening mind
For even a single instant—
Even the conquerors cannot measure
The magnitude of his merit.[586]

In particular, nothing is more excellent than the exchanging of self and others. (*A Guide to the Bodhisattva's Way of Life* states:)

He who wishes to quickly rescue
Both himself and others
Should practice the secret instruction:
The exchanging of self and others.[587]

If this is so, one might ask, are not Hevajra,[588] great seal,[589] or emptiness more excellent? Once in India, a Hevajra yogi once attained the "stream enterer's" stage, reportedly prompting Atiśa to remark: "This is not too bad an outcome. At its worst, his practice could have gone [totally] wrong." Potowa made similar statements, which vexed some people; they [subsequently] asked Chengawa if Atiśa did in fact make such statements.

Chengawa replied, "Of course it's true. Without awakening mind, Hevajra meditation can lead to the hells. It can lead you to the realm of the hungry ghosts and to the animal realm. Without the awakening mind, it can become a condition for these [types of birth]. Emptiness, too, is a causal condition for all states, from the hells to the state of the self-realized ones. The awakening mind, on the other hand, never turns into something else. Since it brings about all the characteristics of buddhahood, it is like a seed. Like the father's seed, it is the unique cause of buddhahood and can therefore never become otherwise."[590] Many excellent benefits such as these have been described.

Therefore no spiritual practice is more excellent than this. Other spiritual practices might become remedies if, as a result of deliberate thought

processes, they arise in your mental continuum. In contrast, by mere recollection of its name this [awakening mind] can turn into a remedy. You
proceed with joy, and you do not stray into [the paths of] disciples and
self-realized ones. Rather, your activities become a bodhisattva's magnificent
deeds.

Since it is not possible to have the initial desire to reflect on this mind, be
inspired by it, and uphold it without contemplating the preliminary practices, you must first appreciate the difficulty of obtaining a human life of
leisure and opportunity and [219] recognize its impermanence through its
susceptibility to disintegration. Following death, you do not become nothing; you have to take birth and this, too, you do through karma. With negative karma you are born in the lower realms, where all the corresponding
sufferings befall [you]. With positive karma, although you attain the state of
gods and humans, you are still caught within the bounds of suffering. Since
the awakening mind arises from seeing as unbearable the desperate suffering
condition of all beings of cyclic existence—beings who are all kind and dear
mothers—all the lower stages of the path are preliminaries [to developing
the awakening mind].

[B. The main practice]

So what is the main practice that you must undertake? This is presented in
the following line:

> For the main practice, train alternately in giving and taking.

Without taking, a practice does not constitute an exchange, and without
giving, your accumulations cannot be accomplished. Thus there are both
giving and taking.[591] This is what is meant by the following:

> Should practice the secret instruction:
> The exchanging of self and others.[592]

As explained before, although some traditions have you first meditate on
the two selflessnesses and then engage in this practice [of the awakening
mind], here we have the tradition of the teacher Serlingpa. According to
this, you begin practicing [the awakening mind] when you [still] possess
self-grasping [undiminished]. Among the two—giving and taking—you

first practice taking. There are various suggestions for the object of practice, such as the recommendation that you focus [first] on an enemy or someone you dislike, the understanding being similar to the idea that if you can defeat the most powerful opponent, you will then be able to defeat all of them. Master Kamalaśīla, on the other hand, says you should begin by focusing on an ordinary person.[593] Atiśa's standpoint, however, is to begin your [taking] meditation with your real-life mother, because that is easier to cultivate. With respect to the immeasurable motivating thoughts, Kamalaśīla's recommends proceeding from the cultivation of the equanimity that is like the ease of drawing water into a ground well leveled.[594] There is also the approach whose root is the glorious *Fortunate Era Sutra*[595] in which you proceed from compassion. Atiśa's standpoint is to proceed from the practice of loving-kindness.

[TAKING]

For this, contemplate in the following way: Right at the start, if your real-life mother is alive, visualize her at her actual present location. If she is not alive, [220] visualize her in front of you. Reflecting upon her kindness in this and previous lives, generate feelings of closeness, intimacy, and endearment, and then cultivate the thought "How I wish my dear mother were endowed with happiness. I will lead her to happiness. I will gather for her all benefits and happiness." Thus, from the depth of your heart, you cultivate clearly and earnestly the thought of loving-kindness.

"Although she desires happiness, she is caught within the bounds of suffering. How I wish she were free from suffering and its causes. I will endeavor to free her from all suffering." Thinking thus, cultivate compassion. It is said that the great Naljorpa stated that if you have no memory of your mother, you can visualize your uncle or whoever has extended you the greatest kindness.[596] This is similar to what Neusurpa[597] said about Geshe Ngaripa's[598] focusing on his aunt in his efforts to absorb this [thought] into his heart.

Motivated by such a thought, you take upon yourself the suffering and its origin that are present in your mother's mental continuum. *Resultant suffering* is suffering such as that subsumed into the eight or three categories that obstruct the attainment of enlightenment—from the suffering of birth, aging, sickness, and death to coldness, being fried and burnt, hunger and thirst, and so on. Imagine that such sufferings are sliced off, as if by a sharp razor, from your mother's mental continuum and are then placed at the center of your heart. In other words, do not merely leave them nearby as if you are making sure that they do not befall you. Rather than simply leaving them on another part of your body, take them into the very kernel of your heart. Take them unconditionally and with no expectation of benefit for yourself.

Karma and mental afflictions are the cause, or origin, [of suffering]. Of these, karma as origin is composed of the ten nonvirtuous actions, the five heinous acts, the five approximations, and the four conditions of downfall, such as transgressing the three [sets of] vows you have taken, which propels you to the hells like the shooting of an arrow. Afflictions as origin include the three poisons or the six primary afflictions, the twenty derivative afflictions, the eighty-four thousand afflictions, and the million permutations that are mentioned, such as those to be eliminated on the path of seeing and on the path of meditation—take all of these. You thus take all the objects to be relinquished below [the level of] the diamondlike [meditative absorption]. Thus by freeing [your mother] of all objects to be relinquished—such as suffering and its origin, and the two defilements together with their residual imprints—imagine that she attains buddhahood. [221] Then extend this to your father, to your siblings and so on, such as those close and related, and from your neighbors to the entire trichiliocosm. As for the boundary [of this visualization], this is as found in the hidden teachings.[599]

Then, as the line "Generate this by drawing parallels to [the metaphor of the earth] being filled with mustard seeds"[600] indicates, you should contemplate in the following manner: If the entire trichiliocosm is filled with mustard seeds, and if each trichiliocosmic world in the east is equivalent to a single mustard seed, mustard seeds will become exhausted, yet the trichiliocosmic worlds in the east would not be exhausted. You should extend this [same calculation] to all the ten directions and then practice [taking] in relation to all sentient beings, extending to the limits of space.

Then turn to the three lower realms. With regard to the suffering of the hells, take those sufferings that arise from fire, weapons, illness, thoughts, and from the blistering hell up to the greatly cracking-open-like-lotus hell. In terms of the origin of that suffering, take the afflictions, such as hatred, and also all acts of grave negative deeds. Take from the hungry ghosts all their sufferings of hunger and thirst and their afflictions, such as attachment, and all their middling negative deeds. Take from the animals their suffering of one devouring another, their afflictions such as delusion, and all their lower-level negative deeds. Of the higher realms, take from the humans their birth, aging, sickness, and death; from the gods of the desire realm take their portents of death and so on; and from the two higher states[601] take their death, transition, descent, and so on.

Sometimes, you should meditate in relation to [the entire] spectrum of sentient beings, and other times, you should take from each class of beings separately, and then, too, from each individual being. Without this [kind of approach], your practice will remain superficial and ineffective. At times you should focus simultaneously on all sentient beings equal to the limit of space; if you fail, your attitude will lack a firm grounding. At times, you can imagine your body in each of the hell realms and through this do the taking. You should sometimes take all the sufferings upon this single body. Sometimes, as explained before, proceed taking from the grosser; yet at other times, you can take whatever you might perceive. On other occasions, focus on those for whom you may harbor the feeling "I don't need to extend [my practice of taking] to them at all." At times, you should take those of the hell beings; and from the self-realized ones[602] to the bodhisattvas. Take from each and every being until their buddhahood—that is, from the hell beings through to the hungry ghosts, from there to the animals, to the humans, from there to the six classes of gods of the desire realm, then to the seventeen levels of the form realm, then to the four levels of the formless realm, then from disciples and self-realized ones and, in their respective sequence, from the bodhisattvas on the ten levels. [222]

At times, you should take the afflictions by distinguishing them each individually; at other times, you should take karma; and at other times, you should take the sufferings by distinguishing them individually. At times, you should take all the forces opposing the path, from grasping at permanence to grasping at substantial reality [of things], and so on. At others, you should take the forces opposing the six perfections, such as miserliness. At yet other times, take all the forces opposing the factors of enlightenment, such as grasping at purity [of phenomena]. At others, take the forces opposing the ten bodhisattva grounds. Sometimes you should take the various distorted conceptions up to all afflictive obscurations, such as those to be eliminated on the paths of seeing and of meditation. Yet at others, you should take all obscurations to knowledge, such as the four-times-nine equals thirty-six conceptions[603] to the subtle concepts.

As a result of pursuing various avenues for contemplation, you will enjoy the following benefits: You no longer become disheartened, you achieve ascertainment and arrive at your goal, your mind becomes susceptible to training, and you achieve a breadth of learning. As a by-product, the other aspects of Dharma practice [also] become present [in your mind]—including even [the knowledge of] their enumeration—much negative karma is purified, and the conditions for perfecting a great accumulation of merit come about.

Since [taking] does not come about by viewing others as enemies or as ordinary beings, you view them as your kind mothers. This is not a case of viewing someone who is not a mother as a mother. Rather, it is viewing those who have been your mothers since beginingless time as mothers. Through the impetus of such a clear and palpable loving-kindness and compassion, you take from them [their sufferings and so on].

Is there something to be taken from the two noble ones, disciples and self-realized ones? Yes. [In general,] all phenomena that share the nature of dependence are [in the nature of] suffering; these [noble ones] have fear toward cyclic existence; also since their aggregates are [in the nature of] suffering, [they possess] resultant sufferings. Furthermore, it is maintained that except for the aggregates of arhats, suffering and its origin pervade the same domain.[604]

Also, as the line "Conceptualizations are the afflictions of the bodhisattva"[605] indicates, the higher [Buddhist schools of thought] maintain that conceptual thoughts are afflictions, and that [bodhisattvas] possess obscurations to knowledge. Alternatively, you can take the remaining objects to be relinquished, those present primarily on the path of accumulation up to the subtle obscurations to knowledge—such as those on the ten levels—which resemble the progressive releasing of chains within a prison. Take these too in their respective order, from the five paths, the ten levels, and the four states of fruition.[606] As before, at times take from them individually, and at others, take from them simultaneously.

You might entertain the thought "If these are taken, [sentient beings] will then be placed in the state of buddhahood. Is this not presumptuous? [223] Given that I myself am not free from bondage, how could I possibly achieve this?"

Since you took a pledge at the time you generated the awakening mind, you cannot shy away from this task. How have you taken the pledge? By stating "I will liberate those beings not yet liberated," you vowed to free all beings from the suffering of cyclic existence and lead them to the first bodhisattva level. By stating "I will release those not released," you vowed to release them from the bondage of grasping at signs and to place them on the seventh bodhisattva level. By stating "I will give relief to those unrelieved," you vowed to place them on the three resultant levels, beginning with the eighth bodhisattva level, as if navigating a ship across an ocean. By stating "I will thoroughly take beyond sorrow those who have not transcended sorrow," you vowed to help even those who are abiding in the diamondlike [meditative absorption]—the last stage of the continuum—to transcend "sorrow." This refers to the obscuration to knowledge—slight imprints of grasping at real entities. Practice in this manner, the master taught.

The following is the way to practice taking in general: In particular, you should take upon yourself this very instant all the harms that can be seen, heard of, and so on. This includes the loss of lives and property due to conflicts; grave illness, such as from epidemics; leprosy; the death of dzos and bulls for those engaged in [animal] trade in the hope of making a profit; the aging of cattle such that they can no longer be put to work; being reduced to something like a rotten carcass of a dead dog as a result of losing monastic vows; not meeting [with loved ones]; harm from humans and nonhumans; deficient faith, intelligence, and so on; not understanding the teachings however many times they are heard; inability to undertake the reflections; an increase in attachment, anger, and so on; being bullied by father, siblings, or equals because of a humble demeanor; and so on. Take all of these occurrences and the fear of these occurrences; [in addition] take upon yourself excessive desires; being at haunted places; contamination by corpses or the fear of being stained by impurities; bad dreams, negative signs, and portents; and the fear of being a victim of others' spells, harmful magic, expulsion rites, and rites of exorcism; and so on. When you take these, do so without expecting any reward for yourself. [224]

You should then train the mind by taking upon yourself all the negative aspects of the external environment, such as terrifying gorges, high cliffs, and thorns. Take the unappealing forms, unmelodious sounds, unpleasant odors, and so on and imagine them to be appealing forms and so on. In brief, take upon yourself all the defects of the environment and beings within, with the exception of the buddhas and your spiritual teachers. The buddhas have eliminated all defects and have perfected all higher qualities.

I asked [my teacher], "Although no taking is to be done in relation to my spiritual teacher, can I take his old age, his weakening physical strength, and so on, which are real in relation to the perspective of ordinary beings?" I was told that it is inappropriate to think in such terms. Since in all the teachings he is described as no different from the buddhas, you must not practice taking [in relation to the spiritual teacher], he said. This is, then, [the practice of] taking.

[GIVING]
Without [practicing] giving, your accumulations will be incomplete. It is more important than the practice of taking. [*A Guide to the Bodhisattva's Way of Life* states:]

> My body and my material resources
> And my virtue engendered in the three times—
> Without reserve I will give these away
> To fulfill the wishes of all beings.[607]

[In *A Guide to the Bodhisattva's Way of Life*] the giving of these three [factors], the awakening mind that exchanges self and others, and the going to the hells for the sake of sentient beings and most practices are mentioned. However, there is no systematic presentation [of these practices], such when such and such should be practiced at such and such time, and so on.

As you give your body, wealth, and roots of virtue, imagine that sentient beings receive the causes and conditions of buddhahood and attain full enlightenment. When you give your body in this context, you cannot give the past; it is the present and all future bodies you are likely to obtain that you give. Three [methods], however, are prohibited: Giving [your body] while visualizing yourself as a meditation deity, giving it [conceived] as ordinary flesh and blood, and imagining that your giving uses it up. The first, giving it while visualizing yourself as a deity, shows disrespect for the deities. It also breaks a root precept. In the best case—for those who understand all beings as deities—there is no fault, for it is like dissolving deities into deities. Regarding the second [prohibition], some proceed in the manner of "Those who desire flesh take away my flesh" and so on, but this is inappropriate. It is not permitted in general, and moreover, some [recipients would] dislike this. You must also not give by visualizing the body as poison or as a weapon, for these are harmful to sentient beings, the exception being when they [poisons and weapons] can be conditions for benefit and happiness [for others]. [225]

So in what manner should you give? *Array of Trees Sutra* states:

> May my body become a wish-fulfilling jewel, a source of daily
> sustenance for all beings.[608]

Or the *Dedications of Vajradhvaja Sutra* states:

> Just as the four great elements sustain all sentient beings through
> diverse avenues, diverse manifestations, and diverse ways, in the
> same way may the bodhisattva's body, too, be transformed into a
> source of daily sustenance for all beings.[609]

And *A Guide to the Bodhisattva's Way of Life* states:

> To fulfill the needs of all beings,
> May my body become a wish-fulfilling jewel.[610]

Thus you give your body by transforming it into a wish-fulfilling jewel (that
is, by imagining your body, your resources, and your virtues as wish-fulfilling
jewels). It is not necessary to visualize [your body's] color, shape, and so on;
the point is rather to grant whatever is desired.

In the procedure for giving, you first visualize in your presence your real-
life mother. As you give [your body] to her, imagine that she attains faith,
ethical discipline, joyous effort, wisdom, the awakening mind, and so on,
which are the substantial causes for attaining buddhahood. In terms of contributory conditions, imagine that she encounters a spiritual teacher and the
scriptures, obtains all (external and internal conditions), such as food, clothing, and so on, and that she becomes fully enlightened. Then extend this to
your father and so on, to all sentient beings pervading the reaches of space.
As you give [to the beings] in the three lower realms, to the disciples, to the
self-realized ones, and to the bodhisattvas on the ten levels, imagine they
attain complete enlightenment.

Also, just as from one wish-fulfilling jewel emerge whatever things sentient beings may desire, such as food, clothing, and so on, in the same manner imagine that from your single body emerge—for sentient beings equal to
the limit of space—food, clothing, shelter, bed, country, farmland, friends
and family, servants, work animals, and so on, all the elements of mundane
happiness. Imagine that from it also emerge preceptors, instructors, and the
scriptures and so on—the causes and effects of supramundane happiness.
Also, just as the wish-fulfilling jewel grants the wishes of sentient beings
through its many manifestations, such as the king of jewels, imagine that,
in the same manner, your body appears in front of each and every sentient
being [226] and, as before, (whatever is wished for by each being comes

about and that they become fully enlightened). Then visualize your body appearing in front of each sentient being as composed of corporeality, as natural elements like water, and so on. Give [your body] away in its entirety at times; and at other times, give it away as if dissecting its individual parts—the head, the legs, the hands, and so on.

Again, as before, take [upon yourself] the despair wrought by suffering and all negative omens and give your body and imagine that sentient beings achieve happiness and experience positive omens. Eventually, by training your mind through such thought processes, your mind training will no longer be a combative act, as if slaying Māra, and you will be free of despair, fear, and apprehension, even when encountering situations where no escape is possible. As you practice giving to the external environment, imagine that the external world turns into pure realms, such as the Blissful or the Lotus-like,[611] where the golden ground is decorated with patterns of lapis lazuli and other [precious stones]. This is what the scriptures refer to as cultivating the buddha fields,[612] the master said.

Giving can be extended to spiritual teachers and buddhas as well. Thus, as you visualize unimaginable multitudes of offering clouds [to these holy beings], as described in the preface to the *Flower Ornament Scripture*,[613] imagine that all their aspirations are fulfilled and that all their enlightening activities flourish, are enhanced, and become pristinely pure. As you give to the disciples, the self-realized ones, and the bodhisattvas, they overcome their remaining objects to be relinquished, perfect their two accumulations, and become fully enlightened. Imagine that these offering clouds help them realize whatever aspirations they may have.

The giving of resources refers to horses, elephants, grains, jewels, food and clothing, land, houses, retinues, servants, and so on—all that you may possess. You should not give things that do not belong to you, for this would constitute stealing. Forests, flowers, precious jewels, and so on, which are not owned by any specific individual and which are the results of the collective karma of sentient beings, belong to you as well. So these can be given. Beings who inhabit [the environment], because they are owned by their own selves, should not be given. This is like the saying that even when offering music [for instance, offering a melodious song of a goose] it is the goose's sound that is being offered, [227] but the goose's body is owned by the goose herself. This is relevant to those with weaker mental faculties. Those with higher mental faculties and those who are free from bondage to self-centeredness, however, can give other beings for the benefit of others. This is similar to your meditation deity and teacher offering a multitude of non-humans to the Three Jewels and binding the nonhumans with pledges. Also, a servant who utilizes the resources of the master out of concern for the accomplishment of the master's own objectives garners no fault.

Philosophically speaking, if in accordance with the Disciples' school you understand all appearances to be the fruits of your own mental afflictions, then nothing that is being given [truly belongs] to others. Therefore everything can be given. If, in accordance with the Mind-only school, you recognize that it is your own consciousness that manifests as external reality, again nothing that is [truly] others' is being given away. Thus everything can be given. The follower of the Middle Way can give by recognizing [all things] as illusionlike; for the perception as separate of self and others, which are nondual, is false.

This analysis of what is or is not an appropriate resource to be given is relevant to the mind of an ordinary person. Once you attain a deeper understanding of the teachings, you can freely give everything that is an object of your six sense faculties. For each [type of] phenomenon—for example, form—there are three: attractive, unattractive, and neutral. And with relation to each of these [three], the [fields of] five or six sensory experiences are present. Giving the attractive gives rise to joy, and giving the unattractive provides the condition for disillusionment. Also, within each object such as form, the [fields of] five or six sensory experiences are complete. Thus you give, from among the objects of your eyes, such things as colors, shapes, and so on, [up through the other sense objects] to the characteristics of phenomena, which are objects of the mental faculty. In each case, you can give an incalculable variety of forms, an incalculable variety of sounds—that of drums, conches, and so on—as described in the sixth dedication of Vajradhvaja.[614] Imagine that immeasurable resources of both the mundane and supermundane levels arise from each of these; thus all the conditions for attaining buddhahood emerge, and [sentient beings] become fully enlightened.

To relate this to each individual trainee, imagine that each sentient being who desires wealth experiences receiving wealth; that is, they experience obtaining whatever they wish for, such as food and clothing, houses, grain, horses, elephants, countries, farms, parents, friends, relatives, retinues, subjects, absence of illness, freedom from malevolent forces, and so on. They also experience obtaining things they desire—places of worship, [228] monasteries, colleagues, scriptures, objects of veneration, articles for offering, and so on.

Imagine that they experience obtaining whatever they aspire to, whatever they have interest in, whatever helps tame them, such as the human life of leisure and opportunity as the basis for practice, the seven noble riches—faith and so on—the three higher trainings, the stages of the path such as impermanence, the four immeasurable thoughts, the two awakening minds, the practice of the six perfections, the four means to attract others, the thirty-seven limbs of the path to enlightenment, the various levels of vows, the four classes of tantra, the enlightened activities, and the characteristics and qualities of the buddhas. Imagine that all of these become conditions for attaining buddhahood and that all sentient beings become fully enlightened. You should apply this same contemplation to other sense objects, from sound to mental objects, both in general and in specific instances—even when giving a single morsel of dough.

In general, regarding offerings to the teachers and the Three Jewels, it is stated:

> Recognizing three types of forms,
> Offer them to all meditation deities.[615]

You can offer all three in the same manner as before. Specifically, imagine each object—material possessions, land, houses, food, clothing, bedding, cushions, and so on—to be immeasurable, that in each are present all five [or six fields of experience], and of immeasurable quantity within each of the [sense] objects. For example, imagine that a butterlamp's illumination radiates beams of precious jewels in all the buddha fields, the sound of the burning wick produces music, [the butterlamp's] odor emits the perfume of incense, its taste becomes food, and its texture becomes garments, and that all of these arise without interruption and immeasurably. Offer these in accord with their respective sensory functions. Also, you should give (your body and resources), for which you may have attachment (as nonattachment is a virtue) and from which you find it difficult to part. In truth, you should give away everything except the three robes.[616]

As for virtues, you should give those of all three times. *A Guide to the Bodhisattva's Way of Life* states:

> The virtues engendered in all three times,[617]

And Nāgārjuna states:

Both what I have done and not done,
The virtues...[618]

Also the commentary on *Eight Thousand Verses* states that you should dedicate the virtue of the three occasions.[619] To illustrate, by giving the roots of virtue derived from offering food, [imagine that] sentient beings are no longer attached to food; finding the food of ambrosia, sentient beings obtain nourishing wisdom endowed with supreme flavor. By giving the roots of virtue [acquired] through offering drink, sentient beings are no longer attached to any taste; they no longer grasp at signs, [229] and they become sated with the unsurpassed bliss and power of Dharma practice. In this manner, as described in the sixth dedication of Vajradhvaja, you should give bedding, cushions, and so on [as well].[620]

The *Questions of Gaganagañja Sutra* states:

Whatever roots of virtue I may possess and whatever expertise in Dharma I may have, may none not turn into an everyday source of sustenance for all sentient beings.[621]

Similarly, as described in the first dedication of Vajradhvaja, in the *Bodhisattva Levels,* in the *Precious Garland,* and in *A Guide to the Bodhisattva's Way of Life,* imagine that all the virtues within your mental states—from a momentary arising of faith to the powerful realization of the awakening mind—all your practical implementations [of Dharma]—from giving a morsel of dough to an animal up to the four means of attracting others—your three categories of merit, and each and every instance of your virtue belonging to the contaminated and uncontaminated classes, produce for sentient beings whatever they wish. Gathering all the conditions of buddhahood, they become fully enlightened. During this process, you should give each sentient being your body, your material resources, and your roots of virtue, each in their entirety. Since this alone will not take you anywhere, you must give the three [body, resources, and virtues] of the buddhas and the bodhisattvas of all three times, as well as those of your teachers, including their entire lineage. If you wonder whether it is appropriate to give these, it is so. [These sublime beings] have relinquished self-grasping, and when they first generated the awakening mind, they dedicated everything to sentient beings.

Imagine transforming these [bodies, resources, and roots of virtue] into wish-fulfilling jewels. Among objects for giving, these are immeasurable. For they include the set of one hundred and twelve qualities[622] possessed by bodhisattvas on the first level up to the level of the Buddha, where within a single instant, immeasurable enlightened activities occur. Even a person in the lineage of the bodhisattvas who first generates the awakening mind acquires merit so immeasurable that it cannot be contained within the expanse of space. Furthermore, [the scriptures] speak of the immeasurable merits that are necessary to [attain the physical qualities of the Buddha], such as the pores of the Buddha's body or the major and minor noble marks. Since giving has immeasurable factors, and since all the conditions for bringing about the welfare of sentient beings will be complete, your accumulations will be perfected; you will experience no difficulty in working for others' welfare; and you will help fulfill the noble aspirations [of the buddhas], the master said.

In the giving of all three, you can do so in a gradual sequence or all at once. [The sequential approach is] from your real-life mother to all sentient beings [230] or from the Avīci hells to the stage of the buddhas. You can also imagine that all three—body, resources, and so on—arise from each one; you can give by giving all three each in their entirety; or you can multiply the body and so on and give to each sentient being individually, [thinking] that this alone causes sentient beings to become satiated, just as you have done with relation to [the meditation on] taking.

If you wonder, "Even if I contemplate along these lines, since others do not [actually] receive these gifts, there is no benefit," it has been stated:

Be not concerned, but train in the various ways;
Analogies such as the seven shallow crossings abound.[623]

Or:

The more a person analyzes a fact,
Because of the thought abiding upon it,
The more his mind will rest on that fact.[624]

Furthermore:

Even if you have no capacity to perform altruistic deeds,
Always cultivate the thought to do so.
For whoever has the intention
Will actually engage in the deeds.[625]

Train your mind in such manner. Since you are [at present] in the phase of experiencing by means of imagination, train on the level of imagination. Subsequently your mind will be so immersed in the [altruistic deeds] that you will then engage in the actual acts. After attaining [a bodhisattva] level, you will possess one hundred and twelve qualities and engage in fulfilling others' welfare through such deeds as giving away your head, legs, hands, and so on. After you become fully enlightened and attain inconceivable enlightened qualities, your altruistic deeds will no longer require any exertion and will become uninterrupted. Through training in such causes, all the enlightened qualities and the enlightened activities will come about. (The *Thorough Exposition of Valid Cognition* states:)

> From the gathering of causes, effects arise.[626]

And:

> Effects follow from causes.[627]

In accordance with commensurate causes, effects arise, while effects arising in the absence of causes are like sky flowers.[628]

If you possess this [practice of giving and taking], it serves every purpose—view, action, meditation, as well as the three fruits.[629] It is like the white medicine that is a remedy for all sicknesses. Since from this very moment you can implement everything into actual practice—from the deeds of a bodhisattva who has attained [a bodhisattva] level up to the enlightened activities of the Buddha—there is no greater teaching than this [giving and taking], the master said. This alone is the main practice.

Since training in either element alone may lead to discouragement, it has been taught that you must "train" or practice "the two alternately." [231] Within each meditation session, you intersperse taking the suffering and its origin of all sentient beings into the very kernel of your heart with giving your body, resources, and roots of virtue to them.

This should proceed, as explained before, from reflecting on your real-life mother and so on with [the two elements] in alternation. (At times, you should proceed toward all beings in a gradual sequence; at others, you should focus on beings with [strong] negative karma, and sometimes on only those ridden with afflictions. Sometimes you should practice taking in the first instant and giving in the second instant.) If you conduct yourself like this, your mind will become receptive to training, your thoughts will focus on the intended purpose, and the bones of your effort will touch your aims.[630] When this condition is met, you will have no difficulty accomplishing the accumulations and purifying the obscurations. No matter how much negative karma you may have, like the fire at the end of the universe annihilating a bird's carcass with no trace of flesh left behind, these too will disappear without a trace. Due to the diverse inclinations and aptitudes of sentient beings, some, merely by hearing about this, might develop the thought "Ah, this is the most appropriate cause [to cultivate] to achieve buddhahood," and engage in it with great joy. Others, reacting with the thought "Such thought processes are ridiculous," may have no admiration for this [practice] and may in fact experience fear and apprehension toward it. There is no certainty with respect to [beings' reactions].

Of course, you cannot accomplish this [training] by simply following your own whims. You need to train decisively using such factors as your teacher's instructions and extensive merit, and through such forces as faith, joyous effort, and wisdom, reversing as well your negative traits and so on. Pursuing this as a mere obligation will not lead to success on the path; you need to train with great effort and courage. Rejoice at times for the opportunity to engage in the deeds of the bodhisattvas on the ten levels. At others, pray to realize this [giving and taking] in your mental continuum. Purify the obscurations that deflate your enthusiasm for its practice and impede its realization in your mental continuum. Accumulate its conducive factors—the merit—appeal for intervention from the doctrine protectors, make aspiration prayers, read and listen to only those texts that pertain to this practice, and associate only with friends who engage in this practice. Do not associate with those who would advise you against this practice or with those who say "but...." Engage in this meditation therefore by bringing all the parts together on the very cushion where you undertake your Dharma practice.

Where are such practices described? All the scriptures describe them— the sutras, the tantras, and the commentarial treatises. In the liberating story of Maṇibhadra in the *Flower Ornament Scripture,* for example, it states:

> I yearn for the sufferings of all sentient beings to befall me. I will transform myself into a form that is the source of everyday sustenance for all beings.[631] [232]

Thus the two—giving and taking—are mentioned. In the *Aspiration Prayers for Supreme Conduct* it states:

Be they the sufferings of hell beings, of animals, and of yamas,
Of the animal realms, and the sufferings of humans—
Countless aggregates, the suffering of all beings;
May they fall upon me, and may others enjoy happiness.[632]

Also *The Aspiration Prayers of Granting the Gift of Loving-kindness* states:

Below the peak of existence and above the Avīci hells
are countless world systems;
Gods, demigods, and the great belly-crawlers—
May they enjoy happiness, for I will take their sufferings.[633]

Also master Nāgārjuna states:

May their negative karma sprout upon me;
May all my positive karma ripen upon them.[634]

Master Śāntideva, too, states:

I will equalize self and others
And exchange self and others.[635]

And:

Recognizing myself as flawed
And others as an ocean of virtues,
I will thoroughly discard self-grasping
And practice cherishing others.[636]

And:

He who wishes to quickly rescue
Both himself and others
Should practice the secret instruction:
The exchange of self and others.[637]

And:

If I fail to thoroughly exchange
My own happiness with others' suffering,
I will not become a buddha,
And even in samsara there will be no joy.[638]

And:

> So, to assuage my own injuries
> And to allay the suffering of others,
> I will devote myself to others
> And protect others as myself.[639]

And:

> Whatever sufferings there are of others,
> May all of them fall upon me.[640]

The most holy Maitreya, too, states in his *Ornament of Mahayana Sutras:*

> Having found the path equalizing self and others
> And the beauty of cherishing others more than oneself,
> What, then, is one's own interest? What is others' interest?[641]

Also:

> As much as the compassionate endure for others' sake
> The intense pain of unbearable suffering,
> That much do they also, having endured the world's agony,
> Engage others, even their enemies, with intense caring.[642]

Master Aśvaghoṣa's *Seventy Stanzas of Aspiration* states:

> Beings bewildered by poisonous afflictions, [233]
> Whatever nonvirtues such beings may possess,
> For their sake I will joyfully descend alone
> Into the hells in whatever way I can.
>
> Sated with blissful calming nectar,
> May their minds be fused with joy;
> Whatever sufferings beings have,
> May I voluntarily embrace them.[643]

Master Vasubandhu states in his *A Discussion of Merit Accumulation:*

> As for my body, life, and so on,
> I will give these to all sentient beings;

Toward all beings I will extend
Thoughts of loving-kindness and compassion.

I yearn to experience in my own mind
the fruition of all negative karma;
I rejoice in all meritorious deeds
And contemplate the greatness of the buddhas.[644]

And:

As for my body and life
I will give them mentally by following my thought.[645]

And:

May all negative karma of living beings
Be realized upon me;
I will take their nonvirtues;
I will take those from the destitute beings.[646]

And:

I will view all others as my own self
And my own self as the other.[647]

Master Asaṅga also makes similar statements in his *Bodhisattva Levels*. Also the *Extensive Daily Confessions of Cakrasaṃvara [Practice]* states:

May the sufferings of all beings ripen upon me;
Through my virtues may they all achieve happiness;
May my three doors become throughout all lives
A precious jewel, an excellent vase, and a wish-fulfilling tree.[648]

Numerous statements such as these have been made.

Again you might wonder, "Beings described as not likely to attain buddhahood—such as those who lack buddha nature, the disciples, and the self-realized ones—surely they cannot be led to buddhahood."

This has been stated for the benefit of the feeble-minded. In reality, it is inconceivable that they cannot be led to buddhahood. So when engaging mind training [practices] such as this, do so with deep conviction and certainty. It has been stated:

The tathāgata essence permeates all beings;
So generate the vast mind that is most excellent;
Since all beings without exception are causes of buddhahood,
No sentient being is not a [receptive] vessel.[649]

Also it has been stated:

Since no distinctions exist within the ultimate expanse,
Differences of lineage are untenable.[650]

And:

Although no difference exists
in the suchness of all beings,
Through its purification one becomes a tathāgata; [234]
All beings are endowed so with this essence.[651]

Also it has been stated:

The buddha bodies radiate to all;
There are no distinctions in suchness;
There are natural lineages; thus all beings are
Endowed always with the essence of buddhahood.[652]

As stated in these lines, you must direct your contemplation toward all beings, especially those beings who indulge in such negative acts as the ten negative actions, and the five heinous acts, and [among the five heinous acts] particularly those who create a schism within a monastic community, destroying it from the foundation. Reflect in the following manner:

As a mother serves
Her ailing child with extra care,
So, too, should the bodhisattvas
Be especially kind toward the wicked.[653]

Or:

That samsara is sought by the great beings—
This I have failed to recognize.
Alas! I have failed, too, to recognize
That beings who lack the lineage are the key targets.[654]

Understand [the question about those beings said to lack buddha nature] in accordance with these statements. Since all the conditions for attaining buddhahood are complete in these two—giving and taking—imagine that all beings become fully enlightened, the master said.

As for the procedure for taking, this is presented in the following line:

Commence the sequence of taking from your own self.

Those whose mind is not trained through study and reflection and whose self-cherishing is strong may develop fear around taking on others' suffering. Because of this you train first in taking your own sufferings. For example, you make such aspirations as "May all the determinate karma[655] I have accumulated since beginingless time and all the fruitional effects that are certain to come into being be realized [upon me] in this lifetime." Here you also take [upon yourself] in the early part of the life what otherwise might come to fruition toward the later part of your life, and so on. Proceeding from this, you extend the taking to your real-life mother and then to all sentient beings—from the Avīci hells to disciples, self-realized ones, and the bodhisattvas. This is as stated in the *Ornament of Mahayana Sutras:*

> Who've fallen prey to the intensely fierce enemies,
> Who are burdened by misery and obscured by darkness,
> Who are trapped in hazardous paths,
> Who thoroughly possess the great fetters of bondage,
> Who cling to nourishment laced with poison,
> And who have totally lost their way—
> For all these beings, you must have compassion.[656]

The following line is directed to those individuals who, because of excessive conceptualization, cannot harness their thoughts, to help them maintain their mental focus on the object and make their mind more susceptible to training:

Place the two astride your breath.

(At first, you should practice giving and taking in combination for a long time. Afterward, shorten the duration [of this combination practice], and as you become very trained, place them astride the breathing.) [235] So as your breath exits, give the three—your body, material resources, and [roots of] virtues—to sentient beings. As you inhale, take upon yourself the negative karma, the suffering, the ill repute, and so on of sentient beings. It has been taught that it is possible for you to achieve through this the ability to stabilize your mind. Similarly you should place astride your breath whatever activities you engage in, such as eating or drinking, engaging in conversations, and so on. These [then] are [the practices during] the meditation session.

The method of how to engage in the practice during the subsequent periods is presented in the following lines:

> **There are three objects, three poisons, and three virtues—**
> **This, in brief, is the subsequent instruction.**[657]

These refer to the methods for training your conduct during the subsequent periods. Since afflictions such as attachment, hatred, and delusion (the three poisons, which are transformed into the three roots of virtue) arise in our mental continuums in relation to attractive, unattractive, and neutral objects of the six senses, the instruction for the subsequent periods is to engage in the training with the thought "May the three [afflictions] of all sentient beings ripen upon me; may all sentient beings possess the virtues of nonattachment, nonhatred, and nondelusion."

> **In brief the essence of instruction is this:**[658]
> **In all deeds train by means of the words.**

These lines indicate that in the activities of the subsequent periods, mind training is undertaken by means of words. So, during all your activities, such as when traveling, strolling, sleeping, sitting, and so on, you should train by means of words, as if repeating an essence mantra [of a meditation deity]. Atiśa states that all over eastern India there are people who recite, "This is the noble truth of suffering; this is the noble truth of origin," and so on, thus contemplating the four [noble truths] by means of words. Geshe Dromtönpa, too, to help trample upon the eight mundane concerns, would sometimes recite, "When obtained or failed to obtain," and at other times would utter, "When praised or belittled." Yet at other times he would recite, "When pleasant or unpleasant," and at other times he would utter, "When renowned or unknown." He would leave out the beginning or [sometimes]

356 Mind Training

the end of such verses as "The knower of the world...."[659] Phuchungwa
would also repeatedly refer to the death of Gyal Lhakhang's spouse and
[often], every time he took a step, he would repeat, "Death, death." Langri
Thangpa, too, would always exclaim, "I will offer gain and victory to the dear
sentient beings. [236] Why? Because all joys and excellent qualities originate in dependence upon them. I will take upon myself all loss and defeat.
Why? Because all faults and negative events originate in dependence upon
self-grasping."[660]

So, in all your deeds, train by means of words, repeating the following as if
it were an essence mantra:

> May the negative karma and suffering of sentient beings ripen
> upon me. May all my happiness and excellent qualities ripen
> upon sentient beings.

Or:

> May their negative karma ripen upon me;
> May all my virtues ripen upon them.[661]

Or:

> May the sufferings of all beings fall upon me;
> Through my virtues, may they all attain happiness.[662]

Or:

> Whether through seeing, hearing, or thinking about,
> Through contact or through exchange of words—
> May I always engage in deeds that bring
> Happiness and benefits to sentient beings.[663]

If you train [along these lines] by means of words, eventually you will
engage in the actual deeds; [the realization of] these will arise in your
mental continuum without any contrivance. The Old Tantra school's
"meditation through chanting" is based on the same principle.[664] At the
beginning, you might worry that the words simply won't come to your
mouth. However, as you become habituated, it may become as Chekawa
states: "Among all sounds perceived or possible, none is more melodious
than that of mind training. Since my strength does not permit me, can you
recite this for me?"[665]

If you wonder, "Can such things be achieved by means of words?" Neusurpa said, "By repeating the mantra *Candra Mahārakṣa,* the wrathful deity Acala appears vividly. So why is this not possible on the [sutra] path?" (Method and wisdom are present on the first bodhisattva level, it has been stated.) Because of this, it has been taught, you will not fall under the power of sleepiness and mental dullness, and this in itself constitutes a benefit. These, then, are the main body or the actual practice of mind training.

[PART II: THE BRANCH PRACTICES]

Now, to present the elaborate explanation of the branch practices, this is in two parts: (1) verses and (2) prose lines.

First present the subject matter of the verses. With these, the master said, there is no definite number or any [strict] sequence, so you simply train in them until their meanings are realized in the mind. There is thus no [definite] causal sequence [for the branch practices], the master said. [Chekawa's] own essential instructions contain some limited comments [to the verses], and my teacher's words, too, provide some limited explanations. My presentation of a brief commentary to help convey [the points] more clearly has three topics:

A. How to engage in the training
B. The measure of being trained
C. The purpose of training

The first is composed of three parts:

1. The causes for [the realizations to] arise
2. The means of guarding them against degeneration
3. The factors for enhancing them

The first is threefold:

a. Motivation, the preliminary practice
b. The actual deeds, the main practice
c. Joyfulness, the concluding practice

a. Motivation, the preliminary practice

There are two tasks—one at the start and one at the end.

At the start, when you get up from bed, cultivate the thought "Today I will subdue my self-grasping and make sure I am not polluted by self-cherishing; I will make sure that my cherishing of others does not degenerate." Before going to bed at night, while in the meditative absorption of the lion's majestic equipoise, reflect, "Today I did this first, then I did that afterward," and, enumerating them individually, examine each of these [acts]. If you find that you have done something contrary to the teachings in general, and to mind training practice in particular, then as the advice goes, "At that instant I will enumerate my flaws/ And recollect the teacher's instructions,"[666] think, "What kind of a person am I who wastes the precious human existence of leisure and opportunity and brings harm to myself?" Request forgiveness, declare these [wrongdoings] and purify them, and resolve "I will never again indulge in acts such as these."

If, on the other hand, you have acted in accordance with the teachings, rejoice with the thought "I have made the human life of leisure and opportunity meaningful; I have spent my time usefully," and make the following aspirations: "Due to this virtuous karma, may Dharma realizations arise in me; may I never be separated from the awakening mind throughout all lives."

Again, when you rise up the next morning, it is important to cultivate your motivation projecting the thought "Today I will conduct myself as excellently as I did yesterday." Do not merely utter that you will act in such manner; rather train your thoughts in that way alone. [238] When you encounter enemies, become afflicted by serious illness, and so on, practice as before. Examine which of the following are present—(1) the blessings of your teachers and the Three Jewels, (2) the might and power of the Dharma protectors, (3) your own virtues of the three times, and (4) the collective merit of all sentient beings—and reflect, "By means of these four factors, I will engage in this [mind training] practice during all four occasions [when getting up in the morning, when going to bed in the evening, when encountering enemies, and when afflicted by sickness] and enhance it like throwing new logs onto a blazing fire."

b. The actual deeds, the main practice

After putting on this kind of armor of motivation, the actual practice has three points:

    i. What are to be understood
    ii. What are to be relinquished
    iii. What are to be adopted

i. What are to be understood

The first, what are to be understood, has three parts—understanding what is an enemy and what is a friend, understanding what is erroneous and what is not erroneous, and understanding the meaning of the treatises. First, what is to be understood is presented in the following lines:

> **Banish all blames to the single source;**
> **Toward all beings contemplate their great kindness.**

Since beginningless time we haves failed to recognize our enemies and have failed to distinguish between what is to be relinquished and what is to be adopted. As such, all our pursuits of Dharma practice have turned into endeavors of self-grasping, and we have thus erred. We have failed to draw any closer to liberation and omniscience by building upon some past familiarity. So, today, we must recognize what is our enemy and what is our friend. How does we do this? There is nothing to do other than viewing our own self as the enemy and relinquishing it and viewing sentient beings as friends and cherishing them. For this, viewing self-grasping as the enemy is presented in the line "Banish all blames to the single source."

Thus whatever undesirable events occur, do not place the blame on others. Don't be like the great hermit who lives alone with no one around who, when the clarified butter he is making overflows and spills due to excessive cooking, curses, "This is the work of wretched demons!" At present, we tend to blame other factors whenever an undesirable event befalls us, saying, for instance, that a place is haunted, that we have been targeted by the demons, that we have displeased the spiritual teachers, and so on. This is a mistake. You must instead recognize your own self-grasping as the target of all this blame. It has been stated:

On the basis of grasping at self
Perceptions of self and others arise;
From this division arise grasping and hatred,
And through their chain, all negative consequences.[667]

Since, as stated here, all faults and negative consequences originate from this [self-grasping], if you experience calamities caused by the external environment or by the beings within it, if you suffer the displeasure of elevated and excellent sources like the buddhas or the Dharma protectors, if [you have misfortunes] caused by lowly beings, such as beggars, or by a multitude of sentient beings, or if you are harmed by nasty lice or by the bodily elements like wind, bile, phlegm, and so on, recognize that the root of all of these lies in self-grasping.

All the disharmony that exists today—between communities, between spiritual teachers, between parents, between relatives, between a master and his servants, between teachers and their students, between followers of the Kadam tradition, not to mention the lack of harmony between benefactors and their beneficiaries—the root of all of this is self-grasping. To grasp onto [the self] as real, to cherish this "real I" alone and disregard all other beings, is the natural characteristic of all ordinary, childish beings. It is on the basis of this that all afflictions and suffering arise. It has been stated:

Whatever harms exist in the world,
Whatever dangers and sufferings are in the world—
All of these arise from grasping at self,
What use is this great demon for me?[668]

All undesirable events in the world stem from self-grasping. Wherever you have been born, you have grasped that body as "mine," and where no "I" has existed, you have clung to an "I." For its sake, in the pursuit of likes and dislikes through either affirmation or negation, you have committed acts of dishonesty, deceit, and treachery against others and, as a result, have accumulated all kinds of afflictions and negative karma. So this [self-grasping] has caused all your sufferings since beginingless time, whether the sufferings of cyclic existence in general or those particular to the three lower realms. (*A Guide to the Bodhisattva's Way of Life* states:)

O mind, countless eons have passed
In your pursuit of self-interest;
Yet through such great hardships
You have sought only suffering.[669]

All the sufferings of the present are caused by this [self-grasping] as well. Do not fail to view it as your enemy, for in its quest for happiness, it will compel you to accumulate negative karma and wander in the limitless cycle of existence for an eternity with ever more intense suffering. So you must recognize your own self as the enemy and contemplate as stated in the following:

Throughout hundreds of eons in cyclic existence
It has injured you; [240]
Therefore, recalling all your grievances,
Today vanquish this thought of self-centeredness.[670]

As stated in the following, it is not appropriate to remain relaxed:

This enemy that has settled in me for so long,
The sole cause of a proliferation of harms—
How can I remain fearless and joyful in cyclic existence
When it is definitively established in my heart?[671]

The locus of this defect is the very body in which you are born, and to cherish this cluster of pus and blood, a sack of mucus, is like carrying thorns while naked. It is as stated:

Whatever suffering is in the world
Arises from desiring one's own happiness.[672]

You must despise that which makes you suffer; if you can recognize this [self-grasping] as the enemy, you will denigrate your own self and speak ill of it. In particular, if, from the depth of your heart, you discern that [others] speaking ill of you actually helps you subdue the enemy, [real] happiness has dawned.

In all the teachings of the Great Vehicle, there is no subject matter apart from these two themes: discarding the self and cherishing others. Furthermore, the entire doctrine [of the Buddha] is for eliminating the afflictions. The root of all afflictions is the "I" and self-grasping, so if your conquest of this is vast, vast will be your happiness; for the middling it will be middling; for the minimal it will be minimal; and those who have pacified none at all will have no happiness. Therefore it is vital that you view this root of all sufferings and negative events as your enemy. In the past, you have failed to recognize this. Today, as stated in the following, you recognize your enemy thanks to the teacher's instruction:

> The old days when you could
> Ruin me at will are now gone.[673]

In this way, it has been taught, you will soon become a genuine Dharma practitioner, one who has been rescued from the hazardous gorges of adversities and has arrived on the open plains of the remedies. These, then, are the points related to recognizing self-grasping as your enemy.

Viewing others as friends is presented in the line "Toward all beings, contemplate their great kindness." In general, all sentient beings are a source of great kindness, as stated in the following from the *Commentary on the Awakening Mind*:

> Those who've been your parents in the past,
> Or your siblings, friends, or those labeled otherwise—
> With all these sentient beings,
> Interact only to repay their kindness.[674]

In particular, the contemplation of enemies as embodiments of kindness is [241] as stated in the following (in *A Guide to the Bodhisattva's Way of Life*):

> Like discovering a treasure in the home
> Without having to seek it through adversity,
> I am delighted to find my enemy,
> Who helps me pursue awakening.[675]

In general, without accomplishing the six perfections, buddhahood cannot be achieved. Just as generosity and morality are perfected in dependence upon beggars, ordination masters, preceptors, and transmitters of the scriptures, forbearance too is perfected in dependence upon perpetrators of harm;

hence the contemplation of all beings who harm you as sources of kindness. For this, you should reflect as follows:

"Since beginingless time all these humans and nonhumans who inflict me with harm have been my mothers greater in number than the *kolāsita* nuts necessary to cover the face of the earth. They have continuously looked after me with loving eyes; they have held me constantly with affection in their hearts; they have consistently protected me against harms and unhelpful situations. They thus embody great kindness, having brought me all kinds of benefits and happiness." Thinking thus, cultivate a sense of endearment and loving-kindness, wishing for their happiness.

[Then] reflect, "The harms they are currently inflicting on me are being perpetrated out of delusion. Since beginingless time they have pursued my interests without regard to negative karma, pain, ill repute, and so on, and because of this they have accumulated negative karma and have thus wandered endlessly, undergoing suffering, in the cycle of existence. So the blame for all of this lies in me. Even today, while I am pursuing enlightenment for the benefit of self and others, my negative karma stirs the dear mothers and compels them to create impediments that obstruct the happiness of all beings. So the blame for their descending to the hells in their future lives also lies in me. O dear, how disheartening!"

In general, you should recognize that all beings have been your mother since beginningless time; recognize especially that those who inflict harms at present are friends assisting you in the pursuit of enlightenment; and recognize, too, that you already gave away your body, resources, and roots of virtue to others when you generated the awakening mind. It has been stated:

> I have already given this body
> To all beings to do with as they please;
> Let them do whatever they wish with it—
> Whether they slay it, deface it, or beat it.[676]

So, as stated here, you should not become hostile toward the perpetrators of harm; rather, you should recognize them as a source of kindness. [242]

Given that it is the failing of your teacher if you lack the knowledge of how to distinguish between your enemies and friends in this manner, and given that it is the student's, that is your own, failing if you fail to successfully make such a distinction, open your eyes to this and embrace what is to be adopted and discard what is to be abandoned. Master Śāntideva states:

> Recognizing myself as flawed
> And others as an ocean of higher qualities,
> I shall thoroughly discard grasping at self
> And practice embracing others.[677]

And:

> Whatever suffering is in the world
> Arises from desiring one's own happiness;
> Whatever happiness is in the world
> Arises from cherishing others' well-being.

> What need is there to say more?

> The childish pursue their own interests
> While the buddhas pursue the welfare of others:
> Observe the difference between these two.[678]

Many statements such as these have been made for the purpose of recognizing enemies and friends.

Langri Thangpa, too, is said to have remarked, "Of all the profound scriptures I have opened, I have found none that does not suggest that all shortcomings are our own and that all positive qualities belong to sentient beings. Given this, we should think to offer victory and benefit to others and accept loss and defeat upon ourselves."[679]

He would repeat the following, it is said, as if it were an essence mantra: "I will offer gain and victory to the dear sentient beings. Why? Because all joys and excellent qualities originate in dependence upon them. I will take upon myself all loss and defeat. Why? Because all faults and negative events originate in dependence upon self-grasping."[680]

Whenever positive events occurred, Potowa too would exclaim, "Look at the strength of this novice. He has such strength!" and, when adverse situations arose, he would utter, "I shall immerse myself in this."[681] In brief, it is impossible to attain freedom from cyclic existence as long as your self-grasping has not become extinct; without cherishing others, it is impossible to attain buddhahood. To understand this point is to [truly] recognize enemies and friends.

Understanding what is erroneous and what is not erroneous in your mind training is presented in the following lines:

> **Train constantly in the three general points;**
> **Transform your thoughts, but remain as you are.**

Ensuring that your mind training is not erroneous means ensuring [1] that it does not contradict your pledges, [2] that it does not turn into an affront, and [3] that it is not biased. If it does contradict these three general points, then it is erroneous.

The first refers to relinquishing conduct that defies the law of karma and its effects. [243] Because you are practicing mind training and there is no need for anything else, you might believe you can transgress the minor precepts without causing harm. In fact, you must relinquish all conduct that contradicts the practices of the three scriptural collections. With your mind you engage in mind training, but in your conduct you do not violate any of the vows and precepts—from [the opening] stanzas[682] [of the discipline collection] up to the Vajrayana—but instead maintain their purity. You should thus be free of conflict with the scriptural collections in general.

The second refers to avoiding all offensive behavior, such as sleeping in haunted sites, cutting down vital plants, visiting areas where you may contract contagious diseases, consorting with people who are degenerate in their commitments, with lepers, with demons, and so on. You should avoid acting in a manner that contradicts the way of life of the Kadampa, the great custom initiated by Geshe Dromtönpa at Radreng, according to which the doctrine [of the Buddha] is upheld from all four corners simultaneously. You should also conduct yourself like the master in the story who, when informed "There appear to be [instructions] such as the 'adornment of pristine cognition,'" replied, "This is not my path; mine is the tradition of Radreng."[683]

The third refers to engaging in a comprehensive training—not falling prey to partial approaches [in your mind training]—and thus being free of error. There are countless examples of such partial practices. For instance, some, though capable of undertaking a single practice—like subduing self-grasping, countering miserliness, or cultivating forbearance—nonetheless lack the capacity for other practices. Some, though capable of practicing forbearance toward humans, are not able to do so toward nonhumans and remain deeply superstitious, while others are the reverse. Some are respectful toward important people but despise the weak, while others are the reverse.

So if you have become more hostile toward your own son but kinder toward the wolves, your mind has not become trained. (You should train consistently with equanimity.)

Furthermore, if, in your action, you conduct [only] your body and speech in the manner [described earlier], this is an erroneous practice. It is your attitude that must be transformed from a self-centered one into one that aspires for the well-being of others. With your physical and verbal actions, do not be ostentatious around others. To [openly recite,] "O take my flesh, take my blood"; to give away your monastic robes; to act in public with pretensions of deep compassion for the lepers and so on; to remove spears equal to the number of deer [slain]; or to claim, "As I have subdued my self-grasping, I have no need for anything else"—all this contradicts the Vinaya discipline teachings, and constitutes offensive behavior besides. Therefore, it has been taught, all your mind training practices should remain discreet but their actual impact should progress with great strides. [244] Therefore, if you display your mind training with body and speech but fail to actually train your mind, or if you act contrary to the scriptural collections, act in an unbecoming manner, or engage in pointless acts even though you may have achieved a slight degree of training, since all of this constitutes offensive conduct, your method of mind training has become erroneous.

"Understanding the meaning of the treatises" is presented in the following lines:

> Like a diamond, like the sun, and like a [medicinal] tree—
> Understand the meaning of the treatises and so on.[684]

For example, the diamond, which is reputed chief among stones with its crystalline form and various qualities, does not lose its [natural] crystalline shape—its facets—or its qualities, even when cut into a hundred or a thousand pieces. In the same manner, whether you partake of it from its beginning or from its end, this mind training [instruction] remains mind training. In each and every word of its explanations, the content of mind training remains intact and undamaged.

Similarly, when a single ray of sun shines, all the rays shine at the same time. Likewise, when the meaning of a single word of mind training dawns in your mind, the meaning of all the words arises in your mind. So there is no need for a [fixed] enumeration [of points] or a particular sequence, and in terms of practice, you can begin wherever most appeals to your mind.

Again, every part of the medicinal tree—its root, its main trunk, its branches, its leaves, its bark, and its flowers—can cure all four hundred and twenty-four classes of disease without exception. This [medicine] wards off all these [diseases]. In the same manner, each and every word of this mind training subdues afflictions and self-grasping. Through this [training] all of these are warded off. Since mind training is effective even without a [fixed] causal sequence [to its points], you should engage in its practice until its realization arises in your mental continuum. These are, then, the principal points to be understood, [which have been presented here] merely by [listing] their names.

ii. What are to be relinquished

This has four parts: (1) relinquishing mental afflictions, (2) relinquishing partialities, (3) relinquishing expectations, and (4) relinquishing dependencies.

The first, relinquishing mental afflictions, is presented in the following line:

> **Purify first whichever affliction is strongest.**[685]

Or:

> **Purify first whichever is most coarse.**

The mental afflictions are the root of all obstacles to practicing Dharma, and the root of the afflictions is self-grasping.[686] It is this that has made you suffer since beginningless time in the cycle of existence. Even today, when you hear the squeaking noise of a rat, he [the self] fears that his ears might be bitten.[687] When it thunders, he fears that [lightning] might strike his head. When there is a rumor of an epidemic in the region, he fears he might contract it. When a site is said to be haunted, he fears being taken away to the rocky cliffs. Similarly, some suffer from fear of bad reputation; others suffer from worries of not being able to look after their family and friends. There are thus countless sufferings, and the root of all of them is self-grasping.

All ordinary beings share this nature—whatever they do is driven by this grasping at self. So it is this that you must subdue. Vanquishing it, however, cannot be done through occasional practice; rather, you must train persistently. If you can subdue it, you will experience a blissful relief, like relieving an intestinal pain caused by food poisoning. Until this occurs, even if you have worn through a dzo-load of monk's lower garments, placed [conse-crated] vases on your head,[688] or dedicated your entire life in pursuit of learn-ing, none of this will be of any avail and will lead nowhere. There is thus not a single moment of happiness. If, on the other hand, you succeed in hammer-ing down the head of this self-grasping a little, your Dharma practice will then become a true remedy, and you will experience a blissfulness. In addi-tion, if you can embrace sentient beings into the depths of your heart, this then becomes what is called the "great vehicle" or the "great container."

To accomplish this, harboring the thought "I have time" will certainly not suffice. You must exert yourself from this very moment. If you take upon yourself what is undesirable and give to others what is desirable, you have subdued self-grasping. Thus taking this as a basis, discern whichever afflic-tion is strongest—attachment, hatred, and so on—and focus primarily on purifying that.

Some can relinquish an affliction [246] simply through analysis and dis-cernment. For others, there is no certainty that discernment alone will lead to relinquishment; for them, relinquishing occurs after cultivating the anti-dotes. Since your teachers and colleagues can discern [which affliction is strongest in you], allow them to determine this. There is a story of Chekawa requesting Sharawa to please him by making this determination, and also encouraging colleagues such as Lungmepa, when he was residing at Neusur, to offer such discernment. So at all times, and in all four everyday activities, allow yourself and others to examine your mental states and, having made the diagnosis, apply the remedies. For the time being, leave your other afflic-tions as they are.

When you feel this [affliction] is now subdued, [deliberately] distort your thought processes and examine whether it arises again. If it does, you have still not attained the actual realization and must therefore continue with your practice. If, on the other hand, you encounter the objects or con-ditions but the affliction still does not arise, then you have subdued it. After you have defeated it, you might experience [its resurgence] like the birth of a new tooth when one is broken, but you will easily overcome it. This is analogous to subduing all other wrestlers with ease once you have defeated the strongest man.

As for the procedure for purifying first whichever [affliction] is the coars-est, the beginner's approach is to avoid the adverse conditions, or if you can, combating [the affliction head-on]. This is as stated in the following:

> The wise will refrain from it well;
> Or the wise will combat it excellently.[689]

Or:

> Until stability is achieved, adverse conditions may harm;
> Once stability is achieved, adverse conditions become aids.[690]

As for turning adversities into favorable conditions, master Nyalpa and his spiritual children would say, "Once something is upheld from within, [favorable conditions] proliferate greatly."[691] When the teacher Sengé Gyaltsen was at Langri Thang [Monastery], because Seberé and others challenged him, his training was more effective. These days, he said, without those demands, the strength of his training is not as great. Such instances have occurred.

Since in some cases a simple encounter with the circumstances can undermine you, avoidance may not be reasonable. So, if you can, combat [the affliction] head-on. Like a skilled falcon trainer who says, "If you send this, I will counter it with this," apply whatever remedy is most appropriate to the affliction, and, as stated in the following, fortify yourself with the antidotes:

> I do not care if I'm burned alive
> Or if I am beheaded—
> Never will I bow down before
> My enemy, the afflictions.[692]

As for these being the enemies, [*A Guide to the Bodhisattva's Way of Life* states]:

> The enemies, such as hatred and craving, [247]
> Do not have legs, arms, and so on;
> They are neither courageous nor intelligent;
> So how is that they have enslaved me?[693]

Also:

> Attachment, hatred, and delusion—
> Summoning these three deep into my heart,

The robbers mushroom in my own mind.
There is no greater thief than this![694]

Contemplate these and many other [similar statements].
The second, relinquishing partialities, is presented in the following line:

Forsake all forms of partiality.[695]

Do not limit your training to specific places, times, and objects. Instead, extend it to all—to the entire universe of the external environment and its inhabitants, to the noble ones, and to all sentient beings both appealing and unappealing. Naturally equanimity toward all will arise once the training is effected.
The third, relinquishing expectations, is presented in the following line:

Forsake all expectations of reward.

If, because of engaging in this practice, the following expectations arise in you—to not be harmed by humans and nonhumans, to be famous, to be respected by your teachers and students, to have abundant food, clothing, and so on, to receive rewards for helping others, to be known as a genuine spiritual practitioner, even to attain buddhahood—[contemplate what] the most holy Maitreya has stated: "Toward conquerors and so on one [still] has subtle attachments."[696]
If you fail to train unconditionally, free of expectations of rewards pertaining to this life and the hereafter, then one aspect of your spiritual practice becomes blind. It is critical, therefore, to train without any hope of reward. If you harbor expectations for this life, [your training] is not even a Dharma practice; harboring expectations for the future life precludes it from becoming a practice of the bodhisattvas. Even if your aspiration for buddhahood is for your own benefit, [your training] becomes a cause for attaining [only] the state of a self-realized one.
The fourth, relinquishing dependence, is presented in the following line:

Do not depend on other conditions.

Generally speaking, it is impossible for hearing, reflection, and meditation and all ten types of spiritual practices not to depend upon other factors. So you do need to depend upon other conditions. It is necessary to gather such favorable conditions as food, clothing, shelter, assistants, articles for retreat, sound health, and so on, and also to ensure the absence of enemies and malevolent forces.

Once Potowa asked Jangpa Sherap if he were able to reflect on the teachings. Jangpa replied, "If my stomach is full and my thirst is quenched, and if my friends do not disturb my mind, it seems that I can to a limited degree."[697] [248] [Chekawa once said:] "At Chenga Monastery there were limited offerings and resources. Thinking, 'I shall go into the countryside to obtain these,' I went to Yarlung, but failed to find them there either. Because of my ignorance I had failed to understand. For 'cyclic existence' is a name for deficiency."[698] Khün said that amenities were not available at Kamapa's, so he went to Tsang, where he found the favorable conditions and was able to make offerings to the Three Jewels, nurture his own health, and get well, thus becoming able to receive great benefits. A student of Kharak's who was served melted *dri* butter when he lost his appetite, exclaimed, "I did not realize there was a spiritual practice on the nipples of a dri."[699] Atiśa, too, would show the wrinkles on his feet and say, "I have reached this stage; now I will not become a highly realized being." Whenever he saw a youth with red cheeks, Shetön Jangbar would say, "Yes, there is something I can do to help you," but when he saw an old and decrepit person, he would say, "You have experienced [life] until the tone of your skin color has changed; now, even if you stay here at my place, it will not be of much benefit."

Some assert that they have been able to cultivate the [mind training] thoughts as a result of occasionally associating with a colleague with strong concentration. Others assert that they failed because some colleagues disturbed them. Still others say that they fail because of being in haste, but when they have leisure, they are more successful. Yet others say that they fail when distracted but succeed in solitude.

Nyak Sengé Drak once remarked, "Kadampas say that they meditate on karma and its fruits, yet without mastering my higher knowledge texts, how can they meditate [on karma]? Do they simply repeat [the words] 'karma and its fruits'?" For this [mind training practice], you don't need to rely on [extensive] studies such as this.

If the amenities are present, you can use them as the basis [for practice]. However, if they are absent, or if people are hostile[700] or kind, if you are hungry, cold, prosperous, impoverished, sick, or not sick, if you are old or young, hungry or full, if you are assailed by enemies or disturbed by demonic spirits, if you enjoy the approval of your spiritual teacher or do not enjoy the approval of your spiritual teacher, or if you are being mentally disturbed by your colleagues, take all of these as the very rationale [for practice] and engage in [mind training] practice.

The precious spiritual teacher used to make each of the family members of Langthang, whose nephews and nieces were not many in number, sit for a session of meditative practice. This is also like the stories of José and of Sengé Gyal, as narrated before.[701] Therefore this can be practiced amid all activities (such as when traveling, when going for a walk, when sleeping, and when sitting). [249] It can be practiced at all times, when busy or when relaxing. For this, the only necessary condition is your determination. It has been stated:

> This mind that is full of defects
> Has nonetheless a multitude of qualities:
> Whatever is cultivated, that comes to be.[702]

To the extent that you persevere, you will succeed. This is not like baked clay [which can no longer be reshaped]. You can train to the best of your capacity. It does not do to think "For when I teach others in the future, this is how it is"; but if you think "I must put this into practice and meditate," you will soon receive the blessing of Dharma. For this [mind training practice], it is said, you must practice [with the intensity of] propitiating a god and until the substances are fully consumed by the ritual fire.[703] Thus, forsaking these four factors is critical.[704]

iii. What are to be adopted

This has three parts: (a) The practice to be undertaken, (b) the method by which this is practiced, and (c) the method of undertaking the practice.

(a) The practice to be undertaken

The first, the practice to be undertaken, is presented in the following lines:

> Engage in the principal practices right now.[705]
> Adopt what is of greatest significance.[706]

Reflect, "Since beginingless time, I have wandered through the three lower realms as if they were my old home. Today, at this juncture, when owing to some meritorious deeds I have obtained the human life of leisure and opportunity so rare to find in even hundreds and thousands of eons, it is more important to pursue the well-being of my future lives rather than that of this present life. Of the two aspects of Dharma—exposition and meditative practice—the latter is more important. Within meditative practices, too, training the mind is more important than external conduct. This is as stated in the following:

> Of the conduct of the bodhisattvas,
> Which has been described as immeasurable,
> You should definitely first engage in
> The conduct of training the mind.[707]

Of the various methods for training the mind, training in the awakening mind is the principal one. This is as stated in the following:

> The awakening mind is described
> As the supreme great vehicle,
> So with efforts grounded in equipoise,
> Generate the awakening mind.[708]

As for the awakening mind, too, exchanging is more important than equalizing self and others. This is as stated in the following:

> He who wishes to quickly rescue
> Both himself and others
> Should practice the secret instruction:
> The exchange of self and others.[709] [250]

For this, too, it is more important to train internally by yourself than to manifest this exchange externally in physical and verbal actions, merely imitating others' behavior. Furthermore, it is more important to train with perseverance on the basis of your teacher's instructions than to train by employing the paddles of scriptural quotations and reasoning. In terms of daily activities, too, it is more important to train this [while seated] on your bed than when on a journey or while going for a walk. Therefore engage in your practice in such a manner.

To ensure that your method does not meet with dangers, it is stated:

Adopt what is of greatest significance.

This means that an ordained practitioner should avoid performing virtuous activities that create a material legacy. This is the task of kings and householders—the inscription of the *Perfection of Wisdom in a Hundred Thousand Lines* in gold, the construction of temples, and so on. The instant [a monk] engages in them it constitutes a degeneration of his precepts. Transgressing these [precepts] gives rise only to the accumulation of anger [within], as a result of which much harm will ensue for others. This will undermine a monk's seeking of solitude and Dharma practice, for he will have to associate with inappropriate companions, such as those who are morally degenerate, those who are captives of demons, and those who have violated their oaths. On this basis, disputes within a community and so on will occur. Many [of these deeds] can therefore turn into conditions that harm the body and life of self and others. Thus you are advised to not engage in meritorious activities that leave a material legacy.

What activities must you engage in, then? You should guard the purity of the precepts you have taken. This is critical. You should purify negative karma, receive the rite for consecrating your speech, dedicate your virtues toward the attainment of enlightenment, make supplications to the teachers and their lineage, meditate on the stages of the path, and ensure that your sacred bond to your spiritual teacher remains inviolate. You should cultivate loving-kindness, compassion, and the awakening mind. You should practice emptiness and compassion in union, recite the essence mantra of your meditation deity, and constantly meditate on your spiritual teacher, who is the foundation for accomplishing all of these. You should associate with good friends, accumulate merit through propitiating the deities and so on, and purify the defilements. You should endeavor in these, it has been taught.

Regardless of your mental capacities and of whether you are entering Tantra or Perfection [Vehicle], none of these [practices enumerated above] lies beyond your scope. Thus they are of great significance.

(b) The method by which this [mind training] is practiced

Second, the method by which this [mind training] is practiced is presented in the following lines:

> **Train constantly in the three difficult challenges;**
> **Train in both the main and the secondary practices;**[710]
> **Apply rejection and affirmation forcefully with regard to the fierce**
> **one. [251]**

The three difficult challenges are that, first, this method is difficult to recall; second, it is difficult to overcome the afflictions; and finally, it is difficult to exterminate the continuum [of the afflictions].

First, when others are not disturbing your mind and your stomach is full and your thirst is quenched, your practice might flow like a torrential river. However, when confronted with adversities, the master said, it is difficult to even remember the remedies. Even if you do remember the remedies, in the intermediate stage, it is difficult to overcome [the afflictions], as if your throat has become dry [and your cannot utter a sound]. At that point you should coordinate your efforts. Even so, it remains difficult to overcome [the afflictions]. Even if you succeed in overcoming them once, when you observe [the object's] features or recall it, you tend to reexperience the angry disturbance. Thus it is difficult to sever the continuum for even that [level of affliction] that was overcome, it is said. So you should cultivate the antidotes, and when adverse conditions arise, strive to recall the remedies. It has been stated:

> In this endeavor, I will be tenacious.
> With a strong grudge, I will battle against it.[711]

As stated here, you should overcome [the afflictions] in the intermediate stage and strive to ultimately exterminate their very continuum.

Make aspiration prayers for such outcomes. This way, even if you have some doubts about [the likelihood of] this [happening], [your aspiration] can become a condition for its realization to arise at a later point. If you develop some conviction, even a close friend mentioning this in conversation could become a condition for the realization to arise at a later point. If you can strive in this for a few years and a few months from this moment, you will triumph over the three difficult challenges. If you recall it during the day, you remain as a bodhisattva during the day; if you recall it during the night, you remain as a bodhisattva during the night. Therefore recall this [application of remedies], overcome the opposing factors, and exterminate their continuum. If your insight is strong, observe the different connections among your thoughts; if your perseverance is strong, observe what kind of joyfulness is present; and if your meditation is excellent, observe whether your mind succumbs to mental dullness.

If you take the line "Train in both the main and the secondary practices" to refer to the main [mind training] practice, then all subsequent practices, including that of [meditation on] no-self, can be regarded as its branches. If, on the other hand, you take this [mind training] to be a branch of the path, then this serves as an antidote against whichever mental affliction [might happen to arise]. So when difficult situations arise—such as when food and clothing are not present, when you are afflicted by illness or enemies, or when a forceful, enflaming emotion arises—if you cannot remain unperturbed through striving in this remedy, you have utterly failed in this spiritual practice. For success in this practice means that regardless of what situation arises, you remain unperturbed. The suggestion is not that this [application of remedies] is relevant only in the context of training the mind in the awakening mind. Practices common with disciples and self-realized ones also exist for subduing the afflictions, self-grasping, and so on. [252] This [application of remedies] alone is not sufficient, however.

Do not say aloud that those who disparage you and so on are a source of great kindness and are your spiritual teachers. Rather, cultivate these thoughts but make sure not to fall prey to the afflictions as a result. Having identified [the afflictions], the procedure for relinquishing them is presented in the line:

Apply rejection and affirmation forcefully in defeating the fierce one.

This [fierce one] refers to the mental afflictions. It is vital that all your practices become antidotes for the afflictions. At present your learning and so on succumb to such thoughts as "No one is greater in learning than me," and so afflictions beget [further] afflictions, and you have thus failed to identify the demon. This is like calling the nose *yuk*,[712] and like the wife of the layman Jangchup Ö placing her nipples into the eyes [of her infant child]. When subduing the afflictions, whose roots are in self-grasping, you must therefore apply the antidotes with great force.

(c) The method of undertaking the practice

Third, the method of undertaking the practice has four parts: (i) the practice of a lifetime, (ii) the conduct of a day, (iii) taking onto the path whatever circumstance you encounter, and (iv) transforming adversities into favorable conditions.

(i) The practice of a lifetime

The first, the practice of a lifetime, is presented in the following line:

Train in the five powers.[713]

It is by means of this practice [of five powers] that you conduct the activities of an entire lifetime. This, in turn, is twofold: (1) that to be undertaken during your entire lifetime and (2) instruction to be undertaken at the point of death.

In the context of the five powers to be practiced during the entire lifetime, the line "In brief the essence of instruction is this" is sometimes inserted before the line "Train in the five powers," and the two lines become a pair. [The five powers are:] (1) the power of propelling intention, (2) the power of the positive seed, (3) the power of eradication, (4) the power of acquaintance, and (5) the power of aspirational prayer.

1) The *power of propelling intention* refers to propelling your thoughts by cultivating the following thoughts: "From here on until buddhahood, I will never be divorced from mind training; I will never be divorced from mind training in this short lifetime, in this very year, and in this very month. Today in particular, whatever harms befall me, such as being disparaged, despised, and so on, I will make sure to not fall prey to self-grasping, but instead to subdue it. Having subdued it, I will not let go again in the future."

This is like projecting the thought "When daylight breaks, I will go fetch some wood," [253] and then waking up [on time] as a result. Likewise, through the power of propelling intention, the mindfulness of remedies arises when you encounter adverse circumstances.

2) The *power of the positive seed* refers to the following: In order to assure

the mind training realization that has not yet arisen and to enhance that which has arisen, even in the periods between meditation sessions, you should strive in accumulation of merit, purification of defilements, supplication to the teachers, requesting intervention from the Dharma protectors, endeavoring in study, reflection, and meditation, and in spiritual activities. All this should be dedicated to ensuring the realization of mind training within your mental continuum.

3) The *power of eradication* refers to eradicating the grasping onto [the notion of] self. Since beginningless time you have wandered through cyclic existence in general and the three lower realms in particular, all due to your self-cherishing, which yearns for your own well-being. In this life, too, all undesirable events that befall you, including the inability to live in harmony with a spouse, the failure to live up to your promises, and so on, are all due to this. Your reluctance to secure realization of [the path], from impermanence to the ultimate nature of reality, is also due to this. Instead of your wisdom, industry, ethical conduct, great learning, and stages of meditative practice becoming antidotes to mental afflictions, they beget further afflictions by giving rise to such thoughts as "No one is more learned than me" and "No one is more industrious than me." All of this is due to your failure to subdue self-grasping.

Also your failure in pursuit of human norms or divine spiritual laws, your failure to get anywhere, or [wasting your life in] the least useful pursuits—such as moving toward the [state of] elders, such as a disciple or a self-realized one, even though it is buddhahood that you seek—all of this is due to your desire to gain victory and defeat others because of self-grasping. You must therefore eradicate this. You should reflect on the verse "Whatever harms are in this world...."[714] As the line "I do not care if I am burned alive..."[715] states, you should cultivate the remedies.

4) The *power of acquaintance* refers to acquainting yourself on a regular basis with the exchange of self and others. If you do not engage in this practice with prolonged, fervent, and uninterrupted enthusiasm and aspiration, you will be unable to relinquish your cherishing of self, [which has persisted] from beginningless time, and the cherishing of others will not arise. Therefore cultivate familiarity with this [exchanging of self and others] on a regular basis. When, as a result of your acquaintance with this, you do gain the realization of mind training within your mental continuum, you will experience the meditative absorption known as "traversing all phenomena with ease,"[716] or you will experience universal joy, for the gods will be happy, the

nāgas will be content, and everyone will enjoy happiness. Reflect therefore upon the lines "Whatever happiness is in the world,"[717] [254] and cultivate acquaintance [with this mind training practice] on a regular basis.

5) The *power of aspirational prayer* refers to praying—at the end of whatever virtuous deed you have performed and at all times—for self-grasping to be subdued and for it not to resurface following its conquest. It refers also to making the various aspirations found in the Mahayana sutras and treatises, such as the following:

> Whatever sufferings beings have,
> May all come to be realized upon me.[718]

If you train in these five powers, it has been taught, all your lifetime activities will therefore be accomplished; the mind exchanging self and others will arise and will become enhanced, producing all the excellent qualities.

If you particularly wish to practice this as an instruction to be applied at the time of death, the following has been stated:

> **As Mahayana's transference method is**
> **The five powers alone, their practice is vital.**[719]

1) First, as for the *power of the positive seed,* offer your belongings to the teachers and the Three Jewels as gifts of the deceased. It is inappropriate to give them to beings whom you cling to. Make arrangements so that in your wake your possessions do not become conditions for accumulating negative karma. Make excellent offerings to those who are worthy of such veneration. It is not appropriate to offer only substitutes of your possessions to the embodiments of kindness. Then, without attachment to any objects of this life, generate an attitude of not fearing the future life.[720]

2) Next *the power of aspirational prayer* is as follows: Lay out the offerings, purify [negative karma] and make a resolve, and request forbearance for any shortcomings. Also review your pledges, such as going for refuge and so on. Then make offerings to the Three Jewels, offer torma cake to the Dharma protectors, and pray that you will recall the two awakening minds during the intermediate state and the next life and also meet with a teacher who will reveal this teaching (and who practices this teaching and trains his own mind) and so on.

3) Next, *the power of eradication* is as follows: "Grasping at self has caused me to suffer from beginningless time to this present moment. Until it is extinguished, it will lead me only to suffering and will ruin me. That ruination is due to clinging to this body as 'mine.' I will [therefore] not assume a body in the intermediate state and I will make this body exist no more." Think also, "I will make this mind that grasps at self, too, vanish into space."[721] With these thoughts you should eradicate self-grasping.

4) Next, the *power of propelling intention* refers to [255] repeatedly cultivating the thought "I will recall this practice during the intermediate state."

5) Next, the *power of acquaintance* refers to a special recollection of what you have gained familiarity with in the past. Since the transference [of consciousness] takes place through the force of your conduct, lie on your left side while placing the right palm under the cheek. With your small finger blocking the right nostril, breathe [normally] through the left nostril. As you exhale, train in giving and taking on the basis of exhalation [and so on]. While in this state, recall the ultimate awakening mind, which is the state of immortality. It is in such a state [of mind] that you ensure the transference [of consciousness].

(ii) The conduct of a day

The second, the conduct of a day, is presented in the following line:

Accomplish all yogas through a single means.

Other teachings describe a variety of practices, such as the yoga of eating. Here, however, all yogas pertaining to food, clothes, and so on are performed through a single means. How? They are performed by the following meditative practice: When you have all the amenities, such as food, clothing, and so on, you think, "Through this good fortune of mine may all beings enjoy happiness." And if these are lacking, you think, "May all the suffering that beings have due to lacking these amenities ripen upon me." Learn to purify all the objects of the senses in this way during the four everyday activities with the twin practice of giving and taking as described in the sutra of *Thoroughly Pure Spheres of Conduct*[722] or the *Clouds of Jewels Sutra*,[723] or as stated by the savior Maitreya in the following:

The more you engage in the deeds of the bodhisattva,
The more diverse the objects entering your sense fields;

Recognizing these as they are and through appropriate words,
Embrace that which you perceive to help sentient beings.[724]

With such understanding, pursue everything by means of the yoga of training in the awakening mind.

(iii) Taking onto the path whatever circumstance you encounter

The third, taking onto the path whatever circumstance you encounter is presented in the following line:

Relate whatever you encounter to your meditation right now.[725]

Whatever you encounter, such as an unexpected interaction with humans,
nonhumans, or animals, or any encounter within the field of your six senses,
purify it right there and then. All types of occasions, joyful and miserable;
all types of places, alien and native; all types of dwellings, such as monasteries, learning centers, and so on; [256] all types of activities, such as traveling, going for a walk, and so on; toward all things that are objects of your six
senses—seeing, hearing, and so on—determine that each of these are of two
kinds: desirable and undesirable. Having made this distinction, train yourself to give the desirable to sentient beings and to take the undesirable upon
yourself.

Just like the saying "When your stomach is full and the sun is warm, everyone seems capable of heroic deeds," when favorable conditions are present,
even your teacher seems to issue affirmations such as "okay" and "excellent."
And when colleagues raise disturbing challenges, you feel capable of handling
them. However, when you come face to face with a crisis or when a heavy
negative karma comes to fruition, you lose your vow, and others view you as
polluted, like the carcass of a dead dog. [For example,] if you had visible scars
of leprosy, others would see you as repulsive. They might cover their noses the
moment they see you. As a result, you would likely suffer such deficiencies as
the lack of a spouse, a home, and so on, and you would suffer ill repute and
disdain. However, when such things do occur, feel compassion and cultivate
the thought "The world is filled with similar situations." (When such events
occur,) make the aspiration "May all undesirable events be realized upon me;
may sentient beings never undergo such suffering." Give all the factors—your
body, material resources, and roots of virtue—to others and imagine that all
beings enjoy happiness, prosperity, and renown.

Even in this life (since you have not acquired any irrevocable realization) you do not know what might befall you. You don't know what kind of karma you have accumulated, so even if suffering befalls you like a mountain crushing down upon you, remain indifferent. To cope with misery when in misery, it is vital not to lose your spiritual practice, and to cope with happiness when happy, it is vital not to lose your spiritual practice. If you lack this [resilience], whether it is one summer to the next, one winter to the next, or one day to the next, [your happiness] will be unreliable. If you are a fully ordained monk, you will fail to find an attendant; if you are a novice monk, you will fail to find a master.

What is responsible for all of these events? It is your lack of [resilience]. It's all due to your desire to achieve higher status, to enjoy fortune, and to obtain victory for yourself alone, the master said. Observe the necessity for forbearance even in seeking a roommate. What hardship is greater in this life than when nobody desires your presence? Recognize that no shortcoming is greater than this. So long as you fail to dispel even a small part of this self-grasping, then it is just like in the saying "No comfort is there if you use a saddle for a pillow." In other words, you find only unhappiness no matter what you do. This all comes from the inability to bear whatever situation arises. [257]

If you do not engage in this [mind training] practice now, you will fail to achieve it in the future as well. This [practice] does not require great visualization [skills], nor excellent meditation or mastery of the mantras. Even someone who does not know the alphabet can engage in this practice. Furthermore, the moment you reflect upon this, there ease arises in your mind, and you experience increased happiness; it acts as a remedy against mental afflictions. This practice is therefore called the meditative absorption "traversing all phenomena with ease." It is as stated in Atiśa's *Songs of Blissfulness*:

> Whether someone is a foe or a close friend —
> These objects that give rise to afflictions—
> He who sees them as spiritual teachers
> Shall be joyful wherever he resides.[726]

Or you will experience something akin to the following:

Wherever you reside is a celestial palace;
Whomever you associate with is a meditation deity;
The mind is the primordial expanse of reality;
The teacher merely brings them to light.[727]

Without this [practice], even if you learn all kinds of sciences and knowledge, you will be disappointed. You will remain vulnerable to malevolent forces and negativity. It is necessary therefore to train decisively the moment your throat tightens and becomes dry. Nothing will be realized if you postpone it. If, however, you can practice in this manner, you will succeed in what is referred to as "The right teaching for the right person; and the right teaching serves the right purpose." This cannot occur if you undertake the practice as an obligation. You must sharpen the tip of your heart, and being your mother's tough son, you must attack the afflictions head-on with the thought "You shall die!"

In all interactions with others, accept the loss and offer them the gain. If you grant others what is most desirable among the mundane excellences and accept upon yourself what is least desirable, then even if you experience disappointments like the person who goes to the land of jewels but fails to find even a piece of rock that can be used against a dog, this [act of giving and taking] will still become a cause for buddhahood. In this sense, whatever you encounter is immediately applied to your practice. In contrast, if you lack this [habit], all your vast learning, refined meditation, and so on become endeavors of the "I." This will lead to your erecting an "I" fortress and complaining, "They hate me," and making such statements as "No one is more learned than I." When this happens, you become like what Ligom Shönu Drak says, "The 'I' and my loyalty to it make me suffer." All your spiritual practices become tools for your rivalries, and you always want to be on the top, which, in addition to dooming your spiritual practice, is misery in itself. If, on the other hand, you take your hat off to everyone and take upon yourself the loss, this increases your happiness. It does not take long; this [effect] will manifest the instant you engage in the reflections. [258]

(iv) Transforming adversities into favorable conditions

Fourth, taking adverse conditions onto the path is threefold: (1) taking suffering, (2) taking the unfortunate era, and (3) taking deficiencies.

(1) Taking suffering

Taking suffering is presented in the following line:

When both are present, take them all.

When you are driven to despair by suffering and its origin, do not cry out, "How will I ever succeed in my spiritual practice?" and become disheartened and demoralized. Instead take the sufferings of others and add these onto your own. Countless sufferings are likely to affect you personally, such as the inability to bear hardships due to old age; attacks by enemies, malevolent forces, or illness; being let down by wealth, friends, and family; and so on. There is the tragic story about two novice monks of Shang, the Chim brothers. They went to Tsang province to study only to die, one day apart, upon their return, while their third brother was left remaining [alone] at Yarlung. Furthermore when you are oppressed by afflictions, such as intense hatred, generate love and compassion for those beings with similar afflictions, and with this thought, take upon yourself their sufferings and their sufferings' origins. (If you train, the master said, your mind training can penetrate into the depths of your mind. But if you do not train in such manner, you merely chip the surface.)

For this [practice] you do not need qualities such as great learning; what is required, instead, is great courage. (You need a well-honed heart.) You can achieve this if you undertake the task right now; you will not succeed through prolonged procrastination. Act according to the saying "If it is white treat it as yogurt, and if it's red treat it as blood."[728] If you are capable of proceeding [on your path] with ease so that whenever afflictions and sufferings arise, your practice reaches there too, then [true] Dharma practice has arisen. To bear the title of a noble one yet be abjectly deficient in virtuous activity is worse than being a non-Buddhist heretic.

(2) [Taking the unfortunate era]

The second, taking the unfortunate era onto the path, is presented in the following lines:

**This proliferation of five degenerations,
Transform it into the path to enlightenment.**

At this time, when only undesirable events reign in this last five-hundredth period,[729] an era degenerate in terms of sentient beings' lives, afflictions, and views, when the pursuit of Dharma practice, such as the seeking of enlightenment, remains difficult, this mind training helps transform all of these into the path to enlightenment. [259] For whatever remains unbearable, make that the entity you transform on the path to enlightenment.

Therefore you must ensure the arising of the awakening mind exchanging self and others where it has not arisen and enhance it where it has already arisen. As it is said, "Apply the nine conditions admired by all."[730] You should (1) seek a teacher who reveals this kind of teaching, (2) associate with friends who engage in this practice, (3) listen to teachings that present this practice, (4) purify the defilements, the obstacles, (5) gather the conducive conditions, the accumulations, (6) make supplications, (7) invoke intervention by the Dharma protectors, (8) reflect upon the [merit] and shortcomings of either possessing or not possessing this realization within, and (9) recognize the afflictions and their root, the grasping at self, as enemies. In this way, whenever afflictions arise in your mind, they become pacified. When you recognize [the true nature of] conceptualizations, you experience a confidence akin to someone who, having recognized the thief, remains immune to any harm. Even if you remember to do this once, or develop the aspiration for it once, or experience joyful admiration for it once, it will become a remedy. Even were you to interview a hundred people, you'd find no meditation to practice other than this. Even were I to bare my heart to you, the master said, nothing [else would be revealed] but red pulsating flesh.

(3) [Taking deficiencies]

The third, taking deficiencies onto the path, is presented in the following line:

Adopt the three principal conditions.

There are three principal conditions for the practice of Dharma. They are as follows: (1) Among primary causes are such perfect conditions as faith, joyous effort, and so on, which make your thoughts susceptible to the realizations [of the path], from the [realization of] impermanence to the ultimate nature of reality. (2) The contributing condition is that you are in the heart of

the perfect, qualified spiritual teacher such that no dog could drive a wedge
between the two of you. Such a spiritual teacher possesses the instructions
to help enhance the student's realizations and has the realizations himself.
(3) Finally, there is a coming together of such favorable conditions as food,
clothing, and so on, not acquired through wrong means of livelihood, and
you are not dependent upon anyone else.

With these three conditions present, you will have no difficulty in your
pursuit of buddhahood, and it will be like the uniting of master Atiśa and
Geshé Dromtönpa. At present, however, you have not fulfilled these three
conditions. Either something of the mountains or something of the plains
is missing.[731] For most people, all three are missing. Relating this to your
own experience and stirred by compassion, take upon yourself other sentient beings' [deficiency in] these three conditions. [260] Also, some who
are with you listening to the teachings may lack the desire to listen, some
who received their vows and precepts together with you may be incapable
[of guarding them], and some who received many practice instructions with
you may have never practiced in the past, never practice at present, and will
never practice in future; they are paralyzed. Take all of these [shortcomings]
upon yourself. Imagine that all beings possess the three conditions and attain
full enlightenment.

c. Joyfulness, the concluding practice

Thus, preceded by the presentation of the main topics such as the three
[points]—what is to be understood and so on—the concluding practice is
presented in the following line:

Cultivate constantly the joyful mind alone.

This means experiencing the taste of mind training and, with the attitude
that "Whatever adversities befall me, I can practice mind training," ensuring that your mind remains free of distress. Even arhats undergo [the prob-
lem of] finding and not finding and so on. Many stories are told [in the
sutras] of arhats contracting leprosy, dying of starvation, and becoming the
victim of bad reputation, and so on, yet there is no unhappiness in their
minds. In contrast, the state of mind of ordinary sentient beings is by nature
unhappy. Even now, because you are still an ordinary being, you yearn for a
circle of friends and for material possessions, and it is difficult, therefore, to

prevent self-grasping from surfacing. So free yourself of likes and dislikes.

Atiśa states that the descent of [vital drops within the] central channel is not so serious; becoming ill is.[732] Analogously, for those engaged in mind training, undesirable occurrences are not so serious; experiencing dislike is. This is similar to Shapopa's statement, "There is no greater insult than to say 'My spiritual teacher is unhappy at heart.'"[733]

Of the four desirable and four undesirable mundane factors, if you deliberately train the mind in relation to the four undesirable phenomena, then everything will become desirable. Regardless of whatever difficult situations and obstacles occur, if your mind does not experience distress, the realization of giving and taking practiced during meditative sessions will then be established during the postmeditation periods [as well]. This is also the meaning of the following lines:

> Riding the awakening mind horse
> And traveling from joy to joy....[734]

Also, as stated in the following lines, you should put on the armor of protection:

> Even if you enjoy the perfections of gods,
> Pray be not conceited;
> Even if you are destitute like the hungry ghosts,
> Pray be not disheartened.[735]

Also:

> Not delighted when praised
> And not perturbed when belittled—
> This is the mark of a sublime being.[736]

[261] You need to contemplate this point free of distraction, on the basis of [pure] ethical discipline and commitments to your teacher. If you find this not to be the case, reflect, "Either I am bereft of Dharma practice or I am someone who merely pretends to be a practitioner and have therefore failed in my practice. I have indulged in this pretense of Dharma practice for a long period. Such is my fate!" You should lament thus.

In brief, whatever undesirable situations befall you, without any distress, learn to turn them into conditions favorable for training the mind, and whatever adversities occur, abide in joy so that its impact is magnified by your meditative equipoise.

2. The means of guarding [mind training] against degeneration

This has three parts: (a) in relation to others, (b) in relation to yourself, and (c) in relation to self and others. The first is threefold: (i) in relation to the objects, (ii) in relation to your attitudes, and (iii) in relation to actions. The first, in relation to objects, is presented in the following line:

Train constantly toward those chosen objects.

In general you might sense you can achieve [mind training], but if you don't train with respect to these [objects], your training will degenerate. There are five chosen objects toward whom you must undertake constant meditative practice. First are your preceptor, your master, your parents, and so on, who are sources of kindness, and toward whom, if you commit any nonvirtuous act, you incur dishonor in this life and lose the very purpose of mind training as well. You must therefore practice with special emphasis toward these embodiments of kindness.

Second, because you risk using inappropriate speech toward those with whom you live and interact frequently, such as people in the same community, you must pay them special attention and constantly practice in relation to them.[737]

Third are those you naturally compete with. On the mundane level, this includes your paternal [and maternal] relatives, and in the religious realm, this includes your peers. Single these out for special attention and constantly practice in relation to them. If you fail, no matter how much you may engage in Dharma practice, your efforts will bear no fruit, like spitting into the ocean. Someone who writes the name of his colleague and places it under his cushion [and sits on it], or someone who rejoices at a former friend's misfortune, uttering, "How satisfying! The nasty person got what he deserved," cannot possibly train the mind. Since such a person cannot possibly achieve even a general realization of mind training, it is important to train by paying special attention to this type of object.

Fourth is the class of individuals who harbor ill-will toward you even though you have done them no harm. [262] They may do so because of your aggression in past lives. As the saying goes, "When thoughts of anger explode, the thread of compassion snaps."⁷³⁸ Thus you should select these as special objects and constantly practice in relation to them.

Fifth are people everyone dislikes although they have done nothing against others. In Tsang province a monk was once told by someone he had never met before that the person disliked him. Also, in Kyimé, someone once said, "I have never met anyone I have disliked as much as I dislike this person."⁷³⁹ Take the negative karma and suffering of these beings and give them your happiness and virtues. It may be very difficult to give these without hesitation. Many monks are happy when they themselves can benefit [others] but are not so happy when others prove beneficial. Laypeople [often] hope to acquire the house of someone who has died, while some monks look forward to inheriting a [deceased monk's] domain.⁷⁴⁰ So it is critical to contemplate as Phuchungwa states, "If you do not constantly practice by choosing such objects for special attention, you will fail [even] to detect when the root [of virtues] has been cut."

The second, [guarding your mind training] in relation to your attitudes, is presented in the following line:

Do not dwell on others' shortcomings.

Do not dwell on or speak of shortcomings—whether in relation to mundane norms or to the sacred Dharma—of sentient beings in general, of those who have entered the order in particular, and especially of your friends. If you happen to perceive such failings, recognize them as your own flaws or delusions.

The third, [guarding your mind training] in relation to actions, is presented in the following line:

Do not speak of the defects [of others].

Calling others "sickly," "blind," and so on in worldly terms, or calling them "ignorant," "morally degenerate," "breakers of oaths," and so on from the perspective of the transworldly [Dharma], makes it impossible to achieve realization such as that of mind training. Such acts are called "carrying a spear pointing [at others]." Conceivably, too, the [monastic] custom of enumerating each other's transgressions may [sometimes] be inappropriate.⁷⁴¹

(b) Guarding [mind training] in relation to yourself

Second, [guarding] in relation to oneself is twofold: (i) In relation to attitudes, and (ii) in relation to actions. The first is presented in the following line:

Destroy all rationalizations.

Rationalizations like "This individual did this unjust act to me" and so on undermine your mind training. You must discard all such negative thoughts.

The second, [guarding] in relation to actions, is presented in the following line:

Whichever of the two arises, bear them both.

[263] Since you risk giving up Dharma practice if you have no forbearance when either of the two situations—prosperity or misfortune—arises, it is crucial that you be able to bear them. If you were to suddenly enjoy great prosperity, you might think "I have accomplished all of this myself. There is no one above me." With such thoughts, you might indulge in draping yourself in new felt robes, constructing temples, and so on. Some people might even step on their companions' lotus [heart]; one [who does these things] lacks mindfulness, the master said.[742] Some become conceited when they attract disciples, material gifts, and honors, and then they belittle others, indulging in abusive behavior. These things happen when you fail to bear prosperity; never become conceited by prosperity or become attached to it. Make sure you don't to fall prey to the eight mundane concerns, but instead take them as factors conducive to [mind training] practice. When your fortune increases, it is important to stay humble, the master said.

Alternatively, when, as a result of a misfortune, you become so impoverished that [you feel] the only thing lower than you is the river flowing under [the bridge], you might become desolate and think, "Why is this happening to me?" You might despair and become incapable of engaging in any virtuous acts and think, "How is Dharma practice possible in my condition?" As in the saying, "Being impoverished, negative karma naturally proliferates," you risk losing your spiritual practice when this happens. Since all this comes from a lack of forbearance, reflect, "Compared to the gulf between the happiness of the higher realms and the suffering of the lower realms, there is not much difference between happiness and suffering within the human realm." So determined to avoid such distraction in the future, endeavor to enhance your virtuous activities. You should be capable of bearing both happiness and suffering just like Langri Thangpa. Whichever of the two arises [prosperity or misfortune], have the thought "If I do not engage in Dharma practice at such times, when, then, do I do so?" This is as stated in the following:

> Even if you are prosperous like the gods,
> Pray be not conceited;
> Even if you are destitute like the hungry ghosts,
> Pray be not disheartened.[743]

(c) Guarding [mind training] in relation to both self and others

Third, [guarding mind training] in relation to both self and others is presented in the following lines:

> **Learn to ensure ease in your practice.**
> **Overcome all errors through a single means.**[744]

If you develop the feeling, "I cannot engage in practices such as this," you might give up [mind training practice]. To counter this, cultivate thoughts such as "I need not endure any hardships of body or speech, for I can train in all [aspects of] the practice by means of my thoughts. It's simple. I don't even have to prepare the meal for a single household." Other spiritual practices require many conditions for their correct implementation—the right environment, the right companions, and so on. Here, however, you don't need any conditions in particular, for you are not dependent on either fortunate or unfortunate circumstances. (Whether you have prosperity or misfortune, whether you acquire all the right conditions or lack some of them, whatever occurs, you can take that very situation [264] as favorable for practice. This practice is extremely easy to implement.) Whatever causes your error [or regression], whether your loss of enthusiasm for training, your failure to gain its realization even though you have engaged in the training, and so on, [willingly] embrace that [circumstance] and use it to further your practice.

3. The factors for enhancing the realizations of mind training

The factors for enhancement are threefold: (a) conduct of the three doors, (b) conduct that prevents degeneration, and (c) training without partiality. The first, conduct of the three doors, is presented in the following line:

Be endowed with the three inseparable factors.

Being a Mahayanist does not mean you have no tasks to do. (You should be overcoming the errors by practicing giving and taking.) Your body should not be divorced from such [activities] as circumambulation, prostrations, and serving your teacher and the Three Jewels. Your speech should not be separated from [reciting] going-for-refuge [stanzas], mantra repetitions, recitation of sutras, and so on, while your mind should not be divorced from the practice of mind training. Mentally engaging in this [mind training] and undertaking mantra repetitions will keep you alert; and employing this [mind training] as a walking staff will help you maintain your thought processes, the master said. This is not to suggest that declaring and purifying infractions of ethical precepts is unnecessary and that taking others' [suffering] is [somehow] a substitute for this. While taking [the suffering] of others, you need to forsake even your most minute infractions.

You need the courage that eliminates negative thought processes the moment they arise. This is analogous to a non-Buddhist [rite master] performing black magic that kills all the animals who appear within his vicinity. You should do the same to whatever conceptualizations arise in you. Thus through striving in virtue with your three doors [of body, speech, and mind], your practice of mind training will become greatly enhanced, like adding fresh logs to a fire.

The second, conduct that prevents degeneration, is presented in the following line:

Contemplate the three, which are free of degeneration.

By ensuring your reverence for the spiritual teachers remains undiminished, your enthusiasm for mind training remains undiminished, and your conscientiousness in [observing] the precepts remains undiminished, your mind training develops to ever higher levels. Since all the positive qualities of the Mahayana [path] depend upon faith and respect for your spiritual teacher, cultivate the mindfulness of recognizing him as an actual buddha, [265] thus ensuring that your faith and respect for him remain undiminished. For if these diminish, you will become just like a pond whose source stream has dried up. Just as a breach of an arm's length can destroy a canal, if you lose your faith and respect for even one of his instructions, the stream of wisdom will not flow in your heart. When faith and respect are damaged, the sacred bond [between teacher and student] degenerates, but even more importantly, the growth of higher qualities ceases, and this is like the violation of a sacred oath. Strive therefore in [guarding your mind training] to the best of your ability. This is not achieved through thoughts alone; rather, it is done through nurturing compassion, even in small degrees. In fact, regardless of who you interact with, let alone your spiritual teacher, it is vital that you be not divorced from respect [for that person]. You should contemplate, the master said, as stated in the following:

> Whoever I interact with I will regard myself as the lowest;
> Like the son of a beggar, I will take the place of the humble.[745]

This cannot be achieved by merely harboring the thought "I will cultivate faith and respect." You need to contemplate the advantages and disadvantages of cultivating faith and respect and, on this basis, cultivate respect for all, regardless of their status. Being incapable of befriending anyone, failing to find attendants, and so on, are all due to lack of faith and respect. Since, as it is said, all positive qualities of the Mahayana degenerate on the basis of [interactions with] friends, cultivating respect for them is critical.

(It is impossible for [mind training] to arise if your enthusiasm for it is lost, thus it is vital that this remains undiminished.) Ensuring this is so is as follows: With the thought "This is the innermost essence of Mahayana, the potent seed of buddhahood," engage (with enthusiasm and joy) in its practice without equating it with any other teachings. (Even when you interact with a dog, for example, you should cultivate faith and respect for it; otherwise it is impossible to succeed in this practice.) Merely thinking "I will be enthusiastic," however, is not sufficient; you need to contemplate the advantages and the disadvantages. Inability to comprehend the teachings initially, forgetting them once you have gained comprehension, lacking the desire to train in the teachings when you have not forgotten them—all these are due to lack of enthusiasm. So it is necessary to engage in the practice with enthusiasm all the time, the master said.

Preventing degeneration of conscientiousness with respect to the precepts is as follows: From [the precepts of] going for refuge to those of a lay practitioner, a novitiate, and finally a fully ordained monk, and on through to the "aspiration" and "engaging" [aspects of the awakening mind] and the empowerments, in regard to each of the vows and ethical disciplines you have adopted, there should not be a single moment of relapse. That realizations fail to arise in you at present with respect to genuinely pure precepts, even though you have anointed yourself with the teachings, is due to destroying the very root [of pure morality] through loss of conscientiousness. Because of this you fail in whatever spiritual practices you undertake. [266] Without genuine conscientiousness you [might] travel to be in the presence of a yogi and then, openly waving a jug of beer, make claims such as "O all householders, I have a profoundly advanced meditation practice." You [may thus] engender wrong views in [others] and lead them to the hells, so be careful here. In this respect, you also need colleagues with whom you can regularly interact. If you seek the company of those who say, "This much cannot be harmful," those who are foolhardy, or those who are reluctant to partake in this [mind training], your [mind training] will conceivably suffer degeneration. Once in Tsang a Kadampa practitioner and a logician went on a journey together. At first the Kadampa did not like the logician's habit of verbosity; later, however, he became worse himself. He would speak only in terms of "I" and exclaim "some assert," "if I am thirsty," and so on.[746] Such things can happen, the master said.

The third, training without partiality toward anyone, is presented in the following lines:

Train without partiality toward [any] object.
Cherish your training, all its breadth and depth.

Since no training can be achieved through a biased approach, if you train without partiality, your practice will develop and progress.[747] All those who say, "I have greater forbearance toward ghosts while he has greater forbearance toward humans; I am stronger with respect to emptiness while he is stronger on compassion," are biased in their approach. It is quite natural for the qualities of the noble ones to be complete while the qualities of ordinary beings are partial. Furthermore, for some individuals, [mind training] occurs when they suffer misfortune; others, when prosperous, have thoughts such as "No man is above me, no dog superior to Gongkar,"[748] and they become an object of ridicule like someone who, with great effort, bends a bamboo stick but later lets go of it.

Some succeed while prosperous but, when misfortune strikes, exclaim, "You don't understand; my situation is desperate," and are incapable of withstanding calamity.[749] Similarly some, when praised, hop around like a rooftop pigeon whose beak has been pierced by a splinter. And when belittled, they can't bear it and act as if they might poison someone. Again, some are measured when it comes to food but are unbalanced about clothing. Some have less attachment to inner [experience] but stronger attachment to external objects; others are the reverse. Some, though lacking in knowledge, are pompous and cannot bear to see others show them disrespect.[750] Some lose their Dharma practice while remaining in their own country, while others lose it away from home. Some are capable of dying for the sake of their group or for the sake of the monastic life, some out of miserliness, envy, or anger, [267] and some for the sake of wealth. Even if you were to list [scenarios] for eons, the master said, the possibilities would not be exhausted.

Make sure all your activities—listening to and teaching the Dharma, [cultivating the] view, and meditating on sublime Dharma—all become remedies against your afflictions; and since the root of all afflictions is self-grasping, it is crucial you train in its antidotes comprehensively, without omitting any elements. To do this, you must settle all qualms through the wisdom of discriminative awareness; and if you possesses a teacher's special instructions, you must apply them concertedly against whatever afflictions, such as miserliness, happen to be most intense. If whatever activity you engage in becomes an antidote to self-grasping, that indicates you have not erred; you will then subdue self-grasping, subdue the three realms, and subdue the entirety of the three states of existence. Then you will have succeeded. You'll not get more than a full plate by relying on one *sang* of meat, the master said.[751]

This yoga pervades all yogas, such as those pertaining to food and so on. And unlike visiting the temple [only] during the daytime, you should engage in this training from the very bones of your heart. You should train like Langthangpa,[752] who dedicated his merit toward being reborn in the hells, and like Chekawa, who is said to have rejoiced in taking the suffering of others. To engage in Dharma practice, you can't merely sit upright and understand the words; you must implement the meaning of the words as an inner practice, the master said.

B. *The measure of being trained*

This is threefold: the actual measure, its signs, and the witness. The first is presented in the following line:

When it is reversed, this is the measure [of being trained].[753]

The beginner's stage is the period of training by means of imagination. The measure of being trained through imagination is when your attachment and clinging to the external world of environment and the internal world of sentient beings—the natural bases [of our clinging]—are discarded and reversed. It is stated:

> When the pangs of attachment grip tightly,
> Even feeling good is held to be erroneous.[754]

And:

> Those sentient who are attached to samsara spin around constantly.[755]

And:

> Touch the conquerors' enlightenment, which is free of attachment.[756]

As stated in these lines, it is essential to practice without being attached to anything. All the teachings of the Buddha were taught as a means to overcome attachment and clinging. All teachings on the stages of the path taught by Atiśa, too, were presented as stages to relinquishing clinging. [268] These include the stages from the overcoming of clinging to this life by reflecting on death to the overcoming of clinging to real entities and their characteristics by reflecting on the two selflessnesses.[757] Therefore, it has been taught, even to attain the liberation of a disciple or a self-realized one, you have to be free of clinging and attachment, as stated in the following lines:

> By giving up everything, one attains nirvana.
> So my mind seeks the transcendence of sorrow.[758]

Only the buddhas have totally eliminated attachment and clinging. All the teachings taught [by the Buddha]—the three higher trainings, the two accumulations, the six perfections, the five paths, the ten [bodhisattva] levels—are methods to eliminate clinging.

There are two avenues through which we cling to this life: the body and things other than the body. The first, attachment to the body, has been described as a source of many disadvantages. It is stated:

> Because of attachment to my body,
> I fear even the least frightening thing.[759]

Attachment to "things other than the body" refers to attachment to things, material possessions, friends, family, and so on. As stated in the following, you should overcome your clinging by reflecting on the disadvantages:

> Those distracted by attachment to wealth
> Have no chance to gain freedom from the suffering of existence.[760]

There are also two avenues through which we become attached to the bodies of future lives. First is the craving for a specific body, such as the desire to obtain an excellent body in the next life, and there is also the arising of craving for no specific body, such as when we become aware of being dead and that we no longer possess a body and we experiences the fear of falling off a cliff. In this respect, consciousness departs [the body] when, in conjunction with exhalation, a craving arises for the body of where we are likely to be born [next].

Some disciple schools do not accept the intermediate state; those that do do not accept the accumulation of karma during this state. They maintain that the form first obtained in the intermediate state changes into something different. Mahayanists, however, accept the accumulation of karma during the intermediate state. They maintain that during this intermediate state you can accumulate karma by following the traces of earlier virtuous and negative actions. They [thus] accept that the perceptions prior to death are vivid and, as you live in their traces, the awareness of the moment of your death arises.

For seven weeks you remain in the intermediate state, and every seven days a different body is assumed, they maintain. Even when entering the mother's womb, those who experience pleasing visions feel as if they are entering a beautiful mansion, and those who experience unpleasant visions feel as if they are entering a swamp. The bodies of the intermediate-state beings are said to be visible only to their own kind and to those with perfect celestial eyes; [269] others cannot see them. All five senses are intact and are not obstructed by barriers such as walls; they consume smell for nourishment. They are, however, obstructed by the [walls of the] mother's womb.

There are differences between male and female bodies, and if you are female, you become attached to your father and jealous toward your mother; and if you are male, it is the reverse. In this manner the link [to the next life] is forged and, sealed by your parents' seeds, you suffer a loss of consciousness for a while. Then the shoots of name-and-form[761] come into being. Those who do not accept the intermediate state maintain that it is through the craving for the body of the next life that the link is forged. If you are to be born in the formless realm, grasping as self the basis of name lying at the core of your heart forges the link. From long past, it is said, the beings of the intermediate state are obstructed by Vajra Seat [Bodhgaya].[762] Since all cultivation of cyclic existence takes place through clinging, it is crucial that you do not cling to the intermediate state, and for that it is crucial to avoid clinging at the moment of death as well. To succeed, it has been taught, you need to train the mind not to cling to anything starting now.

As the tantric adepts train in this manner free of clinging, it is said, they realize the higher attainment of the great seal as knowledge bearers during the intermediate state. They assume a visionary rainbowlike body that does not belong to any of the six realms of migrations. All the bodies of sentient beings, therefore, are rooted in karma and attachment. In the case of the birth of bodhisattvas who have attained the [higher bodhisattva] levels, their compassion substitutes for the afflictions, while their aspirations substitute for karma.[763] In this manner, they take birth to benefit sentient beings.

The second, the signs of being trained, is presented in the following line:

> The sign of being trained is when you are endowed with five [marks of] greatness.[764]

Once your minds become trained in this manner, (1) you will become a great bodhisattva; (2) since you will refrain from even the slightest transgressions, you will become a great upholder of monastic discipline; (3) since on encountering others your forbearance will be as firm as a mountain, you will become a great ascetic; (4) since you will always possess faith and joyous effort in relation to the virtuous actions of body and speech, you will become a great practitioner of virtue; and (5) since you will have mastered the principal subject matter of all the scriptures and treatises and your mind will be trained, you will become a great yogi.

It is vital to train persistently, however. Your effort is not adequate if you remain the same person compared to yesterday or last year; instead, you must look for progress from the earlier session to the later session [270] and from the earlier part of the session to the later part of the same session. Some results may be achieved through learning and reflection; however, this alone will not bear much result, so it is necessary to ensure the consolidation [of learning and reflection within meditation] at the same time. Since it will be vital in the future [as well] to constantly armor yourself, do this by taking sentient beings' negative karma and sufferings upon yourself and giving others your virtue and happiness. Cultivate therefore the following thoughts: "From this very day, whenever harms caused by humans or nonhumans befall me, I resolve to endure whatever I will experience in the future. I will never be divorced even for a single instant from the vows and precepts I have taken. I will forbear whatever befalls me, be it insults, envy, or denigration." If you armor yourself in this manner, in the future you will succeed in enduring whatever experience you encounter. More importantly, you should armor yourself with the intention to never act contrary to the Dharma when encountering situations that might conflict with it. It is stated:

> Toward whom even causing harm leads you to happiness;
> To those sources of happiness I go for refuge.[765]

And:

> He who sees as spiritual teachers
> The objects that engender afflictions—
> Be they enemy or friend—
> Will remain content wherever he is.[766]

And:

> Those who abuse you, belittle you,
> Disparage you, or harbor envy against you—
> O hero, vanquish them with your brilliance.[767]

And:

Even if your kindness is repaid with harm,
You should cultivate compassion in response.
Most excellent being of the world,
Respond to even the negative with goodness.[768]

And:

Even if others cause me harm
Or speak of me disparagingly,
May all possess the fortune of enlightenment.[769]

As stated in these lines, you should train your mind.

With this [mind training], even if you lack everything else, you will become fully enlightened. Toward the end of this very life, it has been taught, your mental continuum could become something extraordinary. And even if actual realizations do not arise, you will experience tranquillity the instant you reflect on the words. Stories, such as those pertaining to the quote, "Those who aspire to swiftly attain full enlightenment must train in the precious awakening mind,"[770] refer to this [mind training], the master said.

However much you wish to cease birth and death, to that same extent you must engage in a spiritual practice such as this. Take the attitude that "This can be realized." [271] If you have the attitude "I will engage in its practice if [its realization] dawns, if everything is okay, if this pleases my teacher's heart, or if other people accord me respect, but if these are absent, I will not do so," then you have already abandoned the teachings, the master said. Those who abandon the teachings when they are successful and powerful will receive no blessings during Dharma practice, the master said. Therefore, it has been taught, you should pray that, from now until [the end of] this life, during the intermediate state, and in future lives up until the attainment of buddhahood, you are never divorced from this teaching but find spiritual teachers who reveal this teaching.

The third, the witness for the arising [of mind training], is presented in the following line:

Of the two witnesses, uphold the principal one.

Others might say of you, "Oh, he has gained Dharma realizations; having subdued self-grasping, he has truly become gentle and tender like a piece of wool taken out of water [and dried]," while in your own conscience, you could be thinking such thoughts as "At such and such a time I was deceitful; at such and such a time self-grasping thoughts arose in me." The principal [witness] is, in contrast, yourself and [the capacity] to sustain the thought within yourself, "Even were I to fall headfirst into the hells, I would have nothing to regret." It is crucial to channel all your abilities through faith, intelligence, perseverance and so on, through sustained effort, without falling prey to distraction and diversion for even a single instant. As if the blood in your heart were being washed away by [clean] water, you should be able to feel "Even were I to die this instant, I would have nothing more to prove." At such a point, your practice attains a high level.

Others may be impressed by observing in you a few excellent qualities and a few acts of kindness, but this is not of primary importance. Likewise, in the context of activities such as giving expositions and engaging in mantra recitations, sharing these with others and helping to dispel harms is of principal importance. It is conceivable that manifest conceit, such as desiring scholarly achievement and power, can be [the motive instead]. There are inexhaustible examples like this one. To accord great importance to external [appearance] is also a function of your inner [mental] state. Sometimes positive conduct and gentle speech may garner recognition of Dharma realization. Pretending to relinquish self-grasping, you may give away some possessions, and when disputes arise, you might respond, "You are right, you are right; it is all my fault." Because of this behavior, you might be recognized as having gained realization of Dharma. This, however, is not the principal witness.

It is necessary to have a [witness] in your own mind. In terms of general Dharma practice, [272] your success can be judged on the basis of others' observations of your body, speech, and mind. Here, however, others' perceptions of your body and speech are immaterial; you should observe your mind alone. And this can only be undertaken by someone who has had all the instructions revealed to him by a teacher and who possesses a courageous will. It is crucial [that such a person] engages in the practice until realizations become manifest. Strive therefore in supplicating the deities and teachers from your heart, in requesting enlightened activities from the Dharma protectors and so on, and in endeavoring to achieve authentic realization of this [mind training].

C. *The purpose of training*

The third, the purpose of training, is presented in the following lines:

> The intent of all teachings converges on a single point.
> It greatly surpasses [all] other qualities.[771]

The purpose of all the scriptures and treatises is to attain liberation, and for this it is necessary to subdue self-grasping. Therefore all activities of study, reflection, and meditation are for the sake of subduing self-grasping. If even the liberation of a disciple and a self-realized one cannot be achieved without eliminating self-grasping, what need is there to speak of omniscience. If your endeavors, such as training your mind with skillfulness, observing ethical discipline with industry, and so on, become aids to the self, giving rise to such thoughts as "None is one more learned than I," you have erred. If they turn into remedies against self-grasping, then the purpose of mind training has been fulfilled.

Because this [mind training practice] does not rely on other favorable conditions, it possesses extraordinary qualities. Other spiritual practices are dependent upon many other factors: good health, youth, solitude, practice at the feet of a spiritual teacher, freedom from illness, and so on. There is also the need for a formless object of cognition, and so on.[772] For this [mind training], however, only two [conditions] are indispensable—the common ethical discipline and the uncommon commitments of the Mahayana [teachings]. If these two are lacking, this is said to be analogous to removing the roots, making it impossible to attain [realization]. If these two are present, then you need not depend upon any other conditions; this mind training is therefore endowed with qualities that greatly surpass other practices. [273] If being independent of other conditions is taken as the criterion for its possession of extraordinary qualities, [the question becomes] why is mind training not dependent on other conditions? This is explained in the following line:

> The adversities are transformed into meditative practice.[773]

This line can also be appropriately applied in the section on transforming adversities into the path. Here it is presented as a reason [demonstrating why mind training possesses extraordinary qualities]: All events—intense suffering, forceful afflictions, deficient amenities, and so on—are turned into factors [that enhance the practice]. Leave aside all other practices in this life, and from today on, engage in this practice [of mind training]. I, for one, cultivate admiration for this and you, too, can attain its realization.

Without this [practice], the moment adversities are encountered, those who claim to be excellent in meditation either fail to understand them [adversities] as remedies or fail to turn [their meditation] into direct antidotes or indirect antidotes. The strength [of their meditation] fails to reduce the force of the afflictions and instead appears to help increase arrogance or conceit. The moment this [mind training] is recalled or cultivated once in your heart, however, the continuous waves of afflictions appear to gently subside. Therefore, when the desire for not encountering undesirable events or the fear of these occurring arises in your heart, take upon yourselves the similar feelings of all sentient beings. When this is understood, the understanding of emptiness, too, arises naturally. Without this, all who claim to have high philosophical views and to be skilled in meditation can fall into intoxicating pride. This [practice] is especially indispensable for helping for taking responsibility for the general well-being [of others]. Sporadic virtuous actions are analogous to dusting a conch.[774]

If so, then by what means are these [adversities] transformed into aids to meditative practice? This is explained in the following line:

Everything is transformed into the Mahayana path.[775]

In this era when the five degenerations are in ascendance, when all types of negative acts are present, when (even in terms of your life) there is no leisure to undertake Dharma practice, and when all varieties of destructive philosophical views are rife, we must train in the two practices of giving and taking, transforming whatever we do into [an aspect of] the Mahayana path.

With these, the presentation of the meaning of the verses is complete.

Now begins the prose section, which gives counsel to the heart:

Do not boast of your good deeds.

Do not boast aloud or harbor feelings of entitlement because of having done some act of kindness to others, because you may be learned, industrious, or skilled in meditation, on the grounds that you are an important person, or for any other reason. [274] Since even those practicing meditation in caves are likely to be boastful, it is especially important to be vigilant against this flaw. Even with your altruistic acts, no one forced you to do them; you pledged yourself to them, so there is really nothing to boast about. Never be like the person who, while shedding tears, boasts to his friend of how he has tended the cattle, protected them against thieves, and so on; particularly avoid acting in such a manner toward your parents, your teachers, or any other person. For if you do this habitually, you run the perilous risk of tormenting others through malicious banter. So it is stated:

Do not torment with malicious banter.

Even for ordinary laypeople, malicious banter is unacceptable, especially for the person it is directed toward. If this is so, a Dharma practitioner who jokingly torments others cannot be a true practitioner. If someone engaged in mind training in particular indulges in malicious humor, this contradicts [the practice of] giving and taking, so abandon it. Don't act like a long-bladed chisel that digs deep into others' shortcomings, with your afflictions pursuing malicious banter about your supposed innocence and another's guilt. It is critical that you not indulge in malicious humor no matter what your regional and family background. Refraining from such banter requires the following:

Do not be ill-tempered.

Most [malicious banter] takes place on the basis of some mental construct, so you can talk [yourself] out of it. Sometimes it can arise without your control due to others' influence; but if you fail to control it the first time, it becomes harder to do so the next time. Conversely, if you refrain from it once, you are more eager to resist [in the future]. [For example,] if you have no plate now, you will not [go and] fetch your meal. Don't act like someone who, just because he has refrained from a few negative acts, believes that his advice is a suitable substitute for offering of a cup of tea.[776]

Whatever harmful acts may be committed against you, such as contempt or verbal abuse, accept the blame [for these] upon yourself. Do not respond in kind or lose your temper. At present, your Dharma practice has failed to become a remedy, and thus the strength of your forbearance is weaker even than a deer calf, and your ill temper more intense than that of a *tsen* spirit[777] from Tsang province. Your practice of Dharma fails to achieve its purpose. You must therefore ensure that it becomes a remedy against self-grasping. Aspire to emulate the great Naljorpa, who said, "[I don't care] if I am elevated as high as the winds or thrown deep down in the sea."[778] Without this root, mind training is impossible.

You must fortify the entrance to your mind at all times. [275] If you succeed in this life-supporting vein of Dharma practice, all other aspects of mind training will arise naturally. When this is lacking, you are liable to engage in malicious banter and remain dissatisfied regardless of whom you interact with, all because of being ill-tempered. So whatever situations arise—good or bad—abide [unperturbed] and uncomplaining. Otherwise, you may be drawn to commit the four negative deeds, such as forsaking sentient beings; and you might lose the precepts of going for refuge and the four qualities that make a person a paragon of virtue.[779] This [ill-temperedness] also causes the degeneration of the sacred bond between teacher and student; it undermines harmony between spouses; and it prevents you from finding cell mates. It is essential therefore to remain free of ill temper at all times. Don't lose your temper over the amount of tea served or the order of seating [assigned to you].[780]

On some occasions, however, you need to be overly sensitive. If harm comes to the Radreng way of life,[781] not only should you express your anger, in fact you must, the master said. It is essential that you show outrage when aspects of [Radreng's] liberating way of life are violated. These include refraining from the [mundane] activities, such as farming, that are the purview of laypeople, not consuming alcohol even at the threat of your life, not forsaking the ten virtuous deeds. Doing this [successfully], however, requires the following:

Do not be boisterous.

When we benefit someone, if they reciprocate in kind, we tend to appreciate this and exclaim, "Not many people are as decent as you." However, if our good deeds are not acknowledged, we tend to react, "Even though I have done so much, and done it all despite hardship, I do not hear even one acknowledgment emerge from that person's mouth. It's no use doing anything for others." Do not think this way. Since this [equanimity] cannot be maintained with a constantly changing mood, the following is stated:

Do not be fickle.

You will not succeed if you act sometimes one way and sometimes another. Some people act overenthusiastically and then, as if frustrated, give up [easily]. When relating with others, do not act as if you are never tired of forging intimacy and engaging in conflict; rather, like a perfectly strung bow, engage in your [mind training] practice with finesse and firmness, free of fatigue or vexation.

Since it is inappropriate to respond negatively when an opportunity arises, the following is stated:

Do not lie in ambush.

The following stories illustrate what this means. Once when Tönpa Dharma Bar was ill, it is said that a tax was levied on the people of Lhodrak for the performance of rites to heal him. [One person thought,] "When will the day come that Dharma Rinchen stops squeezing my mouth?" [276] Once a man from the Phen region[782] was visiting Nyal, and as he went to wash himself, a novice monk squeezed him between the [two panels of a] door. Later the novice was present at a large gathering in Phen. The man, remembering what had happened to him, approached the novice and said, "We know each other, don't we?" to which the novice replied in the negative. So the man squeezed the novice in the same way to remind him and to humiliate him in return. These are examples of "lying in ambush." If you are cultivating an awakening mind and practicing mind training, there is simply no room for such thoughts. As long as you harbor vengeance (acting out a grudge against others because of harms they did to you), it is impossible for the two [giving and taking] to arise.

Also, do not transfer your flaws to others. This is stated in the following:

Do not place the load of a dzo onto an ox.[783]

Mind training is impossible for those who, fearing undesirable circumstances, cast the blame onto others. It's not that [mind training] is impossible for an ordinary being, however; it is that [this tendency to pass blame to others] must be rooted out by means of its antidote. For example, once when Chekawa was residing at a scholastic monastery, his friend Tönpa Dadrak, who was preparing his bed on the rooftop of his host's house, accidentally dropped a rock through the window, and it fell on a porcelain jar, breaking it into pieces. Chekawa did not speak of it; this is because putting the blame on others is inappropriate. So when utensils break and things burn, do not transfer the blame onto others. You should also not pass chores and so on to others.

Also, when obtaining whatever you wish for, it is stated:

Do not sprint to win a race.

When your object of desire is within reach of many, it is not only those with negative character who sprint to win. The danger of this [common human tendency] rearing its head exists also in those with good character, individuals with a degree of mindfulness and introspective vigilance. When he was in his old age, the great Geshe Drolungpa[784] gave away all his valuables to the populace of Yortsang and Phenpo. Now, even if you cannot act in this manner, [try to] follow the example of masters like him. Though old people may endeavor in this manner [in giving away their possessions], the young [their children] might object.

Do not maintain [inappropriate] loyalty.

Hold no grudge against others for harming you, and if others do not heed you when you give them helpful counsel, do not react by exclaiming, "I have done so much [for you], but to no avail; so now just do whatever you wish!" [277] Your current failure to detect the arising of afflictions is due to your inability to apply the antidotes; for if you apply antidotes, afflictions turn out to be like ripples in water. You must therefore vanquish them, the master said.

Do not strike at the heart.

This refers to telling someone they are bad because of their paternal lineage or because their preceptor is degenerate in his or her own vows, or it is like saying to an ordained monk, "You are devoid of vows." This includes loudly declaring in public that someone committed a murder when few knew [simply to hurt the perpetrator]. Although you are not poisoning anyone or using weapons, from the point of view of mind training, nothing is more negative than this [kind of malice]. It is more damaging to the other person than even killing him.

In some remote past, when Gyatön was a young boy, he startled someone's horse on the edge of a cliff, causing the horse to jump off and die. His parents beat him, and in return he threw stones in his mother's face, whereupon he was cast out of his home. He then shouted aloud, "My parents stole a dri[785] from their landlord Dorjé Wangchuk." Because of this they were forced to pay both for the horse and the dri. There is no graver negative act than this kind [of spiteful malice], the master said.

Do not apply misplaced understanding.

There are six kinds of misplaced understandings—aspiration, rejoicing, satiety, dedication, compassion, and forbearance.[786]

Misplaced *aspiration* refers to aspiring for mundane things and not for Dharma practice after entering the spiritual order. Misplaced *rejoicing* refers to rejoicing in the misfortunes of those who are unpleasant toward you instead of rejoicing in those who engage in genuine Dharma practice. It is inappropriate to harbor thoughts such as "The negative karma he committed has borne its fruit; he is himself to blame; this is a just outcome," as when Gyajang fell on a rock at Yor and a youth exclaimed, "Wonderful, wonderful, it is satisfying to see negativity purified. Has his face turned ashen yet?"

Misplaced *savoring* refers to recalling and savoring memories of defeating enemies and indulging in sensual pleasures, as opposed to savoring the experience of true Dharma practice, of extraordinary realization, or of virtues that are consonant with the awakening mind. Understand that when [indulging in sensual pleasures] arouses your bodily elements and awakens you from sleep, you will depart to the hells.

Misplaced *dedication* refers to being dedicated to leading others to the accumulation of wealth, to protecting their loved ones, and to the mundane pursuits of this life instead of being dedicated to leading those under your guidance to Dharma practice. (Among sentient beings equal to the expanse of space, none has not been your mother. So the endeavor of a bodhisattva is to help free all beings from suffering and lead them to buddhahood—the supreme happiness—motivated by the fear that these kind mothers might otherwise suffer in the hells.) [278] Since the dedication of someone who has generated the awakening mind is to lead all beings to happiness, gaining realization of mind training is impossible for those who are jealous of others' happiness or who fear others may surpass them.

Misplaced *compassion* refers to feeling compassion for those enduring the hardship of Dharma practice instead of generating compassion for those caught in suffering and its causes.

Misplaced *forbearance* refers to being able to bear the various hardships involved in farming, subduing [outer] enemies, and protecting loved ones instead of the forbearance involved in being able to endure hardships for the sake of Dharma practice.

Do not turn the gods into demons.

When displeased, the worldly gods cause harm; this is [a situation of] the gods having turned into demons. It is analogous to becoming conceited about your practice of mind training. (Examples of this are despising others with thoughts such as "Apart from me no one understands the basic truths, and since they are not training their mind, none of them will attain buddhahood" and so on. This is like looking for the footprints of a thief on a rocky mountain while letting him escape in the forests. Forsake these attitudes and make sure the medicine is applied to the right ailment.) Humiliate the self-grasping in you, and abide as if you are the lowest of servants compared to all [other] beings. Since it is difficult to predict when this [skill] will be required, it is stated:

Be capable of all.[787]

As long as they are not distracted, people well trained in horse riding are not thrown off, even when traversing difficult terrain. When distracted, however, they can fall off even on a gentle plain, for instance when the horse is startled. Likewise, if you apply the remedies, even the most adverse conditions will not undermine your mind training. However, during moments without application of the remedies, even the slightest [adverse] condition can make you lose your practice. It is therefore necessary to train constantly without distraction. Cultivate the motivation "Today, to subdue self-grasping, I will remain mindful and free of distraction. I will not digress into afflictions." At the same time, discerningly probe whether you are contaminated by negative actions. (At all times you should ensure, through such a probe, that you don't lose [your mindfulness] and that you remain undistracted.) Erect such a wall of fortitude persistently. Without this, you are nothing more than an ordinary layperson. Thus it is essential to practice without distraction. [279]

Again, it is stated:

Do not be sporadic.

This refers to those who sometimes practice mind training but search for something else at other times because they lack conviction. Some scholastic monks, though possessing vast knowledge of the scriptural collections, feel that this is not effectual and thus seek the counsel of married shamans when they become aware of death. Similarly, some, out of fear of spirits and possessors, engage only in mantra recitations. Some engage [only] in the giving and taking meditation. Some pursue mundane greatness at times and at other times work for the welfare of their future life. However, if you try to ride two mounts at the same time, you risk falling off. Some claim that if you meditate, you don't need to recite the essence mantras or confess and purify the infractions of precepts; they challenge this necessity by asking, "Do infractions injure the body or the mind?" Some, when making offerings to the Three Jewels, wish to be seen by other people, and when seen, feel delighted, thus destroying the very ground [of their practice]. All of these [ways of thinking and behaving] are declared to be wrong.

How should you properly conduct yourself, then? Ensuring that erroneous views do not contaminate your body and speech, pursue what has been taught in the scriptures by the Buddha, what has been prescribed in the monastic discipline texts, and what is found in the pith instructions of the three teachers—Atiśa, Dromtönpa, and Potowa—intact and without degeneration, and train in this [awakening] mind alone.

Some, because their views color their conduct, become entangled in the knots of conceptualization. Some, on the basis of tantra, dismiss the teachings of monastic discipline, while others, on the basis of monastic discipline, dismiss tantra. Sangphupa reportedly asserted that it is from none other than our Indian teacher [Atiśa] that the knowledge has emerged to embrace all the teachings [as one integrated whole] as if lifting [a rug] from all fours corners at once.[788]

In relation to this practice, if you fail to arrive at a conviction through critical understanding or fail to ensure that nothing [in the teachings] remains unfamiliar, you risk being hesitant when some urge you in one direction while others urge you in another. Therefore be sure you clarify all your doubts until this [mind training practice] has firmly taken root, and then implement it within your meditative practice. Engage in all the yogas, such as those pertaining to food, clothing, and so on, by means of this [mind training]. At the moment of death, too, you should engage in the training with the thought "May all the suffering of others' birth and death be realized upon me." Forsaking all pondering about whether you have the necessary amenities, engage in this practice alone.

Do not abuse this [practice] as a rite.

All the sick people who send away ritual effigies [of themselves] and have rites performed because of their fear of death do so out of the hope that they might not have to die. Similarly, in the context of general Dharma practice, too, many hope to achieve their own well-being by taking others' suffering and hope to increase their own happiness by giving a fraction of it to others. [280]

Shawopa says, "Those who portray themselves as Dharma practitioners make token offerings of tea to all the good practitioners and claim 'We are colleagues'; they hold on to substantial estates as their residence; they covertly seek interest on loans from some benefactors; and they occasionally repeat segments of *ati*.[789] Through these four acts they aspire to reach the summit of spiritual practitioners. These [types of behaviors] can be found [even] in someone who fears losing his cows or being swept away by a river. Here, we need to discern what the defining characteristics of the Buddha are, what is their significance, and what are their primary causes, and, penetrating these essential points, we need to engage in the practice. Otherwise [our practice] will be like the method of investigation that asserts that because certain omens appeared this morning, the negative aspects have been cleansed.[790] Were this a valid means of enquiry, [you could then assert,] 'I have achieved this much without having to do anything. We, both master and servant, have prospered.'"[791]

So, as stated, if your engagement in study, reflection, and meditation becomes the same as a vase ritual or a rite for restoring life force, you have then been swept away by the winds. It is therefore critical that you do not remain ensnared by this mundane life and by the grasping at self. To succeed, however, the following is required:

[Guard] the two even at the cost of your life.[792]

"The two" are the general and the specific commitments. The first refers to not violating even at the cost of your life the precepts, such as those of going for refuge, that you have received, and the commitments related to your teacher. The second [the specific commitments] refers to activities like publicly disclosing others' infraction of precepts as done by the monks, and thereby uncovering a sharp spear, or exhibiting through your body and speech your exchanging of self and others. Such activities are contrary to the commitments of this practice for they violate the precepts outlined in such [mind training] lines as "Do not speak of the defects [of others]," and "Transform your attitudes, but remain as you are." Given that public disclosure of [others'] infractions of precepts dwells on [others'] shortcomings alone, this prevents mind training. So in terms of your body and speech, it is taught, make sure the main edifice of your pledges, such as going for refuge and so on, remains undamaged and its corners unchipped. Succeeding in this, however, requires the following:

Be released through the two, examination and close analysis.

By determining which affliction is dominant in your mind, strive with special emphasis to eliminate it through applying its antidotes. Thoughts such as "He is to blame" are errors related to the past; if this kind of error should arise in the future, armor yourself with the thought "I will apply the antidotes."

Regarding your past experiences, whatever you have undergone, such as illness, harm from enemies and malevolent forces, [281] failure in finding life partners, being called unreliable, theft, beatings, and so on, train your mind toward them by aspiring "Through these [events], may all that I owe since beginningless time—debts, dues, vengeance, and so on—be purified."

Regarding your future, whatever may befall you, such as being abused by others who say, "I will expel you to such and such a place this evening, at dawn tomorrow, or in the morning," or being accused of theft, being cast out, or becoming afflicted by acute illness, armor yourself by thinking, "I will engage in this practice of the awakening mind exchanging self and others." Potowa asked, "What if a prostitute were to come to you and hand over a little boy...and so on,"[793] to which Chengawa responded, "I would feel saddened," while Phuchungwa said, "I would rather nurture life [by bringing up the child] than die."

As all this illustrates, you should extend your practice to both past and future. (You should thus be released through investigation and close analysis and overcome the entanglement of self-grasping.) Since [all of] this should take place concurrently, it is stated:

Train with decisiveness.

Just as cutting a vein for blood extraction is called decisive,[794] likewise when afflictions arise, you should crush them there and then by means of their counterforce, without hesitation or reservation. To do this, however, it is crucial to be unsoiled by self-centeredness. Therefore it is stated:

Discard poisonous food.

Although good food nourishes the body, if it is mixed with poison it can cause death. Likewise although buddhas originate from the awakening mind, if this is mixed with grasping at real entities, then, like poisonous food, it can give rise to the sufferings of cyclic existence. Furthermore, in the context of mind training, the [thought seeking merely the] happiness of future lives—that of humans and gods—and the bliss of the disciple's and self-realized one's liberation are poisons as well, and must therefore be abandoned.

Also those who wish to achieve happiness must not harbor ill will toward others, as stated in the following:

Do not seek suffering as a means to happiness.

If your enemy dies, to think, "There will be no more harm"; if your relative dies, to hope "I shall obtain his belongings"; if your meditator colleague passes away, to hope "I shall receive all the offerings of the region"; [as well as] to hope for happiness through pursuing a layperson's four [seasonal] activities of farm work[795]—all of these constitute aspiring for happiness by pursuing misery. Langri Thangpa's personal physician, Jotsün Rinjang, and his apprentices received yogurt from their sponsors, yet in place of happiness, they sought misery. Wishing for more yogurt, they acquired a dzo. As a result, the continuum of people bringing yogurt came to an end, [282] and the dzo got lost in the fields in the summer, which kept all the apprentices occupied. Abandon all such endeavors where misery is sought as a means of achieving happiness. Rejoice when sentient beings are happy. He who is joyous when happy is called warm-hearted; you should behave in that manner.

With these the practice of conventional awakening mind, which is the method aspect, has been presented.

[*The practice of the ultimate awakening mind*]

Now, to present in a condensed manner the practice of the ultimate awakening mind, which is the wisdom aspect, it is stated:

When stability is attained, reveal the secret.[796]

The practice of the ultimate awakening mind has three sections: (1) the preliminary practices, (2) the main practice, and (3) the concluding practices.

The first refers to the following. Make offerings and supplications to the deities and the buddhas inside the prayer room of the Three Jewels, and then, seated cross-legged on a comfortable cushion inside a meditation chamber, count your respiration twenty-one times. Then make your body, speech, and mind a fit vessel for the meditative concentrations. Then, preceded by the conventional awakening mind, the main practice [of the ultimate awakening mind] is as follows:

All these practices [of mind training] adhere to the tradition of simultaneous engagement, thus during the actual session you should meditate on the absence of selfhood of all [phenomena] simultaneously. During the preparation stage, however, you should relate to them in a gradual order through the wisdom that discerns the individual characteristics of reality. This allows the moisture of tranquil abiding to give birth to the shoots of realization, the master said.[797]

For this, the meditation on the absence of the intrinsic existence of perceived objects is first presented in the following:

Contemplate all phenomena as dreamlike.[798]

This entire world of external environment and the beings within, which are by nature mere appearances, are nothing but apparitions of your own mind. Not even a single atom exists [substantially] independent of the mind. Reflect that, when examined by awareness, the object of analysis is found to be devoid of substantially true existence.[799]

Next, the meditation on the absence of intrinsic existence of the perceiving subject is presented in the following:

Experience the nature of unborn awareness.[800]

As stated here, you should contemplate regarding this mind, too, that its past is no more, its future is yet to be, and even its present is composed of three parts.[801] It is unborn and does not exist at all in terms of possessing characteristics such as abiding in a certain space or having color, shape, size, and so on. [283]

Next, the meditation on all phenomena lacking intrinsic existence is presented in the following:

> The remedy, too, is freed in its natural place.[802]

Likewise, the mind that probes into the emptiness of everything—[both] the objects and the mind—and acts as the remedy does not exist. For nothing is not subsumed within either [perceived] objects or [the perceiving] mind, and both have been determined to be devoid of intrinsic existence. Rest [your mind] with ease in this state of nonapprehension, for nothing exists in any mode, and do not allow this lucid and nonconceptual awareness to fall prey to mental laxity or excitement. This is stated in the following:

> Place your mind on the "basis of all," the actual path.[803]

It is stated that since the seven [kinds of consciousness] are conceptual processes of the mind, they must be relinquished. (Since these seven classes are conceptualization derived from the mind, and since conceptual thoughts do not purify the subject by themselves, observe them with awareness and let them rest in the expanse of suchness.)[804] In the future, too, whatever conceptualizations of the external world arise, observe them as one awareness observing another awareness, and allow them to rest and be freed in the expanse of suchness. (Since the fundamental ground of all phenomena is ineffable, inconceivable, and free of conceptual elaboration, in concord with this natural state, discard [these elaborations]. Settle your mind in this manner and undertake the practice.) In this respect, you should do short but frequent sessions, for as the saying goes, "It's best to end sessions on a positive note."

The activities to be undertaken at the conclusion are presented in the following:

> In the intervals contemplate the person as illusionlike.[805]

Recognizing the five aggregates, the six sense faculties, and the four types of everyday activities as apparitions of dependently originated aggregations, make sure you don't to pursue grasping at the true existence of things and the afflictions, but instead generate compassion toward all beings who fail to recognize this; and without losing the impact of the meditative session, abide in the expanse of the great union.

It has been stated:

> Ensuring that all your practices remain
> Untainted by clinging to substantial reality,
> Spread them across the spacelike great primordial void
> And journey to the great bliss of immortality.[806]

Colophon

The path of all the buddhas and their children of the three times,
The distilled essence of all Mahayana scriptures,
And the principal heart practice of all spiritual teachers is this—
The profound instruction of mind training.

To integrate all the various presentations into one, [284]
To understand the distinct characteristics of the various divisions,
To help understand with ease the facts concerning the two,
And to bring joy to my heart, I have composed this.

Ratnaguru relied on his teacher's words;
I, too, have applied the meaning a little in my mind;
So through [showing the] interrelations, sequence, and essential
   instructions,
I here present this [instruction on] training the mind.

For any contradictions and mistakes,
I seek forbearance from the teachers and their lineage.
If some see this and lose faith,
I seek forbearance for this, too, for I have explained the reasons.[807]

May this flower of virtue I have created
Be enjoyed by the beings of six realms, the honey bees;

May they feed on the single taste of the honey of [wanting] others'
welfare,
And engage in this practice for the sake of space[like infinite beings].

This is Sangyé Gompa's *Great Public Explication,* which is also the basis of
the guide on mind training composed by the great bodhisattva [Könchok
Gyaltsen].

Jagatam

35. Yangönpa's Instruction on Training the Mind[808]

[285] No composite thing has permanence,
So cut your ties to them and be free of clinging.
There is no joy in the cycle of existence,
So engender the disenchantment of renunciation.

Mundane existence has no essence,
So place not your trust in falsehood.
Your own mind is the Buddha,
So recognize this and behold its face.

So it was taught.[809] Again:

Step outside the shadows of this life
And grab the rope of the liberating path.
The chains of distracting thoughts are long;
Make short the chains of procrastination.

Even if you wish to, you've no power to remain;
Think of what is most beneficial for your future.
Difficult indeed it is to consistently attain a human existence;
So take its essence when you have obtained it once.

Habituation to delusion comes easily,
So send forth the spy of mindfulness.
Skilled you may be in gliding along on sensory objects;
Wake up, for they are of no use.

Nonvirtuous [mindstates] are without essence;
So discard them completely, one by one.

Death will crush you from the depths;
So swiftly destroy this covetous desire.

Again:

Keep death in your heart; this essential point
Ensures your joyous effort remains free of overexertion and lapses.

Reflect on the defects of cyclic existence; this essential point
Ensures you experience disillusionment from the depths of your heart.

Train your thoughts to ponder others' well-being; this essential point
Ensures that everything you do becomes Dharma practice.

Make the teacher the focus of your thoughts; this essential point
Ensures that your mind and his fuse into one.

Train [to view] the environment and the beings within as meditation
    deities;
This essential point ensures you avert ordinary perceptions and identities.

Whatever appears to your perceptions, leave them as they are;
This essential point ensures cyclic existence is liberated naturally.

This is the instruction on the six essential points. The four kings are as
    follows:

Being mindful of death is the king of faith;
Giving up the mundane life is the king of spiritual practice;
Seeing your teacher as a buddha is the king of devotion and respect;
Exhausting the food of dualistic perceptions is the king of realizations.

Again it was taught:

If you aspire to enjoy all happiness, apply the antidotes to attachment;
If you aspire to be free of suffering, apply the antidotes to anger;
If you aspire to attain the state of unexcelled enlightenment, apply the
    antidotes to delusion;

If you aspire to self-mastery, [286] apply the antidotes to pride;
If you aspire to overcome all obstacles, apply the antidotes to jealousy.

No essential points of the profound teachings remain unencompassed
   by these practices. Therefore make supplications [to gain their
   realization] and endeavor to establish them firmly, the master said.

Again:

Send forth the spy of impermanence to [watch] your faith;
Strike your virtuous actions with the iron rod of joyous effort;
Attest your commitments with the witness of your own mind;
Keep fixed on your enemy, the five poisons, while looking inward.

Again:

The root of divine Dharma is faith;
The root of being carefree[810] is disillusionment;
The root of others' welfare is compassion;
The root of blessing is devotion and respect;
The root of buddhahood is authentic realizations.

These are the five roots. The five transformations are as follows:

Transforming apprehension of permanence into [mindfulness of] death;
Transforming the mind of attachment into illusory perceptions;
Transforming the mind of anger into compassion;
Transforming conduct into Dharma activities;
Transforming false conceptions into the [profound] view.

So it was taught. Again:

Dwelling on the past brings turbulent regret and clinging in the future,
   so let go of it;
Anticipating the future extends the boundaries of hope and fear in the
   mind, so let go of it.
Tending to the present incites a circus of attachment and anger, so let go
   of it.

Leaving unaltered whatever appears to your perception is the
   introduction to dharmakāya, so nurture it.

So it was taught. Again:

This illness does not exist as an absolute reality, so pierce your grasping;
On the conventional level, karma and its fruition remain infallible, so
   purify negative karma, nonvirtue, and defilement;
The nature of reality is devoid of intellect, so place your mind in the state
   of nongrasping;
Self-grasping is the progenitor [of all ills], so cut the chains of hope and
   fear;
Your self-nature is dharmakāya, so behold pain as your own face;
Whatever events occur are blessings, so view occurrences as higher
   attainments;
Reflect upon everything and cause no harm to anyone.

Take these seven practices to heart and train in these as inner spiritual practice.

So it was taught.

Sarvaśubham

36. Guide to the Heart of Dependent Origination[811]

[287] I prostrate at the feet of the sublime teachers!

The sole lord master Atiśa's mind training has three lineages, which are the traditions of Dharmarakṣita, of Maitrīyogi, and of Atiśa's teacher Serlingpa, the master said. Here [for this specific instruction], however, there are three parts:

    A. The preparation
    B. The main practice
    C. The conclusion

A. The preparation

First, the preparation is as follows. Visualize, in the space in front of you, your teacher together with the lineage masters and Avalokiteśvara; perform a seven-limb practice of whatever length; and, if possible, make a mandala offering. [Then] make the following supplications:

> Bless me to transform all my aims in life into Dharma practice;
> Bless me so that loving-kindness, compassion, and awakening mind arise in me;
> Bless me so that realizations and meditative states take birth in me;
> Bless me to perceive all sentient beings as my mothers.

B. The main practice

The main practice refers to (1) the meditation on loving-kindness, (2) the meditation on compassion, and (3) the meditation on the awakening mind.

1. The meditation on loving-kindness

The meditation on loving-kindness is as follows.

> Loving-kindness is the sap of the compassion [tree],
> It arises perfectly in relation to suffering.[812]

The meaning of these lines suggests that you should cultivate loving-kindness first toward your mother of this life, for loving-kindness arises by recognizing her kindness and [wishing to] repay it. At the beginning, when you were in the womb, she refrained from [eating] unsuitable food and so on out of fear of miscarriage, and she nurtured you and thus extended great kindness. Then, following birth, she held this wormlike creature with her ten fingers, fed you food with her tongue, wiped your excrement with her bare hands, held you close to her flesh, and nursed you with her breasts. In these ways, she looked after you with tremendous kindness. As you grew up, she gave you food, clothing, and all her wealth. In short, she protected you with the attitude that even the entire resources of the kingdom of a universal monarch would not be too much for you, her child. Contemplate therefore, from the depths of your marrow and bones, "I will lead this mother, who has nurtured me with such kindness, to the cause of happiness." [288]

The thought "I will lead her to loving-kindness" is loving-kindness associated with armorlike [joyous effort]; the thought "May this be so" is loving-kindness associated with an aspiration; and the thought "How joyful would it be if all sentient beings could enjoy happiness and possess its causes!" is loving-kindness associated with rejoicing, the master said.

Then take a little break, let your mind rest at ease, and place it in an uncontrived state. In this way you perform supplications, meditate on loving-kindness, and put your mind at ease, even if it is only for the duration of a single meal, the master said. This, then, is how you should first meditate on loving-kindness toward your mothers.

Regardless of whether [genuine] compassion has arisen or not, extend loving-kindness to your friends and relatives as follows. For all the practices from this point onward, the preliminaries and conclusions remain the same as before. As for the main practice, [reflect] that there is no one among your father, relatives, and friends who has not been your mother. From the beginning to the present you have only relinquished and taken births in the cycle of existence. In that time, each of these sentient beings has been your mother and has helped you and protected you from harm. So you should reflect, "I will cultivate, from the depth of my heart, the thought to lead these kind mothers to the cause of happiness."

The contemplation in relation to the beings of the [entire] human realm is as follows: Do this contemplation in relation to your fellow countrymen; to your neighbors; to two, three, or four people of your region; to the entire world; and to each of the three [remaining] continents.[813] Then cultivate loving-kindness toward the beings in the hell realms, toward the hungry ghosts, toward the animals, and toward the celestial gods. Contemplation on humans was done earlier. As for the celestial gods, reflect on their immeasurable suffering, such as death and downfall, sluggishness caused by epidemics of intense heat, and the pains of battle with the demigods. The contemplation on the demigods contains no points specific to that realm to focus on.

As for animals, there are eighty thousand billion species. In the vast oceans of the external world, below the depth of about twelve outstretched arms, there are [animals] as dense as grains in a fermentation for beer. Every time a whale[814] or sea monster swallows a drop of water, infinite numbers of large and small fish enter its belly and die. Also, many small fish eat away at the sides of large fish as if creating cavelike holes on the face of large rocks. Without neither animosity nor friendship, their minds obscured, animals undergo the immeasurable suffering of one devouring another. [289] Reflect upon the immeasurable suffering of eating one another among the migratory land animals, such as the wild beasts, birds, insects, and so on. Contemplate that even the [domesticated] animals that surround humans face immeasurable suffering. They are forced to carry loads until old age and death, their wool sheared and milk sucked, and they are slaughtered and eaten.

There are thirty-six species of hungry ghosts, falling into five classes. Bring these to mind and meditate on them. To cultivate loving-kindness in relation to the hell realms, call to your mind the sufferings of the eighteen hell realms.

2. The meditation on compassion

If compassion does not arise [naturally] through loving-kindness, the second [practice], the meditation on compassion, is as follows. As for preparation and conclusion, undertake them as before. The cultivation of compassion toward your actual mother, the main practice, is as follows:

Contemplate as before and think, "How joyous it would be if this kind, dear mother enjoyed happiness and were free of suffering. It is tragic indeed that she wanders in this ocean of suffering in cyclic existence." You should cultivate compassion in this way. From this point onward [in the practice], except for your intention, ensure that all other aspects, such as the focus, are fully present as in the meditation on loving-kindness.

Having generated compassion, as before, in relation to either of the two kinds of loving-kindness,[815] in order to generate great compassion, undertake the following. Disciplining your body with specific postures, adopt such postures as sitting cross-legged and so on. Insert a finger between your teeth and support your cheek with your hand, and to discipline your speech through your body, utter, "Mother, mother" like an incantation. To discipline your mind through your speech, develop compassion toward the sentient beings of the six realms—the hell realm and so on. Since no one in these realms has not been your mother, cultivate strong compassion for them from the depth of your heart. This is not a case of contemplating someone who is not actually your mother as your mother. As the treatise *Dispelling Sorrow* states:

> Even if you were to count beads the size of *kolāsita* nuts,
> The earth would fail to measure the extent of your mothers.[816]

3. The meditation on the awakening mind

The third, the meditation on the awakening mind, is as follows.[817] It is not adequate simply to be compassionate; you need to practice giving and taking. Draw forth the sufferings of those mothers who are in the hells and other realms. Imagine that as you give your happiness to them, they achieve all temporary and ultimate happiness. Since sufferings hurt and the origin of sufferings prevents freedom, take from sentient beings onto yourself all sufferings and their origins, [290] as if you sheared them off with a sharp razor. As you give them all your happiness, imagine that sentient beings enjoy immediately the gathering of all the conditions conducive to Dharma practice and, ultimately, the fully enlightened state of buddhahood. Engage in this contemplation even in your dreams, and also under whatever circumstances befall you, such as being swept away by a flood, the destruction of your house, or an attack by armed assailants.

There are two elements—compassion [itself] and the meditative absorption [of compassion]. The spontaneous arising of compassion toward a chosen object of meditation is the actual compassion. Placing your mind in this state [of compassion] with ease on the basis of the meditation on giving and taking, without being distracted by extraneous objects, is a meditative absorption on compassion, the master said. Furthermore, the teacher said, if the meditative absorption of tranquil abiding arises as a meditative state, you should integrate this [into your practice], as described in the tantra of Amoghapāśa.[818]

As for the focus of this meditation, again right from the beginning you should generate compassion and in this way cultivate immeasurable compassion and practice giving and taking. In order to master this, maintain your focus on all objectives. Generally speaking, these are fourfold: (1) taking illnesses, (2) taking malevolent forces, (3) taking obstacles, and (4) taking karma and afflictions.

The first, [taking illnesses] refers to the following: Whatever illness befalls you, absorb the illness of all sentient beings into yourself and imagine that all sentient beings are free from sufferings and that your own illness becomes more intense. You should not contemplate fervently only once or twice; rather, you should do so repeatedly, absorbing the sufferings into you.

The second, taking the possession of malevolent forces, is as follows: As in the *Amoghapāśa Tantra,* whatever malevolent spells befall you, whether from male possessor spirits, such as the custodian of local sites, or female possessor spirits, absorb the malevolent spells [that befall] all sentient beings. Contemplate the possessor spirits themselves as your mothers and imagine giving your own happiness to these mothers. In this way, you practice awakening mind through giving and taking. Seeing the possessors as your mothers and seeing yourself as their child, the mothers are happy and the child is contented. Just as in "cutting off" practice, fears and so on do not arise in your mind, the master said.

The third, taking obstacles, is as follows: Whatever obstacles you encounter, collect together the obstacles of all practitioners and all sentient beings. And as you give your happiness to them, imagine that they all become free of obstacles. Contemplate this repeatedly.

The fourth, taking karma and afflictions, has two parts: taking the afflictions, the cause, and taking karma, the effects. The first is as follows: [291] Take initially whatever afflictions are grossest; anger is probably the easiest. Gross anger arises when you generate the intention to brandish swords and so on, while subtle levels arise when you harbor animosity and when such thoughts as "Should I use this weapon?" arise. Delusion is a harder affliction to take. Nevertheless, the teacher said, with contemplation you will over time be able to do this. Other afflictions vary.

When taking an affliction, do not apply the practice the moment the affliction arises. Rather, do this when its force becomes spent. This is illustrated by the following example. If you are planting crops in a field and bushes are also growing in the field, you do not cut these bushes the moment they sprout, for they would not be destroyed and their roots would not be extracted. On the other hand, if the stumps are pulled out once their force is fully spent, they come out easily, thus improving [the soil for planting crops]. Thus whatever affliction arises, [make sure that] its force is spent and that you dissolve into yourself all of sentient beings' afflictions, such as anger. Imagine that as you give your happiness to all sentient beings, they become free of afflictions.

Second, taking karma—the effects—is as follows: Whenever you experience perceptions of the hells, the three lower realms of existence, and so on, repeatedly dissolve into yourself all the sufferings of the three lower realms. Whatever desperation befalls you, collect upon yourself the desperate situations of all sentient beings, and practice giving and taking.

Generally speaking, there is the search for meditation through experience and the search for experience through meditation, the master said. The first refers to enhancing and cultivating whatever experiences may have arisen with respect to the object [of your meditation] by means of loving-kindness, compassion, and the awakening mind, as described earlier. [Second,] searching for experience through meditation refers to practicing the awakening mind through giving and taking and sustaining its experience alone, as in the practice of "cutting off." Also, if reluctance toward meditation practice arises, think that there is no end to the periods when you are not engaged in meditation in the expanse of the universe. Allow your mind to rest sometimes in this way.

Again, the teacher taught how to practice as follows: Generally speaking, transferring your focus of attention and engaging in the contemplation is like extracting a boulder; you need to examine the situation from all directions to find the easiest spot and then grab it from there, the master said.

All phenomena are dependently originated, and the root, or heart, of this [dependent origination] is the practice of loving-kindness, compassion, and the awakening mind. Therefore this practice is called the heart of dependent origination. [292] This is the practice of the teacher Serlingpa's awakening mind [through] giving and taking.

The lineage of this [instruction] is as follows: our teacher the Buddha, Maitreya, Serlingpa, the great Atiśa, master [Drom]tönpa, Potowa, Gya Chakriwa, Naljorpa Chö Yungdrung, Gyergom Shikpo, Gyagom Ripa, Bodongwa, Lama Wangpo, Nyenpopa. It stems from these masters.

To retain these as notes for myself,
The diamond words, free of exaggeration and omission—
I have penned [here] the words of my teacher.
Through this may all mothers gain buddhahood.

Sarvamaṅgalaṃ

37. Supplement to the "Oral Tradition"[819]
Könchok Gyaltsen (1388–1469)

PART ONE

[293] To the conquerors and their spiritual children,
I respectfully pay homage through all three doors;
I shall present here briefly the four preliminaries,
Which are the bases of the path of Mahayana mind training.

The presentation of the four preliminary practices, which constitute the
basis of Mahayana mind training, has four parts.

A. Reflection on the difficulty of obtaining a human existence of leisure and opportunity

First, reflection on the difficulty of obtaining a human existence of leisure
and opportunity is as follows: In order to become liberated from the ocean
of cyclic existence and attain the state of omniscience, you need to engage
in its cause, which is the perfect Dharma practice that unites method and
wisdom, and to engage in such Dharma practice it is necessary to possess as
its support the perfect human existence of leisure and opportunity. *Letter to
a Student* states:

> That which illuminates the Sugata's path and helps you embark on
> saving beings,
> A powerful, courageous spirit found by humans:
> Gods, nāgas, or demigods cannot find this path,
> Nor can garuḍas, smell-eaters, human-or-what, or belly-crawlers.[820]

Therefore, as stated above, we should contemplate by cultivating the
thought "It is extremely difficult to obtain this human existence of leisure

and opportunity, which is ideal for the practice of Dharma. So today, when I have found this once, I must undertake perfect Dharma practice."

Why is a human existence of leisure and opportunity so hard to find? This is fourfold:

1. From the point of view of its cause
2. From the point of view of its very nature
3. From the point of view of numbers
4. By means of analogy

1. Reflecting on the difficulty of obtaining it from the point of view of its cause

In order to obtain this human existence of leisure and opportunity, which is the ideal basis for engaging in Dharma practice, it is necessary to have perfect Dharma practice as its cause. Śāntideva states:

> I have not engaged in the virtuous acts
> But have amassed negative deeds;
> So for a hundred billion eons,
> I'll not even hear the name of the higher realms.[821]

If you have failed to engage in the virtuous acts and have amassed only negative karma, it will be difficult to even hear the term *higher transmigration,* let alone obtain a human existence of leisure and opportunity. [294] Observing the conduct of sentient beings, if you examine with a critical mind, [you will find that] those engaged in perfect Dharma practice are extremely rare. Therefore its effect, which is the attainment of a human existence of leisure and opportunity, is [also] extremely rare.

2. Reflecting on the difficulty of obtaining it from the point of view of its very nature

So what is this existence of leisure and opportunity? There are eight conditions of leisure and ten aspects of opportunity, and the existence that possesses these eighteen qualities complete is known as the "existence of leisure and opportunity."

The eight conditions of leisure are the overcoming of four conditions pertaining to the nonhuman realm that lack leisure and four conditions pertaining to the human realm that lack leisure. The four conditions pertaining to the nonhuman realm that lack leisure refer [to being reborn in the] three lower realms and as a long-life god. The three lower realms, for most sentient beings, provide not even the sound of Dharma teaching to be heard. Tormented by the sufferings of the lower realms, sentient beings who live there direct all their time and effort to coping with suffering. They have thus no leisure to pursue Dharma practice. As for long-lived gods, since they suffer from excessive, manifest conceit, and since theirs is a realm where wrong views, which are adverse conditions, take root, they too lack the leisure to pursue Dharma practice.

The four conditions of the human realm that lack leisure are as follows: (1) birth as a human in a barbarian borderland, (2) birth in a world where the Buddha has not appeared, (3) harboring wrong views, and (4) birth with a cognitive deficiency. All of these lack the leisure to pursue Dharma practice.

A "barbarian borderland" is an area where not even a sound of Dharma teaching can be heard and where people engage in customs, such as taking one's own mother as a bride, that contradict the norms of ethics. In realms where a buddha has not appeared, no Dharma teaching revealed by a buddha can be found, and as for wrong views, they sever the roots of Dharma practice. Those with cognitive deficiencies possess damaged faculties; and as for those whose mental faculty is damaged, since they remain ignorant of the distinctions between what is ethically sound and what is unsound, they remain outside the scope of Dharma practice. It is extremely difficult to be free of the eight conditions of nonleisure, and most sentient beings of the six classes fall into one of these categories of nonleisure.

The ten aspects of opportunity comprise five pertaining to others and five pertaining to yourself. The first five are the following:

1. That a buddha has appeared in the world
2. He has taught the Dharma
3. The teaching is still extant
4. There are others who follow the teaching
5. There exists the sense of caring for others

The second five are the following:

1. You are born as a human being
2. You are born in the central region [295]
3. You possess reversible karma

4. You possess complete sensory faculties
5. You possess faith in the sacred objects[822]

(1) It is rare for a buddha to appear in the world. Generally speaking, an era during which a buddha appears is called an "era of light," while an era during which [a buddha] does not appear is called an "era of darkness." As a thousand buddhas will appear in our present era, it is called a "fortunate era of light." It is said that after this will come sixty eons of darkness; after that, one light era called the "array of enlightened attributes," after which will come ten thousand eons of darkness. After that will come one light eon called the "greatly famed one"; after this, three hundred eons of darkness; after which will appear one light era known as the "exemplary starlike eon." Thus during four eras of light, it is said, will appear 10,360 eras of darkness. Even within an era of light, which has two parts—one part when the life spans of the people are on the rise and the other when they are on the wane—it is said that the buddhas do not appear when the life span is on the rise. The *Individual Liberation Sutra* states:

The appearance of a buddha in the world is once in a million.[823]

Also the *Enlightenment of Vairocana* states:

The appearance of an omniscient in the world
Is like the blossoming of an *uḍumbara* flower.
If at all, it occurs once in a hundred eons,
Never to reappear again.[824]

(2) It is also rare that a buddha has revealed the Dharma. Even following his full awakening, it is stated that the teacher required repeated supplications to turn the wheel of Dharma.

(3) It is rare, too, for his teaching to remain extant. Even this fortunate era contained an extremely long gap when the teaching was not present between the completion of the period of Buddha Krakucchanda's teaching and the emergence of the teaching of Buddha Kanakamuni. Similarly, in the interval between the cessation of the teaching of an earlier buddha and the emergence of the teaching of a later buddha, almost always the teaching remains absent. So most times go by without the abiding of the teaching.

(4) It is also rare for there to be others who continue to follow the teaching.

Among those who have faith in the Buddha's teaching, who have entered its door, and who engage in its meditative practice, many, not having heard even the name of the three scriptural collections, the classes of tantra taught by the Buddha, or their authoritative commentaries, which are the valid treatises, [296] engage in the study, reflection, and meditation of works composed by fools, which are not in accord with the intention of these authorities. So it seems there are extremely few who actually engage in the study, reflection, and meditative practice of the genuine teachings.

(5) Rare also are those who have a sense of caring for others. The situation is none other than what the spiritual master Sakya Paṇḍita has stated:

> Among precept holders, few are revered;
> Of those revered, few strive in their precepts.
> Among the wealthy, few have faith in the Dharma;
> The offerings of the faithful are of poor quality.
>
> These offerings are a cause for wrong livelihood.
> He who does not consume wrong livelihood,
> Such a practitioner is viewed as an inferior![825]

[Now the five aspects of opportunity related to yourself:] (1) It is extremely rare also to be born as a human being, since to be born human, you must cultivate pure, virtuous karma as its cause. That it is rare to accumulate virtuous karma has been explained earlier. (2) Rare, too, is it to be born in a central region. Asaṅga defines "central region" as those regions where the four disciples are present.[826] Regions where the four disciples are absent appear to equal the expanse of the sky, while the regions where they are present seem as small as the area of a carriage wheel. (3) "Having no irreversible karma" means not having committed any of the heinous acts, which, though they are comparatively rare, obstruct the pursuit of Dharma practice. (4) It is also rare to possess complete sensory faculties, and (5) having faith in sacred objects is rare too. It is extremely rare to find someone who has acquired faith from the depth of his or her heart in the three higher trainings taught by the Buddha.

So if it is extremely difficult to obtain each of these eighteen qualities of leisure and opportunity individually, inevitably the convergence of all of these in a single bodily existence is bound to be rare indeed. If even one of the eighteen qualities is absent, your existence is not one of leisure and opportunity.

For example, although the non-Buddhists who live in Bodhgaya in India, who are all believers in karma and its effects, may possess seventeen of the qualities, because they lack faith in the sacred objects, which is one of the five aspects of opportunity pertaining to oneself, they remain outside the existence endowed with leisure and opportunity. The *Array of Trees Sutra* states:

> Difficult indeed is it to achieve the status of being human; difficult indeed is it also to achieve perfection of the qualities of leisure.[827]

Śāntideva states:

> This existence of leisure and opportunity so hard to find.[828]

[297] So, since your present bodily existence possesses just about all the eighteen qualities of leisure and opportunity, do not allow it to go to waste; and by cultivating the thought "I must definitely undertake Dharma practice," engage in meditative practice from the very marrow of your bones.

3. Reflecting on the difficulty of obtaining it from the point of view of number

If the thought arises "That there are so many people obviously proves that it is not that difficult to obtain a human existence of leisure and opportunity," you have failed to probe well on the basis of settled, careful thinking. For if you examine the realm of sentient beings in general, let alone the human existence of leisure and opportunity, it is extremely difficult to obtain even a full bodily existence. The *Scriptural Collection of the Bodhisattva* states that countless sentient beings are perceived by the wisdom mind of an omniscient but not by others.[829] In the intermediate state alone, it seems, are more beings yet to achieve bodily existence than have realized this state already. In the spring, for example, on a carcass of an animal left lying for three days emerge inconceivable numbers of insects. However many carcasses there are, there are that many more insects inhabiting them, and also there are correspondingly that many beings of the intermediate state destined to be reborn as those insects. If this is so, the same is true of the intermediate-state beings of other classes of transmigration. Therefore the statement "The intermediate state exists for an extremely long time"[830] appears to accord with reality.

Even among those who do attain full embodiment, more are sentient beings of the nonhuman classes, while the number of humans is relatively small. The scriptures of the discipline[831] state that the number of beings who transmigrate from the higher realms to the lower realms resembles the number of dust particles that exist on the face of this great earth. The number of those who depart from a higher realm to another higher realm resembles the dust particles on the face of a fingernail, and the number who transmigrate from the lower realms to a higher realm [also] resembles the particles of dust on the face of a fingernail. Furthermore, the number of sentient beings in the animal realm resembles the [quantity of] grains fermented for beer, while the number of hungry ghosts resembles [the number of flakes in] a heavy snowstorm. The hell realms contain [beings] equal to the dust particles on the face of this great earth.

So when compared to the other classes of sentient beings, it appears as if almost no one obtains human existence. Even if you consider only the random animals you can actually see with your eyes, it seems impossible to obtain a human existence. [298] If you observe the varieties of small insects that appear in the summer, they defy imagination, for you find countless animals in each species. Even among humans, those who possess leisure and opportunity are rare. That this is so can be understood by reflecting on the difficulty of obtaining a human existence of leisure and opportunity from the perspective of its very nature. You should therefore draw the following conclusion: "Today, when among such numerous sentient beings I have now obtained this existence of leisure and opportunity, I must not let it go to waste. I must engage in perfect Dharma practice."

4. Reflecting on the difficulty of obtaining it by means of analogy

Śāntideva states:

> For this reason the Blessed One has stated,
> Like a turtle's neck entering the hole
> Of a yoke afloat a vast, open ocean,
> So rare is it to find human existence.[832]

Imagine with careful attention that this great trichiliocosm universe is one massive ocean and on this floats a wooden yoke with a single hole. Then imagine that there is a blind turtle living on the bottom of the ocean and it surfaces briefly once every hundred years. Now contemplate the probability of the turtle's neck entering the hole of the yoke, which is, of course, minuscule. The possibility is extremely rare. The ocean surface is so vast and its depth great; there is only one hole in the floating yoke, and the turtle surfaces once every hundred years. Furthermore, since the yoke does not lie still at one location but floats wherever the wind carries it, the turtle might be in the east while the yoke is being blown westward by the wind, and so on. It is thus extremely difficult for the two to coincide. Even a slight variation in timing or a spatial difference of only an arm's length will prevent the entry, yet such disjunction of timing and spatial location occurs so easily.

Just as in this analogy, if a slight disruption occurs in the conditions required for attaining human existence, you will not obtain the human existence of leisure and opportunity, yet such disruption can occur very easily. This is because the propensities you possess within yourself for taking rebirth in the realms of other classes of sentient beings far exceed the quantity of water that exists in an ocean, while your propensities for attaining a human existence of leisure and opportunity remain merely the size of a hole in a yoke. As for the conditions activating these propensities, [299] more conditions give rise to a birth in other realms and very few for the human birth. Furthermore, even a slight shift in your thought processes has the ability to adversely affect the propensities for taking birth as a human.

Ascertain the difficulty of obtaining a [human existence of leisure and opportunity] by means of other analogies as well, and on such basis, generate within your heart the spontaneous wish to extract the essence of this human existence of leisure and opportunity. Thus, as a consequence of such reflections, if you develop the thought "It may be true that this human existence of leisure and opportunity is extremely hard to obtain, but obtaining it brings such benefits," this definitely has great merit. For in dependence upon this existence of leisure and opportunity you can cross the ocean of suffering, the cycle of existence. You can also on this basis cultivate the great excellences of the higher realms, such as those of the humans and celestial beings. You can also achieve the states of definite goodness, such as the enlightenment of disciple and self-realized one. Even the ultimate state of buddhahood can be realized in dependence upon it. Therefore, since in dependence upon this existence of leisure and opportunity you can accomplish all levels of temporary and ultimate goodness, it has tremendous merit.

Śāntideva states:

> Relying on this boat of human existence,
> You can cross the ocean of suffering.
> Since this boat is hard to find again,
> Ignorant one, sleep not at this moment![833]

Also *Letter to a Student* states:

> This human existence that is better than a wish-fulfilling jewel—
> Once found, one can cross the ocean of births
> And plant the excellent seed of supreme enlightenment.
> Who would make it bereft of fruits?[834]

Births such as those of the celestial gods and so on are the fruits of an inconceivable amount of virtuous karma, and the bodies themselves are extraordinary. On the basis of such bodies, however, the beneficial qualities of the [human] existence of leisure and opportunity cannot come about. So among the forms of sentient beings, none is a greater source of benefit than this human existence of leisure and opportunity. It is crucial, therefore, not to waste even a single moment in this existence that is so hard to find yet is a source of great benefits. Reflect, "If this human existence of leisure and opportunity is present today, all will be well, and if it is not present today, nothing will be achieved today. On the basis of this bodily existence, I must therefore seek to reach whatever stages I can toward my ultimate goal." As to how you extract your life's very essence by seeking its ultimate aspiration on the basis of this human existence of leisure and opportunity, this is as found in the *Oral Tradition*.[835] [300]

With this, the presentation on the difficulty of obtaining a human existence of leisure and opportunity is concluded.

B. Reflection on death and impermanence

You might entertain the thought "Yes, it is true that I must engage in a perfect Dharma practice on the basis of this human existence of leisure and opportunity. But I can do this later, when I am less busy and will have more free time." If such thoughts arise, then with forceful perseverance and action, strive in the practice without delay, for you might die soon. This is threefold:

1. Reflecting on the inevitability of death
2. Reflecting on the uncertainty of the time of death
3. Reflecting that at the time of death, nothing but Dharma is of benefit

1. Reflecting on the inevitability of death

Rinpoché Sönam Drakpa states:

> These days when people discuss things, they say that they will do this or that unless they die first. Such statements are utterly misguided. We must keep him—death—who will definitely come, deep in our guts.[836]

To this, the great bodhisattva Chöjé responded:

> This is very true. We know that he—death—will definitely come.[837]

If you think that maintaining the thought "Unless I die first, I will do this or that" is to keep death in your guts, [this is wrong]. Keeping death deep in your guts means making preparations from this very instant for a positive death by reflecting "I know that he—death—is certain to come. So I will, with conviction in my own mortality, make sure to experience death in such and such manner."

Generally speaking, death and impermanence need not be established by means of scriptural citations and logical reasoning. The reason you do not fear death even when you see it with your own eyes is that you have failed to contemplate it in relation to yourself. You should therefore contemplate now:

"What is this thing called death?[838] All of this vivid perception of the external world and the beings within it [301] that I experience today—such as being alive; tangibly experiencing the texture of clothes, food, and shelter in the company of friends and family; and participating in all kinds of conversations about various plans for remaining long in this life—I must leave all of this behind. I will have to abruptly leave all of this unfinished, even while my eyes actively shift their glance toward a multitude of objects. I will have to journey alone, with no power to stay for even a single additional moment. In a blackout, the perceptions of this life will cease. I will hear nothing of my friends, family, and material possessions, nor will they hear of me. Such will be the extent of our lasting separation! I will have to venture alone, aimlessly, in a terrain deeply despairing and utterly alien."

It is certain that such events will occur. For example, Śāntideva writes:

> Caught in the snare of afflictions,
> One is trapped in a birth's ensnarement
> And will approach the mouth of the death lord.
> Do we still not know this?[839]

You are born due to the power of karma and mental afflictions, and anything that is born is bound to die. It has been stated:

> The end of meeting is separation;
> The end of hoarding is depletion;
> The end of growth is decay;
> And the end of birth is death.[840]

Dispelling Sorrow states:

> Have you ever seen or heard of,
> Or harbored speculations of, someone—
> Whether on earth or in the heavens—
> Who was born but did not die?[841]

So, whether it is the elevated human world or the higher world of the celestial gods, has anyone seen someone who was born but has not died? Where could such a being be? Has anyone heard of it by means of a reliable anecdote? There is not even room to doubt whether someone not dying is possible. Such a phenomenon cannot be seen or heard of, nor is there ground even for speculation. Death resides in the face of anyone who is born.

Furthermore, it is stated:

> From the very evening of their entry
> Into the mother's womb, all beings of this world
> Enter a road and, with no false turns,
> Move ever closer to the lord of death.[842]

So right from the moment of your conception in the mother's womb, you have entered a road that leads to the lord of death. Without taking as much as a single false step away onto another road, it is said, you move extremely fast and tirelessly toward the lord of death, without pausing for even a moment.

Furthermore, you may be able to avert external enemies through force, but the enemy of death cannot be averted by any means. [302] A lion, which is the king of animals, might be strong enough to overwhelm even an elephant, and by its mere roar may inspire fear in the hearts of other animals. Such is its power that even its roar is unbearable. Yet it cannot shake even a single hair on the body of the lord of death. Moreover, when the lord of death strikes, the lion will have to die, with all its power and haughtiness diminished. The *Garland of Birth Stories* states:

> With their sharp claws, lions overwhelm elephants' might;
> They tear at the elephants' heads with claws and cut deep wounds;
> With their terrifying roar they strike fear in the hearts of others.
> But upon the lord of death's arrival they lie defeated, their strength
>   and haughtiness crushed.[843]

Similarly, the external enemy can be overcome through material resources; the lord of death, however, cannot be averted through such means. Even the god Vaiśravaṇa, who is capable of bestowing wealth on others, is himself bound to die, despite his riches. Similarly, certain harmful spells cast by humans and nonhumans can be averted through mantras, medicine, and ritual substances; the harmful spell of the lord of death, however, cannot be averted through such means. The *Garland of Birth Stories* states:

> O seekers of truth, those with fortitude and goodness
> Can overcome the harmful spells of Indra's approach
> And the spells cast by those adept in incantations;
> Yet it is not possible to avert the lord of death.[844]

Also some external enemies can be overcome through other various means; however, death cannot be overcome by any method. For example, a skilled illusionist might be able to deceive most beings, except the buddhas, with his conjuring. Yet he cannot deceive the lord of death. The *Garland of Birth Stories* states:

In the midst of a crowd, a skilled magician
Fools the eyes of the spectators;
Yet Yama has a power more amazing than this.
For even these magicians cannot deceive his eyes.[845]

So as far as the lord of death is concerned, no means whatsoever exists to avert him. Furthermore, you can escape from external enemies by running away or by moving to a place that is free of them. As for the lord of death, however, you cannot escape him even by running away quickly. Neither can you reach a place where he is absent. [303] It is stated:

Even great sages with five types of clairvoyance,
Who can venture afar in the vast skies,
Cannot journey even if they wish
To a place free of death.[846]

Also:

Wherever you may go,
No place not subject to death exists:
It is not in the skies or in the ocean depths,
Nor is it found in the crevices of mountains.[847]

So the demon, the lord of death, exists and will strike you; and furthermore there are no means of averting him. Since it is impossible to escape from him, there is nothing but death's absolute certainty. Kharak Gomchung states:

He, the death demon, does not stop but comes ever closer;
There are no means whatsoever to escape him.
So if I fall prey to sleep and procrastination today,
A time will soon come when I might be utterly lost.[848]

There is no dispute that death will happen to ordinary sentient beings. And even bodhisattvas, disciples, and self-realized ones have to discard their exalted bodily existence. It is stated:

If conquerors' children and self-realized ones,
And the disciples of the buddhas as well,

Discard their exalted bodies,
What need is there to speak of ordinary beings?[849]

Also to help ascertain that since you are born, you must necessarily die, our teacher the Blessed One, after having displayed the deed of taking birth, displayed the act of entering nirvana. It is stated:

If even the adamantine bodies adorned with
Major and minor noble marks are transient,
What question is there of the embodied beings,
Who resemble coreless banana trees?[850]

Therefore anything born is certain to die. This is analogous to a clay pot. Having been created, the pot will one day break. Depending upon the quality of kneading and firing of the clay, some pots will break after lasting a long time, and others, due to poor kneading and poor response to firing, will break sooner. Nevertheless all will eventually disintegrate.

Furthermore, you should contemplate impermanence by means of analogy. For example, you are like (a) a prisoner on death row, (b) a pond whose source stream has dried up, (c) a sheep in a butcher's corral, (d) a torrential river rushing down the face of a steep mountain, and (e) the white and black rodents in the story. [304]

a. Like a prisoner on death row

After being handed over to the executioner, the prisoner on a death row walks toward the site of his execution. Every step he takes brings him closer to his death, and every two steps he takes brings him still closer. Eventually he arrives at the site of execution, where he is summarily killed by the executioner. In the same way, with each day's passing, you also draw closer to death and that much closer every two days. Contemplate, in relation to your everyday chores, that with the ending of each activity you have drawn closer to your end, and with the ending of two activities you have come even closer. Even with spiritual practices, such as the recitation of mantras, you should contemplate that with every repetition, you are closer to death, and with two repetitions are that much closer. The *Collection of Aphorisms* states:

The person on death row,
With however many steps he takes,

Approaches ever closer to the lord of death;
This is true too of the life of humans.[851]

b. Like a pond whose source stream has dried up

If you cut off by piercing a hole in it the stream that feeds into a pond, water will quickly leak out. Life, too, is like a pond whose source stream had dried up, because no extension is forthcoming. And like the pond whose banks are ruptured, the years, months, and days never stand still but diminish continuously. So there is no other conclusion than that death is inevitable. Śāntideva writes:

> With no power to remain for even a day or a night,
> This life of mine continuously ebbs away.
> Since no extension is possible,
> How is it that I will not die?[852]

c. Like a sheep in a butcher's corral

A butcher puts those sheep earmarked for culling inside a corral where no escape is possible and slaughters them one by one, leaving none behind. Similarly, you are caught in the corral of birth, where you observe the butcher, the lord of death, slaughtering your friends and family members one by one. Despite knowing that your own turn will come as well, if you continue to think [only] of food, drink, and sleep with no sense of fear, that is indeed most foolish. This is analogous to water buffaloes that, while seeing their companions being slaughtered by the butcher, carry on eating and drinking with no sense of fear. On this point Śāntideva writes:

> Do you not see that your own kind [305]
> Is being slaughtered one at a time?
> How is it that you still seek to sleep?
> This is like the tale of the butcher and his buffaloes.
>
> All your paths of escape have been blocked,
> And while the lord of death stares down,
> How can you be attached to eating?
> How can you be attached to sleeping too?[853]

d. Like a torrential river rushing down the face of a steep mountain

A torrential river rushes down the face of a steep mountain as if afraid that the latter parts of its water will not catch up to its earlier parts. Life, too, moves swiftly, as if the subsequent moments wish to catch up with their preceding counterparts. Life ebbs quickly in this manner.

This analogy is suitable only to illustrate swiftness; it cannot represent the rate of exhaustion of human life. If for example a skilled archer were to shoot arrows in all four directions simultaneously and a person with extremely great athletic prowess were to catch them all before they touched the ground, such a person would indeed be extremely fast. Yet the temporal exhaustion of human life is even faster than this. The *Vast Manifestations Sutra* states:

> All three worlds are transient like clouds in autumn;
> The birth and death of beings resemble scenes in a play;
> Life's passage is like lightning in the sky;
> Like torrents rushing down a steep mountain, swiftly we depart.[854]

e. Like the white and black rodents in the story

Imagine that a cluster of grass grows hidden somewhere in the crevice of a steep cliff and a person falling off the cliff manages to grab on to this cluster of grass. However, a white and a black rodent are taking turns nibbling at the grass. If the person strives hard before the grass is completely eaten away, he might be able to pull himself up to safety. If, on the other hand, he procrastinates until the grass is eaten, he will fall off the cliff. Since no one is outside the boundary of death, there is no room for thoughts of laziness and procrastination, such as "There will be a time later" and "I shall do this and that then." In the case of ourselves, we are hanging precariously at the mouth of a cliff facing the lower realms and we are holding on to the grass of what is left of our life span. However, the white and black rodents of day and night are nibbling, not pausing for a single instant, at what little life we have left. In the face of this situation, if we do not demonstrate our vigor and make an effort, and if the grass of our remaining life span disappears and we fall down into the gorge of the lower realms, there is almost no escape from this. Therefore strive with all your effort. *Letter to a Student* states:

If the conduct of a foolish man resembles that of a hell guardian
And causes him to be born in the realm of the animals, [306]
Where one devours the other, why engage in conduct
That will cast you into the deep gorges?[855]

Also, Śāntideva states:

With no power to remain either day or night,
Always does this life ebb away...[856]

The *Friendly Letter* states:

The body ends in ashes; it is a temporary guest;
Becoming no more, it is certain to cease and turn into filth.
Recognize that it will disintegrate into its own constituents.[857]

So as stated here, you should sometimes contemplate in the following manner: "I may nurture this body today with great care. However, following my
death, which of the following situations will occur: Will my body be burned
in fire and reduced to ashes? Will it be buried under ground and rot? Will it
be buried inside a wall and become desiccated? Will it be cast into the water
and be eaten by fish and otters? Or will it lie abandoned at a cemetery and be
devoured by vultures and wild animals that leave nothing behind?"

At other times you should reflect as in the sutra entitled *Advice to a
King*:[858] When you are in the midst of conversations with your family and
friends, reflect, "Today, I may be in the company of my friends and so on,
yet a time will come when I am permanently separated from them." Similarly, when you eat, think, "Today I may be enjoying good food, yet a time
will come when, instead of eating food, I will be eating bitter medicine, and
that too with no benefit. In such a manner I will have to die." When you get
dressed, reflect, "Today I may be wearing beautiful clothes, yet a time will
come when I will be wrapped inside a smelly sheet and discarded." When
you sit on a comfortable throne or a cushion, reflect, "Today I may be sitting
on a comfortable cushion such as this, yet a time will come when I will have
to depart hoisted above four wooden poles." When you ride an attractive
mount, reflect, "Today I may be riding an attractive mount such as this, yet a
time will come when I will be transported by a repulsive-looking corpse han-
dler." When you wash yourself, reflect, "Today I may be taking hygienic care

through such acts as washing, yet a day will come when my own waste will be smeared over my body and I will be discarded in an unclean environment such as a cemetery." [307]

By means of these various contemplations, meditate until a deep sense of conviction arises in your mind concerning the inevitability of death.

2. *Reflecting on the uncertainty of the time of death*

If the thought arises "It is true that death will definitely occur, however, it may not do so for a while," then second, reflecting on the uncertainty of the time of death, is threefold: (a) There is no guaranteed life span, (b) there are more conditions adverse to life than favorable to it, and (c) since the lord of death has no mercy, the separation of mind and body comes most easily.

a. *There is no guaranteed life span*

Some people think that they will pursue mundane goals early in life and only later engage in Dharma practice. Other people might think that this year they will gather favorable conditions, such as provisions, and then from next year on engage in Dharma practice. Such plans are realized only rarely. It is difficult to determine which of the two—next year or next life—will come first. It is difficult even to determine which of the two—next month or next life, next day or next life—will appear first. This is because your life span is not guaranteed. The *Treasury of Higher Knowledge* states:

> Presently there is no certainty, though in the end
> It will be ten; originally it was countless.[859]

There are two parts to this reflection: (1) uncertainty from the point of view of time frame, and (2) uncertainty from the point of view of beings.

First, in the case of beings of the northern continent, their life span is definite, for they invariably live one thousand years. However, the life span of the beings of [this southern] Rose Apple continent has no such certainty. In the beginning [of this era], people could live for countless years; however, toward the end, ten years will become the longest life span.

Second, the life span of beings of the northern continent is fixed for one thousand years: Beings do not last longer than this, nor does anyone die before this life span is exhausted. As for the life span of beings of this Rose Apple continent, there is no certainty at all. Some exhaust their life span and die when they are still in their mother's womb, some immediately after birth, some when just starting to crawl, some when just beginning to walk, some in the prime of their youth, while some die after old age. The *Dispelling Sorrow* sutra states:

Some will die in the womb; [308]
Likewise some instantly after birth;
Some when they start to crawl;
Some when they are able to sprint.

Some die in old age and some in youth;
Some die when they're in their prime;
Like the falling of ripened fruits,
In turn [everyone] will depart.[860]

So there is no indisputable ground of certainty for believing that this year your life span will not reach its end or that your next life will not dawn the next day. Śāntideva states:

To live confidently with the thought
"I will not die today" is unwise;
Without doubt the time will come
When this self will be no more.[861]

Although this is so, certain factors in you may continue to inspire hope and make you feel that you will not die for some time. For example, you may be young and free of illness at present, you may have gathered well such amenities for sustenance as food, clothing, and so on, and you may be free of threats from enemies or malevolent forces. Because of these you might feel, "I will not die for a long time." None of these factors justifies such confidence, however. Youth, for example, cannot justify this confidence, for many young people who are stronger die before old people who are at the stage when they need to rely on others. This is an observed fact. The *Collection of Aphorisms* states:

Of the many people we see in the morning,
In the evening we do not see some;
Of the many people we see in the evening,
In the morning we do not see some.

If many men and women
Die while in their prime,
Why are you certain that
"I will live because I am young?"[862]

Absence of sickness cannot justify such confidence. You see many instances where, before a sick person who is gripped by harmful spells and cannot even walk or sit down by himself and needs others' assistance to roll over dies, a person who is strong and young and free of illness suddenly dies first. Having good sustenance does not warrant such confidence, for you can observe instances where, before the poor person who searches for today's food today and tomorrow's food tomorrow dies, the rich person who is surrounded by wealth dies first. The absence of enemies' harm, too, cannot justify such confidence. You see many occasions where, before someone besieged in a courtyard by enemies dies, someone who has not even heard the name of an enemy dies first. Freedom from harms caused by malevolent forces, too, cannot warrant such confidence. You see numerous instances where, before someone whose mind is afflicted by harmful spells and who has lost control over his mind [309]—engaging in self-destructive activities—dies, someone who is free of harms caused by malevolent forces dies first. Even if you are free of all these adverse factors, this still cannot justify confidence. You can observe many instances where although someone may be free of these conditions at present, he or she suddenly dies due to some other circumstance. Our teachers dare not place their confidence in such factors as young age and so on. For us, too, there is no particular basis for placing our confidence in them. Śāntideva states:

Even if, like this day, you're free of sickness,
Have food, and are devoid of harms,
Life can suddenly let you down;
Your body resembles an object on loan.[863]

b. More conditions are adverse to life than are favorable to it

Given that there are more circumstances causing death than sustaining life, even if you possess some residual life span, there is no guarantee that you will be able to live this out. This is because there are such abundant conditions adverse to life. It is analogous to an oil lamp exposed to a strong wind.

The oil and the wick may not be exhausted, but because of the wind, it is impossible for the flame to stay lit for even a short time. Thus the *Precious Garland* states:

> Like an oil lamp in the midst of a storm,
> We stand in the midst of death's causes.[864]

Also, *Letter to a Student* states:

> Like the flame of a lamp flickering due to a violent wind,
> There is no certainty this life will remain even for an instant.[865]

There are innumerable circumstances that can cause death. The four external elements, for example, can become conditions for death. The conflict between the four internal elements causes illness and can act as a cause of death. Four hundred and twenty-four classes of diseases cause death; so, too, do the classes of eighty thousand obstructive forces that lead to false paths. Humans, such as enemies and friends, can become a cause of death; so can other classes of sentient beings, such as animals. Furthermore, what are considered factors for sustaining life, such as your house, family, food, and clothing, can become conditions for death as well. Even your own self, which is dear to you, can cause your death. You have seen and heard of unimaginable situations where these factors have turned into conditions of death. [310] There are no flawless reasons [for believing] that although these factors may have been conditions of death for our teachers, they will not act as such for us.

Therefore contemplate in the following manner: "Nothing among the internal and external phenomena of this world can be excluded as a potential cause of death. It is impossible to escape to a place that is without the conditions of death, and each condition is individually capable of causing death as well. Furthermore, there is no guarantee that I will not encounter one of these circumstances, so I could die today or tomorrow. I must therefore engage in perfect Dharma practice." On this point, Nāgārjuna states:

> Conditions for death are so numerous;
> While those sustaining life are few;
> Yet these, too, are conditions for death.
> So constantly practice Dharma.[866]

c. *The separation of mind and body occurs extremely easily*

The separation of body and mind occurs extremely easily, for they are more fragile than bubbles in water. Given the ease with which body and mind can separate, it is a wonder we wake up after falling asleep and that we can inhale after having exhaled. On this point, Nāgārjuna states:

> If life has many adversities and is more transient
> Than water bubbles blown by a storm,
> Amazing indeed it is that we inhale after exhaling,
> And that we wake up after going to sleep.[867]

Also, since the lord of death has no mercy, the time of death cannot be predicted. You cannot negotiate with the lord of death by appealing, "Spare me today out of mercy," or "Spare me today, for I am busy." Imagine your situation to be like the animal that is being chased by a hunter: Anything may lead to its capture, and with no time intervening, its slaughter. To be unaware of this status and to make myriad sequential plans related to matters of this life is said to be looked at with displeasure by Yama, the lord of death. *Letter to a Student* states:

> When someone thinks, "I'll do this tomorrow and that afterward,
> And this I shall do some other time later on,"
> Sideways the club-bearing Yama glares at them,
> With fierce and bloodshot eyes, and scorns with laughter.[868]

Therefore do not think, "I shall do this today and do that tomorrow." Prepare instead, from this very moment, to acquire the confidence to be able to think, "I will conduct myself in this manner if I am to die today, and in that manner if I am to die tomorrow." In this respect the spiritual master Yangönpa states:

> The lord of death demon cares not whether you are busy;
> No timing can be arranged for a life with no fixed span; [311]
> If today the four elements and consciousness were to part ways,
> Think whether you are well prepared with confidence.[869]

Master Atiśa states:

> Life is short and the field of knowledge vast;
> The length of your life span, too, cannot be known;
> Just as swans extract milk poured into water,
> Embrace first those [aims] that you [really] aspire to.[870]

Reflect, "There is no valid reason to believe my life will not come to an end this very day. Even if it doesn't, the potential for an untimely death is always present. It is also hard to find any factor that cannot become a hazard; furthermore, these adverse conditions never stop causing obstructions. My body and mind, for which they create these adversities, are so easily separable. Thus I have no confidence that I will not die even before the sun sets. Were I somehow to die today or tomorrow, I would have failed to accomplish any task that requires keeping [the awareness of] death deep in my guts. Alas! What would happen to me after death? I therefore resolve today: 'I will let go of this life. From today onward, I will instead undertake Dharma practice that is beneficial for the time of death.'"

3. Reflecting that at the time of death, nothing but Dharma is of benefit

When death arrives, nothing of this life's mundane advantages will be of benefit. No matter how many friends and family members you have, you cannot avert the lord of death by combating him, nor is it possible to gain even a single moment of reprieve by having your loved ones acting as guarantors. There are no "joint lives"—when you depart to the other shore, no one can take even a single step with you. On this point, *A Guide to the Bodhisattva's Way of Life* states:

> When seized by Yama's messengers,
> What good is a relative, what good is a friend?[871]

Also:

> Though I may lie in my bed
> Surrounded by all my family and friends,
> I alone must endure the experience
> Of my life being snapped.[872]

Similarly, however abundant your material resources are, such as food, cattle, and wealth, none will be of any use. You cannot buy even a short amount of time by making gifts to the lord of death. [312] It is impossible to extend your lifespan by even a moment; not even a small part of it can be taken to the other shore. Similarly, whatever desirable qualities associated with the eight worldly concerns you may possess, such as forceful speech, formidable authority, and so on, they will be of no help. They might in fact do you [more] harm. *A Guide to the Bodhisattva's Way of Life* states:

> "I have great wealth and I am honored,"
> "There are many who adore me,"
> If you harbor such conceited thoughts,
> Terror will strike you following your death.
>
> For the mind that is thoroughly deluded,
> Whatever things it becomes attached to,
> By many thousandfold,
> All these will rise as suffering.[873]

The sutra entitled *Advice to a King* states:

> O great king, at that point and at such time, there is no refuge or protector other than the Dharma.[874]

So what is of benefit at this time? If you have engaged in a perfect Dharma practice, this will help.

A Guide to the Bodhisattva's Way of Life states:

> If at that time it is merit alone that saves....[875]

The sutra *Advice to a King* states:

> At that point and at such time, it is the Dharma that is your refuge, your protector, your support, your locus, and your great ally.[876]

If the thought occurs that even if you practice Dharma, you are still going to die, [understand] that there are differences in the manner of dying, and so on. These should be understood as explained in the *Oral Tradition*.

Death is inevitable, there is no certainty of its time, and only the Dharma is of help in the face of it. It is therefore extremely inappropriate to remain unperturbed, with the confidence of someone who has no fear of death. *A Guide to the Bodhisattva's Way of Life* states:

> Who will grant me fearlessness?
> If it is beyond doubt
> That there is no escape from it whatsoever,
> How can my mind remain in peace?[877]

The *Four Hundred Stanzas* states:

> Among those who rule over the three worlds,
> None can be their own lord of death;
> If, knowing this, you still sleep peacefully,
> What is more unbecoming than this?[878]

Yangönpa advises:

> Those with courage should ensure their own long-term welfare;
> Without deceiving yourself, practice sacred Dharma from your
>   depth.[879]

Similarly it is critical to undertake Dharma practice that forsakes the concerns of this life. With this point, the presentation of the meditation on death and impermanence is now complete.

When death arrives, if nothing of this life, such as your wealth, follows after you, [313] you might wonder, "Does nothing at all follow me after my death?" The virtuous and nonvirtuous karma that you have created are not left behind. They do not depart elsewhere, nor do they cease to exist. They follow you just as a shadow follows a body. The *Advice to a King* sutra states:

> When time calls for you, the king, to depart,
> Your wealth, loved ones, and friends will not follow;
> Yet wherever this person [you] journeys to,
> [Your karma] will follow like the body and its shadow.[880]

C. Cultivation of faith in [the law of] karma—cause and effect

This is fourfold: (1) Contemplating the definitions of virtuous and nonvirtuous karma, (2) contemplating their effects, (3) the classifications of karma, and (4) a concise summary.

1. Contemplating the definitions of virtuous and nonvirtuous karma

The first is twofold, nonvirtuous karma and virtuous karma. With respect to the first, Nāgārjuna states:

> Attachment, anger, and delusion—
> Those generated by these are nonvirtuous.[881]

This refers to actions motivated by afflictions in which the basis, the state of mind, the execution of the act, and the culmination are all complete.

> Nonattachment, absence of anger, and nondelusion—
> Those generated by these are virtuous.[882]

This [second] refers to actions motivated by nonattachment and so on in which the basis, the state of mind, the execution of the act, and the culmination are all complete. Nonvirtuous actions are divided into ten—three nonvirtuous actions of the body, four nonvirtuous actions of speech, and three nonvirtuous actions of mind. Each requires the complete presence of its basis, state of mind, execution, and culmination.

a. The ten nonvirtuous actions

(1) The *basis* of the first, killing, is a sentient being other than yourself. [314] The *state of mind* is twofold: recognition and intention. [Of these] the first, "recognition," refers to the recognition of the object of killing, which in turn is of two kinds—when a particular object is specified and when it is not specified. The first of these is when a specific sentient being is determined as the object of killing and has been accurately recognized. The second is like determining a flock of sheep as the object of killing. Wishing to kill Devadatta, if you mistake Dharmadatta for him and accidentally kill Dharmadatta this does not become a [complete] nonvirtuous karma of killing. A "particular

specified object" means that the object of killing is accurately identified as such. In cases where a particular [object] is not specified, then even when you are mistaken about the object of killing, the act nonetheless becomes a [full] karmic act of killing. [The "intention" refers to] the intention to kill, motivated by any of the afflictions. As for the actual *execution* of the act, this can be by using a weapon, [applying] poison, pushing off a cliff, and so on; it suffices whether you commit these by yourself or you appoint someone else to do them. *Culmination* is when, as a consequence of your act, the other dies before you. Taking life "through attachment" is when you kill because of attachment for the meat or other possession of the object of your killing. "Through anger" is when you despise the other [and take his life], and "through delusion" is [like] when a barbarian kills out of a wish to save old parents from the pain of old age. Its completion is brought about by anger.

(2) The *basis* of the second—taking what is not given—is an object owned by someone other than you. Within the *state of mind,* "recognition" here refers to recognizing the object of theft. This, too, is of two kinds: when a particular object is specified and when it is not specified. As for afflictions, stealing is motivated by any of the three poisons. The "intention" is the desire to take what is not given. As for *execution,* it can be forcible theft using the threat of harm, theft through deception, refusing to return what has been left for safekeeping, and so on. These acts may be committed either by you or by someone assigned by you. *Culmination* is when either of the following two situations arises in the aftermath: the object is removed from its site or the thought of obtainment occurs in your mind. Stealing "through attachment" is when you are attached to the object, "through anger" is when it is done in order to strike at the object's owner, while "through delusion" is when it is done with the thought "There is nothing wrong with taking what is not given." Its completion is brought about by attachment.

(3) The *basis* of sexual misconduct refers to partners of other people, [315] blood relations fewer than seven times removed, or prostitutes who have not been paid for their service. "Inappropriate places" refers to in front of representations of the Three Jewels, at your parents' place, at sites with crevices, where there is light, and so on. "Inappropriate times" refers to during a late stage of pregnancy, during menstruation, and when afflicted with grief. "Inappropriate bodily parts" refers to mouth, anus, and so on.[883] Within the *state of mind,* "recognition" refers to the perception of the object as such. For this act, some say that there is no distinction between specified or unspecified objects. However, the master said, Ārya Asaṅga does accept the

distinction of specification or the lack of it for this act. The "intention" refers to a desire to engage in sexual misconduct that is motivated by one of the three poisonous afflictions. As for *execution,* the preliminary actions include getting up from your seat and so on, while *culmination* is the enjoyment of the pleasure. Here, too, motivated "by attachment" refers to the desire to experience the pleasure of orgasm; "through anger" is with an intention to hurt others, such as by abusing their wife and so on; while "through delusion" refers to things such as when barbarians take their own mothers as brides and commit sexual misconduct. Its completion is brought about by attachment.

(4) The *basis* of telling lies is someone who can speak and comprehend the meaning. Within the *state of mind,* "recognition" refers to stating something contrary to what you believe to be true. The "intention" refers to a desire to modify the listener's perception, and is motivated by any of the afflictions. The *execution* is when the utterance has taken place, and the *culmination* is when the listener has understood the meaning. Its completion is brought about by any one of the three afflictions.

(5) The *object* of divisive speech is a pair of individuals. The *state of mind* refers to the recognition of them and, motivated by any of the afflictions, the desire to cause division between the two people. The *execution* of the act occurs the moment the words are uttered, and its *culmination* takes place so long as the two persons hear the words, regardless of whether the words are true. Finally, its completion is brought about by any one of the three afflictions.

(6) The *object* of harsh speech is someone for whom you harbor ill will. Within the *state of mind,* "recognition" refers to recognizing the object as such, while "intention" refers to the desire to utter words that strike at the heart of the other person, and is motivated by any of the afflictions. [316] The *execution* is constituted by the act of speaking, and it *culminates* when the other person understands the meaning. Its completion is brought about by anger.

(7) The *basis* of engaging in frivolous speech is any class of sentient beings. The *state of mind* is recognizing the basis and, motivated by any of the afflictions, desiring to engage in frivolous speech. Its *culmination* takes place when the words are uttered. Its completion is brought about by any one of the three poisons.

(8) The *object* of covetousness is the same as the basis of stealing. The *state of mind* is recognizing the basis and, motivated by any of the afflictions, having

as your intention the desire to inappropriately make the object your own. *Culmination* takes place when you decides to own the object. Its completion is brought about by attachment.

(9) The *basis* of harmful intent is someone you harbor ill will for. The *state of mind* is recognizing the basis and, motivated by any of the afflictions, having the intention to do harm. The *execution* of the act is thinking, while the *culmination* takes place when you determine to cause harm by either eventually killing the person or separating him from his material resources. Its completion is brought about by anger.

(10) The *basis* of wrong views refers to the law of karma and so on. Within the *state of mind,* recognition is the recognition of the object, and the intention, motivated by any of the afflictions, is the desire to denigrate. The *execution* is having the denigrating thought or arriving at the conclusion that the law of karma and its effect does not exist. Its completion is brought about by delusion.

b. The ten virtuous actions

Second, the virtuous actions are tenfold—three actions of body, such as refraining from killing and so on; four actions of speech, such as refraining from telling lies and so on; and three actions of mind, such as refraining from covetousness and so on. As for their identifications, they are opposite the ten nonvirtuous actions described above. To illustrate with one example, the *basis* of refraining from killing is the same as that of killing. [317] The *state of mind* refers to the recognition of the basis as such and, motivated by nonattachment, nonanger, or nondelusion, to have the intention to refrain from taking life. The *execution* is the giving up of actions, such as striking with a weapon, that cause the other's death. The *culmination* takes place when you have refrained from taking the life of the basis [the object of killing]. Discern the rest [of the virtuous karmic acts] by extending this explanation.

2. Contemplating their effects

Second, contemplating their effects is as follows: Each of these nonvirtuous actions has three types of effects: (1) fruitional effects, (2) causally concordant effects, and (3) environmental effects. As for the fruitional effects of the ten nonvirtuous actions, committing them to great degree causes you to be reborn as a hell being, committing them to a medium degree causes you to be reborn as a hungry ghost, and committing them to a lesser degree causes you to be reborn as an animal. Some sutras also contain statements to the effect that committing nonvirtuous actions to a medium degree causes rebirth as an animal, while the commitment to a lesser degree causes rebirth as a hungry ghost. This does not contradict the first [teaching], the master said, for this is intended to be understood as stating that committing these acts to a medium degree can lead to birth as an animal with intense suffering, while a lesser degree can lead to birth as a hungry ghost with less suffering. Therefore, by committing [this act] to a medium degree you are born as a hungry ghost or as an animal with intense suffering, while by committing to a lesser degree you are born as an animal or as a hungry ghost with less suffering. Given these fruitional effects of indulging in the ten nonvirtuous actions, it is impossible for those who indulge in them to be reborn in any realm higher than the three lower realms.

The causally concordant effects of killing has two aspects: (1) the causally concordant behavioral effects and (2) the causally concordant experiential effects.[884] The first refers to being attracted to the act of killing even though you have escaped the lower transmigration and have taken birth as a human. So you should recognize those who delight in acts of killing today as [experiencing] the causally concordant behavioral effects of the past. Similarly, the causally concordant behavioral effects of other nonvirtuous actions is the attraction you feel for committing these acts again. [318]

The causally concordant experiential effects of killing are that, even though born human, your life is short and you are afflicted with many illnesses. The causally concordant experiential effects of stealing are that, even though born human, you are deprived of material resources, and even if you possess such resources, you have no freedom to enjoy them, for they are forcibly taken away by others. The causally concordant experiential effect of lustful misconduct is, if you are a householder, that your spouse is uncooperative or that you have to share [him or] her with others.

The causally concordant experiential effects of telling lies, when you are a human, are that many will denigrate you, deceive you, and so on. The causally concordant experiential effects of divisive speech are that you have few friends and even the few you have part from you quickly. The causally concordant experiential effect of harsh speech is that you find others' words hurtful even when their motivations are not negative. The causally concordant experiential effect of engaging in frivolous speech is that even though you may say something true, others will not believe it, and thus your words will be ineffective and will not be honored.

The causally concordant experiential effect of covetousness is that you become greedy and incapable of contentment. The causally concordant experiential effect of harmful intent is inclination to violent anger. The causally concordant experiential effect of wrong views is deficient intelligence and ignorance of whether an action is appropriate or inappropriate. All the faults just described should be recognized as the causally concordant experiential effects [of nonvirtuous actions].

The environmental effects arise in the external world. Because of killing, your physical environment will be lackluster and unappealing. Stealing leads to a profusion of adverse conditions, such as crops being assailed by hailstorms and so on. Because of lustful misconduct, your surroundings will be filled with dust, and because of telling lies[885] your surroundings will be mired in mud and will stink. Divisive speech will make your surroundings uneven, and harsh speech will surround you with heat waves. Frivolous speech will bring unpredictable fluctuations [of events] over time. Covetousness will diminish harvests, and because of harmful intent the crops will taste terrible. Because of wrong views you will be reborn in an environment where crops do not grow at all. So in whatever environment you find yourself, recognize the nonvirtuous actions and their [corresponding] environmental effects. [319]

3. The classifications of karma

Third, the presentation of the classifications of karma has five parts:

    a. Presentation in terms of the five mental states
    b. Presentation in terms of the strength and weakness of karma
    c. Presentation in terms of the projecting and completing factors
    d. Presentation in terms of the fruitional effects
    e. Presentation in terms of the time frame of the fruition of the effects

a. The classification of karma in terms of the five mental states

First, through what process is virtuous and nonvirtuous karma accumulated? It is said that [karma] is accumulated by means of five types of mental states. Take killing, for example. A *mental state derived from being decreed* refers to the [instance where], although the killer may deeply disapprove of killing a sentient being and is wary of it, he has no choice but to kill because of a forceful decree from someone such as a king. A *mental state derived from being pleaded with* refers to the [instance where], although you disapprove of taking life, because your friends or relatives beg you and you are incapable of disappointing them, you commit an act of killing. A *mental state derived from ignorance* refers to people such as children, who do not know the destructive effects of taking life, and although they do not possess forceful afflictions, through play and so on they may kill insects, birds, and other small animals. A *mental state derived from manifest grasping at the root* refers to those instances where you take a life while motivated by a strong affliction and with all three elements—preliminary, actual execution of the act, and culmination—complete. A *mental state derived from distortion* refers to instances such as the killing of goats, buffaloes, and so on for the purpose of attaining salvation.[886] Extend this [classification in terms of the five mental states] to the other nonvirtuous actions as well.

Among these [five, those acts of killing committed] through the first two mental states are said to be karma that, though committed, is not accumulated. Because of this, you are not certain to experience its effects. The last two, however, are karma that is both committed and accumulated, and you are therefore certain to experience its effects. Furthermore, rejoicing when calamities befall those you dislike and relishing the harms inflicted upon your enemies are karmic actions accumulated though not actually committed. They are described, therefore, as sources of grave consequences. Since such actions arise easily [320] but are sources of such grave consequences, you need to guard against them vigilantly.

With respect to the virtuous actions, "that which is committed but not accumulated" refers to [acts] such as reciting mantras while your mind is distracted by scattering thoughts. *A Guide to the Bodhisattva's Way of Life* states:

> Though you may engage for long periods
> In mantra repetitions and ascetic practices,
> If these are done with a distracted mind,
> The Knower of Truth declared these to be meaningless.[887]

"That which is [both] committed and accumulated" refers to the following. Motivated by fervent faith and so on, and not distracted by afflictions and mundane thoughts pertaining to this life, you engage from the depth of your heart in any of the virtuous activities of the three doors and subsequently rejoice in them. "That which is accumulated though not committed" refers to rejoicing in deeds performed by others.

O people, direct your mind inward. You will discover that your positive actions of body, speech, and mind, those you identify as virtuous, turn out in most cases to be karmic actions committed but not accumulated. Regarding nonvirtuous actions, however, you have, motivated by intense anger, uttered harsh words certain to strike at the heart of the other. If you have relished these with the thought "I have struck him hard," this constitutes a grave nonvirtuous act known as an *nonvirtuous act manifestly grasping at the root*. This alone is sufficient to cast you into the hells. However, this kind of karma seems to arise many times over the course of even one day. Therefore, if you do not apply your mind with refined intelligence and fail to act correctly with respect to what is to be affirmed and what is to be rejected, even a slight deed can become a tremendous source of regret. So it is vital that you be sustained by mindfulness. The spiritual teacher Phuchungwa exclaimed:

> Our virtuous actions lean on mere words, while our nonvirtuous actions relate efficaciously to the facts.[888]

The spiritual teacher Khamlungpa states:

> If today we fail to engage in a meaningful virtuous activity, we will be returning empty-handed after having been to the land of jewels.[889]

The spiritual teacher Kamapa states:

> You risk visiting the land of jewels and returning with a poisonous plant.[890]

b. The classification of karma in terms of strength and weakness

Although there seem to be many different schools of thought on this, Nāgārjuna writes:

> Permanence, clinging, and lacking in antidotes—
> Deriving from these primary attributes are

Five great virtuous and nonvirtuous deeds; [321]
So strive to accumulate that which is virtuous.[891]

I will explain this classification in accordance with the above quote. From the perspective of *time,* those [actions] that are committed constantly are greater in strength. This is like the nonvirtuous action of a king, for instance, who on a daily basis pledges to kill such and such people and issues the orders to do so. Although killing one sentient being generally and doing so on the basis of a pledge are equal insofar as they entail killing a single being, the nonvirtuous karma of killing on the basis of a pledge on a regular basis is greater in strength.

This is true also of the virtuous karma of daily engaging in ethical actions on the basis of a pledge. Engaging in spiritual practices one day fervently and doing so on the basis of a pledge may be, given the similarity of their motivations and so on, equal in being practices of spirituality for a single day, yet the virtuous karma of the single day of inner reflection that is part of a regular spiritual practice is greater in strength.

From the point of view of the *state of mind,* an action motivated by intense clinging is greater in strength. Some nonvirtuous actions, for example, involve strong clinging to the roots. For virtuous karma, virtuous actions of the three doors that are motivated by such potent attitudes as fervent faith or compassion become greater in strength.

From the perspective of the *antidotes,* nonvirtuous actions that are committed without regret and are accompanied in fact by the rejoicing thought "I have done this and that" are greater in strength. Likewise, in the case of virtuous karma, those committed with rejoicing, thinking, "Yes, I have done this and that," are greater in strength. So if regret arises, even the most powerful nonvirtuous karma can become weaker. Therefore, whatever nonvirtuous actions you happen to commit, it is crucial that you subsequently generate remorse and ensure that this is purified. The same is true of virtuous karma. Even if the karma is not powerful, if you subsequently rejoice, its strength increases. You should therefore, after engaging in any virtuous action, cultivate a special sense of rejoicing, free of any self-importance.

With respect to being greater in strength from the point of view of the *field,* there are two kinds. First any action committed in relation to the Three Jewels, whether virtuous or nonvirtuous, is greater in strength. For example, if with a harmful intention you cause the body of a blessed one[892] to bleed, this constitutes a heinous transgression. The destruction of a blessed one's images or reliquaries [322] is said to approximate the karma of such an act. As for those [actions] pertaining to the Dharma, it is stated, if you accumulate the karma of abandoning the Dharma, this is like the nonvirtuous karma accrued from being devoid of antidotes. If you create a schism in the spiritual community, this is a heinous transgression. If you steal offerings made to the spiritual community, this carries grave nonvirtuous karma. In brief, if your slightly nonvirtuous karmic action is done in relation to the Three Jewels, it becomes greater in strength.

Likewise in the case of virtuous karma, even if you toss a flower in the direction of the Buddha, it is stated, this constitutes a virtuous karmic act of immeasurable merit. Similarly, it is stated that even slight accumulation of virtuous actions in relation to the Three Jewels is powerful. Furthermore, the sutra [entitled] the *Seal Entering the Definitive and Nondefinitive* states:

> Compared to the nonvirtuous karma of a person who plucks out the eyes of every human being in the world and steals all their belongings, harming a bodhisattva out of belligerence is said to be more grave.[893]

Therefore acting against a bodhisattva is said to be a graver negativity. Since it is difficult to know where a bodhisattva might be, it is critical to be mindful on this matter. Similarly, it is stated, more merit is gained in gazing reverently on a bodhisattva once than is gained in offering eyes and material resources to all whose eyes have been plucked out. Committing even a slightly nonvirtuous act toward your parents, who are the source of great kindness—by speaking harshly to them, for instance—is said to constitute powerful nonvirtuous karma. Likewise, it is stated, even the slightest virtuous acts, such as serving them or looking after their welfare, constitute powerful virtuous karma.

Each of these avenues that increase the potency of nonvirtuous actions is capable of casting you into the hells as its fruitional effect, and your own mental continuum must certainly contain many such avenues. For example you might rejoice upon hearing someone belligerently denigrate the spiritual community. Since this karmic act is certain to lead to the suffering of the hell realms, [323] it is extremely inappropriate to remain calm after having accumulated such an act. Śāntideva states:

Having created karma for the hells,
How can I remain tranquil at heart?[894]

For a nonvirtuous karmic act to definitely cast you to the hells does not depend on myriad causal factors, intense exertion, or long stretches of time. For if any of the avenues referred to above that make an act potent is present, even uttering a single [negative] word or shifting your thoughts ever so slightly can cast you to the hells. Therefore the sutras have stated that even a few mildly harsh words can cause the various sufferings of the lower realms, such as those of the hells.

The preceding presentations on classifying powerful nonvirtuous actions have been made in relation to matters shared in common with the lay householders. As for ordained monks, it seems, the very basis of your adopted lifestyle increases the strength of whatever nonvirtuous act you commit.

The four hell-projecting karmic actions that resemble the shooting of an arrow and that have been mentioned in *Maitreya's Great Lion's Roar Sutra*[895] are the following: (1) for an ordained person, consuming the offerings made to the monastic community when your vows have been damaged; (2) deliberately defying, despite knowledge, what the Blessed One has described to cause infractions; (3) not declaring and purifying infractions immediately after they have occurred but remaining with them for a day; and (4) being jealous of others' accomplishments.

Some people do not hesitate whatsoever to indulge in transgressive acts and never purify the infractions when they do occur. Their destination appears to be none other than the three lower realms. Likewise, if you contemplate the fruits of transgressing [even] the minute precepts of the three vows, even those behaviors described earlier as grave negativities seem extremely minuscule [in comparison]. It is in consideration of this point that the great spiritual teacher Tönpa Rinpoché stated, "Compared to nonvirtuous acts committed in relation to the Dharma, all other nonvirtuous acts are [only] indirect causes [of grave consequences]."[896]

Likewise, in the case of virtuous acts, a sutra states the following: Imagine that a householder bodhisattva turns the entire universe of trichiliocosm into one huge lamp, fills it with clarified butter, erects a wick the size of mount Meru, lights it, and offers it in the presence of the Buddha's reliquary. Then imagine another bodhisattva who, after leaving behind his home and taking the life of a thorough renunciate [monk], simply moistens a [tiny] wick with some oil, lights this, and [324] illuminates merely the steps of the

Buddha's reliquary. Compared to the former, the latter [act] is said to be of greater merit. The basis for this [difference] is the way of life. Here [in the second case] the object, attitude, and articles are far superior to those in the first case [because they are based on the monastic vows]. So for ordained members, both loss and gain are tremendously greater. Therefore, with respect to even subtle and minute ethical decisions about what to affirm and what to reject, it is critical that you strenuously avoid all errors.

Also, an act committed by *many together* is said to be greater in strength. For example, if a hundred people share a common objective and with this kill one sheep, each person accrues the negative karma of killing a sheep. If a single person with no partner kills a sheep, he accrues the negative karma of killing a sheep [as well]. However, the negative karma accrued by each person in the former case is greater in strength, and the negative karma of the sole individual is weaker in comparison. Likewise, comparing the construction of a reliquary stupa by a hundred people with construction by a single individual, both are similar insofar as each person accrues the merit of constructing one reliquary stupa. However, the former is greater in strength, while the latter is weaker.

On this point, some who are learned in the scriptural collection of higher knowledge[897] assert that compared to an individual monk reciting the sutras alone in his cell, the recitation of the sutras by each in an assembly of monks is greater in strength. Thus, on the basis of critical examination, recognize as either weak or mediocre [in strength] those virtuous and nonvirtuous actions that lack any of these factors that render them greater in strength.

c. The classification of karma in terms of projecting and completing factors

The nonvirtuous and virtuous karma presented above can also be subsumed into the two categories of projecting and completing factors. Projecting karma is said to be analogous to making line drawings, while completing karma is like applying paint. Among these, nonvirtuous projecting karma propels only the births of the three lower realms and never those of the higher realms. Similarly, virtuous projecting karma will propel only the births of higher realms [325] and never those of the lower realms.

Nonvirtuous completing karma may mature while you are in a lower realm of existence, but it could also mature while you are in a higher realm existence. Similarly, virtuous completing karma may mature while you are in a higher realm of existence, but it could also mature while you are in lower of realm existence.

There are thus four possible permutations: (1) That which is [both] propelled by nonvirtuous karma and also completed by nonvirtuous karma is, for example, the suffering of the hell realms. Being propelled by nonvirtuous karma the bodily existence of a hell being arises, and being completed by nonvirtuous karma you suffer intense heat and cold. (2) The great affluence of wealthy nāgas and the riches rivaling the chief of gods Indra enjoyed by Yama—the lord of death, who is the king of hungry ghosts—are examples of that which is propelled by a nonvirtuous karma but completed by virtuous karma. In brief, any happiness that exists for beings of the lower realms is the result of virtuous completing karma. (3) That which is [both] propelled by virtuous karma and completed also by virtuous karma is, for example, the universal monarch reigning over a thousand kingdoms. Because he has been propelled by virtuous karma, he has attained the existence of a higher realm, and because he has been completed also by virtuous karma, he enjoys unimaginable wealth and power over his dominion. (4) That which is propelled by virtuous karma yet completed by nonvirtuous karma is when you, being propelled by virtuous karma, attain a human existence but, completed by nonvirtuous karma, your life is short, you suffer a host of illnesses, and you are stuck in poverty. In brief, all sufferings that exist in the higher realms of existence are due to nonvirtuous completing karma.

There are instances where one nonvirtuous karma propels multiple lifetimes in the lower realms, and likewise there are instances where one virtuous karma propels multiple lifetimes in the higher realms. There are also cases where multiple karmic seeds propel only one lifetime. People today believe that in order to accumulate karma sufficient to experience the hell realms, they need to commit acts such as killing over a long period of time, or that they need to strive with many companions in acts such as war, or that they have to commit grave nonvirtuous acts such as the destruction of towns and so on, [326] or that they must kill many sentient beings. They feel that only through such acts will they go to the hells and be reborn in specific hell regions. This indicates inadequate familiarity with the teachings. Certainly, these karmas would definitely propel you to the hell realms. It has been stated, however, that each of the powerful karmic acts just described can propel many lower-realm lifetimes. To accumulate karma sufficient to propel a lifetime [in the lower realms] does not depend on forceful exertion and so on. The Blessed One has stated in the sutras that for every nonvirtuous act, you will be reborn in the hells sixteen times. Understand that each karmic act can individually cause infinite sufferings of the lower realms, and strive to relinquish nonvirtuous actions.

d. *The classification of karma in terms of the fruitional effects*

There are four permutations: (1) that which is positive and has a positive fruitional effect, (2) that which is positive yet has a negative fruitional effect, (3) that which is negative and has a negative fruitional effect, and (4) that which is negative yet has a positive fruitional effect.

(1) The first is, for example, making offerings to the Three Jewels out of fervent devotion. This is described as a "positive action with a positive fruitional effect" because both aspects of its motivation—the causal motivation and the concomitant mental state—are positive. (2) Drawing images of buddhas and so on with the aim of obtaining things such as food and wealth because of your craving for these is described as a "positive action with a negative fruitional effect." For though these actions may appear to have a positive concomitant state of mind, their causal motivation is in fact negative. (3) Taking a life for the sake of food is an example of a "negative action with a negative fruitional effect," for both its causal and concomitant motivations are negative. (4) A parent's spontaneous striking or scolding his or her beloved children out of love and in order to protect them against harm may appear to have a negative concomitant mental state, but because its causal motivation is positive, it is a "negative action with a positive fruitional effect."

So in order to posit an act as virtuous or nonvirtuous, the motivation is primary and not the actual nature of the act. [327] For example, the slaying of the spear-wielding dark-skinned man by the skilled captain may, in terms of the actual nature of the act, appear to be [the nonvirtuous karma of] killing.[898] Nevertheless because the motivation was noble, it is said, this helped accumulate many eons' worth of merit. Engaging in virtuous actions with your three doors in order to obtain material gifts, honor, and so on, or to attract others' trust is referred to as "distractions of [external] signs" and is considered nonvirtuous. Guarding your senses for the sake of these [mundane] purposes is said to be a "pretense of ethical discipline," using gentle speech as "false politeness," and obtaining material resources and honor through such means is described as "wrong livelihood." Therefore Śāntideva states:

"Where is my mind straying?"
Observe your mind thus.[899]

So, before engaging in any actions of the three doors whatsoever, examine your motivation critically and act unerringly with respect to what is to be relinquished and what is to be affirmed. If you fail to do this, you might assume that you are engaging in Dharma practice, but there is no guarantee that this really is the case. Kharak Gomchung states:

> Engaging in study with a motive to compete,
> Giving feasts with a craving for a good harvest,
> Displaying pride with an ambition for becoming learned—
> Alas consider, can these become Dharma practice?[900]

e. The classification of karma in terms of the time frame of the fruition of the effects

In terms of time, when do you experience the fruits of karma? There are three kinds [of karma with respect to the time of fruition]: (1) those that will be experienced here and now [in this lifetime], (2) those that will be experienced in other lifetimes [generally], and (3) those that will be experienced after rebirth [in the next lifetime]. As for the first, the *Treasury of Higher Knowledge* states:

> Due to such factors as the field and the state of mind,
> Karma whose fruits can be seen here and now [exists].[902]

If you make offerings of extraordinary articles such as the elaborate perfect offerings to such extraordinary objects as the Three Jewels and inspired by such extraordinary mental states as fervent devotion, the fruits of this action will be experienced in this very life. Similarly, if, motivated by a powerful mental affliction, you accumulate grave negative karma in relation to a holy object, the fruit of that action too will be experienced in this very life. In brief, powerful actions—whether virtuous or negative—whose fruits are realized in this lifetime are described as "karma [whose effects] will be experienced here and now." [328]

The second [category] refers to such [karma] as the accumulation of a heinous karmic act. An action whose fruition is certain to be experienced in the life following its execution is called "karma [whose effects] will be experienced after rebirth." Those actions whose karma will be realized even later than the next life are called "karma [whose effects] will be experienced in other lifetimes." For this [last category] it is not possible to specify an [exact] timeframe or indicate that the effects will come to be by such and such time. The scriptures of discipline make statements such as the following:

> As for the karma of embodied beings,
> Even in a hundred eons it will not go away;
> When all [conditions] are gathered and the time comes,
> Beings will certainly reap the effects.[903]

Many people appear to believe that the relative status of their next life's existence, higher or lower, is determined by the greater and lesser negative karma of their present life. While the greater and lesser negative karma of this life can indeed become a cause for the higher or lower status of the next life's existence, this is not certain. For example, your negative karma of this life may be weak and you may also have engaged in some virtuous actions. But in the next life you still have to experience that karma—which you have been accumulating since beginningless lifetimes—whose imprints lead to certain rebirth in the hells.

Therefore it's impossible to discern whose accumulation of nonvirtuous karmic imprints since beginningless time is denser between the two—a person who commits grave negative acts in this life or a person who engages in an occasional virtuous action. Knowing this, it is wholly inappropriate to ridicule someone who commits grave nonvirtuous acts and with a complacent heart harbor the pride "I do not possess such karma." You do not know how many karmic imprints you have accumulated since beginningless time that are certain to lead to the hell realms. You cannot measure this, for you have neither a basis for confidence nor a reason [to believe] that the karmic propensity to wander in the infinite cycle of existence does not exist within your mental continuum.

You cannot put faith in the fact that you have committed no great negative act in this life and that you have performed occasional virtuous deeds. [The scriptures] state that sentient beings wander in the infinite cycle of existence. On the basis of this [fact] alone, you must endeavor even more than before to relinquish negative karma and accomplish that which is virtuous. If it is difficult for our virtuous karma to even bring rebirth as a human, [at

the same time] there are also countless instances when we have attained birth
as celestial beings [because of] the other [karmic imprints, suggesting that
there are infinitely more imprints of nonvirtuous karma within us]. [329] So
even though you may pride yourself on being good and lofty, *A Guide to the
Bodhisattva's Way of Life* states:

> If you can get stuck in the Avīci hells for an eon
> Through an evil act committed in a single instant,
> What need is there to say that no good migration comes
> Through evil acts amassed since beginningless time?[904]

[So contemplate,] "I have accumulated nonvirtuous karma during beginningless lifetimes in the cycle of existence, as if without respite for even a
single day. In all of this reaping [nonvirtuous karma] upon myself, not even
the slightest will be reaped by others. I should not proceed any further by
even a single step without purifying these [karmic] imprints. It is necessary
to disclose and resolve purely, generating intense remorse for all [the nonvirtuous actions] I have committed in the past, declaring and purifying them
and resolving never to commit them again, even at the cost of my life."

If both virtuous and nonvirtuous karmic imprints are present, which
ripen first? On this point, the elder Bodhibhadra states:

> As for karma's fruition, [it's] those that are weightier,
> Those that are closer, those most habituated toward,
> And those committed earliest—
> Of all [karma] these are reaped first.[905]

Thus, if there is a difference in strength between the virtuous and the nonvirtuous karma, that which is greater in strength is reaped first. If they are
of equal strength, the closer—whichever is more manifest at the time of
death—will be reaped first. If the evidence of a karmic imprint and its
absence are equal [between the virtuous and the nonvirtuous], whichever
was committed first will be reaped first, within which the most habituated
to will be reaped first. If even the degree of habituation is equal, then that
which was accumulated earlier will be realized first or, as the *Compendium of
Higher Knowledge* states, "alternately."[906] What has just been described represents one hypothetical situation as opposed to something definite. Whatever the case, as far as our own mental continuum is concerned, many sound

reasons exist why in our next life the fruits of our nonvirtuous karma may be realized first.

4. A concise presentation of these points by means of a summary

To illustrate concisely the above presentations of karma and its effects by means of a summary, the Buddha states in a sutra, "These beings are [330] inhabitants of karmic birth; they experience their share of karma and make karma their own."[907]

"Inhabitant of karmic birth" implies that the environment and the beings within, as well as all diverse appearances of happiness and suffering, do not come about due to an eternal self, as postulated by the non-Buddhist Indian schools. Nor do they come into being from themselves. They come into being from [the coming together of] sufficient and unmistaken causes [and conditions]. All the appearances of happiness and suffering—the manifestations of your karma—have come about due to the accumulation of karma that gives rise to their experience. *The One Hundred Rites* states:

> The happiness and suffering of all beings
> Are due to karma, the Sage taught;
> Karma arises from diverse acts,
> Which in turn create the diverse classes of beings.[908]

If all happiness and suffering arise from karma, you might wonder, does one karma—virtuous or nonvirtuous—give rise to all the happiness and suffering? Or is it that all karma gives rise to all happiness and suffering? Neither is the case. "They experience their share of karma" [suggests] that happiness arises from its cause, virtuous karma, and never from nonvirtuous karma. Suffering arises from its cause, nonvirtuous karma, and never from virtuous karma. Therefore virtuous causes give rise to happiness; it is impossible for them to produce suffering. Nonvirtuous causes give rise to suffering; it is impossible for them to produce happiness. So "they experience their own share of karma" means that the causes and effects of virtuous and nonvirtuous karma are individually determined, and it is impossible for these two to be conflated.

If this is so, you might wonder, what virtuous karma is responsible for the fact that those who engage in virtuous actions often suffer greatly in this life, while those who commit grave negative acts often enjoy such advantages as attractiveness, wealth, and so on? It is conceivable that after engaging in virtuous actions, you might experience an increase in illness or a decrease in material resources, but this is not because the fruits of that pure virtuous action have ripened as suffering. This is instead the suffering effect of some nonvirtuous karma created in the past. In particular, when a thoroughly pure virtuous act occurs in your heart—such as the arising of the awakening mind—sufferings such as illness can arise. It is said that this is due to karma you accumulated in the past, but due to the power of such a virtuous act, it has now ripened as mere human suffering, instead of as birth in the hells. [331] The need to experience birth in the lower realms has thus been preempted. The *Diamond Cutter Sutra* states:

> Beings who practice the perfection of wisdom will
> experience torments.[909]

A Guide to the Bodhisattva's Way of Life states:

> If someone on death row can be spared
> By having his hands cut off, is this not better?
> So if by small human sufferings,
> You are spared the hells, is this not better?[910]

The fruits of today's pure virtuous karma will [definitely] appear in the future. Likewise, happiness experienced by those who commit serious negative karma does not indicate that the fruits of such negative karma are being reaped as happiness. [Their happiness] is the fruit of causes—virtuous karma—accumulated in the past. It has been stated that when people who have committed powerful negative acts [appear to] enjoy a great degree of happiness, it is a sign that, due to the force of their powerful negative karma, the extensive merit they accumulated in the past that would [otherwise] give rise to higher states is being exhausted in the trivial pleasures of this life, and that from this point onward they will endure only suffering. Once in the past, in the land of Aparānta, famine struck a town where powerful negative acts had been committed. First a rain of rice fell for seven days; second, a rain of barley fell for seven days; then a rain of precious gems fell for seven days, and with these, the great stores of merit that had been accumulated in the past [by the people] were exhausted. Following this, a rain of sand fell for seven days and the town was destroyed. This is recorded [in the scriptures].[911]

So it is impossible for happiness to arise from negative karma; however, powerful negative karma can even destroy past virtuous karma. *A Guide to the Bodhisattva's Way of Life* states:

> Accumulated over a thousand eons
> Through giving, venerating sugatas, and so on,
> Whatever acts of goodness there are,
> An instant of anger destroys them all.[912]

You might think, "Sure, the fruits of that nonvirtuous karma will come about later. That said, although happiness is the fruit of virtuous karma and suffering is the fruit of negative karma, it still may be possible for suffering to arise from virtuous karma and happiness from negative karma. I observe the following situations with my own eyes, for example: When engaging in virtuous deeds, some people suffer pain due to ascetic discipline and hardship, [332] yet because of nonvirtuous activity such as stealing some enjoy great prosperity, and because of killing animals some enjoy meat and fat."

In the case of austerities and hardships when engaging in virtuous deeds, here the virtuous behavior simply triggers these [painful] experiences. The [actual] causes for these [painful] experiences are nonvirtuous deeds committed in the past. The fruits of the austerities and hardships will be realized later. Similarly, prosperity due to stealing arises because of some past nonvirtuous karma, such as giving charity, which gives rise to material resources, and the [act of] stealing is a mere trigger. For example, even though [people may] acquire cattle in equal numbers, due to differences in the force of their past giving, the cattle herd prospers for some while for others it quickly disappears. Virtuous and negative karma never violate the natural order with respect to their effects.

Can you experience the fruits of someone else's virtuous karma? Can the fruits of someone else's nonvirtuous acts ripen upon you? This cannot happen. The statement "They make karma their own" indicates that whatever degree of happiness, great or small, befalls an individual is the effect of virtuous karma created by the individual himself. Likewise, whatever suffering befalls an individual is the effect of negative deeds committed by the individual himself. Your virtuous and negative karma will come to fruition upon you and not upon others.

You might ask, "If this is so, does the virtuous karma created by children for their parents' benefit not bear fruit for the parents?" Some people believe that only the parents experience the fruits of the virtuous deeds done on their behalf, and that [such fruits] are never realized upon the agent of the act himself. This is not so. To the extent that you engage in virtuous deeds for the sake of your parents, to that extent you accrue powerful merit. This benefits the mental continuum of the parents, the master said, by triggering conditions and activating imprints of past virtuous karma and so on, thus serving as empowering conditions for [the parents'] virtuous activities.[913] Therefore, whatever nonvirtuous deeds you have committed in this life, their fruitional effects cannot possibly be experienced by others but only by you.

Since your virtuous and nonvirtuous deeds [333] bear fruit upon your own self, when death arrives, making even a single prostration to the Three Jewels out of fervent faith will be of greater benefit than possessing wealth filling this entire world. Compared to having the whole world rise up as your enemy, uttering out of affliction a single harsh word—and if you are ordained, engaging in a slight misdeed—are greater enemies. Recognizing this, understand that whatever virtuous deeds you commit benefit your own self and whatever nonvirtuous deeds you commit injure you alone. With this understanding correctly follow the discipline of what is to be affirmed and what is to be relinquished, heeding even the subtlest and most minute aspects of karma.

You might think, "There are cases where nonvirtuous acts committed by one being causes harm to another. For instance, the butcher's nonvirtuous act of taking life causes animals like sheep to suffer being slain. Also there are cases where one being's virtuous act causes happiness to another. For instance, the benefactor's virtuous acts of accumulating merit with respect to the monastic community [leads the members of] the community to enjoy material comforts."

This is not a correct [analysis], however. The sheep's suffering of being slain by the butcher is not the fruit of that negative act of killing by the butcher. It is [in fact] the fruit of nonvirtuous deeds committed by the sheep itself in the past. The butcher's nonvirtuous act will ripen in future upon the butcher himself. Similarly, the comfort enjoyed by the monks from the gathering of [material] resources is not the fruit of the benefactor's merit accumulation. Rather it is the fruit of virtuous deeds performed by the monks in the past.

In brief, the meaning of "making karma their own" is this: Any deed performed, whether virtuous or negative, will definitely ripen upon the individual who does it. [These actions] can be a source of benefit and harm for others, too, through being empowering conditions [for their own karma to ripen].

At present we tend to believe that whatever undesirable events befall us are caused by others, and so we blame others. Similarly, we tend to believe that whatever desirable events befall us are due to our own achievements in this life. This is not the case. Since these experiences are the fruits of our own past karma, there is simply no basis for blaming others for the undesirable events that befall us. And as for the fruits of the karmic deeds performed in this life, these will be reaped in the future.

Furthermore, karma increases exponentially. In the realm of external cause and effect, the increment between effect and cause can be as great as that which occurs in the case of the Nayagrota tree, [334] in which the seed is as small as a mustard grain, but the tree it grows into can extend to an area of a three square *yojanas*.[914] This is stated [in the scriptures].[915] The exponential increment of inner cause and effect is even greater. It has been stated that even a slight nonvirtuous act can lead to enormous suffering. For instance, because of saying "you bitch" to her friends, a fully ordained woman was reborn as a female dog for five hundred lifetimes. There is [also] the story of the short hunchback maid who became a servant for others and how this unfortunate woman acquired her hunchback appearance. She was reborn as an unfortunate servant because once, when she was born as a princess, she insulted her attendants by calling them "you [miserable] servants." She acquired her hunchback in the following way. The king had many arhats as his revered guests. Once when they were invited for a feast, one arhat who had a hunchback did not attend. When the king asked his daughter if any of the revered guests were missing, the princess aped the appearance of hunchback and said that the one like this was missing. As a consequence, it is said she was reborn with a hunchback. Although this was neither a karma of deliberate insult to an arhat nor an act committed out of an afflicted motivation, the master said, this was the fruit of mimicking the appearance of an arhat with respect to a defect.

Atiśa's teacher, the great Avadhūtipa, would often refuse to teach when requested and would do so often when not requested. One time, when the teacher and his disciple were crossing a narrow bridge, as they reached the middle of the bridge, the teacher turned his face around and taught the following: "O son, until self-grasping has ceased, shy away from even the minutest aspects of [negative] karma and its effects." When they had crossed the bridge, Atiśa asked his teacher why. The teacher then told him how a particular yogin with such and such meditative absorptions was now in the hells undergoing great suffering as a result of a slight nonvirtuous act; and how a scholar learned in such and such fields of knowledge was now in the hells undergoing such and such degree of suffering as a result of another slight nonvirtuous act. He told Atiśa these stories along with their underlying reasons.

Also, once at Vikramaśīla [Monastery] a hungry ghost with back-facing feet was living in the pit for [disposing] ritual torma cakes. [335] The young novices would throw stones at him, and once he caught one. Many people gathered, and some recited wrathful mantras to try and tame him through fierce means, but this provoked him to fight back. A yogi living nearby heard what had happened. Amused, he went to see for himself, but the ghost did not attack him. So the yogi asked, "Why do you attack others and not me?" to which the ghost replied, "Others come here to provoke me, so I fight them, but you came out of curiosity, so I do not target you." "If this is so, then who are you?" asked the yogi. "Send the young novices away," replied the ghost. When they left, he declared, "I was an elder from Vikramaśīla. Thinking myself to be important and powerful, I used some of the resources of the monastery without permission. Although I [actually] did this for the benefit of the community, I was nonetheless reborn as a hungry ghost. And because I once failed to take my shoes off when walking inside the monastery's temple, my feet are [today] back to front. Because I abused my power a little, I have been born as the least powerful among the hungry ghosts. Therefore I seek shelter here in the pit for ritual torma cakes."

When asked why he requested that the young novices be sent away, he replied that they were [formerly] his students and that he felt ashamed in their presence. For a while he fell asleep but then returned to continue the discussion. When asked, "Why were you were silent for a while?" he said that he went to create obstacles for someone practicing the Dharma. When asked, "You are learned; why do you commit nonvirtuous acts?" he replied, "This is true. But as a hungry ghost, I simply have no control over my mind." So told the master.

A yogi performing the rite of torma offering was attracting many hungry ghosts. One day a hungry ghost appeared in the form of the meditation deity Yamāntaka and demanded that the torma be given to him quickly. When asked his identity, the ghost replied, "I am a Yamāntaka yogi. Because I used a small portion of the monastic community's resources to benefit the community itself but without seeking prior permission, I was reborn as a hungry ghost. Because of my stable self-visualization as the deity Yamāntaka, however, my physical appearance has assumed this form." When asked, "Why didn't you reveal yourself before today?" he answered, "Until yesterday I was too embarrassed; [336] I came today because I was so hungry." So, the master said, the yogi cooked some rice and quickly offered him a ritual cake. The spiritual teacher Sharawa said, "It is clear that we must cook rice and so on and perform the rite of torma offering. Even though he [the ghost] was very hungry, rice was cooked and then offered as a torma."[916]

Therefore, if even this kind of single, slight transgression of secondary precepts can lead to rebirth as a hungry ghost and cause that much suffering, what need is there to speak of the great suffering caused by other more grave nonvirtuous deeds. It is critical, therefore, to refrain from even slight and minute nonvirtuous acts. Similarly, even modest virtuous acts can bring tremendous happiness, such as in the tale of Prince Chiwokyé.[917] Thus, contemplating deeply the presentation of karma and its effects as explained above, meditate on it until an uncontrived conviction in the law of karma and its effects arises. Meditating in this manner is most critical. *A Guide to the Bodhisattva's Way of Life* states:

> The root of all virtuous forces
> Is aspiration, the Sage taught;
> The root of aspiration in turn is
> Constant meditation on [karma's] fruitional effects.[918]

What is the measure of being convinced of the law of karma and its effects? The *Precious Garland* states:

> If you do not breach the teachings
> Through aspiration, hatred, fear, and confusion,
> You are said to have faith.[919]

Thus, as stated, some avoid transgressing the teachings out of aspiration, some out of hatred, some out of fear, and others out of ignorance. Of these four, not transgressing the teachings out of aspiration refers to this. There are some who could not comply when told that they would be given great

wealth, such as dominion over a kingdom, if they committed the nonvirtuous karma of a slight misdeed. The spiritual teacher Potowa said, "Certainly,
if you have conviction in the law of karma and its effects, such things do
occur."[920]

It has been stated that committing slight misdeeds causes rebirth as a
hungry ghost, and committing slight nonvirtuous acts cause rebirth in the
hells. Therefore, if you have to undergo the sufferings of the hungry ghost
and hell realms as a human being even for a brief moment, no amount of
prosperity—even dominion over a kingdom and so on—can in any way
compensate for even a portion of such suffering. [337] The spiritual master
Kamapa said:

> Today, if someone were to promise "If you put your hand in the
> fire and leave it there for a while, I shall transform you into a
> universal monarch reigning over a thousand world systems," no
> one would accept this offer, because everyone knows that the
> fire will burn the hand. Equally, to give up Dharma practice for
> the sake of a slight fluctuation in others' estimation is to lack
> conviction in the law of karma and its effects.[921]

Not transgressing the teachings out of hatred refers to the following. *A Guide
to the Bodhisattva's Way of Life* states:

> Even if all the gods and demigods
> Rise against me as my enemies,
> They cannot drag and deliver me
> Into the fire of the Avīci hell.
>
> Yet this powerful enemy, the afflictions,
> Can cast me in a single instant
> Into the fire that, once taken hold,
> Leaves not even an ash from Mount Meru.[922]

As stated here, regardless of how much others harm your body and resources,
knowing the destructive consequences of hatred and so on, make sure that,
in response to their harm, not even a single instance of afflictions such as
anger arises in you. This is possible if you have developed conviction in the
law of karma and its effects, and if you recognize the destructive nature of

afflictions. It is analogous to the following: Imagine a furnace blazing with intense fire that burns instantly anyone who opens its door, without leaving even an ash, with the powerful flames pouring out of it. Despite threat or entreaty, no one would volunteer to open the door. Those who out of intense hatred retaliate against mere variations in words do so because of their lack of conviction in the law of karma and its effects and their failure to understand the destructive nature of the afflictions.

Not transgressing the teachings "out of fear" refers to the following: Even though the entire human population becomes powerful universal monarchs and commands "You must commit a minor nonvirtuous act" or, if you are ordained, "You must commit the infraction of a slight misdeed," and "If you do not obey, we will kill you by slicing off small pieces of your flesh every day," you do not commit such an act. If you have conviction in the law of karma and its effects, this too is certainly possible. However intense the sufferings described above may be, they are still sufferings of the human realm. [338] In contrast, the fruitional effect of nonvirtuous acts and pledge infractions is the suffering of the lower realms. It is analogous to this: If you are threatened with fists or clubs and told to extract the tip of your heart and hand it over, you would never cut out the tip of your heart and give it away.

Not transgressing the teachings "out of ignorance" refers to the following: Ascertaining all gross and subtle nonvirtuous karma to be causes of suffering, and determining from the depth of your heart that all suffering is the fruit of nonvirtuous karma, you do not transgress the teachings. Say a person has to travel to another place and hears that on the way is a massive fire pit the size of Mount Meru. He would ask those who are familiar with the road such questions as "Where is this fire pit? How wide is its circumference? How should I proceed on the road?" He would be sure to understand the advantages and risks of the road he is traveling on and would traverse the road avoiding the fire pit. In the same manner, when someone who reflects on the law of karma and its effects hears that all sufferings arise from nonvirtuous karma, he will ask those who are learned and who understand correctly the nature of the law of karma and its effects such questions as "What are some examples of nonvirtuous karma? What types of suffering will I experience if I engage in certain nonvirtuous acts? How can I eliminate nonvirtuous karma?" He will interrogate in great detail and learn well. Even if someone were to assert that certain slight nonvirtuous acts do not matter so much for a monk, such as eating in the evening, he would not dare to transgress the precepts.

If you understand well the presentations of karma and its effects and if you have developed deep conviction in them, such restraint is possible. If someone gives you virulent poison and asks you to take it, saying that it won't matter much, you won't take it. In the same way, [with conviction in the law of karma] you won't transgress even the minor precepts. Again, if you are about to cross the sea on a raft and someone asks you to give him a small piece of the raft, a hole only large enough for a finger, asserting that this can hardly matter, you would never give such a piece. Giving even this much would compromise the safety of the raft and you would not be able to get to the other shore. The precious higher trainings are the raft that can carry you across the ocean of cyclic existence. [339] Therefore cultivate the conviction "With even a slight tear or breakage, I will be unable cross the ocean of cyclic existence."

The spiritual teacher Öjowa says:

> Some say that people today are ignorant of Dharma practice and suffer even when no one is harming them. If such an adversary did exist, you could recite the *maṇi* [mantra]. It is so unfortunate when people are ignorant of Dharma practice. Most people these days seem to transgress the teachings out of ignorance. Therefore, even if you don't know the extensive treatises that present karma and its effects, make sure you at least know *The Differentiation of the Five Aggregates* and have a correct understanding of at least one presentation of karma and its effects.[923]

Similarly, with virtuous karma, if you have the conviction that it produces all immediate and lasting happiness, naturally you will persevere in it. If people hear that a joyous festival is taking place behind a hill, they will go even if it involves crossing passes and rivers. And seeing benefits such as abundant harvests, people toil in fields.

This, then, concludes the presentation of the law of karma and its effects.

D. Reflection on the defects of cyclic existence

If, as it is said, indulging in nonvirtuous acts leads you to wander in the lower realms of cyclic existence, what are the defects of falling into the lower realms? The consequences are grave. The *Close Placements of Mindfulness [Sutra]* states:

Hell denizens are impaired by the fires of hell,
Hungry ghosts are impaired by hunger and thirst,
Animals are impaired by devouring each other,
Humans are impaired by life's brevity.

The gods are impaired by their heedlessness—
There is no joy ever in the cycle of existence,
Not even as much as the tip of a needle![924]

As this states, there is no space for joy in the cycle of existence, not even the size of the tip of a needle, and in terms of time not even a single instant [of real joy] exists, and so you remain within the bounds of suffering. [340] You might think "Yes, there is suffering in the lower realms, but humans and gods have happiness." Even were this true, they, too, are ultimately subject to the suffering of change. For example, when you are hungry and you eat, it may seem pleasurable, but overeating can lead to the suffering of death. So seeking joy in cyclic existence is like seeking perfume in excrement! The *Sublime Continuum* states:

As no fragrant odor exists in excrement, no joy exists in the five classes of beings.[925]

Sufferings such as these are intense and powerful. The master Dampa states:

Contemplating the sufferings of samsara pierces my heart;
People of Dingri, laugh not at these matters![926]

Similarly, the spiritual guide Langthangpa states:

People complain that Langri Thangpa's face looks downcast, but how can anyone who contemplates the sufferings of the three realms of cyclic existence maintain a cheerful expression?[927]

This is very true. For if you examine the sufferings of cyclic existence with an uncontrived and focused mind, it is impossible to maintain a cheerful face. Imagine you possess a cherished object with the value of a *shoghang* coin.[928] Although the pain of losing this article is one of the smallest among the sufferings of cyclic existence, this will [still] prevent you from adopting a cheerful expression. This suffering [of cyclic existence] endures long, and without some means of release, then even if each and every sentient being undergoes every possible suffering within the higher and lower realms of cyclic existence, suffering will persist. Whatever suffering has existed from beginningless time up to the present, every sentient being has undergone it innumerable times. But this has not led to even a slight reduction in suffering, let alone its cessation! On this point, the *Friendly Letter* states:

> Each of us has drunk milk
> Exceeding the volume of the four great seas,
> Yet if we follow the pattern of ordinary beings,
> We will drink still greater amounts in cyclic existence.[929]

Like this, contemplate well the general and specific sufferings of cyclic existence as described in the *Oral Tradition*. And like a bird [fleeing] a burning garden or a frozen lake, [341] forsake all your hopes for cyclic existence and seek the means to escape it. The moment to strive for freedom from cyclic existence is now. Today you have found the precious human existence of leisure and opportunity so difficult to obtain; not only that, you have the fortune of having entered the monastic order by relinquishing the life of a householder; you have met with a spiritual teacher and have also encountered the profound and vast teachings of the Mahayana. You thus enjoy the convergence of many essential conditions.

So how do you strive in this? Some might say, "Our spiritual guide and teacher possesses the three qualities of learning, industry, and kindness and is wise in both spiritual and mundane matters. Through these [qualities] he will fulfill all the aspirations of his students and benefactors. What a wonderful teacher we have!" Commenting on this [kind of complacency], the spiritual teacher Shawo Gangpa states:

> One person cannot accomplish two [objectives], one dog cannot catch two foxes [at the same time], and one cannot extract two skins from one fox. It is also not possible to get from the slaughter of a single sheep both a wool cloak that can barely be lifted and a leather sack capable of transporting water. Likewise, it is impossible to leave the patterns of your mundane life unchanged and, at the same time, accomplish a spiritual practice capable of leading you to freedom from cyclic existence and to full enlightenment.

For instance, it is not possible to take one road to travel both to the Mön region[930] in the south and to the salt regions in the north. For if you are traveling south to Mön, you need to gather merchandise appropriate for Mön, such as yak tails, and accordingly turn in that southerly direction. With every step you take as you travel south, you get farther and farther from the salt regions of the north. On the other hand, if you are traveling to the salt regions of the north, you need to gather supplies necessary for going to the salt regions, such as roasted barley flour, and turn toward the northern direction. With every step you take as you travel north, you get farther and farther from the Mön region of the south.

Likewise, one person traveling from cyclic existence toward the city of liberation and omniscience and another wishing to prevent the mundane aspirations of this life from being undermined cannot have the same destination. For to travel to the city of liberation and buddhahood, one must traverse via perfect Dharma practice, relinquishing all forms of self-grasping, such as the eight worldly concerns, [342] and cherishing the path of the three precious higher trainings. As your levels and paths ascend progressively higher, the heads of self-grasping, such as the eight worldly concerns, become correspondingly lower. On the other hand, if your goal is to ensure that the mundane aspirations of this life are not undermined, you will then be motivated by the three poisons. You will need to affirm the practice of defeating your adversaries and tending your friends. The three higher trainings and perfect Dharma practice have no relevance in that situation.

However attractive your behavior appears, however much you try to tame your minds, and however gentle you are in your speech, so long as you allow your mind to be obscured by a single mundane success of this life or be cowed by a single misfortune of this life, it is impossible for even a single positive quality described in the teachings to arise in your mind. Today, in this short life, when many of the essential conditions have come together, it is not the time to view the desires of this life as higher attainments. It is not the time to extend the hub and spokes of the eight worldly concerns, nor is it the time to buttress the citadel of self-grasping. Rather, it is time to engage in Dharma practice, the path pertaining to our next life and beyond. Therefore discard all mundane aspirations.

Just as a drawing of armor on canvas is cast from among the collection of armor, exclude yourself from the ranks of the mundane people. Now is the moment to view your afflictions and self-grasping as your worst enemies and to make sure that whatever spiritual practices you engage in become a remedy against afflictions and self-grasping. The time has now arrived to strive your best to subdue, as much as possible, your afflictions and self-grasping.[931]

You should implement the practices above. Middling nonvirtuous actions and the factors that motivate them, which give rise to cyclic existence, are all present today. Their fruits are hunger and thirst, mental disturbances, persecution, and so on. All the causes of [birth as] animals arise within [as well]. [For instance,] there are the slight nonvirtuous acts together with their motivating factors described above, which consist of karma and the afflictions. Their fruits are the sufferings [of the animal realm], such as stupidity and delusion and devouring one another. Strive to be free from such [miseries].

I have penned these words from memory. If you find any mistakes, such as errors in [the wording of] the scriptural citations, please correct them and use this much [the citations] as a seed [for your contemplations]. By critically determining the [meaning,] put this [instruction] into practice. This was written by the hermit (Könchok Gyaltsen).[932]

Part Two

1. Training in the two awakening minds, the main practice

In general, the great Atiśa possessed three different traditions, or instruction lineages, of training in the awakening mind. There is the lineage stemming from his teacher Dharmarakṣita, who, through the power of his compassion, was capable of giving away parts of his body by slicing them off; there is the lineage stemming from his teacher Maitrīyogi, who was capable of actually taking the suffering of others upon himself; and there is the lineage stemming from his teacher Serlingpa.

Of these, the method of training according to the first two is to engage first in the practice of the ultimate awakening mind, and then with respect to the conventional awakening mind, practice equalizing self and others and then exchanging self and others. This is difficult for a beginner, the master said. According to the tradition of teacher Serlingpa, however, you undertake the practice of conventional awakening mind while remaining in your present state—with self-grasping still manifest—and do not first practice the ultimate awakening mind. Here, too, you engage in the practice of exchanging self and others right from the start. This method is far superior, it is taught, because it is easier to foster in the heart of a beginner and since it yields great benefits.

The practice of the conventional awakening mind according to the tradition of the teacher Serlingpa has three parts:

A. Cultivating loving-kindness and compassion, the preparation
B. Cultivating awakening mind through exchanging self and others, the main practice
C. Transforming the three poisons into the three roots of virtue, the conclusion

A. Cultivating loving-kindness and compassion, the preparation

As for the first, this should be practiced as described in the *Oral Tradition*. [344]

B. Cultivating awakening mind through exchanging self and others, the main practice

[TAKING]

First visualize your real-life mother in front. Although you have earlier completed the visualization of generating loving-kindness and compassion, in order to cultivate joy in taking upon yourself the suffering of your mother, you need to generate at this point a clear and palpable compassion. Then round up into your heart all of your mother's karma and afflictions—her negative karma, such as the ten nonvirtuous actions; all her afflictions, such as those of the three times; all her sufferings, such as birth, aging, illness, and death; all undesirable circumstances; in brief, all the causes that prevent her full awakening and all the obstacles to buddhahood. Take these from your mother as though slicing them off with a sharp razor. You should not do this thinking that these [sufferings] can't befall you or that after taking them, they will simply lie discarded beside you. Take them instead by discarding even lingering anxiety about the risk. Take them from the start right into the very kernel of your heart. When taking in this manner, do so unconditionally with no expectation for reward. Thus it is taught.

Extend this [meditation] to your parents, to your relatives, to your neighbors and friends, to the people of your region, to those of your country, of the world, the four continents, and the eight subcontinents, to those in the three lower realms, and to the gods of the desire realm. Add to these the beings of the small chiliocosm, the beings of the middle chiliocosm, and the beings of the entire trichiliocosm universe, including the inhabitants of the two higher realms. If the entire trichiliocosm were filled with mustard seeds and a single mustard seed were placed in each trichiliocosm in the eastern direction until the entire heap of mustard seeds was exhausted, the trichiliocosms in the east would not be exhausted or even approach near exhaustion, nor would the number of trichiliocosms increase. This is because space has no limit. Every direction, wherever these realms reach, is pervaded by sentient beings as well. Take the [sufferings] of these sentient beings pervading the entire expanse of space in the ten directions.

The hell realm, the first of the three lower realms, is composed of eighteen—eight hot hells, eight cold hells, random hells, and adjoining hells— and the causes of all these are the true origins [of suffering].[933] In the case of the first, for example, [345] [the cause] is either a karmic act motivated by hatred or it is indulgence in a grave nonvirtuous act carried out through an intense affliction. Here [in the context of meditation on taking], however, no actual act of killing is [taken]; but all other nonvirtuous acts are said to be present. The fruit of all of these is suffering. So, as before, take all the sufferings into the very kernel of your heart, such as those caused by fire and those arising from sentient beings, from [falling] weapons, from bursting blisters, from [blisters] cracking open in the shape of lotuses, and so on. When taking these, do so unconditionally with no expectation or hopes of benefit for yourself, not even the hope of purifying your negative karma and perfecting your merit. Do so solely with the wish for [the hell denizens] to attain buddhahood.

Similarly, the causes of hungry ghost birth, too, are the true origins [of suffering], specifically the middling degree of nonvirtuous karma motivated by past attachments and their [underlying] mental states, which are said to be present [in our minds] even at this moment. The effects of these are sufferings such as hunger and thirst, perpetually agitated mental states, assaults by others, and so on.

The causes of animals, too, are the true origins [of suffering], specifically the lesser nonvirtuous actions and the underlying mental states motivated by delusion. Within these [true origins], both karma and afflictions are said to exist. The fruits of these are the sufferings of confusion and delusion, and eating and being eaten by others.

Among the higher realms, the true origin of the humans is as described earlier. Their sufferings include the birth, aging, sickness, and death, not finding what is sought, encountering what is undesirable, and having to part from cherished belongings. In brief, the five appropriated [mental and physical] aggregates are suffering. From the gods of the desire realm, take their heedlessness, their early portents of death, their signs of imminent death, and their intimidation of others. From beings in the two higher realms [the form and formless realms], take their transition into the passage of death, their descent [into lower realms], and their intoxication with meditative absorption.

At times contemplate this in relation to the sphere of all sentient beings and at other times in relation to each class of beings, while on other occasions with regard to each being within a class. For if you lack this [contemplation] in your mind, your practice will remain superficial and you will fail to realize the actual purpose of mind training. At times contemplate all these [sufferings] simultaneously and take into the very kernel of your heart the cause, the true origins, their effects—all the sufferings of sentient beings—to the limitless extent of space, with no partiality based on closeness or distance or judgments of good or bad. Without doing this, there will be no impact on your mind.[934] [346] At times visualize your body facing each sentient being, such as in the hells, and then perform the [meditation of] taking. At other times, visualize taking everything upon this single body of yours. Take in a gradual progression on some occasions, from the grosser to the subtle as described above, while on other occasions take whatever you happen to perceive in whatever direction. In such manner, you should sometimes take the *afflictions* of the six realms by distinguishing them individually; while on other occasions you should take their *sufferings* by distinguishing them individually. On other occasions you should take, simultaneously, all the sufferings and all the afflictions of each and every individual sentient being.

Contemplating in these various ways, you will enjoy benefits, such as not becoming discouraged from taking suffering and afflictions, being able to ascertain [your purpose well] and achieve it, and becoming more receptive to training. If you engage in taking by relating to others as enemies or ordinary beings, the [practice of] taking will not be successful. So, when taking, think of all beings as your kind parents, who are a source of help, and be stirred from your depths by clear and distinct loving-kindness and compassion. Certainly your meditating on giving and taking will affect your enemy, for you will be cherishing others and injuring only your self-grasping.

[GIVING]

What is to be given? *A Guide to the Bodhisattva's Way of Life* states:

> My body and my material resources
> And my virtue engendered in three times—
> Without reserve I will give these away
> To fulfill the wishes of all beings.[935]

As stated here, you give your body, material resources, and the roots of virtue of all three times. When giving the body, do so free of the three imperfections—giving it while visualizing yourself as a meditation deity, giving it as mere flesh and blood, or allowing it go to waste after having given it. Similarly, with material resources, too, do not give, from among ordinary objects, things such as poison and weapons, which are destructive to others. You should also be free of letting [resources] go to waste after having given them.

In what manner should you give, then? The *Array of Trees Sutra* states:

> May my body become a wish-fulfilling jewel, a source of daily nourishment for all beings.[936]

The *[Dedications of] Vajradhvaja Sutra* states:

> Just as the four great elements sustain all sentient beings through their diverse avenues, diverse manifestations, and diverse ways, in the same way the bodhisattva's [347] body, too, transforms into a source of daily sustenance for all beings.[937]

A Guide to the Bodhisattva's Way of Life states:

I will transform it into a wish-fulfilling body.⁹³⁸

So you should give away your body by transforming it into a wish-fulfilling jewel. These citations are not suggesting that you should give your body by visualizing it with the physical shape and color of a wish-fulfilling jewel. The point is that this [body] inexhaustibly fulfills whatever wishes sentient beings have, encompassing their every need. Through such means you should give it.

In terms of the procedure for giving, first visualize your real-life mother in front of you. Imagine that by focusing on her as you give your body to her, all the substantial causes for her buddhahood arise—faith, ethical discipline, perseverance, wisdom, awakening mind, and so on, which are the inner conditions. In terms of contributory conditions, imagine that from your body originate [her encountering] a spiritual teacher, the sacred texts, the articles of worship, a temple, shelter, the company of fellow monastics, and so on. From it [also] emerge all the internal conditions of Dharma practice and, having generated the [awakening] mind, she attains buddhahood. Extend this [meditation] to your father, to friends and family, and to all sentient beings pervading the reaches of space—from the three lower realms, to the disciples and self-realized ones, to the bodhisattvas on the ten levels. As you give to them, just as before, imagine that they, too, generate awakening mind, train in the precepts, and, having perfected the two accumulations, attain buddhahood.

Also, just as from one wish-fulfilling jewel arise whatever things sentient beings may desire—for food, clothing, and so on—in the same manner imagine that from your actual body alone emerge for sentient beings equaling the expanse of space food, clothing, shelter, bed, country, land, friends and family, a circle of subjects, work animals, and so on—all the elements of mundane happiness. Imagine that from it also appear preceptors, instructors, and the sacred texts and so on, constituting the causes and effects of supramundane happiness.

Also, just as the wish-fulfilling jewel grants the wishes of sentient beings through many manifestations, such as the king of jewels, imagine that in the same manner your body, too, stays present in front of each sentient being and, as before, fulfills their aspirations. [348] Also, as your body appears in front of each being, composed as it is of material elements such as earth, water, fire, and so on, imagine that it becomes all the everyday objects that sentient beings use. At times give your body in its entirety; at other times give it away as if dissecting the individual parts—the head, legs, hands, and so on.

As the expression "This is the general rule and there are exceptions" goes, some perceive even flesh and blood as appealing, and others see them as objects of great sensual pleasure. In tantra, too, you [visualize] the body lying on its back in a ritual pit and give it away by slicing off its parts.[939] First transform your body into a wish-fulfilling jewel. Then, later, even if you view it as composed of flesh and blood, giving it will come [spontaneously] from the depths of your heart. Our master states, "There is nothing I have not visualized myself as—long-lasting ponds, pools, open fields and meadows, and even a cave of Cheka."[940]

Also, during a consecration ceremony when you are exorcising a ghost inhabiting an icon, you can imagine your body as statues of various forms and exhort the ghost, "Take these [instead] and do not be displeased. This icon is being consecrated for use as an object of veneration." Similarly, when performing healing rites and torma rituals for the sick, you can place your body into a ritual cake and summon whatever may be causing harm to the individual from all directions, urging, "Take these—my food, my happiness, my sickness—and do not harm this patient. I am a neutral person here to mediate by offering you a gift of gold." When walking at the head of a line, give your body by spreading around its components and conducting yourself in the manner [of giving]. At haunted places, offer your body to the interfering spirits as a collection of offerings, and do the same to both humans and nonhumans as well.

And as you take upon yourself, just as before, all the inauspicious signs—intense craving, bad dreams, ill omens, and harmful spirits—and as you give [your body, resources, and virtues] to beings, you endow them with joyfulness, auspiciousness, wondrous signs, good omens, and so on. In this way you absorb into your heart all the fears and anxieties of others regarding harmful spells, black magic, [harmful] astrological calculation, spirits, zombies, contamination, and so on. As you give away your body and so on, they [the recipients of your giving] become pleased and content, and their harmful intentions and so on become pacified. With all the causes and conditions gathered, imagine that they attain buddhahood. [349] The instant they become cleansed and aware, imagine that they experience bliss and attain the higher qualities that come from being cleansed of all negative actions.

Furthermore, as you extend your giving to those visibly undergoing unwanted events this very moment—death of a loved one, loss of material resources, leprosy or another grave illness, all suffering of aging, intensification of craving, not hearing the Dharma, and so on—imagine that these beings all become free from these [sufferings] and, acquiring qualities contrary to these [adversities], they attain buddhahood. Extend this same [approach] to all [other practices] as stated in the line "Accomplish all yogas through a single means." If you possess this [practice of mind training] alone, you do not become disheartened by any situation, it has been taught. So with respect to practicing mind training in haunted sites and so on, if you train by means of your thoughts, your conduct will not turn into offensive behavior like someone who is within the sphere of Māra's activity. Also when you encounter unavoidable tragedies, distance yourself [mentally] from these without becoming disheartened or terrified, as explained above.

Similarly, with material resources, as you give them away by transforming them into wish-fulfilling jewels, imagine that from each of the objects arise countless mundane and supramundane objects. From these arise wealth for those who desire wealth, and food, fruit, horses, elephants, and so on in accordance with whatever is desired. In relation to the sublime Dharma arise all the factors conducive to buddhahood, such as faith, ethical discipline, and wisdom. Also, whatever object you feel attached to—your body, material resources, and so on—focus on that very object and transform it into a wish-fulfilling jewel, giving it to all sentient beings. By viewing these offerings as measureless as Samantabhadra's clouds of offerings, offer these to your teachers and the buddhas, the master said.

As for your virtues, give everything you have accumulated throughout the three times, from the root of virtue of giving a thin strip of dough squeezed in your hand to an animal, to the practices of the six perfections and the four factors of attracting others, including all deeds that generate merit. In brief, as you give all your virtuous karma, tainted and untainted, from these arise whatever sentient beings desire, require, and most benefit by. And as all the causes and conditions of buddhahood are gathered, imagine that [sentient beings] become fully enlightened. In the immediate term, as you give away your body, material resources, and virtues of the three times by bringing them simultaneously to all sentient beings—good or bad, infinitesimal or gigantic—pervading the expanse of space, undertake the same reflections as before.

To summarize, as you engage in giving in such a manner with respect to all three [body, material resources, and virtues], you can give them sequentially—from your real-life mother to all sentient beings, and from [the denizens of] Avīci hell on up to the buddhas. You can bring all three together and give them simultaneously, or you can give each in turn in its entirety. Or, as with taking, you can contemplate multiplying your body and so on and giving it to each sentient being, or imagine giving this [one body] alone to all beings without the slightest hesitation.

Thus you should practice giving and taking by interspersing [1] taking the undesirable factors of every sentient being—their negative karma and sufferings—into the very kernel of your heart and [2] giving your body, resources, and the virtues of the three times to all beings. As explained above, you should sometimes start with your real-life mother and then give sequentially to every sentient being, and on other occasions you should give to all sentient beings at once. Sometimes you should only give to those with negative karma, and at other times only to those with mental afflictions. Meditate on the basis of such selections. When you practice meditation, do not remain merely on the surface or pursue it as an obligation. Practice with full attention. As you practice in a way that leaves a deep impact upon your heart, your mind will become more receptive to training, your thoughts will turn toward the purpose, and you will touch the heart of the stone,[941] it has been taught.

As for the other [instructions], such as "Commence the sequence of taking from your own self," these are as found in the *Oral Tradition*.

TRANSFORMING ADVERSE CONDITIONS INTO AWAKENING MIND BY MEANS OF THE THOUGHTS OF THE CONVENTIONAL AWAKENING MIND

[351] **Banish all blames to the single source.**

At present, whatever suffering or adversities we encounter, we tend blame others for all of this and view ourselves as innocent and free of blame. This, however, is not right. No matter what sufferings and adverse circumstances arise, the blame for all of this lies solely on self-grasping. The reason is the following: Since beginningless time, this self-grasping has clung to a self where there is none. In order to nurture it and for its sake, we have harbored jealousy toward our superiors, derision toward those who are inferior, and rivalry toward those who are equal. And through acts such as attacking our enemies and tending to our friends, we have committed nonvirtuous acts that are harmful to others. As a consequence, sufferings and adverse conditions befall us. *A Guide to the Bodhisattva's Way of Life* states:

> Countless eons have passed
> In your pursuit of selfish ends.
> Yet through your great hardship
> You have sought only suffering.[942]

All the times you have been cast into suffering by some adverse circumstances, it is [actually] self-grasping that has been the culprit. For example, if there is rumor of a plague in the land, you suffer from the fear that he [this self] might contract it. Other sufferings include the fear of being destroyed by enemies, the fear of being possessed by malevolent spirits, and so on. In brief, these thoughts cause you pain because they conflict with "my" desires to be superior, to be prosperous, and to be happy.

The causes for all suffering and adverse conditions to arise are first accumulated on the basis of self-grasping; and what appear as [adverse] circumstances ultimately materialize on the basis of self-grasping, too, because they conflict with his [the self's] desires. So every single adverse circumstance can be traced to self-grasping.

Toward all beings contemplate their great kindness.

This line states that all sentient beings are solely embodiments of kindness. Since beginningless time they have brought you only benefits and protected you from all kinds of danger, and from this standpoint, their kindness is great indeed. Furthermore, for those who aspire to attain buddhahood, they are an immense source of kindness, for it is on the basis of them that you can cultivate the awakening mind, the primary cause of buddhahood. [352] Demons and malevolent forces that create adversities for you are particularly great sources of kindness. They serve to trigger your karma to encounter adverse conditions, thus helping you exhaust your negative karma. They are also eminently kind because you need adversities to practice forbearance. Therefore all sentient beings are nothing but sources of kindness.

As for the other points pertaining to transforming adverse conditions into the path of enlightenment, they are as found in the *Oral Tradition*.

Relate whatever you encounter to your meditation right now.[943]

The meaning of this is as follows: Relate to [your mind training] and engage in its practice at all times: when joyful or tragic, when prosperous or not; in all places—in your own country or in others; in all contexts—when in a monastery or at home or in other environments; during all activities, such as walking, sleeping, and so on; and toward all things that are objects of your six senses, such as your sight, hearing, recollection, and mental engagement. Within the objects of your six senses are two kinds—those that are desirable and those that are not. Ascertaining these two classes, give that which is desirable to sentient beings and take the undesirable upon yourself. So when engaging in any activity—traveling, going for a walk, and so on—whatever you encounter, on the basis of these two, even in bed before falling asleep, think "I will take upon myself all the sufferings and their origins of sentient beings; I will give them my body, material resources—everything—and will help them all attain buddhahood." Because of this all your sleeping moments will become [part of] the mind exchanging self and others; this training can be in effect even in your dreams, just as described in the sutras, the master said.

The presentation of a lifetime's practice in summary is as found in the *Oral Tradition*.

THE MEASURE OF HAVING TRAINED THE MIND

As for the measure of having trained your mind, the following is stated:

The intent of all teachings converges on a single point.

The intent of all the teachings of the Great and Lesser Vehicles converges on the subduing of self-grasping; [353] the focus of mind training in particular is subduing self-cherishing and cherishing others. Therefore if your spiritual practice in general, and your practice of mind training in particular, fail to counteract self-grasping, then [the realization of] mind training has not arisen in you. For whether mind training has arisen in your heart is determined by whether it has become an antidote to self-grasping. This is the scale to measure spiritual practitioners, the master said.

Of the two witnesses, uphold the principal one.

Others may say, "Dharma realization has arisen in all these spiritual brothers. Here we have 'good spiritual practitioners,'" but those who say that are not the principal witness. Others may recognize you as a good practitioner merely on the basis of some positive behavior or some pleasant speech or because you happen to conform to their expectations. Of the two witnesses, therefore, the principal one is the assurance that you are not faulted by your own mind. This [conscientiousness] is the principal witness. Others may allege "There is no Dharma realization in him," but when you leave your mind in an unbiased state, you are free of self-reproach and possess the sense, "Now even if I were to fall headlong into the hells, I would have no regrets." These two factors [conscientiousness and freedom from self-reproach] constitute the principal witnesses.

Cultivate constantly the joyful mind alone.

When mind training arises in you, you will be joyful, for you will feel that "Whatever adverse situations arise, I can incorporate them into the path of mind training." This is not a question of merely cultivating the thought— when no adversities are afflicting you—"If adversities befall, I shall take them onto the path." Rather it means that in the face of an actual adversity, you view it not as a suffering but relate to it with a mind of ease and joy.

If this can be done even when distracted, you're trained.

This does not refer merely to not being overtaken by adversities you encounter through the deliberate practice of mind training. Rather it refers to the ability to practice mind training spontaneously, without the need for deliberate effort as an antidote, when obstructions arise suddenly and unexpectedly. With deep familiarity, this is certainly possible. For do not afflictions like anger arise spontaneously due to the force of your beginningless habituation to self-cherishing? Do not the afflictions arise immediately in response to any old circumstance?

Although this is called the "measure of having trained the mind," it refers to a measured level of mind training arising in your mental continuum. This is not the sign that you have perfected your training and no longer require further training. [354]

THE COMMITMENTS OF MIND TRAINING

As for the commitments of mind training, there are the following lines:

> **Train constantly in the three general points;**
> **Transform your thoughts, but remain as you are;**
> **Do not speak of the defects [of others];**
> **Do not reflect on others' shortcomings.**

These are as found in the *Oral Tradition*.

> **Purify first whichever affliction is strongest.**

Or:

> **Purify first whichever gross element is greater.**[944]

The meaning of this line is as follows: Examine whichever affliction is strongest in you—attachment, anger, delusion, conceit, envy, and so on—and pacify and vanquish that one. The basis, or root, of all afflictions is self-grasping, and in general their power is great. Since all ordinary beings possess these afflictions, however, then in whatever they attempt, they are obstructed because of their self-grasping; this has caused them to suffer since beginningless time. It is necessary, therefore, to pacify this first. It is stated:

> This enemy that causes my destruction—
> Would any [sane] person cultivate it?
> Alas, I can bear it no more![945]

Also:

> If there is self, there is the thought of other.
> From division of self and other arise grasping and anger;
> And from the interrelation of all of these
> Arise all negative consequences.[946]

Also:

> This enemy that has settled in me for so long,
> This sole cause of a proliferation of harms—
> How can I remain fearless and joyful in cyclic existence
> When it is definitively established in my heart?[947]

As it states here, self-grasping is to blame for all such things as creating enmity and becoming a victim of suffering in this beginningless cyclic existence. When rats squeak, you fear that his [the self's] nose will get cut off; when someone says there is thunder, you fear it will strike his head; when you hear there is an epidemic in the region, you fear he will get infected; and if the terrain is said to be hostile, you fear that he will get snatched away. Likewise, we sometimes suffer for fear of negative publicity. Strike, strike this self-grasping on the head. Shawo Gangpa states:

> I have no more vital task than to press down on what falls squarely under my thumb and to stand guard at the entrance [of my mind] by firmly holding a short spear.[948]

Langthangpa states:

> Offer gain and victory to others;
> Take loss and defeat upon yourself.[949]

Or, as it is stated:

> The king of all male demons, take my head![950] [355]

It has been taught that you must train effectively in this practice.

If you train in this manner, then like recovering from food poisoning, it is said, this [training] can turn what is seemingly painful into something joyful. Until this [ability] is achieved, even if you wear monastic robes the weight of a yak's load, place empty vases on your head,[951] and dedicate your entire life to learning, all of these will become misplaced and will become [nothing but] distractions. Also, when he [the self] is deprived of happiness even for a single moment, he becomes restless like a brooding woman obsessed with having a child. It is important, therefore, to make sure you press down on what fits under your own thumb[952] so that it does not escape. If you can succeed in this, at some point in the future you will achieve what is called "the great vehicle," "the great expanse," "the great capacity," and "the great intelligence."[953] This, of course, cannot be achieved by simply wishing that one day this might happen; you must strive from this instant forward.

So take upon yourself all that is undesirable and give to all sentient beings the three factors [your body, material resources, and virtues] that constitute the desirable. In this respect, train as stated in the following:

> Be it by seeing, hearing, or thinking,
> By coming into contact or uttering words,
> In all possible ways may I always pursue
> That which is of benefit to beings.⁹⁵⁴

Then, taking this as the basis, [recognize that] for some attachment is stronger, for others anger, and for others envy. In your own mind each of the afflictions generally arises like bees washing themselves.⁹⁵⁵ Even though all the afflictions arise, examine which specific affliction is the strongest and subdue that one first. Those of higher intelligence will swiftly discern on their own which of the afflictions is stronger. Of course, mere discernment does not guarantee you will follow the discipline of what is to be affirmed and what is to be discarded. Some may relinquish [their strongest affliction] the moment it is identified, while others will cultivate the antidotes and relinquish [the afflictions] later. Most, however, will need help from their teachers or colleagues to discern this. Once, when Lungmepa was residing at Neusur, he stated:

> Most [of the afflictions among the inhabitants of Neusur] seem to be undetectable; but pride seems rather strong. Because of the proud thought "He does not have this and that [teaching] lineage" some would not bow to another. I felt there was a fair bit of this emotion. Therefore I encouraged fellow practitioners to observe each other.⁹⁵⁶

[356] Therefore it is others who should examine your four everyday activities. [Having discerned] what is coarsest or strongest, train by concentrating on its antidote. Set the other [practices] aside for the time being and train in this [antidote] at all times. When you begin to feel that it has been successfully subdued, observe whether distorted thoughts arise in you. If so, apply the main practice and cultivate the antidotes to prevent their occurrence. Watching in this manner, make sure you subdue, as much as possible, your objects of engagement or adverse conditions. Even when you have successfully subdued an affliction, you will sense that another one emerges [in its place]. As the saying goes "From underneath a broken tooth a new

one grows." However, just as when you have succeeded in subduing the strongest wrestler, you can subdue the others more easily, in the same manner you will no longer have any difficulty [in subduing the other afflictions], the master said. As for those at the beginner's stage, it is stated:

> The wise will refrain from it well,
> Or the wise will combat it excellently.[957]

As it states here, those at the beginner's stage should simply avoid the objects that give rise to the afflictions. Alternatively, the instruction is to combat [the afflictions] with the antidotes. So if avoidance does not help, combat the afflictions as the following lines suggest:

> I shall argue with it,
> Begrudge it, and combat it.[958]

Even if this does not work [completely], simply combat [the afflictions with] whatever antidotes you can muster, just like planting [seeds] in the earth and into the rocks.[959]

Just like Migmang, who when fighting would say, "If you hit me here, I'll hit you there,"[960] apply whatever antidote is appropriate, just like hitting the snout of a pig with a club, striking it every time it sticks its head out. It is stated:

> I may be slain or burned alive;
> Likewise I may be decapitated;
> Under no circumstance shall I
> Bow before my enemy, the afflictions.[961]

Also:

> The enemies, such as hatred and craving,
> Do not have legs, arms, and so on;
> They are neither courageous nor intelligent.
> So how is that they have enslaved me?[962]

Also:

> Attachment, hatred, and delusion—
> Summoning these three deep into my heart,

The robbers mushroom in my own mind.
There is no greater thief than this![963]

As stated in these lines, you should contemplate the destructive effects [of the afflictions].

Shawopa suggests that you should imagine being dragged around while the rope of distorted thoughts is tied around your neck. Ben Gungyal grabbed his own hand and shouted, "Get out of this door!" while Langri Thangpa stated, "Compared to this...."[964] Therefore engage in your practice in terms of all the aspects such as taking—applying the antidotes, being seated on a cushion [where] the four practices [making offerings to meditation deities and teachers, purifying negative karma, making offerings to the harmful forces, and propitiating the Dharma protectors are undertaken], and so on. [357]

However, if you feel that once they have arisen the afflictions will [naturally] subside after a while, it is stated:

The enemy of affliction destroys me,
It destroys sentient beings and ethical discipline.[965]

As the saying goes, "Go away! This battle within us men is hard indeed."[966] Relinquish the afflictions the instant they arise.

With respect to the adversities, too, it is stated:

Until stability is achieved, adverse conditions may harm;
Once stability is achieved, adverse conditions become aids.[967]

As stated in these lines, some can turn adversities into the factors of the awakening mind.

Nyalpa states, "If all of us, the elders and their spiritual children, possess a firm grounding from within, our spiritual practices will become greatly enhanced."[968] It is also as the teacher Sengé Gyaltsen states:

When I was at Langri, my training was more effective because people like Seberé would test my mind. Now, because there is no one who tests my mind to such a degree, the pace of my mind training is not as great. Sometimes, however, when I am sleeping and someone quietly approaches the door and shouts, 'Aha!' I experience powerful bursts of mind training.[969]

It is possible that for some the mere occurrence of adversities results in [their mind training] becoming degenerated. The reason for this is the two demons, Nyawo and Hakpo. It is said that even if you could escape the mouth of Rohipa, the bird of prey, you cannot escape from the mouth of the volcano. Therefore combat the afflictions by exerting great endurance.[970]

Forsake all expectations of reward.[971]

Should the following expectations arise in you because of engaging in this practice—to not be harmed by humans and nonhumans, to be famous, to be respected by your teachers and students, to have abundant food, clothing, and so on, to receive rewards for helping others, to be known as a genuine spiritual practitioner, even to attain buddhahood—[contemplate what] the most holy Maitreya has stated: "Toward conquerors and so on subtle attachments persist."[972]

If you fail to train unconditionally, free of expectation of rewards pertaining to this life or the hereafter, then one aspect of your spiritual practice becomes blind. It is critical, therefore, to train without any hope of reward. If you harbor expectations for this life, [your training] is not even Dharma practice; harboring expectations for the future life precludes it from becoming a practice of the bodhisattvas. Even when you aspire for buddhahood, if it is for your own benefit, [your mind training] becomes a cause for attaining [only] the state of a self-realized one.

Discard poisonous food.
Do not maintain inappropriate loyalty.
Do not torment with malicious banter. [358]

These are as found in the *Oral Tradition*.

Do not lie in ambush.

This is like the following stories. Once, when Tönpa Dharma Bar was ill, it is said that a tax was levied on the people of Lhodrak for the performance of healing rites, [and some harbored the thought] "When will Dharma Rinchen come under my power?" Also, once a man from the Phen region was visiting Nyal [Monastery], and as he went to wash, a novice monk squeezed him between [the panels of] a door. Later, at a large gathering in Phen, the novice happened to be there. So the man, remembering his experience of being squeezed between the [the two panels of] a door, approached the novice and said, "We know each other, don't we?" to which the novice replied in the negative. So the man squeezed the novice between the doors to remind him who it was that was humiliating him now. These are examples of "lying in ambush." If you are cultivating the awakening mind and practicing mind training, there is simply no room for such thoughts. As long as you harbor such vengeful thoughts (including acting out a grudge against others to repay previous harms), it is impossible for the two [giving and taking] to arise. You must therefore discard this.

Do not strike at the heart.

This includes [insulting someone by] saying, "You are bad because of your paternal lineage," or saying to an ordained member, "Your preceptor is degenerate in his own vows," or to the monk himself, "You have no vows," or proclaiming in a public gathering [the news of] a murder not known by many. Although these acts do not involve poison or weapons, from the point of view of mind training, nothing is more negative than such acts. It is [in some sense] graver than actually killing the person.

A long time ago, when Gyatön was a young boy, he startled someone's horse on the edge of a cliff, causing the horse to jump off and die. [When] his parents beat him, he threw stones at his mother's face, and because of that he was banished from home. He then shouted aloud that his parents stole a *dri* [female yak] from their landlord Dorjé Wangchuk. Because of this they were forced to pay both for a horse and for the dri [as well]. There is no graver negative act than this, the master said.

> **Do not place a dzo's load on an ox.**
> **Do not abuse this [practice] as a rite.**
> **Do not sprint to win a race.**
> **Do not turn the gods into demons.**
> **Do not seek misery as a means of happiness.**

These are as found in the *Oral Tradition*.

THE PRECEPTS OF MIND TRAINING

Accomplish all yogas through a single means.[973]

Other teachings present a variety of practices, such as the yoga of eating and so on. Here, however, all yogas pertaining to food, clothes, and so on [359] are performed through a single means. How? They are undertaken by the following meditative practice: When you have all the amenities such as food, clothing and so on, available, you think, "Through this good fortune of mine may all beings enjoy happiness." If these are lacking, think, "May all the suffering that beings have due to lacking these amenities ripen upon me." Learn to understand in earnest how to purify all the objects of the senses in this way during the four everyday activities, as described in the sutra *Thoroughly Pure Spheres of Conduct,*[974] or as stated by the savior Maitreya in the following:

> The more you engage in the deeds of the bodhisattva,
> The more diverse the objects entering your sense fields;
> Recognizing these as they are and through appropriate words,
> Embrace that which you perceive to help sentient beings.[975]

With such understanding, pursue everything by means of the yoga of training in the awakening mind.

Overcome all adversities through a single means.

This is as found in the *Oral Tradition.*

There are two tasks—one at the start and one at the end.[976]

At the start, when you get up from bed, cultivate the thought "Today I will subdue my self-grasping and make sure I am not polluted by self-cherishing; I will make sure that my cherishing of others does not degenerate." Before going to bed at night, while in the meditative absorption of the lion's majestic equipoise, reflect, "Today I did this first, then I did that afterward," and, enumerating them individually, examine each of these [acts]. If you find that you have done something contrary to the teachings in general, and to mind training practice in particular, then as the advice goes, "At that instant I will enumerate my flaws / And recollect the teacher's instructions,"[977] think, "What kind of a person am I who wastes the precious human existence of leisure and opportunity and brings harm to myself?" Request forgiveness, declare these [wrongdoings] and purify them, and make the resolve "I will never again indulge in acts such as these."

If, on the other hand, you have acted in accordance with the teachings, rejoice with the thought "I have made the human life of leisure and opportunity meaningful; I have spent my time usefully," and make the following aspirations: "Due to this virtuous karma, may Dharma realizations arise in me; may I never be separated from the awakening mind throughout all lives."

Again, when you rise up the next morning, it is important to cultivate your motivation projecting the thought "Today I will conduct myself as excellently as I did yesterday." Do not merely utter that you will act in such manner; [360] rather train your thoughts in that way alone. When you encounter enemies, become afflicted by serious illness, and so on, practice as before. Examine which of the following are present—(1) the blessings of your teachers and the Three Jewels, (2) the might and power of the Dharma protectors, (3) your own virtues of the three times, and (4) the collective merit of all sentient beings—and reflect, "By means of these four factors, I will engage in this [mind training] practice during all four occasions [when getting up in the morning, when going to bed in the evening, when encountering enemies, and when afflicted by sickness] and enhance it like throwing new logs onto a blazing fire."

Whichever of the two arises, bear them both[978]

Since you risk giving up Dharma practice if you have no forbearance when either of the two situations—prosperity or misfortune—arises, it is crucial that you be able to bear them. If you were suddenly to enjoy great prosperity, you might think "I have accomplished all of this myself. There is no one above me." With such thoughts, you might indulge in draping yourself in new felt robes, constructing temples, and so on. Some people might even step on their companions' lotus [heart], so bereft of mindfulness are they, the master said.[979] Some become conceited when they attract disciples, material gifts, and honors, and then they belittle others, indulging in abusive behavior. These things happen when you fail to bear prosperity, never become conceited by prosperity or become attached to it. Make sure you don't fall prey to the eight mundane concerns, but instead take them as factors conducive to this [mind training] practice. When your fortune increases, it is important to stay humble, the master said.

Alternatively, when, as a result of a misfortune, you become so impoverished that [you feel] the only thing lower than you is the river flowing under [the bridge], you might become desolate and think, "Why is this happening to me?" You might despair and become incapable of engaging in any virtuous acts and think, "How is Dharma practice possible in my condition?" As the saying goes, "Being impoverished, negative karma naturally proliferates," you risk losing your spiritual practice when this happens. Since all this comes from a lack of forbearance, reflect, "Compared to the gulf between the happiness and suffering of the higher realms and the suffering of the lower realms, there is not much difference between happiness and suffering within the human realm." So with the determination not to be distracted by this in the future, you should endeavor to enhance your virtuous activities. You should thus be capable of bearing both happiness and suffering just like Langri Thangpa. Whichever of the two arises [prosperity or misfortune], you should have the thought "If I do not engage in Dharma practice at such times, when, then, do I do so?" This is as stated in the following:

> Even if you prosper like the gods,
> Pray be not conceited;
> Even if you are destitute like the hungry ghosts,
> Pray be not disheartened.[980] [361]

Guard the two even at the cost of your life.
Train in the three difficult challenges.
Adopt the three principal conditions.
Contemplate the three that are free of degeneration.

These are as found in the *Oral Tradition*.

Be endowed with the three inseparable factors.[981]

Being a Mahayanist does not mean you have no tasks to do. Your body should not be divorced from such [activities] as circumambulation, prostrations, and serving your teacher and the Three Jewels. Your speech should not be separated from [reciting] going-for-refuge [stanzas], mantra repetitions, recitation of sutras, and so on, while your mind should not be divorced from the practice of mind training. Mentally engaging in this [mind training] and undertaking mantra repetitions will keep you alert; and employing this [mind training] as a walking staff will help you maintain your thought processes, the master said. This is not to suggest that declaring and purifying infractions of ethical precepts is unnecessary and that taking others' [suffering] is [somehow] a substitute for this. While taking [the suffering] of others, you need to forsake even your most minute infractions.

You need the courage that eliminates negative thought processes the moment they arise. This is analogous to a non-Buddhist [rite master] performing black magic that kills all the animals who appear within his vicinity. You should do the same to whatever conceptualizations arise in you. Thus through striving in virtue with your three doors [of body, speech, and mind], your practice of mind training will become greatly enhanced, like adding fresh logs to a fire.

> **Train without partiality toward [any] object.**
> **Cherish your training, all its breadth and depth.**[982]

Since no training can be achieved through a biased approach, if you train without partiality, your practice will develop and progress.[983] All those who say, "I have greater forbearance toward ghosts while he has greater forbearance toward humans; I am stronger with respect to emptiness while he is stronger on compassion," are biased in their approach. It is quite natural for the qualities of the noble ones to be complete while the qualities of ordinary beings are partial. Furthermore, for some individuals, [mind training] occurs when they suffer misfortune; others, when prosperous, have thoughts such as "No man is above me, no dog superior to Gongkar,"[984] and they become an object of ridicule like someone who, with great effort, bends a bamboo stick but later lets go of it.

Some succeed while prosperous but, when misfortune strikes, exclaim, "You don't understand; my situation is desperate," and are incapable of withstanding calamity.[985] Similarly some, when praised, hop around like a rooftop pigeon whose beak has been pierced by a splinter. And when belittled, they can't bear it and act as if they might poison someone. [362] Again, some are measured when it comes to food but are unbalanced about clothing. Some have less attachment to inner [experience] but stronger attachment to external objects; others are the reverse. Some, though lacking in knowledge, are pompous and cannot bear to see others show them disrespect.[986] Some lose their Dharma practice while remaining in their own country, while others lose it away from home. Some are capable of dying for the sake of their group or for the sake of the monastic life, some out of miserliness, envy, or anger, and some for the sake of wealth. Even if you were to list [scenarios] for eons, the master said, the possibilities would not be exhausted.

Make sure all your activities—listening to and teaching the Dharma, [cultivating the] view, and meditating on sublime Dharma—all become remedies against your afflictions; and since the root of all afflictions is self-grasping, it is crucial you train in its antidotes comprehensively, without omitting any elements. To do this, you must settle all qualms through the wisdom of discriminative awareness; and if you possesses a teacher's special instructions, you must apply them concertedly against whatever afflictions, such as miserliness, happen to be most intense. If whatever activity you engage in becomes an antidote to self-grasping, that indicates you have not erred; you will then subdue self-grasping, subdue the three realms, and subdue the entirety of the three states of existence. Then you will have succeeded. You'll not get more than a full plate by relying on one *sang* of meat, the master said.[987]

This yoga pervades all yogas, such as those pertaining to food and so on. And unlike visiting the temple [only] during the daytime, you should engage in this training from the very bones of your heart. You should train like Langthangpa,[988] who dedicated his merit toward being reborn in the hells, and like Chekawa, who is said to have rejoiced in taking the suffering of others. To engage in Dharma practice, you can't merely sit upright and understand the words; you must implement the meaning of the words as an inner practice, the master said.

Train constantly toward those chosen objects.[989]

In general you might sense you can achieve [mind training], but if you don't train with respect to these [objects] your training will degenerate. There are five chosen objects toward whom you must undertake constant meditative practice. First are your preceptor, your master, your parents, and so on, who are sources of kindness, and toward whom, if you commit any nonvirtuous act, you incur dishonor in this life and lose the very purpose of mind training as well. You must therefore practice with special emphasis toward these embodiments of kindness.

Second, because you risk using inappropriate speech toward those with whom you live and interact frequently, such as people in the same community, you must pay them special attention and constantly practice in relation to them.⁹⁹⁰

Third are those you naturally compete with. [363] On the mundane level, this includes your paternal [and maternal] relatives, and in the religious realm, this includes your peers. Single these out for special attention and constantly practice in relation to them. If you fail, no matter how much you may engage in Dharma practice, your efforts will bear no fruit, like spitting into the ocean. Someone who writes the name of his colleague and places it under his cushion [and sits on it], or someone who rejoices at a former friend's misfortune, uttering, "How satisfying! The nasty person got what he deserved," cannot possibly train the mind. Since such a person cannot achieve even a general realization of mind training, it is important to train by paying special attention to this type of object.

Fourth is the class of individuals who harbor ill-will toward you even though you have done them no harm. They may do so because of your aggression in past lives. As the saying goes, "When thoughts of anger explode, the thread of compassion snaps."⁹⁹¹ Thus you should select these as special objects and constantly practice in relation to them.

Fifth are people everyone dislikes although they have done nothing against others. In Tsang Province a monk was once told by someone he had never met before that the person disliked him. Also, in Kyimé, someone once said, "I have never seen anyone I have disliked as much as I dislike this person."⁹⁹² Take the negative karma and suffering of these beings and give them your happiness and virtues. It may be very difficult indeed to give these without hesitation. Many monks are happy when they themselves can benefit [others] but are not so happy when others prove beneficial. Laypeople [often] hope to acquire the house of someone who has died, while some monks look forward to inheriting a [deceased monk's] domain.⁹⁹³ So it is critical to contemplate as Phuchungwa states, "If you do not constantly practice by choosing such objects for special attention, you will fail [even] to detect when the root [of virtues] has been cut."

Do not depend on other conditions.⁹⁹⁴

Generally speaking, it is impossible for hearing, reflection, and meditation and all ten types of spiritual practices not to depend upon other factors. So you do need to depend upon other conditions. It is necessary to gather such favorable conditions as food, clothing, shelter, assistants, articles for retreat, sound health, and so on, and also to ensure the absence of enemies and malevolent forces.

Once Potowa asked Jangpa Sherap if he could reflect on the teachings. Jangpa replied, "If my stomach is full and my thirst is quenched, and if my friends do not cause disturbance to my mind, it seems that I can to a limited degree."[995] [Chekawa once said:] "At Chenga Monastery there were limited offerings and resources. Thinking, 'I shall go to the countryside to obtain these,' I went to Yarlung, but failed to find them there either. Because of my ignorance I had failed to understand. For 'cyclic existence' is a name for deficiency."[996] Khün said that amenities were not available at Kamapa's, so he went to Tsang, [364] where he found the favorable conditions and was able to make offerings to the Three Jewels, nurture his own health, and get well, thus becoming able to receive great benefits. A student of Kharak's, who was served melted dri butter when he lost his appetite, exclaimed "I did not realize there was a spiritual practice on the nipples of a dri." Atiśa, too, would show the wrinkles on his feet and say, "I have reached this stage; now I will not become a highly realized being." Whenever he saw a youth with red cheeks, Shentön Jangbar would say, "Yes, there is something I can do to help you," but when he saw an old and decrepit person, he would say, "You have experienced [life] until the tone of your skin color has changed; now, even if you stay here at my place, it will not be of much benefit."

Some assert that they have been able to cultivate the [mind training] thoughts as a result of occasionally associating with a colleague with strong concentration. Others assert that they failed because some of their colleagues disturbed them. Still others say that they fail because of being in haste, but when they have leisure, they are more successful. Yet others say that they fail when distracted but succeed in solitude.

Nyak Sengé Drak once remarked, "Kadampas say that they meditate on karma and its fruits, yet without mastering my higher knowledge texts, how can they meditate [on karma]? Do they simply repeat [the words] 'karma and its fruits'?" For this [mind training practice], you don't need to rely on [extensive] studies such as this.

If the amenities are present, you can use them as the very basis [for practice]. However, if they are absent or inadequate, if they dissipate, if you are cold, prosperous, impoverished, sick, or not sick, if you are old or young, hungry or full, if you are assailed by enemies or disturbed by demonic spirits, if you enjoy the approval of your spiritual teacher or do not enjoy the approval of your spiritual teacher, or if you are being mentally disturbed by your colleagues, take all of these as the very rationale [for practice] and engage in [mind training] practice.

The precious spiritual teacher used to make each of the family members of Langthang, whose nephews and nieces were not many in number, sit for a session of meditative practice. This is also like the stories of José and of Sengé Gyal, as narrated before.[997] Therefore this can be practiced amid all activities (such as when traveling, when going for a walk, when sleeping, and when sitting). It can be practiced at all times, when busy or when relaxing. For this, the only condition necessary is your determination. It has been stated:

> This mind that is full of defects
> Has nonetheless a multitude of qualities:
> Whatever is cultivated, that comes to be.[998]

To the extent that you persevere you will succeed. This is not like baked clay [which can no longer be reshaped]. You can train to the best of your capacity. It does not suffice merely to think, "This is how it is, so [if] I have to teach others in future [I will know what to say]." [365] But if you think "I must put this into practice and meditate," you will soon receive the blessing of Dharma. For this [mind training practice], it is said, you must practice [with the intensity of] propitiating a god and until the substances are fully consumed by the ritual fire.[999] Thus, forsaking these four factors is critical.[1000]

Engage in the principal practices right now.
Do not apply misplaced understanding.

These [lines] are as found in the *Oral Tradition*.

Do not be sporadic.[1001]

This refers to those who sometimes practice mind training but search for something else at other times because they lack confidence. Some scholastic monks, though possessing vast knowledge of the scriptural collections, feel that this is not effectual and thus seek the counsel of married shamans when they become aware of death. Similarly, some, out of fear of spirits and possessors, engage only in mantra recitations. Some engage [only] in giving and taking meditation. Some pursue mundane greatness at times and at other times work for the welfare of their future life. However, if you try to ride two mounts at the same time, you risk falling off. Some claim that if you meditate, you don't need to recite the essence mantras or confess and purify the infractions of precepts; they challenge this necessity by asking, "Do infractions injure the body or the mind?" Some, when making offerings to the Three Jewels, wish to be seen by other people, and when seen, feel delighted, thus destroying the very ground [of their practice]. All of these ways of thinking and behaving are declared to be wrong.

How should you properly conduct oneself, then? Ensuring that erroneous views do not contaminate your body and speech, pursue what has been taught in the scriptures by the Buddha, what has been prescribed in the monastic discipline texts, and what is found in the pith instructions of the three teachers—Atiśa, Dromtönpa, and Potowa—intact and without degeneration, and train in this [awakening] mind alone.

Some, because their views color their conduct, become entangled in the knots of conceptualization. Some, on the basis of tantra, dismiss the teachings of monastic discipline, while others, on the basis of monastic discipline, dismiss tantra. Sangphupa reportedly asserted that it is from none other than our Indian teacher [Atiśa] that the ability has emerged to carry all the teachings squarely as one [unit].[1002]

In relation to this practice, if you fail to arrive at a conviction through critical understanding or fail to ensure that nothing [in the teachings] remains unfamiliar, you risk being hesitant when some urge you in one direction while others urge you in another. Therefore be sure you clarify all your doubts until this [mind training practice] has firmly taken root, and then implement it within your meditative practice. Engage in all the yogas, such as those pertaining to food, clothing, and so on, by means of this [mind training]. At the moment of death, too, you should engage in the training with the thought, "May all the suffering of others' birth and death be realized upon me." [366] Forsaking all pondering of whether you have the necessary amenities, engage in this practice alone.

Train with decisiveness.

This is as found in the *Oral Tradition*.

Be released through the two, examination and close analysis.[1003]

By determining which affliction is dominant in your mind, strive hard to eliminate it through applying its antidotes. Thoughts such as "He is to blame" are errors related to the past; if this kind of error occurs in the future, armor yourself with the thought "I will apply the antidotes."

Regarding your past experience, whatever you have undergone, such as illness, harm from enemies and malevolent forces, failure in finding life partners, being called unreliable, theft, beatings, and so on, train your mind toward them by aspiring, "Through these [events], may all that I owe since beginningless time—debts, dues, vengeance, and so on—be purified."

Regarding your future, whatever may befall you, such as being abused by others who say, "I will expel you to such and such a place this evening, at dawn tomorrow, or in the morning," or being accused of theft, being cast out, or becoming afflicted by acute illness, armor yourself by thinking, "I will engage in this practice of the awakening mind exchanging self and others." Potowa asked, "What if a prostitute were to come to you and hand over a little boy...and so on,"[1004] to which Chengawa responded, "I would feel saddened," while Phuchungwa said, "I would rather nurture life [by bringing up the child] than die." So, as illustrated by these, you should engage in your practice by extending it both to the past and the future.

> **Do not boast of your good deeds.**
> **Do not be ill-tempered.**
> **Do not be fickle.**
> **Do not be boisterous.**

These are as found in the *Oral Tradition*.

> **Through the proliferation of five degenerations**
> **Transform [every event] into the path of enlightenment.**[1005]

At this time, when only undesirable events reign in this last five-hundredth period,[1006] an era degenerate in terms of sentient beings' lives, afflictions, and views, when the pursuit of Dharma practice, such as the seeking of enlightenment, remains difficult, this mind training helps transform all of these into the path of enlightenment. For whatever remains unbearable, make that the entity you transform on the path to enlightenment.

Therefore you must ensure the arising of the awakening mind exchanging self and others where it has not arisen and enhance it where it has already arisen. As it is said, "Apply the nine conditions admired by all."[1007] You should (1) seek a teacher who reveals this kind of teaching, (2) associate with friends who engage in this practice, (3) listen to teachings that present this practice, (4) purify the defilements, the obstacles, (5) gather the conducive conditions, the accumulations, (6) make supplications, (7) invoke intervention by the Dharma protectors, (8) reflect upon the [merit] and shortcomings of either possessing or not possessing this realization, and (9) recognize the afflictions and their root, the grasping at self, as enemies. In this way, whenever afflictions arise in your mind, they become pacified. Similarly, when you recognize [the true nature of] conceptualizations, you experience a confidence akin to someone who, having recognized the thief, remains immune to any harm. Even if you remember to do this once, or develop the aspiration for it once, or experience joyful admiration for it once, it will become a remedy. Even if you were to interview a hundred people, you'd find no meditation to practice other than this. Even were I to bare my heart to you, the master said, nothing [else would be revealed] but red, pulsating flesh.

This essence of ambrosia of instructions
Is transmitted from [master] Serlingpa.[1008]

These are as found in the *Oral Tradition*.[1009]

These oral explanations of the Mahayana training of mind, which are found elucidated clearly in Sangyé Gompa's *Public Exposition,* have been committed to letter as a supplement to the oral tradition by the hermit Könchok Gyaltsen.

Sarvajagatam

38. Root Lines of "Parting from the Four Clingings"[1010]

[368] *Oṃ svasti siddhi*

When the great Sakyapa reached the age of twelve, he undertook an approximation retreat on Mañjuśrī for six months. One day he experienced a direct vision of yellow Mañjuśrī, who was seated on a jewel throne in the posture of a peaceful deity amid a mass of light, with his hands in the gesture of teaching, and flanked on each side by a bodhisattva. The central deity then uttered the following lines:

> If you cling to this life, you are not a practitioner;
> If you cling to the three realms, that is not renunciation;
> If you cling to self-interest, you are not a bodhisattva;
> If grasping arises, it is not the view.

As he [the great Sakyapa] perused the meaning of these utterances, he realized that all the practices pertaining to the path of the Perfection Vehicle converge on this training of mind by means of parting from the four clingings. He thus attained extraordinary ascertainment of all the teachings.

Sāptamiti

39. Parting from the Four Clingings[1011]
Drakpa Gyaltsen (1147–1216)

[369]

1

My teachers, who are so kind,
Meditation deities so compassionate—
To you I go for refuge from my heart;
Pray, bestow your blessings upon me.

2

Conduct contrary to the teachings has no use;
Thus to act in accordance with the teachings,
There is the instruction on parting from the four clingings;
I offer this to your very ears.[1012]

3

If you cling to this life, you are not a practitioner;
If you cling to the three realms, that is not renunciation;
If you cling to self-interest, you are not a bodhisattva;
If grasping arises, it is not the view.

4

First, not clinging to this life:
Ethical discipline, study, reflection, and meditation—
He who pursues these for this life's sake
Is not a practitioner; so cast this aside.

5

First to explain ethical discipline:
It's the root of higher transmigration;

It's the staircase to liberation;
It's the antidote to suffering;

6
So you cannot succeed without ethical discipline.
As for ethical discipline that clings to this life,
Its root is in the eight worldly concerns;
It attracts accusations of immoral behavior;

7
It makes you jealous of those with ethical discipline;
It makes your own discipline a mere pretense;
It's the seed that creates lower transmigration;
So cast aside the pretense of morality.

8
He who engages in study and reflection
Is enriched by resources that enhance knowledge;
He is endowed with the light that dispels ignorance;
He is familiar with the road to guide sentient beings;

9
He is endowed with the seed of the dharmakāya;
So you cannot succeed without study and reflection.
As for the study and reflection that clings to this life,
It provides resources that produce conceit;

10
It causes contempt for those inferior in learning and reflection;
It causes envy toward those who possess learning and reflection;
It causes you to seek retinues and wealth;
It's the root that brings forth lower transmigration.

11
So cast aside study and reflection driven by the eight concerns.
All who undertake meditative practice are
Endowed with the antidote to the afflictions;
They possess the root of the path to liberation;

12
They possess the seed of buddhahood;
So you cannot do without meditative practice.
As for meditative practice pursued for this life's sake,
It brings distractions when residing in solitude;

13
It makes you adept in the art of empty chatter;
It makes you defame those engaged in study and reflection; [370]
It makes you jealous toward other meditators;
So cast aside the meditative concentration of the eight concerns.[1013]

14
To seek nirvana, the state beyond sorrow,[1014]
Relinquish clinging to the three realms.
To relinquish clinging to the three realms,
Reflect on the defects of cyclic existence.

15
First is the suffering of suffering—
This includes the sufferings of the three lower realms.
If you contemplate these well, fear will arise,
For if ripened upon you, they are indeed unbearable.

16
Not gathering the virtuous karma that overcomes these
And continuing to cultivate the fields of lower realms—
Wherever such conduct exists, spit on it.

17
Reflect on the suffering of change—
From higher realms you can fall to the lower realms;
The god Indra can be reborn as a mere earthling;
Sun and moon can turn into darkness;

18
The universal monarch can be reborn as a servant.
These can be known by means of scripture,

But cannot be perceived by ordinary beings.
Therefore, observe your own experience of human-level changes:

19

A rich man turns into a poor man;
A confident man changes into an anxious one;
Many people unite together as one;
This list of such phenomena is inconceivable.

20

If you reflect on the suffering of conditioning,
Karmic deeds are endless—
You suffer with too much, you suffer with too little;
You suffer if rich, you suffer if starved.

21

We wastes our entire lives in preparations;
While in preparation we all die.
Even in death there is no end to the preparations,
For we begin preparations for the next life.

22

Spit on those who continue to cling to
This mass of suffering called cyclic existence.
When freed of this clinging, you go beyond sorrow;
When gone beyond sorrow, you attain happiness.

23

Freedom from these two clingings is the experience of expanse.
Your individual freedom alone is of no value.[1015]
Beings of the entire three realms are your parents;
Spit on those who leave their parents behind
In the storm of suffering and seek their own happiness.[1016]

24

May the sufferings of the three realms ripen upon me;
May sentient beings take away all my merit;

Through the blessings of this meritorious act,
May all sentient beings become fully enlightened.

25

In whatever way you abide in reality[1017]
There is no release so long as you grasp.
To explain this, as well, in greater detail:

26

There is no liberation for those who grasp at existence;
There is no higher rebirth for those who grasp at nonexistence;[1018]
And those who grasp at both are ignorant;
So place your mind freely in the nondual sphere.

27

All things are but objects of the mind;
Without searching for a creator of the four elements,
Such as a wise diviner, Īśvara, and so on, [371]
Place the mind freely in the sphere of mind-itself.

28

The illusory nature of [all] appearances
And [the truth of] dependent origination as well—
One cannot[1019] describe their true mode of being;[1020]
So place the mind freely in the ineffable sphere.[1021]

29

Through the merit derived from this virtue
Of presenting parting from the four clingings,
May all beings of seven classes without exception
Be led to the ground of buddhahood.[1022]

This instruction on parting from the four clingings was composed by the yogi Drakpa Gyaltsen at the glorious monastery of Sakya.

40. Unmistaken Instruction on "Parting from the Four Clingings"[1023]

Sakya Paṇḍita (1182–1251)

[372] Homage to the feet of the sublime teachers!

Having obtained the human existence endowed with leisure and opportunity, encountered the precious teachings of the Buddha, and cultivated a genuine, uncontrived [awakening] thought, it is now vital that you engage in an unmistaken Dharma practice. For this you need to engage in the practice of parting from the four clingings. What are they? They are the following:

1. Not clinging to this life
2. Not clinging to the three realms of cyclic existence
3. Not clinging to your self-interest
4. Not clinging to things and their symbols[1024]

Now I will explain these in more detail. Since this life resembles bubbles in water, the time of death is uncertain. Thus clinging to this life is pointless.

This entire cyclic existence of the three realms is like a poisonous fruit: although it may be tasty in the moment, ultimately it destroys. He who clings to the three realms is therefore deluded.

If you cling to your own self-interest, it is like nurturing the son of your enemy. Although he might show affection in the short run, in the long run he is certain to bring ruin. So if you cling to self-interest, you might gain something temporarily, but in the long run, you will migrate to the lower realms.

Clinging to things and their symbols is like grasping at a mirage that appears to be water. It may look like water right now, but you cannot drink it. Although this cyclic existence appears to your deluded mind, if you analyze it with wisdom, you find nothing that exists by means of its own nature. Therefore cultivate the understanding that does not dwell on the past, become immersed in the present, or project into the future, and in this way recognize all things as free of conceptual elaborations.

By conducting yourself in this manner, not clinging to this life, you will avoid rebirth in the lower realms. By not clinging to the three realms of cyclic existence, you avoid rebirth in cyclic existence. By not clinging to self-interest, you avoid rebirth as a disciple or a self-realized one. By not clinging to things and their symbols, you quickly attain perfect enlightenment.

This completes the unmistaken instruction on parting from the four clingings composed by Sakya Paṇḍita, embodying the import of the enlightened intention of the great and glorious Sakyapa.[1025]

41. An Instruction on "Parting from the Four Clingings"[1026]

Nupa Rikzin Drak (thirteenth century)

[373] *Namo Guru*

The great venerable master Sakyapa[1027] states that all those who wish to seek the supreme state of great bliss beyond sorrow need to part from the four clingings: (1) clinging to this life, (2) clinging to cyclic existence of the three realms, (3) clinging to self-interest, and (4) clinging to things and their symbols.

The antidotes to these are four as well: (1) The antidote to the first clinging is meditation on impermanence; (2) the antidote to the second is reflecting on the defects of cyclic existence; (3) the antidote to the third is recalling the awakening mind; and (4) the antidote to the fourth is reflecting on all phenomena as like dreams and illusions, devoid of self-existence.

Engaging in such reflections and cultivating familiarity with them brings four effects: (1) Your Dharma practice will become genuine Dharma; (2) your Dharma practice will become successful; (3) you will dispel errors of the path; and (4) as the fruit of such understanding and familiarization, you will attain buddhahood, which is [the transformation of all] delusions into perfect wisdom.

First, meditation on death and impermanence, the antidote to clinging to this life, refers to (a) contemplating the unpredictability of the time of death, (b) contemplating the multiplicity of circumstances that can cause death, and (c) contemplating extensively how, at death, nothing is of benefit. As you contemplate in this manner, an eagerness to practice Dharma will arise from the depth of your heart, and at that point your practice becomes true Dharma practice.

Next, reflecting on the defects of cyclic existence, the antidote to clinging to cyclic existence of the three realms, is as follows: You might have the thought, "Yes, this life is flawed because of such and such defects; but other lives—of the universal monarch, of Brahma, of Indra, and so on—represent supreme happiness," but this is not correct. They, too, are within the bounds of suffering. Although their life spans and resources are greater and last for many eons, they all eventually die, become annihilated, and suffer from the threat of rebirth in the Avīci hell. Thus, as you contemplate all of these to be within the bounds of suffering and cultivate your familiarity with the contemplation, your Dharma practice will become successful. You will recognize that the three realms are not outside the bounds of suffering, [374] and on that basis generate the thought, "I must seek the bliss of nirvana" and then strive to accomplish all the aspects of the path for this purpose.

You may have attained these realizations within your mind, but if you lack the awakening mind—if you seek your own happiness alone—you will only become an arhat or a self-realized one. The antidote to clinging to own self-interest, recollecting the awakening mind, is as follows: Reflect "It is useless if I alone gain freedom from this world of three realms, [a state that] is within the bounds of suffering. For from among these sentient beings—each and every one of them—not one has not been my parent. Therefore it is better that they attain the supreme bliss of nirvana, even if I have to be reborn in the hells for eons and eons." As you generate such an attitude and gain familiarity with it, you will dispel the clinging to self-interest, which is the first delusion pertaining to the path.

Even though you might attain such a realization and gain familiarity with it, if you grasp at the true existence of things, you cannot attain omniscience. Therefore, as the antidote to clinging to things and their symbols, it is necessary to reflect that all phenomena are devoid of self-existence. This means that all things share the nature of not existing in any [definable] mode of being. Thus if grasping at their true existence arises, this is a view that grasps at self-existence; clinging to their emptiness, on the other hand, is a nihilistic view. So contemplate all things as dreamlike. Reflect, "As I merge dreams with appearances and meditate on this, appearances too become unreal; yet, while unreal, they still appear [to my mind]." As you continually reflect on this and meditate, you dispel clinging to things and their symbols, which is the second delusion pertaining to the path.

In this manner, when all the delusions are dispelled and perfected, you will attain what is known as "the dawning of delusions as wisdom," which is the supreme happiness constituted by such inconceivable enlightened attributes as the buddha bodies and wisdom.

This is an instruction on parting from the four clingings, which is the teaching of the great master yogi Drakpa Gyaltsen.

Iti

42. A Key to the Profound Essential Points: A Meditation Guide to "Parting from the Four Clingings"
Goram Sönam Sengé (1429–1489)[1028]

[375] Like the sky, your wisdom-mind pervades all objects of knowledge;
Like moon rays, your compassion adorns beautifully the crown of all
beings;
Like a wish-fulfilling jewel, your activities are a treasure and a source of all
wishes—
O lion of the Śākya clan, unexcelled savior, bestow auspiciousness on all
beings.

You're Mañjuśrī, who embodies in one the wisdom of all conquerors,
You're Avalokiteśvara, who has pledged to save all beings of the three
realms,
O Sakyapa, you who've assumed the human form to guide beings of this
degenerate age—
To you, whose name is hard even to utter, I respectfully pay homage.

I shall explain here the unique instructions on Mahayana's essential points
In response to queries posed by someone[1029] with a thoroughly pure mind,
Who, due to past merit, has attained an existence ideal for Dharma practice.
And who glorifies the teaching and its upholders with abundant resources.

Every teaching of the perfectly enlightened Buddha—who is endowed with
a heart that naturally pursues the well-being of the entire universe—was
taught in accordance with spiritual aspirants' natural inclinations, mindsets,
and dispositions and falls into the two categories—that of the Perfection
Vehicle and that of the Adamantine Vehicle [the Vajrayana]. Within the
first class are two kinds: practices based primarily on the major treatises and
practices based on the essential pith instructions.

[I. Stages of the path presented in the major treatises]

The treatises include teachings, as found in the *Ornament of Clear Realizations*,[1030] on the stages of the path of eight clear realizations presented in the Perfection of Wisdom scriptures. In the presentation of the stages of the path found in the *Ornament of Mahayana Sutras*,[1031] the subject matter of various Mahayana scriptures is explained in terms of buddha nature, the natural inclinations toward spiritual teachings, and so on. In his *Precious Garland*,[1032] Nāgārjuna presents the stages of the path whereby the two aspirations—for higher rebirth and for definite goodness—are cultivated by means of the factors of faith and wisdom. [376] Āryadeva presents the stages of the path whereby, taking [the attainment of] buddhahood that is free of the four erroneous views as your goal, you cut off all the afflictions together with their causes that obstruct your perfecting the bodhisattva ideal and turn yourself into a receptive vessel for true suchness, while the ambrosia of true suchness is revealed to you as the actual instruction.[1033]

Master Śāntideva presents the stages of the path for achieving buddhahood within which, on the basis of this human existence endowed with leisure and opportunity, you undertake the practice of the six perfections—the bodhisattva ideal—and complement it with thoroughly pure aspiration prayers.[1034] The great Atiśa taught the stages of the path of the three capacities:[1035] initial capacity whereby you relinquish clinging to this life and pursue the welfare of the next life alone, middling capacity whereby you forsake the pleasures of cyclic existence and pursue mere liberation, and great capacity whereby you pursue buddhahood for the benefit of [all] sentient beings. The glorious Candrakīrti presented the stages of the path establishing the buddha bodies whereby you practice compassion, the awakening mind, and nondual awareness while at the level of ordinary beings, and after you attain the ground of a noble ārya being, you traverse the ten bodhisattva levels by means of the ten perfections.[1036] Although all of these are excellent and wonderful systems elucidated perfectly by realized masters who have actualized the intention of the Mahayana scriptures, they are meant to be cognized by those who have trained their minds in the tradition of the major treatises. They cannot be realized here by means of a brief summary.

II. How to practice the import of these [major treatises] by means of the essential points of the pith instructions

Second is how to practice the import of these [major treatises] by means of the essential points of the pith instructions. Generally speaking, there are numerous approaches. Of these, the principal ones are the one conferred to master Atiśa by Serlingpa and the one conferred to the Sakyapa teacher by Lord Mañjuśrī.

In the first [approach], you begin by creating the basis for your generation of the awakening mind through cultivating four [meditations]: (1) [reflection on] the difficulty of obtaining a human existence of leisure and opportunity, (2) reflection on death and impermanence, (3) reflection on karma and its fruits, and (4) reflection on the defects of cyclic existence. And to prepare for the main practice, you train in loving-kindness and compassion for a long period of time; then for the actual practice you cultivate principally the awakening mind of exchanging self and others. Then, when the conditions arise, you cultivate the ultimate awakening mind as well. Complements to this path include the transformation of adverse conditions into the path of enlightenment, presentation of a lifetime practice in summary, [377] the measure of having trained the mind, the commitments of mind training, and the precepts of mind training. This most excellent method is inconspicuous but highly effective for making huge strides. In Tibet Atiśa gave this only to the spiritual teacher Dromtönpa and to no one else, and the precious spiritual teacher, too, in turn conferred it only upon the three precious brothers.[1037] After that, it spread widely and became, in this land of snows, a path as well known as the sun and moon. For these practices, consult the writings of the bodhisattva Chözong[1038] and his disciples and the works of the great bodhisattva Shönu Gyalchok[1039] and others.

I will now present what Lord Mañjuśrī bestowed upon the Sakyapa teacher, which in terms of the essential points of practice is similar to the practices referred to above, but in terms of its division of the subject matter and its arrangement of the essential points, it is superior. At the age of eleven the great Sakyapa teacher undertook a retreat of Mañjuśrī, and within six months he experienced a vision of Mañjuśrī, whereupon Lord Mañjuśrī uttered the following lines:

If you cling to this life, you are not a practitioner;
If you cling to the three realms, that is not renunciation;

If you cling to self-interest, you are not a bodhisattva;
If grasping arises, it is not the view.

These lines encompass all the practices of the Perfection Vehicle. The meaning of these lines has are four parts:

A. Parting from clinging to this life and directing your mind to Dharma practice
B. Parting from clinging to cyclic existence and ensuring success in Dharma practice
C. Parting from clinging to self-interest and eliminating delusions of the path
D. Parting from clinging to the four extremes and ensuring the dawning of delusions as wisdom

The first has three parts:

1. The preliminary: meditation on the difficulty of finding the human existence of leisure and opportunity
2. The main practice: meditation on death and impermanence
3. The complementary path: meditation on karma and its fruits

1. The preliminary: meditation on the difficulty of finding the human existence of leisure and opportunity

Seated on a comfortable cushion, [378] go for refuge many times to your teacher and the Three Jewels and make supplications to realize the four objectives, such as turning your mind to Dharma practice. After generating the thought "I will attain buddhahood for the benefit of all beings," cultivate the following thought:

"From the point of view of its nature, this human existence endowed with leisure and opportunity—the convergence of the eight aspects of leisure and the ten opportunities—is hard to find indeed. Its cause is the accumulation of virtuous karma, and since virtuous karma is so rare in this mindstream of mine, this human existence will be hard to find from the perspective of cause as well. And from the point of view of numbers, we can perceive directly that among the six classes of sentient beings, the lower classes generally outnumber the higher classes. For example, the number of insects in a single swamp or a single pile of wood during the summer exceed the number of human beings on this earth. So this [human existence] is hard to find indeed.

From the point of view of metaphors, too, it is as rare as peas sticking to the wall when you toss some of them against it; obtaining this [human existence] is more rare than the neck of a turtle chancing to enter the hole of a yoke adrift on a vast windswept ocean. I will therefore not waste this human existence of leisure and opportunity that I have obtained this once. I will endeavor to accomplish the well-being of my next life and beyond." Meditate in such a manner.

2. The main practice: meditation on death and impermanence

As before, having gone for refuge and generated the awakening mind, contemplate in the following manner:

"Since no one has remained without dying after being born, my own death is certain. Furthermore the time of my death is uncertain, for I cannot say that I will die at such and such a time or that I will not die before a particular span of time is finished. Also, since many circumstances cause death and few sustain life, my death is definite, and when the time of death [truly] arrives, no medication or healing rites can avert it. Nothing is of benefit when death arrives. After my death, only my Dharma practice—and none of my circle of friends and none of my possessions—can follow me."

Meditate in this way and ensure you are free of clinging to this life. As this is the principal means for turning your mind to Dharma practice, whenever you enjoy good food, or wear valuable clothes, or are surrounded by a wonderful circle of friends, think, "Yes, right now I am enjoying these things. However, a time will one day arrive when I will have to leave them behind and depart alone. So these things have no essence." Meditate in this manner and make certain you are free of clinging to the affairs of this life. [379]

3. The complementary path: meditation on karma and its fruits

Having gone for refuge and generated the awakening mind as before, contemplate in the following manner:

"I have obtained the human existence of leisure and opportunity that is so rare to find. It is transient, however, and so I shall relinquish all nonvirtuous acts and endeavor to undertake virtuous acts to the best of my ability before I die. For the fruitional effect of indulging in the ten nonvirtuous actions is rebirth in the three lower realms. And the causally concordant experiential effect is, for taking a life, that my life span will be short, for stealing, that I will be bereft of material resources, and so on. As for the causally concordant habitual effect, I will take delight in again indulging in which-ever of the nonvirtuous acts I am habituated to, which will cast me to the lower realms and so on, where I will have no chance for freedom. As for environmental effects, I will be born in places polluted by terrible odors and dust storms. Therefore I must definitely forsake these [nonvirtuous acts].

"Similarly, the fruitional effect of virtuous acts is birth in the higher realms. As the causally concordant experiential effect of not killing, I will enjoy long life, and as the causally concordant habitual effect, I will delight in performing this or that virtuous act. As for environmental effects, I will be born in a place with a pleasant odor and so on. Therefore I must perform these [virtuous acts]." Contemplate in such a manner. It is critical that you understand these essential points about karma and its fruits and integrate them into your practice.

B. Parting from clinging to cyclic existence and ensuring success in Dharma practice

For this you must contemplate the defects of the three realms of cyclic existence. Having gone for refuge and generated the awakening mind as before, contemplate in the following manner:

"This cyclic existence constituted by the three realms lies within the bounds of suffering. In the hot hells are the sufferings of having your body burned and being sliced by sharp weapons and so on, while the cold hells are extremely cold and you suffer having your flesh and bones split open. The random hells include such sufferings as living immersed in lava and so on. If some of these sufferings [380] were to happen to my body today, I would be unable to withstand even a fraction of them. The hungry ghost realm has the sufferings of hunger, thirst, heat and cold, exhaustion, and also fear. Animals in the wild suffer from one species devouring another, while those scattered [domesticated animals] suffer constant hard labor and exploitation. Humans suffer becoming high and low, failing to obtain what is sought, encountering what is unpleasant, being separated from loved ones, and so on. We observe these sufferings directly this very moment. The gods of the desire realm suffer too when they experience early portents of death, which are more mentally painful than the sufferings of the hell beings. The gods of the form and formless realms, too, although at present free from any manifest level of suffering, will one day descend and have to undergo the sufferings of the lower realms. So this entire cycle of existence constituted by the three realms does not lie outside the bounds of suffering. I will therefore entirely forsake this cyclic existence and make sure to attain the state of liberation."

Up to this point, among the stages of the path of the three capacities, the paths of the initial and middling capacities are complete, and with respect to Serlingpa's approach, the four preliminary practices are complete.

C. Parting from clinging to self-interest and eliminating delusions of the path

This has three parts:

1. Meditation on loving-kindness
2. Meditation on compassion
3. Meditation on the awakening mind

1. Meditation on loving-kindness

Reflect, "It is not appropriate for me to seek freedom from cyclic existence for myself alone. All sentient beings within the three realms have been my parents many times and have thus been a source of kindness to me." Reflect in particular that "My mother of this life first carried me in her womb, and after my birth, she protected the life of something resembling a naked insect. Then she nurtured me with food, clothing, and so on." Reflecting on these acts of kindness, cultivate the wish "I will lead her to happiness, for she has been a source of great kindness."

Next, reflect on the kindness of your other family members, enemies who cause you harm, [381] even suffering sentient beings, such as those in the three lower realms, who have all been your mother many times over since beginningless time. Engage in this meditation until loving-kindness, which is the wish to lead them to happiness, arises in your mind.

2. Meditation on compassion

Recollecting all the acts of kindness your mother has done for you, cultivate the thought "Although my mother, who has been so kind, must be freed from suffering, how tragic it is that she is presently caught within the bounds of suffering. How I wish she were free from suffering! I will lead her from suffering to freedom."

As before, you should reflect similarly on the kindness of other sentient beings and meditate on compassion, aspiring that others be freed from suffering. If loving-kindness and compassion are not generated in your heart, the genuine awakening mind cannot arise. Therefore endeavor [in the practice of] these two roots of all Mahayana spiritual practices.

3. Meditation on the awakening mind

This has three parts:

    a. The aspirational awakening mind
    b. The awakening mind equalizing self and others
    c. The awakening mind exchanging self and others

a. The aspirational awakening mind

Cultivate the following thought: "Although my kind parents in the three realms must be endowed with happiness and overcome suffering, I have no power to bring this about. Not only that, even the great worldly beings, such as Brahma and Indra, and those who have transcended the world, such as the disciples and the self-realized ones, do not possess this. Who, then, has this power? Only the fully enlightened buddhas possess this. I will attain the state of buddhahood in order to benefit all beings and rescue my kind parents from the ocean of cyclic existence."

This is an indispensable cause for the attainment of buddhahood. Furthermore, if you possess this thought, all your roots of virtue will become causes of full enlightenment. Therefore numerous praises of this are sung in the scriptural collections of the Great Vehicle.

b. The awakening mind equalizing self and others

"Just as I desire happiness, so too do all sentient beings; therefore just as I pursue my own happiness, so must I seek the happiness of all beings. [382] Just as I shun suffering, so too do all sentient beings; therefore just as I alleviate my own suffering, so must I alleviate the suffering of all beings." Meditate in this manner.

c. The awakening mind exchanging self and others

Visualizing your real-life mother in front of you, reflect, "Though my mother is indeed kind, she is caught within the bounds of suffering. May the sufferings of my mother together with all their causes—the nonvirtuous karma—ripen upon me, and may I myself undergo these experiences. May all my happiness and virtues ripen upon her, and may she, my mother, attain buddhahood." Meditate in this manner.

Likewise meditate individually with respect to your other family members and relatives; every being you have ever seen or heard of; your enemies, who cause you harm; and all the suffering sentient beings, such as those in the three lower realms. Eventually, you should collect upon yourself in a single gesture the sufferings of all beings and give them all your happiness and virtues in the form of whatever goods they desire in the short term. In the ultimate term, these become the cause for attaining buddhahood.

Since this is the heart of Mahayana spiritual practice and [also] the secret of all the buddhas of the three times, I would ideally present the reasons for the necessity of its practice, [give] supporting scriptural citations, provide critical analysis of its meditation procedure, and so on. However, fearing this would lead to excessive length, I have chosen not to elaborate these here.

For the aspirational awakening mind up to this point, you definitely need the preliminaries of going for refuge and generating the awakening mind, as described above. Meditation on guru yoga is also recommended. At the end of each session of all these cycles of visualizations, seal it with dedication and aspiration prayers; moreover, recall these practices throughout your everyday activities.

D. Parting from clinging to the four extremes and ensuring the dawning of delusions as wisdom

[383] The other tradition of pith instructions contains [the practices of] tranquil abiding and penetrative insight. And the latter of these includes meditation on the selflessness of persons and meditation on the selflessness of phenomena and so on. In the present tradition, however, you engage in the following three meditative practices during meditative equipoise: (1) establishing appearances as [aspects of] the mind, (2) establishing the mind as illusion, and (3) establishing illusion as devoid of intrinsic existence. During the postmeditation periods you practice viewing everything as illusions

and dreams, free of clinging. However, if you undertake these meditative practices without relying on a teacher's instruction, you risk becoming confused. Furthermore, since these cannot be learned merely through words, I will not elaborate further.

Nevertheless, what is beneficial in the short term is the following: Whatever roots of virtue you cultivate, it is important you do so free of any conceited thoughts, such as, "*I* am performing a virtuous deed. *These* are virtuous actions. Therefore I have done *this* virtuous act." There is no fault, of course, in proclaiming that you have done such and such virtuous deeds if you do so to encourage others to engage in virtue. When establishing the roots of virtue and when engaging in everyday mundane tasks, bring to the fore the thought "Is it an illusion? Is it a dream?" These factors lead to realizing the [profound] view. Sustain [these practices] with mindfulness.

Thus there are four stages to this path. The first is known as *turning your mind to Dharma practice* since you strive to achieve the welfare of the next life and beyond. The second is known as *ensuring success in your Dharma practice* since you relinquish cyclic existence and seek liberation. The third is known as *eliminating delusions of the path* since you relinquish the attitudes of the Lesser Vehicle and prepare for the Great Vehicle. The fourth is known as *ensuring the dawning of delusions as wisdom* since you eliminate all conceptual elaborations of grasping at extreme views and engage with the truth of the ultimate mode of being.

While practicing these principal aspects of the path, in order to make your body meaningful, perform prostrations and circumambulations; to make your speech meaningful, recite hymns to the buddhas and bodhisattvas and read the profound scriptures; and to make your mind meaningful, meditate on loving-kindness, compassion, and the awakening mind. To make your wealth meaningful, make offerings to the Three Jewels, offer food to the monastic community, and so on. If you perform these with pure aspiration prayers, you will attain perfect buddhahood, which is free of faults and endowed with all higher qualities.

III. Recapitulating the essential points in verse

Rare indeed is it to find this existence ideal for Dharma practice; [384]
Recognizing well that it is transient and disintegrates easily,
The first stage is to maintain heartfelt adherence
To the ethical norms of affirmation and rejection.

Seeing that infinite beings are trapped in the mouth
Of a sea monster called suffering in this ocean of cyclic existence,
The second stage is to generate true renunciation,
Aspiring for the dry shores of freedom beyond the states of sorrow.

Recollecting the kindness shown to you by beings equal to the reach of
 space,
Who have been your father and mother again and again,
The third stage is to accomplish the welfare of others
Through love, compassion, and the supreme awakening mind.

All that you perceive is your own mind.
Like an illusion, the mind is but a composite of causes and conditions.
The fourth stage is to contemplate the ultimate mode of being,
Recognizing that this illusion is devoid of all elaborations.

If you make offerings to the Three Jewels at all times,
If you gradually relinquish nonvirtuous acts,
And if you succor the poor and the unprotected through charity,
Your immediate and ultimate aims will definitely be realized.

I offer this gift wanting to be of some benefit,
Summarizing the essential points of Mahayana for you
As your heart practice, O benefactor of Dharma.
Please put these into practice and accomplish all the points.

The lay bodhisattva Ralo Dorjé, who has indivisible faith in the precious
Dharma and is a great benefactor of the upholders of the teachings, asked
for an instruction, an advice that will be beneficial for the [practice of]
divine Dharma. At his behest I, Sönam Sengé, a monk in Śākyamuni's order,
wrote this piece on the third day of the waxing moon of *kārttika* month[1040]
at the sublime retreat of Dokhar. Subsequently, I will send some essential
points concerning karma and its effects together with [the relevant] scriptural citations.

Maṅgalam bhavantu!
May auspiciousness prevail!

43. A Concise Guide to "Parting from the Four Clingings"

Künga Lekpai Rinchen (fifteenth century)[1041]

[385] Respectfully I pay homage to the teachers and Lord Mañjuśrī.

"For the benefit of all sentient beings, I will attain the state of the perfectly enlightened Buddha. To this end I will listen to the sublime teachings and put them into practice." With this thought generate the awakening mind and cultivate the attitude and conduct appropriate to listening to the teachings, and with these, please listen.

Here, to practice the instruction on parting from the four clingings, the sole path trodden by all the tathāgatas of the three times, embodying into a single unit the essential points of practice of all the sutras, the profound scriptures of the Buddha, there are two sections:

I. A history of the lineage of the teachers to ensure the authority of its sources
II. The actual instruction

I. History of the lineage of the teachers

When the accomplished yogi, the great Sakyapa, reached the age of twelve, he sought the embodiment of compassion, Bari Lotsāwa, as his teacher and received teachings from him.[1042] The teacher advised, "Since you are the son of a great master, you must study, and for this it is crucial to have intelligence, so you should undertake a retreat on Mañjuśrī." With this advice, the teacher conferred upon him the blessings and oral transmission of Mañjuśrī Arapacana. The teacher also served as an assistant for this retreat, which was undertaken at the old quarters of the labrang.[1043] There were a few portents of obstacles, which were averted by means of visualizations and mantra recitations of [the deity] Blue Acala and through the water rites of protection.

After six months had passed, he [the great Sakyapa] experienced a vision of holy Mañjuśrī seated with a peaceful demeanor on a jeweled throne and flanked by two bodhisattvas. At that time, holy Mañjuśrī uttered the following lines:

> If you cling to this life, you are not a practitioner;
> If you cling to the three realms, that is not renunciation;
> If you cling to self-interest, you are not a bodhisattva;
> If grasping arises, it is not the view. [386]

As the great Sakyapa reflected on their meaning, he realized that the essential points of all the practices pertaining to the Buddha's sacred words, the sutras, are encompassed in them, and appreciating this profundity, he undertook these as his heart practice.

The great Sakyapa bestowed this to Lopön Rinpoché; he to Jetsün Rinpoché; he to the master of the teachings glorious Sakya Paṇḍita; he to the protector of beings Chögyal Phakpa; he to Shang Könchok Pal; he to the master of the teachings Drakphukpa; he to the master of the teachings glorious and kind Sönam Gyaltsen; and he bestowed it to our glorious sublime teacher Künga Sangpo.

II. The actual instruction

This has three sections:

    A. The preliminaries
    B. The main practice
    C. The conclusion

A. The preliminaries

The first is composed of two parts, and the first, going for refuge, is the following:

1. Going for refuge

The Mahayana approach to going for refuge has four distinguishing features, and the following are its objects of refuge.[1044] The Buddha Jewel refers to an unexcelled person whose enlightened attributes are inconceivable and who is free of even the slightest defects. The Dharma Jewel refers to all the scriptural and realization Dharma that resides in the hearts of the buddhas and bodhisattvas who are beyond the stage of regress. The Sangha Jewel refers to bodhisattvas beyond the stage of regress who have correctly accomplished these [Dharma] realizations. It is to these we go for refuge.

It is not that you alone go for refuge from this moment until the attainment of enlightenment, but rather that all sentient beings equal to the expanse of space, including your parents, go for refuge for the sake of all beings and out of a desire to attain the state of buddhahood. So, reflecting on this point, and without distraction, utter the following words:

All mother sentient beings—myself and all others, extending to the limits of space—go for refuge to the blessed buddhas of the ten directions; [387]

We go for refuge to the sublime Dharma, which is the embodiment of scriptures and realizations;

We go for refuge to the noble Sangha members, who are the children of the conquerors.

At the end of as many repetitions as possible of going for refuge, recite:

Through the blessings of the Three Precious Jewels may I be blessed so that my thoughts turn toward Dharma practice;

May I be blessed so that my Dharma practice is successful;

May I be blessed so that the delusions of the path are eliminated, so that delusions dawn as wisdom, so that not a single instant of thought contrary to Dharma arises in me, and so that I swiftly attain buddhahood.

Make supplications in this manner.

2. Generating the awakening mind

Second, generating the awakening mind, is as follows:

To the Buddha, Dharma, and the excellent community,
I go for refuge until my enlightenment;
Through the merits of engaging in giving and so on,
May I swiftly achieve buddhahood for the benefit of all beings.

For the sake of all sentient beings I will attain the state of buddhahood, and to this end I will strive with my body, speech, and
mind in virtuous deeds.

Cultivate these thoughts and express them in words as well.

B. *The main practice*

This has four parts.

[*1. Practicing the first meditation*]

To engage in the first meditation, sit cross-legged and adopt whatever posture is most comfortable for your body, and going for refuge and generating
the awakening mind as preliminaries, [contemplate]:

If you cling to this life, you are not a practitioner.

The meaning of this is that you must not cling to this life, for if you do, then
just as clinging to a mirage does not quench your thirst, whatever you engage
in—ethical discipline, study, reflection, and meditation—all will become
merely means to mundane advantages. They will not be genuine Dharma
practice. So it is stated:

Apply yourself excellently to a meditation
Endowed with ethical living, study, and reflection.[1045]

So, with pure ethical discipline as a foundation, first engage in study, then
reflect on the meanings and arrive at critical conclusions, and then meditate
on the conclusions arrived at through study and reflection. For this, there
are two parts: (a) in order to cultivate the desire to engage in Dharma practice where it has not arisen, [388] reflect on the difficulty of finding the
human existence of leisure and opportunity, and (b) in order to enhance

your enthusiasm for Dharma practice to its optimal level, reflection on death and impermanence.

a. The difficulty of finding the human existence of leisure and opportunity

First is as follows:

> This life of leisure and opportunity so hard to find—
> With it one can accomplish the great welfare of beings.
> If I fail to reap benefits on the basis of this,
> How will I ever find such good fortune again in the future?[1046]

As stated here, reflect, "Since it will be difficult indeed to obtain once more this human existence of leisure and opportunity—an existence ideal for engaging in the practice of the sublime Dharma, I must, on the basis of this existence I have found once, engage in perfect Dharma practice." To explain this [point] in a little more detail, there are:

(1) Reflecting on the difficulty of obtaining it from the point of view of its cause

(2) Reflecting on the difficulty of obtaining it from the point of view of numbers

(3) Reflecting on the difficulty of obtaining it from the point of view of analogy

(4) Reflecting on the difficulty of obtaining it from the point of view of its nature

(1) To obtain this perfect human existence of leisure and opportunity, you must accumulate its cause—virtuous karma—through ethical discipline and all virtuous actions. However, among the sentient beings of the three realms, extremely few accumulate virtue, while a great number indulge in nonvirtuous actions. Reflect on the difficulty of finding it from the point of view of its cause, and meditate [on this].

(2) When you observe the world of sentient beings, the number of hell beings rivals the number of particles of dust that exist on earth, while the number of hungry ghosts resembles snowflakes in a snowstorm, and animals are as numerous as the fermented grains of a potent beer. In contrast, those who obtain perfect human existence are extremely few. Reflect upon

the difficulty of finding it from the point of view of numbers and meditate [on this].

(3) It is stated:

> For this reason the Blessed One has stated,
> Like a turtle's neck entering the hole
> Of a yoke afloat on a vast, open ocean,
> So rare is it to find human existence.[1047]

As stated here, for the neck of a blind turtle, who lives underneath a vast ocean and who surfaces once every hundred years, to enter the single hole of a golden yoke adrift upon turbulent waves is the merest possibility. Likewise, although incalculable classes of sentient beings exist, birth as a human being is the merest possibility. Reflect on the difficulty of finding it from the point of view of analogy as well and meditate.

(4) It is rare indeed to be free from such aspects of nonleisure as being born mute or being born in a land far from Dharma, and it is rare, as well, to have the ten aspects of opportunity arise together. Reflect upon the difficulty of finding [a perfect human rebirth] from the point of view of its nature and meditate. [389]

b. Reflecting on death and impermanence

It is stated:

> Death lies ahead for all things born.[1048]

As it is said, the end of having been born is certain death. Meditate on this with the thought "I must swiftly engage in Dharma practice." To explain this further, there are:

(1) Reflection on the certainty of death
(2) Reflection on the unpredictability of the time of death
(3) Reflection on how, at the time of death, nothing except Dharma is of benefit

(1) Reflection on the certainty of death

In general, because all composite phenomena are by nature impermanent, they must all eventually disintegrate. It is stated, for example:

> All three worlds are transient like clouds in autumn;
> The birth and death of beings resemble scenes in a play;
> Life's passage is like lightning in the sky;
> Like torrents rushing down a steep mountain, swiftly we depart.[1049]

In particular, it is stated:

> The form bodies of the Buddha
> Adorned with the major and minor noble marks—
> If even these diamond bodies are unstable,
> What need is there to speak of this bubblelike body,
> Which is in constant flux and devoid of essence?[1050]

Reflect that if even the fully awakened buddhas, who have attained the state of immortality, display the deed of entering nirvana, what need is there to mention the certainty of death for ordinary sentient beings. It is stated:

> Even if they wish to, the great sages
> With five types of clairvoyance,
> Who can venture afar in the vast skies,
> Cannot journey to a place free of death.[1051]

As it is stated, no place is free of death, no matter where you are born in the three realms. Therefore meditate by reflecting, "Definitely, I will die." You will also certainly die because many conditions can cause death but few factors sustain life. It is stated:

> Conditions for death are so numerous,
> While those sustaining life are few,
> Yet these, too, are conditions for death.
> So constantly practice Dharma.[1052]

As this states, among conditions recognized as factors sustaining life—such as shelter, food, and certain behaviors—some can become conditions for death. Thus you should meditate on your certain death.

(2) Reflection on the unpredictability of the time of death

Since some die in their mother's womb, some die at the moment of birth, and you can see with your own eyes how the death of the elderly, middle-aged, and youth has no definite order, meditate by reflecting on the unpredictability of when you will die.

(3) Reflection on how, at the time of death, nothing except Dharma is of benefit

Thus when the time of death arrives—even if you possess great authority and power, abundant wealth, a large circle of friends, or heroic courage— nothing can avert it. [390] [Everyone] dies. And when you die, apart from the Dharma, nothing is of benefit. If you have engaged in Dharma practice your entire life, you will not regret it when death arrives, and because you will be confident of rebirth in a fortunate realm, your mind will be at ease. Therefore reflect and meditate, "I must undertake Dharma practice, and because the time of my death is not certain, I must undertake Dharma practice soon."

2. Practicing the second meditation

If you cling to the three realms, that is not renunciation.

The meaning of this line is as follows. If you cling to the cyclic existence of the three realms, even Dharma practice does not become a path to enlightenment. Therefore you need to abandon clinging to cyclic existence. The defects of cyclic existence are explained for this purpose. By seeing the entire cycle of existence as suffering, the thought to forsake it and seek liberation arises. To cultivate the realization of this thought, there is (a) the reflection on the defects of cyclic existence, and (b) the reflection on karma and its effects. [The purpose of the second reflection is] to understand the causality underpinning birth in the cycle of existence and the discipline regarding what is to be affirmed and what is to be rejected.

a. Reflection on the defects of cyclic existence

It is stated:

> The desire realm is afflicted with flaws;
> The form realm is flawed as well;
> Even the formless realm is flawed;
> Nirvana alone is flawless.[1053]

As stated here, any place you might be born in the three realms is flawed. It is stated:

> Hell denizens are impaired by the fires of hell,
> Hungry ghosts are impaired by hunger and thirst,
> Animals are impaired by devouring each other,
> Humans are impaired by life's brevity.
>
> The gods are impaired by their heedlessness—
> There is no joy ever in the cycle of existence,
> Not even as much as the tip of a needle![1054]

As this states, you should reflect, "No matter which of the three realms or the six classes of beings I am born into, I am bound within the nature of suffering; and whatever resources I enjoy, I remain only within the bounds of suffering. To gain freedom from this, I must engage in perfect Dharma practice that becomes a path to enlightenment." [391] To explain this [point] further, there are:

(1) Reflection on the suffering of suffering
(2) Reflection on the suffering of change
(3) Reflection on the suffering of pervasive conditioning

[(1) Reflection on the suffering of suffering]

The first has three:

(a) Reflection on the suffering of the hell realm
(b) Reflection on the suffering of hungry ghosts
(c) Reflection on the suffering of animals

(a) Reflection on the suffering of the hell realm

The first, the reflection on the suffering of the hell realm, is threefold:

(i) Reflection on the suffering of the cold hells
(ii) Reflection on the suffering of the hot hells
(iii)Reflection on the suffering of the random and adjoining hells

(i) Reflection on the suffering of the cold hells

The first has eight, and they are as follows: (1) In the *blistering hell* you are born in the crevices of mountains or glaciers, devoid of sunshine or protection, and extremely cold winds torment your body. Due to the bitter cold, your entire body becomes covered with blisters. (2) An intensification of frigidity bursts these blisters open, and they drip mucus and pus; thus there is the *popping blisters hell*. (3) Due to an even greater intensity of cold, you experience acute suffering and are forced to weep and cry out, "I am cold! I am cold," so this is known as the *crying out "I'm freezing" hell*. (4) Even greater frigidity afflicts you with so much pain you can't even scream aloud, so you emit from your throat a muffled "Alas!" Therefore this is known as the *moaning hell*. (5) A still greater intensity of cold makes you incapable of crying at all, and your entire body is reduced to a mass of shivering. This is known as the *clattering of teeth hell*. (6) Tormented by even more intensely bitter winds, the color of your skin turns blue and [your body] splits open into eight pieces. This is known as *splitting open like a water lily hell*. (7) Your skin, now blue, cracks open and is blown away by the winds, thus revealing the bare red flesh, which then splits into many pieces like a lotus. This is known as *splitting open like a lotus hell*. (8) Again, because of the bitter cold, your entire body, both exterior and interior, freeze over as solid as a rock. It splits into sixteen pieces and so on, and as the body's exterior cracks open, the internal organs—the intestines, viscera, and guts[1055]—each crack open and turn into something like a large lotus flower. This is known as *splitting open like a large lotus flower hell*.

Recognize the suffering of these [hells] and reflect upon them repeatedly. If you were to experience them, you would find them utterly unbearable. Think, "To ensure that nothing like these befall me, I must undertake a Dharma practice that will become a path to enlightenment." [392]

(ii) Reflection on the suffering of the hot hells

The second has eight: (1) The *reviving hell* is where, due to the power of your karma, you are born where the ground is burning iron. You have a delicate youthful body that you are acutely attached to, but whatever object you pick up turns into a weapon while everyone you see will appear as an enemy; everyone will attack each other with weapons, cutting them into pieces. Then, as a voice from the sky shouts, "Revive!" a cool breeze hits your body and revives it to its former delicate, youthful form [and the process begins all over again]. (2) The *black-lined hell* is where the hell guardians mark your body with 116 lines and cut it into pieces with a saw or an ax, causing unimaginable suffering. (3) The *crushing hell* is where your delicate youthful body is crushed like mustard seeds between mountains shaped like goat and sheep heads, causing extreme pain. (4) In the *howling hell,* as hell guardians chase you on the burning iron ground, you spy a one-story house and run toward it thinking you will be safe there. However, as you enter, the door shuts behind you, trapping you inside a burning metal house. There is no door you can open, nor is there any means of escape. As the fire burns, you are tormented by excruciating pain, compelling you to howl and wail for help. (5) The *great howling hell* has identical features to the preceding hell, except here the house has two stories. (6) The *hot hell* is where your body is pierced by the hell guardians with a spear from your anus to the crown of your head, and you suffer enormously. (7) The *extremely hot hell* is where your body is pierced with a trident from the anus to the crown and from the midpoint to the right and left arms, and you suffer desperately. (8) In the *unrelenting hell* you are burned amid the fire of the blazing iron ground, and your body and the flames become indistinguishable, such that one cannot say this is your body and that is the fire. The howling alone indicates the presence of a hell being.

(iii) Reflection on the suffering of the random and adjoining hells

The third has four, and in the first, (1) the *pit of embers,* which is on the edge of the eight hot hells, you are caught in pits filled with burning embers. All your limbs are being burned. [393] When you lift your right leg, the burning is healed, but your left leg is burned. And when you lift your left leg, it is healed, but the right is burned. Your internal organs, the intestines and viscera, are burned as well, and smoke emerges from your orifices. (2) In the *swamp of putrid filth* you roll around on a ground filled with putrid filth; all the openings of your sense organs become blocked by filth and you suffer in this manner. (3) The *road of razors* lies beyond the edge of the swamp of putrid filth. As you walk across a surface sprouting razors, your feet are rent to the bones, and you suffer in this manner. "And so on" includes the "forest of branches with razor leaves," where the trees have leaves made of razors and to which, by the force of your karma, you are drawn to seek shade from the scorching heat. As one stand below it, wind convulses the trees, causing the weapons to fall, slicing your limbs into pieces, and in this manner you suffer intensely. The tree of sharp glass mountains is where you have the wish to climb to the summit of a towering mountain. As you ascend, iron forks with eight or six sharp downward-facing points pierce your body, causing agonizing pain. As you arrive at the summit, crows and vultures poke out your eyes, slice your tongue, and gouge your brain, causing immense pain. As you descend the mountain hoping to return to the base, the sharp forks turn upward and pierce your body once again. Animals such as wolves, dogs, and foxes that live at the base of the mountain eat and tear flesh from your limbs, pulling them back and forth and slicing you to pieces. In this way you suffer inconceivably. The sufferings of having your body stretched with pegs on a burning iron ground, your tongue stretched by an iron peg and plowed over, and so on, are part of the random and adjoining hells. (4) The *boiling river of mud with no ford* is on the other side of the razor fields. Here your body is caught in a boiling mud that burns through both the exterior and the interior of your body, while the hell guardians keep vigil on the sides. [394] In this manner you suffer horribly.

Reflect on these sufferings and think, "To escape from these [sufferings], I must engage in a practice of sublime Dharma."

(b) Reflection on the suffering of the hungry ghosts

There are hungry ghosts with external obscurations, those with internal obscurations, and those with obscurations in relation to food and drink (also known as those obscured by obscuration). Thus there are three kinds of obscuration.

(i) With the first, due to miserliness and so on, you are born in the realm of the hungry ghosts, and though desperate with hunger and thirst, your eyes cannot perceive food or drink. Thinking a mountain of cooked rice and a vast expanse of water are in the distance, you approach these, and because of the long distance your body and mind become exhausted. When you arrive, what appeared to be a mountain of rice turns into a [mountain of] white stones or a large heap of whitish earth, and what previously looked like water turns out to be a mirage or a bluish plain or [a sea of blue] slate. Able to enjoy neither food nor drink, you suffer even more than before.

(ii) With an internal obscuration, in addition to the sufferings already described, as you finally take what little food and drink you can find, you are unable to get them through your mouth because it is too small, causing much pain through tearing and bleeding. Next [the food and drink] cannot get through your throat, which is as thin as a hair from a horse's tail. In addition, the food becomes prickly and tears your throat, causing sharp pain. And because your belly is as large as a the base of a mountain, even if food reaches it, the food cannot satisfy, thus perpetuating your misery.

(iii) Obscuration in relation to food and drink is the following: Wandering in all directions searching for food, you are terrorized and beaten by dominant hungry ghosts. Even if you find a little food, you suffer fear of theft, and as you eat what little food you have found, you suffer the pains described above of the food not getting through your mouth and so on. When food reaches your stomach, it turns into fire due to the force of your karma, and burns your intestines and viscera, reducing them to burning cinders. In this manner, you suffer greatly.

Reflect and meditate, "Though I may suffer intensely, until my karma is exhausted, I will continue to undergo such experiences of suffering. Therefore, in order not to be born as such a being, I must undertake a perfect Dharma practice that becomes a path to enlightenment." [395]

(c) Reflection on the suffering of the animals

Some dwell in oceans and some dwell in scattered habitats [above ground]. In the great oceans, creatures such as sea monsters equal the density of [a heap of] fermented grains of a potent beer, leading to the suffering of overcrowding, as one crushes another. Because the currents force them in all directions, they have no fixed dwellings, and as they cannot know what creatures they will meet or what friends they will make, they have no sense of being settled. Furthermore, the larger ones eat the smaller ones, and even the larger animals, such as the sea monsters, suffer from being pierced by sharp conches and so on. Those that live in darkness between the continents lack any light and cannot see one another. Because of overcrowding, one sits above the other, and this extreme lack of space causes constriction, rotting their bodies and breaking them into pieces, and they have no time even to search for food. In this manner, these animals suffer.

The animals [dwelling above ground] that are domesticated by humans suffer from being forced to carry loads beyond their capacity, having to plow fields, being milked, being chained with irons, being struck with rods and hooks, being exploited through various activities, and eventually being slaughtered for their meat. Or else they are sold and kept in captivity and suffer being killed for the sake of pearls, wool, bones, and skin. Wild animals not dependent on human beings suffer having no fixed habitat, being hunted with arrows for the sake of their meat, being chased by dogs and forced to jump off crevices and cliffs, so that even if they escape being struck by a weapon, they are killed and caught nonetheless.

Reflect upon these specific sufferings as well as the general animal suffering of being ignorant and confused. Meditate by reflecting, "I must undertake a practice of perfect Dharma."

(2) Reflection on the suffering of change

The suffering of change is illustrated by the lives of the gods. Due to their karma, gods can cause clothes and beautiful houses to appear simply by wishing. They enjoy limitless pleasures, such as the pleasures of the goddesses. However, when the five early portents of death and the signs of imminent death appear, their mental pain is more acute than even the sufferings of the hells. After death, even the chief among the gods, such as Indra, [396] can be born in the human realm as a lowly servant and so on. Even the gods of the sun and moon, whose residence once illuminated the four continents, can be reborn in the darkness between continents and there suffer being unable to see even the stretching and gripping of their own fingers.

In the case of human beings, someone articulate and expressive may become incoherent; the rich may become poor. You encounter aggressors or fear such encounters; you are separated from loved ones or fear such separation; you fail to obtain what you seek; your hopes end in failure; and so on. The possibilities for suffering are inconceivable.

Demigods, too, suffer from combat and armed attacks, severed limbs, and a propensity for rage. Their envy toward the prosperity of the gods also induces inconceivable mental suffering.

(3) Reflection on the suffering of pervasive conditioning

Human beings pursue infinite tasks but never find an end to them. Those efforts go to waste, and people spend their lives in constant preparation, thinking, "I must do this and that." Since these pursuits are endless, they arrive at death's door with intense suffering, for they have failed to realize their goals. The rich suffer being robbed of their possessions, either by thieves or by others through a show of force, and the poor suffer extreme fatigue as a result of scavenging. Thus you should reflect and meditate, "Whichever of the six classes of beings I am born as within the three realms, none is outside the bounds of suffering. I must practice perfect Dharma to ensure that I do not experience such sufferings."

b. Reflection on karma and its effects

Birth in cyclic existence, which is characterized by the sufferings described, results from nonvirtuous actions; therefore you must relinquish these. In brief, you should meditate by reflecting, "I will forsake all nonvirtuous acts and accumulate even a single virtuous act to the best of my ability." To elaborate further, there are:

(1) Reflection on nonvirtuous karma
(2) Reflection on virtuous karma
(3) Reflection on neutral karma [397]

(1) Reflection on nonvirtuous karma

The first has three parts:

(a) Reflection on the nature of nonvirtuous karma
(b) Reflection on its effects
(c) Advice for relinquishing nonvirtuous acts

(a) Reflection on the nature of nonvirtuous karma

The first is tenfold. *Taking a life* means killing a sentient being, from a small ant to a human or a human-to-be, with full cognizance and motivated by one of the three poisons. *Taking what is not given* refers to stealing what others consider to be their own, including even a husk of a grain. *Sexual misconduct* refers to engaging in sexual intercourse with women who belong to others (excepting those procured as a sexual partner through payment), with those upholding the victorious banner of Dharma such as nuns, with those who have taken a daylong vow of celibacy, with those under a guardianship such as that of their parents, and even with your own partner if it is during daytime hours.[1056] These are the three nonvirtuous actions of body.

Telling lies refers to deceiving others and changing their perceptions by false words and actions, motivated by attachment. *Divisive speech* is speech that drives a wedge between people; its motive is the wish to sow dissension among close friends and family members. *Harsh speech* refers to barking hurtful words to others while stirred by anger, whether or not what you say is true. *Frivolous speech* means indulging in meaningless babble, thus hindering the spiritual activities of self and others. There are thus four nonvirtuous actions of speech.

Covetousness refers to desire for the wealth of others, or the wish to possess others' resources and knowledge. These thoughts are motivated by attachment. *Harmful intent* refers to malicious wishes, motivated by anger, for someone to suffer intensely at the hands of others. *Wrong views* refers to views doubting the existence of the Three Jewels and views doubting whether virtuous acts cause happiness and nonvirtuous acts cause suffering, even though the teachers have said so. These are the three nonvirtuous mental acts. Thus there are [altogether] ten [nonvirtuous actions].

(b) Reflection on its effects

As for the effects, there are two: the immediate effects and the ultimate effects. [398] The immediate effects include a short life span, poverty, an antagonistic marriage, insults, disharmonious friendships, unpleasant news, mistrust due to allegations that your words cannot be trusted, unfulfilled hopes, grave dangers, and distorted views. As for the ultimate effects, a slight nonvirtuous act throws you into the animal realm, a middling nonvirtuous act casts you into the hungry ghost realm, and a great nonvirtuous act propels you into the hells.

(c) Advice for relinquishing nonvirtuous acts

The consequence of engaging in these nonvirtuous acts while motivated by the three poisons is nothing but the three lower realms. Therefore mentally vow to avoid these acts even at the cost of your life, and then relinquish doing them.

(2) Reflection on virtuous karma

The second, the reflection on virtuous karma, has the following:

    (a) Reflection on the nature of virtuous karma
    (b) Reflection on its effects
    (c) Advice for cultivating virtuous acts

(a) Reflection on the nature of virtuous karma

By relinquishing the ten nonvirtuous actions described earlier, engage, to the best of your ability, in the ten virtuous acts, motivated by nonattachment, nonanger, and nondelusion.

(b) Reflection on its effects

There are two effects: immediate and ultimate. The immediate effects include long life, abundant resources, a compatible spouse, renown in all directions, harmonious friendships, sharp sense faculties, trusted words, fulfilled hopes, freedom from danger, and thoroughly pure views. As for the ultimate effects, engaging in the ten virtuous actions to a slight, middling, and great degree, you attain the enlightenment of disciple and of self-realized one, and the unexcelled enlightenment [of buddhahood], respectively.

(c) Advice for cultivating virtuous acts

Reflect, "By engaging in virtuous deeds I will achieve one of the three enlightenments. Even the state of disciple would free me from the dangers of cyclic existence and the lower realms. I must therefore accumulate virtuous karma to the best of my ability."

(3) Reflection on neutral karma

The third, reflection on neutral karma, also has three parts. The first, the nature of the karma, refers to eating, creating artifacts, and so on with neither virtuous nor nonvirtuous thoughts as motivation. Second, the effects, means joyfully embracing neutral crafts incapable of producing either happiness or suffering.[1057] Third, you can transform these [neutral activities] into virtuous karma through the power of your motivation. Therefore, when eating, reflect that you are nourishing the tiny insects within your body, and also that by nurturing this body, you [are enabling it to] engage in study, reflection, and so on. When engaging in such activities as walking and sitting, think that you are doing so for the sake of the sublime Dharma. Or else visualize the enlightened buddhas and bodhisattvas on your right, thinking that you are showing them the best side of your body, which is the right side, and circumambulating them as you walk, and so on.

3. Practicing the third meditation

If you cling to self-interest, you are not a bodhisattva.

Having seen the entire cycle of existence as suffering, as described above, you may have engaged in virtuous deeds of small, middling, and great degrees in order to gain freedom from it. You may achieve the state of a disciple or a self-realized one, but at these levels your personal welfare is still not fully accomplished: You are not capable of great altruistic deeds and [still] possess hindrances to attaining complete buddhahood.

Do not aspire in this manner therefore for yourself alone. Seek instead to attain buddhahood for the benefit of all beings, which cannot come about from incomplete or incorrect conditions. For example, during the winter, when heat and moisture are lacking, if you plant rice seeds, they will not grow. Similarly, if while wishing for rice crops you sow barley seeds, you cannot reap a harvest of rice. However, when the cause—rice seeds—and the conditions—heat and moisture—are present, rice will grow for those who desire a harvest of rice. In the same way, it has been stated, perfect enlightenment originates from its cause—compassion—and from its root—the awakening mind—and it is perfected by its conditions—the skillful means. [400]

To implement the meaning of this statement, there are the following:

    a. Meditation on loving-kindness
    b. Meditation on compassion
    c. Meditation on the awakening mind
    d. Training in their conduct

a. Meditation on loving-kindness

The first, meditation on loving-kindness, has four parts: meditation on friends and family, meditation on neutral people, meditation on your enemies, and meditation on all sentient beings. The first in turn has three: (1) recognizing [all beings as] your mother, (2) recollecting their kindness, and (3) cultivating loving-kindness toward them.

(1) Recognizing all beings as your mother

For the first, take your own mother as the example. She is not only your mother in the present life, she has been your mother in many lives. It is stated:

> Even if you were to count beads the size of *kolāsita* nuts,
> The earth will fail to measure the extent of your mothers.[1058]

And also:

> The amount of milk fed to me by one being
> While serving as my mother cannot be found;
> Not even the four great oceans [can match it].
> The horses and elephants given as gifts
> By one being while serving as my father
> Transcend even [those in] the world of Brahma.[1059]

(2) Recollecting their kindness

The second, recollection of their kindness, is as follows: Every time a sentient being has been your mother, she has done you immeasurable kindness. For example, after conceiving you in her womb, she suffered from the weight of her body and fatigue. At the time of delivery, she endured such pain as though her mind and body were being torn apart. After birth, when you were incapable of speech and looked like an earthworm, she nurtured you with a tender heart, looked after you with loving eyes, fed you nutritious food with her tongue, cleaned your excrement with her hands, picked you up in her ten fingers, and provided you with food and clothing to the best of her ability. She protected you from all harm and injury, and as you grew older she gave you material possessions she had accumulated at the cost of her life. She taught you all kinds of knowledge, such as reading and writing. In brief, reflect upon all her acts of kindness in protecting you from all possible harm.

(3) Cultivation of loving-kindness

> To bring about beings' welfare,
> This is called great loving-kindness.[1060]

The definition of loving-kindness is "a mental state that wants sentient beings to enjoy happiness." Combine this with the awakening mind by thinking "I will enable my kind mothers to possess the cause of happiness." Combine this with intention by thinking "How I wish that they could possess the cause of happiness." And combine this with aspiration by thinking "May they possess the cause of happiness." [401] In this manner, engage in meditation free of distraction, and express these [thoughts] in words as well.

Just as you recognize your real-life mother as your mother, recollect her kindness, and cultivate loving-kindness for her, shift your focus and do the same toward the neutral people in your life, toward your enemies, and finally toward all sentient beings. When you become trained well in meditation on loving-kindness, the power of this will cause compassion to arise. For it is stated:

> Loving-kindness is the sap of the compassion [tree].[1061]

b. Meditation on compassion

To meditate on compassion, it is stated:

> To thoroughly protect those with suffering,
> This is called great compassion.[1062]

The definition of great compassion is "a mental state that is unable to bear the sight of the suffering of its objects and wishes them to be free of suffering." For this, too, there is the meditation on friends and family, the meditation on neutral people who are neither friends nor enemies, the meditation on enemies, and the meditation on all sentient beings. The first in turn has three parts: (1) recognition of [all beings as] your mother, (2) recollection of their kindness, and (3) cultivation of loving-kindness. These should be undertaken just as they were in the context of meditation on loving-kindness.

Meditation on compassion is as follows: For example, whether she is alive or dead, vividly visualize your own mother in front of you and reflect, "Tragic indeed is it that my kind mother has been afflicted with suffering and bereft of happiness. She must be freed from suffering and its causes. Observing her state of being, I see she possesses suffering and its causes and remains at their mercy. How sad indeed! I will therefore free her from suffering." Meditate on this by combining it with the awakening mind and so on,[1063] as in the context of meditation on loving-kindness.

Then shift your focus to the neutral people in your life, to your enemies, and finally to all sentient beings in general, and meditate until authentic, spontaneous compassion arises in you. When compassion arises in you in this manner, its power will cause the awakening mind to arise. For it is stated:

> Compassion is accepted as the root.[1064]

c. Meditation on the awakening mind exchanging self and others

It is stated:

> May the sufferings of all beings ripen upon me;
> Through my virtues may they all achieve happiness.[1065]

As stated here, you should recite orally, and contemplate from the depth of your heart as well, the following: "May whatever suffering and mental unhappiness that all sentient beings equal to space possess now ripen upon me. May all sentient beings obtain whatever virtues, happiness, and advantages I possess." [402]

d. Training in their conduct

As for training in the conduct of a bodhisattva, generally speaking this means forsaking harm to others and, as much as you can, trying to help them. Specifically, you enhance yourself through practicing the six perfections and you enhance others through the four factors of attracting others.

Elaborations on implementing these are found in the *Ākāśagarbha Sutra,* the *Compendium of Trainings, A Guide to the Bodhisattva's Way of Life,* and the advice to a king entitled the *Precious Garland.*[1066]

4. Practicing the fourth meditation

If grasping arises, it is not the view.

The meaning of this line is as follows: Even if the conventional awakening mind has arisen well, if you grasp at self-existence, you will fall into the abyss of absolutism and nihilism and will be unable to gain freedom. As an antidote to grasping at things and their symbols, you need to cultivate tranquil abiding and penetrative insight. It is stated:

> Knowing that through insight, perfectly endowed
> With tranquillity, the faults of the afflictions are destroyed....[1067]

This has three parts:

a. The meditative practice of tranquil abiding
b. The meditative practice of penetrative insight
c. The meditative practice of their union

a. The meditative practice of tranquil abiding

The first is as follows: Sit on a comfortable cushion in a quiet and pleasant environment that is within the dominion of a spiritual king, free of physical danger, and devoid of such thorns of concentration as the traffic of people moving about, excessive noise, and so on. [Then,] preceded by taking refuge and generating the awakening mind, which are preliminaries to all sessions, sit with your legs crossed in the vajra [lotus] position. With your hands in the meditative gesture, tongue touching the upper palate, neck slightly bent, spine upright, and your eyes in an appropriate degree of openness, engage in meditation. On this point, it is stated:

> Abiding in perfect truth,
> Place your mind in the mind and....[1068]

As instructed here, place your mind single-pointedly on the object of focus, whether external or internal; this is tranquil abiding. The master

Bodhibhadra the elder, in his *Chapter on the Requisite Conditions of Meditative Absorption,*[1069] speaks of two types of tranquil abiding—one externally oriented and [403] one internally oriented. In the first you focus on an external object, such as a pillar or a black pebble, and place your mind on it, directing your attention single-pointedly to it. "Internally oriented" is what is indicated in the line "Cease the flow of thoughts of the three times":[1070] you don't dwell on the past, anticipate the future, or construct the present, and relinquishing distractions to the objects, you observe the mind's own nature and place your attention upon it single-pointedly.

The *King of Meditation Sutra*[1071] presents this [tranquil abiding] on the basis of focusing on an image of the Buddha. Both this, as well the cultivation on the basis of focusing on a pebble mentioned above, can be used to develop single-pointed abiding. Nevertheless, focusing on an image of the Buddha serves also as a recollection of the Buddha and therefore creates greater merit.

For this you should visualize Buddha Śākyamuni in front of you, seated on a cushion of lotus and moon disk upon a throne of various precious stones. His body is the color of refined gold. His right hand is in the gesture of pressing the earth while his left hand is in the gesture of meditative equipoise. Clad in saffron robes, he is seated in the cross-legged vajra position. Meditate by focusing your attention on this image, and on his forelock in particular. Alternatively, the master said, you can visualize Amitābha as your focus. His body is red, and his hands are in the gesture of meditative equipoise. His seat and so on is the same as described for Buddha Śākyamuni. Cultivating tranquil abiding in this way prior to seeking penetrative insight is the meaning of the phrase "Search for tranquil abiding first."[1072]

As you become well acquainted with tranquil abiding, your mind becomes capable of abiding on a chosen object of meditation for months and even years. This is not sufficient, however. You must also practice penetrative insight, which is the antidote that eradicates the afflictions. *Penetrative insight* is the awareness that—through analyzing the ultimate mode of being of external and internal phenomena using the wisdom that discriminates the individual characteristics of phenomena—cognizes them to be devoid of [all] extremes, such as existence and nonexistence, and absolutism and nihilism. Tranquil abiding, which was explained earlier, is the method for ensuring the single-pointed abiding of the mind. Later, however, you must use tranquil abiding to place your mind single-pointedly on the very point seen through penetrative insight.

b. *The meditative practice of penetrative insight*

The meditative practice of penetrative insight has three parts:

(1) Establishing the appearances[1073] of objects as mental constructs
(2) Establishing perceptions as illusions
(3) Establishing illusions as devoid of intrinsic existence

(1) Establishing the appearances of objects as mental constructs

The first is as follows: Every object that appears [404]— horses, elephants, men and women, walls, vases, woolen fabric, and so on—none of these diverse appearances comes into being from no cause; they are not created by a diviner or by the god Īśvara, they do not originate from the four elements or from atoms, nor are they conjured by the buddhas, and so on. They come into being due to the power of propensities for this or that, impressions that have been left upon your mind since beginningless time. Meditate that mind is the creator of all of these and that, apart from the mind, there is no other creator.

(2) Establishing perceptions as illusions

As for the second, it is stated:

> The magician conjures forms,
> Creating horses, elephants, and various carriages.
> Though appearing real, none exists as it appears.
> Understand that this is true, too, of all phenomena.[1074]

As stated here, all the diverse appearances of objects described above are dreamlike and illusionlike. Like a dream, even though you undergo various experiences of suffering, when you wake up, you realize that these experiences were unreal. Meditate by contemplating, "They appear as mere conventional truths; they are like the reflection of forms in a mirror," until ascertainment arises.

(3) Establishing illusions as devoid of intrinsic existence

The third is as follows: Meditate by reflecting, "These appearances of objects resemble illusions. They arise as diverse appearances merely on the conventional level; therefore appearance itself is not being negated. When analyzed, however, not even a thickness of a hair split into a hundredth fraction is established on the ultimate level."

c. The meditative practice of their union

Having affirmed the points in their respective sequence, such as establishing the appearance of objects as constructed by the mind and so on, realize and ascertain emptiness, which transcends every extreme of conceptual elaboration. With your mind abiding single-pointedly, meditate on [the point] where the mind that cognizes in such manner and the object, which is the ultimate mode of being, have fused indivisibly into a single taste, like water poured into water or the absorption of melted butter into melted butter. As you persistently cultivate familiarity with this, your acquaintance will grow. Driven by [your understanding of] emptiness, compassion will arise toward those sentient beings who have failed to understand this to be so. The delusion of grasping at substantial entities will be dislodged, and the state of perfect buddhahood—the embodiment of three buddha bodies—known as the "dawning of delusions as wisdom" will become manifest.

C. The conclusion: Sealing with dedication

The sealing with dedication should be performed at the end of all sessions. [405] What are to be dedicated here are the virtues of your practice of the profound meditative absorptions. Whatever roots of virtue, such as these, you and others may have created that fall within the class of conditioned things, you should dedicate them all. Also bring to mind the ground of the Buddha [mind], which is thoroughly cognizant of all the aspects of dedication. In terms of objective, dedicate this for the benefit of all sentient beings equal to the expanse of space. While recognizing these aspects as dreams and illusions and first calling out the attention [of the buddhas], you should perform dedications, such as the following one found in the scriptures, to the best of your capacity:

Through this virtue may all beings
Accumulate merit and wisdom;
May they attain the two sublime buddha bodies,
Which arise from merit and wisdom.[1075]

Colophon

Urged by the great knowledge bearer, the tantric adept Künga Lekpa, who is accomplished in the precious knowledge of numerous scriptures and realizations and, after having listened twice to this teaching from the all-knowing spiritual master Künga Sangpo, the monk Künga Lekpai Rinchen—who takes upon his crown [even] the particles of dust under the feet of this sublime teacher—penned these notes. The notes were then submitted to the teacher, the spiritual master, for his perusal to ensure their accuracy. Wönpo Losal, known also as Drakpa Gyaltsen, who is devoted to this teaching and has keen admiration for it, procured the paper.

May it be auspicious!

Table of Tibetan Transliteration

PHONETIC SPELLING	WYLIE TRANSLITERATION
Amdo	A mdo
Bangala	Bhang ga la
Bari Lotsāwa	Ba ri lo tsa ba
Bawa	Ba va
Belpo Che	'Bal po che
Ben Gungyal	'Ban gung rgyal
Bodongwa	Bo dong ba
Butön Rinchen Drup	Bu ston Rin chen grub
Chak Lotsāwa Chöjé Pal	Chag Lo tsā ba Chos rje dpal
Chakshingwa	Lcags zhing ba (Lcags shing ba)
Chegom Dzongpa	Lce sgom Rdzong pa
Chekawa	'Chad ka ba
Cheka	'Chad ka
Chekapa Yeshé Dorjé	'Chad ka pa Ye shes rdo rje
Chenga Lodrö Gyaltsen	Spyan snga Blo gros rgyal mtshan
Chenga Rinpoché	Spyan snga Rin po che
Chengawa (Chengapa)	Spyan snga ba (Spyan snga pa)
Chil	Spyil
Chilbupa, Sé (Kyilbu, Sé)	Spyil bu pa, Se (Skil bu pa, Se)
Chim	Mchims
Chim Namkha Drak	Mchims Nam mkha' grags
Chiwokyé	Spyi bo skyes
Chöding	Chos sding
Chögyal Phakpa	Chos rgyal 'phags pa
Chöjé Gyalwa Sangpo	Chos rje Rgyal ba bzang po
Chöjé Sönam Rinchen	Chos rje Bsod nams rin chen

Chomden Rikral	Bcom ldan rigs ral
Chözong	Chos rdzong
Chudakzin	Chu bdag 'dzin
Dakpo Lhajé	Dvags po Lha rje
Dampa Sangyé	Dam pa sangs rgyas
Dergé	Sde dge
Dharma Rinchen	Dhar ma rin chen
Dharma Yönten	Dhar ma yon tan
Dingri	Ding ri
Dokhar	Mdo mkhar
Dölpa Sherap Gyatso	Dol pa Shes rab rgya mtsho
Dombipa	Dom bhi pa
Dönshap (Dönyö Shap)	Don zhabs (Don yod zhabs)
Dönyö Shakpa	Don yod zhags pa
Dorjé Wangchuk	Rdo rje dbang phyug
Drai Sothangpa	Gra'i so thang pa
Drakmarwa	Brag dmar ba
Drakpa Gyaltsen	Grags pa rgyal mtshan
Drakphukpa	Brag phug pa
Draktön Sherap Rinchen	Brag ston Shes rab rin chen
Dre	'Dres
Dreksum	Breg gsum
Dreurap	Dre'u rab
Drogön Palden Yeshé	'Gro mgon Dpal ldan ye shes
Drompa	'Brom pa
Dromtönpa	'Brom ston pa
Drowa Sangpo	'Gro ba bzang po
Dzechenpa	'Dzed chen pa
Dzeng Wangchuk Gyaltsen	'Dzeng Dbang phyug rgyal mtshan
Gampopa	Sgam po pa
Gangma Githok	Gangs ma gi tog
Gegong	Dge gong
Geluk	Dge lugs
Gendün Drup	Dge 'dun grub
Geshe Chöbar	Dge bshes Chos 'bar
Geshe Drolungpa	Dge bshes Gro lung pa
Geshe Dromtönpa	Dge bshes 'Brom ston pa

Geshe Ngaripa	Dge bshes Mnga' ris pa
Geshe Nyek	Dge bshes Snyegs
Gewachen	Dge ba chen
Godrakpa (Kodrakpa)	Go drag pa (Ko brag pa)
Gongkar	Gong dkar
Gönpapa (Gönpawa)	Dgon pa pa (Dgon pa ba)
Gönpawa Wangchuk Gyaltsen	Dgon pa ba Dbang phyug rgyal mtshan
Goram Sönam Sengé	Go rams Bsod nams seng ge
Götsangpa Gönpo Dorjé	Rgod tshang pa Mgon po rdo rje
Gya Chakriwa	Rgya Lcags ri ba
Gya Gomriwa Shikpo	Rgya sgom ri ba Zhig po
Gyajang	Rgya byang
Gyakhar Ri	Rgya mkhar ris
Gyal Lhakhang	Rgyal lha khang
Gyaltsen Pal	Rgyal mtshan dpal
Gyalwa Sangpo	Rgyal ba bzang po
Gyalwa Yangönpa	Rgyal ba Yang dgon pa
Gyamapa Tashi Gyaltsen	Rgya ma pa Bkra shis rgyal mtshan
Gyatön Jangchup Gyaltsen	Rgya ston Byang chub rgyal mtshan
Gyatso Balap	Rgy mtsho rba rlabs
Gyatsoi Dül	Rgya mtsho'i rdul
Gyen	Gyen
Gyergom Sangyé Wön	Gyer sgom Sangs rgyas dbon
Gyergom Shikpo	Gyer sgom Zhig po
Hakpo	Hakpo
Hortön Namkha Pal	Hor ston Nam mkha' dpal
Jamgön Amé	'Jam mgon A mes
Jamgön Kongtrül Lodrö Thayé	'Jam mgon kong sprul Blo gros mtha' yas
Jamyang Khyentsé	'Jam dbyangs mkhyen brtse
Jangchup Ö	Byang chub 'od
Jangchup Rinchen	Byang chub rin chen
Jangpa Sherap	Byang pa Shes rab
Jayülwa (Jayülpa)	Bya yul ba (Bya yul pa)
Jayülwa Shönu Ö	Bya yul ba Gzhon nu 'od
Jetari	Dze ta ri
Jetsün Ḍombipa	Rje btsun Ḍom bhi pa

Jetsün Matipa	Rje btsun Ma ti pa
Jetsün Ravaintapa	Rje btsun Ra bain ta pa
Joden Lungshöpa	Jo ldan Klung shod pa
Jömo Keru	'Jod mo ke ru
José	Jo sras
Jotsün Rinjang	Jo btsun Rin byang
Jowo	Jo bo
Kadam	Bka' gdams
Kagyü	Bka' brgyud
Kalden Gyatso	Skal ldan rgya mtsho.
Kamapa	Ka ma pa
Kangyur	Bka' 'gyur
Karmapa	Kar ma pa
Khamlungpa	Khams lung pa
Kharak	Kha rag
Kharak Gomchung	Kha rag Sgom chung
Khedrup Chöjé	Mkhas grub Chos rje
Khedrup Sangyé Yeshé	Mkhas grub Sangs rgyas ye shes
Khenchen Dewa Jamchenpa	Mkhan chen Bde ba byams chen pa
Khenchen Lhodrakpa	Mkhan chen Lho brag pa
Khenpo Chöden	Mkhan po Chos ldan
Khenpo Martön	Mkhan po Dmar ston
Khenpo Sherap Dorjé	Mkhan po Shes rab rdo rje
Khenpo Shönu Jangchup	Mkhan po Gzhon nu byang chub
Khenpowa	Mkhan po ba
Könchok Bang	Dkon mchog 'bangs
Könchok Gyaltsen	Dkon mchog rgyal mtshan
Künga Gyaltsen	Kun dga' rgyal mtshan
Künga Lekpai Rinchen	Kun dga' legs pa
Künga Nyingpo	Kun dga' snying po
Künga Sangpo	Kung dga' bzang po
Kyeuchung	Khe'u chung
Kyimé	Skyi smad
Kyormo Lung	Skyor mo lung
Lama Dampa Shönu Gyaltsen	Bla ma dam pa Gzhon nu rgyal mtshan
Lama Könchok Jangchup Pal	Bla ma dkon mchog Byang chub dpal

Lama Wangpo	Bla ma Dbang po
Lama Yeshé Shap	Bla ma Ye shes zhabs
Langlungpa	Glang lung pa
Langri Thangpa	Glang ri thang pa
Langthang (monastery)	Glang thang
Langthangpa	Glang thang pa
Lechen Kunga Gyaltsen	Las chen Kun dga' rgyal mtshan
Lha Chakriwa	Lha lcags ri ba
Lha Chenpo	Lha chen po
Lha Drowai Gönpo	Lha 'Gro ba'i mgon po
Lhadingwa	Lha sdings ba
Lhari Tsagyepa	Lha ri rtsa brgyad pa
Lhasa Shöl	Lha sa zhol
Lhodrak	Lho brag
Ligom Shönu Drak	Li sgom Gzhon nu grags
Loden Sherap	Blo ldan shes rab
Lodrö Jungné	Blo gros 'byung gnas
Loi Gönpa	Lo'i dgon pa
Lo Lotsāwa	Glo Lo tsā ba
Longdöl Lama	Klong rdol Bla ma
Longdöl Ngawang Lobsang	Klong rdol Ngag dbang blo bzang
Lopön Chöchok	Slob dpon Chos mchog
Lopön Lha	Slob dpon Lha
Lopön Shākya Tashi	Slob dpon Shā kya bkra shis
Lopön Shang	Slob dpon Zhang
Lopön Tsültrim Pal	Slob dpon Tshul khrims dpal
Lugu	Lu gu
Lumpipa	Lum pi pa
Lungmepa	Lung smad pa
Lungnangpa Khenpo Rinpoché	Lung nang pa Mkhan po Rin po che
Lungshö Gegong	Klung shod Dge gong
Maldrowa	Mal gro ba
Martön Chökyi Gyalpo	Dmar ston Chos kyi rgyal po
Matön	Rma ston
Migmang	Mig mang
Mipham Chöjé	Mi pham Chos rje
Mön	Mon

Mü	Mus
Mukhyüzin	Mu khyud 'dzin
Naljorpa Amé Jangchup	Rnal 'byor pa A mes byang chub
Naljorpa Amé Shap	Rnal 'byor pa A mes zhabs
Naljorpa Chö Yungdrung	Rnal 'byor pa Chos gyung drung
Naljorpa Sherap Dorjé	Rnal 'byor pa Shes rab rdo rje
Namdak Tsuknor	Rnam dag gtsug nor
Namkha Pal, Hortön	Nam mkha' dpal, Hor ston
Narthang	Snar thang
Neusur	Sne'u zur
Neusurpa Yeshé Bar	Sne'u zur pa Ye shes 'bar
Ngaripa	Mgna' ris pa
Ngok Lekpai Sherap	Rngog Legs pa'i shes rab
Ngülchu Dharmabhadra	Dngul chu Dhar ma bha dra
Ngülchu Thokmé Sangpo	Dngul chu Thogs med bzang po
Nupa Rikzin Drak	Nub pa Rig 'dzin grags
Nup Chölungpa Sönam Rinchen	Snubs chos lung pa Bsod nams rin chen
Nyak Sengé Drak	Gnyags Seng ge grags
Nyal	Gnyal
Nyalpa Yönten Sherap	Gnyal pa Yon tan shes rab
Nyang Chakshingwa	Nyang Lcags shing ba
Nyawo	Nya bo
Nyek brothers	Snyegs mched gnyis
Nyen	Mnyan
Nyenpopa	Nyan po pa
Öjopa (Öjowa)	'Od 'jo pa ('Od 'jo ba)
Paṇchen Śākyaśrī	Paṇ chen Shā kya shri
Paṇchen Sönam Drakpa	Paṇ chen Bsod nams grags pa
Pawo Rölpa	Dpa' bo rol pa
Pawo Tsuklak Trengwa	Dpa' bo Gtsug lag phreng ba
Phabongkha Dechen Nyingpo	Pha bong kha Bde chen snying po
Phakmo Drupa	Phag mo gru pa
Phegöl Rapjom	Phas rgol rab 'joms
Phenpo	'Phan po
Phuchungwa	Phu chung ba

Pön	Dpon
Potowa	Po to ba
Radreng	Ra sgreng
Radrengpa (Radrengwa)	Ra sgreng pa
Ralo Dorjé	Ra lo rdo rje
Rampa Lhadingpa	Ram pa lha sdings pa
Rampopa (Rampowa)	Ram po pa (Ram po ba)
Rangjung Dorjé	Rang byung rdo rje
Rinchen Drakmarwa	Rin chen Bbrag dmar ba
Rinchen Drakpa Shenyen	Rin chen grags pa Bshes gnyen
Rinchen Jungné	Rin chen 'byung gnas
Rinchen Lama	Rin chen bla ma
Rinchen Naburpa (Rinchen Naburwa)	Rin chen Sna bur pa
Rinchen Sangpo	Rin chen bzang po
Rinpoché Sönam Drakpa	Rin po che Bsod nams grags pa
Rirap Gyalpo	Ri rab rgyal po
Ritrö Rechen	Ri khrod ras chen
Rohipa	Ro hi pa
Sachen Kunga Nyingpo	Sa chen Kun dga' snying po
Sakyapa	Sa skya pa
Sakya Paṇḍita (Sapaṇ)	Sa skya Paṇḍita (Sa paṇ)
Samtsé Rinsangpa	Zam tse Rin sangs pa
Sangchenpa	Zangs chen pa
Sang Gönpa	Zang dgon pa
Sangphupa	Gsang phu pa
Sangpoi Pal	Bzang po'i dpal
Sangyé Gompa (Sengé Kyap)	Sangs rgyas bsgom pa (Seng ge skyabs)
Sangyé Gompa Jangchup Kyap	Sangs rgyas bsgom pa Byang chub skyabs
Seberé	Se be re
Sé Chilbu Chökyi Gyaltsen	Se Chil bu Chos kyi rgyal msthan
Sengé Gyaltsen	Seng ge rgyal mtshan
Serlingpa	Gser gling pa
Serthok	Ser thog
Serwakha	Ser ba kha

Shākya Chokden	Shā kya mchog ldan
Shang Drakarwa	Zhang Brag dkar ba
Shang Köchok Pal	Zhang Dkon mchog dpal
Shang Drakmarwa	Zhang Brag dmar ba
Shang Ratnaguru	Zhang Rat na gu ru
Shangshung	Zhang zhung
Shangtön Chökyi Lama	Zhang ston Chos kyi bla ma
Sharawa	Sha ra ba
Shawo Gangpa (Shapo Gangpa)	Sha bo sgang pa (Sha po sgang pa)
Shawopa (abbr. Shawo Gangpa)	Sha bo pa
Sherapbar	Shes rab 'bar
Sherap Sangpo	Shes rab bzang po
Sherap Sönam	Shes rab bsod nams
Shetön Jangbar	Gshe ston Byang 'bar
Sho	Gzho
Shönu Drak	Gzhon nu grags
Shönu Gyalchok	Gzhon nu rgyal mchog
Shönu Samten	Gzhon nu bsam gtan
Sönam Gyaltsen	Bsod nams rgyal mtshan
Sönam Lhai Wangpo	Bsod nams lha'i dbang po
Sönam Rinchen	Bsod nams rin chen
Sönamzin	Bsod nams 'dzin
Sumpa Lotsāwa	Sum pa lo tsa ba
Sumpa Yeshé Paljor	Sum pa Ye shes dpal 'byor
Tengyur	Bstan 'gyur
Thokmé Sangpo	Thogs med bzang po
Thöpa Ka	Thos pa dka'
Thuken Chökyi Nyima	Thu'u kan Chos kyi nyi ma
Tongkhün	Stong khun
Tönpa Dadrak	Ston pa Zla grags
Tönpa Dharma Bar	Ston pa Dhar ma 'bar
Tönpa Rinpoché	Ston pa Rin po che
Trijang Rinpoché	Khri byang Rin po che
Trophu Lotsāwa Jampa Pal	Khro phu Lo tsā ba Byams pa dpal
Tsang	Gtsang
Tsangpa Rinpoché	Gtsang pa Rin po che
Tsarna	Mtshar sna
Tsipkyi Mukhyü	Rtsibs kyi mu khyud

Tsöndü	Brtson 'grus
Tsongkhapa	Tsong kha pa
Tsotrangwa	Mtsho 'phrang ba
Tsültrim Bar	Tshul khrims 'bar
Tsültrim Dar	Tshul khrims dar
Tsültrim Pal	Tshul khrims dpal
Uru	Dbu ru
Wönpo Losal	Dbon po Blo gsal
Yagepa	Ya gad pa
Yakdé Paṇchen	G.yag sde Paṇ chen
Yangönpa, Gyalwa	Yang dgon pa, Rgyal ba
Yarlung	Yar lung
Yeshé Döndrup	Ye shes don grub
Yeshé Jangchup	Ye shes byang chub
Yeshé Shap	Ye shes zhabs
Yongzin Yeshé Gyaltsen	Yongs 'dzin Ye shes rgyal mtshan
Yortsang	Gyor rtsang
Zemey Rinpóche	Dze smad Rin po che

Notes

1 For a clear and succinct explanation of the theoretical understanding of the process of such transformation of the mind and its basis, see H.H. the Dalai Lama, *Transforming the Mind,* pp. 1–19.

2 Tib. *theg pa chen po'i blo sbyong* (pronounced *thekpa chenpoi lojong*). In fact, our volume contains a beautiful, succinct exposition of the "root lines" of mind training entitled *Root Lines of Mahayana Mind Training* (see text 4).

3 This story of how Chekawa sought hard and found the mind training teaching through Sharawa is often repeated in the later commentarial literature on mind training.

4 For details on these scriptures, see the bibliography.

5 Entry 19 of the present volume is an exposition of Śākyaśrī's mind training instruction as encapsulated in these four lines.

6 The Dalai Lama's lecture in Central Park can be found in *Open Heart* (New York: Little, Brown, 2002). Three years later the Dalai Lama returned once again to Central Park. This time he chose to teach Atiśa's *Bodhisattva's Jewel Garland* to a gathering whose size exceeded even the previous meeting. A separate commentary by the Dalai Lama on the *Eight Verses* can be found in *The Compassionate Life* (Boston: Wisdom Publications, 2003).

7 Strictly speaking, the term *mind training* appears to have been retroactively added on to the title of *Eight Verses.*

8 See p. 285 of the present volume. These lines appear to be a slight variation of Nāgārjuna's *Ratnāvali,* 5:83ab. In Nāgārjuna's text, the lines read: "May their negativity ripen upon me, / And may my virtues ripen upon them."

9 The full text of this letter is cited in Yeshé Döndrup's *Treasury of Gems* (p. 169).

10 See, for example, Lechen's *History of Kadam School,* p. 6a:3. This tradition of identifying three main Kadam lineages appears to have been well established by the fourteenth century. Even the brief outline of the history of Kadam in Tsalpa Künga Dorjé's *Red Annals* (pp. 61–66) explicitly divides the account of the Kadam tradition into transmission of these three distinct lineages. Since *Core Teachings of the Book of Kadam* will be a separate volume in *The Library of Tibetan Classics,* the detailed discussion of the history of the Kadam school will be addressed in the introduction to that volume.

11 For a critical analysis of the role of Dharmarakṣita as Atiśa's teacher, especially on the awakening mind, see the introduction by Michael Sweet and Leonard Zwilling in Geshe Lhundub Sopa et al., *Peacock in the Poison Grove*, pp. 4–8, where they opine that there were two distinct traditions within the Kadam school with respect to Dharmarakṣita's role. One, stemming primarily from Dromtönpa through to Chekawa, lists Dharmarakṣita as one of the three teachers of awakening mind, while another tradition accords that teacher only the role of instructing Atiśa in the tenets of the Vaibhāṣika school. To what extent this conjecture of there being two distinct traditions with respect to Dharmarakṣita's role is justified is open to question.

12 Cited in Yeshé Döndrup (*Treasury of Gems*, p. 96) from an old text found at Chöding retreat.

13 See the present volume, p. 89, as well as Thokmé Sangpo, *Commentary on the Seven-Point Mind Training*, in *Treasury of Instructions*, vol. 2 *(kha)*, p. 542.

14 For a detailed analysis of the identity of Serlingpa (literally, the man from Suvarṇadvīpa, or "Golden Island") and this so-called Golden Island, see Alaka Chattopadhyaya, *Atiśa and Tibet*, pp. 84–95.

15 There are several "biographies" of Atiśa, the most well known being the *Source of Teachings (chos kyi 'byung gnas)*, which is attributed to Dromtönpa, as well as the *Extensive Biography (rnam thar rgyas pa)* and the *Standard Biography (rnam thar yongs grags)* of Chim Namkha Drak (thirteenth century). For a critical analysis of the tradition of Atiśa's biographies, see Helmut Eimer, "The Development of the Biographical Tradition Concerning Atiśa (Dīpaṃkaraśrījñāna)."

16 See pp. 57–70.

17 Rahul Sankrityayan asserts that Serlingpa was "famous for his scholarship throughout the Buddhist world." See P. V. Bapat, ed., *2500 Years of Buddhism*, p. 202.

18 Yeshé Döndrup provides a useful list of the key mind training and stages of the path works of the early Kadam masters, in which he refers to several early Tibetan mind training works, such as Langri Thangpa's *Eight Verses* and its commentary by Chekawa as well as a text entitled *Multicolored Udder*, which contains Langri Thangpa's instructions given to Shang and Shawo Gangpa. In fact, in his book, Yeshé Döndrup provides extensive extracts from many early Tibetan mind training texts.

19 In fact, according to Shönu Gyalchok (*Compendium of Well-Uttered Insights*, p. 96b), the organization of the themes of mind training teaching within the framework of seven key points is based upon Sharawa's instructions.

20 Shönu Gyalchok, *Compendium of Well-Uttered Insights*, p. 96b, also writes: "This root text [of the *Seven-Point Mind Training*] is drawn from those composed by Atiśa with minor modifications of wording to help make them easier to understand. This is not an independently authored work." That the tradition of compiling the miscellaneous instructions of the Kadam masters existed very early in the history of the Kadam school is evidenced from the well-known *Miscellaneous*

Sayings of the Kadam Masters, compiled and edited by Chegom Sherap Dorjé (twelfth century).

21 Sönam Lhai Wangpo, *A History of the Precious Kadam Tradition,* p. 383. Interestingly, the author does not mention the *Seven-Point Mind Training* by name, although Langri Thangpa's *Eight Verses* and its commentary by Chekawa are listed. However, there is a mention of certain "scattered Kadam [instructions]," which probably refers to the root lines of mind training that form the basis of the *Seven-Point Mind Training.*

22 Sangyé Gompa alludes to a wonderful story about Chekawa sharing the mind training instruction with individuals suffering from leprosy. Word spread within the lepers' community, and more and more lepers gathered to listen to Chekawa's teaching and engage in the practice, such that the teaching came to be referred to as "teaching for the lepers" *(dze chö).* See *Public Explication,* p. 318, of the present volume.

23 Lechen Künga Gyaltsen, *Lamp Illuminating the History of the Kadam Tradition,* p. 8a. Sumpa Yeshé Paljor (*An Excellent Wish-Granting Tree,* p. 393) also speaks of two transmissions of the teaching of *Seven-Point Mind Training.*

24 See Yeshé Döndrup, *Treasury of Gems,* p. 512. Lechen (p. 8b) makes a similar point about Shönu Gyalchok's approach.

25 Due to the divergences among the various redactions of *Seven-Point Mind Training,* a student of Phabongkha Dechen Nyingpo (1878–1941) requested that he produce a "critical" edition. Comparing the various extant redactions and on the basis of consultation with numerous commentaries, Phabongkha produced a version that is consonant with the approach of Tsongkhapa. This version of the root text can be found in volume 5 *(ca)* of his collected works, and a beautifully concise annotated version of this root text exists in volume 3 *(ga)* of the collected works of Kyapjé Trijang Rinpoché.

26 On the whole, the Geluk authors use the root text embedded in Namkha Pal's *Rays of the Sun,* which accords with the tradition of Sangyé Gompa, while most non-Geluk authors use the root text embedded in Thokmé Sangpo's commentary. In this latter text, the training in the ultimate awakening mind comes earlier.

27 *A Useful List for Those Who Uphold the Geden Tradition and Aspire to Vast Learning* in the *Collected Works of Klong rdol ngag dbang blo bzang,* vol. 2, p. 316.

28 Yeshé Döndrup, *Treasury of Gems,* p. 514.

29 Yeshé Döndrup (*Treasury of Gems,* p. 42) mentions seeing a handwritten copy of the anthology and a so-called Mongolian blockprint version. Hopefully at least one of these versions is extant and may come to light so that we can compare the present version against it.

30 Shönu Gyalchok, *Compendium of Well-Uttered Insights,* pp. 106a–124a. Interestingly, Shönu Gyalchok lists in this final category of mind training texts what he refers to as the "scattered sayings of Kadam, the mind training instructions of yogi Chegom," which may be a reference to the famous *Miscellaneous Sayings of*

580 Notes to pages 15–24

the Kadam Masters compiled by Chegom in the twelfth century. Phabhongkha Dechen Nyingpo, who was one of the greatest custodians and teachers of mind training between the end of nineteenth century and the first part of twentieth century, provides (*Collected Works,* vol. *ka*) a highly useful list of the lineage of the transmissions of the individual texts featured in our mind training anthology. I have provided observations on authorship together with an overview of principal themes in my annotations to the individual texts.

31 A fuller treatment of this question can be found in my introduction to the Tibetan edition of this volume. It is curious that hardly any of the post–fifteenth-century histories of the Kadam school refer to this anthology. The compilation of the volume may have been too close to the writing of Sönam Lhai Wangpo's *History of the Precious Kadam Tradition* (1484) and Lechen's *Lamp Illuminating the History of the Kadam Tradition* (1494), but the anthology should have found its way into at least two later histories, Paṇchen Sönam Drakpa's *History of Old and New Kadam Schools* (sixteenth century) and Jamgön Amé's *Ocean of Wonders* (seventeenth century). The later copies almost verbatim the brief section on mind training texts listed in Sönam Lhai Wangpo. In fact, in many sections of this work, Jamgön Amé copies directly from Sonam Lhai Wangpo without any acknowledgment. Thuken (*Crystal Mirror of Philosophical Schools,* pp. 96–100) gives a succinct yet highly informative discussion on the mind training instructions yet never mentions our anthology by name. So the question of when and by whom the earliest version of our anthology appeared must remain open until further textual resources come to light.

32 Two variants of this title exist. The alternative title, not chosen, is *Jewel Garland of Bodhisattvas.* Although there is no substantial difference between them, the latter title can also be read to mean a garland made of bodhisattvas' qualities rather than a jewel garland for the bodhisattvas. Although this text appears in the Tengyur (Toh 3951) as a self-standing work, it also exists almost in its entirety in another of Atiśa's works, entitled *Letter of Unblemished Precious Jewels* (Toh 4188), a letter sent by Atiśa to the Indian Bengali royalty Nayapāla from Nepal. Noting this, the Tibetan historian Pawo Tsuklak Trengwa asserts that *Bodhisattva's Jewel Garland* may actually have been compiled by Dromtönpa by drawing from Atiśa's writings. See his *Joyful Feast for the Learned (Mkas pa'i dga' ston),* p. 709.

33 "Faith" here refers to a profound faith in the law of karma.

34 The Tibetan term *khenpo* (spelled *mkhan po*), which is translated here as "preceptor," can also mean an abbot of a monastery. Here the term refers to spiritual masters who have conferred vows and precepts upon you.

35 Dergé Tengyur: "Dispel the ground of hostility and unpleasantness."

36 "Both" here refers to the two ends of the spectrum of one's fluctuating state, namely, self-importance (which arises when one's state of mind is overly excited) and discouragement (which arises when one's state of mind becomes too deflated). Dergé Tengyur edition: "Always meditate on emptiness."

37 Dergé Tengyur: "Strive diligently, with no distinction of day and night."

38 The two defilements are the obscuration of afflictions and the subtle obscurations to omniscience.

39 Dergé Tengyur: "Are the seven inexhaustible treasures."

40 This short ode appears as the first entry in the *Father Teachings,* volume 1 of *The Book of Kadam,* and that is probably where the editors of the *Mind Training: The Great Collection* got it for our present anthology.

41 Dromtönpa's dates are taken from *The Blue Annals.* Lechen, Panchen Sönam Drakpa, and Sumpa give 1004 C.E. as his year of birth, though only Sumpa agrees with *The Blue Annals* on the year of Dromtönpa's death. The other two say it was 1063.

42 Alaka Chattopadhaya (*Atiśa and Tibet,* pp. 63–66) provides a brief survey of the various attempts by modern writers at understanding the meaning of this word and concludes that the Tibetan term *zahor* is Persian in origin and is a corrupt form of the word *śahor,* which literally means "city." *The Extensive Tibetan-Chinese Dictionary,* on the other hand, provides a somewhat straightforward meaning for the term when it states that *sahor* (spelled *za hor*) is a degeneration of an Indian word and refers to what is the modern state of Bengal.

43 Although "Bangala" is the old Indian way of writing "Bengal," the two terms do not refer to exactly the same thing. "Bengal" is the name of a state in modern India that borders Bangladesh in the east, Orissa in the south, Madhya Pradesh in the west, and Bihar in the west and northwest. In contrast, "Bangala" in its old usage seems to have covered a larger area, which included large parts of what today comprises the central Indian state of Bihar. In this text, however, the author appears to be using the term as the name of a city where the royal palace of Atiśa's parents was said to be located.

44 Dergé edition: "His wealth and power resemble that of China's Tongkhün." The Tibetan term *tongkhün* (spelled *stong khun*), which I have translated here as "Eastern," is, as suggested by Stein *(Les Tribus Anciennes),* probably a degeneration of the Chinese term *T'ang kiun* ("sovereign of T'ang"). For an alternative meaning of this term, see Tsong kha pa, *The Great Treatise,* vol. 1, chap. 1, n. 8.

45 This is probably a reference to the legendary city of Ghandara, which is mentioned in various Buddhist sources and thought to have been "located in an arc reaching from the western Punjab through the northwest frontier to Kabul and perhaps into southern Afghanistan" (Keay, *India: A History,* p. 58).

46 Dharmodgata *(chos 'phags)* is often cited as an example of a bodhisattva who possesses enormous resources to make offerings to the spiritual teachers.

47 Dergé edition: "Stories of the three are found in brief elsewhere."

48 Dergé edition: "The youngest, who is known as Candragarbhā...."

49 This probably refers to Vikramaśīla, which later became the monastic university where Atiśa became a prominent master. To date, although no conclusive archeological site of this famous Buddhist monastery has been found, it is widely believed

that it existed somewhere on the shores of the Ganga in modern Bihar. Cf. Keay, *India: A History,* p. 193.

50 This is an abbreviation of Vikramalaśīla.

51 Here we follow the Dergé edition.

52 Dergé edition: "Twenty-one girls of noble patronage."

53 Dergé edition.

54 Since the events being described are supposed to have taken place in India, wherever possible, I have attempted to give the names referred to in the text written in Sanskrit. Those that I have failed to reconstruct in Sanskrit, I have left them as they are in the Tibetan original. I would like to thank Acharya Lobsang Dorjé Rabling of the Central Institute of Higher Tibetan Studies, Sarnath, for helping with the reconstruction of many of the Sanskrit names.

55 The names of the ministers have been left as they appear in the Tibetan text.

56 Dergé edition: "Who were all at the threshold of betrothal age."

57 Dergé edition.

58 Siddhārtha is the name of the historical Buddha before he attained full enlightenment under the Bodhi tree.

59 The father of the historical Buddha Śākyamuni.

60 The "twelve great deeds" refer to the key events of the historical Buddha's life as recounted in the Buddhist texts. These are often the subject of mural paintings in the Buddhist temples in India, Tibet, Sri Lanka, China, and other traditionally Buddhist countries in Asia.

61 The more one drinks salt water, the more one feels thirsty; in the same manner, the more one indulges in the sense objects, the more one craves them.

62 "The king of the Śākyas" is an epithet for Śākyamuni, the historical Buddha.

63 Dergé edition.

64 Dergé edition.

65 Dergé edition.

66 Dergé edition.

67 "Other shore" refers to existence beyond this present life, such as future lives. This expression is also often used to refer to liberation, the "other shore" *(pha rol),* as opposed to cyclic existence, which is "this side of the shore" *(tshu rol).*

68 Dergé edition.

69 The term *three spheres (khorsum;* spelled *'khor gsum)* normally refers to the three key elements of a given act—the object of the act, the doer, and the act itself—but this does not make much sense here. Most probably it is a typographical error, and the Tibetan expression should read *khornam ('khor rnams),* which refers to the

prince's retinue. So here the text probably states that the prince offered his entire retinue to the master.

70 Dergé edition.

71 Dergé edition.

72 Dergé edition.

73 Vaiśravaṇa is a god of wealth in the classical Indian Buddhist pantheon and also the guardian of the western direction. He is depicted holding in his right hand a mongoose that is spewing out wish-fulfilling jewels.

74 This is a reference to what are known as the "seven riches of a noble one." The seven riches are are listed by Atiśa at the end of his *Bodhisattva's Jewel Garland:* (1) faith, (2) morality, (3) giving, (4) learning, (5) conscience, (6) a sense of shame, and (7) wisdom.

75 Body, speech, and mind—the three "doors" through which beings perform actions.

76 Yama is the lord of death in ancient Indian mythology, in both the Buddhist and non-Buddhist traditions. His abode is thought to be in the southern direction, and he is often depicted, especially in the Tibetan tradition, with a buffalo head.

77 "The eight mundane concerns" are the four pairs of contrasting reactions that reflect a deep-seated attachment to the concerns of this life. They are (1) being elated when one finds resources and dejected when one does not, (2) being elated when hearing pleasant words and dejected when hearing unpleasant words, (3) being elated when praised and dejected when belittled, and (4) being elated when enjoying happiness and dejected when undergoing unhappiness.

78 This appears to be a paraphrase rather than a direct quote. Most probably, "Nāgārjunagarbha" refers to the famous second-century Buddhist thinker Nāgārjuna, the author of the highly influential *Fundamental Wisdom of the Middle Way.*

79 This is the second in the fivefold topology of the path to enlightenment.The other paths are the path of accumulation, the path of insight, the path of meditation, and the path of no more learning.

80 Dergé edition.

81 A unit of measurement for distance in the classical Indian system, the value of which varies according to the particular source consulted. In the standard *Abhidharmakośa* system, it is roughly equivalent to five standard miles. For a discussion of the conflicting values of this unit of measurement, including a general discussion of the classical Indian methods of computation, see McGovern, *A Manual of Buddhist Philosophy,* pp. 39–48.

82 Monier-Williams, *A Sanskrit-English Dictionary,* p. 307, identifies *kṛṣṇasāra* as the spotted antelope.

83 This expression alludes to the yogi's profound meditative realization, in which his

entire perspective is free of duality between dichotomous categories like subject and object, the external environment and the beings within, and so on.

84 Dergé edition.

85 A major center of Vajrayana Buddhism in ancient times that modern writers identify as the Swat Valley of modern Pakistan.

86 This is the realm where, according to Mahayana Buddhism, all the buddhas attain their full enlightenment in the form of the saṃbhogakāya, the buddha body of perfect resource.

87 The celestial realm where Maitreya, the future Buddha, is believed to reside at present.

88 The pure land of Buddha Amitābha.

89 In classical Indian and Buddhist mythology, the king of Gandharva is identified to be the most skilled musician.

90 An important meditation deity belonging to the class of "mother tantras" of Vajrayana Buddhist teachings. An English translation of this deity's root text can be found in *The Hevajra Tantra,* a two-volume study of the tantra by D. L. Snellgrove.

91 The Sanskrit term *tirthika,* when found in Buddhist texts, usually refers to the non-Buddhist schools of ancient India. In this usage, the term refers to the "upholders of extreme views," such as those of absolutism or nihilism.

92 Dergé edition.

93 Known also as Cakrasaṃvara, Heruka is an important meditation deity belonging to the category of "mother tantras" in the highest yoga class of tantra.

94 Dergé edition.

95 The term *vajra,* which can be translated as "diamond" or "adamantine," connotes indivisibility and indestructibility.

96 Dergé edition.

97 This prose "colophon" appears in the Dergé edition of *The Book of Kadam* in verse with three lines. It was most probably added by a subsequent editor.

98 The full title of this work is *The Liberating Story of Master Atiśa's Meeting with the Peerless Serlingpa Dharmakirti (Jo bo rjes mnyam med gser gling pa chos kyi grags pa dang mjal ba'i rnam thar).* Serlingpa literally means the "one from Serling," the Sanskrit for which is *Suvarṇadvipa,* which in turn literally means a "land of gold" or an "island of gold." Modern scholars identify *Suvarṇadvipa* as the Indonesian island of Sumatra.

99 Monier-Williams, *Sanskrit-English Dictionary,* p. 771, identifies *makara* as: "a kind of sea-monster (sometimes confounded with the crocodile, shark and dolphin &c....)" In the context of the story, it could refer to some kind of whale.

100 This is probably a reference to Atiśa himself, who was a teacher of the learned Kṣitigarbha.

101 The garuḍa is the mythological king of birds in the classical Indian mythology and also the mount of the scepter-wielding Vedic god Indra. It is often depicted devouring serpents and is considered to be the counterforce of nāgas, the serpentine spirits.

102 Yamāntaka, literally meaning "the enemy of Yama," refers to a class of meditation deities regarded as the counterforce of Yama, the lord of death. Vajrabhairava is the most well-known Yamāntaka in the highest yoga class of the Vajrayana.

103 Acala is one of the four principal meditation deities of the Kadam school, and is the guardian protector. The other three divinities are Buddha Śākyamuni as the master of the teachings, Avalokiteśvara as the buddha of compassion, and Ārya Tārā as the buddha of enlightened activity.

104 This is a reference to the Buddhist goddess Tārā, whose key feature is her protection against "eight dangers": (1) lions and the associated emotion of conceit, (2) elephants and the associated emotion of delusion or bewilderment, (3) fire and the associated emotion of anger, (4) poisonous snakes and the associated emotion of jealousy, (5) robbers and the associated mental states of destructive views, (6) the chains of bondage and the associated emotion of miserliness, (7) water and the associated emotion of attachment, and (8) ghosts and the associated emotion of wavering doubts. The close association of the name of Tārā with protection against these dangers seems to have been part of the myth of Tārā from the earliest stages of the evolution of her rites. For a contemporary analysis of Tārā, including translations of some liturgical texts connected with her meditative practice, see Stephen Beyer's *The Cult of Tārā*.

105 This expression "father and son" is probably a reference to Atiśa and his spiritual teacher Serlingpa. If this is correct, then it is interesting to note that even though, at this point in the narrative, Atiśa and Serlingpa haven't met yet, the learned Kṣitigarbha refers to Serlingpa and Atiśa as "father and son."

106 Dergé edition.

107 I have translated the Tibetan expression *mo bön*, which is an abbreviation of the two terms *mo* and *bon*, as "divination and animism." Although the second term, *bön* (spelled *bon*), can also refer to Tibet's pre-Buddhist religion of Bön, I believe that it refers more broadly here to some kind of animistic or shamanistic rites. Interestingly, the expression "divination and animism" *(mo bön)* appears quite frequently in many early Kadam writings.

108 It is difficult to speculate on the meaning of the rather intriguing expression "Nepalese ship" *(bal po'i zings)*. Given that Nepal is a landlocked country, it is highly unlikely that it had any history of maritime activity. It is conceivable that the Tibetan word *belpo* (spelled *bal po*), which is an adjectival form of the noun *belyul* (spelled *bal yul;* "Nepal"), once had a wider meaning that encompassed other ethnic groups. However, given the geographical proximity of Bengal and Nepal, we cannot rule out the possibility that there may have been a tradition of Nepalese craftsmen skilled in shipbuilding at some point in the past.

109 It is difficult to speculate about the identity of this city or whether there even was such a historical place. In the Dergé edition, the name of the city is "Svabhāthana."

110 In the Lhasa Shöl edition of this text in the *Mind Training: The Great Collection* and the Lhasa Shöl and Dergé editions in *The Book of Kadam*, this line reads, "Throw this sky-flower and strike..." *(nam mkha'i me tog 'di...)*. This, I think, is a typographical error.

111 The act of striking the heretics' city with a lightning bolt might entail transgression of the Buddhist precepts of going for refuge and generating the awakening mind. When generating the mind of awakening, one vows never to abandon the well-being of other sentient beings even at the cost of one's life.

112 This is a reference to the central Asian Turks, who had, by the eleventh century, already begun their frequent raids into the vast Indian subcontinent, especially in the northern and central parts of India.

113 This allusion to Bön and its principal center of activity, the land of Shangshung, is most intriguing given that, at the supposed time of the events narrated in this story, Atiśa had not yet made his journey to Tibet. It is, however, conceivable that Atiśa and his student Kṣitigarbha are familiar with Bön as being the pre-Buddhist religion of Tibet, since by the eleventh century the tradition of Tibetans coming to study and translate the major Buddhist texts at the feet of Indian masters was already well established.

114 It seems that leprosy had been a major health concern during the lifetime of the early Kadam masters such as Dromtönpa and his immediate disciples in the eleventh and twelfth centuries in central Tibet. Thus, countering people's prejudices against lepers features prominently in their teachings. According to Tibetan sources, Dromtönpa was so deeply affected by people's prejudices against those suffering from the disease that he dedicated the latter part of his life to nursing many lepers, eventually losing his own life to the illness.

115 *Rākṣasa*, or the Tibetan equivalent *sinpo* (spelled *srin po*), refers to an ogrelike monster. The reference to Laṅka as the kingdom of *rākṣasas* draws from the Indian mythology found in the ancient Hindu Purāṇic literature.

116 Dergé edition.

117 This mantra appears differently in all the various editions of the text, including the Lhasa Shöl and Dergé edition of *The Book of Kadam*.

118 Atiśa's full name is Dīpaṃkaraśrījñāna.

119 This reference is intriguing. If true, it suggests that there was communication between Tibet and Indonesia in the first millennium, something unheard of in the traditional Tibetan historical writings.

120 In opting for *monks* instead of *spiritual friends (geshe)*, as found in the original Tibetan, we are following the Dergé edition.

121 It's difficult to speculate what this monster is.

122 The expression *sky treasury (namkha dzö;* spelled *nam mkha' mdzod)* alludes to a

common legend in Buddhist literature of an inexhaustible treasure. It is said that the one who has mastered this wealth can pull material objects from the sky as if it were a treasury. This power is seen as one of the marks of a bodhisattva who has fully mastered the perfection of giving, which takes place on the first bodhisattva level.

123 This is an allusion to the meditators' failure to recognize Atiśa when he first arrived.

124 Known as *khakkhara* in Sanskrit and *kharsil* (spelled *'khar gsil*) in Tibetan, this staff is one of the "thirteen articles of sustenance" of a fully ordained Buddhist monk. For a drawing and description of this staff, see Willson and Brauen, *Deities of Tibetan Buddhism,* p. 568.

125 I was not able to clarify how large this is.

126 Since all the named monks are Indians, wherever possible I have attempted to reconstruct the probable Sanskrit name.

127 Meaning, perhaps, that it is disrespectful to the Dharma to interrupt a teaching, even in order to pay respect to a noble one who has appeared unexpectedly.

128 Sanskrit: *Abhisamayālaṃkāra*. This is a highly influential classical Buddhist text attributed to Maitreya (c. fourth century) that systematically expounds the themes of the *Perfection of Wisdom* scriptures.

129 The wording of this "colophon" is much shorter in the Dergé edition of the text in *The Book of Kadam.*

130 This entire section, which is effectively a supplication to master Atiśa followed by an aspiration prayer, does not exist in *The Book of Kadam.* Most probably it was added by one of the editors of our present anthology.

131 For problems pertaining to the authorship of this text, see my introduction. As indicated there, this root text sometimes diverges from *Annotated Root Lines of Mahayana Mind Training,* the commentary that follows it in this anthology. The divergences are detailed in my notes to *Annotated Root Lines.*

132 The Tibetan original uses the instrumental case after the *two,* giving the following reading: "Be upheld principally by the two witnesses." However, we have chosen here to follow the more established reading, which is consonant also with the version of *The Root Lines* found in the Dergé edition of Jamgön Kongtrül's *Treasury of Instructions.*

133 For comments pertaining to the authorship of the "root lines" embedded in this annotated text and their relation to *The Root Lines* and the root text of *Seven-Point Mind Training,* see my introduction.

134 In the Tibetan annotation system, the lines of the "root text" are in a larger font while the annotations are smaller. Similarly, to help maintain a clearer separation between the two, we have set the lines of the root text in bold. My own additions, introduced to clarify the meaning, are provided within brackets. The Arabic numbers for the stanzas and Roman numerals for the prose are not part of the original text but have been inserted to make references easier.

135   Lines b, c, and d in this stanza are not found in the *Root Lines*.

136   The next two lines of this stanza are not found in the *Root Lines*.

137   Lines a, b, and c of this stanza are not found in the *Root Lines*.

138   In various commentaries, this line reads: "Relate to your meditation whatever you encounter right now." This variance is caused by a difference in the spelling of a single verb. When spelled with the suffix *b,* as is done here, i.e., *gang thub,* it gives the reading "whatever you can," and when spelled with the *g* suffix as *gang thug,* it gives the reading "whatever you encounter." Judging by its context, and more importantly, following the reading of the early commentarial literature, the second reading seems to be more accurate.

139   The next two lines of this stanza are not found in the *Root Lines*.

140   This line, though consonant with *Seven-Point Mind Training,* reads in the *Root Lines* as follows: "Train in the five powers." This is due to a variation in a single letter of the verb. When written *jarwa* (spelled *shyar ba*), as is the case here, it means "to apply," whereas when written *jangwa* (spelled *shyang ba*), it means "to train."

141   This first line of the stanza is not found in the *Root Lines*.

142   Three general points are (1) that your mind training does not contradict your pledges, (2) that your behavior does not become sarcastic, and (3) that it does not become biased.

143   A dzo, a cross between a yak and a cow, is a domestic animal capable of carrying heavy loads for long distances.

144   This line does not appear in the *Root Lines*.

145   This line does not appear in the *Root Lines*.

146   This line does not appear in the *Root Lines*.

147   Lines xi and xiii do not appear in the *Root Lines*.

148   The first two lines of this stanza are not found in the *Root Lines,* and the last two lines do not match up exactly. In the *Root Lines,* we read: "This proliferation of five degenerations / Is transformed into the path of enlightenment." This variant reading is, interestingly, due to a simple change in case. In the *Root Lines,* the case is genitive, while here the case is instrumental.

149   This entire stanza does not appear in the *Root Lines*.

150   This entire stanza does not appear in either the *Root Lines* or the *Seven-Point Mind Training*. "Fierce one" here refers to the mental afflictions that are powerful and vicious in their destructiveness.

151   Lines a, b, and d of this stanza do not appear in the *Root Lines*.

152   Lines b and c of this stanza do not appear in the *Root Lines*.

153   Lines xix to xxii are not found in the *Root Lines*.

154   The following text has been extracted from Sé Chilbu's commentary (text 7 in

this volume), which is the earliest commentary on Chekawa's *Seven-Point Mind Training*. Interestingly, the compilers chose not to include any root text entitled *Seven-Point Mind Training* attributed to Chekawa in this collection. This is probably because they felt that Sé Chilbu's commentary on the *Seven-Point* is as much Chekawa's as it is Sé Chilbu's, since it was essentially compiled from the notes taken at Chekawa's oral teachings. For convenience's sake, and because of the importance of this particular redaction of the root text of *Seven-Point Mind Training*, I have added this text in the volume. For variants among the different redactions of *Seven-Point Mind Training*, see my introduction and annotations to the two *Root Lines* included in this volume.

155 As noted by the Mongolian Buddhist author Yeshé Dhöndrup (1792–1855) in his *Treasury of Gems*, p. 434, this work represents the earliest commentary on the highly influential mind training work entitled *Seven-Point Mind Training*. Although in the original version of this anthology, of which our volume is a translation, no name is given for the authorship of this commentary, I concur with Shönu Gyalchok (*Compendium of Well-Uttered Insights*, p. 192b) that its author is without doubt Chekawa's own student, Sé Chilbu Chökyi Gyaltsen. For more comments on the antiquity of this commentary and its relation to the "root text" of the *Seven-Point Mind Training*, see my introduction. In this translation, the lines of the "root text" of *Seven-Point Mind Training* are indented and provided in bold.

156 Serlingpa's personal name is Dharmakīrti, which literally means "the fame of Dharma."

157 "Mantra" here refers to the entire system of Buddhist thought and practice known as *Vajrayana*, while "Perfection" refers to the general Mahayana tradition known as the sutra or "perfection" system.

158 The six parameters constitute the boundaries within which a correct reading of a Vajrayana text of the highest yoga class must take place. For an exposition in contemporary language of Vajrayana hermeneutics, see Thurman, "Vajra Herme-neutics."

159 Tib. *Dbyug pa gsum gyi phreng ba*. As rightly noted by Shönu Gyalchok (*Compendium of Well-Uttered Insights*, p. 3a), this sutra does not appear to have been translated into Tibetan. Shönu Gyalchok writes the first word of the title as *gbyig pa*, as opposed to *gbyug pa*.

160 Tib. *Mdo sde rgyan;* Skt., *Sūtrālaṃkāra*. There is no such entry under Aśvaghoṣa's name in the Tengyur. However a Chinese translation of the text exists under the title *Kie man louen*. Modern scholars dispute the ascription of this work to Aśvaghoṣa, and some, who identify this text with *Kalpanāmaṇḍaṭikā*, believe it to be written by Kumāralāta (c. third century), who was the teacher of Harivarman. For a discussion of the authorship of this work and, more importantly, a brief survey of the contemporary academic scholarship on this text, see *Encyclopedia of Indian Philosophy*, vol. 7, p. 237, and endnote 257.

161 *Jātakamālā;* Toh 4150. In the Tengyur catalog, this text is attributed to Āryaśūra, a noted fourth-century Buddhist writer, who the Tibetan tradition identifies with Aśvaghoṣa. According to Tibetan hagiographical sources, Aśvaghoṣa converted to

Buddhism following a series of debates with Āryadeva (c. second century C.E.), the principal student of the great Madhyamaka thinker Nāgārjuna (c. second century). Although Aśvaghoṣa wrote several works, including some philosophical treatises, he is known primarily for his poetic text on the life of the Buddha entitled *Deeds of the Buddha (Buddhacarita)*.

162 Literally, a yogi of loving-kindness.

163 *Ākāśagarbhasūtra;* Toh 260 Kangyur, mdo sde, *za,* 264a–83b.

164 *Bodhicaryāvatāra;* Toh 3871 Tengyur, dbu ma, *la,* 1b–44a.

165 *Śikṣāsamuccaya;* Toh 3939 & 3940 Tengyur, dbu ma, *khi,* 1b–3a and 3a–194b.

166 *Vimalakirtinirdeśasūtra;* Toh 176 Kangyur, mdo sde, *ma,* 175a–239b.

167 *Bodhisattvabhūmi;* Toh 4037 Tengyur, sems tsam, *wi,* 1b–213a. This is one of the most important classical Indian Buddhist texts on the topic of the bodhisattva ideal. A brief summary of this work in English is found in *Encyclopedia of Indian Philosophy,* vol. 7, pp. 415–26. For more information, see bibliography.

168 *Vimalakirtinirdeśasūtra;* Toh 176 Kangyur, mdo, *ma,* chap. 7, 215a:5.

169 For information on the three brothers, who later became the chief custodians of the so-called three lineages of Kadam teachings, see my introduction.

170 This is a reference to Dromtönpa, who founded the famous Kadam monastery of Radreng.

171 "Chamber of divinities" *(lhai khangpa;* spelled *lha'i khang pa)* here refers to one's meditation space, where the practitioner would have images of divinities, such as the Buddha, installed on the altar. In general usage, the abbreviated form of this word, *lhakhang,* is often translated in English as "temple."

172 Throughout this commentary, the author frequently inserts the verb *sung* (spelled *gsungs*), which can be translated as "said" or "taught," at the end of a sentence or paragraph. This is quite characteristic of a specific genre of Tibetan spiritual writing called *sindri* (spelled *zin bris*), which is effectively lecture notes taken at a live teaching or teachings and later compiled into a coherent narrative. If this convention applies here, then the verb "said" or "taught" at the end of a sentence or paragraph can be read as "the master taught" or "the master said," and *master* here refers to Chekawa, who was the teacher of Sé Chilbu, the compiler of the present text.

173 The wording of this line is slightly different in the version found in the *Annotated Root Lines.* There this line reads: "Contemplate all phenomena as dreamlike."

174 In *Annotated Root Lines* this reads: "Experience the unborn nature of awareness."

175 Interestingly, this line is not found in either the *Root Lines* or the *Annotated Root Lines.*

176 Source unidentified.

177 *Bodhicaryāvatāra,* 8:120; Toh 3871 Tengyur, dbu ma, *la,* 28a:5.

178 *Bodhicaryāvatāra,* 8:131; Toh 3871 Tengyur, dbu ma, *la,* 28b:4.

179 *Bodhicaryāvatāra,* 8:136; Toh 3871 Tengyur, dbu ma, *la,* 28b:7.

180 The metaphor implied here is that of grabbing a dog by its snout.

181 *Bodhicaryāvatāra,* 5:70; Toh 3871 Tengyur, dbu ma, *la,* 13a:1.

182 "The great lord of the ten levels" is an epithet of the fully enlightened Buddha, who has perfected all ten bodhisattva grounds *(bhūmis).*

183 Bhūripa's *Extensive Daily Confessions of Cakrasaṃvara [Practice];* Toh 1533 Tengyur, rgyud 'grel, *za,* 95a:4.

184 The four daily activities are walking (to a specific destination), strolling, sleeping, and sitting.

185 There seem to be slight variations in the reading of these two lines in the different versions of the *Seven-Point Mind Training.* In particular, these lines are significantly different in the *Annotated Root Lines,* where they read: "The negativities of the world and beings within cyclic existence/ Transform the adverse conditions into the path of enlightenment."

186 This subheading is missing in the original Tibetan. However, since its counterpart, which is "recognizing sentient beings as friends and cherishing them" is introduced later in the text as subheadingb, a subheading has been inserted here for the sake of consistency.

187 *Bodhicaryāvatāra,* 8:134; Tengyur, dbu ma, *la,* 28b:5.

188 *Pramāṇavārttika,* Pratyakṣa:221; Tengyur, tshad ma, *ce,* 116a:1.

189 *Bodhicaryāvatāra,* 8:113; Tengyur, dbu ma, *la,* 28a:1.

190 *Bodhicaryāvatāra,* 8:155; Tengyur, dbu ma, *la,* 29b:3.

191 This is a reference to a facial expression that is recognized in Tibetan society as demonstrating a determination and courage in the face of an enemy's challenge. Warriors from the Gesar epic are often depicted with this expression while wielding their swords.

192 *Bodhicaryāvatāra,* 4:34; Tengyur, dbu ma, *la,* 9a:7. The reading of the last line is slightly different in this citation from that of the version found in the Dergé edition of the Tengyur.

193 This is probably an old Tibetan saying. A slightly different version of this saying reads: "Though living on the head yet throwing mud into the eyes." The saying describes the ingratitude of someone who deliberately harms those from whom he or she has received benefits.

194 *Bodhicaryāvatāra,* 8:129 & 130; Tengyur, dbu ma, *la,* 28b:3.

195 In Tibetan folk belief, the howling of owls at night is considered a bad omen. It is often seen as an early intimation of misfortune, such as the death of a loved one.

196 *Bodhicaryāvatāra*, 8:154; Tengyur, dbu ma, *la*, 29b:3.

197 *Bodhicaryāvatāra*, 8:169; Tengyur, dbu ma, *la*, 30a:4.

198 I have failed to locate the source of this enumeration system.

199 *Bodhicaryāvatāra*, 8:121; Tengyur, dbu ma, *la*, 28a:5. The reading of the first line in the citation here in the Tibetan text is slightly different from the version found in the Tengyur. Here, I have chosen to follow the edition in the Tengyur.

200 Shawopa is an abbreviation of Shawo Gangpa. He was a student of the famous Kadam master Gönpawa Wangchuk Gyaltsen (1016–82), who was, in turn, a prominent student of both Atiśa and Dromtönpa. The source of this citation from Shawopa remains unidentified. A brief biographical sketch of Shawopa and a selection of his teachings can be found in Yeshé Döndrup, (*Treasury of Gems*, pp. 331–38).

201 The reading of this line in both the Lhasa Shöl and *Treasury of Instructions* editions appear to be corrupt. I have chosen to read this line as follows: *de tsam na zin par blab pa'o.*

202 When one becomes a monk, as part of a public declaration of the fundamental change in one's way of life, one takes a new ordination name. So an ordained person has two names—his or her original name given at birth, which is the person's lay name, and the new name received at the time of ordination.

203 The spiritual master Ben refers to Ben Gungyal, who was a student of the Kadam master Gönpawa. A brief biographical sketch, as well as selections of some of Ben Gungyal's teachings can be found in *Treasury of Gems*, pp. 249–51.

204 Source of this citation remains unidentified.

205 Tib. *sha khyer khrag khyer gyi chos.*

206 Tib. *ltas ngan gyang du len pa'i chos.*

207 This metaphor is found in Nāgārjuna's *Suhṛllekha*, 69cd; Toh 4182 Tengyur, spring yig, *nge*, 43b:7. Lokesh Chandra provides *kolāsita* as the Sanskrit equivalent of the Tibetan word *rgya shug gi tshig gu*. Since I have failed to identify what this tree is supposed to be, I have left its Sanskrit name in my translation here.

208 *Prajñāpāramitāsaṃcayagāthā;* Toh 13 Kangyur, sher phyin, *ka*, 12b:6.

209 The Tibetan word *dzené* (spelled *dze nad*), which is often translated as leprosy, might also be interpreted as referring to some kind of highly contagious severe skin disease. This illness appears to have been a major health concern during the time of the early Kadam teachers in the eleventh and twelfth centuries in central and southern regions of Tibet. Legend has it that even Dromtönpa himself, one of the founding fathers of the Kadam school, devoted the latter part of his life to nursing lepers and eventually became himself a victim of the disease.

210 I have not identified the source of this citation.

211 *Bodhicaryāvatāra*, 3:12a, b, d, and 13d; Toh 3871 Tengyur, dbu ma, *la*, 7a:3.

212 Source unidentified.

213 Given that Chekawa was a student of Langri Thangpa and that furthermore this commentary represents a compilation of notes from Chekawa's teachings, this citation from Langri Thangpa can be viewed as an instance of direct oral tradition.

214 Source unidentified.

215 The first two lines of this stanza do not appear in either the *Root Lines* or the *Annotated Root Lines*. Interestingly, they are also not found in many subsequent editions of the *Seven-Point Mind Training*.

216 This expression "the object of impairment and the agent of impairment" *(gnod bya gnod byed)* refers to a relation of two opposing forces, where one undermines the other. Everyday examples from the physical world include heat and cold and light and darkness. In the mental world, this includes such forces as love and hate, attraction and repulsion, grasping at permanence and the understanding of the transient nature of phenomena.

217 *Vajrapanjaratantra (Vajra Peak Tantra);* Toh 480 Kangyur, rgyud, *nya,* 205b:2.

218 In other words, one's obstructions are baseless.

219 I have failed to discern what list this is. Vasubandhu gives a list of ten consciousnesses in his *Treasury of Higher Knowledge,* but I don't think this is what the author has in mind here. The ten consciousnesses in the *Treasury* are mental qualities of the Buddha's mind, while our text suggests experiences related to anxiety, fear, and psychological trauma.

220 *Bodhicaryāvatāra,* 6:21b; Toh 3871 Tengyur, dbu ma, *la,* 15a:7.

221 *Bodhicaryāvatāra,* 6:21c; Toh 3871 Tengyur, dbu ma, *la,* 15a:7.

222 Source unidentified.It may simply be an aspiration verse by the author of this commentary himself or by Chekawa, on whose lectures this text is based.

223 We follow the reading of the *Treasury* edition for this sentence.

224 Tib. *lhogö* (spelled *lhog rgod*). The *Extensive Tibetan-Chinese Dictionary* says this term refers to a class of infectious diseases related mostly to inflammation of limbs.

225 Source unidentified. It is possible that Chekawa, who was a student of Langri Thangpa, may be citing an oral instruction here.

226 Readers will notice that the order of the five powers in this section is different from the one presented immediately before. While the former presents the standard sequence of the five powers, here the sequence is transferring consciousness at the time of death.

227 "Gifts of the deceased" *(pongthag;* spelled *spong thag,* literally, the "mark of renunciation")* are articles belonging to a deceased person that are offered to a lama or a monastery, or sometimes to the poor, when requests for the performance of the death ritual are made. It became customary in Tibet, especially for dedicated religious practitioners, to make such offerings even before their death. This is to encourage acceptance of the reality of your death so that you can let go of

attachment to your possessions and concentrate on meditative practice, such as mind training, with increased urgency.

228 The meaning of this sentence is obscure. It may be an allusion to a Tibetan "death deception" *('chi bslu)* ritual, where a dough likeness of a sick person is outfitted with make-believe possessions, including, among other things, cloth from the person's clothes. If this interpretation is correct, the author is here underlining that the offerings being made to "embodiments of kindness," namely one's spiritual teachers, monastic community, and so on, should be real possessions, not facsimiles.

229 The Tibetan text of this sentence may be corrupt. Instead of reading *'khor 'das rang bzhin thams cad sems 'khrul pa'i rtsa ba yin* it may be *'khor 'das rang gzhan thams bcad.* In this latter case, the translation would read: "Everything—samsara and nirvana, self and others—is rooted in the deluded mind." This is, in my opinion, a better reading.

230 Just as in the *Root Lines,* the instrumental case appears after the *two,* giving the reading: "Be upheld principally by the two witnesses." Consonant with the commentary, I follow here the more established reading, where the particle is instead read as genitive.

231 In Tibetan, one word, *jampa* (spelled *'jam pa*), is used for both the quality of gentleness, as in the case of a person's heart, and the quality of softness, as in the case of soft wool. Thus the comparison here.

232 This is a peculiar expression. The point is to indicate a visceral quality of the strength of one's single-pointed perseverance in spiritual practice.

233 All the behaviors listed here are, in one way or another, considered dangerous and out of the ordinary. The point is that the practitioner of mind training should not indulge in these to show off his or her courage and sense of invulnerability.

234 Source unidentified.

235 Atiśa, *Bodhisattva's Jewel Garland,* stanzas 17c and 13d respectively; Toh 3951 Tengyur, dbu ma, *khi,* 295a.

236 Nāgārjuna, *Ratnāvali,* 3:73; Toh 4187 Tengyur, skyes rabs, *ge;* 117a5.

237 Sé Chilbu explained above this line from the "root text."

238 It is not clear what authority, whether text or person, the author is citing here.

239 The commentary does not make explicit the correlation between the two methods of applying antidotes—namely, investigation and close analysis—and the present and future afflictions. It is clear, however, that "investigation"—discerning the affliction most dominant in your mind and striving to diminish its force—relates to present afflictions, and "close analysis"—the detailed casual analysis of the afflictions upon which you strive to prevent their arising in the first place—relates to future afflictions.

240 The English word *boastfulness* does not fully convey the Tibetan word *yü* (spelled *yud*). *Yü,* strongly abhorred in Tibetan culture, refers to deliberate, excessive

expectation of recognition for some beneficial or kind act one has performed. It might involve constantly reminding others of the act done, or certain attitudes or bodily expressions that draw attention to it. Since *yü* comes from craving recognition, it involves self-cherishing, which is a key target of attack for the practitioner of mind training. There is a well-known Tibetan saying: "For he who boasts of his acts, no recognition is due" *(las byas yud can la byas ngo med)*.

241 Radrengpa here refers to Dromtönpa, the principal student of Atiśa and a cofounder of the Kadam school. Because he founded Radreng Monastery near Lhasa, Dromtönpa is sometimes referred to as Radrengpa, "the man from Radreng." I have so far failed to locate the earliest appearance of this quotation, which is part of oral tradition.

242 "Author" here refers to Chekawa, the author, or more correctly the compiler, of the root text of *Seven-Point Mind Training*.

243 An epithet for bodhisattvas.

244 On the authorship of this text and the other purportedly Indian works on mind training, see my introduction. In organizing the lines of the poem into stanzas and introducing numbers for them, I have consulted primarily Trichen Tenpa Rapgye's *Notes on the Wheel of Sharp Weapons (Notes)* and the topical outlines found in Lopsang Tamdrin's *Annotations on the Wheel of Sharp Weapons (Annotations)*. In finalizing my translation of this poem and the next one, *Peacock's Neutralizing of Poison*, I have benefited from the translations prepared by Geshe Lhundub Sopa and Michael Sweet in *Peacock in the Poison Grove*, as well as the much earlier translation of the *Wheel of Sharp Weapons* published by the Library of Tibetan Works and Archives.

245 The Buddha Jewel, Dharma Jewel, and Sangha Jewel. In Buddhism, these three, which are likened to wish-fulfilling jewels, constitute the refuge of a spiritual aspirant.

246 Literally meaning "enemy of Yama," who is the lord of death in the Buddhist pantheon, Yamāntaka refers to a meditation deity who is often seen as a wrathful manifestation of Mañjuśrī, the Buddha of wisdom.

247 Sopa et al. *(Peacock in the Poison Grove*, p. 61) reads this line as "If they involve themselves in other afflictions as well...." However, it seems fairly clear from the context that the author meant to extend the same analogy to other afflictions, such as anger. This is par9ticularly clear from the use of the verb *jarwa* (spelled *sbyar ba*), which literally means "to connect or to link," and here is translated as *extend*. Furthermore, Trichen's *Notes* (p. 11:2) also reads this line in the manner suggested here.

248 Trichen (p. 15a:5) reads this line as "From now on I shall condemn all my flaws." However, he acknowledges that other versions give the present reading.

249 The original Tibetan terms I have translated here as "deceit and guile" are, respectively, *mukyo* (spelled *mug skyo*) and *gyunam* (spelled *rgyu nam*), which Trichen (p. 20b:3) identifies to be archaic Tibetan for *yo* (spelled *gyo*) and *gyu* (spelled *sgyu*).

250 "Insights of learning and so on" refers to the three levels of understanding as

described in classical Buddhist texts: understanding derived from (1) learning, (2) reflection, and (3) meditation.

251   Both Tenpa Rapgyé (p. 24b:6) and Lopsang Tamdrin (p. 3a:7) have "all conceptualizations" in the place of "all negative conceptions."

252   In Tibetan Buddhist practice, these two—giving material things to the poor and making offerings to the Three Jewels—are known as the twin activities of giving.

253   Here I have followed the reading of Tenpa Rapgyé and Lopsang Tamdrin. In the original Tibetan of the text the final line reads: "From now on I shall extirpate you, the 'I.'"

254   Tenpa Rapgyé (p. 28a:6) gives the following reading for the last line: "From now on I shall minimize attachment toward everything."

255   Tenpa Rapgyé (p. 29b:4) writes this line as follows: "From now on I shall honor the embodiments of great kindness with my crown."

256   Although the Tibetan text gives this last line as "Therefore I shall be heedful against negative acts," here I have followed the reading of Tenpa Rapgyé and Lopsang Tamdrin, which is more consistent with the rest of the text.

257   My reading of this line, substantially different from Geshe Lhundub Sopa et al., is based on *Notes* (p. 36a). Tenpa Rapgyé reads the line to demonstrate the contradiction between someone who aspires for resources, which according to Buddhist teachings come about as a consequence of giving, yet indulges in such negative acts as stealing and extortion.

258   The Tibetan terms I have translated here as "divination" and "shamanism" are *mo* and *bön*. Although the term *bön* later became established as the name of Tibet's pre-Buddhist religion (Bön), the term can also simply refer to some form of village shamanism or animism. This idea of not relying on *mo* and *bön* appears to be an important theme in the early Kadam writings. For to do so is, according to the Kadam masters, to contradict the Buddhist practice of seeking refuge only in the Three Jewels.

259   Tenpa Rapgyé (p. 41b:1): "Forsaking ethical discipline, the liberation path, I uphold the household."

260   The Tibetan word *satha* (spelled *sa mtha'*), which literally means "remote areas," connotes areas that are outside the bounds of Dharma civilization. The connotation of remoteness is thus primarily in terms of the area's distance from Dharma and not in geographical terms from some "central land." Hence my choice of the term "wilderness."

261   The Tibetan expression *phasé* (spelled *pha zas*), literally "one's father's food," refers to one's inheritance.

262   This is a sarcastic remark that turns on the contradiction between not having any endurance for long-term meditative practice and professing powers of accurate clairvoyance, for in actual fact, clairvoyance can only arise from prolonged meditation practice.

263 Here "well-spoken words" *(legs bshad)* refers to the teachings of the Buddha and their subsequent commentarial treatises.

264 Sanskrit: *sugata*. An epithet of the Buddha, the fully awakened one.

265 The Tibetan original has the following reading: "O wielder of club, the weapon of no-self action." Here I have followed Tenpa Rapgyé and Lopsang Tamdrin, since this reading appears clearer.

266 These two lines resonate very closely with the two very famous lines from *Root Lines* and *Seven-Point Mind Training*.

267 "Existence and pacification" refers to the well-known Buddhist dichotomy of samsara (cyclic existence) and nirvana (its pacification).

268 In Tenpa Rapgyé this line is missing, which ensures that the stanza has four lines just like others and seems also to give a better reading of the stanza. Here, however, I have chosen to leave the original Tibetan text as it is.

269 This line is missing in the Lhasa edition and has been supplemented from the editions found in Tenpa Rapgyé, Lopsang Tamdrin, and the *Treasury of Instructions*.

270 Here I have chosen to follow the readings of Tenpa Rapgyé (p. 56a:6) and Lopsang Tamdrin (p. 7a:4).

271 The three wisdoms or understandings are: (1) understanding derived from learning, (2) understanding derived from reflection, and (3) understanding derived from meditation.

272 Here we follow the reading of Tenpa Rapgyé (58a:6) and Lopsang Tamdrin (p. 7a:6).

273 In the Tibetan original, the verb *spyad pa,* which means "to experience" or to "enjoy" is used here instead of *dpyad pa,* "to examine," which is most probably an error. Here, I have chosen to follow Tenpa Rapgyé (p. 58b:3) and Lopsang Tamdrin (p. 7a:7).

274 This appears to be an alternative title of the text.

275 This is an allusion to a story in the famous collection of Buddhist tales known as the *Jātakamālā,* which narrates many of the Buddha's previous lives. In the Pali canon, or Tipiṭaka, of the Theravada tradition, there are 547 Jātaka stories, and they are contained in the second division of the canon. Complete translations of these stories were published between 1895 and 1907 by Cambridge University Press in six volumes under the title *The Jātaka, or Stories of the Buddha's Former Lives.* In the Tibetan tradition, the Jātaka tales come primarily from Sanskrit sources. The Tengyur contains five volumes on the Jātaka cycle, which comprises eight individual works, among which Āryaśūra's *Garland of Birth Stories (Jātakamālā)* is the most well known. Āryaśūra's *Garland* contains only thirty-four tales, and a later supplement by the Third Karmapa Rangjung Dorjé in the fourteenth century brought the collection up to one hundred stories. The new anthology was named *Hundred Jātaka Tales.* My reference numbers follow this anthology. The story of Viśvāntara is number 9 in *Hundred Jātaka Tales,* pp. 59–76.

276 Jātaka tale 1; *Hundred Jātaka Tales,* pp. 2–7.

277 Jātaka tale 8; *Hundred Jātaka Tales,* pp. 46–59.

278 Jātaka tale 54; *Hundred Jātaka Tales,* pp. 371–78.

279 The identity of this story in the Jātaka tale remains uncertain.

280 Jātaka tale 24; *Hundred Jātaka Tales,* pp. 176–84.

281 An epithet for the Buddha.

282 This appears to be another alternative title for this short work.

283 Sanskrit: *prātimokṣa.* Set of ethical precepts, such as the full ordination vows of a monk, taken within the context of a formal ceremony conducted by a master in Buddhist ethical practice. There are eight categories of individual liberation vows: (1) full ordination of a monk, (2) full ordination of a nun, (3) novitiate precepts of a monk, (4) novitiate precepts of a nun, (5) probationary nun's precepts, (6) layman's vow, (7) laywoman's vow, and (8) one-day layperson's vow.

284 "Aspiration" *(mönpa;* spelled *smon pa)* and "engagement" *(jukpa;* spelled *'jug pa)* refer to the two progressive stages of the generation of awakening mind. The former refers to the initial stage of the awakening mind, when the intention to attain buddhahood for the benefit of all beings remains only at the stage of aspiration, albeit a powerful one. In contrast, "engagement" refers to the same altruistic intention when it is accompanied by a deep commitment to implement this ideal through the practice of the six perfections—generosity, morality, forbearance, joyous effort, concentration, and wisdom. Such a commitment is formalized by taking the bodhisattva vows. For a description of the characteristics of these two aspects of awakening mind, see the *Bodhicaryāvatāra,* 1:15–16.

285 One of the five original disciples of the Buddha, Upāli is known for his exemplary dedication to his life as a monk.

286 One of the five original disciples of the Buddha, Aśvajit is known for his single-pointed dedication to practice.

287 One of the most important of Vedic Hindu gods, Viṣṇu is recognized in the Hindu tradition as having ten incarnations. For a detailed description of the myth of Viṣṇu and his ten incarnations drawn from old Indian sources, see O'Flaherty, *Hindu Myths,* pp. 175–237.

288 "Vajra holder" is an epithet for a realized adept of Vajrayana practice. This stanza makes an allusion to what is a Buddhist equivalent of the rite of exorcism, whereby the malevolent forces are summoned by a highly realized tantric adept and ritually burned.

289 This is probably a reference to personal guardians who are born with individual human beings and are thought to shadow them, which in some ways represents the individual's conscience.

290 The class of eighteen possessors are those of (1) gods, (2) demigods, (3) smell-eaters, (4) serpentine nāgas, (5) yakṣa spirits, (6) Brahma, (7) ogres, (8) flesh-eating ghosts,

(9) hungry ghosts, (10) *kumbhāṇḍa* demons, (11) *kaśoka* demons, (12) distraction makers, (13) zombies, (14) *tshünlai* gods, (15) gurus, (16) sages, (17) elders, and (18) realized mystics.

291 Lobsang Tamdrin (p. 7b: 7) has the following reading: "Ask about this to all the chiefs, grasping at real and six classes of consciousness."

292 This stanza echoes the theme of chapter 24 of the *Collection of Aphorisms,* which are attributed to the Buddha. This text, which is entitled *Udānavarga* in Sanskrit, though similar in style and content to *Dhammapada,* is significantly longer.

293 Here I have chosen to follow the reading of Lobsang Tamdrin (p. 8a:2).

294 Lobsang Tamdrin (p. 8a: 4) has the following reading: "It's the demon of self-grasping, so vanquish it."

295 Here, for the first lines of the stanza, I have chosen to follow the reading of Lobsang Tamdrin (p. 8b:1).

296 Here I have chosen to follow the reading of Lobsang Tamdrin (p. 8b:2).

297 Here, too, I have chosen to follow the reading of Lobsang Tamdrin (p. 8b:2).

298 Lobsang Tamdrin has the following reading: "Integrate all conventional facts into one ultimate truth."

299 Here I have chosen to follow the reading of Lobsang Tamdrin (p. 8:b:4).

300 The Tibetan term *gyerwa* (spelled *gyer ba*) means "to chant something in songs, or sing something as a song." So I have translated the expression *gyergom* (spelled *gyer sgom*) as a "chanting meditation." Although the Tibetan edition of this work, as found in our present anthology, does not provide any note on its authorship, the Tibetan tradition generally attributes this short text to one Maitrīyogi, literally "a yogi of loving-kindness," who is recognized as one of the three principal teachers of Atiśa on mind training. Ostensibly, the work is a series of ecstatic, spontaneous songs sung in a dialogical structure by Maitrīyogi and Maitreya, the future Buddha. There is, however, a third voice, namely that of an interlocutor. This is probably the voice of the person who first compiled the songs together to weave them into a single narrative. Unfortunately, the identity of our editor remains anonymous. Although Tibetan authors identify Maitrīyogi as the younger of the two Kusalī brothers, "Kusalī" is probably a degeneration of Koṣala, the Tibetan equivalent of which is Gewachen (spelled: *dge ba can*), the name Yeshé Döndrup (*Treasury of Gems,* p. 48) gives to Kusalī Jr.

301 This last line suggests that the above song was sung as a self-exhortation by Maitrīyogi.

302 Source unidentified.

303 This work, as noted by Shönu Gyalchok (*Compendium of Well-Uttered Insights,* p. 48), is generally attributed to Serlingpa, Atiśa's principal teacher on the awakening mind. Interestingly, the nineteenth-century Mongolian author Yeshé Döndrup (*Treasury of Gems,* p. 48) attributes this text to Maitrīyogi. On the basis of intratextual considerations, some of which I shall note in the course of the translation,

the case for the first attribution appears stronger. This said, without additional textual evidence, the question of authorship of this poem must remain open. The stanza numbers do not appear in the Tibetan original and have been introduced here to help with the reading of the translation. I was not able to find any Tibetan commentaries on this work to help with this numbering.

304   This line could be read as paying homage to Maitrīyogi, who is, as observed earlier, recognized as one of the three main teachers of Atiśa on awakening mind. Alternatively, "yogi of loving-kindness" can also be read as a generic epithet, which may here refer to Serlingpa. Yeshé Döndrup reads this as the former and therefore chooses to attribute this work to Maitrīyogi. He must have felt that this homage verse acknowledges the source of the mind training instruction contained in this poem.

305   This poem has the rare feature of having a verse of homage at the beginning of each chapter, giving the impression that each chapter is a stand-alone teaching.

306   This is probably a reference to Jātaka tale 81, in which a young prince gives his body to a starving tigress about to devour her young cubs.

307   This stanza appears to be an allusion to Atiśa's hazardous voyage to the island of Sumatra to see Serlingpa.

308   This idea of enduring "beings of ingratitude" in the most compassionate way is a recurring theme in another well-known short mind training work attributed to Serlingpa, namely *Leveling Out All Conceptions*, text 12 of this present volume.

309   Although the Tibetan original gives this line as "To this Vajragarbha replied," I have chosen to follow the edition of *Treasury of Instructions*. "The great compassionate one" here probably refers to Serlingpa, in which case we can read this poem as, at least purportedly, an instruction conferred upon Atiśa by Serlingpa when the former arrived in Sumatra. The opening verses can then be attributed to Atiśa, who is narrating this instruction as he received it.

310   This stanza echoes a central theme of Serlingpa's *Leveling Out All Conceptions*.

311   "Mirror-image practitioners" refers to those who appear to be genuine spiritual practitioners but are not. Like reflections in a mirror, they are nothing but an appearance.

312   You remember the leper's body to remind yourself that there is no qualitative difference between the actual constituents of your own body and that of someone suffering from a contagious disease like leprosy, which drives people to avoid contact with you.

313   The Tibetan expression *gnyan dgu* (pronounced *nyengu*), which I have translated here as "numerous hazards," is somewhat obscure. Furthermore, in the original the expression is spelled *gnyen dgu*, that is with vowel 'e', which gives the reading "numerous blood relations," a seemingly meaningless expression in the context.

314   The earliest possible source for this enumeration of fifteen major possessions of children I have located is *Mahāsahasrapramardanasūtra* (Toh 558 Kangyur, rgyud 'bum, *pha*, 63b–87b). Though bearing the word *sutra* in its title, the work is found

in the tantra section of the Kangyur. There are several sādhana texts in the Tengyur connected to this sutra and a ritual text to help free children from possessions entitled *Secret Wheel of Fire* (Toh 3000 Tengyur, rgyud, *pu,* 60a–60b). Interestingly, there is also a similar text attributed to Atiśa in a popular anthology entitled *Collection of Dhāraṇis (sungdü,* spelled *gzungs bsdus)* or *Numerous Sutras (domang;* spelled *mdo mang).* Although there are two volumes entitled *Collection of Dhāraṇis* in the Kangur (Toh 846–1107 Kangyur, gzungs bsdus, *e* and *vam),* the popular version of *Collection* appears to be substantially different from the canonical edition. The version popular among the laity, which includes several texts, does not appear to enjoy any canonical recognition.

315 The translation of this root text is based on the version found in Yeshé Döndrup's *Treasury of Gems* (pp. 41–42), which its author asserts is a critical edition based on consultation with the commentary found in our present volume. He maintains that the version of this root text found in at least two editions of the *Great Collection*—a handwritten edition and a Mongolian blockprint edition—and also the version found in Sumpa Yeshé Paljor's collected works, all suffer from corruptions of spelling.

316 It is difficult to determine how far the attribution of this short text to Serlinga goes. Judging by the colophon of the commentary on this work, which is also contained in our present volume, the reader is given the impression that this attribution is based on an account given by Atiśa himself. The text possesses a decisively authoritative voice, and its literary style suggests a certain antiquity. Interestingly, if the attribution to Serlingpa is correct, it suggests that this teaching was given at the behest of Atiśa as he was planning to go to Tibet. The expression "to tame the barbarian borderlands" is probably an allusion to Tibet. Interestingly, the kernel of the instructions found in this short work is found also in chapter 14 of the father teachings of *The Book of Kadam* (pp. 790–93), where Atiśa is portrayed as citing these instructions as stemming from Avadhūtipa.

317 The listing of these four antidotes seems to differ slightly in different texts. Here, in this short text, they are listed as: (1) a counterpoint to happiness, (2) a successor to misery, (3) a charm to attract misfortunes, and (4) an additional wish on top of those that are least useful. For additional explanations of these, see the commentary on *Leveling Out All Conceptions* contained in this volume (text 32). Some editions list the third item as "bringing closure to your miseries," which is probably incorrect, an error perpetuated by a corrupt spelling. The gist of this verse is as follows: The practice of mind training is the greatest counterpoint to happiness, which, when not regulated, often leads to excessive attachment. It is also a successor to misery in that, just as suffering can motivate you to practice, training your mind can produce a similar effect. In addition, the practice of mind training resembles a charm that attracts all types of misfortune, for through this practice you deliberately call forth misfortune. Finally, mind training is an addition, albeit a contrary one, to all the useless wishes we harbor within. In other words, mind training represents one genuinely meaningful wish among myriad utterly meaningless ones.

318 The act of sealing your spiritual practice with meditation on emptiness is a common

Mahayana practice. For example, according to Mahayana teaching, the practice of each and every one of the six perfections must be completed with a meditation on the emptiness of what is known as the three factors—object of the action, the agent, and the action itself. This is to ensure that your spiritual practice does not fall prey to the deeply ingrained tendency to grasp at things as possessing some kind of enduring reality, thus reinforcing further your bondage to cyclic existence. The four acts of sealing referred to in this text, however—(1) casting away decisively, (2) letting go, (3) dismantling, and (4) letting be—appear to be a unique approach, possibly suggesting some textual and historical relationship influence of the spontaneous songs *(dohā)* literature, such as that of the Indian Buddhist adept Saraha. Both the mind training texts and the doha teachings emphasize eliminating all forms of conceptualization.

319 It is unfortunate that the compilers of our volume do not provide any information concerning the authorship of this work or the source of the instructions presented here. Since the text is briefly referred to in Shönu Gyalchok's *Compendium of Well-Uttered Insights* (p. 245), it is unlikely that either Shönu Gyalchok or Könchok Gyaltsen themselves wrote this piece. Future research may shed light on who is the "teacher" referred to in the colophon of this work.

The core instruction in this text relates to the mind training practice of taking, undertaken here in relation to others' afflictions, and to dismantling the solidity of the afflictions by contemplating their empty nature. As stated in the opening paragraph, the instruction for taking afflictions onto the path presented here is non-Vajrayana in its orientation.

320 Although the compilers of our volume do not provide any information on the authorship of this guru yoga text, textual evidence suggests that this is a slightly abbreviated guru yoga instruction found in Shönu Gyalchok's *Compendium of Well-Uttered Insights* (pp. 23–27). All the passages of this guru yoga mind training are verbatim extracts from this latter work, including the concluding remark: "This guru yoga is drawn from my teacher's words and put into letter." That this is Shönu Gyalchok's work is reinforced by the lineage of the transmission given here, where we read the name of Puṇyaratna as the last to hold this lineage. "Puṇyaratna" is the Sanskritized version of the Tibetan name Sönam Rinchen, who was from Nup Chölung, a person who figures in another mind training text as the one who transmitted the lineage to Shönu Gyalchok.

321 Despite repeated search, this citation could not be found in the *Gaṇḍavyūhasūtra*. However, as cited by Shönu Gyalchok (*Compendium of Well-Uttered Insights,* p. 23), the stanza is found in Indrabodhi's *Jñānasiddhi (Establishment of Wisdom);* Toh 2219 Tengyur, rgyud, *vi,* 51a:2.

322 Source unidentified.

323 This is Sé Chilbu, a principal student of Chekawa and the author of the earliest commentary on the *Seven-Point Mind Training* (text 7 in this volume). The textual source of this quotation remains unidentified.

324 "Teacher" here refers probably to Shönu Gyalchok's teacher, Tsultrim Pal, who is

explicitly acknowledged as the principal source of his teachings on mind training. See Shönu Gyalchok, *Compendium of Well-Uttered Insights,* p. 23.

325 The compilers of our volume provide no information on the authorship of this text nor do they provide us any indication of the source of the instruction presented here. Furthermore, this work does not feature in the list of mind training texts enumerated in the *Compendium of Well-Uttered Insights* by Shönu Gyalchok or *Memorandum of Teachings Received* by Longdöl Lama. The instruction in this short work is interesting in that it involves the recitation of the three syllables of *Oṃ Āḥ Hūṃ.* But since it pertains only to purification of negative karma and obscurations, its inclusion in an anthology of mind training texts is intriguing.

326 This is the mantra of the meditation deity Akṣobhya *(mitrukpa;* spelled *mi 'khrugs pa),* who belongs to the action class of tantra and is especially associated with the purification of negativity.

327 This is a reference to the hundred-syllable mantra of the meditation deity Vajrasattva, a deity of special significance in the practice of purification.

328 Although the compilers of our volume do not provide any information on the authorship of this short work, the text is listed in both Shönu Gyalchok's *Compendium of Well-Uttered Insights* and Longdöl's Lama's *Useful List [of Texts].* The core instruction in this text is a meditative practice in which, on the basis of the Vajrasattva meditation, you purify grudges you might harbor toward others, as well as overcoming malevolent forces, harmful intentions, jealousy, and rivalry with others. You then train the mind so that you are able to view all sentient beings as your dear parents.

329 This story of Atiśa's meeting with two yoginīs is found also in Chim Namkha Drak's (1210–85) well-known *Biography of Master Atiśa* (p. 95), which is probably the source used by the Tibetan editors of our volume. It is difficult to conclusively determine whether this story existed as an independent piece prior to the compilation of our volume, as suggested by the presence of a lineage at the end of the text. My own guess is that Shönu Gyalchok, one of the two compilers of our volume, was responsible for creating this short excerpt as an independent piece. Whatever the case, it seems fairly safe to assume that the story of Atiśa's encounter with the two yoginīs is an old one, perhaps dating back to Atiśa himself. From the earliest biographical accounts of Atiśa's life, we know that Atiśa is believed to have experienced numerous visions of the goddess Tārā. In fact, according to these biographies, it is eventually at Tārā's urging that Atiśa finally consents to the behests of its Ngari rulers and visits Tibet.

330 The actual instruction on mind training, which, according to this story, was conferred to Atiśa by the two yoginīs, appears as the next entry in our volume under the title *Kusulu's Accumulation Mind Training.*

331 In *Compendium of Well-Uttered Insights* (p. 245), Shönu Gyalchok states that this is the practice of training in the awakening mind according to the secret mantra system that the two yoginīs Tārā and Bhṛkuṭī conferred on Atiśa, when he encountered them in the sky to the east of Bodhgaya stupa. This story is recounted in the preceding entry of this volume under the title *Two Yoginis' Admonition to*

604 Notes to pages 209–215

Atiśa to Train His Mind. The present text is probably the one Longdöl Lama refers to as *Secret Mantra Mind Training* in his list (*A Useful List [of Texts]*, p. 316). The central practice echoes the well-known practice of offering one's body found in the "cutting off" (*chö*, spelled *chod*) tradition of Machik Lapdrön. It is difficult to determine what source Shönu Gyalchok is using to attribute this instruction to Atiśa.

332 Source unidentified.

333 Judging by the description that follows later in the text, the yoginī referred to here appears to be the well-known meditation deity Vajrayoginī.

334 Something like this parenthetical sentence is either missing or simply implied in the present edition. Without this additional step in the visualization, it is difficult to make sense of the opening of the next sentence, "On each point."

335 This is a fascinating short text on mind training that employs the well-known Vajrayana meditation of taking death, intermediate state, and rebirth onto the path as the three buddha bodies. The text provides an instruction on how to apply this three-buddha-bodies meditation for the specifically mind training objective of taking everyday experience as one's spiritual path. Interestingly, the root text of this instruction, which Shönu Gyalchok (*Compendium of Well-Uttered Insights*, p. 245) identifies as the four-line stanza attributed to Kashmiri master Śākyaśrī (1127–1225), does not allude to any association with this Vajrayana method. It is probable that the present work, which is essentially an exposition of Śākyaśrī's four lines, was composed by the Tibetan translator Trophu Jampa Pal, who is listed in the text as the inheritor of the lineage of this instruction from the Kashmiri master. Since no work of Trophu's survives today to my knowledge, this attribution must remain only a hypothesis. For a brief account of the Kashmiri master Śākyaśrī, especially his activity in Tibet, see Gö Lotsāwa's *Blue Annals*, vol. 2, (pp. 1237–49); English translation: *The Blue Annals*, pp. 1062–73.

336 "Pure trainees" here refers to those bodhisattvas who have gained direct insight into emptiness, have attained the state of a noble one, and are, as a consequence, on one of the ten bodhisattva levels. "Purity" here connotes the bodhisattvas' transcendence of bondage to karma, for—following their direct realization of emptiness—they are no longer subject to the law of karma. According to the Mahayana scriptures, the Buddha's embodiment as enjoyment body *(sambhogakāya)* is visible only to those sentient beings who are on the bodhisattva levels.

337 "Impure trainees" here refers to all the spiritual aspirants who have not yet gained direct realization of emptiness and thus are not free from bondage to karma.

338 Shönu Gyalchok (*Compendium of Well-Uttered Insights*, p. 245) identifies the root text of this work to be the following four-line stanza, which he attributes to Sumpa Lotsāwa (c. twelfth century):

> If you can tolerate anything, whatever you do brings happiness;
> If your mind rests where it's placed, you can journey anywhere;
> If your mind is fused with Dharma, it's okay even if you die;
> If you have recognized the mind as unborn, there is no death.

Something similar to these four lines is actually cited in our text. So far I have failed to locate any significant information on the life of Sumpa Lotsāwa. In the information on the transmission of the lineage at the end of this short work, it states that Sumpa Lotsāwa himself transmitted the instruction of this practice to the famous Tibetan master Sakya Paṇḍita. Furthermore, there is a brief reference to Sumpa Lotsāwa as Dharma Yönten in *The Blue Annals* (vol. 1, pp. 469–70; English translation: pp. 388–89), where he is listed as having translated several important texts composed by the Indian master Jayasena (Toh 1516 and 1521), from whom the Sakya patriarch Drakpa Gyaltsen received teachings as well. This would place Sumpa Lotsāwa between late twelfth and early thirteenth century, which fits well with the time of Sakya Paṇḍita. As for the identity of the author of this mind training text based on Sumpa Lotsāwa's instructions, the question must remain open.

339 Shönu Gyalchok (*Compendium of Well-Uttered Insights,* p. 216) lists this work alongside *Eight Sessions Mind Training* as representing supplemental instructions to the practice of giving and taking by means of training the mind in the conventional awakening mind. Although he identifies the cultivation of the three thoughts—the expansive thought, the resolute thought, and the diamondlike thought—to be the core instruction of this work, he does not provide any information on the authorship of this text or on the origin of the instructions presented in it. Judging by its literary style, especially the frequent use of the expression "it was taught"(*gsungs,* which I have translated here as "the master said"), we can safely conclude that this text belongs to the genre of *sindri* (spelled *zin bris*), lecture notes taken at an oral teaching.

340 Samantabhadra's expansive aspirations and vows, cited here, are probably drawn from the well-known work entitled *Vows of Good Conduct* (*Bhadracaryāpraṇidhāna;* Toh 1095 Kangyur, gzungs bsdus, *vam,* 262b–266a), which is sometimes identified as the final section of the *Flower Ornament Scripture (Avataṃsakasūtra).* The recitation of this prayer, which has attracted commentaries from numerous Tibetan authors, is highly popular in Tibetan Buddhist communities, including the laity, and is often recited at funerals as well.

341 The obscurations of karma, of afflictions, and of subtle knowledge.

342 This echoes *Bodhicaryāvatāra,* 1:40.

343 For a detailed description of these factors, see Tsongkhapa's *The Great Treatise,* vol. 2, pp. 76–80.

344 *Bodhicaryāvatāra,* 1:9; Toh 3871 Tengyur, dbu ma, *la,* 2a:5.

345 A disciple of the Buddha renowned for the stability of his mindfulness and his effectiveness in spreading the teachings.

346 This is probably a typographical error and should be Neusurpa, who was a principal disciple of Gönpawa.

347 Judging by the entry of the last name in the lineage of the transmission of this instruction, it appears that this work is a *sindri* based on notes taken at a teaching given by one Mipham Chöjé (which is the Tibetan version of Maitreya). This would then explain the significance of the opening salutation, where the author pays homage to his teacher Maitreya. He is probably the fourteenth-century

Kadam/Sakya master Tsultrim Dar, whom Jamgön Amé (*Treasury of Wonders*, p. 150) refers to as the second Maitreya.

348 Although it is difficult to determine the author of this mind training work, both Thuken (*Crystal Mirror*, p. 99) and Yeshé Döndrup (*Treasury of Gems*, p. 105) identify Dromtönpa as the source of the instruction on eight sessions of mind training. More importantly, the text itself refers to the instruction on eight sessions as "Dromtönpa's instruction." Since Khamlungpa specialized in the propagation of this instruction, this particular approach later came to be known as "Khamlungpa's eight sessions mind training." This instruction encapsulates a wonderful method for taking all aspects of everyday activities and experience into your meditative practice.

349 This is Gyalwa Sangpo, whose name appeared in the lineage of other mind training texts above.

350 *Bodhicaryāvatāra*, 8:113; Toh 3871 Tengyur, dbu ma, *la*, 28a1.

351 It is difficult to determine who is being quoted here.

352 The river that flows down from the Himalayas to the Indian plains across many regions of central India, including the famous city of Varanasi. The Ganges appears in many ancient Indian texts, including the early Buddhist scriptures, where the number of grains of sand on its banks is often used as an example of an extremely great number.

353 This is the celestial realm where the future Buddha Maitreya is believed to reside at present. Within the schema of the three realms—desire, form, and the formless— it belongs to the first category.

354 In the ancient Indian Mount Meru–centered cosmology, this is the main continent in the northern direction and is conceived to be a land of great affluence.

355 The title of the chapter here is slightly different from the one at the beginning of the chapter.

356 In general *torma* refers to a ritual cake customarily made of roasted barley dough and decorated with butter at the front, which is then consecrated and ritually offered to all classes of objects, such as the buddhas, meditation deities, and protectors, including the local guardian spirits.

357 The full stanza reads as follows: "Through the power of my thoughts, / Through the strength of the Tathāgata's blessings, / And through the power of the ultimate expanse as well, / Malevolent forces and those who harbor ill will, / Whatever such interferences there are, / May they all be instantaneously vanquished." This six-line stanza is a well-known prayer recited at the end of a torma ritual and represents the invocation of the power of truth, a practice that is frequently referred to in the Mahayana scriptures as an aspect of the buddhas and bodhisattva's skillful means of helping other sentient beings. Here in our text the first line is cited slightly differently.

358 *Bodhicaryāvatāra*, 3:20; Toh 3871 Tengyur, dbu ma, *la*, 7b:1.

359 *Bodhicaryāvatāra*, 3:19; Toh 3871 Tengyur, dbu ma, *la*, 7b:1.

360 This is probably a reference to the three sets of articles a monk possesses, which include, among others, his robes, alms bowl, staff, and so on.

361 For an elaboration of these two sets of four, see the opening passage of text 24 in this volume.

362 The six characteristics of meditative concentration are (1) having no expectations, (2) having no possessions, (3) renouncing home, (4) living in wilderness, (5) having stable focus of mind, and (6) being alone. Yeshé Döndrup (*Treasury of Gems*, pp. 24–25) provides the entire text of a short Indian Buddhist work bearing the title *Presentation of the Six Characteristics of Meditative Concentration* (*Dhyāna-ṣaddharmavyvaasthāna;* Toh 3926 Tengyur, dbu ma, *ki*, 92b–93a), which is attributed to Avadhūtipa and translated into Tibetan by Rinchen Sangpo. Yeshé Döndrup makes the remark that although Chim, probably referring to the famous Chim Namkha Drak, identifies Avadhūtipa to be Śavaripa, Sapaṇ cites this work in his *Elucidating the Sage's Intent* as being that of Maitrīpa.

363 "Unwavering karma" refers to the karma procured through engaging in deep meditative states, which gives rise to rebirth in the form and formless realms. It is called "unwavering" in that the fruition of karmic potentials cannot be redirected.

364 I think that the two things being correlated here are the clear consciousness that dawns at the moment of death and the thought processes involved in the mind training practice as presented in this eighth session.

365 The eight metaphors of illusion are (1) magical illusion, (2) mirage, (3) dreams, (4) mirror reflections, (5) a smell-eater's town, (6) echoes, (7) a reflection of the moon in water, and (8) bubbles. Sometimes ten metaphors of illusion are referred to, in which case, (9) shadows and (10) apparitions are added. When twelve metaphors are enumerated, (11) rainbows and (12) lightning are added to the list.

366 This is probably a reference to the "six conditions" that give rise to an affliction, as identified in Asaṅga's *Abhidharmasamuccaya (Compendium of Higher Knowledge)*, namely (1) basis, (2) object, (3) distracting activities, (4) [false] explanation, (5) habituation, and (6) mental engagement. A succinct description of these six conditions can be found in Tsongkhapa's *The Great Treatise on the Stages of the Path to Enlightenment* (vol. 1, pp. 301).

367 The entire text of this short mind training instruction is found in Shönu Gyalchok (*Compendium of Well-Uttered Insights*, pp. 221–22). Until further textual evidence surfaces, it is difficult to hazard any speculation on the possible authorship of this work. Interestingly, this text provides no information on the lineage of the instruction. In fact, according to Shönu Gyalchok, this and the next entry in our volume form a single work. This is probably the mind training text referred to in Longdöl Lama (*A Useful List [of Texts]*, p. 316) as *Mind Training with Four Appendixes*. My personal opinion based on the current sources is that this work may have been composed by Shönu Gyalchok himself on the basis of specific instructions extracted from a larger work on mind training by earlier Kadam teachers.

368 As in the case of the preceding work, *Mind Training Removing Obstacles*, the

608 Notes to pages 242–247

entire text of this short work is also found in Shönu Gyalchok (*Compendium of Well-Uttered Insights*, pp. 222–29). As I have suggested in my note to the previous work, this and the previous entry appear to form a single text and Shönu Gyalchok himself may have been the actual author. Interestingly, in the colophon of this second work, there is the short statement that the instructions contained here stem from Atiśa, but no further information of the subsequent lineage of its transmission is given. The key concern in this text appears to be to ensure how best to prevent future circumstances from undermining one's mind training practice, and more importantly, how best to prevent the arising of afflictions before they reach a potentially destructive level. Furthermore, unlike other mind training texts, here the practice of giving and taking, *tonglen*, which is the heart of mind training, is presented in the concluding section of the instruction as part of the benefits. This is done on the basis of a four-line stanza, the source of which I have so far failed to identify.

369 It is difficult to determine when the well-known myth of the Mongol taming a tiger may have evolved in Tibet. It is a popular theme in Tibetan murals, especially on the exterior walls of temples.

370 Shönu Gyalchok (*Compendium of Well-Uttered Insights*, p. 226) lists this second purpose as "the great followup to misery" *(sdug gi mjug mthud chen po)*. This appears to be more consistent with *Leveling Out All Conceptions*, which is probably one of the earliest sources of this concept. However, in his concluding sentence of this section later on, Shönu Gyalchok refers to this as "the closure to misery," thus agreeing with the version found in our text here. Perhaps both versions are correct and carry the same meaning.

371 The original Tibetan for these two expressions, which I have translated as to "let go as best as I can" and to "let go so that it is wiped clean" is *gans legs la thong* and *byug legs la thong*. These expressions are somewhat opaque, so my translations are only suggestive.

372 Source unidentified.

373 So far I have failed to locate any explicit reference in earlier sources for these so-called seven points of Atiśa presented in this short mind training work. Curiously, in the lineage of its transmission, the impression is given that this particular instruction was conferred by Atiśa on Gönpawa, with no mention of Dromtönpa as an intermediary, as is the case for most of the mind training instructions. Without further textual sources, especially works attributed to Gönpawa, it is extremely difficult to determine the earliest source of this particular instruction. As for its authorship, my own guess is that Könchok Gyaltsen himself may have penned it, at least in its present form as found in our volume.

374 It is noteworthy that the author uses the term "yogic exercise" (*'phrul 'khor*, literally meaning "magical wheels") here, which is an expression mostly associated with the teachings of the six yogas of Naropa and some tantric exorcism rites.

375 This is the personal name of Gönpawa, a well-known disciple of Atiśa and Dromtönpa.

376 "Me" here refers to Könchok Gyaltsen, one of the two compilers of our volume. This reference to himself suggests that it was he who authored, at minimum, the opening salutation verses.

377 The Tibetan expression I have translated here as "real-life mother" is *tsa wai ma* (spelled *rtsa ba'i ma*), which literally means something like "root mother." This somewhat archaic Tibetan expression is also found in a much earlier mind training work, Chim Namkha Drak's *Mind Training in a Single Session* (text 26 in this volume) as well.

378 Though this citation could not be located in the Tibetan edition of *Parinirvāṇa-sūtra*, these two exact lines are found in Nāgārjuna's *Suhṛllekha*, 69cd; Toh 4182 Tengyur, spring yig, *nge*, 43b:7. See also note 207.

379 Toh 287 Kangyur, mdo sde, *ya*, 82a – *śa*, 229b.

380 The Tibetan text of this sentence is somewhat obscure, so the translation provided here is only suggestive.

381 In the Lhasa edition of the Tibetan original, this subheading is missing. Since the seven points were clearly stated at the beginning of the text, we know that the fifth point introduces to the aspects of the awakening mind. Thus I have inserted the subheading here. In the critical edition of the Tibetan text, however, this subheading was mistakenly rendered as "Practicing taking and giving."

382 This subheading, too, is missing in the Lhasa edition of the Tibetan original. As with the previous subheading, I have inserted it here on the basis of the seven points presented at the beginning of the text. In the critical edition of the Tibetan text, this subheading was mistakenly given as "Determining all appearances to be your own mind."

383 In the Tibetan original, the text reads, "It is at such times I must reinforce my reasoning." This, I believe, is an error caused by a spelling mistake in the Tibetan. Instead of *rigs pa* (that is, with "sa" suffix), this should read *rig pa*, which means "awareness." This same expression appears later in this text with the accurate spelling.

384 In the Lhasa edition of the Tibetan original, there is no title for this text. In its place, the editor provides the following brief note: "This is the mind training of Chim. I have received the oral transmission." This is then followed by an additional note that reads, "I do not have the oral transmission for this; I must search for it again." This second note was probably inserted by a later editor. I find no grounds for disputing the attribution of authorship to Chim Namkha Drak. Shönu Gyalchok (*Compendium of Well-Uttered Insights*, p. 245) also refers to this short work as "the mind training composed by the great Chim."
    Chim Namkha Drak was one of the most well-known Kadam masters of thirteenth century. A student of the famous Kadam teacher Sangyé Gompa, the author of *Public Explication of Mind Training* (text 34 of this volume), Chim became the seventh abbot of Narthang Monastery, occupying the throne for thirty-six years. His students include, among others, the renowned Chomden Rikral and the Sakya patriarch Phakmodrupa, who later became the ruler of Tibet. Among his most

famous works are the "standard biography of Atiśa" (which can be found in *The Book of Kadam*), a commentary on Atiśa's *Bodhipathapradipa (Lamp for the Path to Enlightenment)*, and an exposition of Vasubandhu's *Abhidharmakośa*, the latter two no longer extant. A succinct biography of Chim can be found in Lechen Künga Gyaltsen's *Lamp Illuminating the History of the Kadam Tradition*, p. 255a–b.

385 In *Root Lines*, this line reads, "For the main practice, train alternately in taking and giving."

386 "The three noble beings"—disciples, self-realized ones, and bodhisattvas—are called "noble" because they have gained the direct realization of emptiness.

387 The wording of this line is slightly different in the *Root Lines*, where it reads, "When stability is attained, reveal the secret." Furthermore, as noted in my annotations to the *Root Lines*, it is not found in Chekawa's *Seven-Point Mind Training*.

388 The six directions are the four cardinal directions—east, south, west, and north— and above and below. This alludes to a well-known reductive analysis found in Vasubandhu's *Twenty Verses* (stanza 12) in which he critiques the concept of indivisible atoms. At the heart of the argument is the assertion that, even at the subtle particle level, a material object will possess at least these six directional perspectives, which implies, at least conceptually, that the object in question remains divisible. For an English translation of the section on Vasubandhu's critique of atomism in his *Twenty Verses* and its commentary, see Anacker, *Seven Works of Vasubandhu*, pp. 167–70.

389 As correctly attributed to the Indian Buddhist mystic Saraha by Sumpa Yeshé Paljor (*An Excellent Wish-Fulfilling Tree*, p. 79), these two lines are found in Saraha's *Songs of the Treasury of Dohas;* Toh 2224 Tengyur, rgyud 'grel, *vi,* 73a:4.

390 The full title of this versified work as found in the Lhasa Shöl edition is *Mind Training Bestowed to Namdak Tsuknor by Atiśa (Rnam dag gtzug nor la jo bos gnag ba'i blo sbyong)*. Attribution of this short work to Atiśa is made both in the opening lines and in the colophon of the text and is accepted by Yeshé Döndrup in his *Treasury of Gems*, where he cites the entire piece in the section on the selection of works attributed to Atiśa. Shönu Gyalchok (*Mind Training*, p. 245) lists this work as "Atiśa's Counsel to Namdak Tsuknor." I see no grounds to doubt the validity of this ascription, although its actual composition in verse may have been the work of either Namdak Tsuknor himself, which the colophon in the edition found in *Treasury of Gems* seems to suggest, or a later Tibetan editor. Ostensibly, it was composed as a personal counsel to a close disciple. If, as I suspect, this teaching was given to one Namdak Tsuknor when Atiśa was about to depart to central Tibet, this would mean that he had already been in the western part of Tibet for several years, thus making it possible that the teaching may have been originally composed in Tibetan rather than being translated from Sanskrit, which would explain its absence in the Tengyur. Interestingly, in terms of its theme and style, this oeuvre echoes a well-known Mahayana scripture entitled *Samādhirāja*, or *King of Meditations* (Toh 127 Kangyur, mdo sde, *da*).

     The three redactions of this text I have been able to consult contain numerous discrepancies. The three versions come from (1) the Lhasa edition of our volume,

(2) the *Treasury of Instructions,* and (3) the *Treasury of Gems.* The variant readings have been fully annotated in the critical edition of the Tibetan volume, but I note below only the ones that affect the meaning substantially.

391 These first six lines must have been inserted by Namdak Tsuknor himself, the recipient of this instruction from Atiśa. So far I have failed to locate any further textual information on the identity of this person or his relationship with Atiśa. Although both in the opening lines and in the colophon of the oeuvre a mention is made about the instruction being bestowed as Atiśa was embarking on his journey to Tibet, it need not necessarily imply that the teaching was given outside Tibet. In some ancient writings, the generic word *Tibet (bod)* is also used as a specific reference to the central regions of Tibet. So, it is conceivable that the teaching was given when Atiśa was in the Ngari region of western Tibet.

392 The stanza numbers have been introduced to help with the reading of the translation. Intriguingly, the next five lines are missing in the edition found in *Treasury of Gems.*

393 In the Lhasa edition of the Tibetan original, this line reads, "When probed in any way they are a mere world of dependent origination." Here I have followed the *Treasury of Gems* version, which seems more consonant with the line of thought.

394 The text of the Lhasa edition in the Tibetan original appears to be corrupt here, so I have followed the reading of *Treasury of Gems.*

395 This is the reading from the edition of *Treasury of Gems.* In the Lhasa edition of the Tibetan original, the line reads, "Practice them as the path of concentration through pure yogic exercises." Since the main theme in this stanza is the relinquishing of negative karma and afflictions, the key point appears to be transcending the duality between what is to be relinquished and its antidotes by reflecting upon the emptiness of the three aspects of an action—the object of an act, the agent, and the act itself. This is in perfect consonance with the reading of *Treasury of Gems.*

396 In the *Treasury of Gems* version, this line and the next read slightly differently: "Are attracted to you, is there lightness or heaviness [on your part]? / Do you confuse this with vision of compassion?" Both readings are somewhat obscure.

397 In *Treasury of Gems,* this line has the reading "Likewise I see the countless instants of nonconceptuality," that is, the opposite of "countless instants of conceptualization." I believe that the present reading is more accurate, especially when related to the subsequent stanza.

398 In *Treasury of Gems,* this line reads slightly differently as "I do not see the arising of any conceptualization."

399 "Wilderness" here refers to a place of solitude for intensive meditative practice.

400 Since the text of this line in the Lhasa edition appears to be corrupt, the translation of this line is based on the *Treasury of Gems* edition.

401 Known in Sanskrit as Tuṣita, this is the celestial realm of Maitreya, the future Buddha.

402 This is a reference to the well-known class of Mahayana scriptures, the Perfection of Wisdom sutras, that include, among others, the *Heart Sutra*.

403 This line is missing in the Lhasa edition of the original Tibetan and has been included here from the *Treasury of Gems*.

404 Although this expression "as before" must refer to the statement of the lineage of transmission of a text given earlier, I can't discern what text is meant here.

405 This passage on the lineage of transmission is missing in the *Treasury of Gems* edition.

406 Though attributed to Lo Lotsāwa, the source of the mind training instruction presented here is identified in its "colophon" as one Darpaṇa Ācārya, who, in turn, was presenting the thought of the Indian mystic Virvapa. The text cites first an eight-line quotation and later a six-line quote from Virvapa, which form the "root text" for this work. The instructions are organized within what the author calls the "yoga of unparalleled compassion" and the "yoga of root cause."

It is difficult to identify who this Indian master Virvapa is. The Tengyur contains two entries attributed to one Birbapa (Toh 1744 and Toh 2280), which may be the same person as our Virvapa. If so, then this is probably in fact Virūpa—the author of the famous *Vajra Lines on the Path and Its Fruits*, which is the primary root text for the cycle of teachings known as *lamdré*, or *path and its fruits*. Virūpa is generally recognized to be the same person as the eighth-century Nālandā Buddhist monk-scholar Dharmapāla. As for Darpaṇa Ācārya, there is an extremely short section on him in *The Blue Annals* (pp. 1045–46), where the only substantive information given is that he is the author of an important work on the rite of initiation entitled *Kriyāsamuccaya* (Toh 3305 Tengyur, rgyud 'grel). Lo Lotsāwa, the author of this text, was a Tibetan translator who was born sometime in the latter part of twelfth century. He traveled to Nepal and India and received extensive teachings from many Indian masters. The translations of a number of Vajrayana works are attributed to him. Intriguingly, neither Darpaṇa Ācārya nor the Tibetan lotsāwa (translator) appear in the lineage of this instruction.

407 These two expressions—"continuum of compassion" and "its rationale"—appear to be vocabulary specific to this mind training instruction and are elaborated below.

408 I introduced these arabic numbers to help the reader identify what the text later refers to as the five rationales for cultivating compassion toward those who harm you.

409 This appears to be a citation from Bhūripa's *Extensive Daily Confessions of Cakrasaṃvara [Practice]* (Toh 1533 Tengyur, rgyud 'grel, *za*, 95a:4).

410 This, too, appears to be a citation from Bhūripa's *Extensive Daily Confessions of Cakrasaṃvara [Practice]*, p. 95a:4. This and the line cited earlier appear in numerous Tibetan works on mind training practices.

411 In many later editions of the *Eight Verses*, the expression "I will train myself to" has been changed to "May I," thus transforming the contents of each stanza into an aspiration rather than a vow to practice. According to *Treasury of Gems* (p. 331),

this change was introduced by Sangchenpa (c. twelfth century). Although the Tibetan editors of our volume chose not to include the root text of *Eight Verses* other than embedded in its commentary, I provide the verses separately here for the sake of convenience. Unlike Chekawa's *Seven-Point Mind Training,* there are no variant redactions of this mind training classic.

412 This commentary on *Eight Verses on Mind Training* is attributed to Chekawa in the colophon at the end of the text, an attribution that is affirmed by Yeshé Döndrup in *Treasury of Gems* (p. 513). I see no grounds to question the validity of this ascription. The somewhat archaic literary style of the text suggests that this is one of the earliest commentaries on an explicit mind training text, if not the earliest. It is possible that Chekawa may have composed the work on the basis of oral teachings received from Langri Thangpa himself, the author of the *Eight Verses* root text. For biographical information on Chekawa, see the notes to my introduction.

413 This is how the title of this commentary appears in the Lhasa edition of the Tibetan original. The "story of the origin" of the eight verses probably refers to the account of Chekawa's first encounter with the *Eight Verses,* as narrated at the beginning of this text.

414 Sönam Lhai Wangpo's *History of the Precious Kadam Tradition* (p. 323) lists Chakshingwa as a principal student of Gya Chakriwa, who was in turn an important student of Langri Thangpa. This would place Chakshingwa sometime in the midtwelfth century.

415 In many later editions of the *Eight Verses,* the expression "I shall train" has been changed to "May I," thus transforming the contents of each stanza into an object of aspiration rather than a vow to practice. According to *Treasury of Gems* (p. 331), this change was introduced by Sangchenpa (c. twelfth century).

416 *Bodhicaryāvatāra,* 4:17; Toh 3871 Tengyur, dbu ma, *la,* 8b:5.

417 This story is included in the present volume as text 31.

418 *Prajñāpāramitāsaṃcayagāthā;* Toh 13 Kangyur, sher phyin, sna tshogs, *ka,* 19a:6.

419 Source unidentified.

420 Maitreya, *Mahāyānasūtrālaṃkāra,* 10:81cd; Toh 4020 Tengyur, sems tsam, *phi,* 12a:4. In the Tengyur edition, the last line reads slightly differently: "He is asserted to be far from enlightenment."

421 Walking toward a destination, going for a stroll, sleeping, and sitting—these are referred to as the four everyday activities in the earliest Buddhist scriptures, especially those that relate to the monastic vows.

422 This sutra remains unidentified.

423 *Bodhicaryāvatāra,* 4:44; Toh 3871 Tengyur, dbu ma, *la,* 9b:7.

424 *Bodhicaryāvatāra,* 4:32; Toh 3871 Tengyur, dbu ma, *la,* 9a:6.

425 *Bodhicaryāvatāra,* 4:33; Toh 3871 Tengyur, dbu ma, *la,* 9a:7.

426 *Bodhicaryāvatāra,* 4:30, 31; Toh 3871 Tengyur, dbu ma, *la,* 9a:5.

427   As the subsequent paragraph alludes, countering the afflictions through conduct refers to refraining from their external expression in body and speech. Countering them through meditation means meditation on the three scopes of the stages of the path *(lamrim)* teaching. Countering them through view refers to seeing the emptiness of these afflictions, their lack of any concrete, real object of reference.

428   *Bodhicaryāvatāra*, 4:46d; Toh 3871 Tengyur, dbu ma, *la*, 10a:1.

429   It is difficult to determine what "the king Asaṅga" refers to. It is probably an allusion to a story from the scriptures.

430   *Bodhicaryāvatāra*, 10:56; Toh 3871 Tengyur, dbu ma, *la*, 40a:3.

431   Nāgārjuna, *Commentary on the Awakening Mind (Bodhicittavivaraṇa)*, 106; Toh 1800 Tengyur, rgyud 'grel, *ngi*, 42a:7. The wording of these two lines is slightly different in the Tengyur. An alternative translation of these two lines that leads to a significantly different meaning is found in Lindtner, *Nāgārjuniana*, p. 215: "The Buddhas have to date seen no means apart from the *bodhicitta!*"

432   A more literal translation of the original Tibetan phrase would be this: "I too am in him." This citation is probably from oral tradition.

433   This sentence is somewhat obscure. Probably the author means that to take the defeat upon yourself means to avoid adding to your negative karma by retaliating against others' slander and so on.

434   This citation is probably from oral tradition. The Tibetan word I translate here as "butter-fried delicacies" is *martsö* (spelled *mar tshod*). This is probably the Tibetan snack known as *khapsé*, although I am not certain.

435   *Bodhicaryāvatāra*, 6:111; Toh 3871 Tengyur, dbu ma, *la*, 19a:2.

436   *Bodhicaryāvatāra*, 6:2; Toh 3871 Tengyur, dbu ma, *la*, 14b:4.

437   This is the first of the three aspects of forbearance, the practices of which are explained in detail by Śāntideva in his *Bodhicaryāvatāra*. The remaining two are: the forbearance of voluntarily accepting suffering and the forbearance that results from reflecting on the teachings.

438   Source unknown; it is also difficult to identify who these two Kadam teachers are.

439   This appears to be a slight variation of the first two lines of Nāgārjuna's *Ratnāvali* 5:83. In Nāgārjuna's text, the lines read, "May their negativity ripen upon me / And may my virtues ripen upon them." *Ratnāvali*, 5:84cd; Toh 4158 Tengyur, skyes rabs, *ge*, 125a:6.

440   This citation is probably from an oral tradition. The text of this citation in *Treasury of Gems* varies slightly from this version.

441   *Bodhicaryāvatāra*, 6:42; Toh 3871 Tengyur, dbu ma, *la*, 16a:5.

442   *Bodhicaryāvatāra*, 6:47; Toh 3871 Tengyur, dbu ma, *la*, 16b:1.

443   *Bodhicaryāvatāra*, 3:16; Toh 3871 Tengyur, dbu ma, *la*, 7a:5.

444   Source unidentified.

445 Sangyé Gompa also cites this stanza in his *Public Explication* (pp. 382), but again does not give its source. Despite repeated search, I have succeeded neither in locating this citation nor in identifying the text referred to here as *Songs of Blissfulness (Bde ba'i klu)*. I remember seeing this same stanza cited as from "Atiśa's *Songs of Blissfulness*" in another text. Several songs appear under Atiśa's name in the Tengyur, none of which contains this stanza.

446 "Definite goodness" *(ngelek, spelled nges legs)* is an epithet for the supramundane attainments of liberation from cyclic existence and of buddhahood.

447 *Bodhicaryāvatāra*, 8:131; Toh 3871 Tengyur, dbu ma, *la*, 28b:4.

448 *Bodhicaryāvatāra*, 9:152–53; Toh 3871 Tengyur, dbu ma, *la*, 36b:4.

449 *Bodhicaryāvatāra*, 9:154ab; Toh 3871 Tengyur, dbu ma, *la*, 36b:6. In the critical Tibetan edition, this citation is mistakenly given as *Bodhicaryāvatāra*, 6:2.

450 With respect to the two remaining truths—the true cessation and the true path that leads to cessation—you imagine giving your potential realizations of the two to all sentient beings.

451 Despite its title, this short text includes four different stories, or rather allusions to them. One is, of course, the story of the ugly mendicant; the second is an allusion to the story of an elderly couple who, when robbed, fail to take countermeasures; the third is Atiśa's frequent meeting with a person of evil character; and finally is an allusion to the story of Langri Thangpa being falsely accused of trangressing the cardinal monastic precept of celibacy. Rather than being a coherent single text, the work is more like several extracts loosely compiled as a resource for teaching. In my view, it was probably Könchok Gyaltsen himself, one of the compilers of our present volume, who put these together here.

452 This story is referred to often in the mind training instructions to emphasize the point that you cannot judge the inner realization of a person from his or her external appearance. Given the allusion to the challenge for debate from the proponents of non-Buddhist schools, the story clearly has an Indian origin. Most probably, it comes from the oral teachings of Atiśa.

453 This story is often alluded to in mind training texts to stress the importance of confronting afflictions as soon as they arise rather than allowing them to follow their course.

454 This story probably comes from an oral tradtion that goes back to Atiśa himself.

455 This Dzechenpa, which can literally mean "the great resilient one," probably refers to Langri Thangpa himself. Source of this stanza remains unidentified.

456 *Tarkajvālā;* Toh 3856 Tengyur, dbu ma, *dze*, 175a:2. Although by citing this passage here, the Tibetan editor is making the general point that ordained monks must pay homage to lay bodhisattvas, inavertently it also appears to give the impression that there may have been some truth in the rumor. I do not believe this was the intention of the editor.

457 This sutra does not appear to exist in the Kangyur as such. I have failed to locate

this citation. In fact, it is difficult to surmise the intended significance of this citation here in the text.

458 Since the explicit context here is that of an ordained practitioner who has taken the vow of celibacy, for women practitioners, the advice would be to live far from the presence of men so that there will be no threat to their cardinal precepts.

459 Though this is clearly a commentary on a verse text entitled *Leveling Out All Conceptions*, in the Lhasa edition of the Tibetan original, interestingly, no title is provided at the beginning of this text. In the short colophon at the end of the text, however, this commentary is presented as being composed, or at least narrated, by Atiśa on the basis of receiving the instructions directly from his teacher Serlingpa. It is difficult to assess the true authorship of this commentarial work. However, if the attribution to Serlingpa of its root text, *Leveling Out All Conceptions*, is valid, it is conceivable that Atiśa gave commentaries, or at least explanations, of the instructions contained in the root stanzas. Although the opening two paragraphs of this text are clearly not by Atiśa, as to the main body of the text, I will follow the traditional attribution of this commentary to master Atiśa.

Since the entire text of this commentary appears in Shönu Gyalchok (*Compendium of Well-Uttered Insights*, pp. 216–221, I have chosen to follow the version found there in several instances, especially in places where the Tibetan text of the Lhasa edition appears to be corrupt.

460 Source unidentified. Shönu Gyalchok (*Compendium of Well-Uttered Insights*, p. 217) cites this as well, but with a slightly different redaction. Unfortunately, he too does not give any specific information on the source of the quote.

461 *Samputatantra;* Toh 381 Kangyur, rgyud, *ga,* 158a:3. These two lines are found also in the *Great Tantra of Magical Net (Māyājālamahātantrarāja);* Toh 466 Kangyur, rgyud, *ja,* 131a:3. They are also cited by Atiśa in his *Bodhipathapradipa;* Toh 3947 Kangyur, dbu ma, *khi,* 240b:2.

462 *Madhyamakāvatāra,* 6:117; Toh 3861 Tengyur, dbu ma, *'a,* 210a:1.

463 The four factors of enlightened phenomena are the four enumerated in the first stanza of the root text of *Leveling Out All Conceptions,* namely (1) leveling out all false conceptions, (2) carrying forth the force of all antidotes, (3) concentrating all aspirations into one, and (4) seeking the path where all paths converge.

464 These four antidotes differ slightly in different texts. Here they are listed as: (1) a counterpoint to happiness, (2) a successor to misery, (3) a charm to attract misfortunes, and (4) an additional wish on top of those that are least useful. Some editions list the third item as "bringing closure to your miseries," which is probably incorrect, an error perpetuated by a corrupt spelling. The gist of this verse is as follows: The practice of mind training is the greatest counterpoint to happiness, which, when not regulated, often leads to excessive attachment. It is also a successor to misery in that, just as suffering can motivate you to practice, training your mind can produce a similar effect. In addition, the practice of mind training resembles a charm that attracts all types of misfortune, for through this practice, you deliberately call forth misfortune. Finally, mind training is an addition, albeit a contrary one, to the useless wishes that we harbor within. In other words, mind

training represents one genuinely meaningful wish among myriad utterly meaningless ones.

465 (1) Forbearance that endures injuries from others, (2) forbearance that voluntarily accepts suffering, and (3) forbearance derived from reflecting on the teachings.

466 On sealing spiritual practice with emptiness, see note 318 to the root text.

467 This last sentence is effectively the colophon of this commentary on *Leveling Out All Conceptions,* and therefore the actual body of the text concludes here. The remaining part is composed of several citations from sutras and tantras, all of which underline the point that great compassion is the core practice of a bodhisattva, whose sole aspiration is to bring about the welfare of other sentient beings. These citations may have been added later by a Tibetan editor, perhaps Könchok Gyaltsen himself.

468 *Amoghapāśahṛdayasūtra;* Toh 682 Kangyur, rgyud, *ba,* 281a:1.

469 Buddhaśrījñāna, *Drop of Freedom;* Toh 1859 Tengyur, rgyud 'grel, *di,* 48b:2.

470 *Drop of Freedom,* 48b:5.

471 *Dharmasaṃgītisūtra;* Toh 238 Kangyur, mdo sde, *zha,* 84a:5.

472 This is one of the most beautiful works of the mind training genre. Although both the homage and the end of the text explicitly acknowledge Chekawa (whom the author calls Maldrowa), intriguingly there is not a single allusion to Chekawa's seven-point mind training, nor any indication of the author's knowledge of Sé Chilbu's influential commentary on it. Furthermore, the explanations of the verses are provided in a seamless interconnected teaching, with no clear section divisions, while the root text cited in this work appears to be almost exactly identical to the *Root Lines* attributed to Atiśa (entry 4 of our volume). All this suggests that this commentarial mind training text either predates Sé Chilbu's commentary on *Seven-Point Mind Training* or that it represents a lineage of transmission different from Chekawa's influential seven-points approach.

The mention of Drakmarwa in the opening stanza may be a clue to its origin. Drakmarwa was a student of an influential Kadam teacher Jayülwa Shönu Ö (1075–1138), who was in turn a student of Chengawa, one of the three Kadam brothers. Drakmarwa's lineage is known as the "Kadam lineage of instructions." Chekawa, who is the source of the seven-point instruction, on the other hand, belongs to the lineage of Potowa through to Sharawa, the lineage known as the "Kadam lineage of treatises." Interestingly, in the brief account of Chekawa's discovery of the mind training instruction found in Sangyé Gompa's *Public Explication,* Chekawa is reported as naming Shang Drakmarwa as a possible source when searching for the instruction. This suggests that Drakmarwa was already established as an authoritative Kadam teacher while Chekawa was on his quest.

The Lhasa edition of the Tibetan original of this work unfortunately suffers from a number of spelling corruptions, all of which I have attempted to correct. The spelling errors were preserved in our critical Tibetan edition in the endnotes. Given the absence of any textual support, it is difficult to speculate who the author of this eloquent work might be. The conciseness of its literary style, the extremely practical approach, and the frequent use of archaic Tibetan all seem to confirm its antiquity. Most probably the work was composed by a student of both Drakmarwa and Chekawa. So we can confidently date the text in the latter part of twelfth century at the earliest.

473 Maldrowa is one of the aliases of Chekawa, the author of *Seven-Point Mind Training*. He is so called because Cheka Monastery, which he established, was in Maldro region of central Tibet.

474 According to Sönam Lhai Wangpo (*A History of the Precious Kadam Tradition*, p. 340) and Yeshé Döndrup (*Treasury of Gems*, p. 291), Drakmarwa (twelfth century) was a student of Jayülwa Shönu Ö and is known as one of the eight great "outer" disciples. I have failed to locate any further biographical details.

475 This is most probably a reference to the four directional guardians.

476 This is an allusion to Nāgārjuna's *Suhṛllekha*. Tsongkhapa identifies these seven defects as the defects of (1) uncertainty, (2) lack of contentment, (3) the need for repeated discarding of bodily existence, (4) the need for repeated conception, (5) repeated fluctuations in your fortunes, and (6) having no companions. According to Tsongkhapa, the seventh is merely a restatement of each of the defects. See Tsongkhapa, *The Great Treatise on the Stages of the Path to Enlightenment*, vol. 1, p. 281.

477 In both *Root Lines* and the root text embedded in Sé Chilbu's commentary on *Seven-Point Mind Training*, this line reads, "For the main practice, train alternately in giving and taking."

478 In both *Root Lines* and *Seven-Point Mind Training*, this line reads,"Commence the sequence of taking from your own self." It is conceivable that the variation in this commentary is a result of a scribe's error.

479 On the enumeration of these different world systems, see McGovern, *A Manual of Buddhist Philosophy*, pp. 48–73.

480 The Tibetan text of these two sentences is not only quite obscure but also appears to suffer from spelling corruption, so the translation is only suggestive.

481 There seem to be several different ways of defining "immeasurability" with relation to the four thoughts—immeasurable loving-kindness, immeasurable compassion, immeasurable joy, and immeasurable equanimity. Here it's in terms of what our author calls the reversal of the three—objects, thoughts themselves, and their fruitions. It is difficult to guess, however, what this reversal means. Judging by the immediately preceding sentence, perhaps what the author means by this is that at an advanced stage, these four thoughts—loving-kindness, compassion, joy, and equanimity—arise spontaneously without actually directing one's thought to the objects, and that the fruits of these thoughts can be experienced without having to consciously cultivate these thoughts. In other Mahayana works, "immeasurability" is sometimes defined by whether compassion and so on are grounded in heightened meditative states, such as the mental states of the form and formless realms.

482 *Gocaparisuddhasūtra;* Toh 44 Kangyur, phal chen, *ka*, chap. 16, 210b–219b.

483 In both *Root Lines* and *Seven-Point Mind Training* this line reads, "There are two tasks—one at the start and one at the end."

484 Although these two sentences are unclear in the Tibetan, I believe the key point being made in this: The kindness of the three objects—our parents, our preceptors, and our teachers—is boundless. However, both knowingly and often unwittingly, we have in the past responded to their kindness with negative behavior. You can develop your appreciation for these kind objects by trying to help people whose minds are dominated by strong negative emotions such as hatred. For such kindness is often repaid with belligerence and abuse.

485 Although the text of the commentary fails to state it here, of these two, it is the latter—namely, one's own self-awareness—that must be held as the principal witness. This idea of self-awareness is similar to the role an individual's moral conscience plays in Western ethics. The reason why self-awareness is more important than the judgment of others is that our self-awareness is present at all times.

486 The English word *boastfulness* does not convey the full sense of the Tibetan word *yü* (spelled *yud*). For my comments on the problems pertaining to the translation of this Tibetan term, see note 239.

487 The Tibetan text in the Lhasa edition is corrupt here, which is why the text repeats itself.

488 In the *Root Lines* and *Seven-Point Mind Training* this line reads, "Do not depend on other conditions."

489 This line is missing in *Seven-Point Mind Training*. It reads slightly differently in *Root Lines,* where it appears as "If relapsed, meditate on it as the very remedy."

490 The wording of the Tibetan text here is slightly different from *Root Lines*.

491 *Gurupañcāśikā;* Toh 3871 Tengyur, rgyud 'grel, *tshu,* 10a–12a. This is a classic Mahayana work outlining in detail the manner in which a practitioner must relate to his or her teacher, especially in the context of the Vajrayana tradition. It is attributed to the well-known second-century Buddhist poet Aśvaghoṣa. An English translation of this work along with a commentary by Tsongkhapa can be found in Tsongkhapa, *The Fulfillment of All Hopes*.

492 In *Root Lines* and *Seven-Point Mind Training* this line reads, "Constantly train in the three general points."

493 This metaphor may be an allusion to an ancient battle custom where a captured enemy is nailed to the ground by driving a stake through his heart. The point of comparison here is the necessity for persistence in both acts—driving a stake into an enemy's heart and the practice of training one's mind.

494 The two metaphors illustrate the need to engage in mind training practice decisively. When slaughtering an animal, if a major artery is cut, that strike becomes decisive. Similarly, when you cut the rope of a heavy load suspended from the roof, the load falls with a thud. In the same manner we are advised to pursue mind training practice with decisiveness.

495 Although this line does not exist in *Root Lines,* it appears in both *Seven-Point Mind Training* and *Annotated Root Lines.*

496 This line is missing in *Root Lines, Annotated Root Lines,* and *Seven-Point Mind Training.*

497 This sentence is extremely obscure in the Tibetan original, so the translation here is only suggestive.

498 In *Root Lines* this line reads, "Train in the five powers."

499 This line reads slightly differently in *Seven-Point Mind Training.*

500 This text, widely acclaimed as "The Great Public Explication" *(Tsogs bshad chen mo),* represents perhaps the most extensive early commentarial work of the mind training genre. Soon after its composition, the work appears to have assumed the status of a classic in this genre. Könchok Gyaltsen, one of the compilers of our present volume, felt the need to compose what is effectively a companion to this classic, which he entitled *Supplement to the "Oral Tradition"* (see text 37). Shönu Gyalchok, on the other hand, recognized Sangyé Gompa's text as a somewhat alternative reading to Chekawa's mainstream approach to *Seven-Point Mind Training* expounded in Sé Chilbu's commentary. In *Compendium of Well-Uttered Insights* (pp. 193–211), Shönu Gyalchok provides a detailed outline of *Public Expilication*'s presentation of the mind training instructions. In terms of literary style, although it frequently says "thus taught the master" *(zhes gsung ngo),* the work does not appear to be based on notes taken at an oral teaching. Rather, it seems to have been composed as an independent piece, and this is explicitly confirmed by the author's dedication, where he writes:

> Ratnaguru relied on his teacher's words;
> I, too, have applied the meaning a little in my mind;
> So through [showing the] interrelations, sequence, and essential instructions,
> I here present this [instruction on] training the mind.

On the basis of this stanza, it is evident that the author's frequent statement "Thus taught the master" refers to his teacher Ratnaguru (mid twelfth–early thirteenth century), whose full name is Shangtön Chökyi Lama. Popuarly known as Shang Ratnaguru, he held the abbotship of Narthang Monastery for ten years. According to Sönam Lhai Wangpo, *History of the Precious Kadam Tradition* (pp. 251b–255a), the author of our text, Sangyé Gompa, succeeded his teacher, Ratnaguru, to the abbotship of Narthang and, like his predecessor, held the seat for ten years. In addition to this influential work on mind training, he is also known to have composed a commentary on Atiśa's *Bodhipathapradīpa.*

501 For comments on this work, see note 160.

502 On Aśvaghoṣa, see note 160.

503 In Sé Chilbu's commentary (text 7 of this volume), he writes the title of this sutra as *Garland of Three Clubs.* See note 159.

504 *Ākāśagarbhasūtra;* Toh 260 Kangyur, mdo sde, *za,* 264a–283b.

505 *Śikṣāsamuccaya;* Toh 3939 Tengyur, dbu ma, *khi.* Composed by the noted Maha-yana author Śāntideva (eighth century), the author of the classic *Bodhicaryāvatāra.*

506 *Vimalakīrtinirdeśasūtra;* Toh 176 Kangyur, mdo sde, *ma,* 175a–239b.

507 *Bodhisattvabhūmi;* Toh 4037 Tengyur, sems tsam, *dzi.* Composed by Asaṅga (fourth century), the well-known Mahayana Buddhist thinker and the founder of the Yogācāra school.

508 *Vimalakīrtinirdeśasūtra;* Toh 176 Kangyur, mdo sde, *ma,* chap. 7, 215a:4.

509 *Vimalakīrtinirdeśasūtra,* 215a:7.

510 *Bodhisattvabhūmi;* Toh 407 Tengyur, sems tsam, *vi,* 71a:4.

511 Sé Chilbu, too, cites this quote, which may have been part of an oral tradition.

512 *Bodhipathapradīpa,* 46; Toh 3947 Tengyur, dbu ma, *khi,* 240a:4. The third line of the translation here appears to be corrupted in the Lhasa edition of our text. Here I have translated it from the Tengyur edition.

513 The following paragraphs present an account of Chekawa's discovery of the mind training teachings that is recounted in many subsequent mind training works, especially that of Shönu Gyalchok (*Compendium of Well-Uttered Insights,* pp. 17–22), where the *Public Explication* account is copied almost verbatim. Shönu Gyalchok refers to Sé Chilbu's "annotations" as the primary source for his account of Chekawa's discovery of mind training teachings, a text that may also have been the source for Sangyé Gompa. So far I have failed to identify this "annotations," let alone locate a copy. Given that Sé Chilbu was Chekawa's principal student, it appears that this story evolved on the basis of Chekawa's own oral accounts.

514 Asaṅga, *Abhidharmasamuccaya;* Toh 4049 Tengyur, sems tsam, *ri.*

515 This is probably a reference to the famous *Blue Udder,* composed by the Kadam master Dölpa Sherap Gyatso (b. 1059).

516 This story of Chekawa hearing the *Eight Verses* first from Chakshingwa is found also at the beginning of *Eight Verses on Mind Training* (text 29 of this volume). As I observe in my annotations there, Chakshingwa was a principal student of Gya Chakriwa, who was in turn an important student of Langri Thangpa. This places Chakshingwa sometime in the mid twelfth century.

517 Asaṅga, *Śrāvakabhūmi;* Toh 4036 Tengyur, sems tsam, *dzi.*

518 *Perfection of Wisdom in a Hundred Thousand Lines, Śatasāhasrikāprajñāpāra-mitāsūtra;* Toh 8 Kangyur, shes phyin, *ka–a.*

519 *Bodhicaryāvatāra,* 10:55a; Toh 3871 Tengyur, dbu ma, *la,* 40a:3.

520 *Ratnāvali,* 5:84cd; Toh 4158 Tengyur, skyes rabs, *ge,* 125a:6.

521 The Tibetan original of this saying is very obscure, so my translation must remain provisional.

522 *Gocarapariśuddhasūtra;* Toh 44 Kangyur, phal chen, *ka,* chap. 16, 210b–219b.

523 This is a principal student of Chekawa and the author of the commentary on *Seven-Point Mind Training* contained in our volume (text 7). Chilbu's full name is Sé Chilbu Chökyi Gyaltsen.

524 *White Lotus of Compassion Sutra (Karuṇāpuṇḍarikasūtra);* Toh 112 Kangyur, mdo sde, *cha,* chap. 3, 148a:4.

525 This is a reference to the Jātaka tales, which narrate the previous lives of the Buddha.

526 Cited in Prajñākaramati, *Exposition of the Difficult Points of the "Bodhicaryāvatāra" (Bodhicaryāvatārapañjikā);* Toh 3872 Tengyur, dbu ma, *la,* 45b:4.

527 (1) Living in a conducive environment, (2) relying upon sublime beings, (3) having made excellent aspirational prayers, and (4) having gathered merit in past lives. Nāgārjuna lists these in his *Suhṛllekha,* stanza 62.

528 (1) Having a long life, (2) having an attractive appearance, (3) having an excellent family lineage, (4) enjoying excellent prosperity, (5) enjoying credibility, (6) having a reputation for influence, (7) being male, and (8) possessing power.

529 I have failed to identify these seven higher qualities.

530 *Kusumasañcayasūtra;* Toh 266 Kangyur, mdo sde, *'a,* 288a–319a.

531 Nāgārjuna, *Suhṛllekha,* 59; Toh 4182 Tengyur, spring yig, *nge,* 43b:1.

532 *Bodhicaryāvatāra,* 4:20; Toh 3871 Tengyur, dbu ma, *la,* 8b:6. In the critical Tibetan edition, this is wrongly cited as *Bodhicaryāvatāra,* 3:20.

533 *Bodhicaryāvatāra,* 4:15; Toh 3871 Tengyur, dbu ma, *la,* 8b:4.

534 Candragomin, *Śiṣyalekha,* 64; Toh 4183 Tengyur, spring yig, *nge,* 50a:2. The reading of this stanza is slightly different from the version found in Tengyur compared to that cited by Sangyé Gompa in his *Public Explication* (text 34 of this volume). "Human-or-what" *(kinnara;* Tibetan, *mi 'am ci)* refers to a class of sentient beings thought to be similar to human beings in their appearance, while "belly-crawlers" refers to snakes.

535 *Bodhicaryāvatāra,* 1:4; Toh 3871 Tengyur, dbu ma, *la,* 1b:7.

536 *Gaṇḍavyūhasūtra;* Toh 44 Kangyur, phal chen, *ga,* chap. 44, 381a:7.

537 *Bodhicaryāvatāra,* 4:23; Toh 3871 Tengyur, dbu ma, *la,* 9a:2.

538 *Bodhicaryāvatāra,* 4:18; Toh 3871 Tengyur, dbu ma, *la,* 8b:5.

539 *Śiṣyalekha,* 65ab; Toh 4183 Tengyur, spring yig, *nge,* 50a:3.

540 *Śiṣyalekha,* 63; Toh 4183 Tengyur, spring yig, *nge,* 50a:2.

541 Aśvaghoṣa, *Śokavinodana (Dispelling Sorrow);* Toh 4177 Tengyur, spring yig, *nge,* 33a:4.

542 All text in parentheses is, in the original Tibetan, written in a smaller font embedded within the text. These are notes added by an editor. I chose parentheses to distinguish them from my own additions, which are in square brackets.

543 *Śokavinodana,* 33a:6.

544 *Śokavinodana,* 33b:3.

545 Source unidentified.

546 Despite repeated searches, we have failed to locate this citation.

547 *Udānavarga,* 1:3; Toh 326 Kangyur, mdo sde, *sa,* 209a:2.

548 *Bodhicaryāvatāra,* 4:16; Toh 3871 Tengyur, dbu ma, *la,* 8b:4.

549 *Śiṣyalekha,* 65cd; Toh 4183 Tengyur, spring yig, *nge,* 50a:4.

550 *Suhṛllekha,* 56; Toh 4182 Tengyur, spring yig, *nge,* 43a:4.

551 *Suhṛllekha,* 58 and 56, respectively. The Tibetan critical edition cites these as stanzas 55 and 57.

552 Sangwé Jin, *Saptakumārikāvadāna;* Toh 4147 Tengyur, 'dul ba, *su,* 251b:1.

553 *Abhidharmakośa,* 3:78; Toh 4089 Tengyur, mngon pa, *ku,* 9b:7.

554 The parenthetical annotation cites this as being from the *Ratnāvali,* but we have not found it in the actual text in the Tengyur.

555 *Ratnāvali,* 3:78; Toh 4158 Tengyur, skyes rabs, *ge,* 117b:1.

556 *Bhadrakāratrisūtra;* Toh 313 Kangyur, mdo sde, *sa,* 162b:2.

557 *Bodhicaryāvatāra,* 2:34; Toh 3871 Tengyur, dbu ma, *la,* 5a:4.

558 *Bodhicaryāvatāra,* 2:41; Toh 3871 Tengyur, dbu ma, *la,* 5b:2.

559 *Bodhicaryāvatāra,* 6:49; Toh 3871 Tengyur, dbu ma, *la,* 16b:7.

560 *Saptakumārikāvadāna;* Toh 4147 Tengyur, 'dul ba, *su,* 246b:2.

561 *Bodhicaryāvatāra,* 8:32; Toh 3871 Tengyur, dbu ma, *la,* 24b:3.

562 *Bodhicaryāvatāra,* 2:35; Toh 3871 Tengyur, dbu ma, *la,* 5a:6.

563 *Rājāvavādakasūtra;* Toh 221 Kangyur, mdo sde, *dza,* 82a:1. There are three sutras in the Kangyur that carry the same Tibetan title *Rgyal po la gdams pa theg pa chen po'i mdo:* Toh 214, 215, and 221, the first two bearing the Sanskrit title *Rājadeśasūtra.* Each of these sutras is addressed to a different king, the first (Toh 214) to Bimbisāra, the second (Toh 215) to Udhyāna, while the third is addressed to king Prasenajit of Kośala.

564 *Suhṛllekha,* 77; Toh 4182 Kangyur, spring yig, *nge,* 44a:5.

565 *Suhṛllekha,* 86; p. 44b:4.

566 *Suhṛllekha,* 84; p. 44b:3.

567 *Suhṛllekha,* 91; p. 45a:1.

568 *Suhṛllekha,* 89; p. 44b:6.

569 *Suhṛllekha,* 48; p. 44a:1.

570 *Suhṛllekha,* 98–100; p. 45a:5.

571 *Suhṛllekha,* 102; p. 45b:1. The "migration defilement" refers to obscurants that demigods acquire by their very fact of birth as demigods.

572 *Suhṛllekha,* 103; p. 45b:1.

573 *Suhṛllekha,* 65; p. 43b:5.

574 *Suhṛllekha,* 69; p. 44b:6.

575 *Suhṛllekha,* 66; p. 43b:6.

576 *Suhṛllekha,* 68; p. 43b:7.

577 *Śokavinodana;* Toh 4177 Tengyur, spring yig, *nge,* 34a:5.

578 Nāgārjuna, *Suhṛllekha,* 687; Toh 4182 Kangyur, spring yig, *nge,* 43b:6.

579 *Udānavarga,* 2:17ab; Toh 326 Kangyur, mdo sde, *sa,* 211b:2. The wording of the second line is slightly different here compared to the edition in the Tengyur. According to Tibetan interpretations, *karśapaṇa* is understood to be a kind of shell used widely in ancient India as a substitute for silver coins (e.g., *Tibetan-Chinese Dictionary,* vol. 1, p. 11). There is however no entry for the term in Monier-Williams' *A Sanskrit-English Dictionary,* where we read that a *karśa* is a weight of gold or silver equal to 16 *mārśas,* while a *paṇa* is a weight of copper used as a coin. *Paṇa* also means betting or wagering.

580 *Bodhicaryāvatāra,* 8:23ab; Toh 3871 Tengyur, dbu ma, *la,* 24b:4.

581 *Suhṛllekha,* 69cd; Toh 4182 Tengyur, spring yig, *nge,* 43b:7. See also note 207.

582 *Suhṛllekha,* 58; p. 43b:1.

583 Source unidentified.

584 *Suhṛllekha,* 52; p. 43a:4.

585 *Bodhicaryāvatāra,* 1:9; Toh 3871 Tengyur, dbu ma, *la,* 2a:5.

586 Nāgārjuna, *Bodhicittavivaraṇa,* 108; Toh 1800 Tengyur, rgyud 'grel, *ngi,* 42b:1.

587 *Bodhicaryāvatāra,* 8:120; Toh 3871 Tengyur, dbu ma, *la,* 28a:5.

588 An important highest yoga tantric practice belonging to the mother tantra class.

589 Mahāmudrā practice, which stems principally from the teachings of the Indian Buddhist mystics, such as Saraha. *Mahāmudrā* refers to an advanced Buddhist path that emphasizes recognizing the luminous emptiness of all mental activity, and is particularly privileged by the Kagyü school of Tibetan Buddhism.

590 This obviously comes from an oral tradition.

591 The section on the practice of giving and taking from *Public Explicitation* has been copied almost verbatim in Shönu Gyalchok (*Compendium of Well-Uttered Insights,* pp. 97–117) with only minor additions. A fortunate consequence of this is that we have for comparison another version of this important section.

592 *Bodhicaryāvatāra*, 8:120cd; Toh 3871 Tengyur, dbu ma, *la*, 28a:5.

593 This is probably a reference to Kamalaśīla's *Bhāvanākrama: Middle Section*, where he writes the following: "Then view all beings with an equanimous mind, with no discrimination. And with the thought 'No sentient being has not been my kin a hundred times in this beginningless cycle of existence,' meditate on ordinary sentient beings." Toh 3916 Tengyur, dbu ma, *ki*, 42a–55b.

594 *Bhāvanākrama;* Toh 3916 Tengyur, dbu ma *ki*, 43a. The four immeasurable motivating thoughts are equanimity, loving-kindness, compassion, and sympathetic joy directed boundlessly toward all sentient beings.

595 *Bhadrakalpikasūtra;* Toh 94 Kangyur, mdo sde, *ka*.

596 This great Naljorpa is most probably the highly revered disciple of Atiśa known as Naljorpa Amé Shap (1015–78). According to *History of the Precious Kadam Lineage,* Najorpa's name is Jangchup Rinchen, and he hailed from the Tsongkha region of Amdo Province in northeastern Tibet. At age thirty-one, he went to central Tibet and met with Atiśa when the latter was in Ngari, in western Tibet. Naljorpa was also a student of Dromtönpa and succeeded him in the abbotship of Radreng, which Naljorpa held for twelve years.

597 Neusurpa (1042–1118), whose full name is Neusurpa Yeshé Bar, was a student of Gönpawa and Potowa and held the abbotship of Radreng Monastery for many years. He is accredited with composing a *tenrim* (spelled *bstan rim,* a text on the stages of doctrine) on the basis of integrating the instructions of Gönpawa and the three Kadam brothers. Yeshé Döndrup (*Treasury of Gems,* pp. 206–19) credits him also with being the source of several important Kadam works of the *lamrim* (stages of the path) genre.

598 This is a reference to Ngari Sherap Gyaltsen (eleventh century), who hailed from the Ngari region of western Tibet and was a student of Ngok Lekpai Sherap.

599 This probably refers to an oral tradition according which it is explained that for the practice of taking, since what is being taken are suffering, its origin, negative karma, afflictions, and their propensities, this visualization should not include fully enlightened buddhas. In contrast, for the practice of giving, one can extend this visualization to include the buddhas as well. Since Sangyé Gompa is writing this work as a "public explication," he refers the reader to the oral tradition on certain critical aspects of mind training practice.

600 Source unknown. This is probably a reference to an earlier Kadam text.

601 This is a reference to the form and formless realms.

602 In the Tibetan original this reads "and from the buddhas to the bodhisattvas," which I think is a scribal error. Earlier the author made it clear that the visualization of taking is not to be extended to buddhas. So I have corrected the text here to read as "and from the self-realized ones to the bodhisattvas" by simply adding the word *rang* (self) in the Tibetan text.

603 This is probably a reference to a list of four sets of nine conceptions enumerated in the commentarial literature on the first chapter of Maitreya's *Ornament of Clear*

Realizations (Abhisamayālaṃkāra). This enumeration pertains to grasping at the true existence of object and subject, each in terms of substantial reality and nominal reality, all of which must be eliminated on the path to enlightenment.

604 The meaning here is that, except for the psychophyiscal aggregates of the arhat—which are exclusively resultant sufferings—anything that is in the nature of suffering is an origin of suffering as well.

605 Source unidentified. This is probably a citation from a Mahayana sutra.

606 These are the four stages of fruition of the disciple's path, namely, (1) the stream-enterer, (2) the once-returner, (3) the never-returner, and (4) the arhat.

607 *Bodhicaryāvatāra,* 3:10; Toh 3871 Tengyur, dbu ma, *la,* 7a:2.

608 *Gaṇḍavyūhasūtra;* Toh 44 Kangyur, phal chen, *ga,* chap. 45, 90a:7.

609 *Vajradhvajapariṇāmasūtra;* Toh 44 Kangyur, phal chen, *kha,* chap. 8, 108b:3.

610 *Bodhicaryāvatāra,* 5:70cd; Toh 3871 Tengyur, dbu ma, *la,* 13a:1.

611 These are references to the pure realms of Amitābha and Avalokiteśvara, respectively.

612 "Cultivating the buddha fields" refers to a practice whereby a bodhisattva on a high level deliberately "cultivates" the pure realms, or buddha fields, that he or she is to actualize upon complete enlightenment. This aspect of the bodhisattva practice is described in detail in Maitreya's *Abhisamayālaṃkāra* and its commentaries.

613 *Avataṃsakasūtra;* Toh 44 Kangyur, phal chen, *ka.* An English translation of this preface from the Chinese source can be found in Thomas Cleary, trans., *The Flower Ornament Scripure,* Book One, pp. 55–149.

614 *Vajradhvajapariṇāmasūtra;* Toh 44 Kangyur, phal chen, *kha,* chap. 30, 21a:7.

615 Source unidentified. Again, these three are attractive, unattractive, and neutral forms.

616 The three robes refer to a monk or nun's lower garment *(thang gos),* upper garment *(bla gos),* and ceremonial garment *(rnam sbyar).* This advice is of course for monastics.

617 *Bodhicaryāvatāra,* 3:10c; Toh 3871 Tengyur, dbu ma, *la,* 7a:2.

618 *Ratnāvali,* 5:69cd; Toh 4158 Tengyur, skyes rabs, *ge,* 124b:4.

619 This is probably a reference to Haribhadra's commentary on the *Eight Thousand Verses* entitled *Illumination of the Abhisamayālaṃkāra;* Toh 3791 Tengyur, shes phyin, *cha,* 1b–341a.

620 *Vajradhvajapariṇāmasūtra;* Toh 44 Kangyur, phal chen, *kha,* chap. 30, 21a:7.

621 *Gaganagañjaparipṛcchāsūtra;* Toh 148 Kangyur, mdo sde, *pa,* 278a:5. The wording of the citation here is slightly different from the version in Kangyur.

622 These progressively more excellent qualities of the bodhisattva on the levels are described in detail in *The Sutra of the Ten Levels (Daśabhūmikasūtra).*

623 Source unidentified. The analogy of the seven shallow crossings remains opaque to me.

624 Source unidentified.

625 Source unidentified.

626 Dharmakīrti, *Pramāṇavārttika,* 1:9; Toh 4210 Tengyur, tshad ma, *ce,* 95a:2.

627 *Pramāṇavārttika,* 1:36; Toh 4210 Tengyur, tshad ma, *ce,* 96a:2.

628 Both classical Indian and Tibetan authors use a few stock examples of nonexistent things, including flowers growing in the sky, the horn of a rabbit, and the son of a barren woman.

629 Most probably, "the three fruits" here refers to rebirth in the higher realms, liberation from cyclic existence, and full enlightenment, all of which are fruits of view, conduct, and meditation.

630 "The bones of your effort touching your aims" is my translation of the Tibetan expression *don dang rdo rus thug.* This probably refers to your effort bearing fruit and leading to the accomplishment of your aim.

631 *Avataṁsakasūtra;* Toh 44 Kangyur, phal chen, *a,* chap. 45, 50b:4. The wording in the citation here is slightly different from the version in Kangyur.

632 *Agracayapraṇidhāna;* Toh 4396 Tengyur, sna tshogs, *nyo,* 327b:6.

633 Source unidentified. "Belly-crawlers" is a name for serpents.

634 *Ratnāvali,* 5:84; Toh 4158 Tengyur, skyes rabs, *ge,* 125a:6.

635 *Bodhicaryāvatāra,* 7:16; Toh 3871 Tengyur, dbu ma, *la,* 20b:5.

636 *Bodhicaryāvatāra,* 8:113; p. 28a:1.

637 *Bodhicaryāvatāra,* 8:120; p. 28a:5.

638 *Bodhicaryāvatāra,* 8:131; p. 28b:4.

639 *Bodhicaryāvatāra,* 8:136; p. 28b:7.

640 *Bodhicaryāvatāra,* 10:56; p. 40a:3.

641 *Mahāyānasūtrālaṃkāra,* 6:2; Toh 4020 Tengyur, sems tsam, *phi,* 5b:6.

642 *Mahāyānasūtrālaṃkāra,* 6:3; p. 5b:7.

643 *Praṇidhānasaptatināmagāthā;* Toh 4392 Tengyur, sna tshogs, *nyo,* 321a:4.

644 *Saṃbhāraparikathā;* Toh 4166 Tengyur, spring yig, *ge,* 173b:3.

645 *Saṃbhāraparikathā,* p. 173b:3.

646 *Saṃbhāraparikathā,* p. 174b:5.

647 *Saṃbhāraparikathā,* p. 175a:3.

648 Bhūripa, *Dpal 'khor lo bde mchog gi rgyun gshags rgyas pa;* Toh 1533 Tengyur, rgyud 'grel, *za,* 95a:4.

649   *Samādhirājasūtra;* Toh 127 Kangyur, mdo sde, *da,* chap. 10, 32b:7. The first line of this quote is missing in the edition in the Tengyur. Furthermore, the wording of the third line is slightly different as well.

650   Maitreya, *Abhisamayālaṃkāra,* 1:40; Toh 3786 Tengyur, shes phyin, *ka,* 3b:2.

651   *Mahāyānasūtrālaṃkāra,* 10:37; Toh 4020 Tengyur, sems tsam, *phi,* 10a:5.

652   Maitreya, *Uttaratantra,* 1:28; Toh 1024 Tengyur, sems tsam, *phi,* 56a:2.

653   Āryadeva, *Catuḥśatakaśāstra,* 5:11; Toh 3846 Tengyur, dbu ma, *tsha,* 6b:2. The wording of the lines cited here is slightly different from the Tengyur.

654   Source unidentified. The citation stresses the point that the practitioner of mind training should take those who are less privileged as a key focus of their altruistic action.

655   *las byed nges.* This refers to acts committed whose corresponding karma is accrued as well.

656   *Mahāyānasūtrālaṃkāra,* 18:29 and 30; Toh 4020 Tengyur, sems tsam, *phi,* 26b:1.

657   This second line is not found in *Seven-Point Mind Training,* though it does appear in *Root Lines.*

658   This first line is not found in the *Seven-Point Mind Training,* but it is in the *Root Lines.*

659   We have failed to identify the stanza being alluded to here.

660   This is cited also in Hortön Namkha Pal's *Rays of the Sun.*

661   *Ratnāvali,* 5:84; Toh 4158 Tengyur, skyes rabs, *ge,* 125a:6.

662   Bhūripa, *Extensive Daily Confessions of Cakrasaṃvara [Practice];* Toh 1533 Tengyur, rgyud 'grel, *za,* 95a:4.

663   Though our author does not provide the source of this citation, Yongzin Yeshé Gyaltsen's *Essence of Ambrosia (Blo sbyong bdud rtsi'i snying po)* cites its source in Āryaśūra's *Jātakamālā.* This stanza is found in the first story of Āryaśūra's collection of thirty-four birth stories. This same stanza is cited by Könchok Gyaltsen in his *Supplement* without giving the source.

664   *sngags rnying ma ba'i gyer sgom kun.* It is difficult to infer what the author means exactly by "Old Tantra school's meditation through chanting."

665   This was cited earlier in Sé Chilbu's commentary on *Seven-Point Mind Training* as well.

666   These two lines are from Atiśa's *Bodhisattva's Jewel Garland,* though in that text the lines are not contiguous.

667   *Pramāṇavārttika,* 2:221; Toh 4210 Tengyur, tshad ma, *ce,* 116a:1.

668   *Bodhicaryāvatāra,* 8:134; Toh 3871 Tengyur, dbu ma, *la,* 28b:5.

669   *Bodhicaryāvatāra,* 8:155; p. 29b:3.

670 *Bodhicaryāvatāra,* 8:172; p. 30a:6.

671 *Bodhicaryāvatāra,* 4:34; p. 9a:7.

672 *Bodhicaryāvatāra,* 8:129ab; p. 28b:3.

673 *Bodhicaryāvatāra,* 8:169; p. 30a:4.

674 Nāgārjuna, *Bodhicittavivaraṇa,* 74; Toh 1800 Tengyur, rgyud 'grel, *ngi,* 41a:4. The Dergé Tengyur edition has five lines for this stanza, and the wording is slightly different as well.

675 *Bodhicaryāvatāra,* 6:107; Toh 3871 Tengyur, dbu ma, *la,* 18b:6.

676 *Bodhicaryāvatāra,* 3:12; p. 7a:3.

677 *Bodhicaryāvatāra,* 8:113; p. 28a:1.

678 *Bodhicaryāvatāra,* 8:129–30; p. 28b:3.

679 This is probably a part of an oral tradition.

680 This exact statement was cited earlier in *A Commentary on Eight Verses on Mind Training* (entry 32 of this volume).

681 This is probably a citation from an oral tradition.

682 The Sanskrit word *kārikā,* which I have translated as "stanzas," here refers to the stanzas of the monastic discipline texts known as the Vinaya.

683 Here, too, the author is drawing from an established oral tradition. It is difficult to determine whether the expression "adornment of pristine cognition" *(ye shes kyi rgyan)* refers to a specific text or a meditative practice.

684 These two lines are found in neither the *Root Lines* nor Chekawa's *Seven-Point Mind Training.* However they appear in the *Annotated Root Lines* and in later redactions of Chekawa's *Seven-Point Mind Training.*

685 This line is not found in the *Root Lines* but does appear in the *Annotated Root Lines.* Here, the author provides two different versions of the line.

686 The entire text of the commentary on this line from *Public Explication* appears verbatim in Shönu Gyalchok's *Compendium of Well-Uttered Insights,* (pp. 154–56), which has been used as a basis to detect possible typographical corruptions in the original Tibetan edition of our text. All information related to corrections introduced can be found in the endnotes of the critical Tibetan edition.

687 Here, for rhetorical effect, the author refers to self-grasping using a third-person pronoun, *kho,* which I have translated as "he."

688 This is an allusion to receiving advanced Vajrayana empowerments in which the placing of consecrated vases on the initiate's head is an essential part of the initiation rite.

689 Source unidentified.

690 Source unidentified.

691 Here the author is probably drawing from an oral tradition.

692 *Bodhicaryāvatāra,* 4:44; Toh 3871 Tengyur, dbu ma, *la,* 9b:7.

693 *Bodhicaryāvatāra,* 4:28, p. 9a:4.

694 Source unidentified.

695 Although this line does not exist in either the *Root Lines* or the *Seven-Point Mind Training,* a slightly different version of it appears in the *Annotated Root Lines.*

696 *Abhisamayālaṃkāra,* 3:4d; Toh 3786 Tengyur, shes phyin, *ka,* 6a:6. The point being made in this citation is that, even on some of the levels of bodhisattva, some form of subtle attachment still lingers.

697 Here the author is citing oral tradition.

698 In Shönu Gyalchok's *Compendium of Well-Uttered Insights* (p. 177), where this entire section appears verbatim, this passage remains unattributed to anyone.

699 A *dri* is a female yak.

700 Later in Könchok Gyaltsen's *Supplement,* where in a clearly verbatim copy of this section of Sangyé Gompa's *Public Explication of Mind Training,* this expression appears slightly differently. There, it reads "if they are inadequate" *(mi ldang na),* which would then make the second expression read "if they dissipate." Judging by the context, the reading in Könchok Gyaltsen's *Supplement* appears to be more accurate, which also does not have the repetition "if you are hungry," as is the case here.

701 It is difficult to determine the story being referred to here. In fact, this whole paragraph is somewhat obscure in the original Tibetan, so my translation is only suggestive.

702 Source unidentified.

703 The analogies here are somewhat obscure. In my understanding, the point is the following: Just as when propitiating a hostile god, you ensure that all the elements of the rite are correctly performed, you must do the same in the context of your mind training. Also, just as a successful rite of exorcism or ritual burning of malevolent forces can result in observable signs, such as audible cracking sounds, pursue your mind training practice until you observe signs of success.

704 This is the concluding sentence to the explanation of the four factors to be relinquished: (1) the afflictions, (2) partiality, (3) expectation of reward, and (4) dependence on other conditions.

705 This line does not appear in the *Root Lines* but is found in the *Annotated Root Lines* as well as in the *Seven-Point Mind Training.*

706 This line is not found in any of the three texts—*Root Lines, Annotated Root Lines,*

or *Seven-Point Mind Training*—which suggests that Sangyé Gompa is working from yet another version of the "root lines on mind training."

707 *Bodhicaryāvatāra*, 5:97; Toh 3871 Tengyur, dbu ma, *la,* 14a:2.

708 Nāgārjuna, *Bodhicittavivaraṇa,* 105; Toh 1800 Tengyur, rgyud 'grel, *ngi,* 42a:6. The version cited in our text here is significantly different and reads as follows: "Since it has been revealed that in this vehicle / The awakening mind is most supreme, / Generate the mind for awakening / And strive to remain in equipoise on it. /" Since the reading in the Tengyur seems more coherent, I have chosen to follow it here.

709 *Bodhicaryāvatāra*, 8:120; Toh 3871 Tengyur, dbu ma, *la,* 28a:5.

710 The next two lines do not appear either in the *Root Lines* or the *Seven-Point Mind Training;* however, they are found in the *Annotated Root Lines.*

711 *Bodhicaryāvatāra*, 4:43ab; Toh 3871 Tengyur, dbu ma, *la,* 9b:7.

712 Although it is difficult to precisely determine the full story being alluded to here, it is probably a reference to the well-known story involving an aristrocrat's attendant who wrongly referred to the nose as *uyuk.* The second story, the story of a mother placing her nipples into her infant child's eyes, suggests a mother who does not know the proper way to nurse her child. The point being made here is that without proper identification of what is to be done, the task cannot be successfully accomplished.

713 In the *Annotated Root Lines* this line reads, "Apply yourself to the five powers."

714 *Bodhicaryāvatāra*, 8:134a; The full stanza was cited above.

715 *Bodhicaryāvatāra*, 4:44; The full stanza was cited above.

716 Tib. *chos thams cad bde bar 'gro ba'i ting nge 'dzin.*

717 *Bodhicaryāvatāra*, 8:129; The full stanza was cited above.

718 *Bodhicaryāvatāra*, 10:55ab; Toh 3871 Tengyur, dbu ma, *la,* 40a:3.

719 These two lines appear in both the *Annotated Root Lines* and the *Seven-Point Mind Training,* although not in the *Root Lines.*

720 This whole section on the power of positive seed as part of a death-and-dying instruction seems to be copied almost verbatim from Sé Chilbu's commentary on the *Seven-Point Mind Training.*

721 In the Lhasa edition of the Tibetan original this sentence reads, "I will make this sentient being that grasps at self, too, vanish into space." This is most probably a typographical error where the word *sem* (spelled *sems*), "mind," has been mistakenly written as *semchen* (spelled *sems can*), "sentient being."

722 *Gocarapariśuddhasūtra;* Toh 44 Kangyur, phal chen, *ka,* chap. 16, 210b–219b.

723 *Ratnameghasūtra;* Toh 231 Kangyur, mdo sde, *wa,* 1b–112b.

724 *Mahāyānasūtrālaṃkāra*, 6:9; Toh 4020 Tengyur, sems tsam, *phi,* 6a:4. The wording

of the last line cited here is slightly different from the version found in Tengyur. I have chosen to follow the Tengyur reading.

725   In the *Seven-Point* this line reads, "Relate to your meditation whatever you can right now." This variation results from the difference of spelling the Tibetan word *thug* ("to encounter") as *thub,* which means "can."

726   Atiśa's *Songs of Blissfulness* remains unidentified.

727   Source unidentified.

728   *dkar na zho byas / dmar na khrag byas.* Although this saying is unfamiliar to me, the intended meaning appears to be that instead of wasting time in unending hesitation, you should act decisively.

729   This is a reference to the traditional view that the Buddha Śākyamuni's teaching will last for the duration of five thousand years. Our era is said to be in the last five-hundreth of this period.

730   Source unidentified.

731   *la la'i gang yang ma 'dzoms/ lung lung gang yang m 'dzom.* The expression "Something of the mountains or something of the plains is missing" is probably an old Tibetan saying, possibly from the Phenpo region of central Tibet. The point is that some essential condition is always missing.

732   This oblique expression is probably an allusion to an emission of sexual fluids a celibate monk might experience as an accident, say in a dream. The point is that this is less of an obstruction to your spiritual practice than becoming sick.

733   The author is citing an oral tradition.

734   *Bodhicaryāvatāra,* 7:30.

735   Nāgārjuna, *Ratnāvali,* 3:73; Toh 4158 Tengyur, skyes rabs, *ga,* 117a:5.

736   Source unidentified.

737   For lay practitioners, this second class of objects includes close family members, such as spouse and children.

738   *zhe sdang gi blo rdol na snying rje'i thag pa cad.* It is difficult to discern whether this is a direct citation from a text or a saying from an old oral tradition.

739   The story may have been well known in the region where Sangyé Gompa was teaching during the thirteenth century, but the reference is now obscure.

740   *ban de kun la 'di shi na yul khams 'di cog ge thob.* This is probably an allusion to the fact that when a senior monk passes away, the families for which the monk was serving as their main counsel will then be passed on to other monks.

741   This refers to an aspect of the fortnightly confession ceremony of Buddhist monks where, to be in strict accordance with the prescribed rites, individual members of the order are supposed to remind each other of their possible infractions of precepts during the previous two weeks.

742   This sentence is somewhat obscure in the Tibetan original, and the translation provided here is only provisional.

743 Nāgārjuna, *Ratnāvali,* 3:73; Toh 4158 Tengyur, skyes rabs, *ge,* 117a.

744 This first line does not appear in the *Seven-Point,* while the second line is not found in either of the two versions of the *Root Lines.* And with respect to the second line, interestingly, Sangyé Gompa's reading differs from those of Sé Chilbu and Shönu Gyalchok. The former reads the Tibetan word *log non* as "overcoming regressions," while Sé Chilbu and Shönu Gyalchok read the word as "overcoming errors," such as overcoming erroneous meditative practices.

745 Source unidentified.

746 The point here is that, over time, the Kadampa practitioner became excessive in his use of first-person pronouns in his conversation, suggesting an increase in self-centeredness.

747 This entire section, that is, the two paragraphs of commentary on the two lines, is copied verbatim in Könchok Gyaltsen's *Supplement* and in Shönu Gyalchok's *Compendium of Well-Uttered Insights* (pp. 181–83).

748 This is probably an allusion to a story of someone who had an exaggerated opinion himself as well as his dog named Gongkar ("the white-collared").

749 This long sentence is obscure in the Tibetan original.

750 The Tibetan original of this sentence is somewhat obscure, so my translation is provisional.

751 *sha srang gang la gtad sa sde rtse gang las med gsungs.* A *sang* is a unit of weight. This expression is obscure. Literally, it is saying that a scale full of meat cannot be expected to produce more than one full plate when cooked. The intended meaning appears to be that if your activities become an antidote to self-grasping, all other realizations will follow naturally.

752 Abbreviation for Langri Thangpa, the author of the well-known *Eight Verses on Mind Training.*

753 This line is not found in either the *Root Lines* or the *Seven-Point.*

754 Source unidentified.

755 *Saṃcayagāthā;* Toh 13 Kangyur, shes phyin, *ka,* 175a:5.

756 *Saṃcayagāthā,* p. 164a:5.

757 The *two selflessnesses* are the lack of a personal selfhood and the lack of selfhood, or fundamental essence, in all other phenomena.

758 *Bodhicaryāvatāra,* 3:21; Toh 3871 Tengyur, dbu ma, *la,* 7a:3.

759 *Bodhicaryāvatāra,* 8:121; Toh 3871 Tengyur, dbu ma, *la,* 28a:5.

760 *Bodhicaryāvatāra,* 8:79cd; Toh 3871 Tengyur, dbu ma, *la,* 26b:2.

761 Fourth in the twelve links of dependent origination, referring to the combined mind ("name") and body ("form") in the early stages of fetal development.

762 It is said that there are two things that obstruct access to the beings of the

intermediate state—a mother's womb and "Vajra Seat," which is generally thought to refer to Bodhgaya, the location of Buddha's enlightenment.

763 In other words, ordinary beings take uncontrolled rebirth through the power of their contaminated karma and afflictions, while higher-level bodhisattvas take rebirth through the power of their compassion and altruistic aspirations.

764 This line is not found in the *Seven-Point* or the *Root Lines,* but does exist in the annotated *Root Lines.*

765 *Bodhicaryāvatāra,* 1:36cd; Toh 3871 Tengyur, dbu ma, *la,* 3b:4.

766 Source unidentified.

767 Source unidentified.

768 Source unidentified.

769 *Bodhicaryāvatāra,* 3:16; Toh 3871 Tengyur, dbu ma, *la,* 7a:5.

770 This probably alludes to the story of the two yoginīs admonishing Atiśa to engage in the practice of the awakening mind when the latter was circumbulating the great stupa of enlightenment at Bodhgaya. See p. 207 in the present volume.

771 This second line is not found in the *Root Lines* or the *Seven-Point.*

772 This last point is somewhat obscure. Either the Tibetan text is corrupt here or this is a reference to the meditation on emptiness, wherein the object of medita-tion is necessarily devoid of form (e.g., mahāmudrā practice). Since the line upon which Sangyé Gompa is commenting does not appear in either the *Root Lines* or the *Seven-Point,* I have no commentarial work against which this text can be cross-checked.

773 This is not found in the two versions of the *Root Lines* or in the *Seven-Point;* how-ever, this line does appear in the version of *Root Lines* that is attributed to Atiśa as presented in Shönu Gyalchok's *Compendium of Well-Uttered Insights* (pp. 212–13).

774 This metaphor is obscure; my guess is that the comparison is between the infre-quency of the acts.

775 This line is not found in the *Seven-Point* or in the two versions of the *Root Lines.*

776 This is probably an allusion to an expression that may have once been well-known among the Kadam teachers, but it remains quite obscure today.

777 The word *tsen* refers to the somewhat violent spirit of a dead person that is thought to linger because of the deceased's attachment to some unresolved matters. Often, these *tsen* become tamed and transformed by high lamas, who then assign them the role of powerful Dharma protectors.

778 "The great Naljorpa" refers to Naljorpa Amé Jangchup (1015–78), who was a stu-dent of both Atiśa and Dromtönpa and held the abbotship of Radreng Monastery for twelve years following the latter's death. The source of Naljorpa's quotation remains unidentified.

779 The four qualities that make a person a paragon of virtue are (1) not returning

insults, (2) not returning hostility, (3) not striking back when hit, and (4) not returning humiliation when humiliated.

780 Many of these situations—finding a colleague to share your cell, not losing your temper over the amount of tea served to you, and not getting angry over the order of seating—are relevant to the life of a monk in a monastic community on a day-to-day basis.

781 This is a reference to the Kadampas' spiritual way of life, which is grounded in the practice of mind training as its foundation. Radreng is the name of the first Kadam monastery, founded by Dromtönpa.

782 Phen is an abbreviation of Phenpo, a region in southwestern Tibet where many of the early Kadam masters were most active.

783 A dzo, a cross between a yak and a cow, is a domestic animal capable of carrying heavy loads for long distances.

784 Drolungpa, whose full name is Lodrö Jungné, was a principal student of the great translator Loden Sherap and renowned for his vast scriptural learning. Drolungpa is today best known for his authorship of the great Kadam classic *Great Stages of the Doctrine (Bstan rim chen mo),* which was the model for Tsongkhapa's *Great Exposition of the Stages of the Path to Enlightenment.* The exact dates of Drolungpa's birth and death remain unknown; however, in his *Biograpies of the Lineage Masters of the Stages of the Path,* Yongzin Yeshé Gyaltsen asserts that Drolungpa lived for eighty years.

785 A *dri* is a female yak.

786 In Sé Chilbu's commentary on the *Seven-Point* and here as well, the order of these six is slightly different, and that which appears to be the standard sequence found in most mind training commentaries. The standard sequence is misplaced forbearance, misplaced aspiration, misplaced satiation, misplaced compassion, misplaced dedication, and misplaced rejoicing.

787 This line is missing in both versions of the *Root Lines* and in the *Seven-Point* as well.

788 Sangphupa, a.k.a. Ngok Lekpai Sherap (eleventh century), was a direct disciple of Atiśa and Dromtönpa and founded the famous Sangphu Monastery in central Tibet in 1073.

789 It is difficult to determine what exactly this "repetition of segments of *ati*" is actually supposed to mean. It could be interpreted as a criticism of those who use the rhetoric of the highest *atiyoga* of the dzokchen teachings and dismiss the relevance of ethical practice.

790 *skra 'dzoms pas ngan pa yang dag pa.* This is probably an allusion to the ancient Tibetan divination practice known as "analyzing omens" *(skra srtag pa),* which involves a shaman looking into a silver mirror.

791 The source of this long quote from Shawopa, the text of which is extremely

obscure, remains unknown so far. Shawopa is Shawo Gangpa (1067–1131), the principal student of Langri Thangpa.

792 This line is not found in the *Seven-Point* or the *Root Lines,* but exists in the *Annotated Root Lines,* where the parenthetical word *guard* is explicit.

793 Although I have failed to locate the full text of the quotation, it probably pertains to the hypothetical question of how a mind training practioner, such as one of the three brothers, would respond if, out of the blue, a woman were to accuse him of being the father of her infant child.

794 This is an allusion to a Tibetan medical practice that involves therapeutic bloodletting.

795 This is probably a reference to what are called the "four seasonal tasks of farming," which are (1) collecting fertilizer during the winter, (2) planting in the spring, (3) weeding in the summer, and (4) collecting the harvest in the autumn. Alternatively, the term *sonam* here may refer to mundane activities in general, in which case, the expression the "four aspects of *sonam*" would refer to: (1) agriculture, (2) trade, (3) lending money for profit, and (4) cattle herding.

796 This line does not exist in the *Seven-Point* although it is found in both versions of the *Root Lines.*

797 These two paragraphs are almost identical to the corresponding section found in Sé Chilbu's *A Commentary on "Seven-Point Mind Training."*

798 In the *Seven-Point* this line reads, "Train to view all phenomena as dreamlike."

799 The text of the commentary of this line is nearly identical to the one found in Sé Chilbu.

800 In the *Seven-Point* this line reads, "Examine the nature of unborn awareness."

801 The "three parts of the present" probably refer to the arising, abiding, and cessation of the present moment.

802 This line, though not appearing in the *Root Lines,* is found in both the *Annotated Root Lines* and the *Seven-Point.*

803 This line is not found in the two versions of the *Root Lines,* but is found in the *Seven-Point.*

804 The seven classes of consciousness here refer to five sensory consciousnesses, the mental consciousness, and the afflicted mental consciousness.

805 In the *Seven-Point* this line reads, "In the intervals create the illusionlike person."

806 Source unidentified.

807 This is probably an allusion to the traditional custom of treating mind training practice as hidden and not widely taught in public. As noted by the very title of this work, Sangyé Gompa wrote this text deliberately as an open, public teaching.

808 Gyalwa Yangönpa (1213–58), whose actual name was Gyaltsen Pal, was a highly eclectic master who received teachings from all the principal spiritual lineages

of his time, including Kadam, Dzokchen, Kagyü mahāmudrā, Sakya path and fruits, and the cutting-off teachings of *chöd.* His teachers included the famous Sakya Paṇḍita, Godrakpa, and most importantly, the great Drukpa Kagyü master Götsangpa Gönpo Dorjé (1189–1258). Yangönpa is most remembered for his vast collection of experiential songs and the cycle of three works collectively known as "A Trilogy of Hermetic Teachings," *(ri chos skor gsum).* It is interesting that Könchok Gyaltsen, the editor of our volume, chose to include this piece from Yangönpa in the present collection. Strictly speaking, this work does not belong to the mind training genre, though the resonance of Kadam instructions, especially from the well-known "Miscellaneous Sayings of Kadam Masters" is unmistakably discernible in some of the lists found here. The Tibetan text of this short piece found in the Lhasa Shöl edition, the basis of the critical edition on which this translation is based, has been compared and corrected against Yangönpa's own *Collected Works.*

809   In Yangönpa's *Collected Works,* this appears as "So taught the precious one" *(rin po che'i zhal nas gsungs).* It is difficult to discern whether this refers to a teacher of Yangönpa, in which case he is citing these instructions from a teacher, or to Yangönpa himself. The latter case would imply that the current text was put together later by a student of Yangönpa. This question cannot be settled until more textual resources become available.

810   In the Tibetan original, the term I have translated here as "being carefree" is written as *jo bzangs,* a term not in any of the Tibetan dictionaries available at my disposal, including the various "elucidations" of archaic Tibetan terms. I have read it as *jo bzang,* which means carefree or having a sense of abandon.

811   There is no mention of this particular mind training instruction in Shönu Gyalchok's *Compendium of Well-Uttered Insights.* However, Lechen Künga Gyaltsen's *Lamp Illuminating the History of the Kadam Tradition* (p. 8) identifies Dromtönpa as the origin of this instruction and asserts that Ngülchu Thokmé Sangpo wrote a guide on this instruction. The *Treasury of Gems* (p. 195), on the other hand, recognizes the instruction as being initially developed by the Kadam master Phuchungwa (1031–1106). Phuchungwa, whose actual name was Shönu Gyaltsen, was one of the three famous Kadam brothers and later became the source of the so-called Kadam lineage of pith instructions. It is intriguing to note, however, that in the brief presentation of the lineage of this instruction found at the end of this short work, the author of this text fails to include Phuchungwa on the list, which seems to support Lechen's statement that the instruction originated from Drontönpa rather than Phuchungwa. It is also difficult to speculate who the actual author of this work is.

812   Unless it is an error, which is conceivable, especially if the author is citing these lines from memory, these two lines appear to be a deliberate modification of the *Mahāyānasūtrālaṃkāra,* 18:39ab. In *Mahāyānasūtrālaṃkāra* itself, these two lines read, "Compassion is the juice of loving-kindness. / When suffering then, with a sense of joy,…" See Toh 4020 Tengyur, sems tsam, *phi,* 26b:7.

813   In Abhidharma cosmology, our earth being is the southern continent, and the "three other continents" refers to those of the three remaining cardinal directions.

814 The Tibetan term I have translated here as "large whale" is *ngami chenpo* (spelled *nga mid chen po*), which could literally mean "swallowing fish."

815 This sentence is slightly obscure, and it is not clear what the "two kinds of loving-kindness" refers to. My own guess is that it refers to the cultivation of loving-kindness toward your actual mother and then toward all beings.

816 These lines come not from the *Śokavinodana*, as stated here, but rather from Nāgārjuna's *Suhṛllekha*, 69cd; Toh 4182 Tengyur, spring yig, *nge*, 43b:7. See also note 207.

817 In the Shöl edition, this heading appears as "the second," which is clearly a typographical error and has been accordingly corrected in our critical Tibetan edition.

818 The Tibetan expression translated here as "the tantra of Amoghapāśa" is döngyü (spelled don rgyud), which I have read as an abbreviation of don zhags kyi rgyud, the tantra of Amogapāśa. Although there is no text entitled the *Amoghapāśa Tantra* in the Kangyur, several entries pertaining to the practice of the Amoghapāśa tantra, all of which are in one way or another explicitly related to Avalokiteśvara. It is difficult to discern which text our author has in mind here.

819 "Oral tradition" here refers to Sangyé Gompa's *Public Explication of Mind Training* (text 34). See my comments in the endnote to Sangyé Gompa's text.

820 Candragomin, *Śiṣyalekha*, 64; Toh 4183 Tengyur, spring yig, *nge*, 50a:2.

821 *Bodhicaryāvatāra*, 4:19; Toh 3971 Tengyur, dbu ma, *la*, 8b:6.

822 "Sacred objects," which is the translation of the Tibetan term *ne* (spelled *gnas*), refers to the Three Jewels: the Buddha, Dharma, and the spiritual community.

823 Although this is a well-known line, I have failed to locate this citation. It does not appear in either version—for monks and nuns—of the *Prātimokṣasūtra* found in the Kangyur.

824 *Mahāvairocanādhisaṃbodhi;* Toh 494 Kangyur, rgyud, *tha*, 168a:3. There are frequent references to this mysterious *udumvara* flower in the ancient Buddhist scriptures, and it is often used as a metaphor for extreme rarity. Monier Monier-Williams *(Sanskrit-English Dictionary)* identifies *uḍumvara* as "the tree Ficus glomerata."

825 Sakya Paṇḍita, *An Epistle Appealing to the Buddhas and Bodhisattvas of the Ten Directions,* Collected Works, vol. 2, p. 56a:6.

826 *Śrāvakabhūmi (Levels of the Disciple);* Toh 4036 Tengyur, sems tsam, *dzi*, 2b:6. The four disciples are: (1) fully ordained male and female monks, (2) male and female novices, (3) probationary nuns, and (4) male and female laity.

827 *Gaṇḍavyūhasūtra;* Toh 44 Kangyur, phal chen, *ga*, chap. 45, 381a:7.

828 *Bodhicaryāvatāra*, 1:4a; Toh 3871 Tengyur, dbu ma, *la*, 1b:5.

829 *Bodhisattvapiṭaka;* Toh 56 Kangyur, dkon brtsegs, *ga*, chap. 4, 27b:1.

830 I can't determine whether the author is here citing from a text or from an oral tradition.

831 This is probably a reference to a passage found in *Foundational Discipline (Vinayavastu);* Toh 1 Kangyur, 'dul ba, *ka,* 87b:2.

832 *Bodhicaryāvatāra,* 3:20; Toh 3871 Tengyur, dbu ma, *la,* 8b:6.

833 *Bodhicaryāvatāra,* 7:14; Toh 3871 Tengyur, dbu ma, *la,* 20b:4.

834 Candragomin, *Śiṣyalekha,* 63; Toh 4183 Tengyur, spring yig, *nge,* 50a:2.

835 Throughout this text, the expression *Oral Tradition* refers to Sangyé Gompa's *Public Explication,* the full translation of which is found in this volume.

836 Sönam Drakpa (1273–1345) was an important Kadam master during the fourteenth century. His students include such luminaries as Ngülchu Thokmé Sangpo and the great encyclopedist Butön Rinchen Drup. Yeshé Gyaltsen, in his *Biographies of the Masters of the Lineage of the Stages of the Path,* lists him as number seventy-two in this lineage. This citation probably comes from a well-known oral tradition.

837 The "great bodhisattva Chöjé" probably refers to Ngülchu Thokmé Sangpo (1295–1369), the author of the famous *Thirty-Seven Practices of a Bodhisattva.*

838 In the Lhasa Shöl edition of the Tibetan original, this sentence appears as "This is called death" *('chi ba zhes bya ba yin).* This is most probably a printing error. The sentence should read, as I have corrected here, in the form of a question "What is this thing called death?"

839 *Bodhicaryāvatāra,* 7:4; Toh 3871 Tengyur, dbu ma, *la,* 20a:5.

840 *Advice to King [Bimbisāra] Sutra (Rājadeśasūtra);* Toh 214 Kangyur, mdo sde, *tsha,* 207a:6.

841 *Śokavinodana;* Toh 4177 Tengyur, spring yig, *nge,* 23a:6.

842 *Jātakamālā;* Toh 4150 Tengyur, skyes rabs, *hu,* 129a:4.

843 *Jātakamālā,* p. 129a:4.

844 *Jātakamālā,* p. 130a:3.

845 *Jātakamālā,* p. 130a:4. Yama is the lord of death.

846 *Śokavinodana;* Toh 4177 Tengyur, spring yig, *nge,* 33b:2.

847 *Udānavarga,* 1:27; Toh 326 Kangyur, mdo sde, *sa,* 210a:1.

848 Yeshé Döndrup (*Treasury of Gems,* p. 256) states that this stanza was part of six stanzas Kharak Gomchung wrote, each corresponding to one of the four cardinal directions and the upper and the lower door frames of a temple, when master Potowa asked him to compose some verses of instruction. This particular stanza was inscribed on a post erected in the southern direction. Kharak Gomchung was a well-known eleventh-century Kadam master and a colleague of Potowa. He is best

known for his short poetic work entitled *Mind Training with Seventy Exhortations,*
the entire text of which can be found in *Treasury of Gems* (pp. 257–64).

849   *Udānavarga,* 1:27; Toh 326 Kangyur, mdo sde, *sa,* 210a:1. The wording is slightly
different in the citation given here compared with the edition in the Dergé
Tengyur.

850   *Śokavinodana;* Toh 4177 Tengyur, spring yig, *nge,* 33b:3.

851   *Udānavarga,* 1:15; Toh 326 Kangyur, mdo sde, *sa,* 209b:1.

852   *Bodhicaryāvatāra,* 2:40; Toh 3871 Tengyur, dbu ma, *la,* 5b:2.

853   *Bodhicaryāvatāra,* 7:5–6; Toh 3871 Tengyur, dbu ma, *la,* 20a:6.

854   *Lalitavistarasūtra;* Toh 95 Kangyur, mdo sde, *kha,* 88a:2.

855   Candragomin, *Śiṣyalekha,* 62; Toh 4183 Tengyur, spring yig, *nge,* 50a:1.

856   *Bodhicaryāvatāra,* 2:40; Toh 3871 Tengyur, dbu ma, *la,* 5b:2.

857   Nāgārjuna, *Suhṛllekha,* 56; Toh 4182 Kangyur, spring yig, *nge,* 43a:6.

858   *Rājāvavādakasūtra;* Toh 221 Kangyur, mdo sde, *dza,* 207a:1.

859   Vasubandhu, *Abhidharmakośa,* 3:79; Toh 4089, Tenyur, mngon pa, *ku,* 9b:7. The
meaning of this verse is explicated in the commentary that follows.

860   Although the author cites these quotes as being from the *Śokavinodana,* they are
actually found in the chapter on impermanence in the *Udānavarga.* See Toh 326
Kangyur, mdo sde, *sa,* 9b:7.

861   *Bodhicaryāvatāra,* 2:59; Toh 3871 Tengyur, dbu ma, *la,* 6a:6.

862   *Udānavarga,* 1:7–8; Toh 326 Kangyur, mdo sde, *sa,* 209a:4.

863   *Bodhicaryāvatāra,* 4:16; Toh 3871 Tengyur, dbu ma, *la,* 8b:4.

864   Nāgārjuna, *Ratnāvali,* 4:17; Toh 4158 Tengyur, skyes rabs, *ge,* 118b:7. In the
Tibetan original, the author cites this as being from Śāntideva's *Bodhicaryāvatāra,*
which is an error.

865   Candragomin, *Śiṣyalekha,* 65cd; Toh 4183 Tengyur, spring yig, *nge,* 50a:4.

866   *Ratnāvali,* 3:79; Toh 4158 Tengyur, skyes rabs, *ge,* 137b:1.

867   *Suhṛllekha,* 55; Toh 4182 Tengyur, spring yig, *nge,* 43a:6.

868   Candragomin, *Śiṣyalekha,* 66; Toh 4183 Tengyur, spring yig, *nge,* 50a:4.

869   *Collected Works,* vol. 3, p. 309b:5. In the version found in Yangönpa's *Collected
Works,* the order of the first and second lines is reversed.

870   *Commentary on the Difficult Points of the "Bodhipathapradipa,"* Toh 3948 Tengyur,
dbu ma, *khi,* 280b:2. Atiśa is referring to a belief of his time that swans possess the
ability to extract the milk from a mixture of milk and water.

871   *Bodhicaryāvatāra,* 2:42ab; Toh 3871 Tengyur, dbu ma, *la,* 5b:5.

872 *Bodhicaryāvatāra*, 2:41; Toh 3871 Tengyur, dbu ma, *la*, 5b:3.

873 *Bodhicaryāvatāra*, 8:17, 18; Toh 3871 Tengyur, dbu ma, *la*, 24a:2.

874 *Rājāvavādakasūtra;* Toh 221 Kangyur, mdo sde, *dza*, 82a:1.

875 *Bodhicaryāvatāra*, 2:42c; Toh 3871 Tengyur, dbu ma, *la*, 5b:3.

876 *Rājāvavādakasūtra;* Toh 221 Kangyur, mdo sde, *dza*, 82a:1.

877 *Bodhicaryāvatāra*, 2:60; Toh 3871 Tengyur, dbu ma, *la*, 6a:6.

878 *Catuḥśatakaśāstra*, 1:1; Toh 3846 Tengyur, dbu ma, *tsha*, 1a:2.

879 *Collected Works*, vol. 3, p. 310a:3. The wording is slightly different in the version found there.

880 *Rājāvavādakasūtra;* Toh 221 Kangyur, mdo sde, *dza*, 208a:3.

881 *Ratnāvali*, 1:20ab; Toh 4158 Tengyur, skyes rabs, *ge*, 107b:5.

882 *Ratnāvali*, 1:20cd; Toh 4158 Tengyur, skyes rabs, *ge*, 107b:5.

883 In identifying the "inappropriate" places, times, and bodily parts, the author is most probably following the second-century Indian Buddhist work *Daśakuśala-karmapathanirdeśa* (Toh 4178 Tengyur, spring yig, *nge*, 34b–35b), which is attributed to Aśvaghoṣa.

884 In the Shöl edition of our Tibetan text, which has been kept unaltered in the critical Tibetan edition, these two headings appear in the wrong order, with the following sentence appearing immediately after the headings: "The first refers to the sufferings of lower transmigration that one experiences as fruitional effects, while the second refers to the attraction felt toward killing even when you are born human after gaining release from lower transmigration." This, I think, is a scribe's error. First of all, the scribe erroneously gives rebirth in the lower realms as an example of a "causally concordant experiential effect," which is, as the text itself pointed out earlier, the fruitional effect. Second, later in the same paragraph the text gives an accurate explanation and illustration of the causally concordant experiential effect of killing.

885 From this point onward, the Tibetan text omits the instrumental for some of the subsequent nonvirtuous acts and presents them in their genitive forms, which I think is either a scribe's error or represents a somewhat lax style of writing on the part of the author. Here I have translated all the nonvirtuous acts in their instrumental forms; that is, they are presented as the causal agents for their corresponding effects.

886 This is an allusion to religious practices that involve animal sacrifice.

887 *Bodhicaryāvatāra*, 5:16; Toh 3871 Tengyur, dbu ma, *la*, 10b:6.

888 Yeshé Döndrup (*Treasury of Gems*, p. 497) cites this statement attributed to Phuchungwa as quoted in Chim Namkha Drak's *The Precious Supreme Path of the Great Vehicle (Theg chen lam mchog rin po che)*. The text of the citation is slightly different. In Chim's version, we read the quote as the following: "As for us, we

display virtuous [acts] by [merely] stringing words together, while we display non-virtuous [acts] in their actuality."

889 The text of this citation, too, is slightly different in Yeshé Döndrup (*Treasury of Gems,* p. 497), where it reads as follows: "If we do not engage in the virtuous [acts] through actual implementation, we would be returning empty-handed after journeying to the land of jewels."

890 Yeshé Döndrup (*Treasury of Gems,* p. 271) cites this quotation attributed to Kamapa (1057–1131) from Lumpipa's *Notes on the Stages of the Path (Lam rim zin bris).* Lumpipa, whose personal name was Yeshé Jangchup, was a principal student of Kamapa.

891 In other words, a buddha, the first of the Three Jewels; the second and third are the Dharma and the spiritual community, respectively. *Suhṛllekha,* 42; Toh 4182 Tengyur, spring yig, *nge,* 42b:4. The five ways of differentiating the strength and weakness of karma, as referred to here by Nāgārjuna and explained individually by our author, are from the point of view of (1) time, (2) state of mind, (3) their antidotes or the lack of them, (4) their field or object, and (5) the number of agents involved.

892 "Blessed one" is an epithet for a buddha.

893 *Niyatāniyatagatimudrāvatārasūtra;* Toh 202 Kangyur, mdo sde, *tsha,* 75b:5. There is a difference in the wording of the sutra as cited here and the version found in the Tengyur.

894 *Bodhicaryāvatāra,* 7:12cd; Toh 3871 Tengyur, dbu ma, *la,* 20b:3. The last line appears slightly differently in the Tengyur, where it reads, "How can I remain tranquil in this manner?"

895 *Maitreyamahāsiṃhanādasūtra;* Toh 67 Kangyur, dkon brtsegs, *ca,* 74a:1.

896 Here Tönpa Rinpoché refers to Dromtönpa. This citation is found also in Yeshé Döndrup (*Treasury of Gems,* p. 89) where, however, the text reads slightly differently, as follows: "Next to negative karma [accrued] in relation to Dharma, the karma of ten nonvirtuous actions is [like] pieces of rags."

897 Since the most extensive explanation of the Buddhist theory of karma is found in the scriptural collection of higher knowledge *(Abhidharmapiṭaka),* it is those who are learned in these texts who are most versed in the various aspects of the theory of karma.

898 This is a reference to a well-known story found in the Mahayana sutra entitled *Upāyakauśalyasūtra* (Toh 261 Kangyur, mdo sde, *za*), which is often cited as an example of a bodhisattva's act of compassionate killing. For English translation of the relevant passage from this sutra on the story, see Tatz (1994), pp. 73–74.

899 *Bodhicaryāvatāra,* 5:41; Toh 3871 Tengyur, dbu ma, *la,* 29b:7.

900 *Mind Training with Seventy Exhortations,* 18. The full text of Kharak Gomchung's text is found in Yeshé Döndrup's *Treasury of Gems* (pp. 257–64). The wording of the stanza in Yeshé Döndrup is slightly different.

901 In the Shöl edition of the Tibetan text, this subheading is listed as number 4, which would be (d) according to our system. This is clearly an error and has accordingly been corrected here as well as in the critical Tibetan edition of the text.

902 Vasubandhu, *Abhidharmakośa,* 4:55; Toh 4089. Tengyur, mngon pa, *ku,* 13a:1.

903 *Vinayavastu;* Toh 1 Kangyur, 'dul ba, *nga,* 110a:2. The wording is slightly different in the Kangyur version.

904 *Bodhicaryāvatāra,* 4:21; Toh 3871 Tengyur, dbu ma, *la,* 8b:7.

905 Although our author cites this to be from Bodhibhadra, the passage is actually found, as correctly identified by Tsongkhapa in his *Great Treatise,* in Vasubandhu's *Exposition of the Treasury of Higher Knowledge (Abhidharmakośabhāṣya);* Toh 4090 Tengyur, mngon pa, *khu,* 94b:5.

906 Asaṅga, *Abhidharmasamuccaya,* chap. 2; Toh 4049 Tengyur, sems tsam, *ri,* 86a:3.

907 Source unidentified.

908 *Karmaśataka;* Toh 340 Kangyur, mdo sde, *ha,* 106a:7. The wording of the two lines is slightly different in the Kangyur.

909 *Vajracchedikāsūtra;* Toh 16 Kangyur, sher phyin, *ka,* 127b:4.

910 *Bodhicaryāvatāra,* 6:72; Toh 3871 Tengyur, dbu ma, *la,* 17b:1.

911 This story is probably from an unidentified sutra.

912 *Bodhicaryāvatāra,* 6:1; Toh 3871 Tengyur, dbu ma, *la,* 14b:3.

913 In the Shöl edition, the text of these two sentences appears to be corrupt. Although this corruption is noted in the critical Tibetan edition, the text remains uncorrected; I have corrected it here.

914 On *yojana* (Tib., *dpag tshad*), see note 81.

915 The author is here referring to scriptures in general and probably has no specific sutra in mind.

916 This is probably cited from an established oral tradition.

917 Drogön Palden Yeshé, who was a student of Thokmé Sangpo, narrates the full story of this prince and identifies its source to be the sutra entitled *Wise and the Foolish (Mdzangs blun zhes bya ba'i mdo;* Toh 341 Kangyur, mdo sde, *a).* See Drogön Palden Yeshé, *Beautiful Garland of Stories,* pp. 395–98.

918 *Bodhicaryāvatāra,* 7:40; Toh 3871 Tengyur, dbu ma, *la,* 21b:5.

919 Nāgārjuna, *Ratnāvali,* 1:6; Toh 4158 Tengyur, skyes rabs, *ge,* 107a:4.

920 Chegom Sherap Dorje, *Heap of Precious Jewels: A Teaching by Means of Similes (Dpe chos rin chen spungs pa),* p. 95. Strictly speaking, the author is citing here from Chegom Dzongpa's commentary to Potowa's root-verse text entitled *A Teaching by Means of Similes (Dpe chos).* Potowa's root text, Cegom's commentary, as well as Drogön Palden Yeshé's highly useful narrative of the stories alluded to in Potowa's text can all be found in volume 17 of *Gangs can rigs brgya'i sgo 'byed lde mig,* a

Tibetan-language series specifically for use in higher studies in Tibetan and Buddhist disciplines and developed under the guidance of the late Panchen Lama and published by National Minorities Press in Beijing.

921   The source of Kamapa's quote cited here remains unidentified.

922   *Bodhicaryāvatāra,* 4:30, 31; Toh 3871 Tengyur, dbu ma, *la,* 9a:5.

923   Source unidentified. *The Differentiation of the Five Aggregates (Pañcaskandha-prakaraṇa)* is a treatise by Vasubandhu; Toh 4059 Tengyur, sems tsam, *shi,* 11b–17a.

924   *Smṛtyupasthānasūtra;* Toh 287 Kangyur, mdo sde, *ya,* 285a:7.

925   Maitreya, *Uttaratantra,* 4:50; Toh 4024 Tengyur, sems tsam, *phi,* 69b:5.

926   These two lines, attributed here to the Indian mystic Dampa Sangyé, do not appear in the *Heart Advice of Phadampa Sangyé,* found in volume 9 of Kongtrül's *Treasury of Instructions (Gdams ngag mdzod).* Nor do they appear in the standard redaction of the short advice text entitled *Hundred Verses of Advice to the People of Dingri (Ding ri brgya rtsa).* Either our author, Könchok Gyaltsen, is citing this from heart, as learned from an oral tradition, or he had access to a different redaction of Dampa Sangyé's advice.

927   Yeshé Döndrup (*Treasury of Gems,* p. 329) cites this quotation as found in the *Great Ear-Whispered Mind Training (Snyan rgyud chen mo)* of Radrengpa but does not provide its earliest source.

928   A old unit of Tibetan currency.

929   Nāgārjuna, *Suhṛllekha,* 67; Toh 4182 Kangyur, spring yig, *nge,* 43b:6.

930   The Mön region lies in the Arunachal Pradesh of modern India, where the traditionally Buddhist Mön tribes reside. This region is to the south of Phenpo, from which many of the great Kadam masters hailed.

931   It is unclear whether this long piece is a direct quote or a paraphrase of Shawo Gangpa's advice. The source of this long advice remains unidentified.

932   The Tibetan term *bya bral ba* (pronounced *jadrelwa*), which I have translated here as "hermit," literally means someone who has shunned all mundane activities. It is interesting that Könchok Gyaltsen chose to end this first section with a colophon.

933   "True origin" is the translation for the Tibetan expression *kun 'byung,* which literally means "the origin of all," and refers to karma and afflictions.

934   The Tibetan expression I have translated here as "impacting the mind" is *blo'i 'gram,* which, if spelled correctly, is archaic Tibetan. I have failed to locate this in any of the lexicons at my disposal.

935   *Bodhicaryāvatāra,* 3:10; Toh 3871 Tengyur, dbu ma, *la,* 7a:2.

936   *Gaṇḍavyūhasūtra;* Toh 44 Kangyur, phal chen, chap. 45, 90a:7.

937   *Vajradhvajapariṇāmasūtra;* Toh 44 Kangyur, phal chen, *kha,* chap. 8, 108b:3.

938 *Bodhicaryāvatāra,* 5:70cd; Toh 3871 Tengyur, dbu ma, *la,* 13a:2. The line cited here in the Tibetan text appears to be slightly corrupt, giving the reading: "Through fulfillment of wishes I will transform it into a body."

939 This is probably a reference to a visualization practice in Vajrayana meditation, where you imagine the various parts of your body as ritual offering.

940 It is difficult to discern whom Könchok Gyaltsen is referring to here as "our master" *(slob dpon)*. It may be Shonu Gyalchok, since this was our author's principal mind training teacher. "Cheka" is probably a reference to Chekawa, the author of *Seven-Point Mind Training.*

941 *don dang rdo rus thug pa.* This is probably an allusion to the metaphor of eating a fruit that has a stone inside.

942 *Bodhicaryāvatāra,* 8:155; Toh 3871 Tengyur, dbu ma, *la,* 29b:3.

943 This line reads in the *Root Lines* as "Relate whatever you can to your meditation right now." This variance is due to a simple difference of suffix of a Tibetan verb; when written as *gang thub,* it means "whatever you can," and when written as *gang thug,* it means "whatever you encounter." The reading of this line here agrees with Sangyé Gompa's *Public Explication,* which, as I noted there, appears to be preferable.

944 It is interesting that Könchok Gyaltsen gives both these readings and accepts either as valid.

945 Source unidentified.

946 Dharmakīrti, *Pramāṇavārttika,* 2:221; Toh 4210 Tengyur, tshad ma, *ce,* 116a:1.

947 *Bodhicaryāvatāra,* 4:34; Toh 3871 Tengyur, dbu ma, *la,* 9a:7.

948 Sé Chilbu cites a similar quotation in his commentary on *Seven-Point Mind Training,* the translation of which is found in our volume. He attributes the citation to Ben Gungyal and not to Shawo Gangpa, however.

949 The instruction is found in Langri Thangpa's *Eight Stanzas on Mind Training,* but the wording of these two lines is slightly different there.

950 Source unidentified.

951 This is probably a critical remark on those who put too much hope in Vajrayana empowerment ceremonies, where the placing of consecrated vases on the initiate's head is an integral part of the blessing rite.

952 *mtheb gang po 'di ma shor bar rtse re non pa cig dgos.* This expression "what fits under your own thumb," which appeared in a citation earlier, is somewhat intriguing. My own guess is that it refers to the fact that one can press on one's heart, the seat of one's self-grasping, with a single thumb.

953 All of these epithets probably refer to the state of a bodhisattva.

954 Though our author does not provide the source of this citation, this stanza, quoted in Yongzin Yeshé Gyaltsen's *Essence of Ambrosia (Blo sbyong bdud rtsi'i snying*

po), is found in the first story of Āryaśūra's collection of thirty-four birth stories *Jātakamālā;* Toh 4150 Tengyur, skyes rabs, *hu,* 4a:4.

955   If the Tibetan text is uncorrupted here, the metaphor of bees taking a bath remains quite oblique to me. Perhaps the point of comparison is that just as bees zoom in and out very fast when they wash themselves, in the same manner all the afflictions arise in us very rapidly.

956   The earliest textual source for this citation remains unidentified.

957   Source unidentified.

958   *Bodhicaryāvatāra,* 4:43ab; Toh 3871 Tengyur, dbu ma, *la,* 9b:3.

959   This expression "planting seeds into the earth and into the rocks" remains somewhat obscure to me. Perhaps the suggestion is to strive so hard that even if your effort resembles that of planting seeds into rocks, you should still persevere.

960   So far I have failed to identify the source of this allusion.

961   *Bodhicaryāvatāra,* 4:44; Toh 3871 Tengyur, dbu ma, *la,* 9b:5.

962   *Bodhicaryāvatāra,* 4:28; Toh 3871 Tengyur, dbu ma, *la,* 9a:4.

963   Source unidentified.

964   The source of these three citations—one from Shawopa, the second from Ben, and the third from Langri Thangpa—remains unidentified. Ben Gungyal's advice alludes to his story of instinctively reaching out his hand to steal something because of his past habit of being a thief and then instantly becoming mindful of the act. It is difficult to discern what statement of Langri Thangpa is being alluded to by the opening lines "Compared to this..."

965   Source unidentified.

966   *nged khyo kha'i nang 'thab 'di dka' bar 'dug/ khyod song.* This expression remains obscure.

967   Source unidentified.

968   Source unidentified, possibly part of an established oral tradition.

969   Source unidentified. Most probably Könchok Gyaltsen is citing here from an oral tradition.

970   This entire passage is extremely obscure in Tibetan, and my translation offered here must be taken only as suggestive. I have also failed to identify the two demons referred to in this paragraph. My guess is that they probably invoke certain legends that are part of the widespread popular beliefs in the Phenpo region of central Tibet, from which many of the early Kadam masters hailed. The metaphors refer to the twin forces of self-grasping and self-cherishing.

971   The text of Könchok Gyaltsen's commentary on this line is almost exactly identical to the one found in Sangyé Gompa's *Public Explication.*

972   *Abhisamayālaṃkāra,* 3:4d; Toh 3786 Tengyur, sems tsam, *phi,* 6a:6.

973 The text of Könchok Gyaltsen's commentary on this line is, except for few minor differences, almost identical to the one in Sangyé Gompa's *Public Explication*. For comparison, see pp. 380-81 of this volume.

974 *Gocaraparíśuddhasūtra;* Toh 44 Kangyur, phal chen, *ka,* chap. 16. There is a short commentary on this sutra by Rāhulabhadra in the Tengyur (Toh 3965).

975 *Mahāyānasūtrālaṃkāra,* 6:9; Toh 4020 Tengyur, sems tsam, *phi,* 6a:4. Sangyé Gompa cites this stanza in his *Public Explication,* but there the wording of the last line is slightly different.

976 The text of Könchok Gyaltsen's commentary on this line found here is identical to the one found in Sangyé Gompa's *Public Explication.*

977 These two lines are from Atiśa's *Bodhisattva's Jewel Garland,* though in that text the lines are not contiguous.

978 The text of Könchok Gyaltsen's commentary on this line is exactly identical to the one in Sangyé Gompa's *Public Explication.* Although there are few scribal differences between the two texts, I have here provided a reading that combines both texts so that we have a clearest possible version.

979 This sentence is somewhat obscure in the Tibetan original, and the translation provided here is only provisional.

980 Nāgārjuna, *Ratnāvali,* 3:73; Toh 4158 Tengyur, skyes rabs, *ge,* 117a.

981 The text of Könchok Gyaltsen's commentary on this line is identical to the one in Sangyé Gompa's *Public Explication,* the only difference being the omission of the parenthetical sentence that is found in *Public Explication* and not here.

982 The following commentary on these two lines is identical to the one in *Public Explication.*

983 This entire section, that is, the two paragraphs of commentary on the two lines, is copied verbatim here from Sangyé Gompa's *Public Explication of Mind Training.*

984 This is probably an allusion to a story of someone who had an exaggerated opinion of himself as well as his dog called Gongkar [the white-collared].

985 This long sentence is obscure in the Tibetan original.

986 The Tibetan original of this sentence is somewhat obscure, so my translation is provisional.

987 *sha srang gang la gtad sa sde rtse gang las med gsungs.* A *sang* is a unit of weight. This expression is obscure. Literally, it is saying that a scale full of meat cannot be expected to produce more than one full plate when cooked. The intended meaning appears to be that if your activities become an antidote to self-grasping, all other realizations will follow naturally.

988 Abbreviation for Langri Thangpa, the author of the well-known *Eight Verses on Mind Training.*

989 The commentary on this line found here is identical to the one in Sangyé Gompa's *Public Explication.*

990 For lay practitioners, this second class of objects includes close family members, such as spouse and children.

991 *zhe sdang gi blo rdol na snying rje'i thag pa chad.* This is probably an old saying though I am unfamiliar with it.

992 The story may have been well known in the region where Sangyé Gompa was teaching during the thirteenth century, but the reference is now obscure.

993 *ban de kun la 'di shi na yul khams 'di cog ge thob.* This is probably an allusion to the fact that when a senior monk passes away, the families for which the monk was serving as their main counsel will then be passed on to other monks.

994 Könchok Gyaltsen's commentary of this line is identical to the one in *Public Explication.*

995 Here the author is citing oral tradition.

996 Both in Sangyé Gompa's *Public Explication* and in Shönu Gyalchok's *Compendium of Well-Uttered Insights* (p. 177), where this entire section appears verbatim, this passage remains unattributed to anyone, but oral tradition attributes this statement to Chekawa.

997 It is difficult to determine the story being referred to here. In fact, this whole paragraph is somewhat obscure in the original Tibetan, so my translation is only suggestive.

998 Source unidentified.

999 The analogies given here are somewhat obscure. In my understanding, the point is the following: Just as when propitiating a hostile god, you ensure that all the aspects of the rite are correctly performed, you must do the same in the context of your mind training. Also, just as a successful rite of exorcism or ritual burning of malevolent forces can result in observable signs, such as audible cracking sounds, pursue your mind training practice until you observe signs of success.

1000 As evident from the text so far, the four factors to be relinquished are the following: (1) the afflictions, (2) partiality, (3) expectation of reward, and (4) dependence on other conditions.

1001 The text of the commentary on this line is identical to the one in *Public Explication.*

1002 Sangphupa refers to Ngok Lekpai Sherap (eleventh century), a direct disciple of Atiśa and Dromtönpa who founded the famous Sangphu Monastery in central Tibet in 1073.

1003 The text of the commentary of this line is identical to the one found in *Public Explication.*

1004 Although I have failed to locate the full text of the quotation, it probably pertains to the hypothetical question of how a mind training practioner, such as one of the three brothers, would respond if, out of the blue, a woman were to accuse them of being the father of her infant child.

1005 Although the text of the commentary of these two lines is identical to *Public Explication,* there is a slight variation in the lines themselves. In *Public Explication* the lines read, "This proliferation of five degenerations, transform it into the path of enlightenment," while here the instrumental case in the Tibetan version gives the reading "Through this proliferation of five degenerations..." Interestingly, these two variant readings can also be seen in the various editions of the root text of Chekawa's *Seven-Point Mind Training.*

1006 See my note 729 to Sangyé Gompa's *Public Explication of Mind Training.*

1007 Source unidentified.

1008 These two concluding lines are missing from Chekawa's *Seven-Point* as found in Sé Chilbu's commentary and also from both the *Root Lines* and the *Annotated Root Lines.* They are, however, found in Namkha Pal's *Rays of Sun,* where they appear at the beginning of the text.

1009 It is intriguing that although these two lines do not appear in the "root lines" found in Sangyé Gompa's *Public Explication,* our author, Könchok Gyaltsen, refers his readers to the explanation of these lines in *Public Explication.* This is probably an oversight.

1010 As explicitly mentioned in this brief text, the four lines that present the core instruction of the practice of parting from the four clingings is traditionally recognized as a revelation from Mañjuśrī, the buddha of wisdom. Jamgön Amé, in his *Lineages of the Sakya Family (Sa skya'i gdung rabs,* p. 26), identifies Sachen Kunga Nyingpo as the "great Sakyapa," who experienced this vision of Mañjuśrī and received the revelation. Interestingly, Nupa Rikzin Drak (entry 41 of the present volume) identifies Drakpa Gyaltsen as the origin of this instruction. The explanations of the origin of this instruction may have been added on by an editor or by Könchok Gyaltsen, one of the compilers of our present volume, who was himself an important member of the Sakya school. The four root lines of *Parting from the Four Clingings* appear in volume 4 of the *Collected Works* of Drakpa Gyaltsen, p. 297b.

1011 This short verse work on parting from the four clingings appears in volume 4 of the *Collected Works* of Drakpa Gyaltsen. A succinct biography of this important Sakya master, who was one of the five founding fathers of the Sakya school, can be found in Jamgön Amé's *Treasury of Wonders: The Lineages of the Sakya Family,* pp. 69–84.

1012 In the version found in the *Collected Works,* the following annotation appears in small letters after these lines: "These present the homage and the promise to compose."

1013 In the *Collected Works* version, the following annotation appears in small letters: "These [lines] present explicitly the distinction between correct and incorrect [forms of study, reflection, and meditation] found in the following lines from the *Abhidharmakośa:* 'Apply yourself excellently to a meditation / Endowed with ethical living, study, and reflection.' Implicitly, they present the difficulty of finding a human existence of leisure and opportunity and the procedure for meditating on death and impermanence." *Collected Works,* vol. 4, p. 298a:6.

1014 The presentation of the second freedom from clinging, which is the freedom from clinging to cyclic existence, begins with this stanza.

1015 The presentation of the third freedom, the freedom from clinging at one's self-interest, begins from this line.

1016 The following annotation appears after this line in the version found in the *Collected Works:* "Having explicitly presented the defects of cyclic existence up to this point, [the text now] presents implicitly the discipline of what is to be affirmed and what is to be rejected."

1017 The presentation of the fourth freedom, the freedom from clinging at self-existence, begins from this line.

1018 In the *Collected Works* annotation, we read the following: "Having implicitly presented the meditation on loving-kindness and compassion up to this point, their fruit, which is the exchanging of self and other, is explicitly presented." *Collected Works,* vol. 4, p. 299a:3.

1019 Here the annotation reads, "Having presented the stages of the path common with the bodhisattvas of the Mind-only school, the uncommon path of the Middle Way bodhisattvas is..."

1020 In the annotation we read the following: "Up to this point, it presents the method for relinquishing the views of absolutism and nihilism and placing one's mind in the nondual union."

1021 Here the annotation reads, "Having up to this point presented implicitly the practice of tranquil abiding, now, for the practice penetrative insight, it presents the establishment of appearing objects as the mind, as illusory, as devoid of intrinsic existence, as dependent origination, and as ineffable, thus explicitly presenting the meditation on the union free of conceptual elaborations." *Collected Works,* vol. 4, p. 299a:6.

1022 In the annotation we read, "These [lines] present the dedication and the fruits." *Collected Works,* vol. 4, p. 299b:2.

1023 This short instruction on the parting from the four clingings is found in volume 12 of the *Collected Works of the Masters of the Sakya School,* p. 223b. The author, whose personal name is Kunga Gyaltsen was not only one of the five founding fathers of the Sakya school of Tibetan Buddhism, but he was one of the greatest luminaries in the history of Tibetan Buddhist thought. A clear and extensive biography of Sakya Paṇḍita can be found in Jamgön Amé's *Treasury of Wonders,* pp. 85–149. A brief account of his life written by his student, Martön Chökyi Gyalpo, can be read in English translation in Cyrus Stearns's *Luminous Lives,* pp. 159–67.

1024 To cling to "things and their symbols" refers to grasping at the substantial reality of things and their characteristics, including their causes and effects. As becomes obvious from the text of Sakya Paṇḍita's explanation later on, this idea of gaining freedom from clinging is related to the Buddhist teaching on emptiness and the need to root out our deeply ingrained tendency to grasp at things and their properties.

1025 "The great and glorious Sakyapa" here refers to the Sakya master Kunga Nyingpo, whom we observed earlier to be the recipient of the revelation from Mañjuśrī of this instruction on parting from the four clingings. This colophon, which contains the honorific form of the verb "to compose" *(dzepa;* spelled *mdzad ma),* was probably added by an editor later.

1026 This is a very concise exposition of parting from the four clingings. A unique feature of this teaching lies in the presentation of the instruction in terms of three factors: (1) what are to be relinquished, which are the specific kinds of clinging, (2) what serve as antidotes, which are the specific meditative practices, and (3) the corresponding results. I have failed to locate any biographies of Nupa Rikzin Drak. Jamgön Amé (*Treasury of Wonders,* p. 83) lists him as an important student of the great Sakya master Drakpa Gyaltsen, suggesting that he was a contemporary of Sakya Paṇḍita.

1027 As the colophon of this work explicitly makes clear, "the great Sakyapa" here refers to the Sakya master Drakpa Gyaltsen, who was the main teacher of our author, Nupa Rikzin Drak.

1028 Goram Sönam Sengé, known often in his shorter names as Gowo Rapjampa or simply as Gorampa, was one of the most influential thinkers in the Sakya school during the fifteenth century. Unlike the works of his somewhat controversial contemporary, the brilliant Śākya Chokden, Gorampa's philosophical writings later became the standard textbooks for many of the monastic colleges of the Sakya School. His works, covering a vast area of classical Buddhist scholarship and running into thirteen large volumes, also became recognized as presenting the mainstream Sakya standpoint on many doctrinal and philosophical issues. It is difficult to discern whether it was Könchok Gyaltsen himself who included this short work of Gorampa in the present volume or whether it was added later by a subsequent editor. For Könchok Gyaltsen himself gave the transmission of most of the mind training teachings to Gorampa. Gorampa's text appears in volume 8 of his collected works, which is volume 14 in the *Collected Works of the Masters of Sakya School.*

1029 The colophon of this short work provides the name of the benefactor at whose behest Gorampa composed this guide.

1030 Maitreya, *Abhisamayālaṃkāra.*

1031 Maitreya, *Mahāyānasūtrālaṃkāra.*

1032 *Ratnāvali.*

1033 This is a reference to Āryadeva's *Catuḥśatakaśāstra.*

1034 This is a reference to Śāntideva's *Bodhicaryāvatāra.*

1035 This is a reference to Atiśa's *Bodhipathapradīpa.*

1036 This is a reference to Candrakīrti's *Madhyamakāvatāra,* which is structured in accordance with the ten bodhisattva levels.

1037 Potowa, Phuchungwa, and Khamlungpa, who are known as the three Kadam brothers.

1038 This is a reference to Ngülchu Thokmé Sangpo (1295–1369), the author of the well-known *Thirty-Seven Practices of a Bodhisattva,* who was recognized as a principal custodian of the lineage of mind training teachings during the fourteenth century.

1039 Shönu Gyalchok is one of the compilers of the present volume and the author of *Mind Training: Compendium of Well-Uttered Insights,* which I have cited extensively in my various annotations in this volume. See my introduction for more on his life and work.

1040 "The waxing moon of *kārttika* month" is called *mindruk* (spelled: *smin drug*) in Tibetan. *Mindruk* refers to the period between the sixteenth of the ninth month to the fifteenth of the tenth month in the Tibetan lunar calendar.

1041 Despite effort, I have failed to find any biographical details for Künga Lekpai Rinchen. As indicated in the brief section of the text pertaining to its lineage, our author was a student of the Sakya *lamdré* master Ngorchen Künga Sangpo, from whom he himself received the transmission of this instruction.

1042 Bari Lotsāwa (1040–1111) was an important translator during the eleventh century. The translation of several Vajrayana texts are accredited to him in the Tengyur. *The Blue Annals* (p. 73) gives 1040 as the year of his birth and states that he was born in the same year as the well-known Tibetan poet-saint Milarepa. According to the same source, Bari Lotsāwa met Atiśa at the age of fifteen. The "great Sakyapa" referred to in this passage is Sachen Künga Nyingpo to whom, according to the tradition, the instruction of parting from the four clingings was revealed by Mañjuśrī.

1043 Residential complex of a high lama.

1044 This fourfold formula is elaborated below after the descriptions of the objects of refuge and the visualization.

1045 *Abhidharmakośa,* 6:5ab; Toh 4089 Tengyur, mngon pa, *ku,* 18b:7.

1046 *Bodhicaryāvatāra,* 1:4; Toh 3871 Tengyur, dbu ma, *la,* 1b:7.

1047 *Bodhicaryāvatāra,* 3:20; Toh 3871 Tengyur, dbu ma, *la,* 8b:6.

1048 *Śokavinodana;* Toh 4177 Tengyur, spring yig, *nge,* 33a:4.

1049 *Lalitavistarasūtra;* Toh 95 Kangyur, mdo sde, *kha,* 88a:2.

1050 *Śokavinodana;* Toh 4177 Tengyur, spring yig, *nge,* 33b:3. The wording of the lines here is quite different from their rendering in the Tengyur.

1051 *Śokavinodana,* p. 33b:2.

1052 *Ratnāvali,* 3:79; Toh 4158 Tengyur, skyes rabs, *ge,* 137b:1.

1053 Source unidentified.

1054 *Smṛtyupasthānasūtra;* Toh 287 Kangyur, mdo sde, *ya,* 285a:7.

1055 The Tibetan anatomical terms I have translated here as "intestines, viscera, and guts" are respectively, *rgyu ma, gnye ma,* and *long ga.* Although the first term can be fairly accurately translated as "intestines," the two latter terms are merely suggestive.

1056 For women practitioners, the reader should substitute "men" for "women" and "monks" for "nuns" and so on.

1057 Here the sense of a certain act "producing" happiness or suffering should not be understood in the short term but rather in terms of the karmic result in future lives.

1058 *Suhṛllekha,* 69cd; Toh 4182 Tengyur, spring yig, *nge,* 43b:7. See also note 207.

1059 Source unidentified. Similar sentiments are found in Nāgārjuna's *Suhṛllekha,* 68; Toh 4182 Kangyur, spring yig, *nge,* 43b:6.

1060 *Madhyamakāvatāra,* 6:211cd; Toh 3861 Tengyur, dbu ma, *'a,* 214b:3.

1061 *Mahāyānasūtrālaṃkāra,* 18:39a; Toh 4020 Tengyur, sems tsam, *phi,* 26b:7.

1062 *Madhyamakāvatāra,* 6:212ab; Toh 3861 Tengyur, dbu ma, *'a,* 214b:3.

1063 This is a reference to the practice of combining the cultivation of compassion with the awakening mind, intention, and aspiration as explained above in the section on cultivating loving-kindness.

1064 *Mahāyānasūtrālaṃkāra,* 5:3a; Toh 4020 Tengyur, sems tsam, *phi,* 4b:3.

1065 Bhūripa, *Extensive Daily Confessions of Cakrasaṃvara [Practice];* Toh 1533 Tengyur, rgyud 'grel, *za,* 95a:4.

1066 See bibliography for bibliographical details on these texts.

1067 *Bodhicaryāvatāra,* 8:4; Toh 3871 Tengyur, dbu ma, *la,* 23b:3. The wording of the second line of this quotation is slightly different from the version in the Tengyur, where it reads, "Knowing that insight perfectly endowed with / Tranquillity utterly destroys the afflictions...."

1068 *Mahāyānasūtrālaṃkāra,* 19:67; Toh 4020 Tengyur, sems tsam, *phi,* 31a:2.

1069 *Samādhisambhāraparivarta;* Toh 3924 Tengyur, dbu ma, *ki,* 90a:3.

1070 *Ibid.*

1071 *Samādhirājasūtra;* Toh 127 Kangyur, mdo sde, *da,* 13b:5.

1072 This is a reference to the third line of *Bodhicaryāvatāra,* 9:2. The whole stanza reads as follows: "Knowing that insight perfectly endowed with / Tranquillity utterly destroys the afflictions, / Search for tranquil abiding first. This, too, in its turn, / Is achieved through nonattachment to the world."

1073 The original Tibetan word I have translated here as "appearance" *(snang ba)* has both subjective and objective connotations. When the subjective connotation is implied, the Tibetan term is then better captured by the word *perception.* Hence

I have translated the same word as "perception" in the context of the next stage of the meditation, where, having established all appearances of objects as mental constructs, the perceptions themselves are being established as illusory.

1074 *Samādhirājasūtra*, 4; Toh 127 Kangyur, mdo sde, *da*, 26b:2.

1075 Nāgārjuna, *Yuktiṣaṣṭikā (Sixty Stanzas of Reasoning)*, 61; Toh 3825 Tengyur, dbu ma, *tsa*, 22b:4.

Glossary

adverse conditions/adversities *(rkyen ngan)*. Refers to all types of conditions, circumstances, and events that are detrimental to well-being. These include ill health, tragic events, and harm from others. The mind training teachings focus on how to creatively turn these adversities into conditions favorable to spiritual practice.

advice *(gdams ngag, upadeśa)*. An important aspect of the mind training teaching is to train your mind to understand every word of the Buddha's teaching as an advice or an instruction to help overcome the mental afflictions. The Sanskrit term *upadeśa* is also translated as *man ngag* in Tibetan, which has been translated as "pith instruction" or simply as "instruction." *See also pith instructions*

afflictions *(nyon mongs, kleśa)*. A class of dissonant mental states, including both thoughts and emotions, that have their root in ignorance. They are referred to as "afflictions" because they afflict the individual from deep within. The classical Abhidharma texts list six root afflictions—(1) attachment, (2) aversion, (3) conceit, (4) afflicted doubt, (5) ignorance, and (6) afflicted view—and twenty afflictions that are derivative of these root afflictions.

antidote *(gnyen po)*. Just as a specific medicine is seen as the antidote for a specific illness, in mind training practice, mental states such as compassion and loving-kindness are identified as antidotes against specific mental ills. Since one of the principal objectives of mind training practice is the purification of your mind, applying antidotes is an important recurrent theme in the mind training texts. The Tibetan term *gnyen po* is sometimes translated also as "remedy" or "counter factor" as well.

arhat *(dgra bcom pa)*. Literally meaning "foe destroyer," the term refers to a highly evolved spiritual person who has eliminated all the afflictions and has thus gained victory over them, the afflictions being the "foe" in this context.

aspiration *('dun pa)*. In the context of mind training teaching, the term refers to a fundamental form of aspiration, such as your life's aspiration. One of the mind training precepts is to avoid misplaced aspiration, which means viewing the advantages of this life as admirable and aspiring for them. *See also six misplaced understandings*

aspiration prayer *(smon lam, praṇidhāna)*. In the literary context, aspirational prayers in Tibetan are easily recognized by the presence of their ending particle *shog*, which is translated as "may such and such be." The Tibetan term *smon lam* is sometimes translated simply as "prayer" or "prayer aspiration."

aspiring awakening mind *(smon pa byang sems)*. *See awakening mind*

awakening mind *(byang chub kyi sems, bodhicitta)*. An altruistic intention to attain buddhahood for the benefit of all beings. The awakening mind is characterized by an *objective,* the full awakening of budhahood, and a *purpose,* the fulfillment of others' welfare.

Following the Indian Mahayana classics, the mind training texts speak of "training in the two awakening minds"—the *conventional awakening mind* and the *ultimate awakening mind.* The former refers to altruistic intention as defined above, while the latter refers to a direct realization of the emptiness of the fully awakened mind. In general usage, the term *awakening mind* is a synonym for the conventional awakening mind, which is in turn understood in terms of two levels. First is the *aspiring awakening mind,* which is likened to the intention of a person who wishes to travel somewhere; and the second is the *engaging awakening mind,* likened to the intention of the person who has actually embarked on the journey. This second level is realized when the aspirant commits him or herself, by means of a vow, to the actual fulfillment of the aim of bringing about others' welfare.

basis-of-all *(kun gzhi, ālaya)*. There are two principal interpretations of what is meant by "basis-of-all" in the context of mind training. One interpretation is that it refers to an uncontrived mind *(sems ma bcos pa),* while the second interpretation maintains that it refers to the mind's emptiness. In the context of Yogacāra theory, *basis-of-all (kun gzhi, ālaya)* refers to a foundational consciousness that is thought to be the repository of all our karmic imprints, propensities, and habitual tendencies.

bodhicitta drops *(byang sems)*. The term "bodhicitta drops" is a rendering of the word *bodhicitta* when used in the tantric context, where it refers to the pure essence of the white male and female sexual fluids. These bodhicitta drops are intimately associated with experiences of bliss engendered through deep meditative yogic practices. In this volume, the term appears in those mind training works explicitly associated with the Vajrayana.

bodhisattva *(byang chub sems dpa')*. A person who has cultivated the awakening mind and is on the path to buddhahood.

clinging *(zhen pa)*. A mind or action that grasps to an object, quality, or a mental state. The cycle of mind training teachings revealed to the great Sakya master Künga Nyingpo focuses on parting from four clingings: clinging to this life, to cyclic existence, to your own welfare, and to views.

compassion *(snying rje, karuṇā).* A mental state that wishes others to be free of suffering. *Compassion* is often used in mind training literature as a synonym for "great compassion" *(snying rje chen po).* *Great compassion* is a universal, nondiscriminatory compassion that wishes all beings to be free of suffering.

conceptual elaborations *(spros pa, prapañca).* Conceptual elaborations include all forms of dichotomizing conceptualization, such as subject-object duality, as well as grasping at objects and their characteristics. The direct realization of emptiness is marked by total freedom from all such conceptual elaborations.

conceptualization *(rnam rtog, vicāra).* The Tibetan term *rnam rtog* has been translated as "conceptualization" and carries numerous connotations. (1) It can refer simply to thoughts, which unlike direct sensory experiences are mediated by language and concepts. (2) However, it can also refer specifically to dichotomizing thoughts that lead to the objectification and reification of things and events. (3) Sometimes, the term may be used in the negative sense of "false conceptualization." In the context of this volume, *rnam rtog* (conceptualization) carries more the second and third meaning.

confession/purification *(bshags pa, deśanā).* The practice for cleansing your past negative karma. A successful practice of purification must involve the application of antidotes endowed with four powers: (1) the power of eradication (by means of repentance), (2) the power of applying antidotes, (3) the power of turning away from the errors, and (4) the power of the basis (refuge in the Three Jewels).

conventional awakening mind *(kun rdzob byang chub sems).* See *awakening mind*

conventional truth *(kun rdzob bden pa, saṃvṛtisatya).* See *two truths*

cyclic existence *('khor ba, saṃsāra).* The perpetual cycle of birth, death, and rebirth within an existence conditioned by karma and afflictions. Freedom from cyclic existence is characterized as *nirvāṇa,* the "transcendence of sorrow."

defilement *(sgrib pa, āvaraṇa).* Literally "obscuration," *defilement* refers to the factors (such as mental and emotional states as well as their imprints, propensities, and habitual tendencies) that obstruct you from attaining liberation or the full omniscience of buddhahood. There are two main categories of defilements. The first, "defilements in the form of the afflictions and their seeds," obstructs the attainment of liberation. And the second, "defilements in the form of subtle propensities of these mental states and the deep habitual tendencies for dualistic perceptions," obstructs the attainment of buddhahood.

dharmakāya *(chos sku).* One of the three bodies of buddhahood. *Dharmakāya,* which literally means "truth body," refers to the ultimate reality of a buddha's enlightened mind—unborn, free from the limits of conceptual elaboration, empty of intrinsic existence, naturally radiant, beyond duality, and spacious like the sky. The other two buddha bodies, the buddha body of perfect resource *(longs sku)* and the buddha body of emanation *(sprul sku),* are progressively grosser bodies that arise naturally from the basic dharmakāya state.

disciple *(nyan thos, śrāvaka).* Disciples of the Buddha whose primary spiritual objective is to attain liberation from the cycle of existence. The Sanskrit term and its Tibetan equivalent are sometimes translated as "hearers" (which stays close to the literal meaning) or as "pious attendants." *Disciples* are often paired with *self-realized ones,* who seek liberation on the basis of autonomous practice as opposed to listening to others' instructions.

emptiness *(stong pa nyid, śūnyatā).* According to the Perfection of Wisdom scriptures of Mahayana Buddhism, all things and events, including our own existence, are devoid of any independent, substantial, and intrinsic reality. This emptiness of independent existence is phenomena's ultimate mode of being—the way they actually are. The theory of emptiness is most systematically developed in the writings of the second-century thinker Nāgārjuna, who demonstrated the emptiness of all things and events, both external and internal, through logical reasoning. Since our deeply ingrained tendency is to perceive and grasp a substantial reality in all phenomena, we engender a cycle of conceptualization, objectification, grasping, and bondage. Only through bringing an end to this cycle, Nāgārjuna argues, can we begin the path to liberation.

existing by means of real substance *(rdzas su yod pa, dravyasat).* Although all phenomena exist in dependence upon other factors, particularly their designations within the conventional framework of language and thought, we tend to perceive them as existing by means of real substance because of our deeply ingrained tendency for grasping. The logic of emptiness negates the content of this belief, according to the mind training teachings.

five powers *(stobs lnga).* The powers of (1) propelling intention, (2) acquaintance, (3) positive seed, (4) eradication, and (5) aspirational prayer. The mind training texts describe the application of these five powers as the essence of mind training instruction. The sequence in which they are practiced on a daily basis and their application at the point of death, where the practice functions as a method of transference, are slightly different.

four factors of attracting others *(bsdu ba'i dngos po bzhi, saṃgrahavastu).* (1) Giving what is immediately needed (such as material needs), (2) using pleasant speech, (3) giving sound spiritual advice, and (4) living in accord with what you teach. These four factors are identified as the primary means by which a bodhisattva attracts others and enhances their minds. In contrast, the *six perfections* are said to be the primary factors for the development and enhancement of the bodhisattva's own mind.

freeing the remedy too in its own place *(gnyen po nyid kyang rang sar grol ba)*. This means that, in applying antidotes against the afflictions, you need to avoid grasping at the antidotes themselves. This instruction echoes the Mahayana exhortation to remember that emptiness, too, is empty of intrinsic existence.

ingratitude *(log sgrub)*. Literally, "acting in a misguided manner." In some mind training texts, the term is used to refer to a lack of gratitude for the kindness that has been done by others, a negative trait endemic to beings of a degenerate era. This Tibetan term has also been translated as "misguided ways" in some contexts in this volume.

instruction to be applied at the point of death *('chi ka'i gdams ngag)*. A practice for the point of death to ensure that (1) you die in peace, (2) the process of dying is utilized most efficiently toward furthering your spiritual path, and (3) the transition to next life goes smoothly. In the mind training texts, the application of the five powers is recommended as the best example of this. *See also five powers*

loving-kindness *(byams pa, maitrī)*. As a "mental factor wishing others to achieve happiness," *loving-kindness* is said to be the other facet of compassion. The mind training texts give specific instructions on cultivating loving-kindness. This loving kindness is to be distinguished from the loving-kindness of cherishing others as dear, which is step four in the seven-point cause-and-effect method of cultivating the awakening mind.

Māra's activity *(bdud las)*. In Mahayana thought, often a detrimental thought or action is described as "Māra's activity," implying that it is the product of the beguiling forces of the afflictions. The concept of *Māra* goes back to the earliest Buddhist literature, where it is a personification of the basic obstructive forces—internal afflictions, such as anger, desire, and delusion. In fact, one of the "twelve deeds of the Buddha" is his gaining victory over the forces of Māra. Classical Buddhist texts list four such māras: (1) the māra of afflictions, (2) the māra of death, (3) the māra of conditioned aggregates, and (4) the māra of beguiling desire (literally, the "son of devas").

meditation *(sgom, bhāvanā)*. Both the Sanskrit and the Tibetan terms for meditation connote the notion of cultivation, such as the cultivation of certain mental habit. The Tibetan term in particular carries a strong sense of cultivating familiarity, be it with a chosen object, topic, or a particular way of thinking or being. Principally, there are two kinds of meditation: absorptive meditation *('jog sgom)*, which is characterized by single-pointed focus; and analytic meditation *(dpyad sgom),* which is characterized primarily by deep analysis. There are other types of meditation, too, such as visualization, aspiration, or cultivation. Given this diversity, different words—"contemplate," "meditate," "visualize," and "cultivate"—have been used to translate the Tibetan verb *sgom pa,* depending upon the context.

meditative absorption *(ting nge 'dzin, samādhi).* Meditative absorption refers to the state where the mind is totally focused in single-pointed absorption on a chosen object. The Sanskrit term *samādhi* and its Tibetan equivalent have several different meanings in different contexts. In the context of the Abhidharma taxonomy of mental factors, the term refers to a mental factor whose primary function is to ensure the stability of the mind. This mental factor is part of a group of mental factors present in all unmistaken cognitions. *Meditative absorption* can also refer to a specific advanced meditative state, such as the direct single-pointed realization of emptiness. Finally, the term can refer to a specific meditation practice, such as meditative absorption on compassion.

meditative equipoise *(mnyam gzhag).* A session of single-pointed fusion with the chosen object of meditation. Sometimes *meditative equipoise* is simply a synonym for "meditation session" in contrast with practices of the post-meditation periods. In the *Seven Point Mind Training,* for example, the practices of cultivating the two awakening minds are regarded as practices for the actual meditation session, while all other practices are described as those of subsequent periods.

method *(thabs, upāya). Method* refers to the altruistic deeds of the bodhisattva, including the cultivation of compassion and the awakening mind. In Mahayana Buddhism, the union of method and wisdom is central to understanding the path.

mind generation *(sems bskyed, cittotpāda).* This somewhat awkward term is in fact a synonym for the conventional awakening mind, the altruistic intention to attain buddhahood for the benefit of all beings. Drawing from their Sanskrit sources, classical Tibetan texts use this term often when they refer to the awakening mind. Judging by the past tense of the verb, the term *sems bskyed* can be a shorthand way of writing "the mind that has been generated" and may be better translated as "the generated mind." However the term also refers to the act of generating the mind in the context of a rite or at the beginning of a meditation practice as part of the preliminaries.

negative action *(sdig pa/sdig pa'i las, pāpa/pāpakarma).* Actions of body, speech, and mind that are actually harmful or potentially harmful. Negative actions are motivated by any of the three poisons of the mind—attachment, aversion, and delusion. Though used interchangeably in the texts with *mi dge ba* or *mi dge ba'i las* (Tibetan equivalents for the Sanskrit terms *akuśala* or *akuśalakarma*) and translated as "nonvirtuous action," the Tibetan term *sdig pa* and its Sanskrit equivalent actually carry a heavier, sin-like connotation. Hence I have chosen to distinguish their usage by choosing two different English renderings: "negative" and "nonvirtuous." The classical Buddhist texts list ten classes of negative actions: three actions of body, which are (1) killing, (2) stealing, and (3) sexual misconduct; four actions of speech, which are (4) lying, (5) engaging in divisive speech, (6) using harsh words, and (7) indulging in frivolous speech; and three actions of mind, which are (8) covetousness, (9) ill will, and (10) wrong views. *See unwholesome karma*

noble one *('phags pa, ārya)*. A being on the path who has gained direct realization of the truth. Noble ones are contrasted with ordinary beings *(so so'i ske bo, prathagjana)*, whose understanding of the truth remains bound by language and concepts.

nonvirtuous karma *(mi dge ba/mi dge ba'i las, akuśala/akuśalakarma)*. Although in most Buddhist texts the term *akauśalakarma* (nonvirtuous action) is used interchangeably with *pāpakarma* (negative action), etymologically the Sanskrit term *akuśala* connotes an act that is unskillful rather than negative. Similarly, the Tibetan equivalent of the term *mi dge ba* connotes an act that is not auspicious or virtuous. *See negative action*

penetrative insight *(lhag mthong, vipaśyanā)*. An advanced meditative state where the meditator has successfully attained physical and mental pliancy because of having applied analytic meditation on a basis of tranquil abiding. Sometimes the term is also used generically to embrace all analytic, as opposed to absorptive, meditation practices.

perfection of wisdom *(sher phyin, prajñāpāramitā)*. One of the six perfections that lie at the heart of the practice of the bodhisattva. Classical Mahayana texts apply the term in three principal ways. In the context of the resultant stage, the term refers the perfected wisdom of a fully awakened buddha, who is free of all defilements and directly perceives the two truths—conventional and ultimate—of all phenomena spontaneously in a single mental act. In terms of the path, *perfection of wisdom* refers to the bodhisattva's direct realization of emptiness, a wisdom that is in perfect union with the method side of the path. Finally, this term also refers to a specific subdivision of the Mahayana scriptures that outline the essential aspects of these paths and their resultant state. The *Perfection of Wisdom in Eight Thousand Lines,* the *Heart Sūtra,* and the *Diamond Cutter* are some of the most well-known Perfection of Wisdom scriptures.

pith instructions *(man ngag, upadeśa)*. Sometimes translated simply as "instruction," *pith instruction* connotes a specialized kind of advice. This Tibetan word and the term *gdams ngag,* which has been translated as "advice," are both equivalents of a single Sanskrit term *upadeśa*. *Man ngag* connotes an instruction suited only to select practitioners. Often, *man ngag* also refers to an oral lineage. *See also advice*

pollutants *(dri ma, mala)*. These include all the afflictions that contaminate, pollute, and stain the mind, such as attachment, aversion, and delusion.

pristine cognition *(ye shes, jñāna)*. Often contrasted with ordinary consciousness *(rnam shes)*, pristine cognition *(ye shes)* refers to a buddha's fully awakened wisdom and also to the uncontaminated gnosis of the noble ones that is characterized by the direct realization of emptiness. Some translate the Sanskrit term and its Tibetan equivalent as "wisdom" or "gnosis."

remedy *(gnyen po)*. *See antidote*

self-cherishing *(rang gces 'dzin)*. The deeply ingrained thought that cherishes the welfare of your own self and makes you oblivious to others' well-being. This is one of the "twin demons" *('gong po gnyis)* that lie within our heart and serve as the source of all misfortune and downfall (the other twin demon being grasping at selfhood). These two thoughts—self-cherishing and self-grasping—are the primary focus of combat in the mind training practice.

self-grasping *(bdag 'dzin, ātmagṛha)*. Instinctively believing in the intrinsic existence of your own self as well of the external world. *Self* here means a substantial, truly existing identity. The wisdom that realizes emptiness eliminates this self-grasping. *See also self-cherishing*

self-realized one *(rang sangs rgyas, pratyekabuddha)*. Self-realized ones are those aspiring for their own liberation from cyclic existence who, unlike *disciples,* seek liberation primarily on the basis of their own autonomous understanding rather than relying on instruction from others. In addition, they are said to accumulate both merit and wisdom for a much longer period than disciples. The distinction between the disciple and the self-realized one varies among different philosophical schools.

six misplaced understandings *(go log drug)*. The six misplaced understandings are (1) misplaced forbearance, (2) misplaced aspiration, (3) misplaced savoring, (4) misplaced compassion, (5) misplaced dedication, and (6) misplaced rejoicing.

stages of the path *(lam rim)*. A genre of instruction on the Mahayana Buddhist path that evolved from Atiśa's *Bodhipathapradipa*. This short text lays out the essence of the entire teachings of the Buddha within a graduated framework of practices that are geared to three levels of mental capacity. Tsongkhapa's *Great Exposition of the Stages of the Path* is the most well-known of the later Tibetan works inspired by Atiśa's text.

substantial existence *(bden par yod pa/bden par grub pa)*. A belief that things and events, including your own self, possess a true existence definable in terms of their elementary constituents (atom-like particles) or in terms of characteristics like causes, conditions, and effects.

substantial reality *(bden pa'i dngos po)*. A belief that things and events possess substantial existence.

suchness *(de bzhin nyid, tattva/tathatā)*. The reality of things as they are; often used as a synonym for *emptiness*.

supplication *(gsol 'debs)*. An appeal or request written often in verse and directed to an object of veneration, such as the Three Jewels or your spiritual teacher.

tathāgata *(de bzhin gshegs pa, tathāgata)*. Literally, "thus-gone one"; an epithet for a buddha.

Three Jewels *(dkon mchog gsum, triratna)*. The Buddha Jewel, the Dharma Jewel and the Sangha Jewel together constitute the true object of refuge in Buddhism. You take refuge in the Buddha as the true teacher, in the Dharma as the true teaching, and in the Sangha (the spiritual community) as the true companions on the path.

three scriptural collections *(sde snod gsum, tripiṭaka)*. Literally, "the three baskets," the term refers to a threefold classification of all the teachings attributed to the Buddha: (1) discipline *(vinaya piṭaka)*, (2) discourses *(sūtra piṭaka)*, and (3) higher knowledge *(abhidharma piṭaka)*.

torma *(gtor ma)*. A cake for ritual offerings made from dough; in some contexts, a representation of a deity. Often cone-shaped and composed of yak butter and barley flour, *torma* can be as simple as a dough ball or elaborately crafted with colorful butter ornamentation.

tranquil abiding *(zhi gnas, śamatha)*. An advanced meditative state where the meditator has attained a physical and mental pliancy derived from focusing the mind. It is characterized by stable single-pointed attention on a chosen object with all mental distractions calmed. Tranquil abiding is an essential basis for cultivating *penetrative insight*.

transference *('pho ba)*. An advanced tantric practice whereby the meditator deliberately directs his or her consciousness out of the body. According to the texts, this is to be applied when the practitioner perceives imminent signs of death but the actual dying process has not yet begun. In the context of mind training teachings, the practice of the *five powers* is said to be an ideal method of transference.

two truths *(bden pa gnyis, satyadvaya)*. The concept of two levels of reality, *two truths,* is employed in all schools of Buddhism to explain their understanding of the nature of reality. What constitutes the conventional truth and what constitutes the ultimate truth differs among these schools. According to the Middle Way school, the perspective adopted in most of the mind training texts, *ultimate truth* refers to emptiness—the absence of the intrinsic existence of all phenomena. In contrast, *conventional truth* refers to the empirical aspect of reality as experienced through perception, thought, and language.

ultimate awakening mind *(don dam byang chub sems)*. See *awakening mind*

ultimate expanse *(chos dbyings, dharmadhātu)*. Often used as a synonym for *emptiness* and *suchness,* the term refers to the ultimate underlying truth of all things—namely their empty nature. This ultimate underlying truth constitutes the expanse from which arises the entire world of diversity, cause and effect, identity and difference, and so on, that characterizes our everyday world of existence.

ultimate nature *(gnas lugs)*. Refers to the ultimate mode of being of things, which is *emptiness.* Hence the expression, "emptiness, the ultimate nature of phenomena" *(chos rnams kyi gnas lugs stong pa nyid)*.

ultimate truth *(don dam bden pa, paramārthasatya)*. See *two truths*

virtuous karma *(dge ba / dge ba'i las, kuśala/kuśalakarma)*. Actions of body, speech, and mind motivated by wholesome states of mind, such as nonattachment, nonaversion, and nondelusion; these are actions either actually or potentially beneficial for others and one's own self. *See also nonvirtuous karma*

wisdom *(shes rab, prajñā)*. The Sanskrit term *prajñā* and its Tibetan equivalent *shes rab* have different applications depending upon the context. In the Abhidharma taxonomy of mental factors, *prajñā* refers to a specific mental factor that helps evaluate the various properties or qualities of an object. The term can refer simply to intelligence or mental aptitude. In the context of the Mahayana path, *prajñā* refers to the wisdom aspect of the path constituted primarily by deep insight into the emptiness of all phenomena. Hence the term *prajñā* and its Tibetan equivalent are translated variously as "wisdom," "insight," or "intelligence."

yoga *(rnal 'byor)*. Literally meaning "union," yoga refers to advanced meditative practices, especially in the context of Buddhist tantra. The Tibetan term *rnal 'byor* has the added connotation of "uniting one's mind with the nature of reality."

Bibliography

WORKS CITED IN THE TEXTS

Kangyur *(Canonical Scriptures)*

Advice to a King Sutra. Rājāvavādakasūtra. Rgyal po la gdams pa'i mdo. Toh 221, mdo sde *dza.* P887, *tshu.*

Advice to King [Bimbisāra] Sutra. Rājadeśasūtra. Rgyal po la gdams pa zhes bya ba theg pa chen po'i mdo. Toh 214, mdo sde *tsha.* P215 *tsu.*

Ākāśagarbha Sutra. Ākāśagarbhasūtra. Nam mkha'i snying po'i mdo. Toh 260, mdo sde *za.* P926, *zhu.*

Amoghapāśa Tantra. See *Heart of Amoghapāśa Sutra.*

Array of Trees Sutra. Gaṇḍavyūhasūtra. Sdong po bkod pa'i mdo. Toh 44, phal chen *ga,* P761, *hi.* This is chapter 45 of the *Flower Ornament Scripture* in the Tibetan edition; in Cleary's translation from the Chinese, this is book 39.

Close Placements of Mindfulness Sutra. Smṛtyupasthānasūtra. Dam pa'i chos dran pa nye bar gzhag pa. Toh 287, mdo sde *ya.* P953, *'u.*

Clouds of Jewels Sutra. Ratnameghasūtra. 'Phags pa dkon mchog sprin. Toh 231, mdo sde va, P897, *dzu.*

Collection of Aphorisms. Udānavarga. Ched du brjod pa'i tshoms. Toh 326, mdo sde *sa.* P992, *shu.*

Collection of Flowers Sutra. Kusumasañcayasūtra. Me tog gi tshogs. Toh 266 mdo sde *'a.* P932, *zu.*

Condensed Perfection of Wisdom in Stanzas. Prajñāpāramitāsaṃcayagāthā. Shes rab kyi pha rol tu phyin pa bsdud pa tshigs su bcad pa. Toh 13, shes phyin *ka.* P735, *tsi.*

Dedications of Vajradhvaja Sutra. Vajradhvajapariṇāmasūtra. Rdo rje rgyal mtshan gyi yongs su bsngo ba. Toh 44, phal chen *kha.* P761, *i.* This is chapter 30 of the *Flower Ornament Scripture* in the Tibetan edition; in Cleary's translation from the Chinese it is book 25.

Diamond Cutter Sutra. Vajracchedikāsūtra. Rdo rje gcod pa. Toh 16, sher phyin *ka.* P739, *tsi.* This sutra is also known as the *Perfection of Wisdom in Three Hundred Lines (Sher phyin sum brgya pa).*

Enlightenment of Vairocana. Mahāvairocanādhisaṃbodhi. Rnam snang mngon byang gi rgyud. Toh 494, rgyud *tha.* P126, *tha.*

Flower Ornament Scripture. Avataṃsakasūtra. Sangs rgyas phal po che zhes bya ba shin tu rab tu rgyas pa. Toh 44, phal chen *ka–a.* P761, *yi–hi.*

Fortunate Era Sutra. Bhadrakalpikasūtra. Phags pa bskal ba bzang po zhes bya ba theg pa chen po'i mdo. Toh 94, mdo sde *ka.* P762, *i.*

Foundational Discipline. Vinayavastu. 'Dul ba gzhi. Toh 1, 'dul ba *nga.* P1030, *khe.*

Good Signs Sutra. Bhadrakāratrisūtra. Mtshan mo bzang po. Toh 313, mdo sde *sa.* P979, *shu.*

Great Nirvana Sutra. Mahāparinirvāṇasūtra. 'Phags pa yongs su mya ngan las 'das pa chen po'i mdo. Toh 119 and 120, mdo sde *nya, ta,* and *tha.* P787 and 788, *ju* and *tu.*

Great Tantra of Magical Net. Māyājālamahātantrarāja. Rgyud kyi rgyal po chen po sgyu 'phrul dra ba. Toh 466, rgyud 'bum *ja.* P102, *ja.*

Heart of Amoghapāśa Sutra. (Referred to also as *the Amoghapāśa Tantra.*) *Amoghapāśahṛdayasūtra. 'Phags pa don yod zhags pa'i snying po.* Toh 682, rgyud *ba.* P366, *ma.*

King of Meditation Sutra. Samādhirājasūtra. Ting nge 'dzin rgyal po'i mdo. Toh 127, mdo sde *da.* P795, *thu.*

Mahāsahasrapramardanasūtra. Stong chen mo rab tu 'joms pa. Toh 558, rgyud 'bum *pha.* P177, *pha.*

Maitreya's Great Lion's Roar Sutra. Maitreyamahāsiṃhanādasūtra. Byams pa'i seng ge'i sgra chen po. Toh 67, dkon brtsegs *ca.* P760:23, *zi.*

One Hundred Rites. Karmaśataka. Las brgya tham pa. Toh 340, mdo sde *ha.* P1007, *su.*

Perfection of Wisdom in a Hundred Thousand Lines. Śatasāhasrikāprajñā-pāramitāsūtra. Shes rab kyi pha rol tu phyin pa stong phrag brgya pa. Toh 8, shes phyin *ka–a.* P730, *ra–ji.*

Perfectly Gathering the Qualities [of Avalokiteśvara]. Dharmasaṃgitisūtra. Chos yang dag par sdud pa'i mdo. Toh 238, mdo sde *zha.* P904, *vu.*

Questions of Gaganagañja Sutra. Gaganagañjaparipṛcchāsūtra. 'Phags pa nam mkha'i mdzod kyis zhus pa. Toh 148, mdo sde *pa.* P815, *nu.*

Sampuṭa Tantra. Sampuṭatantra. Yang dag par sbyor ba'i rgyud. Toh 381, rgyud *ga.* P26, *ga.*

Scriptural Collection of the Bodhisattva. Bodhisattvapiṭaka. Byang chub sems dpa'i sde snod. Toh 56, dkon brtsegs *ga.* P760:12, *dzi.* English translation of chapter 11 found in Pagel 1995.

Seal [for] Entering the Definitive and Nondefinitive Sutra. Niyatāni-yatagatimudrāvatārasūtra. Nges pa dang ma nges par 'gro ba'i phyag rgya'i mdo. Toh 202, mdo sde *tsha.* P868, *tsu.*

Skill in Means Sutra. Upāyakauśalyasūtra. Thabs la mkhas pa zhes bya ba theg pa chen po'i mdo. Toh 261, mdo sde *za.* P927, *zhu.* English translation found in Tatz (1994).

Teachings of Akṣayamati Sutra. Akṣayamatinirdeśasūtra. 'Phags pa blo gros mi zad pas bstan pa'i mdo. Toh 175, mdo sde *ma.* P842, *bu.*

Teachings of Vimalakirti Sutra. Vimalakirtinirdeśasūtra. Dri ma med par grags pas bstan pa. Toh 176, mdo sde *ma.* P843, *bu.*

Thoroughly Pure Spheres of Conduct Sutra. Gocarapariśuddhasūtra. Spyod yul yongs su dag pa'i mdo. Toh 44 phal chen *ka.* P761, *i.* This is chapter 16 of *the Flower Ornament Scripture* in the Tibetan edition; in Cleary's translation from the Chinese edition, this is book 11.

Vast Manifestations Sutra. Lalitavistarasūtra. Rgya cher rol pa'i mdo. Toh 95, mdo sde *kha.* P763, *ku.*

Vows of Good Conduct. Bhadracaryāpraṇidhāna. Bzang po spyod paʼi smon lam. Toh 1095, gzungs bsdus *vam.* P716, *ya.* This is found also as part 4 of the *Flower Ornament Scripture.*

White Lotus of Compassion Sutra. Karuṇāpuṇḍarikasūtra. Snying rje pad ma dkar poʼi mdo. Toh 112 mdo sde *cha.* P780, *tsu.*

Tengyur *(Canonical Treatises)*

Aspiration Prayers for Supreme Conduct. Agracaryāpraṇidhāna. Mchog gi spyod paʼi smon lam. Toh 4396, sna tshogs *nyo.* P5939.

Āryadeva. *Four Hundred Stanzas [on the Middle Way]. Catuḥśatakaśās-tra. Bstan bcos Bzhi brgya pa.* Toh 3846, dbu ma *tsha.* P5246, *tsha.* An English translation of this work with extant fragments of the Sanskrit original can be found in Karen Lang's *Āryadeva's Catuḥśataka* (Copenhagen: Akademisk Forlag, 1986). A translation of the root stanzas from the Tibetan edition with Gyaltsap Je's commentary can be found under the title *The Yogic Deeds of Bodhisattvas: Gyel-tsap on Āryadeva's Four Hundred.* Ruth Sonam, trans. and ed. Ithaca: Snow Lion, 1994.

Āryaśūra. *Garland of Birth Stories. Jātakamālā. Skyes rabs kyi rgyud.* Toh 4150, skyes rabs *hu.* P5650, *ki.*

Asaṅga. *Compendium of Higher Knowledge. Abhidharmasamuccaya. Chos mngon pa kun las btus pa.* Toh 4049, sems tsam *ri.* P5550, *li.* For an English translation from Walpola Rahula's French translation, see Asanga, *Abhidharmasamuccaya,* trans. by Sara Boin-Webb. Fremont CA: Asian Humanities Press, 2001.

———. *Levels of the Bodhisattva. Bodhisattvabhūmi. Byang chub sems dpaʼi sa.* Toh 4037, sems tsam *vi.* P5538, *zhi.* For an English translation of the chapter on ethics, see Mark Tatz (1986). The chapter on reality has been translated by Janice Willis in *On Knowing Reality: The Tattvārtha Chapter of Asaṅga's Bodhisattvabhūmi* (New York: Columbia University Press, 1979).

———. *Levels of the Disciple. Śrāvakabhūmi. Nyan thos kyi sa.* Toh 4036, sems tsam *dzi.* P5537, *vi.*

Aśvaghoṣa. *Dispelling Sorrow. Śokavinodana. Mya ngan bsal ba.* Toh 4177, spring yig *nge.* P5677, *nge.*

————. *Revealing the Course of Ten Unwholesome Actions. Daśakuśalakarmapathanirdeśa. Mi dge ba bcu'i las kyi lam bstan pa.* Toh 4178, spring yig *nge.* P5678, *ngi.*

————. *Seventy Stanzas of Aspiration. Praṇidhānasaptatināmagāthā. Smon lam bdun bcu pa.* Toh 4392, sna tshogs *nyo.* P5936, *mo.*

Atiśa Dīpaṃkara. *Bodhisattva's Jewel Garland. Bodhisattvamaṇevali. Byang chub sems dpa' nor bu'i phreng ba.* Toh 3951, dbu ma *khi.* P5347, *ki.* An English translation is found in the present volume (entry 1).

————. *Commentary on the Difficult Points of the "Bodhipathapradipa." Bodhimārgapradipapañjikā. Byang chub lam gyi sgron ma'i dka' 'grel.* Toh 3948, dbu ma *khi.* P5344, *ki.*

————. *Letter of Unblemished Precious Jewels.* Vimalaratnalekha. *Dri ma med pa rin po che'i spring yig.* Toh 4188, spring yig *nge.* P5688, *nge.*

————. *Lamp for the Path to Enlightenment. Bodhipathapradipa. Byang chub lam gyi sgron ma.* Toh 3947, dbu ma *khi.* P5343, *ki.* For an English translation, see Geshe Sonam Rinchen's *Atisha's Lamp for the Path to Enlightenment.* Ruth Sonam, trans. Ithaca: Snow Lion, 1997.

Avadhūtipa. *Presentation of the Six Characteristics of Meditative Concentration. Dhyānaṣaḍdharmavyavasthāna. Bsam gtan gyi chos drug rnam par gzhag pa.* Toh 3926, dbu ma *ki.* P5321, *a.*

Bhāvaviveka. *Blaze of Reasoning. Tarkajvālā. Dbu ma rtog ge 'bar ba.* Toh 3856, dbu ma *dza.* P5256, *dza.*

Bhūripa. *Extensive Daily Confessions of Cakrasaṃvara [Practice]. Dpal 'khor lo mde mchog gi rgyun bshags rgyas pa.* Toh 1533, rgyud 'grel *za.* P2244, *pha.*

Bodhibhadra. *Chapter on the Requisite Conditions of Meditative Absorption. Samādhisambhāraparivarta. Ting nge 'dzin gyi tshogs kyi le'u.* Toh 3924, dbu ma *ki.* P5319, *a.*

Buddhaśrījñāna. *Drop of Freedom. Muktitilaka. Grol ba'i thig le.* Toh 1859, rgyud 'grel *di.* P2722, *ti.*

Candragomin. *Letter to a Student. Śiṣyalekha. Slob ma la springs pa'i spring yig.* Toh 4183, spring yig *nge.* P5683, *nge.*

Candrakīrti. *Entering the Middle Way. Madhyamakāvatāra. Dbu ma la 'jug pa'i tshig le'ur byas pa.* Toh 3861, dbu ma'a. P5262, 'a. An English translation of this work from the Tibetan can be found in C. W. Huntington, Jr. (1989).

Dharmakīrti. *Thorough Exposition of Valid Cognition. Pramāṇavārttika. Tshad ma rnam 'grel gyi tshigs le'ur byas pa.* Toh 4210, tshad ma *ce.* P5709, *ce.*

Jñānavajra. *Secret Wheel of Fire. Gsang ba me'i 'khor lo.* Toh 3000, Tengyur, rgyud *pu.* P3825, *tu.*

Kamalaśīla. *Stages of Meditation. Bhāvanākrama. Sgom pa'i rim pa.* Toh 3916, Tengyur, dbu ma *ki;* P5311, *a.* An English translation of the middle section of this work with the Dalai Lama's commentary can be found under the title *Stages of Meditation,* Ithaca: Snow Lion, 2001.

Maitreya. *Ornament of Clear Realizations. Abhisamayālaṃkāra. Mngon rtogs rgyan.* Toh 3786, shes phyin *ka.* P5184, *ka.*

———. *Ornament of Mahayana Sutras. Mahāyānasūtrālaṃkāra. Theg pa chen po mdo sde'i rgyan.* Toh 4020, sems tsam *phi.* P5521, *phi.*

———. *The Sublime Continuum. Uttaratantra. Rgyud bla ma.* Toh 4024, sems tsam *phi.* P5525, *phi.* An English translation of this work can be found under the title *The Changeless Nature.* Ken and Katia Holmes, trans. U.K.: Karma Drubgyud Dharjay Ling, 1985.

Nāgārjuna. *Commentary on the Awakening Mind. Bodhicittavivaraṇa. Byang chub sems kyi 'grel pa.* Toh 1800, rgyud 'grel *ngi.* P2665, *gi.* An English translation is in Lindtner (1982).

———. *Friendly Letter. Suhṛllekha. Bshes pa'i spring yig.* Toh 4182, spring yig *nge.* P5682, *nge.* English translation in Tharchin and Engle (1979).

———. *Precious Garland. Ratnāvali. Rgyal po la gtam bya ba rin po che'i phreng ba.* Toh 4158, skyes rabs *ge.* P5658, *nge.* English translations in Hopkins (1998) and in Dunne and McClintock (1997).

———. *Sixty Stanzas of Reasoning. Yuktiṣaṣṭikā. Rigs pa drug cu pa.* Toh 3825, dbu ma *tsa.* P5225, *tsa.* For an English translation of this short work see Lindtner (1982).

Prajñākaramati. *Exposition of the Difficult Points of the "Bodhicaryāvatāra."* *Bodhicaryāvatārapañjikā. Byang chub sems dpa'i spyod pa la 'jug pa'i dka' 'grel.* Toh 3872, dbu ma *la.* P5273, *la.*

Sangwé Jin (Gsang bas byin). *The Tale of the Seven Maidens. Saptakumāri-kāvadāna. Gzhon nu ma bdun gyi rtogs pa brjod pa.* Toh 4147, 'dul ba *su.* P5648, *u.*

Śāntideva. *Compendium of Trainings. Śikṣāsamuccaya. Bslab pa kun las btus pa.* Toh 3939 & 3940, dbu ma *khi.* P5336, *ki.* English translation from Sanskrit by Cecil Bendall and W.H.D. Rouse under the title *Śikṣā Samuccaya: A Compendium of Buddhist Doctrine.* Delhi: Motilal Banarsidass, reprint, 1971.

———. *A Guide to the Bodhisattva's Way of Life. Bodhicaryāvatāra. Byang chub sems dpa'i spyod pa la 'jug pa.* Toh 3871, dbu ma *la.* P5272, *la.* Several English translations of this work exist, including Stephen Batchelor's *Guide to the Bodhisattva's Way of Life* (Dharamsala: Library of Tibetan Works & Archives, 1979), the Padmakara Translation Group's *The Way of the Bodhisattva* (Boston: Shambhala Publications, 1997), Alan and Vesna Wallace's *A Guide to the Bodhisattva Way of Life* (Ithaca: Snow Lion Publications, 1997), and Crosby and Skilton (1995).

Saraha. *Songs of the Treasury of Dohas. Dohākoṣagiti. Do ha mdzod kyi klu.* Toh 2224, rgyud 'grel *vi.* P3068, *mi.* English translation in Herbert Guenther, *The Royal Song of Saraha.* Seattle: University of Washington, 1969.

Vasubandhu. *A Discussion of Merit Accumulation. Saṃbhāraparikathā. Tshogs kyi gtam.* Toh 4166, spring yig *ge.* P5666, *nge.*

———. *Treasury of Higher Knowledge. Abhidharmakośa. Chos mngon pa mdzod kyi tshig le'ur byas pa.* Toh 4089, mngon pa *ku.* P5590, *gu.* English translation from La Valleé Poussin's French edition found in Leo M. Pruden, *Abhidharmakośa Bhāṣyam.* Fremont: Asian Humanities Press, 1991.

———. *Exposition of the Treasury of Higher Knowledge. Abhidharmakośa-bhāṣya. Chos mngon pa'i mdzod kyi bshad pa.* Toh 4090, mngon pa *ku* and *khu;* P5591, *gu.* English translation from La Valleé Poussin's French edition by Leo M. Pruden, *Abhidharmakośa Bhāṣyam.* Fremont: Asian Humanities Press, 1991.

————. *Twenty Verses. Vimśatikā. Nyi shu pa' tshig le'ur byas pa.* Toh 4056, sems tsam *shi.* P5557, *si.* English translation in Anacker (1984).

Tibetan Works

The Book of Kadam. Bka' gdams glegs bam. Typeset edition, Kansu: Nationalities Press, 1993, 2 vols.

Chegom Sherap Dorjé (ca. twelfth century). *Heap of Precious Jewels: A Teaching by Means of Similes. Dpe chos rin chen spungs pa.* Typeset edition in *Gangs can rigs mdzod lde mig,* vol. 17, Beijing: Nationalities Press, 1987.

————, compiler. *Miscellaneous Sayings of the Kadam Masters. Bka' gdams gsung bgros thor bu.* Full text in Yeshé Döndrup's *Treasury of Gems,* pp. 562–615.

Chekawa Yeshé Dorjé (1101–75). *Commentary on the Eight Verses on Mind Training. Blo sbyong tshig brgyad ma'i 'grel pa.* This text appears as entry 30 of the present volume.

Dampa Sangyé (d. 1117). *Hundred Verses of Advice to the People of Dingri. Zhal gdams ding ri brgya rtsa.* Typeset edition in *Sgrub brgyud shing rta chen po brgyad kyi bsdus 'grel gangs can rig brgya'i nyin byed skya rengs dang po,* pp. 557–62, Beijing: Nationalities Press, 2000.

Kharak Gomchung (1186–1271). *Mind Training Attached to Six Posts. Blo sbyong tho lcogs drug ma.* Full text cited in Yeshé Döndrup's *Treasury of Gems,* pp. 255–56.

————. *Mind Training with Seventy Exhortations. Blo sbyong ang yig bdun cu ma.* Full text cited in Yeshé Döndrup's *Treasury of Gems,* pp. 257–64.

Potowa Rinchen Sal (1027–1105). *A Teaching by Means of Similes. Dpe chos.* Typeset edition in *Gangs can rigs mdzod lde mig,* vol. 17, Beijing: Nationalities Press, 1987.

Thokmé Sangpo (1295–1369). *Commentary on the Seven-Point Mind Training.* The full text in volume 3 of Jamgön Kongtrül's *Treasury of Instructions.* Delhi: Lungtok and Gyaltsen, reprint, 1971.

Sachen Künga Nyingpo (1092–1158). *Parting from the Four Clingings. Zhen pa bzhi bral.* Full text appears as entry 38 in the present volume.

Sakya Paṇḍita (1182–1251). *An Epistle Appealing to the Buddhas and Bodhisattvas of the Ten Directions. Phyogs bcu'i sangs rgyas dang byang chub sems rnams la zhu ba'i 'phrin yig. The Collected Works of the Masters of Sakya School,* vol. 5, Tokyo: The Toyo Bunko, 1968.

Sé Chilbu Chökyi Gyaltsen (1121–89). *Commentary on the Seven-Point Mind Training. Blo sbyong don bdun ma'i 'grel pa.* Full text appears as entry 7 of the present volume.

Sherap Gyaltsen (b. 1059). *Blue Udder. Man ngag be'u 'bum sngon po.* Typeset edition in *Gangs can rig mdzod lde mig,* vol. 16, Beijing: Nationalities Press, 1987.

Yangönpa Gyaltsen Pal (1213–58). *Garland of Wish- Jewels: The Sacred Writings of the Conqueror Yangönpa. Rgyal ba yang dgon pa'i bka' 'bum yid bzhin nor bu'i phreng ba. The Collected Works of Yangönpa,* vol. 3; reprinted by Kunsang Topgyal in Delhi, 1976.

Translator's Bibliography

Anacker, Stefan. *Seven Works of Vasubandhu, The Buddhist Psychological Doctor.* Delhi: Motilal Banarsidass, 1984.

Atiśa Dīpaṃkara (982–1054). *Letter of Unblemished Precious Jewels. Vimalaratnalekha. Dri ma med pa'i rin po che'i phreng ba.* Toh 4188, Tengyur, spring yig nge. P5688, nge.

Bapat, P. V., ed. *2500 Years of Buddhism.* Delhi: Ministry of Information and Broadcasting, Government of India, 1959; reprinted 1987.

Beyer, Stephan. *The Cult of Tārā: Magic and Ritual in Tibet.* Berkeley CA: University of California Press, 1973; reprinted 1978.

A Biographical Dictionary of Tibetan Scholars and Adepts. Gangs ljongs mkhas grub rim byon gi ming mdzod. Kansu: Nationalities Press, 1992.

The Book of Kadam. Bka' gdams glegs bam. Typeset edition, Xining: Qinghai Minorities Press, 1993, vols. 1 & 2.

Chalmers, Robert et al., trans. *The Jātaka or Stories of the Buddha's Former Lives.* 6 vols. Cambridge: Cambridge University Press, 1885–1907.

Chandra, Lokesh. *Tibetan-Sanskrit Dictionary.* Kyoto: Rinsen Book Co, 1990; compact edition.

Chattopadhaya, Alaka. *Atiśa and Tibet.* Delhi: Motilal Banarsidass, 1967; latest reprint, 1999.

Chenga Lodrö Gyaltsen (1402–72). *Initial Mind Training: Opening the Door of Dharma.* Thog ma'i blo sbyong chos kyi sgo 'byed. Xylograph edition reprinted in Three Texts on Lamrim Teachings. Dharamsala: Library of Tibetan Works & Archives, 1987.

Chim Namkha Drak (1210–85). *Biography of Master Atiśa. Jo bo rje'i rnam thar rgyas pa yongs grags.* In *The Book of Kadam (Bka' gdams glegs bam)*, vol. 1, pp. 44–228. Typeset edition, Kansu: Nationalities Press, 1993.

Cleary, Thomas, trans. the *Flower Ornament Scripture: A Translation of The Avatamsaka Sutra.* Boston: Shambhala Publications, 1993.

Dalai Lama, H. H. the. *Awakening the Mind, Lightening the Heart.* New York: HarperCollins, 1995; reprint, HarperCollins, India, 1997.

———. *The Compassionate Life.* Boston: Wisdom Publications, 2001.

———. *Open Heart.* New York: Little, Brown, 2002.

———. *Transforming the Mind.* Geshe Thupten Jinpa, trans. London: Thorsons, 2000.

Drogön Palden Yeshé (fourteenth–fifteenth century). *Beautiful Garland of Stories. Gtam rgyud rin chen phreng mdzes.* Typeset edition in *Gangs can rigs brgya'i sgo 'byed lde mig*, vol. 17. Beijing: Nationalities Press, 1987.

Dromtönpa (1005–65). *Source of Teachings. Chos kyi 'byung gnas.* In The Book of Kadam, vol. 1, pp. 229–90.

Dunne, John, and Sarah McClintock, trans. *The Precious Garland.* Wisdom Publications: Boston, 1997.

Eimer, Helmut. "The Development of the Biographical Tradition Concerning Atiśa (Dipaṃkaraśrijñāna)." In T*he Journal of the Tibet Society*, London, 2 (1982): 41–51.

The Extensive Tibetan-Chinese Dictionary. Bod rgya tshig mdzod chen mo. Beijing: Nationalities Press, 1993; compact edition, 2 vols.

Gö Lotsawa Shönu Pal (1392–1481). *The Blue Annals. Deb ther sngon po.* Typeset edition in two volumes, Sichuan: Minorities Press, 1984. English translation by George N. Roerich as *The Blue Annals.* Delhi: Motilal Banarsidass; latest reprint 1988.

Goram Sonam Sengé (1429–89). *Ocean of Wonders: The Liberating Life of the Great Mü Master. Rje mus pa chen po'i rnam par thar pa ngo mtshar rgya mtsho.* In *Lamdré Cycle of Texts* (*Lam 'bras chos skor*), vol. ka, pp. 56b–74a. Rajpur: Sakya College, 1983.

Hopkins, Jeffrey, trans. *Buddhist Advice for Living and Liberation: Nāgārjuna's Precious Garland.* Ithaca: Snow Lion, 1998.

Hortön Namkha Pal (1373–1447). *Mind Training: Rays of Sun. Blo sbyong nyi ma'i 'od zer.* Xylograph edition reprinted by Tibetan Cultural Printing Press, Dharamsala, 1986. English translation of this text is available under the title *Mind Training Like the Rays of Sun.* Dharamsala: Library of Tibetan Works & Archives, 1992; translated by Brian Beresford and edited by Jeremy Russell.

Huntington, C. W., Jr., and Geshe Namgyal Wangchen. *The Emptiness of Emptiness.* Honolulu: University of Hawaii, 1989.

Jamgön Amé (1597–1659). *Ocean of Wonders: A History of the Kadam Tradition. Bka' gdams chos 'byung ngo mtshar rgya mtsho.* Typeset edition, Kansu: Minorities Press, 1995.

———. *Treasury of Wonders: A History of the Sakya Family Lineage. Sa skya'i gdung rabs ngo mtshar bang mdzod.* Typeset edition, Beijing: Nationalities Press, 1986.

Jamgön Kongtrül (1831–90), ed. *Treasury of Instructions. gDams ngag mdzod.* Xylograph edition. Delhi: Lungtok and Gyaltsen, reprint, 1971.

Jinpa, Thupten. "Introduction" *(Sngon gleng ngo sprod).* In *Mind Training: The Great Collection. Theg pa chen po blo sbyong brgya rtsa.* New Delhi: Institute of Tibetan Classics, 2004.

Karmapa Rangjung Dorjé (1284–1339). *One Hundred Birth Stories. Skyes rabs brgya pa.* Typeset edition in *Gangs can rigs brgya'i sgo 'byed lde mig,* vol. 22. Beijing: Nationalities Press, 1995.

Keay, John. *India: A History.* Oxford: Oxford University Press, 2000.

Lechen Künga Gyaltsen (fifteenth century). *Lamp Illuminating the History of the Kadam Tradition. Bka' gdams chos 'byung gsal ba'i sgron me.* Xylograph edition published under the instruction of the Fifth Dalai Lama. Text scanned by the Tibetan Buddhist Resource Center (TBRC), New York, at the request of the Institute of Tibetan Classics.

Lindtner, Chr. *Nāgārjuniana: Studies in the Writings and Philosophy of Nāgārjuna.* Delhi: Motilal Banarsidass, 1982; reprint, 1990.

Lobsang Tamdrin (1867–1937). *Annotations on the "Peacock's Neutralizing of Poisons Mind Training." Blo sbyong rma bya dug 'joms kyi mchan. The Collected Works of rje btsun blo bzang rta mgrin,* vol. ka, Delhi: Guru Deva Lama, 1975.

———. *Annotations on the "Wheel of Sharp Weapons Mind Training." Blo sbyong mtshon cha 'khor lo'i mchan.* The Collected Works, vol. ka.

Longdöl Ngawang Lobsang (1719–94). *Staircase to Liberation: A Memorandum of Initiations, Oral Transmissions and Commentaries Received Pertaining to Sūtra and Tantra.* Part 1. *Mdo sngags kyi dbang lung khrid gsum thob pa'i gsan yig thar pa'i them skas. stod cha. The Collected Works of Klong rdol ngag dbang blo bzang.* Xinhua: Tibetan Press for the Publication of Old Tibetan Texts, 1991; vol. 2, pp. 1–176.

———. A *Useful List for Those Who Uphold the Geden Tradition and Aspire Toward Vast Learning* in the *Collected Works of Klong rdol ngag dbang blo bzang,* vol. 2, pp. 307–29.

McGovern, William Montgomery. *A Manual of Buddhist Philosophy.* Lucknow: Oriental Reprinters, 1976; first published, London, 1923.

Meadows, Carol. *Ārya-Śura's Compendium of the Perfections: Text, Translation and Analysis of the Pāramitāsamāsa.* Indica et Tibetica, vol. 8. Bonn: Indica et Tibetica Verlag, 1986.

Monier-Williams, Monier. *Sanskrit-English Dictionary.* Delhi: Motilal Banarsidass, latest reprint 1993.

Ngülchu Dharmabhadra (1772–1851). *Heart Jewel of the Bodhisattvas. Rgyal sras snying nor. The Collected Works of Dngul chu Dharma bhadra,* vol. *cha;* reproduced from a manuscript copy traced from prints of the Dngul-chu blocks by Jampa Öser, New Delhi, 1973.

O'Flaherty, Wendy Doniger, trans. *Hindu Myths*. Penguin Classics; London: Penguin Books, 1975.

Pagel, Ulrich. *The Bodhisattvapiṭaka: Its Doctrines, Practices and Their Position in Mahāyāna Literature*. Tring: The Institute of Buddhist Studies, 1995.

Panchen Sönam Drakpa (1478–1554). *History of the New and Old Kadam Schools: Beautiful Ornament for the Mind. Bka' gdams gsar rnying gi chos 'byung yid kyi mdzes rgyan*. Xylograph edition of Potala Library reprinted in Two Histories of Kadam School published by Gonpo Tseten in Delhi, 1977.

Pawo Tsuklak Trengwa (1504–66). *Joyful Feast for the Learned: A History of Buddhism. Chos byung mkhas pa'i dga' ston*. Typeset edition in two volumes, Beijing: Nationalities Press, 1985.

Phabongkha Dechen Nyingpo (1978–1941). *Memorandum of Teachings Received. Gsan yig. The Collected Works of Pha bong kha*, vol. ka. Xylograph edition. Delhi: Chöphel Lekden, reprint, 1973.

———. *Root Text of the Seven-Point Mind Training. Blo sbyong don bdun ma'i rtsa tshig*. The Collected Works, vol. ka.

Potter, Karl H., ed. *Encyclopedia of Indian Philosophy*, vol. 7: Buddhist Philosophy from 100–350 a.d. Delhi: Motilal Banarsidass, 1999.

Rabten, Geshe, and Geshe Ngawang Dhargyey. *Advice from a Spiritual Friend*. Delhi: Publications for Wisdom Culture, 1977; reprint, Boston: Wisdom Publications, 2001.

Sangyé Gompa (1179–1250). *Public Explication of Mind Training. Blo sbyong tshogs bshad ma*. Entry 34 of the present volume.

Sankrityayan, Rahul. "Ācārya Dīpaṅkara Śrījñāna" in P. V. Bapat, ed. *2500 Years of Buddhism*. Delhi: Publications Division, Ministry of Information and Broadcasting, Government of India, 1959; reprinted 1987.

Śāntideva. *The Bodhicaryāvatāra*. Kate Crosby and Andrew Skilton, trans. New York: Oxford University Press, 1995.

Shönu Gyalchok (fourteenth century). *Mind Training: Compendium of Well-Uttered Insights. Blo sbyong legs bshad kun btus*. Xylograph, Dergé edition. Delhi: Ngawang Topgyal, reprint, 1996.

Snellgrove, D. L. *The Hevajra Tantra.* Sanskrit text, Tibetan version and commentary, and English rendering. London: Oxford University Press, 1959.

Sönam Lhai Wangpo (fifteenth century). *A History of the Precious Kadam Tradition: Sun Illuminating the Liberating Lives. Bka' gdams rin po che'i chos 'byung rnam thar nyin mor byed pa'i 'od stong.* Xylograph edition of Potala Library reprinted in Two Histories of Kadam School, published by Gonpo Tseten in Delhi, 1977.

Sopa, Geshe Lhundub, with Michael Sweet and Leonard Zwilling. *Peacock in the Poison Grove: Two Buddhist Texts on Training the Mind.* Boston: Wisdom Publications, 2001.

Stearns, Cyrus. *Luminous Lives: The Stories of the Early Masters of the Lam 'bras Tradition in Tibet.* Boston: Wisdom Publications, 2001.

Stein, R. A. *Les Tribus Anciennes des Marches Sino-Tibétaines: Légendes, Classifications et Histoire.* Paris: Presses Universitaires de France, 1961.

Sumpa Yeshé Paljor (1704–88). *An Excellent Wish-Fulfilling Tree: History of Buddhism. Chos 'byung dpag bsam ljon bzang.* Typeset edition, Kansu: Minorities Press, 1992.

Tatz, Mark. *Asanga's Chapter on Ethics with the Commentary of Tsong-kha-p*a. Berkeley: University of California, 1986.

———. (Trans.) *The Skill in Means (Upāyakauśalya) Sūtra.* Delhi: Motilal Banarsidass, 1994.

Tendar Lharam, Alaksha (1759-1840). *Essential Points for [Understanding the] Seven-Point Mind Training. Blo sbyong don bdun ma'i nyer mkho. The Collected gSung 'bum of bstan dar lha-rams of A-lag-sha,* vol. 2, entry va. Delhi: Guru Deva Lama, reprint, 1971.

Tharchin, Geshe Lobsang, and Artemus Engle. *Nāgārjuna's Letter to a Friend with a Commentary by Venerable Rendawa Zhon-nu Lo-dro.* Dharamsala: Library of Tibetan Works & Archives, 1979.

Thokmé Sangpo (1295–1369). *Commentary on the Seven-Point Mind Training.* The full text in volume 3 of Jamgön Kongtrül's *Treasury of Instructions.* Delhi: Lungtok and Gyaltsen, reprint, 1971.

Thuken Chökyi Nyima (1737–1802). *Crystal Mirror of Philosophical Schools. Grub mtha' shel gyi me long.* Typeset edition. Kansu: Minorities Press, 1985.

Thurman, Robert. "Vajra Hermeneutics." In Donald S. Lopez, Jr., ed. *Buddhist Hermeneutics.* Honolulu: University of Hawaii, 1988; reprinted in Delhi, 1993.

Trichen Tenpa Rapgyé (1759–1815). *Ambrosia Giving Birth to Shoots of Altruistic Deeds: Notes on the Wheel of Sharp Weapons. Blo sbyong mtshon cha 'khor lo'i zin bris gzhan phan myu gu bskyed pa'i bdud rtsi. The Collected Works of Thri chen Bstan pa rab rgyas,* vol. 3. Dharamsala: Library of Tibetan Works & Archives, 1985.

Trijang Lobsang Yeshé (1901–82). *Annotations on the Seven-Point Mind Training. Blo sbyong don bdun ma'i mchan 'grel. The Collected Works of Skyabs rje Tri jang Rdo rje 'chang,* vol. ga. New Delhi: Lama Guru Deva, no date.

Tsalpa Künga Dorjé (1309–64). *The Red Annals. Deb ther dmar po.* Typeset edition with extensive annotations by Dungkar Lobsang Trinlé. Beijing: Nationalities Press, 1981.

Tsenla Ngawang Tsültrim. *Golden Mirror Unraveling the Terms. Brda dkrol gser gyi me long.* Beijing: Nationalities Press, 1997.

Tseten Shapdrung (1910–98) *Compendium of Chronologies. Bstan rtsis kun las btus pa.* Xining: Qinghai Nationalities Press, 1982.

Tsongkhapa (1357–1419). *The Great Treatise on the Stages of the Path to Enlightenment. Byang chub lam rim chen mo. The Collected Works of Tsongkhapa,* vol. pha. Xylograph edition reprinted by Guru Deva Lama in Delhi, 1978. Typeset edition, Kansu: Minorities Press, 1985. English translation of this work is available as *The Great Treatise on the Stages of the Path to Enlightenment,* vols. 1–3. The Lamrim Chenmo Translation Committee; Guy Newland, ed.; Joshua W. C. Cutler, editor-in-chief. Ithaca: Snow Lion, 2000, 2002, and 2004.

———. *The Fulfillment of All Hopes of Disciples: An Exposition of the "Fifty Verses on the Guru." Bla ma lnga bcu pa'i rnam bshad slob ma'i re ba kun skong. The Collected Works,* vol. ka. English translation of this work by Gareth Sparham is available under the title *The Fulfillment of All Hopes:*

Guru Devotion in Tibetan Buddhism. Boston: Wisdom Publications, 1999.

Willson, Martin, and Martin Brauen. *Deities of Tibetan Buddhism: The Zürich Paintings of the Icons Worthwhile to See.* Boston: Wisdom Publications, 2000.

Yeshé Döndrup (1792–1855). *Treasury of Gems: Selected Anthology of the Well-Uttered Insights of the Teachings of the Precious Kadam Tradition. Legs par bshad pa bka' gdams rin po che'i gsung gi gces btus legs bshad nor bu'i bang mdzod.* Typeset edition. Kansu: Nationalities Press, 1995.

Yongzin Yeshé Gyaltsen (1713–93). *Biographies of the Masters of the Lineage of the Stages of the Path. Lam rim bla ma brgyud pa'i rnam thar.* Collected Works, vols. *nga* and *ca.* Reproduced from a set of Tshe mchog gling blocks. New Delhi: Tibet House, 1979.

———. *Essence of Ambrosia: A Guide on Mind Training. Blo sbyong gi khrid yig bdud rtsi'i snying po.* Collected Works, vol. *ba.*

Zemey Lobsang Palden (1927–96). *An Instruction on Relating the "Eight Verses on Mind Training" to the Bodhisattva Practice of the Six Perfections. Blo sbyong tshigs brgyad ma rgyal sras kyi spyod pa sbyin sogs phar phyin drug dang sbyar ba.* The Collected Works of Kyapjé Zemey Rinpoché. Geshe Thupten Jinpa, ed., vol. *ga* (3). Mundgod: Tashi Gephel House, 1996.

———. *Relating the "Eight Verses on Mind Training" to the Mahayana Path of Equalizing and Exchanging Self and Others. Blo sbyong tshigs brgyad ma theg pa chen po'i lam bdag gzhan mnyam brjes dang sbyar ba.* The Collected Works of Kyapjé Zemey Rinpoché, vol. *ga* (3).

Index

awakening mind
Atiśa's teachers of, 41–44, 207
basis of, 219
excellence of, 333–35
generating, 543–44
meditation on, 426–29, 536–37
See also conventional awakening
mind; giving and taking; two
awakening minds; ultimate
awakening mind

Bangala, 27, 581n43
barbarian borderlands, 195–96, 433,
601n316
bardo. See intermediate state
Bari Lotsāwa, 541, 652n1042
bee analogy, 500
Belpo Che, 318
Ben Gungyal, 103, 502, 592n203,
646n964
Bhṛkuṭi, 207
bias, 118, 365–66, 370, 394–95, 508–9
Birbapa, 612n406
blame, 285, 406–7, 477, 494
Blaze of Reasoning (Bhāvaviveka), 291–92
Blue Udder (Sherap Gyaltsen), 316,
621n515
boasting, 128–29, 403–4
Bodhgaya, 61, 207, 215, 398, 436
Bodhibhadra, 38, 40–42, 472, 563
Bodhicaryāvatāra. See Guide to the
Bodhisattva's Way of Life, A
Bodhisattva Levels. See Levels of the
Bodhisattva
Bodhisattva's Jewel Garland (Atiśa), 6
bodhisattvas
conduct of, 561–62
historical figures, 218–19
karma of, 398, 466–67
karma toward, 465
purity, 604n336
qualities, 347, 348
wisdom of, 315
See also heroes
body
attachment to, 100, 101–2, 189–91, 221,
397

basis for future happiness, 130
countless bodies due to rebirth, 332
offering, 189, 190–91, 230–31, 341–43,
490–92
transforming, 232–34
boisterousness, 129, 405
Bön, 61, 585n107, 586n113
Brahma, 527–28
breathing meditation, 96, 229, 259, 302,
354–55
Buddha. See Śākyamuni Buddha;
Kanakamuni Buddha; Krakucchanda
Buddha
buddha bodies, 107, 108, 347, 604n335
buddha fields, 626n612
buffalo analogy, 445
butcher analogies, 445, 476

Cacika, 61
Cakrasamvara. See Heruka
calm abiding. See tranquil abiding
Candrabhadra, 66
Candragarbhā, Prince. (Later known as
Atiśa), 28–55
Candragomin. See Letter to a Student
Candrakīrti, 294, 530. See also Entering
the Middle Way
celestial beings. See gods
celibacy, 291–92
central region, 435
Chakshingwa, 277, 316, 613n414
Chapter on the Requisite Conditions of
Meditative Absorption (Bodhibhadra),
563
Chegom Sherap Dorjé, 579–80n30,
643n920
Cheka Monastery, 618n473
Chekawa
teaching mind training, 11, 318
life story, 315–19, 371
practice of mind training, 277, 319, 368,
395, 406–7
seeking mind training instruction,
316–18
on sources of mind training, 2, 8, 11
See also Seven-Point Mind Training
Chenga Lodrö Gyaltsen, 13

Sachen Kunga Nyingpo. *See* Sakyapa

Sahor, 27, 39, 581n42

Sakya Paṇḍita, 435, 605n338, 650n1023

Sakya school, 651n1028

Sakyapa, 517, 529, 531, 541–42, 649n1010, 651n1025

Śākyamuni Buddha

expansive thought, 218

life, 66. *See also* Siddhārtha

past lives, 321. *See also Jātaka Tales; Garland of Birth Stories*

powerless to prevent death, 300

teachings, 87, 130, 313, 320, 396, 473, 585n103, 632n729

visualizing, 563

Śākyaśrī, 5, 604n335

Samantabhadra, 66, 218–19, 493

Samantabhadra palace, 40

samsara. *See* cyclic existence, defects of

Samudra Parag, 320

Samudragarbha, 320

Sangphupa, 410, 635n788

Sangyé Gompa, 10, 13, 620n500

Śāntideva. *See Compendium of Trainings; Guide to the Bodhisattva's Way of Life, A*

Sautrāntika school, 314

Scriptural Collection of the Bodhisattva, 436

Sé Chilbu Chökyi Gyaltsen, 8, 11, 201, 320, 319, 588–89n154, 589n155

sea monster. *See* makara

Seal Entering the Definitive and Nondefinitive, 465

Seberé, 369

self as enemy, 98–103, 168, 184

Sengé Gyaltsen, 369, 502

Serlingpa Dharmakīrti

lineage, 225–26, 578n14

philosophy, reasoning and authority, 88, 314–15

sequence of mind training, 487

source of mind training, 8–9, 131, 335

teacher of Atiśa, 8–9, 63, 65–69, 88–89, 225

seven riches, 583n74

Seven-Point Mind Training (Chekawa), 2, 4, 6–7, 9–13, 589n154

Seventy Stanzas of Aspiration (Aśvaghoṣa), 351

sexual misconduct, 457–58, 460, 461, 555–56

shame, 125

Shang Drakmarwa. *See* Drakmarwa

Shangshung king, 61

Sharawa, 2, 11, 315, 316–19, 368, 479

Shawo Gangpa (Shawopa; Shabopa; Shapopa), 103, 105–6, 118, 387, 411, 484–86, 499, 502, 592n200

sheep analogy, 445, 476

Sherapbar, 7, 285

Shetön Jangbar, 371

Sho, 316

Shönu Gyalchok, 10, 12, 13–15, 531

Shönu Gyaltsen. *See* Phuchungwa

sickness. *See* illness

Siddhartha, Prince. (*Later known as* Śākyamuni Buddha), 34, 35

simultaneous engagement, 91

sindri, 590n172

six conditions, 607n366

six directions, 610n388

six misplaced understandings, 127

six perfections, 234–35

sky treasury, 586–87n122

sleep, 228

Sönam Drakpa, 440, 639n836

Sönam Lhai Wangpo, 11

Sönam Rinchen (Puṇyaratna), 602n320

Songs of Blissfulness (Atiśa), 286, 382, 615n445

Sothangpa, 316

southern continent, 448–49, 636n813

spirits, 104–5

spiritual teachers, 125, 199–201, 286, 340–41, 392–93. *See also* guru yoga

sporadic approach, 128, 410

śrāvakayāna. See Disciples' School/ Vehicle

Śrīdevi, 231

Śrīgarbhā (prince), 28

Śrīprabhā (queen), 28, 46, 48, 55

About Thupten Jinpa

THUPTEN JINPA LANGRI was educated in the Tibetan monastic system, where he received the highest degree of *geshé lharam*. Jinpa also holds a BA in philosophy and a PhD in religious studies, both from the University of Cambridge, England. Since 1985, he has been the principal translator to the Dalai Lama, accompanying him on tours throughout the world and translating and editing many books. Jinpa's own works include *Self, Reality and Reason in Tibetan Thought*, several volumes of translations in *The Library of Tibetan Classics*, and the modern biography *Tsongkhapa: A Buddha in the Land of Snows*. He is currently the president and the editor-in-chief of the Institute of Tibetan Classics, based in Montreal, and he also chairs the Mind and Life Institute and the Compassion Institute.

The Institute of Tibetan Classics

THE INSTITUTE OF TIBETAN CLASSICS is a nonprofit, charitable educational organization based in Montreal, Canada. It is dedicated to two primary objectives: (1) to preserve and promote the study and deep appreciation of Tibet's rich intellectual, spiritual, and artistic heritage, especially among the Tibetan-speaking communities worldwide; and (2) to make the classical Tibetan knowledge and literature a truly global heritage, its spiritual and intellectual resources open to all.

To learn more about the Institute of Tibetan Classics and its various projects, please visit www.tibetanclassics.org or write to this address:

Institute of Tibetan Classics
304 Aberdare Road
Montreal (Quebec) H3P 3K3
Canada

The Library of Tibetan Classics

"This new series edited by Thupten Jinpa and published by Wisdom Publications is a landmark in the study of Tibetan culture in general and Tibetan Buddhism in particular. Each volume contains a lucid introduction and outstanding translations that, while aimed at the general public, will benefit those in the field of Tibetan Studies immensely as well."

—Leonard van der Kuijp, Harvard University

"This is an invaluable set of translations by highly competent scholar-practitioners. The series spans the breadth of the history of Tibetan religion, providing entry to a vast culture of spiritual cultivation."

—Jeffrey Hopkins, University of Virginia

"Erudite in all respects, this series is at the same time accessible and engagingly translated. As such, it belongs in all college and university libraries as well as in good public libraries. *The Library of Tibetan Classics* is on its way to becoming a truly extraordinary spiritual and literary accomplishment."

—Janice D. Willis, Wesleyan University

Following is a list of the thirty-two proposed volumes in *The Library of Tibetan Classics*. Some volumes are translations of single texts, while others are compilations of multiple texts, and each volume will be roughly the same length. Except for those volumes already published, the renderings of titles below are tentative and liable to change. The Institute of Tibetan Classics has contracted numerous established translators in its efforts, and work is progressing on all the volumes concurrently.

1. *Mind Training: The Great Collection*, compiled by Shönu Gyalchok and Könchok Gyaltsen (fifteenth century). NOW AVAILABLE
2. *The Book of Kadam: The Core Texts*, attributed to Atiśa and Dromtönpa (eleventh century). NOW AVAILABLE
3. *The Great Chariot: A Treatise on the Great Perfection*, Longchen Rapjampa (1308–63)
4. *Taking the Result As the Path: Core Teachings of the Sakya Lamdré Tradition*, Jamyang Khyentsé Wangchuk (1524–68) et al. NOW AVAILABLE
5. *Mahāmudrā and Related Instructions: Core Teachings of the Kagyü Schools.* NOW AVAILABLE
6. *Stages of the Path and the Oral Transmission: Selected Teachings of the Geluk School.* NOW AVAILABLE
7. *Mountain Dharma: An Ocean of Definitive Meaning*, Dölpopa Sherab Gyaltsen (1292–1361). NOW AVAILABLE
8. *Four Tibetan Lineages: Core Teachings of Pacification, Severance, Shangpa Kagyü, and Bodong*, Jamgön Kongtrül (1813–99). NOW AVAILABLE
9. *The Tradition of Everlasting Bön: Five Key Texts on Scripture, Tantra, and the Great Perfection.* NOW AVAILABLE
10. *Stages of the Buddha's Teachings: Three Key Texts.* NOW AVAILABLE
11. *The Bodhisattva's Altruistic Ideal: Selected Key Texts*
12. *The Ethics of the Three Codes*
13. *Sādhanas: Vajrayana Buddhist Meditation Manuals*
14. *Ornament of Stainless Light: An Exposition of the Kālacakra Tantra*, Khedrup Norsang Gyatso (1423–1513). NOW AVAILABLE
15. *A Lamp to Illuminate the Five Stages: Teachings on the Guhyasamāja Tantra*, Tsongkhapa (1357–1419). NOW AVAILABLE
16. *Studies in the Perfection of Wisdom*
17. *Treatises on Buddha Nature*
18. *Differentiations of the Profound View: Interpretations of Emptiness in Tibet*
19. *Illuminating the Intent: An Exposition of Candrakīrti's Entering the Middle Way*, Tsongkhapa (1357–1419). NOW AVAILABLE
20. *Tibetan Buddhist Epistemology I: The Sakya School* 21. *Tibetan Buddhist Epistemology II: The Geluk School*
21. *Tibetan Buddhist Epistemology II: The Geluk School*
22. *Tibetan Buddhist Psychology and Phenomenology: Selected Texts*
23. *Ornament of Abhidharma: A Commentary on the Abhidharmakośa*, Chim Jampaiyang (thirteenth century). NOW AVAILABLE
24. *Beautiful Adornment of Mount Meru: A Presentation of Classical Indian Philosophies*, Changkya Rölpai Dorjé (1717–86). NOW AVAILABLE

25. *The Crystal Mirror of Philosophical Systems: A Tibetan Study of Asian Religious Thought*, Thuken Losang Chökyi Nyima (1737–1802). NOW AVAILABLE
26. *Gateway for Being Learned and Realized: Selected Texts*
27. *The Tibetan Book of Everyday Wisdom: A Thousand Years of Sage Advice.* NOW AVAILABLE
28. *Mirror of Beryl: A Historical Introduction to Tibetan Medicine*, Desi Sangyé Gyatso (1653–1705). NOW AVAILABLE
29. *Selected Texts on Tibetan Astronomy and Astrology*
30. *Art and Literature: An Anthology*
31. *Tales from the Tibetan Operas.* NOW AVAILABLE
32. *A History of Buddhism in India and Tibet*, Khepa Deu (thirteenth century). NOW AVAILABLE

To receive a brochure describing all the volumes or to stay informed about *The Library of Tibetan Classics*, please write to:

support@wisdompubs.org

or send a request by post to:

Wisdom Publications
Attn: Library of Tibetan Classics
132 Perry Street
New York, NY 10014 USA

The complete catalog containing descriptions of each volume can also be found online at wisdomexperience.org.

Become a Benefactor
of the Library of Tibetan Classics

THE LIBRARY OF TIBETAN CLASSICS' scope, importance, and commitment to the finest quality make it a tremendous financial undertaking. We invite you to become a benefactor, joining us in creating this profoundly important human resource. Contributors of two thousand dollars or more will receive a copy of each future volume as it becomes available, and will have their names listed in all subsequent volumes. Larger donations will go even further in supporting *The Library of Tibetan Classics*, preserving the creativity, wisdom, and scholarship of centuries past, so that it may help illuminate the world for future generations.

To contribute, please either visit our website at www.wisdomexperience .org, call us at (617) 776-7416, or send a check made out to Wisdom Publications or credit card information to the address below.

Library of Tibetan Classics Fund
Wisdom Publications
132 Perry Street
New York, NY 10014
USA

Please note that contributions of lesser amounts are also welcome and are invaluable to the development of the series. Wisdom is a 501(c)(3) nonprofit corporation, and all contributions are tax-deductible to the extent allowed by law.

If you have any questions, please do not hesitate to call us or email us at support@wisdompubs.org.

To keep up to date on the status of *The Library of Tibetan Classics*, visit the series page on our website, and subscribe to our newsletter while you are there.

About Wisdom Publications

Wisdom Publications is the leading publisher of classic and contemporary Buddhist books and practical works on mindfulness. To learn more about us or to explore our other books, please visit our website at wisdomexperience.org or contact us at the address below.

Wisdom Publications
132 Perry Street
New York, NY 10014 USA

We are a 501(c)(3) organization, and donations in support of our mission are tax deductible.

Wisdom Publications is affiliated with the Foundation for the Preservation of the Mahayana Tradition (FPMT).